SUNDAYS AND SEASONS

YEAR A 2017

Sundays and Seasons
2017, Year A
Guide to Worship Planning

The Sundays and Seasons family of resources

Sundays and Seasons: Preaching, 2017, Year A (978-1-4514-9601-7)

Worship Planning Calendar, 2017, Year A (978-1-4514-9598-0)

Words for Worship, 2017, Year A (978-1-4514-9604-8)

Calendar of Word and Season 2017 (978-1-4514-9602-4)

Church Year Calendar, 2017, Year A (978-1-4514-9599-7)

Church Year Calendar, 2017, Year A PDF (978-1-4514-9600-0)

Bread for the Day: Daily Bible Readings and Prayers 2017 (978-1-4514-9603

sundaysandseasons.com

preludemusicplanner.org

Acknowledgments

Copyright © 2016 Augsburg Fortress. All rights reserved. Except as noted herein and for brief quotations in critical articles or reviews, no part of this book may be reproduced in any manner without prior written permission from the publisher. Write to: Permissions, Augsburg Fortress, Box 1209, Minneapolis, MN 55440-1209.

Unless otherwise indicated, scripture quotations are from the New Revised Standard Version Bible © 1989 Division of Christian Education of the National Council of the Churches of Christ in the United States of America. Used by permission. All rights reserved.

Revised Common Lectionary © 1992 Consultation on Common Texts. Used by permission.

The prayers of intercession (printed in each Sunday/festival section) may be reproduced for onetime, non-sale use, provided copies are for local use only and the following copyright notice appears: From *Sundays and Seasons*, copyright © 2016 Augsburg Fortress.

Come, Lord Jesus: Devotions for Advent, Christmas, Epiphany (Augsburg Fortress, 1996): The Advent Wreath; Blessing for a Home at Epiphany, adapt.

Evangelical Lutheran Worship (Augsburg Fortress, 2006): various prayers.

In These or Similar Words: Crafting Language for Worship (Augsburg Fortress, 2015): confession and forgiveness (time after Epiphany, adapt.; Lent, adapt.); thanksgiving for baptism (Easter); offering prayer (Christmas; Summer; November); invitation to communion (Advent, adapt.; Lent, adapt.; Maundy Thursday); prayer after communion (Summer); dismissal (Christmas; time after Epiphany; Easter/Pentecost; Summer).

Music Sourcebook for All Saints through Transfiguration (Augsburg Fortress, 2013): Thanksgiving for Saints of the Congregation.

Annual and seasonal materials

The Year of Matthew: Troy M. Troftgruben

For the Church Universal: Praying in 2017: Gail Ramshaw

Hymn of the Day as Reformation Inheritance: Mark Mummert

Preparing for the Season: Jon Niketh (Advent); Anne Edison-Albright (Christmas); Marissa Sotos (Time after Epiphany); D. Foy Christopherson (Lent); Miriam Schmidt (Three Days); Kevin Anderson (Easter); Alex Raabe (Summer); Craig M. Mueller (Autumn); Karen Bates-Olson (November)

Seasonal Worship Texts: Martin A. Seltz; Bradley E. Schmeling (Autumn).

Seasonal Rites: Emily Hartner (midweek Advent series); Michael Coffey (Blue Christmas Evening Prayer); Richard Bruxvoort Colligan (Christmas Day calls to worship); Lynn Bulock (midweek Lenten series); John Roberts (script for John 20); Gail Ramshaw (thanksgivings at the table for Reformation 500)

Weekly materials

Prayers of Intercession: Jennifer Baker-Trinity, Lynn Bulock, Lawrence Clark, Brett Davis, Julie Kanarr, Jean Larson, Jennifer Manis, Rachel Manke, Kyle Schiefelbein

Images in the Readings and Connections with the Liturgy: Gail Ramshaw

Ideas for the Day: Tim Brown, Michael Coffey, Yehiel Curry, Melody Eastman, Heidi Heimgartner, Jim Honig, Rebecca Liberty, Bekki Lohrmann, Henry Martinez, Lucille Mills, Alissa Oleson, Katya Ouchakof, Julie Seymour, Harvard Stephens, William Storm, Paul E. Walters

Let the Children Come: Sharolyn Browning

Music materials

Assembly Song: Mark Mummert (hymns), Cheryl Dieter (psalmody), Lorraine S. Brugh (global), Omaldo Perez (praise/contemporary)

Music for the Day: Zebulon M. Highben (choral), Andrea Baxter (children's choir), Chad Fothergill (keyboard/instrumental), Michael J. Glasgow (handbell)

Art and design

Cover art: Christina Saj

Interior art: Gertrud Mueller Nelson

Cover design: Laurie Ingram

Interior design: Alisha Lofgren

Development staff

Suzanne Burke, Martin A. Seltz

Manufactured in the U.S.A.

978-1-4514-9597-3

Introduction

Advent

Christmas

Time after Epiphany

Lent

The Three Days

Easter

Time after Pentecost — Summer

Time after Pentecost — Autumn

Time after Pentecost — November

Index of Seasonal Rites

Lectionary Conversion Chart

Time after Pentecost, Year A, 2017

If today is . . .	. . . it falls within this date range.	The "lectionary" number assigned to this date range in *Evangelical Lutheran Worship* is . . .	. . . which is equivalent to "proper ____" in other printed lectionaries.	In 2017, this Sunday is the "____ Sunday after Pentecost."
Sunday, June 18	Sunday between June 12 & 18 (if after Holy Trinity)	Lectionary 11	6	2nd
Sunday, June 25	Sunday between June 19 & 25	Lectionary 12	7	3rd
Sunday, July 2	Sunday between June 26 & July 2	Lectionary 13	8	4th
Sunday, July 9	Sunday between July 3 & 9	Lectionary 14	9	5th
Sunday, July 16	Sunday between July 10 & 16	Lectionary 15	11	6th
Sunday, July 23	Sunday between July 17 & 23	Lectionary 16	11	7th
Sunday, July 30	Sunday between July 24 & 30	Lectionary 17	12	8th
Sunday, August 6	Sunday between July 31 & Aug 6	Lectionary 18	11	9th
Sunday, August 13	Sunday between Aug 7 & 13	Lectionary 19	14	10th
Sunday, August 20	Sunday between Aug 14 & 20	Lectionary 20	15	11th
Sunday, August 27	Sunday between Aug 21 & 27	Lectionary 21	16	12th
Sunday, September 3	Sunday between Aug 28 & Sept 3	Lectionary 22	17	13th
Sunday, September 10	Sunday between Sept 4 & 10	Lectionary 23	18	14th
Sunday, September 17	Sunday between Sept 11 & 17	Lectionary 24	19	15th
Sunday, September 24	Sunday between Sept 18 & 24	Lectionary 25	20	16th
Sunday, October 1	Sunday between Sept 25 & Oct 1	Lectionary 26	21	17th
Sunday, October 8	Sunday between Oct 2 & 8	Lectionary 27	22	18th
Sunday, October 15	Sunday between Oct 9 & 15	Lectionary 28	23	19th
Sunday, October 22	Sunday between Oct 16 & 22	Lectionary 29	24	20th
Sunday, October 29	Sunday between Oct 23 & 29	Lectionary 30	25	21st
Sunday, November 5	Sunday between Oct 30 & Nov 5	Lectionary 31	26	22nd
Sunday, November 12	Sunday between Nov 6 & 12	Lectionary 32	27	23rd
Sunday, November 19	Sunday between Nov 13 & 19	Lectionary 33	28	24th
Christ the King, Nov 26	Sunday between Nov 20 & 26	Lectionary 34	29	Last

Lectionary Color Chart
Year A, 2017

Advent

Nov 27	First Sunday of Advent	Blue
Dec 4	Second Sunday of Advent	Blue
Dec 11	Third Sunday of Advent	Blue
Dec 18	Fourth Sunday of Advent	Blue

Christmas

Dec 24/25	Nativity of Our Lord	White
Jan 1	Name of Jesus	White
Jan 1	First Sunday of Christmas	White
Jan 6	Epiphany of Our Lord	White

Time after Epiphany

Jan 8	Baptism of Our Lord	White
Jan 15	Second Sunday after Epiphany	Green
Jan 22	Third Sunday after Epiphany	Green
Jan 29	Fourth Sunday after Epiphany	Green
Feb 5	Fifth Sunday after Epiphany	Green
Feb 12	Sixth Sunday after Epiphany	Green
Feb 19	Seventh Sunday after Epiphany	Green
Feb 26	Transfiguration of Our Lord	White

Lent

Mar 1	Ash Wednesday	Purple
Mar 5	First Sunday in Lent	Purple
Mar 12	Second Sunday in Lent	Purple
Mar 19	Third Sunday in Lent	Purple
Mar 26	Fourth Sunday in Lent	Purple
Apr 2	Fifth Sunday in Lent	Purple
Apr 9	Sunday of the Passion	Scarlet/Purple
Apr 10	Monday in Holy Week	Scarlet/Purple
Apr 11	Tuesday in Holy Week	Scarlet/Purple
Apr 12	Wednesday in Holy Week	Scarlet/Purple

Three Days

Apr 13	Maundy Thursday	Scarlet/White
Apr 14	Good Friday	None
Apr 15/16	Resurrection of Our Lord	White/Gold

Easter

Apr 23	Second Sunday of Easter	White
Apr 30	Third Sunday of Easter	White
May 7	Fourth Sunday of Easter	White
May 14	Fifth Sunday of Easter	White
May 21	Sixth Sunday of Easter	White
May 25	Ascension of Our Lord	White
May 28	Seventh Sunday of Easter	White
June 4	Day of Pentecost	Red

Time after Pentecost

June 11	The Holy Trinity	White
June 18	Lectionary 11	Green
June 25	Lectionary 12	Green
July 2	Lectionary 13	Green
July 9	Lectionary 14	Green
July 16	Lectionary 15	Green
July 23	Lectionary 16	Green
July 30	Lectionary 17	Green
Aug 6	Lectionary 18	Green
Aug 13	Lectionary 19	Green
Aug 20	Lectionary 20	Green
Aug 27	Lectionary 21	Green
Sept 3	Lectionary 22	Green
Sept 10	Lectionary 23	Green
Sept 17	Lectionary 24	Green
Sept 24	Lectionary 25	Green
Oct 1	Lectionary 26	Green
Oct 8	Lectionary 27	Green
Oct 9	Day of Thanksgiving (Canada)	Green
Oct 15	Lectionary 28	Green
Oct 22	Lectionary 29	Green
Oct 29	Reformation Sunday	Red
Oct 29	Lectionary 30	Green
Nov 5	All Saints Sunday	White
Nov 5	Lectionary 31	Green
Nov 12	Lectionary 32	Green
Nov 19	Lectionary 33	Green
Nov 23	Day of Thanksgiving (USA)	Green
Nov 26	Christ the King (*Lect. 34*)	White/*Green*

Introduction

Welcome to the 2017 edition

With this edition of *Sundays and Seasons* we begin another three-year lectionary cycle. Maybe you have been relying on *Sundays and Seasons* since its inception twenty-two years ago. Perhaps you are encountering it for the first time. You are welcome here! As it has from the beginning, the Sundays and Seasons family of resources continues to support week-by-week planning for Lutherans with content and ideas shaped by the Revised Common Lectionary, the church year, and the assembly gathered around word and sacrament. Or, to say it the way its first editor, Samuel Torvend, said it, "*Sundays and Seasons* points us to that merciful place of encounter where God comes to abide among us in the holy gospel and the sacraments of grace: the worshiping assembly."

Sundays and Seasons has expanded beyond a single print volume into a family of resources that includes a robust online planning tool, sundaysandseasons.com (see a list of the whole family on page 2 of this volume). In 2014, we introduced *Sundays and Seasons: Preaching*, an annual print resource that encourages and provides help for lectionary preaching, taking into account all the readings for the day, in addition to the rest of the service and the day itself in the church year. For each day, someone writing from the perspective of a scholar addresses the question, "What would I want my pastor to know about these readings, this day, in approaching the sermon-writing task?" And a practicing preacher—a different one for each day—provides ideas for ways to craft a sermon that compellingly confronts the worshiping assembly with law and gospel in the vital Lutheran tradition.

Reformation 500

Not only does this year mark the beginning of another lectionary cycle, it also brings us to the observance of the five hundredth anniversary of the Reformation. In this year's edition you will find helps and suggestions throughout the publication that will prepare your worshiping community for this significant moment in the life of the church. The three articles that begin this volume consider various aspects of this observance: how the Gospel of Matthew informs preaching and planning; how we might organize our prayers for the church during this Reformation 500 year; and how the hymn of the day is a particular Reformation inheritance for Lutherans. Each seasonal

introduction also suggests ways in which congregations might prepare to observe this milestone anniversary. Look for the "Reformation 500" section in each. The seasonal materials for Autumn (pp. 249-255) consider Reformation observances in detail and provide many practical helps. This year's prayers of intercession, particularly the petition for the church, have been crafted with Reformation themes in mind.

With the whole church

This resource would not exist without the creative talents of many people across the church. Those who create content for *Sundays and Seasons* are people just like you. They are pastors, musicians, associates in ministry, members of worship committees and altar guilds, seminary professors, visual artists, diaconal ministers, and deaconesses. They work full time, part time, or are volunteers in their churches. They serve large and small congregations and campus ministries in rural areas, small towns, cities, and suburbs in the United States, Canada, and abroad. They come from various cultural contexts, and with different approaches to worship in word and sacrament. Over the past two decades literally hundreds of people have contributed to *Sundays and Seasons*. Here's this year's group.

Visual art

Christina Saj (cover art) has had a longtime fascination with spiritual objects and universal symbols. Using their formal and structural elements as a departure point, she creates paintings in which the symbols can be recognized and reinvented so they may reflect the character of the time in which they were created. Christina lives and works in Cedar Grove, New Jersey. www.christinasaj.com. **Gertrud Mueller Nelson** (interior art) grew up in St. Paul, Minnesota. She is an illustrator, author, speaker, and designer. Montessori, the domestic church and Jung's psychology are often subjects of her lectures and writing. She has written and/or illustrated thirteen books including the best seller *To Dance with God* (Paulist Press, 1986). Best of all, she is the Oma of three grandchildren. Gertrud lives in San Diego.

Annual and seasonal materials

Troy M. Troftgruben (introduction to Matthew) is assistant professor of New Testament at Wartburg Theological

Seminary in Dubuque, Iowa, an ordained minister of the ELCA, and author of the newest Book of Faith study on Matthew (Augsburg Fortress, 2016). **Gail Ramshaw** (praying for the church universal in 2017; thanksgivings at the table for Reformation 500), a Lutheran laywoman, studies and crafts liturgical language from her home outside of Washington, D.C. She recently authored *More Days for Praise: Festivals and Commemorations in Evangelical Lutheran Worship* (Augsburg Fortress, 2016). **Mark Mummert** (hymn of the day as Reformation inheritance) is minister of music and communications at Zion Lutheran, York, Pennsylvania. He was the 2015 distinguished visiting cantor at Lutheran Theological Seminary at Gettysburg. **Jon Niketh** (preparing for Advent) serves as pastor of First Lutheran in Lynn, Massachusetts on Boston's north shore, and chairs the New England Synod's worship team. **Emily Hartner** (midweek Advent series) is pastor of St. Mark's Lutheran in Charlotte, North Carolina. She is married to Ian and her social media posts primarily feature their two adorable French bulldogs. **Michael Coffey** (Blue Christmas) serves as pastor of First English Lutheran in Austin, Texas, and is author of *Mystery without Rhyme or Reason: Poetic Reflections on the Revised Common Lectionary.* **Anne Edison-Albright** (preparing for Christmas) is a pastor celebrating nine years of writing for *Sundays and Seasons*. Next year: cake! **Richard Bruxvoort Colligan** (Christmas calls to worship) is a freelance psalmist bringing adventurous songs to the wider church. He's part of the body at Emanuel Lutheran in Strawberry Point, Iowa. **Marissa Sotos** (preparing for the time after Epiphany) is a graduate of the Lutheran School of Theology at Chicago who loves all things beautiful and liturgical. She lives in Minneapolis. **D. Foy Christopherson** (preparing for Lent) is pastor for worship and the arts, hospitality, and pastoral care at Central Lutheran, Minneapolis. **Lynn Bulock** (midweek Lenten series) is a diaconal minister in Thousand Oaks, California. She is a wife, mother, grandmother, writer, and advocate for mental health issues. **Miriam Schmidt** (preparing for the Three Days) serves as pastor/priest of All Saints in Big Sky (Montana), a shared ministry of the Episcopal and Lutheran (ELCA) churches. **Kevin Anderson** (preparing for Easter) is director for worship and music at St. Philip Lutheran in Mount Dora, Florida. **Alex Raabe** (preparing for Summer) is a church planter at Table of Mercy in Austin, Texas who is passionate about vintage religious kitsch, postmodernity, Jesus, and cream soda. **Craig M. Mueller** (preparing for Autumn) is pastor of Holy Trinity Lutheran in Chicago and is interested in the intersection of liturgy, preaching, virtuality, and outreach to the millennial generation. **Bradley E. Schmeling** (seasonal worship texts for Autumn) serves as senior pastor at Gloria Dei Lutheran in St. Paul. **Karen Bates-Olson** (preparing for November) serves as pastor to the wonderful people of Resurrection Lutheran in Tacoma, Washington. She and her family love the North "wet."

Prayers of intercession

Jennifer Baker-Trinity is an associate in ministry and church musician who leads the people's song at Beaver Lutheran in Beaver Springs, Pennsylvania. **Rev. Dr. Lawrence James Clark II** is senior pastor of St. Mark Evangelical Lutheran in Chicago. **Brett Davis** is associate pastor of Muhlenberg Lutheran in Harrisonburg, Virginia. Pastor **Julie Kanarr** serves Christ Lutheran in Belfair, Washington. In addition to writing, she enjoys bicycling, camping, and sea kayaking. **Jean Larson** lives in Missoula, Montana, with her husband and her horse. After 34 years in ministry, she trained with Auburn Seminary and coaches her colleagues (jeanlarsoncoaching.com). Diaconal minister **Jennifer Manis** serves at Lutheran Campus Ministry in Raleigh, North Carolina. She encounters God's peace in the swimming pool and eating with friends. **Rachel Manke** is a pastor in Richmond, Virginia. She teaches music and plays the ukulele. **Kyle Schiefelbein** earned his PhD in liturgical studies from Graduate Theological Union and is a member of St. Mark's Lutheran in San Francisco. **Lynn Bulock** (see seasonal materials) also contributed prayers of intercession to this volume.

Ideas for the day

Tim Brown is the senior pastor of Good Shepherd Lutheran in Raleigh. He loves beer, writing, his wife and two boys, and brevity. **Yehiel Curry** is the seventh child born to Regina Curry. He has been husband to Lashonda for twenty years and is a proud empty-nesting father of three awesome daughters. **Melody Eastman** is a parish pastor in Illinois. In her spare time she inflicts her bodhrán (drum) playing on tolerant trad Irish music sessions. **Heidi Heimgartner** is a parish pastor in Blooming Prairie, Minnesota. She and her spouse parent two elementary-aged sons who give great sermon feedback. **Jim Honig** is pastor of Faith Evangelical Lutheran in Glen Ellyn, Illinois and loves pastoral ministry, reading, writing, and the outdoors. His new passion is serving as a prairie restoration volunteer at Nachusa National Grasslands. **Rebecca Liberty** has served in congregations and campus ministries in the western United States and is now pastor of Redeemer Lutheran in Bangor, Maine. **Bekki Lohrmann** is serving in her second year as pastor at Faith Lutheran in Joliet, Illinois. She studied at the Lutheran School of Theology at Chicago and Valparaiso University. **Henry Martinez** is country coordinator for the ELCA's Young Adults in Global Mission program in Australia. He loves cooking and being a dad. **Rev. Lucille "Ce Cee" Mills** is program associate for African Descent Ministries for the ELCA. She lives in Greensboro, North Carolina. At press time, **Alissa Oleson** was serving her pastoral internship at St. Paul Lutheran in Arlington, Massachusetts. **Katya Ouchakof** serves as co-pastor of Lake Edge Lutheran in Madison, Wisconsin. She enjoys canoeing, knitting, Star Wars, the Bible, and her family. **Julia Seymour** serves as pastor of Lutheran Church of

Hope in Anchorage, Alaska. Along with family time, she enjoys reading, outdoor walks, and crocheting. **Harvard Stephens Jr.** is dean of the chapel at the Lutheran School of Theology at Chicago. He is also a tai chi instructor and jazz musician. **William Storm** is a first call pastor at Memorial Drive Lutheran in Houston, Texas. He is excited to be a first time contributor to *Sundays and Seasons*. **Paul Walters** is pastor of Lutheran Church of the Master in Troy, Michigan. He is a husband, father of three boys, and a knight of Sufferlandria. **Michael Coffey** (see seasonal materials) also contributed ideas for the day to this volume.

Other weekly materials

Sharolyn Browning (let the children come) is a Godly Play storyteller and trainer. She is awaiting her first call as a pastor in the ELCA, after having worked with children and their families for more than twenty years. She holds a certificate in the spiritual guidance of children. **Gail Ramshaw** (images in the readings; connections with the liturgy), a Lutheran laywoman, is the author of *Treasures Old and New: Images in the Lectionary*, *Christian Worship: 100,000 Sundays of Symbols and Rituals*, and *What Is Christianity?* (Fortress Press, 2002, 2009, 2013).

Music suggestions

Andrea Baxter (children's choir) serves as the associate director for music at Trinity Evangelical Lutheran in Lansdale, Pennsylvania where she directs a graded children and youth music program. **Lorraine S. Brugh** (global) is professor of music and director of chapel music at Valparaiso University. She serves as executive director of the University's Institute of Liturgical Studies, which annually brings church leaders across the country together to study and reflect upon worship practices. **Cheryl Dieter** (psalmody) is minister of worship and music at Trinity Lutheran in Valparaiso, Indiana, and business manager for the Association of Lutheran Church Musicians. **Chad Fothergill** (keyboard/instrumental) is a university fellow and PhD student in musicology at Temple University,

Philadelphia, and has served as keyboardist, conductor, and composer for congregations in Minnesota, Iowa, and Pennsylvania. **Michael J. Glasgow** (handbell) is an award-winning composer and internationally recognized conductor working in handbell, organ, orchestral and choral settings. He is known for his high energy, positive spirit, and musical integrity (www.michaeljglasgow.com). **Zebulon M. Highben** (choral) is a conductor, composer, and Lutheran church musician who teaches at a Presbyterian liberal arts college—Muskingum University in New Concord, Ohio. **Mark Mummert** (hymns) is minister of music and communications at Zion Lutheran, York, Pennsylvania. He was the 2015 distinguished visiting cantor at Lutheran Theological Seminary at Gettysburg. **Omaldo Perez** (praise/contemporary) has served Lutheran congregations in New Jersey, Arizona, Washington, and now Ohio, where he is the music director and organist at Zoar Lutheran in Perrysburg.

You make it happen

Sundays and Seasons continues to be a collaborative endeavor each year. In our editorial conversations here at Augsburg Fortress we regularly evaluate the scope, format, and quality of the content provided in these pages. Your feedback, collected from you firsthand at events around this church, from postings in various forms of social media, from phone calls and emails to our sales and service representatives, and from surveys, helps us make decisions about how to adjust content so it is even more helpful, or, frankly, to leave it alone because it is doing its job. You, dear partners in ministry, make this resource happen. I welcome your ideas for future content, your suggestions for potential contributors (maybe you!), and your constructive feedback. Thank you for the trust you place in the changing roster of contributors who offer their time and talent to the whole church through *Sundays and Seasons*. Even more, thank you for the many and various ways in which you care for the Sunday assembly and its worship of the triune God.

Suzanne K. Burke, general editor

The Year of Matthew

Matthew's gospel—the focus of year A—is often beloved, disliked, or a little of both. It is beloved for how it spotlights Jesus as teacher, gives practical ethical instructions, and includes some of Jesus' most influential statements (e.g., the Beatitudes). It is disliked for how harshly Jesus characterizes religious leaders and how often he speaks of judgment and hell (Gehenna). At the end of the day, Matthew's gospel often plays a significant role in people's experiences of the New Testament and of the Christian faith, and with mixed impressions. Neither as enigmatic as Mark nor as attuned to the Greco-Roman world as Luke, Matthew's most distinctive trait is likely how it highlights the Messiah's Jewish heritage from the very start: "An account of the genealogy of Jesus the Messiah, the son of David, the son of Abraham" (1:1). For this reason Matthew's gospel is a fitting "bridge" between the Hebrew Bible and the New Testament, between the books that precede and follow in the Christian canon.

Selections from Matthew appear on Sundays and festivals in year A more than forty times, depending on one's accounting. Simply by using the assigned readings, one can hear about 60 percent of this gospel over the course of the lectionary year—no small thing since Matthew is one of the longest books in the New Testament. Here are some important considerations for engaging this gospel in the year ahead.

Matthew's Gospel in Historic Use

Throughout history, Matthew has without question been the "First Gospel" for Christians on many levels. Since earliest times it appears first in the canonical order, likely due to the tradition that it was the first gospel written (Irenaeus, *Adv. Haer.* 3.1.1; Eusebius, *Eccl. Hist.* 3.24.5-7; 3.39.16). Matthew also features a great deal of something highly esteemed by early Christians: Jesus' teaching, organized into designated sections (e.g., 5:1—7:28). For these reasons, until just a century ago Matthew received the most historic attention. For example, Augustine's *Harmony of the Gospels* was simply a volume on Matthew followed by another on non-Matthean gospel pericopes. And the medieval lectionary features Matthew more than any other New Testament writing. Martin Luther expressed a preference for John among the gospels ("Prefaces to the New Testament"). But the ecclesiastical culture of Luther's day esteemed

Matthew highly, making Luther very familiar with preaching and teaching the First Gospel (see, e.g., *Luther's Works 68, Sermons on the Gospel of St. Matthew 19–24*).

Background on Matthew's Gospel

Early tradition credits the disciple Matthew with writing this gospel originally in Aramaic, but most scholars today deem this unlikely. The narrative relies heavily on Mark (preserving about 90 percent of it) and shows no evidence of being written in a language other than Greek. More likely, an anonymous Christian steeped in Israel's religious heritage composed the gospel from the context of a Christian community (18:15-22) that valued the abiding significance of the Jewish law (5:17; 17:24-27; 23:2-3). Where this community was located is unknown, but cues in the narrative (2:23; 4:24; 15:22) lead many scholars to suggest Syria, in a city like Antioch. The author likely wrote around 80–90 CE, at a time when Mark's gospel was circulating, deviant teachers were accumulating (Matt. 7:25; 13:21-22; 24:10-12), and interest in Christian teaching was escalating (cf. the *Didache*). Harsh characterizations of religious leaders and "their" synagogues (e.g., Matt. 6:2, 5; 10:17) imply that a rupture between church and synagogue may have recently occurred. These traits make the gospel uniquely poised to navigate the polarities of Jew-Gentile and synagogue-church by embracing both "what is new and what is old" (13:52) in a way that is distinctively Jewish-Christian—or Christian-Jewish.

Themes
Jesus and the heritage of Israel

Unlike other gospels, Matthew engages Jesus' Jewish theological heritage with an eye to prioritizing "the lost sheep of the house of Israel" (10:5). Unique within the New Testament, Matthew's gospel emphasizes that Jesus has not come to abolish but to fulfill the Jewish law (5:17-18; cf. Rom. 3:31; Gal. 5:14). Clues within the narrative even imply that Matthew's community continued to observe the sabbath (24:20) and Jewish dietary laws (15:17; cf. Mark 7:19). Clearly questions regarding the enduring significance of the Torah were of utmost importance to Matthew's community.

The teaching gospel

As many scholars have noticed, Matthew's gospel focuses especially on Jesus' teaching. The narrative revolves around five didactic discourses (5:1–7:27; 10:1-42; 13:1-52; 18:1-35; 24:1–25:46) that all focus on matters of discipleship. Matthew's gospel also models a deliberate catechetical progression: calling disciples (4:18-22), instructing them (5:1ff.), and finally authorizing them to teach others (28:18-20). As Paul Minear observes, these features make Matthew's gospel uniquely designed to be optimally helpful to teachers in Christian congregations (Minear, *Matthew: The Teacher's Gospel* [Eugene, OR: Wipf and Stock, 2003], 3).

The nature of discipleship

If Jesus is the teacher par excellence, then his followers are those trained—or "discipled" (*mathēteutheis*)—for the reign of heaven (13:52). As the narrative shows, Jesus' disciples are not merely informed intellectually but *formed* holistically: to practice humility, authentic piety, service to the "least of these," and aversion to social recognition. As the story of the disciple Matthew shows, Jesus calls followers from among "tax collectors and sinners" as a sign of God's mercy (9:10-13). Unique to this gospel, the disciples are frequently called "you of little faith" (e.g., 8:26), which is not inherently a criticism: they do reflect *some* faith! And ultimately they are called and sent out as those embodying the ministry of Jesus himself (10:24-25a; 28:18-20).

Christian community

Matthew's gospel is the only New Testament writing in which Jesus explicitly names and instructs the "church" (*ekklēsia*), and his instructions are both profound and practical. Jesus "builds" the church with the assurance that "the gates of Hades will not prevail against it" (16:18). But at the same time this community embraces sinners (9:13) and doubters (28:17), who perennially struggle with temptations (18:6-9), disciplinary issues (18:15-20), and challenges extending forgiveness (18:21-35). Indeed, the fact that the teaching discourse most focused on community (18:1-35) devotes so much space to forgiveness is itself instructive. Far from an abstract meditation, Matthew's gospel is at once theological and practical regarding the practice of Christian community.

The abiding presence of God

Matthew's gospel alone calls Jesus "Emmanuel, which means 'God is with us'" (1:23). More than simply giving Jesus a name, this gospel associates God's presence with Jesus so much that he is rightly and regularly worshiped (e.g., 2:11; 8:2; 9:18). Even more, the narrative implies that the divine presence continues in the world long afterward through gathered believers (18:20), "the least of these" brothers and sisters (25:40), and by virtue of Jesus' promise: "I am with you always, to the end of the age" (28:20). In ways that effectively address questions about God's perceived absence in the world, Matthew's gospel professes that God is in fact "with us."

Peter's prominence

Despite the traditional association of Peter with Mark's gospel (Eusebius, *Eccl. Hist.* 3.39.15), Peter plays a more prominent role in Matthew's. In the First Gospel alone does Peter walk on water (14:28-31), raise questions about forgiveness (18:21-22; also 17:24-27), and most importantly stand at the center of Jesus' building his church (16:17-20). What precisely Jesus means by "on this rock (*petra*) I will build my church" (16:18, cf. *Petros*, "Peter") is debated, but at the very least Matthew's gospel portrays Peter as representing both the follies (14:28-31) and future (16:17-20) of Jesus' church.

Areas of Caution and Special Focus
Taking Jesus' countercultural ethics seriously

Many of Jesus' teachings in Matthew—like in the Sermon on the Mount (5:1—7:27)—seem idealistic, if not impossible. And many Protestants respond by evaluating them as "law" that aims simply to foster a keen sense of human incapacity. But this interpretation misses the potential of Jesus' radical ethics for countercultural change. Christian reformers throughout history have regularly found inspiration from Jesus' ethics in Matthew's gospel (especially the Sermon on the Mount) for guiding the values of Christian community: for example, Dietrich Bonhoeffer, André Trocmé, Brother Roger of Taizé, and Martin Luther King Jr. Although these ethics can seem at odds with a theology centered in grace, they inform in remarkable fashion how a graced people can in turn respond by incarnating radical grace in community for others.

Judgment and polemics

Jesus' teachings in Matthew's gospel reflect a more judgment-oriented vision and more references to hell (*Gehenna*) than is common for some modern Christians (e.g., 5:22, 29-30; 13:24-30, 36-43; 23:15, 33). These emphases reflect the promise of an eschatological judgment that will ultimately fulfill God's righteous standards. And while uncomfortable to many moderns, these texts aim less to condemn and more to encourage faithfulness in disciples, whose deeds will ultimately be shown for their true worth. Despite the occasional harshness of such judgment language, Matthew's overarching vision strives primarily to show disciples how to be faithful, not how to fail.

Honoring our Jewish sisters and brothers

Negative characterizations of Jewish religious leaders appear often in Matthew's gospel—associating them with vipers, hell, and the devil (12:34; 15:13; 23:33). There is also the unfortunate response of the crowd to Pilate's resolve to crucify Jesus: "His blood be on us and on our children!" (27:25). These features have played their part in fostering the anti-Semitic sentiments of past centuries among Western Christianity. A poignant example of these sentiments is Martin Luther, who expressed beautifully the nature of Christian liberty ("On the Freedom of a Christian") and later called for violence against Jews ("On the Jews and Their Lies"). In the shadow of the Holocaust, we do well to read Matthew with greater sensitivity. Toward this end, here are some suggestions. First, the Jewish people implicated by Matthew's narrative are a particular group, with no direct correlation to actual people today. Second, the rhetorical aim of Jesus' harsh words is typically not to condemn outsiders but to exhort insiders to live differently (23:1-12). Third, much of the vitriol of these words reflects the pain experienced later by Matthew's community, the product of intrafamilial fighting among Jews of diverging faiths. As social psychologists today observe, sibling conflicts can often be some of the severest—and outsiders have little right to cast stones one way or the other. Fourth, most of Matthew's condemnations of Jewish people come from the mouth of a Jewish man who himself experienced the utmost condemnation for the sake of all humanity. In 2017 as we observe the 500th anniversary of the Reformation, we honor Luther well by honoring the eighth commandment (on bearing false witness) regarding our Jewish siblings better than Luther did in his day.

Troy M. Troftgruben
Wartburg Theological Seminary

For the Church Universal: Praying in 2017

The classic Christian liturgy often replaces one with two. One single word, one short phrase, one biblical reference, is recognized as inadequate, as only half the truth: so the liturgy gives us two words, two phrases, two biblical citations. To celebrate Christmas, the lectionary gives us Luke 2 on Christmas Eve and John 1 on Christmas Day. The twoness helps us enter into the fullness of the mystery. On Passion Sunday, we hear from the synoptic gospels, and on Good Friday, we listen to John. The two gospels deliver a richer testimony to the passion and death of Christ than can any single gospel. At the eucharistic table each week, we sing both the song of the angels—"Holy, holy, holy"—and the chant of the Jerusalem crowd—"Hosanna! Hosanna!" Through the dual song we can envision in the bread and wine on the table both God on a heavenly throne and Jesus on his way to the cross. Many historic prayers incorporated this same double truth by addressing "almighty and merciful God." These adjectives are not meant to be synonymous. Rather, "almighty" and "merciful" suggest opposite qualities that are surprisingly combined in our God.

The prayers of intercession offer more opportunity to enact liturgical twoness. Following the advice of *Evangelical Lutheran Worship*, the prayers of intercession begin with a prayer "for the church universal, its ministry, and the mission of the gospel" (p. 105). This petition may well utilize a printed resource as a starter, like the yeast to your dough. Each assembly will then personalize the text; as the rubric says, the prayers are to be "prepared locally for each occasion." So here is the twoness that characterizes the intercessions: generality and specificity. First comes the universal, then comes

the particular. A broad topic or a petition that was previously crafted serves as the body for the clothing provided each week by the local assembly. The wide generality connects us with everyone else who is praying this petition, while the local application arises from our neighborhood this very week.

The category "the church universal" can be opened up by listing a specific denomination across the sea or across the street that for some reason is in the news; by naming your own and other church's leaders; by commemorating occasions of baptism, confirmation, or ordination in your own or in sister congregations; by citing mission sites here and abroad. "For its ministry" is a skeleton that wants enfleshing: we can name pastors, teachers, diaconal ministers, church musicians, committee members, missionaries, the concerns of old congregations with few members, the hopes of newly established assemblies. "For the mission of the gospel" can invoke the church's many mission activities across town and across the globe, those feeding the hungry or housing the refugee, those serving in care facilities and ecological efforts, those tending the very young or the very old. As in the early church, our prayers must once again include those Christians whose mission brings them face-to-face with persecution and death. The intercessor ought to be sure to check the news on Saturday or even Sunday morning to ensure the prayer about the church universal is not omitting something important.

On many weeks during this new liturgical year, the calendar of commemorations can suggest specificity to the petition for the church. Here are some examples:

12/4/16	John of Damascus	Christian church artists and hymnwriters
2/5/17	The Martyrs of Japan	Christians facing martyrdom
3/12/17	Gregory the Great	Bishops and leaders in all Christian denominations
4/9/17	Dietrich Bonhoeffer	Christians who oppose evil in government policies
4/23/17	Toyohiko Kagawa	Christians who work for peace and justice
5/21/17	Helena	Christians who assist with building new churches
6/25/17	Augsburg Confession	Teachers of Christian theology
7/23/17	Birgitta of Sweden	Christians who provide for the poor
8/13/17	F. Nightingale/C. Maass	Christians who minister as nurses and doctors
8/20/17	Bernard of Clairvaux	For a deepening of our lives of prayer
9/17/17	Hildegard of Bingen	Christians who attend to the health of the earth
10/15/17	Teresa of Avila	Christians who work to reform the church

As well, the liturgical year itself suggests some specifics to add to the "church" petition. The prayers at the Easter Vigil can include all those being baptized that night, and on the Day of Pentecost, petition can be made for all who hear the preaching of the word. So many specifics: and here we are considering only the first petition!

Many suggestions are being made for how during 2017 the worship of Lutherans might be influenced by remembrance of the events of 1517. Here is one listing in which all the eighty-four member churches of the Lutheran World Federation (LWF) are assigned to the intercessions throughout the year. Countries with large Lutheran churches are listed by themselves, and those with a smaller Lutheran population are grouped together. By adding these churches to the "church universal" petition, the year of the commemoration of the Reformation can direct our minds to all the world's Lutherans.

11/26/16	Advent 1	Angola, Zimbabwe
12/4/16	Advent 2	Italy, Croatia
12/11/16	Advent 3	India
12/18/16	Advent 4	Austria
12/25/16	Christmas Day	Israel, Palestine
1/1/17	Name of Jesus	Canada
1/8/17	Baptism of Our Lord	Ethiopia
1/15/17	Epiphany 2	Tanzania
1/22/17	Epiphany 3	Finland
1/29/17	Epiphany 4	Central African Republic
2/5/17	Epiphany 5	Japan, South Korea
2/12/17	Epiphany 6	Serbia, Slovakia, Slovenia
2/19/17	Epiphany 7	Malaysia
2/26/17	Transfiguration	Nigeria
3/5/17	Lent 1	Guatemala, Philippines
3/12/17	Lent 2	Ireland, United Kingdom
3/19/17	Lent 3	Cameroon
3/26/17	Lent 4	El Salvador, Nicaragua, Venezuela
4/2/17	Lent 5	Russian Federation
4/9/17	Passion Sunday	Indonesia
4/16/17	Easter Day	The staff of the LWF
4/23/17	Easter 2	Namibia
4/30/17	Easter 3	Iceland, Lithuania
5/7/17	Easter 4	Hong Kong, Taiwan
5/14/17	Easter 5	Liberia, South Africa
5/21/17	Easter 6	Netherlands
5/28/17	Easter 7	France, Switzerland
6/4/17	Day of Pentecost	Democratic Republic of Congo, Rwanda
6/11/17	Holy Trinity	United States
6/18/17	Lectionary 11	Australia, Eritrea
6/25/17	Lectionary 12	Bolivia, Brazil
7/2/17	Lectionary 13	Papua New Guinea
7/9/17	Lectionary 14	Botswana, Czech Republic
7/16/17	Lectionary 15	Costa Rica, Honduras, Peru
7/23/17	Lectionary 16	Sweden
7/30/17	Lectionary 17	Norway
8/6/17	Lectionary 18	Madagascar
8/13/17	Lectionary 19	Poland
8/20/17	Lectionary 20	Bangladesh, Nepal
8/27/17	Lectionary 21	Ghana, Senegal, Sierra Leone
9/3/17	Lectionary 22	Denmark
9/10/17	Lectionary 23	Colombia, Kenya
9/17/17	Lectionary 24	Belgium, Zambia
9/24/17	Lectionary 25	Myanmar, Thailand
10/1/17	Lectionary 26	Malawi, Mozambique
10/8/17	Lectionary 27	Republic of the Congo, Singapore
10/15/17	Lectionary 28	Argentina, Chile
10/22/17	Lectionary 29	Romania, Sri Lanka
10/29/17	Lectionary 30	Germany
11/5/17	Lectionary 31	Ecuador, Guyana, Suriname
11/12/17	Lectionary 32	Latvia
11/19/17	Lectionary 33	Hungry
11/26/17	Christ the King	Estonia, Mexico

Because leading prayers is not the same as reading a petition, the persons who serve as intercessors will want to practice praying such petitions aloud so that the names are read smoothly and can function as prayer, rather than as the week's geography lesson. Perhaps using this list during 2017 will encourage us to develop an ecumenical list of Christian denominations to pray for during 2018.

Twoness. The intercessions can include both the breadth of the universal and the precision of the particular. In 1 Kings 3, Solomon asks God for the one gift of wisdom, and in 1 Kings 8, he pleads for God's help in times of famine, plague, blight, mildew, locust, caterpillar, siege, sickness, battle, captivity. First comes a broad topic, then follows the list of items. To assist our assemblies in following along in the intercessions, it is helpful to organize our lengthy lists of needs according to the standard categories: the church, the creation, the nations, the needy, all who suffer, and our local concerns, all of which are concluded by thanksgiving for those who have died in the faith. Yet the comprehensive categories call out for precise details, carefully selected so that the hearts and minds of the whole assembly are gathered into the prayer, like fish caught up in the net, like the many fruits on a tree. In John 17, Jesus prays for all those who believe in him. Let us follow Christ in prayer, as best we can.

Gail Ramshaw
Liturgical scholar

Hymn of the Day as Reformation Inheritance

In a Lutheran seminary course on Christian worship, a prominent professor had spent the full semester tracing the historical and theological roots of worship on the pattern of the Sunday assembly. He was particularly convincing with one of his many themes of the course: all Christian worship is derived from a common shape, which is an ecumenical inheritance. On the final day of class, when students were invited to ask any question, a Lutheran student asked, "What, then, makes Christian worship specifically Lutheran?" The professor paused a moment to collect an answer. Then he offered this: "I suppose it is the way Lutherans sing in Christian worship. But by 'the way we sing,' I do not mean necessarily the fervor of our singing or the grand repertoire of song available to us, or even the amount of music we sing in each service. I mean the purpose of our song is perhaps different. For instance, the placement and purpose of the hymn of the day is unique to Lutherans in the ecumenical shape of the Sunday and festival liturgy of Holy Communion."

The placement and purpose of a hymn that unites the proclamation of the scripture texts and preaching for the day with the spirit of the season and the contextual character of each assembly is a Reformation inheritance. This central hymn is a communal proclamation of the gospel, parallel to the proclamation of an address given to those who have been called to speak such a word on our behalf in sermons or homilies. According to the rubrics of *Evangelical Lutheran Worship*, the hymn of the day is a central element of the liturgy of Holy Communion (p. 92).

Before the Reformation, extrabiblical texts were sometimes added to the alleluia that was sung between the reading from the appointed epistles and gospel readings. These texts, called tropes or sequences, formed a repertoire of sung proclamation to be sung by the schola or choir. In Luther's modest reforms of the mass, a hymn to be sung by the assembly invoking the Holy Spirit was placed between the assigned epistle and gospel readings. Further, a primary hymn chosen to correspond to the assigned scripture texts was placed either after the gospel reading and prior to the preaching or after the preaching of the sermon. By the time of J. S. Bach two hundred years later, this calendar of hymns appointed for every Sunday and festival of the one-year lectionary was established, such that the flourishing of works based on these appointed hymns resulted in cantatas and organ preludes.

As we commemorate the anniversary of the Reformation, it seems wise to recover this inheritance as fully as possible. Such a recovery would not mean that every congregation should use the same calendar of hymns at all times. Rather, each assembly could select the primary hymn of the day, chosen with the guidance of worship planning aids like this volume, and commit to singing at least this hymn each week. This primary hymn might also receive the most attention from the musicians and musical groups of the congregation.

In some places, this primary hymn of the day is called a sermon hymn. Such a title is limited, as it implies that the hymn relates only to the sermon and not the whole day's worship. It is easy to imagine, if the worship planning in a congregation is done largely by a pastor who will be asked to spend considerable time preparing a sermon for the liturgy, that he or she might want the hymn to correspond to the sermon as best as possible. However, a preacher cannot fully discern the movement of the Spirit in time to adequately name the primary hymn of the day for a liturgy, particularly if it is to receive the best support, leadership, and rendering of the musicians and the full assembly. It would be better to plan the list of the primary hymn of the day for each Sunday and festival of the year well in advance, even three, six, or ninth months in advance, to allow for thorough preparation. Then, when such a list is determined by the worship planners, a preacher can open the hymnal to the primary hymn and consult it as "richer fare" to open up the scriptures as the sermon is being prepared.

Mark Mummert
Zion Lutheran, York, Pennsylvania

Advent

Preparing for Advent

Lectionary

"You know what time it is" (Rom. 13:11).

The cycle of the church year orders our time in Christian community around the central mystery of our faith: the life, death, and resurrection of Jesus Christ. Our experience of this mystery, however, is not linear—a simple narrative path from beginning to end. Our lives are full of endings and beginnings happening all at once, interspersed with waiting, lament, and hope.

The "now-and-not-yet" nature of the fulfillment of our hope in Christ is never more rhetorically real than in the season of Advent. In its great wisdom, the lectionary launches us into this wheel of time with a season that, much like our own lives, is full of endings and beginnings—and, of course, waiting.

While Advent has often been understood as Christmas's Lenten counterpart—a season of preparation for a particular feast—our readings in this season serve a deeper liturgical purpose than simply helping us resist the commercialization of the holiday season and more reverently celebrate Christmas. Advent is indeed a season of anticipation, but also of revolution: "The world is about to turn," as we sing in Rory Cooney's fiery paraphrase of the Magnificat (ELW 723). The readings in Advent prepare us to receive not only a new baby, but a new world where God's justice and mercy reign.

For this reason, the first Sunday of Advent begins not with a reference to Jesus' impending birth but with the "coming of the Son of Man" at an unexpected hour in Matthew 24. This text disrupts our sense of time by declaring that we don't, in fact, know what time it is—and need time to prepare. The prophecy in Isaiah 2 gives us hope for a world at peace, and Paul's encouragement in Romans 13 tells us "the day is near." And yet references to Noah and a thief in the night in the gospel reading give us the sense that the coming day of the Lord will be so bright it might singe our hair. Of course it won't. But we will be changed.

The readings on the second Sunday further develop this theme of conversion. From Isaiah foretelling a world where the "wolf shall live with the lamb," to Paul's admonition that Christians "live in harmony with one another," the readings this day are full of reconciliations that are impossible without a drastic change in the world order. In fact, the promise held out by these readings sounds perfectly ridiculous if left to human will or strength. But the change at hand is directed and empowered by the "Spirit of the Lord" (Isa. 11), the Spirit given in baptism, and of which John the Baptist is a herald (Matt. 3): Repent! Be cleansed! Bear fruit!

These are not soft and comforting words that echo the sentiments often expressed in the movies constantly rerun on cable television this month. They are piercing and disorienting words. And yet therein lies their beauty, as most people in worship on these Sundays are keenly aware that something is not right in the world—or within themselves, for that matter—and they are longing to be set free. They might also be longing to have language in worship that allows them to pray and sing for that freedom in community, if the church would give them the space and the permission.

This longing is perhaps perfectly captured on the third Sunday: "Are you the one who is to come," John asks through the disciples in Matthew 11:3, "or are we to wait for another?" But on this Sunday, sometimes called *Gaudete*, or "Rejoice" Sunday, the heaviness of our preparatory task begins to lift, and the fear and foreboding of the previous two Sundays starts giving way to joy—joy such that even the creation itself breaks forth into praise (Isa. 35). Mary's Magnificat (Luke 1:46-55) is an option as a response to the first reading on this day, calling us to rejoice with her in God's saving work. While the Mighty One's "bringing down" and "lifting up" may prove unsettling for the powerful, it will be received by the lowly as a blessing and a promise kept.

Only now, on the fourth Sunday of Advent, are we ready to hear of the Child. We have considered our world: its structures of power, its systems of justice and injustice; we have considered the earth: the land, the sea, and their creatures; and we have considered ourselves, and our relationship with the all these powers, places, and living things. We are now ready to be changed and receive the gift, for now we know what to look for: not a new program or politician or product to come and save us, but a sign that says, "God is with us" (Isa. 7, Matt. 1).

It's all here: hope, longing, fear, comfort, repentance, restoration, death, birth, endings, and beginnings. And like our lives, it doesn't all come at us in a tidy package. But over these four Sundays, the arc of the story is clear: the darkness is giving way to the light, the world is being reborn, and God is on the way.

Visual Environment

The readings in Advent are some of the most visually evocative of the entire church year. The prophecies from Isaiah paint a rich picture of a world made new by the promised coming of God: a new branch growing from an ancient tree, predators and prey playing together, weapons and ammunition disfigured into farming tools, crocuses blossoming and waters gushing in the desert, and a major highway construction project. The possibilities for drawing upon these images are seemingly endless. Add in the apocalyptic, baptismal, and birth imagery in the gospels—everything from pyrotechnics to gynecology—and you have a treasure trove of sights, sounds, smells, and other sensations to experiment with.

Rather than attempt to do artistic justice to all of these images—or even some of them—a congregation might adopt the "less is more" approach and focus on one particular image that can be developed and lived into over the course of the four Sundays in much the same way the Advent wreath functions in many congregations.

The worship environment, though, extends beyond symbols and pieces of artwork that exist in the space. The space itself can be a sign. Take, for instance, the image of a road prepared in the wilderness. How might the existing pathways in your worship space—or entire building—be adorned or modified to help the assembly experience this image more deeply? What if the traffic flow in the parking lot was reversed—or more daringly—the line at coffee hour? What if the gathering procession took a different and more extended or circuitous path than on an ordinary Sunday—and if the whole congregation was part of the procession? What if the worship space was reconfigured so that worshipers couldn't find their usual seats but were forced to experience the space in a different way?

While building an actual road through artistic means may be fun and even beneficial, how might this radical reorientation behind this image be practiced in ways that are not only admired by the congregation but that invite its full and active participation?

While much of the world does not observe Advent in cold weather, it will be winter in the United States and Canada when these readings are heard. We often think of bringing foliage, flowers, and other living things into the worship space during the summer. But doing so in the winter—when such bounty is not expected—is a way of lifting up the new and unexpected life prophesied in the Isaiah texts, and gives the assembly a visual focus when it makes its own sung response to this life in the psalms.

Other ideas for visually embodying the new world Christ is coming to create:

- A congregation could sponsor together with the local police department a "Swords into Plowshares Day," on which weapons could be traded in for food, clothing, job training, or access to other community resources that might seem inaccessible.
- A congregation could adopt an actual highway or stretch of road and take turns beautifying it.
- Go on a "crocus crawl" (an idea that first came to life at Valparaiso University through Pastor David Kehret), planting crocuses on the church property—or around the neighborhood with the proper permission—that will bud in unexpected places at springtime. This is also a way to visually connect Advent and Christmas with the promise of Easter.
- If a congregation uses or creates banners or any kind of blue draping materials, consider introducing them progressively. Make whatever is visible on the first Sunday of Advent look intentionally unfinished. People will ask why the altar guild didn't do its job. Such questions are good.

Music

If your congregation has not yet discovered the musical treasures in *Music Sourcebook: All Saints through Transfiguration* (Augsburg Fortress, 2013), do them a favor and stop reading this essay long enough to go purchase it. In the same way that the visual environment of a worship space has the power to inspire, challenge, and transform, so does music—and not just hymns! Rather than introducing more elements into the service, this resource provides musical options for singing what is already there in new and beautiful ways. Among them are:

- Sung prayer responses
- Taizé-style refrains inviting singers to slow down and breathe
- Advent canticles written in plain language with simple melodies
- A litany with the refrain "Stir up your power," drawing from the language in all four prayers of the day in Advent

If your congregation always sings "Let the vineyards be fruitful" as the bread and wine are brought forward, substitute it with "We Are Awaiting the Coming" (S536) or "Now Is the Moment to Wake from Sleep" (S537). If you end each petition in the intercessions with "Lord, in your mercy, hear our prayer," try singing "Maranatha! Come, Lord Jesus" (S532–S534). If your congregation prays evening prayer together during Advent, consider singing "Filled with Hope and Gratitude" (S528) as Mary's Song, or Ike Sturm's amazing jazz setting (S527). Instead of simply lighting a candle on the Advent wreath and speaking a prayer, surround the whole ritual action with Paul Friesen-Carper's "Thanksgiving for Light for Advent" (S524). When we hear familiar words in new ways, ours can be the eyes that are opened, the ears that are unstopped, and the tongues that sing for joy (Isa. 35:5-6).

We should not bemoan that many people want to sing Christmas hymns during this season, for their desire to sing them is a testament to the hymns' durability. Instead of debating whether it is "okay" to sing them, however, consider what could be lost by not singing the hymnody of Advent.

The readings in Advent conjure up a mixture of images and emotions that often intersect with what we are feeling in ourselves this time of year: longing, lament, judgment, hope, and promise. Advent hymns, with their sometimes solemn, sometimes joyful, always hopeful texts and melodies are uniquely poised to give voice to this full spectrum of praise and lament. How unfortunate if a congregation was deprived of the experience of praying and singing with their full hearts—and all that is within them—in order to only celebrate.

For a congregation that especially loves Christmas hymns, consider having a hymn festival on one of the twelve days of Christmas.

Reformation 500

"How is this Advent different from all other Advents?" Perhaps no Advent is ever the same. But this one will usher us into a year of commemorating the 500th anniversary of the Reformation: a global event that will involve not only celebrating the Lutheran theological heritage but also the ongoing work of reformation of our own church and steps toward reconciliation with other churches.

The theme of the report prepared by the joint Lutheran-Catholic Commemoration of the Reformation is titled "From Conflict to Communion." Five hundred years ago, those words would have sounded as impossible to hold together as the wolves sleeping with lambs and streams flowing through deserts that Isaiah prophesied!

It is precisely because of their seeming impossibility that Advent is a perfect time to lift them up. Lutherans and Roman Catholics sharing the eucharistic meal at the same altar? "When hell freezes over," our grandparents might have said. But Advent dares us to hope, to stay awake, and to bear fruit worthy of repentance—including for the unkind words and assumptions we have so often made about each other.

If we can hold out hope that the new world God is bringing about in Jesus Christ is indeed coming—and coming soon!—and with it will come "new highways opened, new protocols declared" (ELW 266), then even to this prayer of unity at the table we can add our own "Maranatha! Come, Lord Jesus."

Seasonal Checklist

- Order candles and greens for the Advent wreath. Consider a smaller, table-sized wreath for gatherings outside the main worship space.
- Recruit volunteers of all ages to decorate the worship space.
- If it is not your practice, try scheduling midweek morning or evening prayer each week in Advent.
- Use the Kyrie. Omit the canticle of praise. Explore and use *Music Sourcebook: All Saints through Transfiguration* (Augsburg Fortress, 2013).
- Select a musical setting of the liturgy that differs in its tone than what you would use during Christmas or Easter.
- Use the O Antiphons of Advent—if not during evening prayer from December 17–23, then at a special Advent vespers.

Worship Texts for Advent

Confession and Forgiveness

All may make the sign of the cross, the sign marked at baptism,
as the presiding minister begins.

Blessed be the holy Trinity, ✝ one God,
who comes to wake us from sleep,
who leads us into the light of grace.
Amen.

Let us prepare the way of the Lord
by confessing our sin against God and neighbor.

Silence for reflection and self-examination.

God of all time,
we confess that we have not prepared
for your merciful reign among us.
We ignore our neighbors in need
and fail in the labor of justice and peace.
In your mercy forgive us.
Grant us wisdom to welcome your light
and to seek the things that will endure
until Christ comes again in glory. Amen.

Comfort, O comfort my people,
says your God.
In ✝ Jesus Christ your sins are forgiven
and all things are made new.
Rejoice in this good news!
Amen.

Offering Prayer

Savior of the nations, come.
Make your home here in us.
Feed us with your love,
that our faith shine ever new
and our lives reveal your light.
Amen.

Invitation to Communion

Rejoice! Emmanuel shall come to you.
Share in the feast of salvation.

Prayer after Communion

God for whom we wait,
you come to us
in the broken bread and the cup we share.
Make us ready always
to welcome Christ into our hearts,
and send us forth to be your people in the world,
announcing your coming among us
in Jesus Christ our Lord.
Amen.

Blessing

May Christ, the Sun of righteousness, shine upon you
and scatter the darkness from before your path.
Almighty God, Father, ✝ Son, and Holy Spirit,
bless you now and forever.
Amen.

Dismissal

Go in peace. Prepare the way of the Lord.
Thanks be to God.

Seasonal Rites for Advent

The Advent Wreath

One of the best known customs for the season is the Advent wreath. The wreath and winter candle-lighting in the midst of growing darkness strengthen some of the Advent images found in the Bible. The unbroken circle of greens is clearly an image of everlasting life, a victory wreath, the crown of Christ, or the wheel of time itself. Christians use the wreath as a sign that Christ reaches into our time to lead us to the light of everlasting life. The four candles mark the progress of the four weeks of Advent and the growth of light. Sometimes the wreath is embellished with natural dried flowers or fruit. Its evergreen branches lead the household and the congregation to the evergreen Christmas tree. In many homes, the family gathers for prayer around the wreath.

First Sunday of Advent

Use this blessing when lighting the first candle.

Blessed are you, O Lord our God, ruler of the universe.
You call all nations to walk in your light
and to seek your ways of justice and peace,
for the night is past, and the dawn of your coming is near.
Bless us as we light the first candle of this wreath.
Rouse us from sleep,
that we may be ready to greet our Lord when he comes
and welcome him into our hearts and homes,
for he is our light and our salvation.
Blessed be God forever.
Amen.

Second Sunday of Advent

Use this blessing when lighting the first two candles.

Blessed are you, O Lord our God, ruler of the universe.
John the Baptist calls all people to prepare the Lord's way
for the kingdom of heaven is near.
Bless us as we light the candles on this wreath.
Baptize us with the fire of your Spirit,
that we may be a light shining in the darkness
welcoming others as Christ has welcomed us,
for he is our light and our salvation.
Blessed be God forever.
Amen.

Third Sunday of Advent

Use this blessing when lighting three candles.

Blessed are you, O Lord our God, ruler of the universe.
Your prophets spoke of a day when the desert would blossom
and waters would break forth in the wilderness.
Bless us as we light the candles on this wreath.
Strengthen our hearts
as we prepare for the coming of the Lord.
May he give water to all who thirst,
for he is our light and our salvation.
Blessed be God forever.
Amen.

Fourth Sunday of Advent

Use this blessing when lighting all four candles.

Blessed are you, O Lord our God, ruler of the universe.
In your Son, Emmanuel,
you have shown us your light
and saved us from the power of sin.
Bless us as we light the candles on this wreath.
Increase our longing for your presence,
that at the celebration of your Son's birth
his Spirit might dwell anew in our midst,
for he is our light and our salvation.
Blessed be God forever.
Amen.

Tidings of Comfort and Joy
A Midweek Advent Series

Overview

The holiday season can stir deep emotions within each of us. Many children greet the advent of Christmas with joy and excitement, whereas those who have lost loved ones during the past year may find great sadness in the very same event. Thankfully, our God meets us wherever we are, both physically and emotionally. This Advent series gives voice to the complex situations and emotions with which we greet the coming Messiah and uses the reactions of those who first received the news of Jesus' birth (Zechariah, Joseph, Mary, and the shepherds) to do so. These services acknowledge responses of fear, confusion, doubt, and curiosity, while the coming of Jesus promises comfort and joy for all of us.

Visual Environment

Since there are many expectations placed on us during the Advent season (particularly, that we *must* be happy as we go about our Christmas shopping and decorating), consider how you might create an environment that welcomes those for whom such cultural expectations create tension. If you expect a smaller crowd than on Sunday mornings, perhaps you might find a different location for these midweek services. If your seating arrangement is flexible, sitting in the round may help individuals feel more invited. These services are probably not the time or place for extravagant Christmas decorations. Simplicity is key: a few candles, including those of the Advent wreath, are adequate to mark the growing promise of comfort. If your congregation is involved in a prayer shawl ministry, consider distributing prayer shawls to those who have attended these services, perhaps during the final week of Advent, as yet another sign of comfort.

For the Reflections

The reflection time may include a traditional homily or other forms of reflection. For Week 1 (fear), use this time to invite participants to jot their fears anonymously on notecards. These fears could be blessed and exchanged for use as prayer petitions during a time of silence or during the following week. For Week 2 (confusion), create two collages from newspapers and/or magazines—one of confusing world events and one of clarifying and hopeful messages. For Week 3 (doubt), engage those present in a conversation about which articles of faith or passages of the Bible they find the most difficult to believe and what they know to be true. For Week 4 (curiosity), do some wondering together. Tell the birth narrative by heart, and in the style of Godly Play (www.godlyplayfoundation.org), pose the following questions at the end of the story: "I wonder what part of the story you like best?" "I wonder what part of the story is the most important?" "I wonder what part of this story is especially for you this year?" "I wonder if there is any part of the story we can leave out and still have all the story we need?" Leave a time of silence for pondering these questions, or invite participants to respond to these "wondering questions" aloud.

Weekly Themes

Week 1 - The Angel Speaks to Zechariah's Fear
Week 2 - The Angel Speaks to Joseph's Confusion
Week 3 - The Angel Speaks to Mary's Doubt
Week 4 - The Angel Speaks to the Shepherds' Curiosity

Gathering Music

Opening Dialogue

Week 1
This season of Advent confronts many of our emotions.
Sometimes we are terrified and overwhelmed with fear.
"Do not be afraid. Your prayer has been heard."
Joy and gladness will come to us.
The Holy Spirit will fill our hearts.
And we will all share tidings of comfort and joy.

Week 2
This season of Advent confronts many of our emotions.
Sometimes we are confused, unsure of what is happening in our lives.
"Do not be afraid. The child is from the Holy Spirit."
God is with us.
The child shall be called Emmanuel.
And we will all share tidings of comfort and joy.

Week 3

This season of Advent confronts many of our emotions.
Sometimes we doubt and fail to trust God.
"Do not be afraid. You have found favor with God."
Nothing is impossible with God.
Let it be with us according to your word.
And we will all share tidings of comfort and joy.

Week 4

This season of Advent confronts many of our emotions.
Sometimes we are curious about what the future holds.
"Do not be afraid. I am bringing you good news of great joy."
Let us go to Bethlehem to see this thing that has taken place.
Let us make known what has been told to us about this child.
And we will all share tidings of comfort and joy.

Gathering Song

Week 1

Come, thou long-expected Jesus ELW 254, LBW 30

Week 2

Lost in the night ELW 243, LBW 394

Week 3

Each winter as the year grows older ELW 252
Unexpected and mysterious ELW 258

Week 4

All earth is hopeful ELW 266, TFF 47, WOV 629

Greeting and Prayer

The grace of our Lord Jesus Christ, the love of God,
and the communion of the Holy Spirit be with you all.
And also with you.

Week 1

O God who brings comfort and joy, when fear overwhelms us
and we cannot see a way out, speak to our fear. Calm our troubled hearts and provide peace in our fearful world. In Jesus'
name we pray.
Amen.

Week 2

O God who brings comfort and joy, when the world baffles us
with conflicting messages and puzzling events, speak to our
confusion. Comfort us with the knowledge that you are with us
in times of clarity and times of confusion. In Jesus' name we
pray.
Amen.

Week 3

O God who brings comfort and joy, when our faith waivers and
we question your word, speak to our doubt. Comfort us with
your promises and renew our trust in you. In Jesus' name we
pray.
Amen.

Week 4

O God who brings comfort and joy, when we wait with anticipation of what will come, speak to our curiosity. Comfort us with
your surprises and give us hearts that are thankful for all that
you provide. In Jesus' name we pray.
Amen.

Reading

Week 1 - Isaiah 2:1-5
Week 2 - Isaiah 11:1-10
Week 3 - Jeremiah 33:14-16
Week 4 - Zephaniah 3:14-20

Gospel

Week 1 - Luke 1:5-20
Week 2 - Matthew 1:18-25
Week 3 - Luke 1:26-38
Week 4 - Luke 2:8-20

Reflection

Song

Week 1

He came down ELW 253, TFF 37

Week 2

He came down ELW 253, TFF 37
Wait for the Lord ELW 262

Week 3

He came down   ELW 253, TFF 37

The angel Gabriel from heaven came   ELW 265, WOV 632

Week 4

He came down   ELW 253, TFF 37

Awake! Awake, and greet the new morn   ELW 242, WOV 633

Prayers

During these weeks of waiting and expecting, where people live in fear of the unknown,

we pray for peace.

Where people are confused about your will for their lives or for the world,

we pray for clarity.

Where people doubt your presence and your word,

we pray for trust.

Where people are curious, and await the future with hopeful anticipation,

we pray for wonder.

Most of all, when the world longs for you,

we pray you help us respond with glad tidings of comfort and joy.

We pray all this in the name of Jesus, our long-expected Savior.

Amen.

Lord's Prayer

Blessing

The peace of God accompany your waiting,

the light of + Christ warm your hearts,

and the joy of the Spirit fill you with hope.

Amen.

Sending Song

Week 1

As the dark awaits the dawn   ELW 261

Blessed be the God of Israel   ELW 250, WOV 725

Week 2

O come, O come, Emmanuel   ELW 257, LBW 34

Week 3

Rejoice, rejoice, believers   ELW 244, LBW 25

Savior of the nations, come   ELW 263, LBW 28

Week 4

Joy to the world   ELW 267, LBW 39

Dismissal

Go in peace. Share the good news.

Thanks be to God.

Sending Music

Longest Night
Blue Christmas Evening Prayer

While Advent is a season of hope and Christmas is a season of joy, not everyone feels hopeful or like celebrating. Grief, illness, aging, depression, loneliness, unemployment, and loss are magnified. Even those who are not struggling with losses may feel the stress of preparations and expectations around Christmas time. A Longest Night/Blue Christmas service may provide a time and place of solace during the often frenetic days surrounding the celebration of Christmas. We come together seeking healing and room to share grief, sadness, loneliness, or confusion when these emotions often feel out of place during the holidays.

In the Northern Hemisphere, December 21 is the longest night, the winter solstice. It marks the shortest day of the year, the official start of winter. Tradition says that nature and all her creatures stop and hold their breath to see if the sun will turn back from its wanderings, if the days will lengthen and the earth will once again feel the sun's warmth. On this darkest day of the year, we come with our honest yearnings seeking the return of light and hope.

Gathering Music

Welcome

Silent Meditation

The silence may begin with a chime. When the chime sounds a second time the assembly stands and faces the processional cross.

Procession

Wait for the Lord ELW 262
In silence we wait SP 17

Greeting

From the one who was, who is, and who is to come:
Grace and peace be with you all.
And also with you.

Hymn of Light

During the hymn, worshipers may light candles in the prayer station.
Christ, mighty Savior ELW 560
Joyous light of heavenly glory ELW 561
Lumière de Dieu/Come, light of God SP 26

Thanksgiving for Light *(ELW, pp. 310–311)*

The assembly is seated.
Silence.

Psalm 27

The psalm may be chanted antiphonally by a cantor and the assembly, or by the assembly divided into two groups.

Prayer
Lord God, our light and our salvation, grant that your servants who seek your face in times of trouble may see your goodness in the land of the living, and that we may be set safely on the rock of our faith, Jesus Christ, our Savior and Lord.
Amen.
Silence.

First Reading Isaiah 9:2-7

The word of the Lord.
Thanks be to God.
Hymn - O come, O come, Emmanuel ELW 257, sts. 1-4; LBW 34, sts. 1-3

Second Reading Isaiah 40:1-11

The word of the Lord.
Thanks be to God.
Hymn - Comfort, comfort now my people ELW 256, LBW 29

Third Reading Matthew 11:28-30

The word of the Lord.
Thanks be to God.
Hymn - O come, O come, Emmanuel ELW 257, sts. 5-7; LBW 34, sts. 4-5

Fourth Reading John 1:1-5, 14

The word of the Lord.
Thanks be to God.
Hymn - Lo, how a rose e'er blooming ELW 272, LBW 58

Reflection

Gospel Canticle

My soul proclaims your greatness ELW 251, WOV 730

Prayer Stations

A chime may call the assembly to prayer, then the songs are sung meditatively. During this time, worshipers may light a candle and place it in a sand-filled container; write a prayer concern on a slip of paper and place it in a designated area; or kneel, sit, or stand for individual prayer. Prayer with laying on of hands and anointing may be offered by prayer ministers to worshipers who desire this form of healing prayer (see Evangelical Lutheran Worship, p. 277).

Songs

O God, we call SP 30
Deep peace SP 7
The Lord is my light SP 41
Come and fill our hearts ELW 528
O Lord, hear my prayer ELW 751

Contemplative Prayer

A time for silent prayer and meditation follows the singing. A chime may signal the end of the prayer time.

Lord's Prayer

Candle Lighting Hymns

During the hymns, individual candles are lighted. Worshipers may pass the light to someone near them.
It came upon the midnight clear ELW 282, LBW 54
Silent night, holy night! ELW 281, LBW 65

Blessing

The Lord bless you and keep you.
The Lord's face shine on you with grace and mercy.
The Lord look upon you with favor and + give you peace.
Amen.
Individual candles are extinguished.

Sending Music

Hospitality

Worshipers are invited to stay for refreshments following the service.

Music Notes

SP indicates *Singing Our Prayer: A Companion to Holden Prayer Around the Cross* (Augsburg Fortress, 2010). Melody lines for these songs are available for download to sundaysandseasons.com subscribers; both accompaniment and melody files are available to preludemusicplanner.org subscribers.

A psalm refrain for Psalm 27 is available in *Psalter for Worship, Year C* (Augsburg Fortress, 2006; see Lent 2). *Psalter for Worship* includes the accompaniment and a reproducible melody file for the assembly. Subscribers to preludemusicplanner.org can download both the accompaniment and melody files. Subscribers to sundaysandseasons.com can download the melody line from the Library > Lectionary and Psalm Resources > ELW Psalm Refrains, Year C > Lent 2C.

November 27, 2016
First Sunday of Advent

The new church year begins with a wake-up call: Christ is coming soon! In today's readings both Paul and Jesus challenge us to wake from sleep, for we know neither the day nor hour of the Lord's coming. Isaiah proclaims the day when God will gather all people on the holy mountain and there will be no more war or suffering. Though we vigilantly watch for the promised day of salvation, we wait for what we already have: Christ comes among us this day as the word and meal that strengthens our faith in the promises of God.

Prayer of the Day

Stir up your power, Lord Christ, and come. By your merciful protection save us from the threatening dangers of our sins, and enlighten our walk in the way of your salvation, for you live and reign with the Father and the Holy Spirit, one God, now and forever.

Gospel Acclamation

Alleluia. Show us your steadfast ˈ love, O Lord,* and grant us ˈ your salvation. *Alleluia.* (Ps. 85:7)

Readings and Psalm

Isaiah 2:1-5

The visionary message presented in this reading focuses on a future day when God establishes a universal reign of peace. Divine decisions will make war obsolete, and the worshiping community responds: "Let us walk in that light of that Lord now!"

Psalm 122

I was glad when they said to me, "Let us go to the house of the Lord." (Ps. 122:1)

Romans 13:11-14

Paul compares the advent of Christ to the coming of dawn. We live our lives today in light of Christ's coming in the future.

Matthew 24:36-44

Jesus describes his second coming as a sudden, unexpected event that will bring salvation or judgment upon people caught up in the usual affairs of daily life. He urges people to be alert and expectant.

Preface   Advent

Color   Blue

Prayers of Intercession

The prayers are prepared locally for each occasion. The following examples may be adapted or used as appropriate.

As we anticipate the fullness of the presence of Christ, we join with the church throughout the world, praying for all who are in need.

A brief silence.

For the church and its leaders, and for all who work for the unity of the gospel; that the compassion of Christ break down all divisions, let us pray.

Have mercy, O God.

For the well-being of creation, for mountains and hills, lakes and rivers, snow and sunshine, plants and animals, and for all who care for the earth; that God raise up stewards to protect this good creation, let us pray.

Have mercy, O God.

For peace among nations, for those who lead all levels of government, for judges and magistrates, and for those who speak for the voiceless; that all are treated with equity and fairness, let us pray.

Have mercy, O God.

For those who are anxious and worried, for the sick and bereaved, for the homeless and imprisoned, for those in any need (*especially*); that the compassion shown by Christ be embodied in caregivers and advocates, let us pray.

Have mercy, O God.

For those who gather for word and sacrament, for those who travel, and for our holiday preparations; that in all our activities we give thanks to the Lord, let us pray.

Have mercy, O God.

Here other intercessions may be offered.

In thanksgiving for those who have died and are at rest; that their witness to the gospel serve as examples of living the life of faith, let us pray.

Have mercy, O God.

Merciful God, hear the prayers of your people, those spoken aloud and those known only to you, and grant us peace through Jesus Christ, our coming Savior.

Amen.

Images in the Readings

The apocalyptic imagery of **the end of the world**, like the flood sweeping all things away, echoes from the Old Testament into the preaching of Jesus and continues in contemporary disaster movies and terrorist activity. For Christians, fear about the end always comes to rest in trust in the presence of God. When all is over, at our end is God.

Today's readings expand and challenge our society's welcome of God arriving as only baby Jesus, for God comes as **judge** and calls us into a life of justice for all, evoking in us both anticipation and fear. Often in classical art, Justice is a towering robed woman who judges right from wrong.

Often in the Bible, God meets with humankind on a **mountain**. Our language even calls "a mountaintop experience" one so overwhelming that it changes one's future. Sinai, Horeb, Jerusalem, the mount of Jesus' sermon, the Mount of Transfiguration, the Mount of Olives, Golgotha, Zion: all are superimposed on our church buildings, for the Christian mountain is wherever we receive the word and sacraments.

In English, the phrase "**swords into plowshares**" indicates the hope for world peace, a hope for which Christians pray to God.

Ideas for the Day

- The end-time imagery of Matthew and Isaiah has often appeared in protest movements. In the 1980s, the Plowshares movement, a pacifist group influenced by Catholicism, became famous when its members were convicted and served prison time for damaging military property in resistance to war. In the American civil rights movement, African Americans chanted, "What time is it?" (The answer: "Nation time!") The spiritual "Down by the Riverside," sometimes used in antiwar protests, uses Isaiah's words to imagine a time when people "study war no more." Recall the ways these scriptures have given hope, concreteness, and urgency to social change efforts, and apply them to your time and place. What are the current and concrete hopes for people struggling in your community? For people you know who are oppressed, "what time is it?"

- "Keep awake," Jesus says, a call echoed in Paul's letter to the Romans: "It is now the moment for you to wake from sleep" (Rom. 13:11). The concepts of spiritual awakening and being fully present attract many people, Christians and non-Christians alike. Many spiritual teachers and counselors have shared advice on living "awake" and in the moment. You might compare and contrast some of those popular teachers with Jesus and Paul. A few places to start include the work of scientist and mindfulness teacher Jon Kabat-Zinn, and two best-selling books, *The Power of Now: A Guide to Spiritual Enlightenment* by Eckhart Tolle (Novato, CA: New World Library, 1999) and *Waking Up: A Guide to Spirituality without Religion* by Sam Harris (New York: Simon & Schuster, 2014). As we begin this Advent season, how do you describe the difference between being "awake" in one's life and being "awake" to Christ's coming?

- In Matthew's gospel, Jesus pictures the Son of Man surprising people in the midst of daily life: while people are in the field, grinding meal, or sleeping at home. Use one or more short skits to imagine contemporary scenes for his coming, such as workers gathered around an office conference table, young people playing video games, or shoppers at a mall preparing for Christmas. Where do we watch for Christ's coming today?

Connections with the Liturgy

The Apostles' Creed anticipates the coming of the judge: I believe in Jesus Christ, who "will come to judge the living and the dead."

Let the Children Come

Advent is our signal that some brand-new thing is about to begin! And yet it feels old and familiar, doesn't it? Some of the children in your community are too young to quite remember last year, or some might be murmuring, "Not this again!" The work of the Christian people is to invite children into our collective memory, but also to learn from children how to see, with new eyes, God's presence animated among us. We all are partners together in the body of Christ. Let us approach Advent, and this year, learning and teaching alongside children in our midst.

Assembly Song
Gathering

Great Litany ELW 238, LBW pp. 168–173
Lo! He comes with clouds descending ELW 435, LBW 27
O Lord, how shall I meet you ELW 241, LBW 23

Psalmody and Acclamations

Hobby, Robert A. "Psalm 122" from PWA.
Long, Larry J. "Psalm 122" from PSCY.
Savoy, Thomas F. "I Rejoiced When They Said to Me." SATB, cant, assembly, org. GIA G-7524.
(GA) Syrian traditional. "Halle, Hallelujah" from *Pave the Way: Global Songs 3*. AFP 9780800676896. Use ELW psalm tone 5 in E minor with verse for Advent 1.

Hymn of the Day

Wake, awake, for night is flying ELW 436, LBW 31, LLC 276
  WACHET AUF
Soon and very soon ELW 439, WOV 744, W&P 128, TFF 38
  VERY SOON
Rejoice, rejoice, believers ELW 244, LBW 25 *HAF TRONES LAMPA FÄRDIG*

Offering

Soon and very soon ELW 439, WOV 744, W&P 128, TFF 38
Come now, O Prince of peace ELW 247

Communion

My Lord, what a morning ELW 438, TFF 40, WOV 627
The people walk/*Un pueblo que camina* ELW 706, LLC 520
Wait for the Lord ELW 262

Sending

The King shall come ELW 260, LBW 33
Lord our God, with praise we come ELW 730

Additional Assembly Songs

I want to be ready TFF 41
O Savior, rend the heavens wide LBW 38
We are awaiting the coming MSB2 S536
⊕ Farrell, Bernadette. "Word of Justice" from *Agape: Songs of Hope and Reconciliation*. 2 pt. Lutheran World Federation. Out of print. Available on Amazon.com.
☼ Corum, Casey. "Kindness" from CCLI.
☼ Kirkland, Eddie. "Hosanna" from CCLI.
☼ Mac, Toby. "Break Open the Sky" from CCLI.
☼ Reeves, Sarah/Jeremy Rose/Sarah Hart. "Awaken" from CCLI.
☼ Smith, Martin/Chris Tomlin/Jesse Reeves. "Waiting Here for You" from CCLI.
☼ Walton, Greg. "Come to Us" from CCLI.

Music for the Day
Choral

♬ Bouman, Paul. "Rejoice, Rejoice, Believers." SATB, org. MSM 50-0004.
Nelson, Ronald A. "A Vision of Peace." SAB, pno. GIA G-7007.
P♬ Nelson, Ronald A. "Rejoice, Rejoice, Believers." SAB, pno or org, opt assembly. AFP 9781451424027.
Leavitt, John. "My Lord, What a Morning." SATB, pno. CPH 98-4157.

Children's Choir

Lindh, Jody. "An Advent Carol." U, kybd. CG CGA648.
P Patterson, Mark. "Advent Prayer" from *ChildrenSing: Seven Anthems for Elementary Age Singers*. U/2 pt, kybd. AFP 9780800677695.
P Schram, Ruth Elaine. "I Was Glad." 2 pt mxd, kybd. AFP 9780800676650.

Keyboard / Instrumental

♬ Krebs, Johann Ludwig (1713–1780). "Wake, Awake, for Night Is Flying" (Wachet auf) from *Eight Chorale Preludes for Organ with Trumpet (or Oboe)*. Tpt or ob, org. PRE 453001070.

Mendelssohn-Bartholdy, Felix (1809–1847). "Andante" from *Sonata No. 6 in D Minor, Op. 65.6*. Org. Various editions.
P♬ Raabe, Nancy. "Rejoice, Rejoice, Believers" with "Come Now, O Prince of Peace" (Haf trones lampa färdig; Ososŏ, ososŏ) from *Grace and Peace, vol. 7: Hymn Portraits for the Christmas Cycle*. Pno. AFP 9781451499124.
P Rowland-Raybold, Roberta. "Creator of the Stars of Night" (Conditor alme siderum) from *Winter Solstice: Carols for Organ*. Org. AFP 9781451499100.

Handbell

♬ Ingram, Bill. "Soon and Very Soon." 3-5 oct, L3-. Ring Praise! RP7624.
P♬ Moklebust, Cathy. "Rejoice, Rejoice" from *Celebrate the Season*. 2-3 oct, L2+, CG CGB785. 3-5 oct, L2+, CG CGB786.
♬ Page, Anna Laura. "Wake, Awake (Wachet auf)." 3-6 oct hb, opt 3-5 oct hc, L4. CG CGB755.

Wednesday, November 30
Andrew, Apostle

Andrew was the first of the Twelve. He is known as a fisherman who left his net to follow Jesus. As a part of his calling, he brought other people, including Simon Peter, to meet Jesus. The Byzantine church honors Andrew as its patron and points out that because he was the first of Jesus' followers, he was, in the words of John Chrysostom, "the Peter before Peter." Together with Philip, Andrew leads a number of Greeks to speak with Jesus, and it is Andrew who shows Jesus a boy with five barley loaves and two fish. Andrew is said to have died on a cross saltire, an X-shaped cross.

Saturday, December 3
Francis Xavier, missionary to Asia, died 1552

Francis Xavier (SAYV-yehr) was born in the Basque region of northern Spain. Francis's native Basque language is unrelated to any other, and Francis admitted that learning languages was difficult for him. Despite this obstacle he became a missionary to India, Southeast Asia, Japan, and the Philippines. At each point he learned the local language and, like Martin Luther, wrote catechisms for the instruction of new converts. Another obstacle Francis overcame to accomplish his mission work was a propensity to seasickness. All his travels to the Far East were by boat. Together with Ignatius Loyola and five others, Francis formed the Society of Jesus (Jesuits). Francis spoke out against the Spanish and Portuguese colonists when he discovered their oppression of the indigenous people to whom he was sent as a missionary.

⊕ = global song   ♬ = relates to hymn of the day
☼ = praise song   P = available in Prelude Music Planner

December 4, 2016
Second Sunday of Advent

At the heart of our Advent preparation stands John the Baptist, who calls us to repent and make a new beginning. As the darkness increases we turn toward the light of Christ's coming. For Christians he is the root of Jesse, the righteous judge who welcomes all, especially the poor and meek of the earth. We wait with hope for that day when the wolf will dwell with the lamb, and there will be no more hurt or destruction. From the Lord's table we are sent in the spirit of John the Baptist to proclaim that in Christ the kingdom of God has come near.

Prayer of the Day

Stir up our hearts, Lord God, to prepare the way of your only Son. By his coming nurture our growth as people of repentance and peace; through Jesus Christ, our Savior and Lord, who lives and reigns with you and the Holy Spirit, one God, now and forever.

Gospel Acclamation

Alleluia. Prepare the way | of the Lord.* All flesh shall see the salva- | tion of God. *Alleluia.* (Luke 3:4, 6)

Readings and Psalm

Isaiah 11:1-10

In today's reading the prophet describes the ideal ruler who will come in the future as a green shoot springing from a dead stump (David's royal line) of Jesse (David's father). Gifted by the Spirit, this messiah will seek justice for the poor, and the reign of this monarch will be experienced as paradise regained.

Psalm 72:1-7, 18-19

May the righteous flourish; let there be an abundance of peace. (Ps. 72:7)

Romans 15:4-13

God's promise to include Gentiles within the circle of God's blessed people has been fulfilled in Jesus Christ. Christians live out their unity by welcoming and encouraging each other just as Christ has welcomed them into God's family.

Matthew 3:1-12

Just before Jesus begins his public ministry, John the Baptist appears, calling people to mend their ways and speaking of a powerful one who is to come.

Preface   Advent

Color   Blue

Prayers of Intercession

The prayers are prepared locally for each occasion. The following examples may be adapted or used as appropriate.

As we anticipate the fullness of the presence of Christ, we join with the church throughout the world, praying for all who are in need.

A brief silence.

For the church throughout the world, for all inspired and led by the Holy Spirit, and for all who proclaim the wondrous deeds of God; that all divisions and disagreements cease, let us pray.

Have mercy, O God.

For the earth and its creatures, for animals of every size, for plants that provide shade and nourishment; that we see God's goodness revealed in every living thing, let us pray.

Have mercy, O God.

For the nations and those in authority, for police officers and firefighters, for social workers and attorneys; that God grant them wisdom to work for peace and justice, let us pray.

Have mercy, O God.

For the poor, the meek, the unwelcomed, those suffering from malaria and HIV/AIDS, the sick and the bereaved (*especially*); that they experience Christ embodied in healthcare workers and caregivers, let us pray.

Have mercy, O God.

For those traveling and those absent from this gathering, for those serving in the military, for those preparing for baptism, and for our congregation; that in all we do we praise and glorify God, let us pray.

Have mercy, O God.

Here other intercessions may be offered.

In thanksgiving for the faithful departed who have died in Christ (*especially the theologian John of Damascus*); that they show us the way of hope through the incarnate Word, let us pray.

Have mercy, O God.

Merciful God, hear the prayers of your people, those spoken aloud and those known only to you, and grant us peace through Jesus Christ, our coming Savior.

Amen.

Images in the Readings

Ancient Near Eastern iconography often depicted the monarch as a **tree of life**, whose successful reign ensured a vibrant life for the people. Both first and second readings rely on this ancient imagery when they refer to the "root of Jesse." In Israelite history, Jesse, the father of the legendary King David, is described as the root of the tree that was King David. John the Baptist warns that some trees will be cut down to make way for Christ, who is our tree of life.

The gospel reading situates John the Baptist in the **wilderness**, baptizing in the Jordan River, the **river** the Israelites crossed on their way into the promised land. Led by Jesus, our Joshua, who entered the wilderness of our lives, Christians too cross a river in baptism and so enter into the kingdom of God.

The lion and the lamb have become a beloved symbol of peace between natural enemies. The toddler is playing with the adder. In Christ is the promise of this extraordinary hope for the world.

Ideas for the Day

- As the first season of a new liturgical year, Advent offers a sense of new beginnings, heightened by John the Baptist's imagery of repentance, cleansing, and preparation. In a sermon, guided meditation, or time of reflection, you could invite people to review the past year through an "examen" (also called "examination of consciousness"), following the practice of Ignatius of Loyola and the Jesuits. To learn about the examen in its daily or yearly form, go to www.ignatianspirituality.com/ignatian-prayer/the-examen or read *Sleeping with Bread: Holding What Gives You Life* by Dennis Linn, Sheila Fabricant Linn, and Matthew Linn (Mahwah, NJ: Paulist, 1995). In the language of Matthew and Romans, questions such as these would be appropriate: Where has love borne fruit in your life, and what could be cleared away to make more space for love? When have you had opportunities to repent and change? When have you noticed the kingdom of God coming near? Where have you found steadfastness and encouragement? What gives you hope for the year to come?
- A call to repentance invites us to reflect not only on our own individual sins but also on the sins of the systems that have shaped us and the ways we can help shape a vision of God's kingdom. Using Isaiah's image of a peaceable kingdom and Paul's call to the Romans to "live in harmony," lift up such a vision for your location. Who would be able to live together in peace? Who would find a new sense of safety? An Edward Hicks painting, *The Peaceable Kingdom*, could provide a starting point (view it at www.worcesterart.org/collection/American/1934.65.html). Read about the ways Hicks was challenged by the systems of his time and place in an art review by Holland Carter,

"Finding Endless Conflict Hidden in a Peaceable Kingdom" (*New York Times*, June 16, 2000).
- Advent first took shape in Christian practice as a "little Lent," during which people prepared for Christ's coming with repentance. As in Lent, a baptismal connection is appropriate in Advent, particularly with this gospel. After confession and forgiveness, consider including a rite of sprinkling.

Connections with the Liturgy

A prayer of confession (*ELW*, p. 95) echoes the preaching of John the Baptist: "Turn us again to you, and uphold us by your Spirit, so that we may live and serve you in newness of life through Jesus Christ, our Savior and Lord."

The passage from Isaiah describing the gifts of the Spirit inspires one of the prayers at baptism (*ELW*, p. 231), as we ask God for the spirit of wisdom, understanding, counsel, might, knowledge, and the fear of the Lord.

Let the Children Come

"My, how you've grown!" Even when children are a little annoyed by the exclamation of an adult they haven't seen in a while, it is still a statement of truth and hope. Growth is the promise of new life to come. It is our hope, though, that growth isn't just about getting bigger. Yes, we want more people in the pews and more children in Sunday school, but numbers alone are not a measure of the abundance of this wild and growing shoot of Jesse. How are children in your community nurtured (and nurturing) in peace, where the wolf shall live with the lamb?

Assembly Song
Gathering

Hark! A thrilling voice is sounding! ELW 246, LBW 37
Come, thou long-expected Jesus ELW 254, LBW 30
Blessed be the God of Israel ELW 250, WOV 725

Psalmody and Acclamations

Bedford, Michael. "Psalm 146" from *ChildrenSing Psalms*. U, kybd, 3 hb. AFP 9780800663872.

Burkhardt, Michael. "Psalm 146" from *Psalms for the Church Year*. U or 3 pt canon a cap. MSM 80-708.

Chepponis, James. "Psalm 146." 2 cant, assembly, opt SATB, kybd, gtr, C inst, hb. GIA G-4227.

(GA) Syrian traditional. "Halle, Hallelujah" from *Pave the Way: Global Songs 3*. AFP 9780800676896. Use ELW psalm tone 5 in E minor with verse for Advent 2.

Hymn of the Day

There's a voice in the wilderness ELW 255 *ASCENSION*

On Jordan's bank the Baptist's cry ELW 249, LBW 36 *PUER NOBIS*

O day of peace ELW 711, WOV 762 *JERUSALEM*

Offering

He came down ELW 253, TFF 37

Comfort, comfort now my people ELW 256, LBW 29

Communion

Come now, O Prince of peace ELW 247

O Lord, how shall I meet you ELW 241, LBW 23

Wait for the Lord ELW 262

Sending

Prepare the royal highway ELW 264, LBW 26

Hark, the glad sound! ELW 239, LBW 35

Additional Assembly Songs

Isaiah the prophet has written of old NCH 108

O God, we call SP 30

Let us prepare MSB2 S545

⊕ Feliciano, Francisco. "Who Will Set Us Free?" from *Sound the Bamboo*. U. GIA G-6830.

⊕ Maraschin, Jaci. "Come to Be Our Hope, O Jesus" from *Global Songs 2*. U. AFP 9780800656744.

☼ Anderson, Jared/Seth Moseley. "The King Is Coming" from CCLI.

☼ Colson, Craig/Kristen Colson. "Justice Shall Flourish" from *Spirit and Song*. OCP.

☼ Evans, Darrell/Eric Nuzum. "Prepare the Way" from CCLI.

☼ Hall, Charlie. "Make Straight" from CCLI.

☼ Smith, Martin. "Did You Feel the Mountains Tremble" from CCLI.

☼ Tomlin, Chris/Jess Coates/Jason Ingram. "Even So Come" from CCLI.

Music for the Day

Choral

Highben, Zebulon M. "The Lord Shall Come and Not Be Slow." SATB. AFP 9781451402520.

P Keesecker, Thomas. "Waiting." 3 pt trbl or mxd, kybd, fl or vln, opt hb. AFP 9781451401769.

♬ Monteverdi, Claudio. "On Jordan's Bank the Baptist's Cry." SAB, kybd, 2 trbl insts. GIA G-2834.

P♬ Organ, Anne Krentz. "There's a Voice in the Wilderness Crying." 2 pt mxd, pno, ob. AFP 9780800676537.

Children's Choir

Bailey, Lynn Shaw. "A Child Will Lead the Way (And We Say Thank You, God)." U/2 pt, opt narr, small perc. LOR 10/4040L.

Bedford, Michael. "Prepare a Way for the Lord!" from *Seven Songs for the Church Year*. U, opt 2 hb. CG CGA693.

Bostrom, Sandra. "Christ Is Coming." U/2 pt, pno. CG CGA691.

Keyboard / Instrumental

P♬ DeJong, Kenneth L. "There's a Voice in the Wilderness" (Ascension) from *Star of Promise: Ten Preludes on Advent Hymns*. Org. AFP 9781451499087.

P♬ Kim, Marianne. "O Day of Peace" (Jerusalem) from *My Soul Proclaims: Piano Meditations for Worship*. Pno. AFP 9781451499131.

P Organ, Anne Krentz. "Comfort, Comfort Now My People" (Freu dich sehr) from *Piano Reflections on Advent Tunes*. Pno. AFP 9781451462647.

Pachelbel, Johann (1653–1706). "Comfort, Comfort Now My People" (Freu dich sehr) from *Selected Organ Works*, vol. 4. Org. ALF 9780769242729.

Handbell

P♬ Afdahl, Lee J. "There's a Voice in the Wilderness" from *Hymn Accompaniments for Handbells: Advent and Christmas*. 3-5 oct, L3+. AFP 9780806698076.

P♬ Krug, Jason W. "Jerusalem." 3-5 oct hb, opt 3-5 oct hc, L3+. HOP 2664.

P Nelson, Susan. "Nativity Carol." 3-5 oct hb, opt 3 oct hc, opt 1-3 oct alt bells, opt sleigh bells, L2+. CPH 977064.

Sunday, December 4

John of Damascus, theologian and hymnwriter, died around 749

Born to a wealthy family in Damascus and well educated, John left a career in finance and government to become a monk in an abbey near Jerusalem. He wrote many hymns as well as theological works. Foremost among the latter is a work called *The Fount of Wisdom*, which touches on philosophy, heresy, and the orthodox faith. This summary of patristic theology remained influential for centuries.

⊕ = global song   ♬ = relates to hymn of the day

☼ = praise song   P = available in Prelude Music Planner

Tuesday, December 6
Nicholas, Bishop of Myra, died around 342

Though Nicholas is one of the church's most beloved saints, little is known about his life. In the fourth century he was a bishop in what is now Turkey. Legends that surround Nicholas tell of his love for God and neighbor, especially the poor. One famous story tells of Nicholas secretly giving bags of gold to the three daughters of a father who was going to sell them into prostitution because he could not provide dowries for them. Nicholas has become a symbol of anonymous gift giving.

Wednesday, December 7
Ambrose, Bishop of Milan, died 397

Ambrose was a governor of northern Italy and a catechumen when he was elected bishop of Milan. He was baptized, ordained, and consecrated a bishop within one week's time. While bishop he gave away his wealth and lived in simplicity. He was a famous preacher and is largely responsible for the conversion of Augustine. He is also well known for writing hymns. On one occasion, Ambrose led people in a hymn he wrote while the church in which they were secluded was threatened by attack from Gothic soldiers. The soldiers turned away, unwilling to attack a congregation that was singing a hymn. Ambrose is credited with authorship of three hymns in *Evangelical Lutheran Worship*, including "Savior of the Nations, Come" (ELW 263).

December 11, 2016
Third Sunday of Advent

A note of joyful expectation marks today's worship. Isaiah announces that the desert shall rejoice and blossom. Jesus points to signs of God's reign: the blind see, the lame walk, lepers are cleansed, the deaf hear. We wait with patience for the coming of the Lord, even as we rejoice at his presence among us this day: in word and holy supper, in church and in our homes, in silent reflection and in works of justice and love. We pray that God would open our eyes and ears to the wonders of Christ's advent among us.

Prayer of the Day

Stir up the wills of all who look to you, Lord God, and strengthen our faith in your coming, that, transformed by grace, we may walk in your way; through Jesus Christ, our Savior and Lord, who lives and reigns with you and the Holy Spirit, one God, now and forever.

Gospel Acclamation

Alleluia. I am sending my messen- | ger before you,* who will prepare your | way before you. *Alleluia*. (Matt. 11:10)

Readings and Psalm
Isaiah 35:1-10

The prophet describes the return from the Babylonian captivity as a joyous procession to Zion. God's coming reign will bring a renewal of creation in which health and wholeness will be restored. There is no need for fear, for God is coming to save.

Psalm 146:5-10

The LORD lifts up those who are bowed down. (Ps. 146:8)

or Luke 1:46b-55

My spirit rejoices in God my Savior. (Luke 1:47)

James 5:7-10

In anticipation of the Lord's coming, Christians are called upon to cultivate patience rather than discontent.

Matthew 11:2-11

John the Baptist expects the Messiah to bring God's judgment upon the earth. From a prison cell, he wonders whether Jesus is the one who will do this.

Preface   Advent

Color   Blue

Prayers of Intercession

The prayers are prepared locally for each occasion. The following examples may be adapted or used as appropriate.

As we anticipate the fullness of the presence of Christ, we join with the church throughout the world, praying for all who are in need.

A brief silence.

For the church and all messengers of the gospel, for all who call upon the name of the Lord, and for congregations throughout the world; that God work through us to bring harmony and reconciliation, let us pray.

Have mercy, O God.

For rain forests and deserts, for wilderness and developed land, and for plants blossoming and dormant; that the splendor and diversity of creation proclaim the glory of the Lord, let us pray.

Have mercy, O God.

For our government, for the military and international relief workers, and for those who care for the stranger, widow, and orphan; that God raise up leaders who work for the protection of all, let us pray.

Have mercy, O God.

For the hungry and homeless, for those in captivity, for the fearful and sorrowful, for those living with HIV/AIDS, and for the sick (*especially*); that those who help others serve with patience and grace, let us pray.

Have mercy, O God.

For all who call this community home, for those visiting from near and far, and for those preparing for the holiday season, that the advent of Christ make our hearts and minds rejoice, let us pray.

Have mercy, O God.

Here other intercessions may be offered.

In thanksgiving for the departed who were faithful to God's word; that their words and actions direct us to the one who prepares a way for us, let us pray.

Have mercy, O God.

Merciful God, hear the prayers of your people, those spoken aloud and those known only to you, and grant us peace through Jesus Christ, our coming Savior.

Amen.

Images in the Readings

The **flowering wilderness** is the image presented in both the first reading and the gospel. Often the Bible uses imagery from nature to celebrate God's presence. All of nature rejoices in God's continuing creation. We are called to ecological care for God's good earth, making literal the symbol of a flowering wilderness.

The **healing of the blind and lame** is a recurring image in the Old Testament to describe the effect of the presence of God. The gospels say that Jesus healed the blind, the lame, the lepers, and the deaf; he raised the dead; and he preached to the poor—thus enacting all the miracles that are cited in the ancient poems.

In the ancient Near East, conquerors built massive **highways** to allow for civic processions so as to display their power. The Bible cites and then transforms this image: there will be a highway on which the people will return in safety to their own city. Might is changed into right.

Ideas for the Day

- In his picture book *The Curious Garden*, Peter Brown writes of a little boy named Liam who discovers new vegetation on an abandoned railway in an otherwise barren city. He is inspired to become a gardener and care for the plants, and as the story unfolds, the garden becomes just as much a character in the story as Liam, exploring even the "old, forgotten things" ([New York: Little, Brown, 2009], 24). The wilderness in Isaiah 35 may also seem like an old, forgotten thing before it is visited by God's glory. And it is that glory that not only brings new life but creates a new opportunity for God's people.

- When John's disciples ask Jesus if he really is the one, they may have a bit of uncertainty regarding his ministry, but the second part of the question, "or are we to wait for another?" (Matt. 11:3), is telling—if Jesus is not the one, they are likely willing to wait for another. Rather than settling for passive waiting, the Baptist's ministry is an example of a hope that persistently challenges the assumption that things are as they should be. Rather than hope being something one simply possesses, what if, instead, hope is itself an action? If hope can be understood in such a way, what can be said about waiting faithfully?

- Will Willimon identifies the church's Sunday worship as the primary source of prophetic conviction, "where the truth keeps being refurbished by a fund of imaginative images, metaphors, and the judgment and forgiveness whereby we are enabled to live the truth in a world of lies" (*Pastor* [Nashville: Abingdon, 2002], 251). Willimon draws attention to the need for communal prophetic practice over and above individual prophetic voices. What difference does it make to think about Sunday worship as the event that inspires prophetic conviction?

Connections with the Liturgy

Recalling the promises of the miraculous presence of God, we pray in the intercessions "for the poor, oppressed, sick, bereaved, lonely, and for all who suffer in body, mind, or spirit," that is, for the ancient poems to be realized today.

Let the Children Come

"Are we there yet?" It is the familiar cry from the backseat on a long car ride, the mutterings of the altar guild getting ready for the festival, and indeed, the existential cry of a world waiting to turn. Waiting. Waiting and preparation give the ultimate goal meaning and dimension. The wider culture doesn't have the same goal as the church this season. The buzz on the street is "Don't wait; buy now!" It is hard to resist the glittery lights of consumption. How can communities nurturing the faith of children help them pace themselves through the journey of Advent and life?

Assembly Song
Gathering

Awake! Awake, and greet the new morn   ELW 242, WOV 633

He came down   ELW 253, TFF 37

People, look east   ELW 248, WOV 626

Psalmody and Acclamations

Bruxvoort Colligan, Richard. "The God of Jacob Hallelujah (Psalm 146)" from *Shout for Joy*. AFP 9780806698632.

Haugen, Marty. "Bless the Lord, My Soul (Psalms 146 and 147)." SATB, cant, assembly, gtr, kybd. GIA G-3339.

ᴾ Friesen-Carper, Paul. "Filled with Hope and Gratitude (Magnificat)." MSB2 S528.

(GA) Syrian traditional. "Halle, Hallelujah" from *Pave the Way: Global Songs 3*. AFP 9780800676896. Use ELW psalm tone 5 in E minor with verse for Advent 3.

Hymn of the Day

All earth is hopeful   ELW 266, WOV 629, TFF 47   *TODA LA TIERRA*

Let streams of living justice   ELW 710   *THAXTED*

Prepare the royal highway   ELW 264, LBW 26   *BEREDEN VÄG FÖR HERRAN*

Offering

My soul proclaims your greatness   ELW 251, WOV 730

Canticle of the Turning   ELW 723, W&P 26

Communion

Light dawns on a weary world   ELW 726

Lost in the night   ELW 243, LBW 394

Wait for the Lord   ELW 262

Sending

Hail to the Lord's anointed   ELW 311, LBW 87

Joy to the world   ELW 267, LBW 39, LLC 288

Additional Assembly Songs

In silence we wait   SP 17

To a waiting world   MSB2 S530

Stir up your power   ASG 38

⊕ Bena tune, arr. Austin C. Lovelace. "Christ the Savior Has Appeared" from *Set Free: A Collection of African Hymns*. SATB. AFP 9780806600451.

⊕ Yanapa, Zoilo. "Sarantañani/Let's Walk Together" from *Sing with the World: Global Songs for Children*. U. GIA G-7339.

☼ Baloche, Paul, et al. "King of the Broken" from CCLI.

☼ Brown, Brenton/Glenn Roberts. "All Who Are Thirsty" from CCLI.

☼ Cooper, Greg [et al.]. "We Are Waiting" from CCLI.

☼ Doerksen, Brian. "Jesus, Hope of the Nations" from CCLI.

☼ Garrard, Stuart/Martin Smith. "My Glorious" from CCLI.

☼ Jobe, Kari/Cody Carnes. "Savior's Here" from CCLI.

⊕ = global song   ♫ = relates to hymn of the day
☼ = praise song   ᴾ = available in Prelude Music Planner

Music for the Day
Choral

Davis, Taylor. "Come, Thou Long-Expected Jesus." SAB, pno. CG CGA1078.

Fleming, Larry L. "Go and Tell John." SATB div. MSM 50-5900.

ᴾ Raabe, Nancy. "Creator of the Stars of Night." 2 pt mxd, kybd. AFP 9781451401622.

ᴾ♫ Shaw, Timothy. "Prepare the Royal Highway." SATB, tamb. AFP 9781451485929.

Children's Choir

ᴾ Helgen, John. "Keep Your Lamps Trimmed and Burning." U, opt desc. AFP 9780800677497.

Hopson, Hal. "Dance and Sing, for the Lord Will Be with Us." U, kybd, opt tamb. CG CGA749.

McRae, Shirley W. "Carol of Prophecy." U, opt hb. CG CGA720.

Keyboard / Instrumental

ᴾ Biery, Marilyn. "He Comes to Us as One Unknown" (Repton) from *A British Perspective: Melodies and Hymn Tunes for Organ*. Org. AFP 9780800663919.

♫ Cherwien, David. "All Earth Is Hopeful" (Toda la tierra) from *O God beyond All Praising*. Org. AFP 9780800657246.

Mendelssohn-Bartholdy, Felix (1809–1847). "Andante tranquillo" from *Sonata No. 3 in A Major, Op. 65.3*. Org. Various editions.

ᴾ♫ Organ, Anne Krentz. "Prepare the Royal Highway" (Bereden väg för Herran) from *Piano Reflections on Advent Tunes*. Pno. AFP 9781451462647.

Handbell

Glasgow, Michael J. "A Child Shall Lead Them." 5-6 oct hb, L4, FTT 20381. Bell tree solo (opt fl), FTT 20381BT.

ᴾ♫ Larson, Lloyd. "O God beyond All Praising." 3-5 oct, L2. HOP 2632.

♫ Wissinger, Kathleen. "Advent Voices." 2-5 oct hb or hc, opt fc, opt wc, L2+. LOR 20/1325L.

Tuesday, December 13

Lucy, martyr, died 304

Lucy was a young Christian of Sicily who was martyred during the persecutions under Emperor Diocletian. Apparently she had decided to devote her life to God and her possessions to the poor. Beyond that, however, little is known for certain about Lucy. However, her celebration became particularly important in Sweden and Norway, perhaps because the feast of Lucia (the name means "light") originally fell on the shortest day of the year. A tradition arose of a girl in the household, wearing a crown of candles, bringing saffron rolls to her family early in the morning on the day of Lucia.

Wednesday, December 14

John of the Cross, renewer of the church, died 1591

John was a monk of the Carmelite religious order who met Teresa of Ávila when she was working to reform the Carmelite Order and return it to a stricter observance of its rules. He followed Teresa's lead and encouraged others to follow her reform. He was imprisoned when he encountered opposition to the reform. His writings, like Teresa's, reflect a deep interest in mystical thought and meditation. In one of John's poems, "The Spiritual Canticle," he cried, "Oh, that my griefs would end! Come, grant me thy fruition full and free!"

December 18, 2016

Fourth Sunday of Advent

Today Isaiah prophesies that a young woman will bear a son and name him Emmanuel. The gospel is Matthew's account of the annunciation and birth of the one named Emmanuel, God-with-us. During these final days of Advent we pray, "O come, O come, Emmanuel," a beloved hymn based on ancient prayers appointed for the seven days preceding Christmas. On this final Sunday in Advent we prepare to celebrate the birth of the one born to save us from the power of sin and death.

Prayer of the Day

Stir up your power, Lord Christ, and come. With your abundant grace and might, free us from the sin that hinders our faith, that eagerly we may receive your promises, for you live and reign with the Father and the Holy Spirit, one God, now and forever.

Gospel Acclamation

Alleluia. The virgin shall conceive and ᐧ bear a son,* and they shall name ᐧ him Emmanuel. *Alleluia.* (Matt. 1:23)

Readings and Psalm

Isaiah 7:10-16

An Israelite and Aramean military coalition presented a serious threat to King Ahaz of Judah. In response, Ahaz decided to secure his throne and kingdom by seeking refuge in Assyrian help. Isaiah reminds Ahaz that human attempts to establish security will fail. The prophet gives the sign of Immanuel that is the only source of true safety: God is with us!

Psalm 80:1-7, 17-19

Let your face shine upon us, and we shall be saved. (Ps. 80:7)

Romans 1:1-7

Most of the Christians in Rome do not know Paul. In this letter's opening he introduces himself as an apostle divinely appointed to spread God's gospel. The gospel's content is the promised coming of Christ, and Paul's mission is to bring about the obedience of faith among all nations, including his Roman audience.

Matthew 1:18-25

Matthew's story of Jesus' birth focuses on the role of Joseph, who adopts the divinely-begotten child into the family of David and obediently gives him the name Jesus, which means "God saves."

Preface   Advent

Color   Blue

Prayers of Intercession

The prayers are prepared locally for each occasion. The following examples may be adapted or used as appropriate.

As we anticipate the fullness of the presence of Christ, we join with the church throughout the world, praying for all who are in need.

A brief silence.

For the church universal and all servants of the gospel, for poets and artists, for musicians and preachers, and for theologians and teachers; that all proclaim that God is with us in Christ, let us pray.

Have mercy, O God.

For all plants and animals, seas and skies, snow and rain, and all of God's marvels; that all of creation grow and thrive as we bless, protect, and use with care what God has made, let us pray.

Have mercy, O God.

For the nations and those in authority, for peace and justice throughout the whole world, and for those who advocate on behalf of others; that all in positions of leadership choose what is good for the community, let us pray.

Have mercy, O God.

For the thirsty and hungry, the weak and fearful, those in childbirth, those who mourn, and the sick (*especially*); that they know Christ the Anointed One who dries up every tear and comforts those who suffer, let us pray.

Have mercy, O God.

For those who travel near and far, for those who prepare our congregation for worship and celebration, and for those who gather around word and sacrament; that all experience welcome and refreshment, let us pray.

Have mercy, O God.

Here other intercessions may be offered.

In thanksgiving for the saints who have died and are now at rest; that the witness of their faith point us to the promises of grace and resurrection in Christ, let us pray.

Have mercy, O God.

Merciful God, hear the prayers of your people, those spoken aloud and those known only to you, and grant us peace through Jesus Christ, our coming Savior.

Amen.

Images in the Readings

In Matthew's narratives, an **angel** figures in the stories of Jesus' birth and resurrection. In our society, many depictions of angels are unfortunately quite cutesy, not very helpful as images of the might of God. The angel is the divine messenger, the extension of the power and mercy of God, and in the Bible often the way that believers encounter the Almighty.

The **pregnant woman** can be a symbol of the life that comes from God. In the Bible, many women, from Eve in Genesis 4:1 on, conceive and bear children with the help of God. When we acclaim God as creator, we attest that God is continually creating life on this earth.

This Sunday it is **Joseph** who hears and receives the word of God. The history of art often depicted Joseph as an old man as a technique to convey that he was not instrumental in Mary's pregnancy. However, often in the Scriptures a woman's pregnancy is seen as a gift from God. We are now Mary, and God is in us. We are now Joseph, receiving from God a gift we cannot have achieved on our own.

Ideas for the Day

- The film *Hugo* (Warner Bros., 2011) tells the story of a young boy who could easily succumb to the nightmare of being orphaned but instead embraces an adventure beyond his imagination. He searches relentlessly for a missing part to a machine that he believes holds a message. In the reading from Isaiah, Ahaz sees only the impending nightmare of armies allied against him. He refuses to "stand firm in faith" (Isa. 7:9) and is thus unable to see what God-with-us could be like. Along with a lack of trust, or maybe because of it, Ahaz lacks the imagination to see a future other than the one he chooses.

- Joseph is resolved. He decides the best course of action, which is consistent with his righteous character. Then he has a dream and changes direction. Instead of resolve being his notable characteristic, Joseph is recognized for doing what "the angel of the Lord commanded him" (Matt. 1:24). Resolve, the unwillingness to back down despite any difficulty, is often lauded as a sign of strength. We don't know if Joseph struggled with this challenge to his resolve, but it is worth considering in terms of faithful decision making. What does obedience look like in a world where resolve is greatly prized?

- The painting *The Sign of Promise*, by landscape painter George Inness, has been lost since the mid-1860s. The most complete description of the painting to date is from an 1863 article in the *New York Evening Post*. However, describing a painting is not the same as seeing it. In the opening of Romans, Paul recognizes the power of a promise and faces the challenge of trying to describe it. He is witness to a story that has been in the making, one that may have looked exclusive to a particular people but now extends to his addressees "who are called to belong to Jesus Christ" (Rom. 1:6). In sharing the gospel, Paul attempts to paint a picture of God's fulfilled promise. How might God's promise be depicted in a way that is powerful and readily accessible in congregational settings?

Connections with the Liturgy

In the Nicene Creed we acclaim: Jesus Christ, "the only Son of God, . . . was incarnate of the Holy Spirit and the virgin Mary."

Let the Children Come

Families are formed in such peculiar ways. If we were to glance at a nativity scene, the surface might reveal a mommy, daddy, and baby—and that baby came about in the biological and magical way that babies happen. Today's gospel should confound that surface way of thinking about family structure. Families come with complexities and unique histories, which are made holy by God's presence at work in them. Joseph adopts Mary's baby as his own, trusting "God is with us." How are families, complex and unique, celebrated and supported in your community? Do the children in your community feel the value of all families?

Assembly Song
Gathering

Creator of the stars of night / O Lord of light, who made the stars ELW 245 / LBW 323

Awake! Awake, and greet the new morn ELW 242, WOV 633

People, look east ELW 248, WOV 626

Psalmody and Acclamations

Furlong, Sue. "God of Hosts, Bring Us Back" from *Psalm Songs 1.* AFP 0800657705.

Haugen, Marty. "Lord, Make Us Turn to You." SATB, cant, assembly, kybd, gtr. GIA G-2884.

Jenkins, Stephen. "An Advent Psalm." SATB, assembly, org, opt U or cant. MSM 80-003.

(GA) Syrian traditional. "Halle, Hallelujah" from *Pave the Way: Global Songs 3.* AFP 9780800676896. Use ELW psalm tone 5 in E minor with verse for Advent 4.

Hymn of the Day

O come, O come, Emmanuel ELW 257, LBW 34, LLC 281 *VENI, EMMANUEL*

Savior of the nations, come ELW 263, LBW 28 *NUN KOMM, DER HEIDEN HEILAND*

Canticle of the Turning ELW 723, W&P 26 *STAR OF COUNTY DOWN*

Offering

He came down ELW 253, TFF 37

Let all mortal flesh keep silence ELW 490, st. 2; LBW 198, st. 2

Communion

Unexpected and mysterious ELW 258

As the dark awaits the dawn ELW 261

The angel Gabriel from heaven came ELW 265, WOV 632

Sending

Fling wide the door ELW 259, LBW 32

Love divine, all loves excelling ELW 631, LBW 315

Additional Assembly Songs

Await the hand of God CBM 57

O Antiphons MSB2 S538

It's Christmas coming again/*Ya viene la Navidad* LLC 282

⊕ Bell, John L. "Carol of the Advent" from *Innkeepers and Light Sleepers: Seventeen New Songs for Christmas.* SATB. GIA G-3835.

⊕ Taulé, Alberto. "All Earth Is Hopeful/*Toda la tierra*." U. ELW 266.

⊕ = global song   ♫ = relates to hymn of the day
☼ = praise song   P = available in Prelude Music Planner

☼ Angrisano, Steve. "God with Us (Emmanuel)" from CCLI.
☼ Egan, John/Mia Fieldes. "Joy Will Come" from CCLI.
☼ Houston, Joel. "Salvation Is Here" from CCLI.
☼ Maher, Matt. "Love Has Come" from CCLI.
☼ Packiam, Glenn. "God Who Comes to Save" from CCLI.
☼ Wesley, Charles/Rowland Hugh Prichard/Paul Baloche/Kathryn Scott. "This Is Love (with Come Thou Long-Expected Jesus)" from CCLI.

Music for the Day
Choral

♫ Bandy, Timothy Lee. "O Come, O Come, Emmanuel." SATB, pno, opt inst. AFP 9780800676551.

♫ Costello, Michael D. "Canticle of the Turning: Magnificat." SATTBB, org, tbn, opt assembly. AFP 9781451401615.

Jean, Martin. "Advent Hymn." SATB. AFP 9780800656621.

P ♫ Organ, Anne Krentz. "Come, My Light." 2 pt trbl or mxd, kybd. AFP 9780800675813.

Children's Choir

P Algozin, Charlotte. "How Will We Know Him?" U, kybd, opt fl. CG CGA634.

P Burkhardt, Michael. "Prepare Thyself, Zion." U, kybd, opt vc/bsn. MSM 50-0415.

♫ Schram, Ruth Elaine/arr. Douglas Nolan. "An Invitation for Advent." U/2 pt, opt egg shaker. SHW HL35029815.

Keyboard / Instrumental

♫ Callahan, Charles. "An Advent Prelude" (Veni, Emmanuel; Conditor alme siderum) from *Advent and Christmas: Two Preludes for Solo Instrument and Organ.* Trbl inst (C or B flat), org. MSM 20-110.

P ♫ Kim, Marianne. "Canticle of the Turning" (Star of County Down) from *My Soul Proclaims: Piano Meditations for Worship.* Pno. AFP 9781451499131.

P Organ, Anne Krentz. "As the Dark Awaits the Dawn" (Lucent) from *Piano Reflections on Advent Tunes.* Pno. AFP 9781451462647.

P ♫ Walther, Johann Gottfried. "Savior of the Nations, Come" (Nun komm, der Heiden Heiland) from *Light on Your Feet, vol. 3: A Collection for Organ with Minimal Pedal.* Org. AFP 9780806698021.

Handbell

P ♫ Geschke, Susan. "O Come, O Come, Emmanuel." 2-3 oct hb, L2. CG CGB857.

♫ Thompson, Karen. "Canticle of the Turning." 3-6 oct hb, opt 3 oct hc, L3. GIA G-8491.

♫ Wagner, H. Dean. "Carillon for Advent." 5 oct hb, opt 2-5 oct hc, L3. HOP 1906.

Tuesday, December 20

Katharina von Bora Luther, renewer of the church, died 1552

Born to an impoverished nobleman, when Katharina (Katie) was five her mother died and she was sent to live in a convent. She later took vows as a nun, but around age twenty-four she and several other nuns who were influenced by the writings of Martin Luther left the convent. Six children were born to Katie and Martin. Though initially Luther felt little affection for Katie, she proved herself a gifted household manager and became a trusted partner. She was so influential that Luther took to calling her "my lord Katie."

Christmas

Preparing for Christmas

At Luther Seminary's Celebration of Biblical Preaching in October 2015, Dr. Karoline Lewis preached about making Christmas last beyond a day and even beyond twelve days. The incarnation deserves more than a short season of our attention. Dr. Lewis said:

> We must preach about the significance of the incarnation in between Christmas and Easter, and in between Easter and Christmas: not as doctrine, but as God's commitment to the inherent vulnerability of humanity, as God's commitment to the entirety of what it means to be human. That God chose to become human should be serious cause for pause. The embodiment of God is frequently left behind, packed away with the Advent candles. Why? Perhaps because God chose to be located within the body of a woman. And so we move on. We move on quickly: out of liturgical necessity, yes, but also out of a desperate need to move away from our discomfort with the bodies of women. We fast-forward to the cross.

> The death of God cannot be the only locus of vulnerability. Life is equally so. This is what God chose. The Word became flesh and dwelt among us.

As worship leaders this time of year, it may feel like we don't have very many choices. Many of the ways we celebrate God's incarnation are set months in advance or repeated the same ways year after year. And yet the event we are gathering to celebrate is anything but traditional. We are coming together—some of us for the only time we will worship with others this year—to celebrate God's choice to be born, *really* born: carried for nine months in an unwed mother's womb, brought into the world through the dangerous, messy, miraculous-yet-common means of labor, and cared for in a state of complete vulnerability—not just on that Christmas night, but through all the nights and days we don't read about in the Bible, but can begin to imagine because of our shared human experience with such nights and days.

And if our incarnational imagination quits at Jesus' birth, if we fast-forward from the manger to the cross in our wonder at the incarnation, we have missed the space that most of us inhabit: that space between life and death where we live, in our bodies, and where Christ also lived, in his body. So, one possibility for preaching, singing, and worshiping together this year would be to take Christmas as a time to look ahead and think about ways to focus on the incarnation all year long.

The first choice comes on January 1: Do we celebrate the Name of Jesus? What a wonderful Sunday to celebrate baptisms, if you do those throughout the year. Do we remember instead the state-sponsored murder of children, the exile of the holy family? In a time when more people, the vast majority of them women and children, are displaced than any time since World War II, this seems very relevant. Do we also mark the secular New Year, somehow? Certainly that will be on people's minds. However we choose to mark the day, the message that *God is with us* is powerful, relevant, and necessary.

Incarnation-focused worship can continue past that first (and last) Sunday of Christmas and into the time after Epiphany, when the fullness of God's promise and incarnation is revealed. The reality of Christ's embodied self can certainly be a connecting thread during Lent, as Jesus turns his eyes toward Jerusalem and to the reality of his own death, all the while using his body to heal, to bring life, to bring hope to humans not in some abstract way, but in the flesh. We can preach the incarnation again on Easter Sunday, not in the abstract as a cool concept, but as the scandalous, incredible, unbelievable-without-the-Spirit's-help choice of God to experience the whole of human life and death. In the season of Easter, on the Day of Pentecost, and in the many green Sundays that follow, we can preach the incarnation as the good news that God isn't far away and disinterested in human life and suffering: God was, is, and will be among us, right in the midst of everything that makes us human.

This short season is a gift because it can give us a sense of focus for the seasons to come. The world today is mostly convinced that the church is irrelevant, and that God, if there is one, is far off and uninvolved. Christmas is a direct contradiction of the far-off God. This is not only good news, this is countercultural news, and this is news that requires a completely different understanding of God and where God chooses to be located. This is theology of the cross, yes. But with help from creative worship planners, this embodied theology can go beyond the manger and the cross and fill in all of those spaces between Easter and Christmas, and Christmas and Easter.

Music

The worst theology ever put to music rose to the top of the charts in 1990, sung beautifully by Bette Midler: "God is watching us from a distance." Although many children today do not know this song, this is still the dominant theology of our culture, what Kenda Creasy Dean calls "moralistic therapeutic deism" in her book *Almost Christian: What the Faith of Our Teenagers Is Telling the American Church* (New York: Oxford University Press, 2010). In addition to tending to strongly worded requests for favorite Christmas hymns this season, anything you can do in your hymn and song choices to counteract this civic theology would support the very different, actual Christian message that God is not far away, God is with us! Emmanuel!

Mark Miller's "All My Days," based on Psalm 139, is a reflection on how deeply we are known and loved by God, and can be sung by a choir or the whole assembly. "O God of light" (ELW 507) would make a great segue into the time after Epiphany, emphasizing God's very present, very active work in the world. As you are able, choose songs that highlight the whole human experience: not only joy, but also loss and struggle. The good news of the incarnation is that God is with us in the midst of everything we experience: the whole breadth of birth, life, death, and life after death.

Environment

A grief counselor shared the story of coming back to church for the first time after her young son died. "I tried to come back at Christmas," she said. "That was a mistake. There were flowers and lights and ribbons everywhere. Everything was celebrating children and what a joy they are. Every song was happy. I didn't come back to church until Lent. Then the poinsettias were gone and there were just these vases full of dry, bare sticks. The sanctuary was wrapped in purple and black. The church looked like I felt. It looked bare and broken. It looked bruised."

The grief people feel at Christmas is real. Marj Leegard wrote about holiday sadness in *Give Us This Day*, a collection of her writings for *Lutheran Woman Today*: "When we are children the family is what it is: family. When we grow older we see the family as fragments, as memories. There are empty chairs. It is difficult to realize that there have always been empty chairs. The family that seemed so complete when we were kids was fragmented to our grandparents" (Augsburg Fortress, 1999).

We can't fill the empty chairs or the empty spaces in the pews. We can't make the altar cloths purple. We can't ban "Joy to the world." But there are some things we can do:

- Spend time during Advent conscientiously reaching out to people who are grieving, homebound, lonely, or sick. Send care packages to college students and missionaries. As part of this outreach, invite these folks to Christmas worship, or let them know you will be keeping them in prayer during worship.
- Incorporate music and other messages during Christmas and the Christmas season that speak to the reality of human loss. The first Sunday of Christmas's gospel is about the death of children. Let people know you will be talking about this, and as Dr. Karoline Lewis says, "Preach from a place of kindness. We live in a vulnerable world."
- Plan a Twelfth Night party at the church, or encourage small groups in the congregation to plan smaller gatherings on Twelfth Night. Activities this night may include a Christmas tree bonfire, singing Christmas carols, eating Christmas cookies—other celebrations that speak to Christmas as a season, the incarnate joy of being together, and ways to build community beyond immediate family during a time that can be isolating even as it is filled with gatherings and events.

The joy of Christmas, like the joy of Easter, is not a shallow joy. It is joy that knows the reality of death, the reality of human suffering, and yet has joy and hope anyway. As we prepare our worship environments for Christmas, we "make [our] house fair, as [we] are able" (ELW 248). But we also name the full reality of what it means to be human, because that is the reality into which Christ was born.

Reformation 500

Martin Luther delighted in the Christmas story, and he is credited with starting many interesting Christmas traditions (including the tradition of the baby Jesus bringing Christmas presents, which is still observed in many places in Europe). For Luther, the manger and the cross were both places that showed the immense grace of God: the last places on earth where you would expect an all-powerful deity to be, and yet these are the places God chooses to go in Christ.

The folktale of "The Three Trees" is available widely in many formats and can be used as a short play in worship or at a Twelfth Night celebration. It takes Luther's wonder at the manger and the cross (and adds a boat in between—an important nod to the fact that Jesus was found in unlikely places during his life on earth too) and turns it into a short story about God defying our expectations.

Seasonal Checklist

- Honor your embodied, incarnate self. Find ways to take a rest, and spend time with family and friends—if not on Christmas Eve or Day itself, then shortly thereafter. Be good to your body and be kind to the bodies and souls of the people who serve and worship with you.
- Publicize Christmas services in outdoor signage, local newspapers, and online listings; on your church website and Facebook page; with postcards or other mailings.
- Make sure your congregation's website is up to date. Visitors are coming!
- Make sure your congregation's Twitter worship hashtag is on the bulletin/screen so people can clearly label their sermon tweets and pictures they take during Christmas worship. Encourage people to help you publicize your worship offerings this way.
- Repair or replace seasonal decorations and materials as needed.
- Is the Christmas tree already up? If not now, when? What's the plan for bringing it down? Maybe a Twelfth Night bonfire?
- If handheld candles are used by worshipers on Christmas Eve, make sure you have enough candles on hand and that fire extinguishers and smoke detectors are up to date. Don't forget to instruct people on proper candle-lighting method (tip the unlit candle, not the lit one).
- Order service folder covers if needed for Christmas Eve, Christmas Day, and Epiphany.
- Design service folders that guests will be able to follow easily, including specific instructions for communion distribution. For tips on preparing excellent worship folders, consult *Leading Worship Matters: A Sourcebook for Preparing Worship Leaders* ([Augsburg Fortress, 2013], 268–272).
- If you project your worship service onto a screen or wall, proofread the text carefully before worship and test it on the screen/wall beforehand to check visibility. Work with musicians to make sure that texts on the screen match what will be led/sung.
- Do a "secret shopper" swap with another congregation a few weeks before Christmas to help each other spot things that church insiders might not see. Ask these guests from outside your congregation to look for things that would be helpful or unhelpful to visitors, especially issues related to accessibility for people with mobility, hearing, and visual impairments, families with young children, and any other areas you think may be a blind spot for your congregation (signage? parking? website?).
- Use the canticle of praise ("Glory to God"). In addition to the form in the communion setting, see options in the service music section of *Evangelical Lutheran Worship* (#162–164).
- Use the Nicene Creed.
- Consider especially Thanksgiving at the Table III in *Evangelical Lutheran Worship*.

Worship Texts for Christmas

Confession and Forgiveness

All may make the sign of the cross, the sign marked at baptism,
as the presiding minister begins.

Blessed be the Holy One of Israel,
the Word made flesh,
the Power of the Most High,
+ one God, now and forever.
Amen.

Gathered in the name of Jesus,
let us confess our sin against God and our neighbor.

Silence for reflection and self-examination.

Gracious God,
in Christ Jesus you come among us
as light shining in darkness.
We confess our failure to welcome this light.
Forgive us and renew our hope,
so that we may live in the light of your grace,
and welcome the truth of Christ the Lord. Amen.

I bring you good news of great joy for all the people:
To you is born a Savior, Christ the Lord.
Your sins are forgiven in + Jesus' name.
Amen.

Offering Prayer

God with us:
You came as a baby to a manger.
You slept on straw and greeted shepherds.
You come again in bread and wine.
Remind us how good you are at blessing ordinary things.
And then, through these gifts,
help us to bless the lives of others
in the strength of your holy name.
Amen.

Invitation to Communion

Joy to the world! The Lord is come.
Let every heart receive your Savior.

Prayer after Communion

On this day, O God, you gave us
Christ the Son to save us.
As you sent the one foretold,
send us now with good news for all people.
Let the gladness of this feast have no end
as we share with others the joy that fills us;
through Jesus Christ, our Savior and Lord.
Amen.

Blessing

May Christ, who by his incarnation
has filled us with grace and truth,
give you peace this Christmas and always.
Almighty God, Father, + Son, and Holy Spirit,
bless you now and forever.
Amen.

Dismissal

Glory to God in the highest!
Peace to God's people on earth!
Go in peace. Share the gift of Jesus.
Thanks be to God.

Seasonal Rites for Christmas

Christmas Proclamation

This contemporary version of an ancient proclamation places the birth of Christ into human history yet avoids a literalistic accounting of time. The last phrase makes it clear that the nativity of Jesus is not only then but now, today, in our own time. The proclamation may be chanted by a presiding or assisting minister, cantor(s), or choir at the beginning of the Christmas Eve or Christmas Day liturgy, perhaps before the gathering hymn. Music Sourcebook for All Saints through Transfiguration (Augsburg Fortress, 2013) includes two musical settings for the Christmas proclamation.

Many ages from the time when God created
the heavens and the earth
and then formed man and woman in his own image;
long after the great flood,
when God made the rainbow shine forth
as a sign of the covenant;
twenty-one centuries from the time the promise was given
to Abraham and Sarah;
thirteen centuries after Moses led the people of Israel
out of Egypt and Miriam danced in freedom;
eleven hundred years from the time of Ruth and the judges;
one thousand years from the anointing of David as king,
in fulfillment of the times and years and months and days
discerned by the prophets;
in the one hundred and ninety-fourth Olympiad;
the seven hundred and fifty-second year from the
foundation of the city of Rome;
the forty-second year of the reign of Octavian Augustus;
while the whole world enjoyed a span of peace,
Jesus Christ, eternal God and Son of the eternal Father,
desiring to sanctify the world by his most merciful coming,
being conceived by the Holy Spirit
and nine months of growth in the womb of his mother—
now in our own times is the nativity of our Lord Jesus Christ,
God made flesh.

Text: Traditional, adapt. Brian T. Johnson

Christmas Day Calls to Worship
Based on Psalm 98 (polite, but loud)

Sing to God something brand new!
For God has done wonderful things!
God has not forgotten to love us all!
Even the ends of the earth have heard!
Make a joyful noise!
Break forth in song!
With strings and horns,
sing praise to the Holy One!
With the roaring sea and everything in it!
With all the land and everything in it!
The floods clap their hands.
The hills sing for joy.
Thank God! God is coming to set everything right:
Justice for everyone, everything fair.
Sing to God something brand new!
For God has done wonderful things!

Based on Psalm 98 (downright unruly)

Hey! Sing to God something brand new!
(Loudly): For God has done wonderful things! Hey!
God has not forgotten to love us all!
Even the ends of the earth have heard!
Make a joyful noise!
Hey! Hey! HEY!
With symphony and band!
All instruments turned up to 11!
With the roaring sea and everything in it!
With all the land and everything in it!
The floods clap their hands!
The hills sing for joy!
Thank God! God is coming to set everything right:
Justice for everyone, everything fair!
Hey! Sing to God something brand new!
For God has done wonderful things! HEY!

Text: Worldmaking adaptation by Richard Bruxvoort Colligan

Blessing for a Home at Epiphany

Matthew writes that when the magi saw the shining star stop overhead, they were filled with joy. "On entering the house, they saw the child with Mary his mother" (Matt. 2:10-11). In the home, Christ is met in family and friends, in visitors and strangers. In the home, faith is shared, nurtured, and put into action. In the home, Christ is welcome.

Twelfth Night (January 5), Epiphany of Our Lord (January 6), or another day during the time after Epiphany offers an occasion for gathering with friends and family members for a blessing for the home. Someone may lead the greeting and blessing, while another person may read the scripture passage. Following an eastern European tradition, a visual blessing may be inscribed with white chalk above the main door; for example, 20 + CMB + 17. The numbers change with each new year. The three letters stand for either the ancient Latin blessing *Christe mansionem benedicat*, which means, "Christ, bless this house," or the legendary names of the magi (Caspar, Melchior, and Balthasar).

Greeting

May peace be to this house and to all who enter here.
By wisdom a house is built
and through understanding it is established;
through knowledge its rooms are filled
with rare and beautiful treasures. *(Proverbs 24:3-4)*

Reading

As we prepare to ask God's blessing on this household,
let us listen to the words of scripture.

In the beginning was the Word,
and the Word was with God, and the Word was God.
He was in the beginning with God.
All things came into being through him,
and without him not one thing came into being.
What has come into being in him was life,
and the life was the light of all people.
The Word became flesh and lived among us,
and we have seen his glory,
the glory as of a father's only son, full of grace and truth.
From his fullness we have all received,
grace upon grace. *(John 1:1-4, 14, 16)*

Inscription

This inscription may be made with chalk above the entrance:
20 + C M B + 17
Write the appropriate character (left) while speaking the text (right).
The magi of old, known as
C   Caspar,
M   Melchior, and
B   Balthasar
followed the star of God's Son who came to dwell among us
20   two thousand
17   and seventeen years ago.
+   Christ, bless this house,
+   and remain with us throughout the new year.

Prayer of Blessing

O God,
you revealed your Son to all people
by the shining light of a star.
We pray that you bless this home and all who live here
with your gracious presence.
May your love be our inspiration,
your wisdom our guide,
your truth our light,
and your peace our benediction;
through Christ our Lord.
Amen.

Then everyone may walk from room to room, blessing the house with incense or by sprinkling with water, perhaps using a branch from the Christmas tree.

An acclamation may be sung during the procession, such as Music Sourcebook for All Saints through Transfiguration #S560.

Adapted from *Come, Lord Jesus: Devotions for the Home* (Augsburg Fortress, 1996). See also "Blessing for a Home" in *Evangelical Lutheran Worship Pastoral Care*, pp. 337–353.

December 24, 2016
Nativity of Our Lord
Christmas Eve

On a long winter evening we gather to proclaim the coming of the light. Isaiah announces that the people who walked in darkness have seen a great light. Paul reminds us that the grace of God has appeared, bringing salvation to all. In the familiar account of Christ's birth, the evening sky is bright with the heavenly host singing, "Glory to God in the highest." Amid our broken world we proclaim that the prince of peace is born among us. God comes to us in human flesh—in Christ's body and blood—so that we may be bearers of divine light to all the world.

I
Particularly appropriate for Christmas Eve

Prayer of the Day

Almighty God, you made this holy night shine with the brightness of the true Light. Grant that here on earth we may walk in the light of Jesus' presence and in the last day wake to the brightness of his glory; through your Son, Jesus Christ our Lord, who lives and reigns with you and the Holy Spirit, one God, now and forever.

Gospel Acclamation

Alleluia. I am bringing you good news of great joy for ⁻ all the people:* to you is born this day in the city of David a Savior, who is the Messi- ⁻ ah, the Lord. *Alleluia.* (Luke 2:10-11)

Readings and Psalm

Isaiah 9:2-7

This poem promises deliverance from Assyrian oppression, a hope based on the birth of a royal child with a name full of promise. While Judah's king will practice justice and righteousness, the real basis for faith lies in God's passion for the people: The zeal of the Lord of hosts will do this!

Psalm 96

Let the heavens rejoice and the earth be glad. (Ps. 96:11)

Titus 2:11-14

The appearance of God's grace in Jesus Christ brings salvation for all humanity. Consequently, in the present we live wisely and justly while also anticipating the hope of our Savior's final appearance.

Luke 2:1-14 [15-20]

God's greatest gift comes as a baby in a manger. Angels announce the "good news of great joy" and proclaim God's blessing of peace.

Preface   Christmas

Color   White

Prayers of Intercession

The prayers are prepared locally for each occasion. The following examples may be adapted or used as appropriate.

Rejoicing in the good news of Christ's birth and dwelling in hope, let us pray for the church, those in need, and all of creation.

A brief silence.

Holy God, from you comes all grace and righteousness. Bind your church together during this Christmas season, that we bear witness to the truth of the gospel throughout the world. Lord, in your mercy,

hear our prayer.

Holy God, all creation reveals your splendor and majesty. Guide us in caring for the earth and all it contains, and bring about favorable weather during this time of travel. Lord, in your mercy,

hear our prayer.

Holy God, in the midst of chaos, your Son was born for us. Instill in politicians, military leaders, and civil servants a desire for justice and peace. Lord, in your mercy,

hear our prayer.

Holy God, you care for your children in this and every place. Grant relief to those in fear, shelter to the homeless, community to the isolated, joy to expectant parents, relief to those who yearn for children, and healing to the sick (*especially*). Lord, in your mercy,

hear our prayer.

Holy God, protect those who travel, comfort those who are alone, accompany those who celebrate, and make your presence known among those who gather around word and sacrament. Lord, in your mercy,

hear our prayer.

Here other intercessions may be offered.

Holy God, your Son became incarnate to provide salvation for all. Lead us by the example of the faithful departed as we await the blessed hope of the life to come. Lord, in your mercy, **hear our prayer.**

Hear the prayers of your people, glorious God, for the sake of the one who took on our nature and form to redeem the whole world, Jesus Christ, our Savior and Lord. **Amen.**

Images in the Readings

Luke's gospel presents images of **the poor**: those oppressed by Roman government, women giving birth in a place that houses both people and barn animals, newborns wrapped only in strips of cloth, the socially despised and religiously unclean shepherds. In our society where Christmas suggests unrestricted spending and continual feasting, Luke's image of the poor is striking.

Both the gospel and the first reading suggest the image of the **mother** bearing new life. Often in the Bible, childbirth is credited to God's power. All Christians are now Mary, bearing Christ for the world.

The Hebrew word ***Bethlehem*** means "house of bread." From this historic city famous for its connection to King David comes the one who will feed the people forever. In the liturgy, we enter that house of bread and eat.

Ideas for the Day

- Consider creating "living luminarias" to welcome neighbors to the worship service. Invite members to make luminarias at home and distribute extras to neighbors with a note inviting them to worship. (Be sure to include the address and time for gathering.) Before the service begins, gather along walkways leading to the church (weather permitting) holding the lighted luminarias. Worshipers may sing carols as the prelude and then process into the worship space while singing "O come, all ye faithful."
- Many congregations traditionally hand out candles to be lit while singing "Silent night" near the end of the Christmas Eve service. If a crèche is present in the worship space, consider filling trays with sand and placing them around the holy family. (Large ceramic saucers for planters work well for this.) If numbers and space permit, the assembly can be invited to gather around the crèche to sing the hymn and then place their candles in the sand trays at the conclusion. Yellow glow sticks may be provided for young children or others who may not be able to handle candles safely.
- For many, Christmas Eve is a time of deep nostalgia. While nostalgia is usually, at root, a longing for an experience, people tend to connect that longing with objects—a tree decorated just so, traditional ornaments or food. This may be a good time to reflect on the difference between longing for "Christmases past" and longing for the experience of God—what C. S. Lewis called "Sehnsucht." In the afterward to the third edition of *The Pilgrim's Regress* (Grand Rapids: Eerdmans, 1943), Lewis described the failures of his own efforts to create experiences of God and how he had to learn to wait for the Spirit to provide them.

Connections with the Liturgy

The standard canticle of praise quotes today's gospel: "Glory to God in the highest, and peace to God's people on earth." Every Sunday that we sing this canticle, we join with the angels at the birth of Jesus.

Let the Children Come

On us light shines and our joy has increased! Indeed, this is the night of joy. The church around the globe rejoices as it welcomes this Christ child! Have you wondered how children express joy compared to how adults express joy? Does your worship support all? Are children treated as objects performing for the gratification of others, or are they welcomed as ones with their own spiritual and worshiping dimensions? This night is about welcoming a poor baby into the world as we welcome God. Does your worshiping community hold in tension the imperfections of runny noses with the perfection of divine love?

Assembly Song
Gathering

Angels we have heard on high ELW 289, LBW 71
Once in royal David's city ELW 269, WOV 643
O come, all ye faithful ELW 283, LBW 45, LLC 309

Psalmody and Acclamations

Jenkins, Stephen. "A Christmas Psalm." SATB, assembly, opt U or cant, org. MSM 80-102.
Ollis, Peter. "Today a Saviour Has Been Born" from *Psalm Songs 1*. AFP 0800657705.
Wetzler, Robert. "Psalm 96" from PWA.
(GA) O come, all ye faithful ELW 283, st. 1 before and st. 3 after the gospel

Hymn of the Day

From heaven above ELW 268, LBW 51 VOM HIMMEL HOCH
Midnight stars make bright the skies ELW 280 HUAN-SHA-XI
Joy to the world ELW 267, LBW 39, LLC 288 ANTIOCH

Offering

'Twas in the moon of wintertime ELW 284, LBW 72
In the bleak midwinter ELW 294

Communion

O little town of Bethlehem   ELW 279, LBW 41
I am so glad each Christmas Eve   ELW 271, LBW 69
Silent night, holy night!   ELW 281, LBW 65, LLC 301

Sending

Hark! The herald angels sing   ELW 270, LBW 60
Joy to the world   ELW 267, LBW 39, LLC 288

Additional Assembly Songs

Before the marvel of this night   WOV 636
Gloria en las alturas/Glory in the highest   LLC 297
I wonder as I wander   WOV 642, TFF 50
⊕ Kwami, Robert M. "Drismas dodzi vo/Christmas Time Is Here" from *World Carols for Choirs*. SATB. OXF ISBN 019353231-X.
⊕ Malawi traditional. "That Boy-Child of Mary" U. ELW 293.
☼ Getty, Keith/Kristyn Getty. "Noel Noel" from CCLI.
☼ Hart, Sarah/Scott Krippayne. "We Adore" from CCLI.
☼ Ingram, Jason/Meredith Andrews. "He Has Come for Us (God Rest Ye Merry, Gentlemen)" trad. 18th century from CCLI.
☼ LeBlanc, Lenny. "Christmas Night" from CCLI.
☼ Morgan, Reuben/Ben Fielding. "Unto Us" from CCLI.
☼ Tomlin, Chris/Matt Maher/Ed Cash. "Born That We May Have Life" from CCLI.

Music for the Day
Choral

℗ Highben, Zebulon M. "My Heart Rejoices." SATB, opt children's choir, org, vla, hb. AFP 9780800664152.
℗♫ Langlois, Kristina. "Midnight Stars Make Bright the Skies." U, Orff, perc. AFP 9780800679309.
♫ Nelson, Ronald A. "From Heaven Above." SATB, assembly, org, fl. MSM 60-1004.
℗♫ Wentzel, Brian. "Silken Sounds." SAB, pno. AFP 9781451462470.

Children's Choir

Brooke, Ashley. "On This Day Earth Shall Ring." U/2 pt, opt tamb. SHW HL 35028259.
℗ Hopson, Hal. "Oh Come, Little Children." U/2 pt, pno, opt hb. CG CGA1366.
℗ Music, David. "How Far Is It to Bethlehem?" U/2 pt, opt fc and claves. CG CGA1378.

Keyboard / Instrumental

Daquin, Louis-Claude (1694–1772). "Noël Étranger sur les Jeux d'Anches" from *French Noëls for Organ*. Org. DOV 0486296962.
♫ Nelhybel, Vaclav (1919–1996). "Joy to the World" (Antioch) from *Festival Hymns and Processionals*. 2 tpt, 2 tbn, opt tba, opt timp, org. AG 750.
℗♫ Rowland-Raybold, Roberta. "Midnight Stars Make Bright the Skies" (Huan-sha-xi) from *Winter Solstice: Carols for Organ*. Org. AFP 9781451499100.
℗ Wold, Wayne L. "On Christmas Night" (Sussex Carol) from *Light on Your Feet, vol. 3: A Collection for Organ with Minimal Pedal*. Org. AFP 9780806698021.

Handbell

♫ Eithun, Sandra. "German Carol Medley." 3-5 oct hb or hc, L2, CG CGB899. Opt SATB vcs, CG CGA1428. Opt full score, CG CGB898.
♫ Morris, Hart. "Midnight Stars Make Bright the Sky." 3-5 oct hb, opt 3 oct hc, opt fl or trbl C inst, L3. CG CGB359.
℗♫ Page, Anna Laura. "Joy to the World" from *I Heard the Bells*. 2-3 oct, L2+, CG CGB860. 3-5 oct, L2+, CG CGB861.

⊕ = global song   ♫ = relates to hymn of the day
☼ = praise song   ℗ = available in Prelude Music Planner

December 25, 2016
Nativity of Our Lord
Christmas Day

On this Christmas morning the people of God gather to celebrate the birth of the Word made flesh, Christ our Lord. Luke recounts the familiar story of shepherds and angels; John's gospel tells of the Word that dwells among us, full of grace and truth. The meaning of Christmas is made clear: the light shines in the darkness. It is in the liturgy that we encounter the Word made flesh—in the people of God gathered together as the body of Christ, and in the meal around the holy table. We go forth to be bearers of light as we proclaim this good news to all the ends of the earth.

II
Particularly appropriate for Christmas Day

Prayer of the Day

All-powerful and unseen God, the coming of your light into our world has brightened weary hearts with peace. Call us out of darkness, and empower us to proclaim the birth of your Son, Jesus Christ, our Savior and Lord, who lives and reigns with you and the Holy Spirit, one God, now and forever.

Gospel Acclamation

Alleluia. A holy day has dawned upon us. Come, you nations, and a- ' dore the Lord.* For today a great light has come up- ' on the earth. *Alleluia.*

Readings and Psalm
Isaiah 62:6-12

The prophet invites the people to give God no rest until God reestablishes Jerusalem. In turn, they will receive names full of promise: Holy People, the Redeemed of the Lord, a City Not Forsaken.

Psalm 97

Light dawns for the righteous, and joy for the honest of heart. (Ps. 97:11)

Titus 3:4-7

God saves us not because of what we do. Rather, God is a God of mercy and salvation who graciously cleanses us in baptism and renews our lives through the Holy Spirit.

Luke 2:[1-7] 8-20

The world's deep night is shattered by the light of God's new day. The glory of God is revealed to poor shepherds, who share the good news with others.

III
Particularly appropriate for Christmas Day

Prayer of the Day

Almighty God, you gave us your only Son to take on our human nature and to illumine the world with your light. By your grace adopt us as your children and enlighten us with your Spirit, through Jesus Christ, our Redeemer and Lord, who lives and reigns with you and the Holy Spirit, one God, now and forever.

Gospel Acclamation

Alleluia. I am bringing you good news of great joy for ' all the people:* to you is born this day in the city of David a Savior, who is the Messi- ' ah, the Lord. *Alleluia.* (Luke 2:10-11)
or
Alleluia. A holy day has dawned upon us. Come, you nations, and a- ' dore the Lord.* For today a great light has come up- ' on the earth. *Alleluia.*

Readings and Psalm
Isaiah 52:7-10

A messenger races home to Jerusalem with the marvelous words: "Your God reigns!" In comforting the people, God proves to be the best brother or sister (redeemer) they have ever known. Everyone will witness the victory (salvation) of God.

Psalm 98

All the ends of the earth have seen the victory of our God. (Ps. 98:3)

Hebrews 1:1-4 [5-12]

This letter opens with a lofty declaration of Jesus' preeminent status as the Son through whom God created the world and through whom our sins are cleansed. God speaks to us now through the Son, who is exalted even above the angels.

John 1:1-14

The prologue to the Gospel of John describes Jesus as the Word of God made flesh, the one who reveals God to be "full of grace and truth."

Preface   Christmas

Color   White

Prayers of Intercession

The prayers are prepared locally for each occasion. The following examples may be adapted or used as appropriate.

Rejoicing in the good news of Christ's birth and dwelling in hope, let us pray for the church, those in need, and all of creation.

A brief silence.

Holy God, you raise up leaders throughout the church to proclaim your word of hope. Unite the church through the good news of salvation, so that all will know and experience your glory. Lord, in your mercy,
hear our prayer.

Holy God, you created mountains and hills, seas and rivers, and all creatures. Reveal to us the goodness of all you have made so that we live wisely with these your gifts. Lord, in your mercy,
hear our prayer.

Holy God, you desire that all people live in peace. Guide all in positions of authority to lead with equity, and give courage to advocates who speak for the voiceless. Lord, in your mercy,
hear our prayer.

Holy God, you sent your Son to be our physician and remedy. Strengthen medical professionals and counselors to care for the sick and grieving (*especially*), so that all people experience healing and consolation. Lord, in your mercy,
hear our prayer.

Holy God, you gather us together in community, blessing us with friends and family. Make yourself known to all who participate in worship today, and send us forth to serve our neighbors. Lord, in your mercy,
hear our prayer.

Here other intercessions may be offered.

Holy God, you show your love and faithfulness in every generation. Through the witness of our ancestors in the faith, you have shown us how to testify to your grace and truth. Lord, in your mercy,
hear our prayer.

Hear the prayers of your people, glorious God, for the sake of the one who took on our nature and form to redeem the whole world, Jesus Christ, our Savior and Lord.
Amen.

Images in the Readings

II

Luke writes that **angels**, messengers from heaven, a link between God and humankind, announce Christ and sing praise to God. Describing and especially depicting angels in a worthy manner is a challenge. Contrary to popular notions, Christian doctrine does not teach that dead Christians become angels, but rather that angels are supernatural beings who signify and convey the power of God. In Luke the angels proclaim the meaning of the incarnation. Recall that in Luke's telling of the annunciation to Mary, the angel is Gabriel, whom Jewish tradition identified as the one who would proclaim the arrival of the eschaton.

Although in some places in the Bible cities are described as evil and filled with temptations, in Isaiah 62 **Jerusalem** symbolizes God's protection, God's very presence on earth. Throughout history, the church has used the image of Jerusalem as a picture of itself: we are like Jerusalem, a magnificent city, protected by the arms of God, thriving on word and sacrament. This imagery might not be clear to all worshipers, who might think we are referring to the actual city of the twenty-first century: sometimes in our worship "Jerusalem" identifies first-century geography, sometimes it is a metaphor for the church, and sometimes it is the name of a current city filled with international religious conflict.

On a day that we think about the **birth** of Jesus, we recall also the water of our rebirth in baptism.

III

During the fourth century, Christians chose the festival at the winter solstice as an appropriate time to celebrate the birth of Jesus. The prologue of John praises the Word of God as this **light** come to illumine the world. What has been born into the darkness on the earth is its light—an image especially appropriate for Christians in the northern hemisphere. The light of Christmas awaits the light of the resurrection.

Too often the church speaks about **creation** as if it were the task of only God the Father. However, the prologue of John and the introduction to Hebrews see the fullness of God as having created the world. Jesus Christ, the Son of God, "the exact imprint of God's very being" (Heb. 1:3), is lauded as creator of all things. For Christians, God is always triune.

The gospel of John demonstrates its Greek context in its reliance on the imagery of Jesus as the **Son of God**. Christian theologians stressed that calling Jesus the Son of God does not mean what it commonly signified in Greco-Roman polytheism, where superhumans were born from a human mother who had been impregnated by a god like Jupiter. Rather, the image is a supreme metaphor for Jesus' origin from God. John also claims that Jesus, as the Father's only Son, makes all believers into children of God.

For John, Christ is the **Word**. When Jesus speaks, we hear God. When God speaks, we encounter Jesus. Worshipers receive this word at Sunday worship.

Ideas for the Day

- Depending on the number of people attending worship on Christmas Day, consider offering a "Dinner Church" service especially geared for people who may not have family or friends to gather with on this day. The worship service can be held in an alternative space that will accommodate tables and chairs. Worship takes place in the context of a shared meal. The homily time becomes space for sacred conversation shared at the table. Links to several examples of complete orders of service from Episcopal and Lutheran congregations can be found at www.diovermont.org/Table/Mission-and-Ministries/Stirrings-of-the-Spirit/.
- The reading from John 1 bridges the immediacy of the incarnation and the cosmic vastness of the divine plan. Worshipers may come with questions about the relationship of faith in the miracle of this birth to scientific understanding of the cosmos. Grace Wolf-Chase, member of St. Paul Lutheran Church in Wheaton, Illinois, and astronomer at the Adler Planetarium in Chicago, speaks to the question, "How do we reconcile faith and science?" in a podcast titled *Balance by Jamie Godfrey* (episode 25, July 15, 2015, available on iTunes). Dr. Wolf-Chase's reflection on this question begins around 00:53:00.
- George MacDonald was a Scottish author, poet, and minister and a primary influence on C. S. Lewis. MacDonald's short story "The Gifts of the Child Christ" draws a powerful and unusual portrait of the divine Love that becomes enfleshed for the sake of a world burdened by grief and death in spite of its good appearances. The complete story can be accessed at www.online-literature.com/george-macdonald/3641/. The story is also in the anthology *The Gifts of the Child Christ: Fairy Tales and Stories for the Childlike* (Grand Rapids: Eerdmans, 1973).

Connections with the Liturgy

II

For the dismissal today, we call out, "Go in peace. Share the good news. Thanks be to God." We are the shepherds.

III

In the Nicene Creed we confess that our one Lord, Jesus Christ, is "the only Son of God, eternally begotten of the Father, God from God, Light from Light, true God from true God."

Let the Children Come

The last time Christmas fell on a Sunday, the church down the street put a banner on its lawn: "Christmas morning: Come as you are . . . wear your pajamas to church." A young girl was mesmerized and wanted to go. Her mother was puzzled and realized it wasn't that she didn't want to go to the family's own church, but she wanted the intimacy, surprise, and ease of worshiping in her pajamas. Somehow the idea encapsulated Christmas morning. We have been invited into the intimacy of the birth of Christ—the warm blankets, the edge between steamy breath and crisp winter air. Do not be afraid to be surprised!

Assembly Song
Gathering

Good Christian friends, rejoice ELW 288, LLC 289, LBW 55
O come, all ye faithful ELW 283, LBW 45, LLC 309
Angels, from the realms of glory ELW 275, LBW 50

Psalmody and Acclamations

Manalo, Ricky. "Be Glad in the Lord (Psalm 97)." Cant, assembly, kybd, C inst, gtr. GIA G-4363.
Roberts, William Bradley. "Psalm 97," Refrain 2, from PSCY.
Behnke, John. "Psalm 98: Sing to the Lord a New Song." SATB, cant, assembly, kybd, 2 tpt, hb. CPH 983666WEB.
(GA) Ferguson, John. "Gospel Processional." SATB, org, tpt, assembly. AFP 9780800677084.

Hymn of the Day

Of the Father's love begotten ELW 295, LBW 42 *DIVINUM MYSTERIUM*
Go tell it on the mountain ELW 290, LBW 70, TFF 52 *GO TELL IT*
Hark! The herald angels sing ELW 270, LBW 60 *MENDELSSOHN*

Offering

What child is this ELW 296, LBW 40
Word of God, come down on earth ELW 510, WOV 716

Communion

Let our gladness have no end ELW 291, LBW 57
Lo, how a rose e'er blooming ELW 272, LBW 58
Love has come ELW 292

Sending

Let all together praise our God ELW 287, LBW 47
The bells of Christmas ELW 298, LBW 62

Additional Assembly Songs

God here among us MSB2 S552
Emmanuel W&P 36
Break forth, O beauteous heavenly light PH 26

- Bell, John, arr. "I Am for You" from *Heaven Shall Not Wait*. SATB. GIA G-3646.
- Kalinga melody. "In the Heavens Shone a Star" from *Glory to God*. U. WJK 0664238971.
- Baloche, Paul/Kathryn Scott. "This Is Love" from CCLI.
- Baloche, Rita. "Prepare Him Room" from CCLI.
- Bruxvoort Colligan, Richard. "Shout for Joy" (Psalm 98)" from *Shout for Joy*. AFP 9780806698632.
- Dell, David/Shirley Erena Murray. "Where Is the Room" from CCLI.
- Hastings, Ben/Seth Simmons/Ben Fielding. "Peace Has Come" from CCLI.
- Herms, Bernie/Stephanie Lewis/Mark Schultz. "When Love Was Born" from CCLI.
- Kendrick, Graham/Paul Baloche. "What Can I Do" (Christmas version) from CCLI.

Music for the Day
Choral

- Crosier, Katherine. "Of the Father's Love Begotten." SATB, hb. GIA G-2837.
- Hovland, Egil. "The Glory of the Father" from *Augsburg Motet Book*. SATB. AFP 9781451423709. Available as octavo from WAL G-W2973.
- Mendelssohn, Felix/arr. Michael Burkhardt. "Hark! The Herald Angels Sing." SATB, SSA, assembly, org, opt br qrt, hb. CG CGA901.
- Nelson, Ronald A. "From High on the Mountain." U, pno, desc. AFP 9780806698366.

Children's Choir

- Bedford, Michael. "Glory to God" from *Seasonal Songs for Young Singers*. U, pno, opt hb or hc. CG CGA1160.
- Patterson, Mark. "Go, Tell It on the Mountain." U/2 pt, pno. CG CGA1038.
- Raabe, Nancy. "Lullaby Carol" from *ChildrenSing in Worship*, vol. 3. U/2 pt, opt fc. AFP 9781451476576.

Keyboard / Instrumental

- Bach, J. S. "Der Tag, der ist so freudenreich," BWV 605, from *Orgelbüchlein*. Org. Various editions.
- Miller, Aaron David. "Of the Father's Love Begotten" (Divinum mysterium) from *Hymns in Jazz Style*. Pno. AFP 9780800678531.
- Turner, John. "Go Tell It on the Mountain" (Go Tell It) from *Jazz Carols for Piano*. Pno. AFP 9781451499117.
- Visser, Larry. "Of the Father's Love Begotten" (Divinum mysterium) from *Paraphrases on Four Gregorian Themes for Organ*. Org. Wayne Leupold WL600091.

Handbell

- Dobrinski, Cynthia. "Hark! The Herald Angels Sing." 3-5 oct, L3+. HOP 1654.
- Eithun, Sandra. "Of the Father's Love Begotten." 3-6 oct hb, opt 3-6 oct hc, L2. GIA G-8715.
- Raney, Joel. "Go, Tell It on the Mountain." 3-5 oct hb, opt 3-5 oct hc, L4-, HOP 2731. Opt synth/perc, HOP 2731P.

Monday, December 26
Stephen, Deacon and Martyr

Stephen was a deacon and the first martyr of the church. He was one of those seven upon whom the apostles laid hands after they had been chosen to serve widows and others in need. Later, Stephen's preaching angered the temple authorities, and they ordered him to be put to death by stoning, with Saul (later Paul) as one of the observers. As he died, he witnessed to his faith and spoke of a vision of heaven.

Tuesday, December 27
John, Apostle and Evangelist

John, the son of Zebedee, was a fisherman and one of the Twelve. John, his brother James, and Peter were the three who witnessed the light of the transfiguration. John and James once made known their desire to hold positions of power in the kingdom of God. Jesus' response showed them that service to others was the sign of God's reign in the world. Tradition has attributed authorship of the gospel and the three epistles bearing his name to the apostle John. John is a saint for Christmas through his proclamation that the Word became flesh and lived among us, that the light of God shines in the darkness, and that we are called to love one another as Christ has loved us.

Wednesday, December 28
The Holy Innocents, Martyrs

The infant martyrs commemorated on this day were the children of Bethlehem, two years old and younger, who were killed by Herod, who worried that his reign was threatened by the birth of a new king. Augustine called these innocents "buds, killed by the frost of persecution the moment they showed themselves." Those linked to Jesus through their youth and innocence encounter the same hostility Jesus encounters later in his ministry.

January 1, 2017
Name of Jesus

From the beginning, by virtue of our baptism, we are called Christian. We were "Christ-ened" at the font. Bearing his name, we share the same Father and are invited to address him intimately: Abba! Jesus bears our sins in humble obedience to the will of the Father. Today we pray that the mind of Christ, whose name we bear, would be our own. It is a good way to begin, again, another year.

Prayer of the Day

Eternal Father, you gave your incarnate Son the holy name of Jesus to be a sign of our salvation. Plant in every heart the love of the Savior of the world, Jesus Christ our Lord, who lives and reigns with you and the Holy Spirit, one God, now and forever.

Gospel Acclamation

Alleluia. At the name of Jesus every ˈ knee should bend,* in heaven and on earth and un- ˈ der the earth. *Alleluia.* (Phil. 2:10)

Readings and Psalm

Numbers 6:22-27

God commanded Aaron to say these words, known as the Aaronic benediction, in blessing the people of Israel. We too are marked with God's name and God's blessing as we are sent from our assemblies into the world.

Psalm 8

How majestic is your name in all the earth! (Ps. 8:1)

Galatians 4:4-7

Paul proclaims the ultimate significance of the nativity: Jesus was born the Son of God so that, because of him, we all may be God's children.

or Philippians 2:5-11

This early Christian hymn points to Christ's self-emptying obedience on the cross as cause for his exaltation by God and worthy of praise by the entire cosmos.

Luke 2:15-21

Eight days after his birth, Jesus is circumcised according to Jewish law and given the name announced by the angel before his conception.

Preface   Christmas

Color   White

Prayers of Intercession

The prayers are prepared locally for each occasion. The following examples may be adapted or used as appropriate.

Rejoicing in the good news of Christ's birth and dwelling in hope, let us pray for the church, those in need, and all of creation.

A brief silence.

Blessed Jesus, your name is proclaimed through preaching, sacraments, music, art, and all forms of creativity. Bring together congregations and leaders from various traditions to make you known. Lord, in your mercy,

hear our prayer.

Blessed Jesus, you reveal yourself through creation, here on earth and throughout the cosmos. Protect endangered species, bring favorable weather, and guide us to be good stewards of all that you have made. Lord, in your mercy,

hear our prayer.

Blessed Jesus, you show nations and leaders the way of the humble servant. Guide all in authority to use power for the benefit of all people throughout the world. Lord, in your mercy,

hear our prayer.

Blessed Jesus, you attend to the needs of your brothers and sisters. Hear the cry of those who call upon your name (*especially*) and send caregivers to provide help to all in need. Lord, in your mercy,

hear our prayer.

Blessed Jesus, you shower us with your grace. Accompany students returning to school, workers who rest from a busy holiday season, and your people gathered here for worship. Lord, in your mercy,

hear our prayer.

Here other intercessions may be offered.

Blessed Jesus, you emptied yourself to take on our likeness and form so we are blessed to become children of God. Inspire us by the witness of the faithful departed to confess your name above all names. Lord, in your mercy,

hear our prayer.

Hear the prayers of your people, glorious God, for the sake of the one who took on our nature and form to redeem the whole world, Jesus Christ, our Savior and Lord.

Amen.

Images in the Readings

We who call the president by his first name are far distant from a culture in which knowing a person's **name** was a sign of having access to that person's inner self. To use a person's first name was a privilege granted to only a few, something like being free to see a person naked. Today's readings include a glossary of divine names; in the Luke reading, "Jesus," which means "the Lord saves"; in Numbers, "Lord," which is a traditional circumlocution for I AM; in Galatians, "Father," since it seems that even Paul could not translate into Greek the surprising endearment of *Abba*; "Father, Son, and Spirit" in Paul's early trinitarian description; and in Philippians, the essential Christian naming, that we call Jesus Lord.

The image of the **shepherds** who come to see Jesus and return to praise God stands at the outset of the new year. We too have been to the stable, we too return to our tasks praising God.

To **bless** people is to call down upon them the goodwill of God. The casual phrase used when someone sneezes—"Bless you!"—is not a polite pleasantry but a prayer for divine visitation. At worship we receive God's blessing from the pastor, who ministers to us in God's name. Perhaps today, January 1, is a good day for all of us to bless one another, marking each other's forehead with the sign of the cross at the start of the new year.

Ideas for the Day

- This Sunday's readings are filled with blessings and provide an opportunity to explore the notion of blessing for this assembly. Liturgical scholar Benjamin Stewart suggests that "blessing is a deliberate act that makes space, a space in which we stop short so as not to be mere consumers but receivers, thankful recipients of holy gifts" (sermon at the Institute of Liturgical Studies, Valparaiso, Indiana, April 16, 2012). On this first day of the new year, consider how a specific blessing might be given in this assembly as worshipers gather full of hopes and dreams for a new year.
- At the naming of Jesus, there was blood—as there is when a male baby's foreskin is removed. The shedding of that blood is a foreshadowing of the blood shed on the cross. John Milton's poem "Upon the Circumcision," written around 1633, contains these lines and images: "He who with all Heaven's heraldry whilere / entered the world, now bleeds to give us ease / . . . but oh! ere long / huge pangs and strong / will pierce more near his heart."
- On the mind of every person at worship today is the passing of time, especially the day-by-day, week-by-week, year-by-year passage of time. That strict keeping of time is evident in Jesus' parents following the prescription to bring their newborn son to the temple on the eighth day. The reading from Galatians calls our attention to a different

kind of time: *kairos* time, the time when things come together in the symbiotic intersection of divine providence. A reflection on specific opportunities for ministry in the local context helps people to look beyond the passage of *chronos* time with a view to how and where God is working—kairos moments when God invites us into God's holy mission in specific and concrete ways.
- A quick internet search of "Wordle for the names of Jesus" results in a variety of collages of the names of Jesus. Many of them are in the public domain and could be useful for projection or bulletin covers. You could also try your hand at creating your own at Wordle.com.

Connections with the Liturgy

Many Lutherans over the centuries have inherited from Martin Luther his preference for the Aaronic blessing as the benediction at the close of the Sunday liturgy (*ELW*, p. 114). Henry Melchior Muhlenberg's 1748 liturgy for the colonial ministerium of Pennsylvania also appointed the Aaronic blessing for regular Sunday use. With this ancient benediction, we begin each week, as we begin each year, under the name of God.

Let the Children Come

Eric Clapton's song "Tears in Heaven" begins with "Would you know my name, if . . . ?" If we know someone's name, we recognize them and claim them as part of us. In today's gospel, the baby is named Jesus, known by his parents, shepherds, angels—and now us. It is our deep longing to know and be known by others. This goes for everyone. Naming the Christ child the common, ordinary name Jesus puts all children on a first-name basis with God. How does your whole community call children by name? Does your community wear name tags or regularly name everyone in prayer throughout the year?

Assembly Song
Gathering

All my heart again rejoices   ELW 273, LBW 46
Once in royal David's city   ELW 269, WOV 643
Jesus, what a wonderful child   ELW 297, TFF 51

Psalmody and Acclamations

Bruxvoort Colligan, Richard. "How Great Is Your Name" (Psalm 8)" from *Shout for Joy*. AFP 9780806698632.
Cherwien, David and Susan. "Two Psalm Settings (Psalm 8)." U/2 pt, kybd, assembly, opt tr, 3 hb or hc. CG CGA1077.
Helgen, John. "Psalm 8" from *ChildrenSing Psalms*. U, kybd, 2 hb, fc. AFP 9780800663872.
(GA) He came down   ELW 253, sts. 1-2 before and sts. 3-4 after the gospel.

Hymn of the Day

That boy-child of Mary ELW 293, TFF 54 *BLANTYRE*
At the name of Jesus ELW 416, LBW 179 *KING'S WESTON*
Love has come ELW 292 *UN FLAMBEAU*

Offering

Blessed be the name ELW 797
How sweet the name of Jesus sounds ELW 620, LBW 345

Communion

O Savior, precious Savior ELW 820, LBW 514
Jesus, the very thought of you ELW 754, LBW 316
Cold December flies away ELW 299, LBW 53, LLC 292

Sending

All hail the power of Jesus' name! ELW 634, LBW 328/329
Good Christian friends, rejoice ELW 288, LLC 289, LBW 55

Additional Assembly Songs

Before the ancient one, Christ stands CBM 13
Greet now the swiftly changing year LBW 181
⊕ Mozambique traditional. "Nzamuranza" from *Pave the Way: Global Songs 3*. SATB, U. AFP 9780800676896.
⊕ Karki, Chitra. "Chitra's Tune" from *One Is the Body: Songs of Unity and Diversity*. U. GIA G-5790.
☼ Alexander, Cecil Frances Humphreys/Laura Story. "Emmanuel" from CCLI.
☼ Cottrell, Angela/Travis Cottrell. "Your Name" from CCLI.
☼ Hall, Charlie/Matt Maher. "Light Has Come" from CCLI.
☼ Maher, Matt. "Great Things" from CCLI.
☼ Nockels, Christy/Nathan Nockels. "His Renown" from CCLI.
☼ Utterbach, Clinton. "Blessed Be the Name of the Lord" from CCLI.

Music for the Day
Choral

P Anerio, Giovanni Francesco. "Christ Humbled Himself" from *Augsburg Motet Book*. SATB. AFP 9781451423709.
♫ Burkhardt, Michael. "At the Name of Jesus." SATB, assembly, org, hb, br qrt, timp. MSM 60-9100.
P♫ Highben, Zebulon M. "Love Has Come." SATB, assembly, org, fl, cl, perc. AFP 9780800679286.
P Raabe, Nancy. "The Everlasting Light." 2 pt mxd, pno. AFP 9781451499001.

Children's Choir

Burkhardt, Michael. "Let Our Gladness Have No End" from *Christmas Songs from Around the World*. U/2 pt, opt Orff inst. MSM 50-1810.
P Miller, Aaron David. "Lift Your Eyes" from *ChildrenSing in Worship*, vol. 1. U/2 pt, pno. AFP 9781451461220.
Spevacek, Linda. "Jesus, Infant Holy." 2 pt, pno. LOR 15/3008H.

Keyboard / Instrumental

P♫ Biery, Marilyn. "At the Name of Jesus" (King's Weston) from *A British Perspective: Melodies and Hymn Tunes for Organ*. Org. AFP 9780800663919.
P Markull, Friedrich Wilhelm (1816–1887). "From Heaven Above" (Vom Himmel hoch) from *Twenty-Four Chorale Preludes, Op. 123*. Org. AFP 9781451401875.
P Maynard, Lynette L. "Cold December Flies Away" (El desembre congelat) from *All Earth Is Hopeful: Piano Preludes for the Christmas Season*. Pno. AFP 9780806697987.
♫ Powell, Robert J. "Love Has Come" (Un flambeau) from *Seven Carols of Christmas*. Fl, cl, bsn, org. CPH 97-5921.

Handbell

P Bettcher, Peggy. "Jesus, Messiah" from *Easy to Ring Praise & Worship VII*. 2-3 oct, L2, HOP 2687. 3-5 oct, L2, HOP 2670.
Cota, Patricia S. "Jesus' Name." 3-5 oct, L3-. HOP 2189.
♫ Mazzatenta, Michael. "Love Has Come." 3-5 oct, L2. SF 201833SF.

⊕ = global song   ♫ = relates to hymn of the day
☼ = praise song   P = available in Prelude Music Planner

January 1, 2017
First Sunday of Christmas

As we celebrate the Twelve Days of Christmas, our gospel today confronts us with the death of innocent children at the hands of Herod. The birth of Christ does not remove the power of evil from our world, but its light gives us hope as we walk with all the "holy innocents" of past generations and today who have suffered unjustly. In our gathering around word and meal, God continues to redeem us, lift us up, and carry us as in days of old.

Prayer of the Day

O Lord God, you know that we cannot place our trust in our own powers. As you protected the infant Jesus, so defend us and all the needy from harm and adversity, through Jesus Christ, our Savior and Lord, who lives and reigns with you and the Holy Spirit, one God, now and forever.

Gospel Acclamation

Alleluia. Let the peace of Christ rule ᴵ in your hearts,* and let the word of Christ dwell ᴵ in you richly. *Alleluia.* (Col. 3:15, 16)

Readings and Psalm

Isaiah 63:7-9

God does not delegate divine intervention to a messenger or angel. God's own presence brings salvation. The prophet and all who read these words join in celebrating God's gracious deeds. God trusts that God's people will not act falsely.

Psalm 148

The splendor of the LORD is over earth and heaven. (Ps. 148:13)

Hebrews 2:10-18

Through Jesus' suffering and death, the trail to eternal salvation has been blazed for us. We do not fear death, because he has conquered the power of death. Thus Christ, our merciful and faithful high priest, has the final say over the destiny of our lives.

Matthew 2:13-23

Matthew relates the slaughter of babies in Bethlehem as one example of evil in the world. Jesus has been born into this world to manifest God's presence and save his people from their sins.

Preface   Christmas

Color   White

Prayers of Intercession

The prayers are prepared locally for each occasion. The following examples may be adapted or used as appropriate.

Rejoicing in the good news of Christ's birth and dwelling in hope, let us pray for the church, those in need, and all of creation.

A brief silence.

Merciful God, make your presence known throughout your church in all its different forms. Guide preachers and teachers to proclaim the work you do in this and every place. Lord, in your mercy,

hear our prayer.

You created the earth and all it contains. Send rain and snow to parched places so that plants and animals thrive. Direct us to be good stewards of all that you create. Lord, in your mercy,

hear our prayer.

You heal what is broken and make all things new. Grant peace in war-torn nations (*especially*), diplomatic wisdom to leaders, and end the torment of violence, so that all people live in safety and security. Lord, in your mercy,

hear our prayer.

You call us as your children and comfort us in our afflictions. Bring patience to the distressed, compassion to the grieving, and relief to the suffering (*especially*), so that all experience your loving care. Lord, in your mercy,

hear our prayer.

You gather us together and feed us with your word and sacrament. Send us forth to make your name known to all in our community by serving our neighbors. Lord, in your mercy,

hear our prayer.

Here other intercessions may be offered.

You give us examples of Christlike living through the witness of the faithful departed. As your beloved called on the name of Jesus throughout their lives, inspire us to call upon him in joy and in need. Lord, in your mercy,

hear our prayer.

Hear the prayers of your people, glorious God, for the sake of the one who took on our nature and form to redeem the whole world, Jesus Christ, our Savior and Lord.

Amen.

Images in the Readings

The image that recurs in the three readings is the **child**. Jesus is the child of God; the children of Bethlehem are slaughtered; God has treated Israel like beloved children; the sacrifice of Jesus makes believers into children of God. The challenge in our culture is to keep this image from shallow sentimentality.

The gospel reading contrasts the protected child with the **victim**. All three readings speak their good news against the backdrop not of joyous Christmas celebration but of endless human suffering. Many medieval churches displayed life-sized depictions of the slaughter of the innocents, with weeping mothers holding bleeding infants. This art hinted at what is to come: Mary weeping over the dead Jesus. Christianity is not for the squeamish.

God, like a **loving parent**, a father, a mother, is carrying the toddler to safety.

Ideas for the Day

- The great hymns of Christmas, replete with boisterous refrains of "Gloria in excelsis Deo," will still be ringing in the ears of worshipers this Sunday. The violence embedded in the gospel reading is no reason to eschew continuing the celebration of good news with great joy. Rather, it's an opportunity to embody in liturgy and preaching the "both/and" truth that the good news is always proclaimed and heard in the midst of human pain and suffering. The holy family looks into the unknown of a future on the run and trusts in God's protection. Tell the stories from your own congregation or community when people have faced a difficult and unknown future and have relied on God's provision to bring deliverance.

- When powerful rulers exercise their authority and exert their might, inevitably their demonstrations of power affect the innocent ones. No doubt this week's news stories provide up-to-the-minute examples of the slaughter of innocents. In our care and compassion for the innocents, we also remember the death of the Innocent One, God among us. For Jesus to live through infancy, innocent children died; for all to have life with God, the innocent Jesus died. Include a petition in the prayers of intercession for those who suffer innocently in the wake of war and violence.

- Matthew frames Jesus' return to Nazareth as fulfillment of the prophecy that the messiah would be called a Nazorean (2:23). While scholars debate the exact source of that prophecy, maybe Matthew is calling our attention to something beyond the rectilinear connection between prophecy and fulfillment. Nazareth was an out-of-the-way place; from there God came to bring salvation to the whole world. Our celebrity culture tends to overlook the tiny backwoods places of no seeming significance. What are the "nowhere" places in our own backyards—places that we have overlooked—where God is already at work? How can we encourage the assembly to be part of that work?

Connections with the Liturgy

As we hear in the second reading, Jesus calls us brothers and sisters, and so in the thanksgiving for baptism we hear, "By water and your Word you claim us as daughters and sons." In the prayers of intercession, we pray for "the poor, oppressed, sick, bereaved, lonely, and all who suffer in body, mind, or spirit," and so we ask God to care for all suffering children around the world.

Let the Children Come

Madeleine L'Engle's book *The Glorious Impossible* (New York: Simon & Schuster, 1990) is illustrated with the hauntingly beautiful frescoes of Renaissance painter Giotto as it depicts the life of Christ. It is categorized as "juvenile literature," and yet most parents and teachers would skip "The Massacre of the Innocents" page. Don't we want to skip the upsetting part of the story? And yet we can't ignore suffering, wherever it is found. Children suffer at the hand of others; genocide in our homeland, school violence down the street, human trafficking in our cities, and abuse in our homes. When we turn our eyes from the suffering of children in the world, we turn our back on the cross.

Assembly Song
Gathering

All my heart again rejoices ELW 273, LBW 46
Once in royal David's city ELW 269, WOV 643
Angels, from the realms of glory ELW 275, LBW 50

Psalmody and Acclamations

Leckebusch, Martin. "Let All Creation's Wonders" (Thaxted) from LUYH.
Mummert, Mark. "Psalm 148" from PSCY.
Praise the Lord! O heavens ELW 823.
(GA) He came down ELW 253, sts. 1-2 before and sts. 3-4 after the gospel.

Hymn of the Day

That boy-child of Mary ELW 293, TFF 54 *BLANTYRE*
Your little ones, dear Lord ELW 286, LBW 52 *HER KOMMER DINE ARME SMÅ*
'Twas in the moon of wintertime ELW 284, LBW 72 *UNE JEUNE PUCELLE*

Offering

In the bleak midwinter ELW 294
From heaven above ELW 268, sts. 1-3, 12-14; LBW 51, sts. 1-3, 12-14

Communion

It came upon the midnight clear   ELW 282, LBW 54
What child is this   ELW 296, LBW 40
Cold December flies away   ELW 299, LBW 53, LLC 292

Sending

Go tell it on the mountain   ELW 290, LBW 70, TFF 52
The bells of Christmas   ELW 298, LBW 62

Additional Assembly Songs

Oh, sleep now, holy baby   WOV 639
Into a time of darkness   CBM 87
María, pobre María/Oh, Mary, gentle poor Mary   LLC 310

⊕ Grau, Alberto, arr. "Niño lindo/Lovely Baby" from *World Carols for Choirs*. SATB. OXF ISBN 019353231-X.

⊕ Lee, Hyun Chul. "Come to the Table" from *Glory to God*. WJK 0664238971.

☼ Cowper, William/Bob Kauflin. "God Moves" from CCLI.

☼ Dawn, Maggi. "Into the Darkness of This World" from CCLI.

☼ Rice, Chris. "Welcome to Our World" from CCLI.

☼ Sons of Korah. "Psalm 148" from 5ive.

☼ Tomlin, Chris/Ed Cash/Scott Cash. "Whom Shall I Fear (God of Angel Armies)" from CCLI.

☼ Townend, Stuart/Keith Getty. "Joy Has Dawned" from CCLI.

Music for the Day
Choral

P ♫ Bedford, Michael. "'Twas in the Moon of Wintertime." U, pno, opt drm, opt fl or rec. AFP 9780800674311.

P ♫ Benson, Robert A. "'Twas in the Moon of Wintertime." SATB, pno. AFP 9781451462517.

P ♫ Denis, Kimberley. "That Boy-Child of Mary." SATB, pno, opt assembly. AFP 9781451485981.

Gelineau, Joseph. "Psalm 148." 2 pt mxd, cant, org. GIA G-2245.

Children's Choir

Berry, Cindy. "Welcome, Lord Jesus." U, pno. CG CGA1157.

Messick, Pat. "Christ Was Born on Christmas Day." U/2 pt, kybd, opt drm, tri, fc, and fl or rec. CG CGA274.

Stroope, Randall. "Sans Day Carol." 2 pt, hp or pno. CG CGA549.

Keyboard / Instrumental

Bach, J. S. "In dulci jubilo," BWV 608, from *Orgelbüchlein*. Org. Various editions.

♫ Biery, Marilyn. "'Twas in the Moon of Wintertime" (Une jeune pucelle) from *Augsburg Organ Library: Christmas*. Org. AFP 9780800659356.

Powell, Robert J. "Cold December Flies Away" (El desembre congelat) from *Instruments for All Seasons*, vol. 2. Cl, org. CPH 97-7255.

P Stevens, Wendy Lynn. "It Came upon the Midnight Clear" (Carol) from *All Is Calm, All Is Bright: 13 Carols for Piano*. Pno. AFP 9780800679040.

Handbell

Glasgow, Michael J. "Gaudete!" 3-7 oct hb, opt 3 oct hc, L4-, CG CGB907. Opt full score (tri/tamb), CG CGB906.

♫ Larson, Katherine. "Children at the Manger." 3-4 oct, L3. AFP 1110623.

P ♫ Moklebust, Cathy. "'Twas in the Moon of Wintertime" from *Celebrate the Season*. 2-3 oct, L2+, CG CGB785. 3-5 oct, L2+, CG CGB786.

Sunday, January 1, 2017
Name of Jesus

The observance of the octave (eighth day) of Christmas has roots in the sixth century. Until the recent past, Lutheran calendars called this day "The Circumcision and Name of Jesus." The emphasis on circumcision is the older emphasis. Every Jewish boy was circumcised and formally named on the eighth day of his life. Already in his youth, Jesus bears the mark of a covenant that he makes new through the shedding of his blood on the cross. That covenant, like Jesus' name, is a gift that marks the children of God. Baptized into Christ, the church begins a new year in Jesus' name.

Monday, January 2
Johann Konrad Wilhelm Loehe, renewer of the church, died 1872

Loehe (approximate pronunciation: LAY-uh) was a pastor in nineteenth-century Germany. From the small town of Neuendettelsau, he sent pastors to North America, Australia, New Guinea, Brazil, and the Ukraine. His work for a clear confessional basis within the Bavarian church sometimes led to conflict with the ecclesiastical bureaucracy. Loehe's chief concern was that a congregation find its life in the holy communion, and from that source evangelism and social ministries would flow. Many Lutheran congregations in Michigan, Ohio, and Iowa were either founded or influenced by missionaries sent by Loehe.

⊕ = global song   ♫ = relates to hymn of the day
☼ = praise song   P = available in Prelude Music Planner

January 6, 2017
Epiphany of Our Lord

Epiphany means "manifestation." On this day we celebrate the revelation of Christ to the Gentiles—that is, to all nations. Some Christian traditions celebrate three great epiphanies on this day: the magi's adoration of the Christ child, Jesus' baptism in the Jordan River, and his first miracle in which he changes water into wine. The word and sacraments are for us the great epiphany of God's grace and mercy. We go forth to witness to the light that shines brightly in our midst.

Prayer of the Day

O God, on this day you revealed your Son to the nations by the leading of a star. Lead us now by faith to know your presence in our lives, and bring us at last to the full vision of your glory, through your Son, Jesus Christ our Lord, who lives and reigns with you and the Holy Spirit, one God, now and forever.

or

Almighty and ever-living God, you revealed the incarnation of your Son by the brilliant shining of a star. Shine the light of your justice always in our hearts and over all lands, and accept our lives as the treasure we offer in your praise and for your service, through Jesus Christ, our Savior and Lord, who lives and reigns with you and the Holy Spirit, one God, now and forever.

or

Everlasting God, the radiance of all faithful people, you brought the nations to the brightness of your rising. Fill the world with your glory, and show yourself to all the world through him who is the true light and the bright morning star, your Son, Jesus Christ, our Savior and Lord, who lives and reigns with you and the Holy Spirit, one God, now and forever.

Gospel Acclamation

Alleluia. We have observed his star ᶦ at its rising,* and have come to ᶦ worship him. *Alleluia.* (Matt. 2:2)

Readings and Psalm

Isaiah 60:1-6

Jerusalem is assured that nations will make a pilgrimage to her, because the light of God's presence is in her midst. The bountiful food of the sea and the profits of international trade will come streaming to Jerusalem and thereby declare God's praise.

Psalm 72:1-7, 10-14

All kings shall bow down before him. (Ps. 72:11)

Ephesians 3:1-12

What had been hidden from previous generations is now made known through the gospel ministry of Paul and others. In Christ both Jews and Gentiles participate in the richness of God's promised salvation.

Matthew 2:1-12

God's promise shines bright in the night as magi follow a star to honor a new king. Strangers from a faraway land, they welcome the long-awaited messiah of Israel.

Preface   Epiphany of Our Lord

Color   White

Prayers of Intercession

The prayers are prepared locally for each occasion. The following examples may be adapted or used as appropriate.

Rejoicing in the good news of Christ's birth and dwelling in hope, let us pray for the church, those in need, and all of creation.

A brief silence.

Gracious God, you reveal yourself to the world in your Son, Jesus. Grant your church throughout the world wise servants of the gospel who proclaim this good news in many ways. Lord, in your mercy,

hear our prayer.

You reveal your goodness through all you have created. Let the beauty of all living things make us yearn to protect the earth and all for whom it contains life. Lord, in your mercy,

hear our prayer.

You reveal your reign of peace through leaders of government at all levels. Guide all in positions of authority to make and uphold laws that are fair for all people. Lord, in your mercy,

hear our prayer.

You reveal your compassion through medical professionals and advocates. Comfort the distressed, tend the grieving, liberate the oppressed, and heal the sick (*especially*). Lord, in your mercy,

hear our prayer.

You reveal yourself through those who are precious in your sight. Strengthen us by your presence in the body of Christ gathered here and in those who are absent from our community, so that all rejoice at the coming of Christ. Lord, in your mercy,

hear our prayer.

Here other intercessions may be offered.

You reveal yourself through generations of faithful people who are now at rest in you. Through their example, lead us to proclaim the gospel with boldness and confidence. Lord, in your mercy,
hear our prayer.
Hear the prayers of your people, glorious God, for the sake of the one who took on our nature and form to redeem the whole world, Jesus Christ, our Savior and Lord.
Amen.

Images in the Readings

The main image is **light**. The star symbolizes a new light in the cosmos. The dawn pierces the thick darkness that has obscured our vision. During January, the northern hemisphere is experiencing a gradual lightening of the darkest time of the year, an appropriate time for the church to praise Christ as the light. This light shines again in the night of the Easter Vigil.

Made popular in hymns, pageants, and crèche sets are the gifts of the magi: **gold**, **frankincense**, and **myrrh**. Gold denotes Jesus as a king. Frankincense and myrrh are sweet-smelling resins that were used in offerings to a god and at status burials. These are symbolic gifts for the divine king who has come to die. The birth narratives contain in them the death of Christ.

The ancient political idea was that monarchs were supposed to ensure safety for their subjects. Christ, not Herod, is the true **king** who gives life, rather than death, to the people.

Ideas for the Day

- The magi had their own plans for their return trip home, which might have included a chat with Herod. However, God had other plans: "And having been warned in a dream not to return to Herod, they left for their own country by another road" (Matt. 2:12). The beginning of the calendar year is often a time for plans. How has God been included in those plans? What other roads might God be suggesting for you, your congregation, and the people you serve?
- *Bethlehem* means "house of bread." How appropriate that Jesus, the bread of life, is born in the house of bread. Consider some of the ways Jesus feeds people today. How do you feed people in your congregation with the word of God? How can you help people feast on the word Monday through Saturday? How does this connect with feeding ministries in your congregation? How does this connect with the feeding ministry of the ELCA World Hunger Appeal? Why might your congregation be called "house of bread"?
- Herod acts in secret while God sends a big, bright star to shine over Jesus. So often in public scandals people get in as much trouble for attempting to cover their deeds as for the deeds alone. In conflicts in churches, keeping secrets does more damage than the secrets themselves. How can

our churches be places where hard truths are spoken? How does the truth of Jesus coming into our world free us to speak truth? How do you speak truth in such a way that you invite others into conversation rather than speaking in such a blunt way that they refuse to hear? How can we speak hard truths while proclaiming the good news of Jesus?

Connections with the Liturgy

Even when contemporary churches encourage parish contributions via automatic withdrawals from individuals' bank accounts, the liturgy hopes to make clear that at every service, whenever believers celebrate God's gift of grace, they make donations for those in need. Our offerings to help those in need and to pay for the ministries of the church are like the magi's gold, frankincense, and myrrh: they are gifts of financial value that come in symbolic praise to God and in recollection of the death of Christ.

Let the Children Come

Finally, the magi arrive! The nativity tableau can be built throughout the Christmas season. For younger children, the story unfolds over time; while for older children, this is a great opportunity to point out how the four evangelists tell the good news, each with a slightly different perspective and details to the story. Matthew's story of the magi is one of Christ: hidden and revealed, precise and ambiguous, near and far. If this little Christ child, this little baby, can be so confounding and amazing to these wise ones, surely it is okay for the little children among us to wonder.

Assembly Song
Gathering

The first noel ELW 300, LBW 56
Bright and glorious is the sky ELW 301, LBW 75
As with gladness men of old ELW 302, LBW 82

Psalmody and Acclamations

Chepponis, James. "Lord, Every Nation on Earth." SATB, cant, assembly, kybd, gtr, C inst, perc. GIA G-6894.
Hobby, Robert. "Psalm 72:1-7, 10-14" from PWA.
Mummert, Mark. "Psalm 72," Refrain 1, from PSCY.
(GA) Ferguson, John. "Gospel Processional." SATB, org, tpt, assembly. AFP 9780800677084.

Hymn of the Day

O Morning Star, how fair and bright! ELW 308, LBW 76, LLC 320 *WIE SCHÖN LEUCHTET*
Brightest and best of the stars ELW 303, LBW 84, LLC 316 *MORNING STAR*
What child is this ELW 296, LBW 40 *GREENSLEEVES*

Offering

Shine, Jesus, shine   ELW 671, WOV 651, TFF 64
This little light of mine   ELW 677, TFF 65

Communion

Come, beloved of the Maker   ELW 306
I want to walk as a child of the light   ELW 815, WOV 649
Drawn to the Light   ELW 593

Sending

Arise, your light has come!   ELW 314, WOV 652
Songs of thankfulness and praise   ELW 310, LBW 90

Additional Assembly Songs

We three kings of Orient are   WOV 646, LLC 321
Los magos que llegaron a Belén   LLC 317
Rise up! Shine!   MSB2 S555

⊕ African American spiritual. "Sister Mary." U. TFF 60.
⊕ Aguiar, Ernani. "Acalanto para o Menino Jesus/Carol for the Baby Jesus" from *World Carols for Choirs*. SATB. OXF ISBN 019353231-X.
☼ Anderson, Jared. "Messiah's Song" from CCLI.
☼ Baloche, Rita. "Follow That Star" from CCLI.
☼ Byrd, Marc/Sarah Hart/Trey Heffinger. "Follow the Light" from CCLI.
☼ Doerksen, Brian. "You Shine" from CCLI.
☼ Hardman, Autumn/Scott Ligetwood/Harrison Wood. "Our King Has Come" from CCLI.
☼ Poythress, Don/Tony Wood/John Wade/C. Frederick Oakeley. "Adore Him" from CCLI.

Music for the Day
Choral

P ♫ Praetorius, Michael. "O Morning Star, How Fair and Bright" from *Chantry Choirbook*. SSATB, opt cont. AFP 9780800657772.
P Cool, Jayne Southwick. "Bright Morning Star." 2 pt, kybd. AFP 9780800664213.
P Thompson, Randall. "Arise, Shine" from *Augsburg Motet Book*. SATB. AFP 9781451423709.
P ♫ Weber, Paul D. "Arise, Shine." SATB div. AFP 9780800677367.

Children's Choir

Burkhardt, Michael. "Kling Glöckchen" from *Come to Bethlehem: Five Carols for Choir and Orff Instruments*. U, sop rec, sop glock, alto and bass metallophones. MSM 50-1120.
P Cool, Jane Southwick. "Bright Morning Star." 2 pt, kybd. AFP 9780800664213.
Mayo, Becki Slagle. "What Shall I Give?" U/2 pt, pno, opt fl. CG CGA1188.

Keyboard / Instrumental

♫ Bender, Jan. *Partita on How Brightly Shines the Morning Star, Op. 102* (Wie schön leuchtet). Org or pno. MSM 10-200.
♫ Manz, Paul O. (1919–2009). "O Morning Star, How Fair and Bright" (Wie schön leuchtet) from *Improvisations for the Christmas Season, Set 3*. Org. MSM 10-102.
P ♫ Markull, Friedrich Wilhelm. "O Morning Star, How Fair and Bright" (Wie schön leuchtet) from *Twenty-Four Chorale Preludes, Op. 123*. Org. AFP 9781451401875.
P Turner, John. "We Three Kings of Orient Are" (Kings of Orient) from *Jazz Carols for Piano*. Pno. AFP 9781451499117.

Handbell

♫ Angerman, David. "Brightest and Best of the Stars of the Morning." 5 oct, L2. SHW HP5408.
P ♫ Cota, Patricia S. "What Child Is This?" from *Twelve Bells +1 for Christmas*. 3 oct (4-6 ringers). HOP 2691.
♫ Moklebust, Cathy. "O Morning Star, How Fair and Bright." 2-3 oct hb, opt 3-5 oct hc, opt perc, L2, CPH 97/7421. 3-5 oct hb, opt 3-5 oct hc, opt perc, L2, CPH 97/7428.

⊕ = global song   ♫ = relates to hymn of the day
☼ = praise song   P = available in Prelude Music Planner

Time after Epiphany

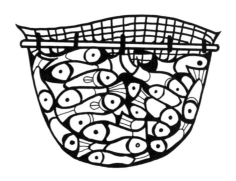

Preparing for the Time after Epiphany

This is bread and butter Christianity. Here we find the foundational stuff of Christian life. Between the high dramas of Christmas and Lent, the time after Epiphany returns to the basics. Basic does not mean unimportant, though. On the contrary, many foundational and well-known texts are packed into these eight weeks: "To do justice, and to love kindness and to walk humbly with your God"; the Beatitudes; "Love your enemies"; "Here is the Lamb of God"; "Jews demand signs and Greeks desire wisdom, but we proclaim Christ crucified"; and many more phrases that you may find yourself reciting as much as reading. Through all eight weeks the texts point again and again to the centrality of Christ, his life and teaching. He is the servant, the lamb, the light, the foundation, and the beloved Son. For us, his disciples, the attention turns to our baptismal identity and activity. We find passages that fill out the image of discipleship in commandments, justice, testimony, and praise, all rooted in the joy and confidence of our baptism into Christ.

This time in the church year is often experienced as a lull, but with that comes the opportunity to scale back and focus intentionally on central things. Let the texts' primary themes—Christ, baptism, discipleship, and light—set the tone for your worship space and music as well as your preaching. Blend the light and joy of the Christmas cycle with the simplicity and intentionality of Lent and allow that to serve as a bridge between the seasons. Lean into the familiarity of the texts, letting your comfort with them become an opportunity to make your preaching deeper and more specific to the people you serve. In one sense these eight weeks are very simple: they focus on Christ and how he has transformed our lives. In another sense that means that all the joy, struggle, and complexity of Christian life can be found here in this little green season.

Lectionary

The time after Epiphany is bookended by the festivals of Baptism of Our Lord and Transfiguration. In the gospel texts for both, Jesus is extolled by a voice from heaven naming him God's beloved Son. These are important high points celebrating Jesus' ministry and festival times to praise incarnation, revelation, and the majesty of God. Between these bookends though, and after John announces him as the one who will baptize with the Holy Spirit, we find Jesus in the trenches, calling the first disciples and preaching the Sermon on the Mount. In fact, the Sermon on the Mount dominates these weeks of year A, paired with readings from 1 Corinthians in the New Testament and Isaiah, Micah, Deuteronomy, and Leviticus in the Old. These partner texts serve to emphasize Christ, his promise and teachings, and give testimony to the goodness and justice of God. Running throughout, the themes of light, baptism, cross, and discipleship appear again and again.

Preaching

Preaching on texts as familiar as the Sermon on the Mount and the Old Testament readings assigned to these weeks is a special kind of challenge. You and your congregation face the danger that, having grown used to the words, you won't hear the radical nature of what is being proclaimed. One way that you and your listeners can literally hear a text in a new way is for you to memorize it. This takes a little time, but as you read the text aloud more intentionally for memory hooks and structure, you will hear fresh details, tones, and patterns in even the most familiar passage. By speaking what you have learned directly to the congregation in the new way you hear it, you will give them new ears for the text as well.

Another way to get new insight into a text is to research it until you find some piece of information that breaks the passage open for you. There are many, many commentaries on the assigned texts, especially Matthew and the Sermon on the Mount, but Frederick Dale Bruner's 2004 revision of his tome *The Christbook* (Grand Rapids: Eerdmans, 2004) has enough exegetical, historical, and theological commentary to get you well on your way.

The Sermon on the Mount can also be approached from much more specific angles. Glen H. Stassen's *Living the Sermon on the Mount* (San Francisco: John Wiley & Sons, 2006) confronts head-on the seemingly impossible moral standards of the sermon with an accessible and gracious everyday approach. For a more varied, and at times radical, discussion of the sermon, David Fleer and Dave Bland's anthology *Preaching the Sermon on the Mount* (St. Louis: Chalice, 2007) gives a variety of preachers' perspectives on communal justice in the text and our own contexts.

Of course the Sermon on the Mount isn't the only text to preach on. David Bartlett and Barbara Brown Taylor's anthology *Feasting on the Word* (Louisville: Westminster John Knox, 2010) provides a variety of perspectives for all of the readings and can be an especially helpful place to start should you choose to preach on an Old Testament reading or epistle text. One note on preaching from the assigned Old Testament readings, especially the Isaiah texts in the first three weeks: while it is important to keep interfaith respect and historical context in mind when preaching from texts like Isaiah, it is also all right to embrace that, for Christians, these readings point to Christ. The Revised Common Lectionary is clearly using the selected Old Testament readings to illuminate Jesus as the long-awaited messiah. So go ahead, use the beautiful images and promises of the Servant Songs and Isaiah 9 in your preaching and liturgy.

Environment

The themes of simple abundance and sturdy symbols will serve you well during this time. As Christmas decorations come down, think about what else you might want to change. Are there ways you can keep the brightness and energy of Christmas while getting rid of some of the excess? What can you do to highlight central symbols while beginning to turn toward the simplicity of Lent?

Light continues to be a prominent image, so make sure that the brightness in the texts shows throughout your space. Baptism and Transfiguration of Our Lord have the advantage of white paraments to make your space feel lighter (but make sure you pull white fabrics out ahead of time to check for stains and wrinkles!). Green paraments can appear brighter with accents of white or gold, and of course actual lights or candles are helpful too. In northern climates a bright green might feel incongruous with the season, but the contrast with drab colors outside can bring energy to the space and help make connections with the other, more summery, green season.

The font and the cross are especially apt to make focal points during this time. Maybe in your space it makes sense to bring them together, letting the primary symbol for Christ and the symbol for baptism together create an image of discipleship. Or maybe in your space they will speak more clearly if emphasized separately. Whichever you do, think about light, color, lines of sight and traffic flow through the worship space as guides to centrally focus the cross and font, and let those criteria help you continue to highlight the table and place of the word as well.

If your congregation has or would enjoy creating art that depicts Jesus' incarnation and the lives of disciples throughout history, this would be a wonderful time to bring that into your worship space, letting it support the central symbols. Icons or other art can be placed with extra lighting or candles around the periphery of the worship space, physically bringing people into the midst of Jesus and the disciples and encouraging them to imagine their own lives alongside faithful Christians throughout the ages.

Music

As you select music for the next eight weeks, keep the Time after Epiphany section of *Evangelical Lutheran Worship* handy for hymns that are especially tied to the texts (#304–318). Don't forget to look beyond it, though, for hymns that proclaim textual themes in slightly broader ways as well, such as many of the hymns in the Holy Baptism section that speak to the entirety of Christian life, and in the Holy Communion section with its strong emphasis on incarnation. You can also find many more hymns that are thematically appropriate for this time filed under Commitment, Discipleship; Hope, Assurance; Justice, Peace; and Witness.

Use this relatively brief stretch of Sundays to consider ways that you would like to expand your assembly's singing and repertoire. Eight weeks is a great amount of time to teach two or three new songs. Use the versatility of themes like discipleship or baptism to think ahead to where in the church year your assembly's song could use more variety. Maybe you can find a hymn in the Commitment, Discipleship section that can reappear several times during Lent or can take a hiatus and then be reintroduced during the time after Pentecost. Or maybe you will find something more specific to introduce, like a gospel acclamation that would be perfect during the Easter season or a baptismal response the congregation could confidently sing at the Easter Vigil.

Children

The festival of Baptism of Our Lord is a natural time to begin or strengthen the practice of gathering children around the font and inviting them to touch the water. A children's time or thanksgiving for baptism is an opportunity to teach children to trace watery crosses on their own or their family's foreheads. Once you have introduced the practice of touching the water or making crosses, find a time in worship when children (and adults!) can easily pass the font and touch the water, perhaps on the way to or from communion. Not only is this a reminder of baptismal identity, but it will draw people's attention to the font as a core symbol of Christian life and discipleship, setting the stage for an even greater emphasis on baptism during Lent.

Reformation 500

As you are likely in the big-picture planning phase for the 500th anniversary of the Reformation this October, now is an opportunity to have congregational conversation about what you will be celebrating and why. Start people talking about what commemorating the Reformation means to them. What are the central things they value from their Lutheran heritage?

What are things they associate with the Reformation that might be more peripheral or local? (For example, putting scripture into conversation with daily life would be a central value; celebrating German ancestry would be a more local one.) Of course both types can be celebrated well, but it can make more detailed planning easier to have the conversation about what your congregation is going to focus on now.

Once you have discussed some of the things about Reformation heritage that you would like to celebrate, move the conversation into the present and future. How does this congregation put those inherited values they have discussed into practice? How do the central things you have discussed appear in your current local context? What are some of the ways that the Reformation is a living tradition that your congregation can celebrate?

Seasonal Checklist

- *Preaching*: Find preaching helps in advance so you can think about these eight weeks as a whole before you get down to the details. Are you going to do a sermon series on the Sermon on the Mount? Would you prefer to focus on the Old Testament readings for several weeks and use those as a lens to illuminate Jesus' life and our discipleship? Whatever you do, it will serve you well to have some continuity in your planning.
- *Environment*: Spend some time in your worship space. What can you do to brighten and simplify it? How can you make central symbols plainly central? Take the time to physically rearrange things and see what works. Pull out candles or small spotlights if you have them. Make sure your white paraments are clean, and find a few colorful items (crosses, art, small banners) to accent your whites and greens.

- *Hymnody*: What new hymns would you like to introduce, and how are you going to teach them? Is there a piece of service music or a hymn that you would love to have the congregation sing confidently during Lent, Easter, or the time after Pentecost? Will you find a "hymn of the month" that can connect with themes over several weeks, introduce a new melody in a prelude or reflection time, or program a new hymn multiple times with a musician who is comfortable leading it?
- *Reformation anniversary*: What can your congregation do now to lay the groundwork for celebrating in October? Are there any logistics you should already be considering? How can you get congregational conversation going? Maybe this is a time to plan some educational opportunities like adult forums, or maybe small groups would like to discuss their Lutheran values and ideas for celebration.
- If you are hosting a catechumenal process and have a group of inquirers, use Welcome to Baptism (*ELW*, pp. 232–233) prior to the beginning of Lent.
- If the alleluia will be symbolically buried or bid farewell on the festival of the Transfiguration, make appropriate arrangements.

Worship Texts for the Time after Epiphany

Confession and Forgiveness

All may make the sign of the cross, the sign marked at baptism, as the presiding minister begins.

Blessed be the holy Trinity, ✛ one God,
who stretches out the heavens,
who sends light to the nations,
who gives breath to us all.
Amen.

Let us confess our sin
in the presence of God and of one another.

Silence for reflection and self-examination.

Loving God,
**we confess that we have turned from your way
to follow our own ways.
Forgive us for the times
we have spoken or acted too quickly;
we have not spoken or acted at all;
we have hurt those closest to us;
we have hurt those we have yet to know;
we have thought more about ourselves than others;
we have thought less of ourselves than we ought.
Turn us around, and give us a fresh start,
so that we can live again as your children. Amen.**

Even when we have done wrong, God makes us right.
Even when we have messed up, God puts us together.
God's love never runs out.
God never tires of calling us beloved children.
Hear God say to you now:
Your sins are forgiven,
for the sake of ✛ Jesus Christ our Savior.
Amen.

Offering Prayer

Merciful God,
receive the gifts we bring,
our selves, our time, and our possessions.
Through this meal unite us as your body,
shining with the light of your justice and mercy;
for the sake of him who gave himself for us,
Jesus Christ our Lord.
Amen.

Invitation to Communion

We who are many are one body,
for we all partake of the one bread.
Come. Be filled with light and life.

Prayer after Communion

O Morning Star, fair and bright,
you have refreshed us again with heavenly food.
You are our dearest treasure.
Go with us now—
today, tomorrow, every day—
that we tell the story of your never-ending love
and sing your praise both now and forever.
Amen.

Blessing

The God of glory dwell in you richly,
name you beloved,
and shine brightly on your path;
and the blessing of almighty God,
the Father, the ✛ Son, and the Holy Spirit,
be upon you and remain with you always.
Amen.

Dismissal

Go in peace. Be the light of Christ.
Thanks be to God.

Seasonal Rites for the Time after Epiphany

Week of Prayer for Christian Unity

At least once a year, Christians are reminded of Jesus' prayer for his disciples that "they may be one so that the world may believe" (see John 17:21). Hearts are touched and Christians come together to pray for their unity. Congregations and parishes all over the world exchange preachers or arrange special ecumenical celebrations and prayer services. The event that touches off this special experience is the Week of Prayer for Christian Unity.

Traditionally the week of prayer is celebrated between January 18 and 25, between the feasts of St. Peter and St. Paul. In the southern hemisphere, where January is a vacation time, churches often find other days to celebrate it, for example around Pentecost, which is also a symbolic date for unity.

In order to prepare for the annual celebration, ecumenical partners in a particular region are invited to produce a basic liturgical text on a biblical theme. Then an international editorial team of World Council of Churches (WCC) and Roman Catholic representatives refines this text to ensure that it can be prayed throughout the world, and to link it with the search for the visible unity of the church.

The text is jointly published by the Pontifical Council for Promoting Christian Unity and the WCC, through the WCC's Commission on Faith and Order, which also accompanies the entire production process of the text. The final material is sent to WCC member churches and Roman Catholic episcopal conferences, and they are invited to translate the text and contextualize or adapt it for their own use. Liturgical resources and materials for use in congregations are available at www .oikoumene.org/en/resources/week-of-prayer/week-of-prayer.

Reprinted from www.oikoumene.org/en/resources/week-of-prayer; accessed January 2016.

Farewell to Alleluia

Congregations that keep the ancient practice of fasting from singing or speaking "alleluia" through the forty days of Lent may consider the practice of "burying" the alleluia at the end of the liturgy on the last Sunday before Ash Wednesday. This might mean simply singing an appropriate song at the end of the service. Or it might include the actual lowering of a visual alleluia (a banner created by children, perhaps) while singing. The alleluia may literally be buried in a box in the church yard or hidden away somewhere in the church (where only the children know where it is!). The alleluia should return with great joy at the first alleluias of the Easter season, perhaps at the Vigil of Easter liturgy.

Hymns and songs

Alleluia, song of gladness ELW 318, WOV 654
Halle, halle, hallelujah ELW 172
Gospel Acclamation / Celtic Alleluia ELW 174
Schwandt, Daniel. "Farewell to Alleluia." *Music Sourcebook for All Saints through Transfiguration* S571.

January 8, 2017
Baptism of Our Lord
Lectionary 1

In the waters of the Jordan, Jesus is revealed as the beloved Son of God. Through this great epiphany, Jesus fulfills all righteousness and becomes the servant of God who will bring forth justice and be a light to the nations. In the waters of baptism we too are washed by the Word, anointed by the Spirit, and named God's beloved children. Our baptismal mission is to proclaim good news to all who are oppressed or in need of God's healing.

Prayer of the Day

O God our Father, at the baptism of Jesus you proclaimed him your beloved Son and anointed him with the Holy Spirit. Make all who are baptized into Christ faithful to their calling to be your daughters and sons, and empower us all with your Spirit, through Jesus Christ, our Savior and Lord, who lives and reigns with you and the Holy Spirit, one God, now and forever.

Gospel Acclamation

Alleluia. A voice from heaven said, "This is my Son, | the Beloved,* with whom I | am well pleased." *Alleluia.* (Matt. 3:17)

Readings and Psalm

Isaiah 42:1-9

God's servant Israel is endowed with the Spirit in order to bring justice to the nations. The servant will not exercise authority boisterously or with violence, nor will weariness ever prevent the fulfilling of the servant's task. God's old promises have been fulfilled; the new assignment of the servant is to bring light to the nations.

Psalm 29

The voice of the LORD is upon the waters. (Ps. 29:3)

Acts 10:34-43

Peter crosses the sharp religious boundary separating Jews from Gentiles and proclaims the good news of God's inclusive forgiveness in Jesus' name to Cornelius, a Roman centurion. As a result of Peter's preaching, Cornelius and his family become the first Gentiles to be baptized in the name of Jesus Christ.

Matthew 3:13-17

Before Jesus begins his ministry, he is baptized by John, touched by the Spirit, and identified publicly as God's child.

Preface   Baptism of Our Lord

Color   White

Prayers of Intercession

The prayers are prepared locally for each occasion. The following examples may be adapted or used as appropriate.

Called to be a light to the nations, let us pray for God's justice, peace, and healing.

A brief silence.

Pour out your Spirit of unity, triune God. Renew our lives in the promises of baptism. Hold us together in the oneness of the body of Christ. Empower us to be one as you are one. Hear us, O God.

Your mercy is great.

Pour out your Spirit of life, eternal God. Move over polluted waters. Breathe on barren fields. Strengthen ancient cedars and oaks. Engage us in your care of sea, land, and sky. Hear us, O God.

Your mercy is great.

Pour out your Spirit of wisdom, holy God. Guide politicians and military officials as they wrestle with complex situations. Grant them courage and compassion to work for peace in every nation (*especially*). Hear us, O God.

Your mercy is great.

Pour out your Spirit of justice, gracious God. Heal the pain of all who are victims of crime. Be present with all who are imprisoned. Reconcile broken relationships within communities. Comfort the sick and their caregivers (*especially*). Hear us, O God.

Your mercy is great.

Pour out your Spirit of love, glorious God. Sustain all who knit prayer shawls, sew quilts, and provide housing for our neighbors who are homeless. Surround those who seek warmth and shelter with grace-filled advocates. Hear us, O God.

Your mercy is great.

Here other intercessions may be offered.

Pour out your Spirit of peace, resurrecting God. Bring all who grieve into a community rooted in you. Uphold them with your grace and keep us all grounded in your promise of life eternal. Hear us, O God.

Your mercy is great.

Receive these prayers in the name of Christ, the light of the world, who is one with you and the Holy Spirit, now and forever.

Amen.

Images in the Readings

There can be no life as we know it without **water**. Christians see in the waters of baptism the matrix of our new life in Christ. The font is like the Jordan, a river of water that leads us to the new land of promise.

The **dove** functions in several biblical stories as a symbol of the presence of God's Holy Spirit. The white color matches the baptismal garment. Secular culture connects the dove especially with peace, which Acts cites as the message of Jesus' preaching.

The gospel reading uses the image of **Son** to describe Jesus' identity; the first reading uses the image of **servant**; and the second reading speaks of Jesus as the **anointed one**. Each of these images conveys something of the meaning of Jesus for believers. It is instructive to think about "Son" and "Christ" as metaphors before these words became literalized as part of Jesus' name.

Once again **light** is an image for the power of God. Early Christians referred to baptism as enlightenment.

Ideas for the Day

- Epiphany is a day in the church year and is also a word used in general conversation. When used generally, *epiphany* can mean a sudden appearance, particularly of a deity, or a sudden insight. Today's epiphany is the Spirit of God appearing on the scene, descending in the form of a dove and heard in a voice from heaven (Matt. 3:16-17). In our lives, God's appearance is rarely as obvious or overt. God's presence can be seen in forgiveness offered after an argument. It can be a sense of peace in spite of bad news delivered by a doctor. It can be the comfort of a hug from a child. What are the little epiphanies made possible by the big epiphany of the God who comes to us through Jesus?

- Baptism of Our Lord always falls early in the new year. Consider using affirmation of baptism with affirmation by the assembly in today's worship following the hymn of the day (*ELW*, pp. 234–235, 237). Sing "I'm going on a journey" (ELW 446) and sprinkle the assembly with water, or invite them to come and mark their own foreheads with a watery cross ("My head is wet . . .") after the affirmation. Begin this new year of grace by remembering and celebrating the gift of baptism and praying for the Holy Spirit to continue to stir up God's gifts in all the baptized.

- In the reading from Acts, Peter makes the case that the gift of Jesus is for all people. It is sometimes tempting to see the church as existing solely to serve those who are already part of the church. If Jesus truly is a gift for the world, how do you share that gift? If you haven't looked at the websites for the ELCA or ELCIC lately, check out ways for your congregation to connect to the church's wider ministry. The "Our Work" section of the ELCA's site (www.elca.org/en/ Our-Work) and the "What We Do" section of the ELCIC's site are good places to start.

Connections with the Liturgy

In the thanksgiving for baptism, we praise God with these words: "At the river your Son was baptized by John and anointed with the Holy Spirit," which Spirit now has anointed us for service.

Let the Children Come

Martin Luther's "flood prayer" invites us to imagine all water as made holy by God's work through it. Our Orthodox Catholic siblings in faith mark this day by "blessing the waters," throwing a cross into the community's major waterway three times, as young people dive to retrieve it. Today we remember not just our own baptisms but Jesus' solidarity with us and with all of creation through the life-giving water. While it may be too cold for "wear your swimsuits to church" today, everyone should get a little wet in thanksgiving for baptism, water, and God's creative and redeeming word.

Assembly Song
Gathering

Songs of thankfulness and praise ELW 310, LBW 90
Hail to the Lord's anointed ELW 311, LBW 87
God, whose almighty word ELW 673, LBW 400

Psalmody and Acclamations

Haugen, Marty. "The Lord Will Bless His People with Peace" from TLP:A.
Mummert, Mark. "Psalm 29," Refrain 1, from PSCY.
Smith, Geoffrey Boulton. "Give Strength to Your People, Lord" from *Psalm Songs 1*. AFP 0800657705.
(GA) Mxadana, George. "Two Songs from South Africa: Alleluia." SATB. GIA G-5286. Use ELW psalm tone 11 in G major with proper verse for Baptism of Our Lord.

Hymn of the Day

I bind unto myself today ELW 450, LBW 188 *ST. PATRICK'S BREASTPLATE*
When Jesus came to Jordan ELW 305, WOV 647 *KING'S LYNN*
Crashing waters at creation ELW 455 *STUTTGART*

Offering

O living Breath of God/*Soplo de Dios viviente* ELW 407, LLC 368
Spirit of Gentleness ELW 396, st. 1; WOV 684, st. 1

Communion

Come, beloved of the Maker ELW 306
I'm going on a journey ELW 446
The only Son from heaven ELW 309, LBW 86

Sending

I'm going on a journey   ELW 446
Oh, love, how deep   ELW 322, LBW 88

Additional Assembly Songs

Come to the water   MSB2 S562
Song over the Waters   W&P 127
Out from your throne, O God   CBM 102

⊕ Belihu, Almaz. "When Jesus Worked Here on Earth" from *Set Free: A Collection of African Hymns*. SATB. AFP 9780806600451,

⊕ Thangaraj, M. Thomas. "Ocean of Love" from *Pave the Way: Global Songs 3*. U. AFP 9780800676896.

☼ Egan, John/Paul Mabury/Mia Fielder. "Take Me to the River" from CCLI.

☼ Hampton, Larry. "Shine upon Us" from CCLI.

☼ Maher, Matt/Chris Tomlin/Audrey Assad. "No Greater Love" from CCLI.

☼ Nuzum, Eric/Chris Springer. "Healing Waters" from CCLI.

☼ Smith, Martin. "Find Me in the River" from CCLI.

☼ West, Matthew/Mark Hall. "Thrive" from CCLI.

Music for the Day
Choral

P Farlee, Robert Buckley. "O Radiant Christ, Incarnate Word." 2 pt mxd, org. MSM 50-9935.

Herman, David. "When Jesus Went to Jordan's Stream." SAB or SATB, org, ob or C inst. GIA G-3421.

Pinkham, Daniel. "For the Gift of Water." SATB, opt org. ECS 5204.

♫ Trapp, Lynn M. "When Jesus Came to Jordan." SATB, org, C inst. GIA G-5266.

Children's Choir

P Highben, Zebulon M. "I'm Going on a Journey." U/2 pt, pno, bass gtr, ten sax, opt assembly. AFP 9781451423693.

P Horman, John. "Jesus Is Baptized" from *Sing the Stories of Jesus*. U, kybd. AFP 9781451460759.

P Patterson, Mark. "I Will Give My Heart to the Lord" from *Young ChildrenSing*. U, kybd, opt Orff inst or hc. AFP 9781451460247.

Keyboard / Instrumental

P Carter, John. "Down to the River to Pray" from *Shall We Gather: Settings for Four-Hand Piano*. Pno (4 hand). HOP 8569.

P ♫ Cherwien, David. "I Bind unto Myself Today" (St. Patrick's Breastplate) from *More Postludes on Well Known Hymns*. Org. AFP 9780800678425.

P Hansen, Sherri. "Baptized and Set Free" (Baptized and Set Free) from *Piano Weavings*. Pno. AFP 9781451497861.

♫ Sedio, Mark. "When Jesus Came to Jordan" (King's Lynn) from *How Blessed This Place: Hymn Preludes for Organ*. Org. AFP 9780800658038.

Handbell

P Page, Anna Laura. "Joys Are Flowing like a River" (Blessed Quietness). 3-5 oct hb, opt 3-5 oct hc, L2+. CG CGB822.

♫ Page, Anna Laura. "Praise the Father." 2-3 oct, L1. ALF 19647.

P Sherman, Arnold/Larry Shackley. "Morning Has Broken." 3-5 oct, L3+. HOP 2634.

January 15, 2017
Second Sunday after Epiphany
Lectionary 2

Today's gospel opens with further reflection on Jesus' baptism. He is the Lamb of God who takes away the sin of the world, and the one anointed by the Spirit. In the liturgy we come and see Christ revealed among us in word and meal. We go forth to invite others to come and worship the Holy One, and to receive the gifts of grace and peace made known among us.

Prayer of the Day

Holy God, our strength and our redeemer, by your Spirit hold us forever, that through your grace we may worship you and faithfully serve you, follow you and joyfully find you, through Jesus Christ, our Savior and Lord.

Gospel Acclamation

Alleluia. In the ᴵ Word was life,* and the life was the light ᴵ of all people. *Alleluia.* (John 1:4)

Readings and Psalm

Isaiah 49:1-7

Here the servant Israel speaks for herself and acknowledges herself as God's secret weapon. Called before her birth like Jeremiah and John the Baptist, the servant is not only to restore Israel itself. The servant's ultimate assignment is to bring news of God's victory to the ends of the earth. God in faithfulness has chosen Israel for this task.

Psalm 40:1-11

I love to do your will, O my God. (Ps. 40:8)

1 Corinthians 1:1-9

Though God's church in Corinth is a fractious congregation beset with many conflicts, Paul opens this letter by spotlighting the multiple ways God has enriched and sustained its life as part of the divine call into the fellowship of our Lord Jesus Christ.

John 1:29-42

John the Baptist's witness to Jesus initiates a chain of testimony as his disciples begin to share with others what they have found.

Preface   Sundays

Color   Green

Prayers of Intercession

The prayers are prepared locally for each occasion. The following examples may be adapted or used as appropriate.

Called to be a light to the nations, let us pray for God's justice, peace, and healing.

A brief silence.

Gather us in, gracious God. Bring together Methodist and Pentecostal, Baptist and Roman Catholic, Lutheran and AME-Zion. Form us in worship into your united people. Send us out as one in you, proclaiming your glory and serving all. Hear us, O God.

Your mercy is great.

Fed with bread and wine, Christ's body and blood, make us eager to care for your good creation. Send us to pick up litter from highways and lakeshores and protect animal habitats. Hear us, O God.

Your mercy is great.

We pray for all the nations of the world (*especially*). Help us to reach out to the places where the scandal of hunger resides. Hear us, O God.

Your mercy is great.

Quell the anxieties of all who wait for test results. Bring hope to all whose life is a struggle and filled with despair. Send us to care for those who suffer (*especially*). Hear us, O God.

Your mercy is great.

Open us to see how our congregation abounds with every spiritual gift. Send us out to share our abundant gifts and proclaim your steadfast love. Hear us, O God.

Your mercy is great.

Here other intercessions may be offered.

We thank you for the faithfulness of your prophets (*especially Martin Luther King Jr.*). Strengthen our faith in you. Send us out to proclaim and live your justice boldly. Hear us, O God.

Your mercy is great.

Receive these prayers in the name of Christ, the light of the world, who is one with you and the Holy Spirit, now and forever. **Amen.**

Images in the Readings

Once again we are given the images of **water**, **light**, and **dove** (see Baptism of Our Lord).

The fourth gospel refers to Jesus as the **Lamb** of God. Several New Testament writers used this image to give salvific meaning to Jesus' execution. The lamb as apocalyptic conqueror, the lamb as suffering servant, and the paschal lamb are all possibilities of what the earliest Christians meant by the image. The medieval church stressed Christ as sacrificial lamb, whose blood takes away sin.

God calls. The scriptures include many **call** narratives in testifying that this God is the kind of deity who knows us by name and calls us into a new identity. All three readings refer to such a call. In the poem from Second Isaiah, the call comes to the prophet even before birth. The church has described baptism as our call to servanthood, and many churches use the imagery of the call in descriptions of their clergy.

Ideas for the Day

- In today's culture we are often told to point to ourselves through our own blogs, Facebook, Twitter, and other social media. John points to Jesus throughout the gospel. How might we, as the body of Christ, be more like John in giving witness to the Lamb of God? Could these same tools that we often use to boost our own statuses and titles also be used to point to Jesus, the light and salvation of the world?

- Titles are often given to people to help others understand their roles. John gives Jesus several titles, which help us understand his identity. Invite those with distinct titles (both officially and unofficially given) to share how these titles have shaped their identity. How have they lived into these identities—or tried to shed them? How does our title as "baptized" challenge, privilege, transform, and shape us? In what ways do Jesus' titles affect how we interact with him?

- In the Gospel of John, Jesus' first words aren't a statement but rather a question: "What are you looking for?" (John 1:38). TED curator Chris Anderson has a show dedicated to questions (http://www.ted.com/talks/questions_no_one_knows_the_answers_to). What might the church look like if it constantly encouraged questions like, "What are you (or we) looking for?" What might we learn by deeply listening to each other, and how might this guide our mission?

- For most churches, this Sunday is a time when the liturgical color changes from white to green, often symbolizing a time of growth. This time after Epiphany reminds us of our own epiphanies, whether sudden, like the call of Andrew and Simon, or gradual. Not only do we learn that Jesus is the light of the world but also that as God's servants we are called to be light to the world. How does living in community, like the early Christians struggling in Corinth, act as an unfolding discovery? What epiphanies have unfolded that might point to our future as light and salvation bearers to the world?

Connections with the Liturgy

Many Christians sing "Lamb of God" when they come forward for communion to receive this blood of mercy and peace. Some clergy begin their sermons by quoting Paul, "Grace to you and peace from God, our Father, and the Lord Jesus Christ."

Let the Children Come

Isaiah's metaphor for Israel of an unborn baby, already beloved by God, will probably float past most in your assembly, unless they are longing to have a child or grieving the loss of a pregnancy. Nothing embodies the words "let the children come" more than a pregnancy. The topic is charged with love and emotion, with a dash of privacy, which creates the perfect environment to avoid talking about infertility and pregnancy loss in your assembly. This can be an isolating environment for ones among us longing for a child. How can you give voice to this longing so that Christ's light can be seen?

Assembly Song
Gathering

Hail to the Lord's anointed ELW 311, LBW 87
Arise, your light has come! ELW 314, WOV 652
O day full of grace ELW 627, alternate text, sts. 2-4

Psalmody and Acclamations

Alonso, Tony. "Here I Am." SATB, cant, assembly, kybd. GIA G-6735.
Haas, David. "Second Sunday in Ordinary Time (A)" from COJ:A.
Haugen, Marty. "Here Am I, O God" from PCY, vol. 2.
(GA) Mxadana, George. "Two Songs from South Africa: Alleluia." SATB. GIA G-5286. Use ELW psalm tone 11 in G major with proper verse for Epiphany 2.

Hymn of the Day

Now behold the Lamb ELW 341, TFF 128 *NOW BEHOLD THE LAMB*
The only Son from heaven ELW 309, LBW 86 *HERR CHRIST, DER EINIG GOTTS SOHN*
He comes to us as one unknown ELW 737, WOV 768 *REPTON*

Offering

Here I Am, Lord ELW 574, sts. 1, 3; WOV 752, sts. 1, 3
This little light of mine ELW 677, TFF 65

Communion

Come, beloved of the Maker ELW 306
Christ, Be Our Light ELW 715
Jesus, come! for we invite you ELW 312, WOV 648

Sending

We are marching in the light ELW 866, WOV 650, TFF 63
Rise, shine, you people! ELW 665, LBW 393

Additional Assembly Songs

Lumière de Dieu/Come, light of God SP 26

You are God's own people MSB2 S566

Yo soy la luz del mundo LLC 319

🌐 Khill, Yusuf. "Holy Lamb of God/Ya hamalallah" from *Glory to God*. WJK 0664238971.

🌐 Rantatalo, Matti. "O Lamb of God/Oi, Jumalan Karitsa." U. ELW 197.

☼ Carson, Daniel/Chris Tomlin/Ed Cash/Jesse Reeves. "Jesus Messiah" from CCLI.

☼ Ligertwood, Brooke. "I Will Exalt You" from CCLI.

☼ Maher, Matt. "Behold the Lamb of God" from CCLI.

☼ Pritzl, Michael J. "Invitation Fountain" from PraiseCharts.

☼ Williams, Hank, Sr. "I Saw the Light" from CCLI.

☼ Zschech, Darlene/Michael W. Smith/Andy Makken. "I Am Yours" from CCLI.

Music for the Day
Choral

P ♫ Ferguson, John. "He Comes to Us as One Unknown." SATB, org, opt assembly. AFP 9780800656003.

P Smith Moore, Undine. "I Believe This Is Jesus." SATB div. AFP 9780800645281.

P Thomas, André. "Walk in the Light." U or 2 pt, pno. CG CGA1062.

Willan, Healey. "Behold the Lamb of God." SATB, org. CPH 981509.

Children's Choir

P Horman, John. "Samuel Listens" from *Sing the Stories of God's People*. U, pno. AFP 9781451460537.

Raabe, Nancy. "Epiphany Counting Carol." 2 pt, pno, vln. AFP 9780800638085.

Wright, Vicki Hancock. "Let Us Walk in the Light of the Lord." U, opt Orff inst, opt rhythm sticks, opt bell tree. CG CGA 1125.

Keyboard / Instrumental

♫ Bach, J. S. "Herr Christ, der einig Gotts Sohn," BWV 601, from *Orgelbüchlein*. Org. Various editions.

P ♫ Farlee, Robert Buckley. "The Only Son from Heaven" (Herr Christ, der einig Gotts Sohn) from *Treasures Old and New: Hymn Preludes for Organ*. Org. AFP 9781451499094.

Organ, Anne Krentz. "I Want to Walk as a Child of the Light" (Houston) from *Woven Together: Reflections and Intonations for Piano and Solo Instrument*. B flat or C inst, pno. AFP 9780800658168.

P ♫ Weber, Jacob B. "He Comes to Us as One Unknown" (Repton) from *Christ Is King: Organ Hymn Preludes*. Org. AFP 9781451486032.

Handbell

P Ingram, Bill. "And Can It Be." 3-5 oct, L2. HOP 2663.

P Ingram, Bill. "Spirituals for Twelve Bells." 3 oct (3-6 ringers), L3. CG CGB848.

♫ Waugh, Timothy. "Repton Reminiscence." 2-3 oct, L2. ALF 42905.

Sunday, January 15
Martin Luther King Jr., renewer of society, martyr, died 1968

Martin Luther King Jr. is remembered as an American prophet of justice among races and nations, a Christian whose faith undergirded his advocacy of vigorous yet nonviolent action for racial equality. A pastor of churches in Montgomery, Alabama, and Atlanta, Georgia, his witness was taken to the streets in such other places as Birmingham, Alabama, where he was arrested and jailed while protesting against segregation. He preached nonviolence and demanded that love be returned for hate. Awarded the Nobel Peace Prize in 1964, he was killed by an assassin on April 4, 1968. Though most commemorations are held on the date of the person's death, many churches hold commemorations near Dr. King's birth date of January 15, in conjunction with the American civil holiday honoring him. An alternate date for the commemoration would be his death date, April 4.

Tuesday, January 17
Antony of Egypt, renewer of the church, died around 356

Antony was born in Qemen-al-Arous, Upper Egypt, and was one of the earliest Egyptian desert fathers. Born to Christian parents from whom he inherited a large estate, he took personally Jesus' message to sell all that you have, give to the poor, and follow Christ. After making arrangements to provide for the care of his sister, he gave away his inheritance and became a hermit. Later, he became the head of a group of monks who lived in a cluster of huts and devoted themselves to communal prayer, worship, and manual labor under Antony's direction. The money they earned from their work was distributed as alms. Antony and his monks also preached and counseled those who sought them out. Antony and the desert fathers serve as a reminder that certain times and circumstances call Christians to stand apart from the surrounding culture and renounce the world in service to Christ.

🌐 = global song   ♫ = relates to hymn of the day
☼ = praise song   P = available in Prelude Music Planner

Tuesday, January 17
Pachomius, renewer of the church, died 346

Another of the desert fathers, Pachomius (puh-KOME-ee-us) was born in Egypt about 290. He became a Christian during his service as a soldier. In 320 he went to live as a hermit in Upper Egypt, where other hermits lived nearby. Pachomius organized them into a religious community in which the members prayed together and held their goods in common. His rule for monasteries influenced both Eastern and Western monasticism through the Rule of Basil and the Rule of Benedict, respectively.

Wednesday, January 18
Confession of Peter
Week of Prayer for Christian Unity begins

The Week of Prayer for Christian Unity is framed by two commemorations, the Confession of Peter (a relatively recent addition to the calendar) and the older Conversion of Paul. Both apostles are remembered together on June 29, but these two days give us an opportunity to focus on key events in each of their lives. Today we remember that Peter was led by God's grace to acknowledge Jesus as "the Christ, the Son of the living God" (Matt. 16:16). This confession is the common confession that unites us with Peter and with all Christians of every time and place.

Thursday, January 19
Henry, Bishop of Uppsala, martyr, died 1156

Henry, an Englishman, became bishop of Uppsala, Sweden, in 1152 and is regarded as the patron of Finland. He traveled to Finland with the king of Sweden on a mission trip and remained there to organize the church. He was murdered in Finland by a man he had rebuked and who was disciplined by the church. Henry's burial place became a center of pilgrimage. His popularity as a saint is strong in both Sweden and Finland.

Saturday, January 21
Agnes, martyr, died around 304

Agnes was a girl of about thirteen living in Rome, who had chosen a life of service to Christ as a virgin, despite the Roman emperor Diocletian's ruling that had outlawed all Christian activity. The details of her martyrdom are not clear, but she gave witness to her faith and was put to death as a result, most likely by the sword. Since her death, the church has honored her as one of the chief martyrs of her time.

January 22, 2017
Third Sunday after Epiphany
Lectionary 3

Jesus begins his public ministry by calling fishers to leave their nets and follow him. In Jesus the kingdom of God has come near. We who have walked in darkness have seen a great light. We see this light most profoundly in the cross—as God suffers with us and all who are oppressed by sickness, sin, or evil. Light dawns for us as we gather around the word, the font, and the holy table. We are then sent to share the good news that others may be "caught" in the net of God's grace and mercy.

Prayer of the Day

Lord God, your lovingkindness always goes before us and follows after us. Summon us into your light, and direct our steps in the ways of goodness that come through the cross of your Son, Jesus Christ, our Savior and Lord.

Gospel Acclamation

Alleluia. Jesus preached the good news ¹ of the kingdom* and cured every sickness a-¹ mong the people. *Alleluia.* (Matt. 4:23)

Readings and Psalm

Isaiah 9:1-4

The northern tribes of Zebulun and Naphtali experienced the gloom of defeat by Assyrian military forces, but they are assured that their condition will be reversed when God makes a light-filled appearance. The joy they will experience will resemble celebrations of great harvests, because God will deliver them from everything that diminishes or oppresses them.

Psalm 27:1, 4-9

The LORD is my light and my salvation. (Ps. 27:1)

1 Corinthians 1:10-18

Paul calls on the Corinthians to end their dissensions and share the unified outlook of the gospel. Discord arises when we forget that we belong not to human leaders or institutions but to Christ. Indeed, the unifying word of the cross is the center of the gospel and the power of God's salvation.

Matthew 4:12-23

Jesus begins his public ministry shortly after John the Baptist is imprisoned by Herod. He proclaims the nearness of God's reign and calls four fishermen to be his first disciples.

Preface   Sundays

Color   Green

Prayers of Intercession

The prayers are prepared locally for each occasion. The following examples may be adapted or used as appropriate.

Called to be a light to the nations, let us pray for God's justice, peace, and healing.

A brief silence.

Holy God, you call us to fish for people. Tear down divisions and unite the church universal in your mission. Make us of the same mind and purpose in service and worship to you. Hear us, O God.

Your mercy is great.

Nurturing God, you call us to care for creation. Breathe into us the joy and beauty of stewardship. Teach us to care for the small seed and the expansive sky. Hear us, O God.

Your mercy is great.

Compassionate God, you call us to care for the stranger in our midst. Sustain refugees from every country (*especially*) and empower organizations that provide food and shelter for them, especially Lutheran Immigration and Refugee Service. Hear us, O God.

Your mercy is great.

Redeeming God, you break the oppressor's rod. Bring an end to tyranny and poverty. Wipe out fear. Uphold all your children who suffer in body, mind, or spirit (*especially*). Heal us with your presence. Hear us, O God.

Your mercy is great.

Triune God, you call us into relationship with you. Raise up leaders in your church who risk looking foolish for the sake of the gospel. Hear us, O God.

Your mercy is great.

Here other intercessions may be offered.

Ever-living God, you call us to rest in you. Keep us faithful on earth and bring us to life everlasting with the saints of every time and place. Hear us, O God.

Your mercy is great.

Receive these prayers in the name of Christ, the light of the world, who is one with you and the Holy Spirit, now and forever. **Amen.**

Images in the Readings

The gospel describes the first disciples as catchers of **fish**. This may be a memory of the profession of some in the Jesus movement. As well, it grounds the early Christian imagery of baptism as water, believers as water dwellers, the net as the gospel, and the boat as the church. The Greek of the early Christian creed "Jesus Christ, God's Son, Savior" presents the acronym *ichthus*, meaning "fish," and fish show up in much Christian iconography.

The gospel introduces the image of "the **kingdom** of heaven." Arguably the most important image in the New Testament, the kingdom invoked Israelite memory of a time of political independence. Yet this kingdom is, according to Matthew, "of heaven," that is, of a realm beyond this earth, and was probably, in accord with Jewish sensibilities, a circumlocution for "God." The designation of Jesus as Christ, that is, the one anointed by God for power to reign, relies on the kingdom imagery. It is not an image easily accessible for twenty-first-century believers. In the New Testament, *basileia*—kingdom—is not solely a reference to either the church or an afterlife.

The poem in Isaiah mentions **Midian**. Israel remembered its oppression by the Midianites and then, under the leadership of Gideon, its victory over them. Invoking this memory, First Isaiah likens God's coming salvation to the military victory that set them free. Even the archetypal practice of warriors **plundering** the vanquished is offered as a positive image.

Ideas for the Day

- It is not uncommon today to be inundated with pleas to "follow" different companies or public figures on social media. The more followers they have, the more easily and cheaply they can disseminate their message or advertise their product. Books and blogs have been written on "how to rapidly build and boost your social media following." How does a culture of consumerism that emphasizes "following" affect the way we understand today's readings from 1 Corinthians and Matthew as Christians? How, as a community, do we help each other differentiate and listen to the call from Jesus over the temptation of so many others?
- Today's gospel is sometimes described as the launch of Jesus' public ministry. In her book *Public Church: For the Life of the World*, Cynthia Moe-Lobeda expands on Martin Luther's words when she says that *public* is the "arena of the church's vocation." She goes on to say, "The public may extend to the vast interrelated household of God's creation" ([Augsburg Fortress, 2004], 9). How might Moe-Lobeda's words help spark our imagination about the church's public ministry to proclaim the good news of the kingdom?
- Today's gospel highlights vocation as Jesus called ordinary fishers to follow him. While it might seem obvious that we *all* are called to be fishers of people in the way we live out our lives, it is important to name this explicitly, as some groups appear to be left out of this text (i.e., women and children). Consider using the affirmation of Christian vocation (*ELW*, p. 84) within the sending rite of today's service to emphasize everyone's call to be fishers of people.
- In times of vocational transition, people may experience a lot of waiting, feelings of anxiety, and doubts about meeting high selection standards. For those who are wondering if they are good enough or have what it takes to follow a certain employer, school, or program, today's gospel might be an important reminder that Jesus doesn't wait for people to apply to him. Jesus calls followers and then uses what they already know. We need not worry if our résumés or letters of recommendation will be good enough; Jesus knows they are.

Connections with the Liturgy

Paul's comments remind us that all Christians are baptized either into the name of our Lord Jesus Christ or into the name of the Father, the Son, and the Holy Spirit. Baptism is into the Christian church as a whole, rather than into its denominational units, and nearly all branches and denominations of the church agree not to rebaptize anyone who has already received baptism.

Let the Children Come

Today's gospel is packed with imagery that will spark a child's imagination! It reads like a child's adventure novel: traveling through strange territories on land and sea, great light, deep darkness, brothers leaving their home, fishing nets . . . and then there is that phrase, "the kingdom of heaven has come near." It is as if some elusive feather is brushing up against your ear. This kingdom sounds so mysterious and intriguing. When we keep the stories of faith open, without moralistic punctuation, we can recognize a living Word among us. How has the "kingdom of heaven" come near with the children in your congregation?

Assembly Song
Gathering

Dearest Jesus, at your word ELW 520, LBW 248

Light shone in darkness ELW 307

Drawn to the Light ELW 593

Psalmody and Acclamations

Browning, Carol. "The Lord Is My Light/El Señor es mi luz." SAB, cant, kybd, gtr, opt vn. GIA G-7256.

The Lord is my light TFF 61

Behnke, John A. "The Lord Is My Light and My Salvation." SAB, assembly, kybd, opt 2-3 oct hb. CG CGA981.

(GA) Mxadana, George. "Two Songs from South Africa: Alleluia." SATB. GIA G-5286. Use ELW psalm tone 11 in G major with proper verse for Epiphany 3.

Hymn of the Day

You have come down to the lakeshore ELW 817, LLC 560, WOV 784 *PESCADOR DE HOMBRES*

The Son of God, our Christ ELW 584, LBW 434 *SURSUM CORDA*

Light shone in darkness ELW 307 *LUX IN TENEBRIS*

Offering

Here I Am, Lord ELW 574, st. 3; WOV 752, st. 3

Listen, God is calling ELW 513, WOV 712, TFF 130

Communion

Will you come and follow me ELW 798, W&P 137

Come, beloved of the Maker ELW 306

I want to walk as a child of the light ELW 815, WOV 649

Sending

Thy strong word ELW 511, LBW 233

I love to tell the story ELW 661, LBW 390, TFF 228

Additional Assembly Songs

Light and darkness SP 24

They cast their nets LBW 449

There's a light in the world ASG 41

⊕ Bell, John. "The Lord Is My Light" from *I Will Not Sing Alone*. SATB. GIA G-6512.

⊕ Czech hymn tune. "The Lord Is My Light" from *Many and Great: Songs of the World Church*. SSATB. GIA G-3649.

☼ Camp, Jeremy. "I Will Follow (You Are with Me)" from CCLI.

☼ Canedo, Ken. "Fish with Me" from OCP.

☼ Hughes, Tim/Martin Smith. "Clinging to the Cross" from CCLI.

☼ Leiweke, Stephen/John Hartley/Kelly Minter/Henk Pool. "We Will Not Go" from CCLI.

☼ Mooring, Leeland/Jack Mooring/Ed Cash. "Follow You" from CCLI.

☼ Smith, Martin. "Message of the Cross" from CCLI.

Music for the Day
Choral

P Johnson, Ralph M. "Sing Hey for the Carpenter." SATB, tri, drm. AFP 9780800621544.

P Keesecker, Thomas. "Jesus Said, Come Follow Me." SATB, ob or C inst. AFP 9781451420746.

P♫ Sedio, Mark. "Light Shone in Darkness." SATB, pno. AFP 9780800678302.

P Simon, Julia. "Follow Me." U or 2 pt, pno. AFP 9780800664046.

Children's Choir

P Anderson, Shari. "I Want to Walk as a Child of the Light" from *ChildrenSing in Worship*, vol. 2. U/2 pt, pno, fl. AFP 9781451461213.

P Horman, John. "Follow Me" from *Sing the Stories of Jesus*. U, kybd. AFP 9781451460674.

P Taylor, Terry. "I Am the Light" from *Shine Your Light*. U, kybd. CG CGA1361.

Keyboard / Instrumental

P♫ Ashdown, Franklin D. "Light Shone in Darkness" (Lux in tenebris) from *Bright and Guiding Star: An Epiphany Collection for Organ*. Org. AFP 9781451462593.

Hassell, Michael. "Come, Follow Me, the Savior Spake" (Machs mit mir, Gott) from *Traveling Tunes: Hymn Arrangements for Solo Instrument and Piano*. Inst, pno. AFP 9780800656195.

P♫ Roberts, Al. "You Have Come Down to the Lakeshore" (Pescador de hombres) from *We Belong to God: Piano Settings of Folk Tunes*. Pno. AFP 9781451451801.

P♫ Titus, Hiram. "The Son of God, Our Christ" (Sursum Corda) from *Glorify! Hymn Settings for Piano*. Pno. AFP 9781451424218.

Handbell

P Moklebust, Cathy. "I Want to Walk as a Child of the Light." 2-3 oct hb, opt trbl B flat or C inst, L2, CG CGB831. 3-5 oct hb, opt trbl B flat or C inst, L2, CG CGB832.

P Rogers, Sharon Elery. "My Heart Ever Faithful." 2-3 oct, L1+. CG CGB522.

♫ Rose, William. "Lord, You Have Come to the Lakeshore." 3-5 oct hb, opt 3 oct hc, L3, GIA G-7036. Opt tpt, perc, gtr, GIA G-7036INST.

Wednesday, January 25

Conversion of Paul
Week of Prayer for Christian Unity ends

Today the Week of Prayer for Christian Unity comes to an end. The church remembers how a man of Tarsus named Saul, a former persecutor of the early Christian church, was turned around by God's grace to become one of its chief preachers. The risen Christ appeared to Paul on the road to Damascus and called him to proclaim the gospel. The narratives describing Paul's conversion in the Acts of the Apostles, Galatians, and 1 Corinthians inspire this commemoration, which was first celebrated among the Christians of Gaul.

⊕ = global song   ♫ = relates to hymn of the day
☼ = praise song   P = available in Prelude Music Planner

Thursday, January 26
Timothy, Titus, and Silas, missionaries

On the two days following the celebration of the Conversion of Paul, his companions are remembered. Timothy, Titus, and Silas were missionary coworkers with Paul. Timothy accompanied Paul on his second missionary journey and was commissioned by Paul to go to Ephesus, where he served as bishop and overseer of the church. Titus was a traveling companion of Paul, accompanied him on the trip to the council of Jerusalem, and became the first bishop of Crete. Silas traveled with Paul through Asia Minor and Greece and was imprisoned with him at Philippi, where they were delivered by an earthquake.

Friday, January 27
Lydia, Dorcas, and Phoebe, witnesses to the faith

On this day the church remembers three women who were companions in Paul's ministry. Lydia was Paul's first convert at Philippi in Macedonia. She was a merchant of purple-dyed goods, and because purple dye was extremely expensive, it is likely that Lydia was a woman of some wealth. Lydia and her household were baptized by Paul, and for a time her home was a base for Paul's missionary work. Dorcas is remembered for her charitable works, particularly making clothing for needy widows. Phoebe was a *diakonos*, a deaconess in the church at Cenchreae, near Corinth. Paul praises her as one who, through her service, looked after many people.

Saturday, January 28
Thomas Aquinas, teacher, died 1274

Thomas Aquinas (uh-KWY-nus) was a brilliant and creative theologian of the thirteenth century. He was first and foremost a student of the Bible and profoundly concerned with the theological formation of the church's ordained ministers. As a member of the Order of Preachers (Dominicans), he worked to correlate scripture with the philosophy of Aristotle, which was having a renaissance in Aquinas's day. Some students of Aristotle's philosophy found in it an alternative to Christianity. But Aquinas immersed himself in the thought of Aristotle and worked to explain Christian beliefs in the philosophical culture of the day.

January 29, 2017
Fourth Sunday after Epiphany
Lectionary 4

Who are the blessed ones of God? For Micah, they are those who do justice, love kindness, and walk humbly with God. For Paul, they are the ones who find wisdom in the weakness of the cross. For Jesus, they are the poor, mourners, the meek, those who hunger for righteousness, the merciful, the pure in heart, the peacemakers. In baptism we find our blessed identity and calling in this countercultural way of living and serving.

Prayer of the Day

Holy God, you confound the world's wisdom in giving your kingdom to the lowly and the pure in heart. Give us such a hunger and thirst for justice, and perseverance in striving for peace, that in our words and deeds the world may see the life of your Son, Jesus Christ, our Savior and Lord.

Gospel Acclamation

Alleluia. Rejoice ˈ and be glad,* for your reward is ˈ great in heaven. *Alleluia.* (Matt. 5:12)

Readings and Psalm

Micah 6:1-8

With the mountains and the foundations of the earth as the jury, God brings a lawsuit against Israel. God has "wearied" Israel with a long history of saving acts. God does not want or expect lavish sacrifices to attempt to earn divine favor. Rather God empowers the people to do justice, to love loyalty to God, and to walk shrewdly in God's service.

Psalm 15

LORD, who may abide upon your holy hill? (Ps. 15:1)

1 Corinthians 1:18-31

According to the world's standards of power and might, the message of the cross seems stupid and offensive. Yet this word reveals the paradoxical way God has chosen to work power and salvation through weakness, rejection, and suffering. Hence the message of the cross becomes true wisdom and power for believers.

Matthew 5:1-12

Jesus opens the Sermon on the Mount by naming those who are blessed in the reign of God.

Preface   Sundays

Color   Green

Prayers of Intercession

The prayers are prepared locally for each occasion. The following examples may be adapted or used as appropriate.

Called to be a light to the nations, let us pray for God's justice, peace, and healing.

A brief silence.

We pray for wholeness in the body of Christ. Bind up fractures within the church. Humble the proud and lift up the lowly. Make us one at your table. Hear us, O God.

Your mercy is great.

We praise you for the beauty of the universe. For the light of the stars, for the majesty of the mountains, we thank you. Mold us into stewards of your creation. Hear us, O God.

Your mercy is great.

We pray for peacemakers around the world. End violence. Restore communities (*especially*). Stop bribery within political systems. Reign with justice and peace and commit us to this act of discipleship. Hear us, O God.

Your mercy is great.

We pray for our neighbors who mourn, who have no clean water, who hunger. Provide their daily bread. Heal the forgotten, the lost, and our enemies, family, and friends (*especially*). Hear us, O God.

Your mercy is great.

We praise you for this congregation. Bless the work and play of young and old. Deepen our faith. Expand our discipleship. Equip us to do justice, love kindness, and walk humbly with you. Hear us, O God.

Your mercy is great.

Here other intercessions may be offered.

We praise you for all the saints who died proclaiming the gospel. Strengthen us through their witness. Hear us, O God.

Your mercy is great.

Receive these prayers in the name of Christ, the light of the world, who is one with you and the Holy Spirit, now and forever.

Amen.

Images in the Readings

Jesus preaches from the top of a **mountain**. In the Bible, significant religious events occur on a mountain because God is described as dwelling above the earth, and still today people climb mountains for an otherworldly experience. In worship, the mountain is here in the church building, on the ambo, in the pulpit, on the altar.

Especially intertestamental Jews wrote about *hokmah*, the **wisdom** of God, personified as a goddess-like figure who accompanied, even governed, the activity of God. Yet Paul criticizes the cultural idea of wisdom as being quite other than the mercy of the cross.

The oracle from Micah includes the imagery of **sacrifice**, that is, burnt offerings of animals or children to prove veneration of the gods. Although Christians never authorized literal sacrifices, the imagery remains, both in the theological proposal that Christ's death was in some way a similar sacrifice and in the church's speech about a selfless life of giving for others.

Ideas for the Day

- In the service of Holy Baptism (*ELW*, p. 227), we ask candidates as well as the parents and sponsors of young children to make some very significant promises. We ask them to do the following: "proclaim Christ through word and deed, care for others and the world God made, and work for justice and peace." Parents are asked to teach their children how to do these things. However, the blessings of baptism are not contingent on being able to do these things. The blessing comes from God's own grace. Living into that grace, however, comes with the more dubious-sounding blessings mentioned in today's gospel. Meekness, thirsting for righteousness, purity of heart, and mourning are mostly unavoidable when living faithfully according to the baptismal promises. Putting our baptized identity first means these "blessings" will come to us, with hope and love poured out on us by the Spirit.
- One month in, New Year's resolutions may already be wearing thin in practice, if they haven't been abandoned outright. Were the Beatitudes part of anyone's goals for the year? It is not too late to take a look at these guides and how they shape our living. Consider rethinking and rewriting new or altered resolutions beginning with "Happy are those. . . ."
- The musical *Annie* includes the song "You're Never Fully Dressed without a Smile." The life of faith does not always lend itself to grinning. Paul reminds the church at Corinth and in the modern day that believers are never fully dressed without the cross. Take time this week to talk about making the sign of the cross as part of a daily practice. As a reminder of Christ's presence and faithfulness, little is closer to the heart in proximity and meaning.

Connections with the Liturgy

In the oracle from Micah, the Lord asks, "O my people, what have I done to you? In what have I wearied you? Answer me!" These words are the inspiration for the Solemn Reproaches, an optional litany for Good Friday, in which Christ on the cross asks, "O my people, O my church, what have I done to you? How have I offended you? Answer me."

Let the Children Come

We live in a rewards-driven culture. Nowhere is this more evident than school: perfect attendance, report cards, honor roll, sports teams—the list goes on. If you can perform at a certain standard, you will be rewarded. This is a theology of glory. Jesus subverts this way of thinking with his grace-filled list of those blessed. Children (and ourselves) don't have to do or be anything to receive God's gifts of grace. Closely examine your children's programming to make sure actions match theology. Rewarding children for behavior, attendance, or performance does not convey the grace of God.

Assembly Song
Gathering

Rise up, O saints of God! ELW 669, LBW 383
O God of mercy, God of light ELW 714, LBW 425
Let streams of living justice ELW 710

Psalmody and Acclamations

Hopson, Hal. "Psalm 15" from TPP. (Note: verses may be spoken or improvised.)
Traditional, arr. Wendell Whalum. "Psalm 15" from PAS 15C.
Webber, Christopher L. "Lord, Who May Dwell within Your House" (Crimond) from LUYH.
(GA) Mxadana, George. "Two Songs from South Africa: Alleluia." SATB. GIA G-5286. Use ELW psalm tone 11 in G major with proper verse for Epiphany 4.

Hymn of the Day

When the poor ones/*Cuando el pobre* ELW 725, LLC 508
  EL CAMINO
Blest are they ELW 728, WOV 764 *BLEST ARE THEY*
Oh, praise the gracious power ELW 651, WOV 750
  CHRISTPRAISE RAY

Offering

Holy God, holy and glorious ELW 637
Jesus, the very thought of you ELW 754, LBW 316

Communion

Thee we adore, O Savior ELW 476, LBW 199
We Are Called ELW 720, W&P 147
We come to the hungry feast ELW 479, WOV 766

Sending

To be your presence   ELW 546

The Spirit sends us forth to serve   ELW 551, LBW 723

Additional Assembly Songs

What does the Lord require of you   MSB1 S444

Hope of the world   LBW 493

Blessed are you   DH 86

⊕ Bell, John, arr. "Hey, My Love" from *Heaven Shall Not Wait*. SATB. GIA G-3646.

⊕ Falam Chin traditional melody. "Lord of Region and of World" from *Sound the Bamboo*. STB. GIA G-6830.

☼ Angrisano, Steve. "Go Make a Difference" from CCLI.

☼ Baloche, Rita/Jamie Harvill. "Arise, Shine" from CCLI.

☼ Drummer, Elias/Nick Herbert/Ben Cantelon. "A City on a Hill" from CCLI.

☼ Greif, Jean Anthony/Tom Tomaszek."We Are the Light of the World" from *Spirit and Song*, vol. 1. OCP.

☼ Hall, Charlie. "Micah 6:8" from CCLI.

☼ Hughes, Tim. "God of Justice" from CCLI.

Music for the Day
Choral

Beck, John Ness. "Offertory." SATB, kybd. BP 1280.

♫ Cherwien, David. "When the Poor Ones." SATB, pno or gtr. MSM 50-5425.

Leavitt, John. "Blessed Are They." U or 2 pt mxd. AFP 9781451423938.

℗ Nelson, Ronald A. "Who May Abide" from *Augsburg Motet Book*. SATB, opt kybd. AFP 9781451423709.

Children's Choir

Bedford, Michael. "Blessed Are They (The Beatitudes)." U/2 pt, org, fl. CG CGA1025.

Haugen, Marty. "Sing for Peace." 2 pt, kybd, opt fl and rec. GIA G-8840.

℗ Wold, Wayne L. "Build New Bridges" from *ChildrenSing in Worship*, vol. 3. U, opt 2 pt, kybd. AFP 9781451476545.

Keyboard / Instrumental

℗♫ Nelson, Ronald A. "When the Poor Ones" (El camino) from *Easy Hymn Settings for Organ*, vol. 4. Org. AFP 9781451486049.

℗♫ Organ, Anne Krentz. "Blest Are They" from *In Heaven Above: Piano Music for Funerals and Memorials*. Pno. AFP 9781451401912.

℗♫ Wilson, Terry D. "When the Poor Ones" (El camino) from *Creative Spirit: Piano Settings*. Pno. AFP 9781451479607.

♫ Wold, Wayne L. "Oh, Praise the Gracious Power" (Christpraise Ray) from *Child of the Light: Preludes on Hymntunes by Women*. Org. AFP 9780800657994.

⊕ = global song   ♫ = relates to hymn of the day
☼ = praise song   ℗ = available in Prelude Music Planner

Handbell

℗ Bettcher, Peggy. "The Power of the Cross." 2-3 oct, L3-, HOP 2629. 3-5 oct, L3-, HOP 2513.

℗ Compton, Matthew. "If Thou But Suffer God to Guide Thee." 3-7 oct, L3+. HOP 2707.

♫ Helman, Michael. "Blest Are They." 3-6 oct hb, opt 3-5 oct hc, opt fl, L3-. GIA G-7043.

Thursday, February 2
Presentation of Our Lord

Forty days after the birth of Christ we mark the day Mary and Joseph presented him in the temple in accordance with Jewish law. There a prophetess named Anna began to speak of the redemption of Israel when she saw the young child. Simeon also greeted Mary and Joseph. He responded to the presence of the consolation of Israel in this child with the words of the Nunc dimittis. His song described Jesus as a "light for the nations."

Because of the link between Jesus as the light for the nations, and because an old reading for this festival contains a line from the prophet Zephaniah, "I will search Jerusalem with candles," the day is also known as Candlemas, a day when candles are blessed for the coming year.

Friday, February 3
Ansgar, Bishop of Hamburg, missionary to Denmark and Sweden, died 865

Ansgar was a monk who led a mission to Denmark and later to Sweden, where he built the first church. His work ran into difficulties with the rulers of the day, and he was forced to withdraw into Germany, where he served as a bishop in Hamburg. Despite his difficulties in Sweden, he persisted in his mission work and later helped consecrate Gothbert as the first bishop of Sweden. Ansgar had a deep love for the poor. He would wash their feet and serve them food provided by the parish.

February 5, 2017
Fifth Sunday after Epiphany
Lectionary 5

Light shines in the darkness for the upright, the psalmist sings. Isaiah declares that when we loose the bonds of injustice and share our bread with the hungry, the light breaks forth like the dawn. In another passage from the Sermon on the Mount, Jesus, the light of the world, calls his followers to let the light of their good works shine before others. Through baptism we are sent into the world to shine with the light of Christ.

Prayer of the Day

Lord God, with endless mercy you receive the prayers of all who call upon you. By your Spirit show us the things we ought to do, and give us the grace and power to do them, through Jesus Christ, our Savior and Lord.

Gospel Acclamation

Alleluia. Jesus says, I am the light | of the world;* whoever follows me will have the | light of life. *Alleluia.* (John 8:12)

Readings and Psalm

Isaiah 58:1-9a [9b-12]

Shortly after the return of Israel from exile in Babylon, the people were troubled by the ineffectiveness of their fasts. God reminds them that outward observance is no substitute for genuine fasting that results in acts of justice, such as feeding the hungry, sheltering the homeless, and clothing the naked.

Psalm 112:1-9 [10]

Light shines in the darkness for the upright. (Ps. 112:4)

1 Corinthians 2:1-12 [13-16]

Though people such as the Corinthians are enamored with human philosophy and wisdom, Paul continuously presents God's hidden wisdom which is Jesus Christ crucified. True spiritual maturity involves judging ourselves and others in light of God's revelation in the cross.

Matthew 5:13-20

In the Sermon on the Mount, Jesus encourages his followers to be the salt of the earth and the light of the world, doing good works and keeping God's commandments.

Preface   Sundays

Color   Green

Prayers of Intercession

The prayers are prepared locally for each occasion. The following examples may be adapted or used as appropriate.

Called to be a light to the nations, let us pray for God's justice, peace, and healing.

A brief silence.

Eternal God, you are one-in-three and three-in-one. Strengthen the ministry of the World Council of Churches and the Lutheran World Federation. Solidify ecumenical partnerships as they work to break the bonds of injustice and let the oppressed go free. Hear us, O God.
Your mercy is great.

Send relief where storms and floods overwhelm. Provide shelter and safe habitat for all creatures. Protect seeds and bulbs for the spring and fall harvest. Hear us, O God.
Your mercy is great.

Ignite the nations with the flame of your justice. Enlighten the leaders of the International Monetary Fund and the World Bank with your wisdom; guide government officials to seek economic justice in their communities. Hear us, O God.
Your mercy is great.

Comfort the afflicted, compassionate God. Accompany all who wait on death row. Reconcile families torn apart by crime or addiction. Heal the brokenhearted, the newly diagnosed, and all who suffer (*especially*). Hear us, O God.
Your mercy is great.

Fill those who form the faith of others with insight and energy. Multiply the fruit of their labor. Grow disciples eager to feast on your living word and embody it each day. Hear us, O God.
Your mercy is great.

Here other intercessions may be offered.

We thank you for all the saints who dared to shine with the light of Christ (*especially the martyrs of Japan*). Compel us to shine freely and witness to your abundant grace each day. Hear us, O God.
Your mercy is great.

Receive these prayers in the name of Christ, the light of the world, who is one with you and the Holy Spirit, now and forever.
Amen.

Images in the Readings

Light is an image on many Sundays. The Sermon on the Mount speaks also of the **lampstand**. Paul would remind us that, contrary to the wisdom of the world, our lampstand is the cross.

Salt is necessary for human life. In recollection of this passage, some early Christian communities placed salt on the tongue of the newly baptized. In the early twentieth century, the British placed an embargo on salt, requiring the Indian people to purchase salt from them, and Gandhi's Salt March became a symbol of the right of Indians to manage their own survival.

The passage from Isaiah speaks about a **fast**. In many religious traditions, people limit or refrain from some necessary human activity as a symbol that their truest life comes only from the divine. In both the Jewish and Christian traditions, fasting must be accompanied with justice for the poor for God to acknowledge its value.

Ideas for the Day

- The film *The King's Speech* (Weinstein Co., 2010) focuses on the relationship between King George VI of England and speech therapist Lionel Logue. The king had a terrible stutter but came to leadership through unexpected events at a critical time. Between the rise of radio as a regular medium of communication and the increasing crisis that became World War II, George VI had to confront his speech difficulties head-on with the help of Logue. The two became deep and lasting friends through their work together, and the king's leadership was a blessing to England during the time of war. The story never would have happened if either man had ignored his situation, hiding his light of vocation, skill, and opportunity. Letting our lights shine means being willing to work to overcome our own difficulties. We also must be willing to accept help from and offer help to others. Letting our lights shine brightens the world so that others may see more clearly and give glory to God.

- Salt comes in many varieties. Pink, black, gray, flaky, crystals, rock, sand, iodized, and uniodized are just a few of the possibilities. Some salts are better used in cooking, while others are best as a finishing touch. Some salts are not edible but are used cosmetically or for chemical purposes. Given the wide variety of salt around the world and its culinary and chemical significance, Jesus' comparison of believers to salt is even more meaningful. We are chemically the same, through the work of the Spirit, but called to different uses and work.

- Light is not just the opposite of dark. It is also the opposite of heavy. Isaiah calls Israel to a fast that is about reducing heaviness. The fast that God has chosen should lessen the burden of oppression and struggle on their neighbors—especially the poor and those on the margins. Lighting the world as children of God should also involve lightening the weight of war, poverty, destruction, and division.

Connections with the Liturgy

At the welcome to the newly baptized (*ELW*, p. 231), we hear reminders of today's gospel reading. Option 1 connects Matthew's words about light with John's: our light comes from the Light that is Christ. Option 2 quotes Matthew 5:16: our light draws people not to ourselves but to our Father in heaven.

Let the Children Come

Salt and light. Nothing could be so different. It is like a strange game of rock-paper-scissors. They don't seem to go together at all; light is just snuffed out by salt. So how can we be both? How wonderful is this riddle to help us expand our understanding of God at work in the world. As children acquire language, they make use of binary thinking: in/out, up/down, light/dark. Ideas are "either/or" instead of "both/and." Here Jesus is inviting us to hold two truths at the same time. This way of thinking expands, instead of limits, our relationship with God.

Assembly Song
Gathering

O God of light ELW 507, LBW 237
God, whose almighty word ELW 673, LBW 400
Lord of light ELW 688, LBW 405

Psalmody and Acclamations

"Take Your Place at the Table." *Psallite* C-176. Cant or SATB, assembly, kybd.
Nelson, Ronald A. "Psalm 112:1-9 [10]" from PWA.
Pavlechko, Thomas. "Psalm 112," Refrain 3, from PSCY.
(GA) Mxadana, George. "Two Songs from South Africa: Alleluia." SATB. GIA G-5286. Use ELW psalm tone 11 in G major with proper verse for Epiphany 5.

Hymn of the Day

This little light of mine ELW 677, TFF 65 *THIS JOY*
Gather Us In ELW 532, WOV 718 *GATHER US IN*
Rise, shine, you people! ELW 665, LBW 393 *WOJTKIEWICZ*

Offering

Light shone in darkness ELW 307
Lord, whose love in humble service ELW 712, LBW 423

Communion

Christ, Be Our Light ELW 715
We Are Called ELW 720, W&P 147
I want to walk as a child of the light ELW 815, WOV 649

Sending

Go, make disciples   ELW 540, W&P 47

Let justice flow like streams   ELW 717, WOV 763

Additional Assembly Songs

Bring Forth the Kingdom   LS 35, W&P 22

You are the seed   WOV 753, TFF 226, LLC 486

Jesus, the Light of the World   TFF 59

⊕ Swaziland traditional. "We Will Walk with God" from *One Is the Body: Songs of Unity and Diversity*. SATB. GIA G-5790.

⊕ Vas, Charles. "Give Us Light/Jyothi dho Prabhu" from *Love and Anger: Songs of Lively Faith and Social Justice*. U. GIA G-4947.

☼ Getty, Keith/Stuart Townend. "Speak, O Lord" from CCLI.

☼ Hughes, Tim/Nick Herbert/Nick Cantelon. "The Way" from CCLI.

☼ L'Ecuyer, Jan/John L'Ecuyer. "Salt and Light" from CCLI.

☼ Mailloux, Greg. "Walk in the Light" from CCLI.

☼ Schwartz, Stephen. "Light of the World" from *Godspell* from Musicnotes.

☼ Story, Laura/Jess Cates/Anthony Skinner. "Keeper of the Stars" from CCLI.

Music for the Day
Choral

♫ Hampton, Keith. "True Light." SATB, pno. EAR.

P♫ Roberts, William Bradley. "This Little Light of Mine." SATB div. AFP 9781451499018.

Routley, Erik. "Light and Salt." SATB, org. GIA G-2300.

P Thomas, André. "Walk in the Light." U or 2 pt, pno. CG CGA1062.

Children's Choir

P Ferguson, John. "Jesus, My Lord and God." U/2 pt, kybd. AFP 9781451476569.

♫ Helgen, John. "This Little Light of Mine." U/2 pt, pno. AFP 9780800675936.

Paradowski, John. "Arise and Shine!" U/2 pt, kybd, opt hb. CG CGA1039.

Keyboard / Instrumental

♫ Burkhardt, Michael. "Rise, Shine, You People" (Wojtkiewiecz) from *Five Hymn Accompaniments for Brass Quartet and Organ, Set 5*. Br qrt, Org. MSM 20-848.

♫ Cherwien, David. "Rise, Shine, You People" (Wojtkiewiecz) from *Augsburg Organ Library: Epiphany*. Org. AFP 9780800659349.

P♫ Childs, Edwin T. "This Little Light of Mine" (This Joy) from *Spirituals for Organ: For Manuals Only*. Org. AFP 9781451401141.

P♫ Linneweber, Edie. "Gather Us In" (Gather Us In) from *Christ Is Near: Hymn Settings for the Church Pianist*. Pno. AFP 9781451401158.

Handbell

♫ Helman, Michael. "Variations on 'Gather Us In.'" 3-5 oct hb, opt 3 oct hc, L4. AFP 0800674928.

♫ Moats, William. "This Little Light of Mine." 2-3 oct, L2+. CG CGB678.

♫ Morris, Hart. "Rise, Shine, You People." 3-5 oct, L3. CPH 97-7471.

Sunday, February 5
The Martyrs of Japan, died 1597

In the sixteenth century, Jesuit missionaries, followed by Franciscans, introduced the Christian faith in Japan. But a promising beginning to those missions—perhaps as many as 300,000 Christians by the end of the sixteenth century—met complications from competition between the missionary groups, political difficulty between Spain and Portugal, and factions within the government of Japan. Christianity was suppressed. By 1630, Christianity was driven underground.

Today we commemorate the first martyrs of Japan, twenty-six missionaries and converts who were killed by crucifixion. Two hundred and fifty years later, when Christian missionaries returned to Japan, they found a community of Japanese Christians that had survived underground.

February 12, 2017
Sixth Sunday after Epiphany
Lectionary 6

In today's reading from Deuteronomy we are called to choose life by loving and obeying God. Much of today's gospel reading echoes portions of the Ten Commandments. Jesus' instructions to the crowd reveal a pattern of behavior that honors both God and the neighbor, resulting in life and health for the whole community. We, too, are invited to embrace these commandments, not out of fear of retribution, but because God has promised that to do so means life for us.

Prayer of the Day

O God, the strength of all who hope in you, because we are weak mortals we accomplish nothing good without you. Help us to see and understand the things we ought to do, and give us grace and power to do them, through Jesus Christ, our Savior and Lord.

Gospel Acclamation

Alleluia. You are the light | of the world.* A city set upon a hill can- | not be hid. *Alleluia.* (Matt. 4:14)

Readings and Psalm

Deuteronomy 30:15-20

The Lord sets before the people of God a clear choice. Life and prosperity will come to the faithful; loss of the land will be the consequence of disobedience. Choosing life entails loving and holding fast to the Lord. Life in God's presence presupposes the promise made to the ancestors.

or Sirach 15:15-20

Wisdom literature has a high estimation of human possibilities. We are God's trusted creatures. Wisdom invites people to choose to keep God's commandments. Contrariwise, God does not command people to be wicked or give them permission to sin.

Psalm 119:1-8

Happy are they who follow the teaching of the LORD. (Ps. 119:1)

1 Corinthians 3:1-9

Human leaders in the church are not the ones who control ministry. Rather they are fellow workers who belong to God, the one who truly controls and continuously empowers the ministry of the church.

Matthew 5:21-37

In the Sermon on the Mount, Jesus exhorts his followers to embrace standards of righteousness that exceed legal requirements and traditional expectations.

Preface   Sundays

Color   Green

Prayers of Intercession

The prayers are prepared locally for each occasion. The following examples may be adapted or used as appropriate.
Called to be a light to the nations, let us pray for God's justice, peace, and healing.
A brief silence.
Holy Lord, you alone are God. Remove jealousy and quarreling between Christian denominations. Hold us in the unity of our baptism as we work together to serve you. Lord, in your mercy,
hear our prayer.
You called into being the first fruits of the earth. Guide gardeners and farmers who till the soil and tend the fields. Bless their work and in due season bring forth the bounty of the land. Lord, in your mercy,
hear our prayer.
Merciful Lord, your love knows no bounds. Break down barriers caused by nationalism. Challenge our stereotypes. Give us courage to engage in difficult conversations with those whose experiences are different from our own. Lord, in your mercy,
hear our prayer.
Pour out your Holy Spirit on all who struggle (*especially*). Ease the pain of families affected by divorce. Grant life-giving work to all who seek employment. Lord, in your mercy,
hear our prayer.
You know every hair on our heads. Yet we do not even know each of our neighbors. Equip our outreach ministry and this assembly to get to know the people in our community. Lord, in your mercy,
hear our prayer.
Here other intercessions may be offered.
Eternal Lord, you are the God of our ancestors in faith. You are our God. Keep us faithful until we join all the saints at your heavenly banquet. Lord, in your mercy,
hear our prayer.
Receive these prayers in the name of Christ, the light of the world, who is one with you and the Holy Spirit, now and forever.
Amen.

Images in the Readings

According to Matthew, Jesus threatened immoral people with **hell**. The idea that God will punish sinners with eternal fire came into intertestamental Jewish tradition from their Zoroastrian neighbors and is included in some New Testament books. Matthew's literalism is seen in the phrase that one's "whole body be thrown into hell." Fear of hell was apparently a central religious motivation during some pieties and periods of the church, and lurid descriptions of torment extended far beyond what many theologians propose: that hell is self-willed distance from God, through life and beyond death. From the second century to the present, some Christians have maintained that eternal punishment contradicts the primary description of a merciful God. The Apostles' and Nicene Creeds speak only of judgment and an everlasting life of the world to come, although according to the later Athanasian Creed, "those who have done evil will enter eternal fire."

The word of God is **milk** to us who are infants. As nursing mothers know, both the infant and the mother need the times of feeding. It is as if God needs to give us the milk we need.

The passage from Deuteronomy evokes the classic *The Pilgrim's Progress*, by John Bunyan, in which the Christian life is described as one **choice** after another. It is God's Spirit who inspires us to choose what God has already chosen for us: in Paul's words, life in God's field, God's building.

Ideas for the Day

- Sometimes it is very difficult to sustain healthy relationships with our "significant others"—spouses, siblings, parents, and even members of our congregations. It is not surprising that when we gather for worship, surrounded by signs and symbols of our unity in Christ, we easily recall our estrangements from other people. The altar is an especially powerful symbol of God's reconciling presence in our world. Jesus says to us, "If you remember that your brother or sister has something against you, leave your gift there before the altar and go: first be reconciled to your brother or sister" (Matt. 5:23-24). How do these words challenge and empower us to seek forgiveness, make amends, and if needed, gracefully seek closure when our ties of intimacy and friendship with others can no longer be sustained?
- Cooking shows on television feature prominent chefs who dazzle their audiences with amazing food creations. How surprising that sometimes their approaches to food preparation affirm what we've already learned to do at home. In today's first reading from Deuteronomy, Moses reminds us of spiritual practices that have been taught among us for generations: *love God, obey God, and stay close to God.* As we lift up what Moses said to prepare God's people to enter the promised land, name and celebrate other faithful leaders who speak to the critical concerns of today's church, offering timeless recipes for faithful living that are essential to our life as Christians.
- Some people are extremely attached to their mobile phones, tablets, and other electronic devices. They can't imagine living without constant access to search engines, wireless communications, and entertainment on demand. Can our dependence on technology erode our sensitivity to what we need to give and receive from God and one another? "If [something] causes you to sin," Jesus says, "tear it out and throw it away" (Matt. 5:29-30). Technology is great, but perhaps we need encouragement from time to time to take a techno-fast. Unplug. Look away from the screen. Spend some quality time offline. We need to affirm that we are children of God and gifted members of the body of Christ, even without our smartphones.

Connections with the Liturgy

In the order for Individual Confession and Forgiveness (*ELW*, pp. 243–244), the penitent can articulate the idea of our choice to live the godly life by using the following words: "I firmly intend to amend my life, and to seek help in mending what is broken."

Let the Children Come

Paul's letter to the Corinthians puts forth a metaphor for new Christians as being like infants or little children. Paul's low view of children, in this text, has (perhaps mistakenly) made Paul out to be a very poor theologian of childhood. If we really look closely, Paul uses imagery of himself as their nursing mother, deeply devoted to this assembly. The pearl of this passage for those working with children and families is the metaphor of a plant growing. While we can nurture faith, guide faith, walk beside in faith, we do not "form" faith in children (or anyone); God does.

Assembly Song
Gathering

Come down, O Love divine ELW 804, LBW 508
O God, my faithful God ELW 806, LBW 504
Jesus, we are gathered ELW 529, TFF 140

Psalmody and Acclamations

"Love the Lord Your God." *Psallite* A-112. Cant or SATB, assembly, kybd.
Burkhardt, Michael. "Psalm 119:1-16" from *Psalms for the Church Year*. U, org. MSM 80-708.
Harmon, Kathleen. "Fifth Sunday in Ordinary Time (A)" from COJ:A.
(GA) Mxadana, George. "Two Songs from South Africa: Alleluia." SATB. GIA G-5286. Use ELW psalm tone 11 in G major with proper verse for Epiphany 6.

Hymn of the Day

O Christ, our hope ELW 604, LBW 300 *LOBT GOTT, IHR CHRISTEN*
In all our grief ELW 615, WOV 739 *FREDERICKTOWN*
God, when human bonds are broken ELW 603, WOV 735
   MERTON

Offering

Come, all you people ELW 819, WOV 717, TFF 138
O Master, let me walk with you ELW 818, LBW 492

Communion

Healer of our every ill ELW 612, WOV 738
Forgive our sins as we forgive ELW 605, LBW 307
Eternal Spirit of the living Christ ELW 402, LBW 441

Sending

Praise the Lord, rise up rejoicing ELW 544, LBW 196
Oh, that the Lord would guide my ways ELW 772, LBW 480

Additional Assembly Songs

Christ, our peace SP 5
Eternal ruler of the ceaseless round LBW 373
⊕ Sosa, Pablo. "Allí está Jesús" from *Éste es el Día*. U. GIA G-7021.
⊕ Swahili, traditional. "Bwana awabariki/May God Bless Us."
   TFF 162.
☼ Butler, Chuck/Moriah Peters/Tony Wood/Ed Cash. "I Choose
   Jesus" from CCLI.
☼ Hall, Mark. "If We Are the Body" from CCLI.
☼ Hall, Mark/Matthew West. "Jesus Friend of Sinners" from
   CCLI.
☼ Ortega, Fernando. "Come Ye Sinners Poor and Needy" from
   CCLI.
☼ Tomlin, Chris/Louie Giglio/Henri Abraham/Cesar Malan.
   "Take My Life" from CCLI.
☼ Zschech, Darlene. "The Potter's Hand" from CCLI.

Music for the Day
Choral

P Buxtehude, Dietrich. "Everything You Do" from *Chantry
   Choirbook*. SATB, org. AFP 9780800657772.
P Hobby, Robert A. "Strengthen for Service." 2 pt mxd, opt assem-
   bly, org. AFP 9780800678265.
   Jennings, Carolyn. "Blessed Are They." SATB, org, opt fl. CG
   CGA896.
P ♫ Keesecker, Thomas. "In All Our Grief and Fear We Turn to
   You." 2 pt mxd, pno. AFP 9780806697352.

Children's Choir

   Cool, Jayne Southwick. "A Prayer for Peace." U/opt 2 pt, opt
      assembly. AFP 9780800664114.
   Lindh, Jodi W. "Ready to Forgive." U/2 pt, pno, fl. CG CGA1145.
P Scroggins, Debra. "An Instrument of Thy Peace." U/2 pt. CG
   CGA1330.

Keyboard / Instrumental

♫ Buxtehude, Dietrich. "Lobt Gott, ihr Christen," BuxWV 202.
   Org. Various editions.
♫ Cherwien, David. "In All Our Grief" (Fredericktown) from *O
   God, Beyond All Praising*. Org. AFP 9780800657246.
P Howarth, Mary. "Come, All You People" (Uyaimose) from *Glo-
   rify! Hymn Settings for Piano*. Pno. AFP 9781451424218.
♫ Organ, Anne Krentz. "In All Our Grief" (Fredericktown)
   from *Woven Together: Reflections and Intonations for
   Piano and Solo Instrument*. B flat or C inst, pno. AFP
   9780800658168.

Handbell

P Bettcher, Peggy. "From the Inside Out" from *Easy to Ring
   Praise & Worship VII*. 2-3 oct, L2, HOP 2687. 3-5 oct, L2,
   HOP 2670.
P Compton, Matthew. "Through the Walk of Life." 3-7 oct, L4+.
   CG CGB813.
P Dobrinski, Cynthia. "Enduring Joy." 3-6 oct, L3-. HOP 2636.

Tuesday, February 14
Cyril, monk, died 869; Methodius, bishop, died 885; missionaries to the Slavs

These two brothers from a noble family in Thessalonika in
northeastern Greece were priests and missionaries. After some
early initial missionary work by Cyril among the Arabs, the
brothers retired to a monastery. They were later sent to work
among the Slavs, the missionary work for which they are most
known. Since Slavonic had no written form at the time, the
brothers established a written language with the Greek alphabet as its basis. They translated the scriptures and the liturgy
using this Cyrillic alphabet. The Czechs, Serbs, Croats, Slovaks,
and Bulgars regard the brothers as the founders of Slavic literature. The brothers' work in preaching and worshiping in the
language of the people is honored by Christians in both East
and West.

⊕ = global song   ♫ = relates to hymn of the day
☼ = praise song   P = available in Prelude Music Planner

Saturday, February 18
Martin Luther, renewer of the church, died 1546

On this day in 1546, Martin Luther died at the age of sixty-two. For a time, he was an Augustinian monk, but it is his work as a biblical scholar, translator of the Bible, public confessor of the faith, reformer of the liturgy, theologian, educator, and father of German vernacular literature that holds him in our remembrance. In Luther's own judgment, the greatest of all of his works was his catechism, written to instruct people in the basics of faith. And it was his baptism that sustained him in his trials as a reformer.

February 19, 2017
Seventh Sunday after Epiphany
Lectionary 7

In today's first reading we hear, "You shall be holy, for I the Lord your God am holy." Yet we know we cannot achieve perfection. Our attempts to love neighbors and even our enemies fall short of what God desires for us. Yet in Jesus we see one who loved even those who persecuted and killed him. We are made holy in baptism, and forgiven at the table of God's mercy. As a people made holy by God, we go in peace to love as we have been loved.

Prayer of the Day

Holy God of compassion, you invite us into your way of forgiveness and peace. Lead us to love our enemies, and transform our words and deeds to be like his through whom we pray, Jesus Christ, our Savior and Lord.

Gospel Acclamation

Alleluia. In those who obey the ¹ word of Christ,* the love of God has ¹ reached perfection. *Alleluia.* (1 John 2:5)

Readings and Psalm
Leviticus 19:1-2, 9-18

The Holiness Code in Leviticus urges people to be holy since God is holy. Holiness is lived out in partiality for and consideration of the poor and the weak. We are to love our neighbors as ourselves.

Psalm 119:33-40

Teach me, O LORD, the way of your statutes. (Ps. 119:33)

1 Corinthians 3:10-11, 16-23

Jesus Christ is the foundation of the church and its ministry. We are God's temple because God's Spirit dwells in us, and we belong to Christ. Hence we are called to build wisely upon this sure foundation not for our own benefit but for others to experience Christ's benefits.

Matthew 5:38-48

In the Sermon on the Mount, Jesus declares an end to the law of vengeance. God's people will respond to evil with love and forgiveness.

Preface   Sundays

Color   Green

Prayers of Intercession

The prayers are prepared locally for each occasion. The following examples may be adapted or used as appropriate.

Called to be a light to the nations, let us pray for God's justice, peace, and healing.
A brief silence.

Make the church in every land holy as you are holy, O God. Join the voices of rich and poor, young and old, friends and enemies, in praise of you. Orchestrate harmony among us. Lord, in your mercy,
hear our prayer.

We pray for clean air, clean water, and clean soil. Renew the sky, land, and waterways. Teach us how to care for the earth as you desire. Lord, in your mercy,
hear our prayer.

We pray for an end to war and for peace throughout the world (*areas experiencing conflict may be named*). Prosper the work of peacemakers, erase hatred, and stop violence. Lord, in your mercy,
hear our prayer.

We pray for all who live with cognitive disorders or eating disorders. Provide them with supportive communities. Restore the forgotten; comfort the mourning; heal the hurting (*especially*). Lord, in your mercy,
hear our prayer.

We pray for all who are discerning a call to ministry and those who accompany them. Empower them with your grace and wisdom to continue building on the foundation of faith we have in Jesus Christ. Lord, in your mercy,

hear our prayer.

Here other intercessions may be offered.

We give thanks for the faithful departed (*especially*) and we pray for those who will die today. Hold them in your loving embrace. Breathe your Spirit of peace into them. Lord, in your mercy,

hear our prayer.

Receive these prayers in the name of Christ, the light of the world, who is one with you and the Holy Spirit, now and forever. **Amen.**

Images in the Readings

The **enemy** is a metaphoric category throughout the Bible. Psychologists tell us that most humans care for only a small "sympathy group," and those further away receive less concern. In extending the Israelite call to love the neighbor, the Matthew reading includes several examples of the outsider—the evildoer, the enemy, the persecutor, the unrighteous, the tax collector—whom we are called to love. Too complete an overlap between the church and the nation makes such love of the enemy nearly impossible, and we need to resist such an overlap.

Leviticus ordered the farmers to leave some produce in the field for the poor to **glean**. The tale of Ruth and Boaz is set in the situation of the poor widows gleaning what the rich man leaves—a sort of ancient rummage sale. Yet Matthew calls us to far more care than this.

Most biblical societies had **temples**, understood as houses of the deities whose protection the people desired. Many were like the Lincoln Memorial: open porticoes with a central statue of the god or goddess. To honor the deity, devotees visited the temple with gifts that supported its staff. Assuming an imminent eschaton, Paul sees no need for any such Christian buildings. Rather, the community is the temple within which God dwells.

Ideas for the Day

- Whenever we experience the power of extraordinary forgiveness, something inside of us changes. Even as we consider what we would do "if we were in their shoes," the witness of those who are truly able to love their enemies astounds us. On June 17, 2015, nine members of Emanuel African Methodist Episcopal Church in Charleston, South Carolina, were shot and killed by a stranger, a young white man who was welcomed into an evening Bible study held in their sanctuary. The slain included the pastor of this historic African American congregation, the Rev. Clementa Pinckney, a prominent community leader and a member of the South Carolina State Senate. The surviving families chose to publicly forgive the one whose hate-filled actions violated the sanctity of their house of worship and caused

unspeakable loss and heartbreak. What impact do events like this have on your perspective of God's grace and justice and on the work of reconciliation entrusted to the whole people of God in Christ Jesus?

- The apostle Paul's image of a master builder affirms how the power of Christ is renewed among the baptized in every generation. Paul also speaks against the distractions of human competitiveness as he celebrates the mission he has in common with Cephas, Apollos, and other leaders of the early church. Who are the master builders who have guided and sustained the work of God's people in your context? How do they embody the continuity of the church as they offer leadership and introduce innovations into ministries first envisioned by others?

- Stephen Covey counsels leaders in *The 7 Habits of Highly Effective People* (New York: Simon & Schuster, 1990) to begin every important task with the end in mind. This approach is paramount to all we do in Jesus' name. Jesus says "be perfect" to remind us that our ministries are not about us but rather are reflections of his presence in our world. As you consider the ministries entrusted to you and others, what gives you confidence that God is at work in the imperfect lives of your sisters and brothers in Christ who are saved by grace through faith?

Connections with the Liturgy

In the prayers of intercession each Sunday, we are asked to pray for the whole world, for the church universal, for peace and justice in the world, for the nations and those in authority, and for the community. By attending to this list, we will regularly pray for those whom we might first think of as evildoers, enemies, persecutors, the unrighteous, and crooked political collaborators.

Let the Children Come

Dennis, Sheila, and Matthew Linn describe in their book *Don't Forgive Too Soon: Extending the Two Hands That Heal* (Paulist Press, 1997) the concept of "creative nonviolence" as something acquired in childhood. When children are nurtured in a culture of forgiveness and empathy, they embody those qualities so deeply they can last their lifetime. In today's gospel text, Jesus' isn't simply teaching the disciples to respond safely to bullies or to be good victims, but is helping them envision a flipping of a whole culture of systemic violence. Don't look for the easy solution by telling children they should just be nice and walk away from injustice.

Assembly Song
Gathering

Built on a rock   ELW 652, LBW 365
Lord of glory, you have bought us   ELW 707, LBW 424
Great God, your love has called us   ELW 358, WOV 666

Psalmody and Acclamations

Burkhardt, Michael. "Psalm 119:33-40" from *Psalms for the Church Year*. U/SATB and org, or SATB a cap. MSM 80-708.

Mummert, Mark. "Psalm 119: 33-40," Refrain 1, from PSCY.

Nelson, Ronald A. "Psalm 119:33-40" from PWA.

(GA) Mxadana, George. "Two Songs from South Africa: Alleluia." SATB. GIA G-5286. Use ELW psalm tone 11 in G major with proper verse for Epiphany 7.

Hymn of the Day

Oh, praise the gracious power ELW 651, WOV 750
CHRISTPRAISE RAY

Goodness is stronger than evil ELW 721 *GOODNESS IS STRONGER*

Lord of all nations, grant me grace ELW 716, LBW 419
BEATUS VIR

Offering

Eternal Spirit of the living Christ ELW 402, LBW 441

Jesu, Jesu, fill us with your love ELW 708, WOV 765, TFF 83

Communion

O Jesus, joy of loving hearts ELW 658, LBW 356

Creating God, your fingers trace ELW 684, WOV 757

Bring peace to earth again ELW 700

Sending

O day of peace ELW 711, WOV 762

The church of Christ, in every age ELW 729, LBW 433

Additional Assembly Songs

Beloved and most loving source CBM 61

Bring your best to our worst SP 4

Now in this banquet W&P 104

⊕ Harling, Per. "You Are Holy/Du är helig." ELW 525.

⊕ Kijugo, Joas, arr. "The Love of God Almighty" from *Set Free: A Collection of African Hymns*. SATB, cant. AFP 9780806600451.

☼ Fielding, Ben/Sam Knock. "The Lost Are Found" from CCLI.

☼ Gate, David. "Teach Me to Love Like Jesus" from CCLI.

☼ Getty, Keith/Stuart Townend. "The Perfect Wisdom of Our God" from CCLI.

☼ Herns, Bernie/Mark Hall. "Love Them like Jesus" from CCLI.

☼ Ingram, Jason/Mia Fielding. "Ashes" from CCLI.

☼ Mooring, Leeland/Jack Mooring/Michael Farren. "All-Consuming Fire" from CCLI.

Music for the Day
Choral

ℙ Attwood, Thomas. "Teach Me, O Lord" from *Augsburg Motet Book*. SATB, opt kybd. AFP 9781451423709.

Bell, John. "Two Songs of Social Justice (Goodness Is Stronger Than Evil)." SATB, cant. GIA G-5671.

ℙ Fleming, Larry L. "Humble Service." SATB. AFP 9780800646226.

Nelson, Ronald A. "If You Love One Another." U or 2 pt, kybd. SEL 422-841.

Children's Choir

Marshall, Jane. "Dear Lord Day by Day." U, kybd, opt fl. CG CGA637.

McClune, Ellen/ A. Steven Taranto. "Let Us Go to the House of the Lord." U, pno. CG CGA872.

Shaw, Timothy. "Teach Me Your Way." U/2 pt, kybd, opt trbl instr. CG CGA1081.

Keyboard / Instrumental

Haan, Raymond H. "Awake, O Sleeper, Rise from Death" (Azmon) from *Five Preludes for Cello and Organ*. Vc, org. MSM 20-985.

ℙ ♫ Nelson, Ronald A. "Goodness Is Stronger than Evil" (Goodness Is Stronger) from *Easy Hymn Settings for Organ*, vol. 4. Org. AFP 9781451486049.

ℙ Raabe, Nancy. "Eternal Spirit of the Living Christ" (Adoro te devote) from *Grace and Peace, vol. 4: Hymn Portraits for Piano*. Pno. AFP 9781451443561.

♫ Sedio, Mark. "Lord of All Nations, Grant Me Grace" (Beatus vir) from *Six Slovak Hymn Improvisations*. Org. MSM 10-833.

Handbell

ℙ Eithun, Sandra. "Holy, Holy, Holy" from *Ring Praises!* 2-3 oct, L1+, CG CGB767. 3-5 oct, L1+, CG CGB768.

Krug, Jason W. "Compassion." 3-7 oct hb, opt 2 oct hc, L3. BP HB382.

ℙ Waldrop, Tammy. "I Want Jesus to Walk with Me." 3-6 oct hb, opt 2 oct hc, L2+. HOP 2635.

Thursday, February 23
Polycarp, Bishop of Smyrna, martyr, died 156

Polycarp was bishop of Smyrna (in present-day western Turkey) and a link between the apostolic age and the church at the end of the second century. He is said to have been known by John, the author of Revelation. In turn he was known by Iranaeus, bishop of Lyon in France, and Ignatius of Antioch. At the age of eighty-six he was martyred for his faith. When urged to save his life and renounce his faith, Polycarp replied, "Eighty-six years I have served him, and he never did me any wrong. How can I blaspheme my king who saved me?" The magistrate who made the offer was reluctant to kill a gentle old man, but he had no choice. Polycarp was burned at the stake, his death a testimony to the cost of renouncing temptation.

⊕ = global song   ♫ = relates to hymn of the day
☼ = praise song   ℙ = available in Prelude Music Planner

Saturday, February 25
Elizabeth Fedde, deaconess, died 1921

Fedde was born in Norway and trained as a deaconess. In 1882, at the age of thirty-two, she was asked to come to New York to minister to the poor and to Norwegian seafarers. Her influence was wide-ranging, and she established the Deaconess House in Brooklyn and the Deaconess House and Hospital of the Lutheran Free Church in Minneapolis. She returned home to Norway in 1895 and died there.

February 26, 2017
Transfiguration of Our Lord
Last Sunday after Epiphany

Today's festival is a bridge between the Advent-Christmas-Epiphany cycle that comes to a close today and the Lent-Easter cycle that begins in several days. On the mount of transfiguration Jesus is revealed as God's beloved Son, echoing the words at his baptism. This vision of glory sustains us as Jesus faces his impending death in Jerusalem. We turn this week to Ash Wednesday and our yearly baptismal journey from Lent to Easter. Some churches put aside the alleluia at the conclusion of today's liturgy. This word of joy will be omitted during the penitential season of Lent and will be sung again at Easter.

Prayer of the Day

O God, in the transfiguration of your Son you confirmed the mysteries of the faith by the witness of Moses and Elijah, and in the voice from the bright cloud declaring Jesus your beloved Son, you foreshadowed our adoption as your children. Make us heirs with Christ of your glory, and bring us to enjoy its fullness, through Jesus Christ, our Savior and Lord, who lives and reigns with you and the Holy Spirit, one God, now and forever.

Gospel Acclamation

Alleluia. This is my ⸗ Son, my Chosen,* lis- ⸗ ten to him! *Alleluia.* (Luke 9:35)

Readings and Psalm
Exodus 24:12-18

At Mount Sinai, Moses experienced the presence of God for forty days and forty nights. The "glory of the Lord" settled on the mountain, and on the seventh day God called out to Moses. On the mountain God gave Moses the stone tablets inscribed with the ten commandments.

Psalm 2

You are my son; this day have I begotten you. (Ps. 2:7)

or Psalm 99

Proclaim the greatness of the Lord; worship upon God's holy hill. (Ps. 99:9)

2 Peter 1:16-21

At the transfiguration, God's voice was heard, declaring Jesus to be the beloved Son. By the activity of the Holy Spirit, God's voice continues to be heard through the word of scripture.

Matthew 17:1-9

Shortly before he enters Jerusalem, where he will be crucified, Jesus is revealed to his disciples in a mountaintop experience of divine glory called the transfiguration.

Preface   Transfiguration

Color   White

Prayers of Intercession

The prayers are prepared locally for each occasion. The following examples may be adapted or used as appropriate.
Called to be a light to the nations, let us pray for God's justice, peace, and healing.
A brief silence.

God of Moses, you revealed your glory on Mount Sinai. Reveal your glory through missionaries and campus ministries. Shine your light through their acts of caring, justice, and mercy. Lord, in your mercy,

hear our prayer.

God of Eve, you create humankind in your image. Cultivate in us a passion for your good creation. Transform our daily routines so that our stewardship reveals your image. Lord, in your mercy,

hear our prayer.

God of David, you equip shepherds to care for your people. Where leaders rule by fear, transform their hearts with compassion and mercy. Send advocates for peace. We pray for your justice in every land (*especially*). Lord, in your mercy,

hear our prayer.

God of Naomi, you care for the widow. Be with all who mourn. Connect children in foster care with loving families. Protect refugees. Heal the sick and strengthen caretakers (*especially*). Lord, in your mercy,

hear our prayer.

God of Zechariah, you invite us to worship. Teach us to sing your praise in all places and in all circumstances. Embolden us to proclaim the joy of your faithfulness with our whole being. Lord, in your mercy,

hear our prayer.

Here other intercessions may be offered.

God of Lazarus, you resurrect the dead. Deepen our trust in the resurrection promise. Grant us peace as we grapple with what it means to die and live in you. Lord, in your mercy,

hear our prayer.

Receive these prayers in the name of Christ, the light of the world, who is one with you and the Holy Spirit, now and forever.
Amen.

Images in the Readings

Once again the readings include the central biblical images of **light** and **mountain**.

Yet God is not only brilliant light: important for the readings is the image of the **cloud**. Although contemporary people tend to think of clouds as relating to weather conditions, in the Bible the cloud is a sign of God's presence. It is as if God covers the earth, brings life, effecting much yet suddenly vanishing. Christians can add that from God as cloud rains down the waters of baptism.

We are so accustomed to the language of being children of a God who is like a Father that we miss the astonishment of the early church, when this imagery was a religious surprise. Christ is to God as a **son** is to a father, and we are not pitiful creatures struggling to live in a hostile environment but rather children cared for by a beneficent God. "Son of Man," on the other hand, is the biblical name for the apocalyptic judge, thus only paradoxically the beloved Son of God.

Ideas for the Day

- Help the congregation to recognize the insertion of God's audible presence in the gospel reading. Ask someone who has a strong, booming voice to proclaim God's line: "This is my Son, the Beloved; with him I am well pleased; listen to him!" (Matt. 17:5). The mountaintop experience is special because of a new view and understanding of God. The experience changes, shifts, and invigorates our vision. Ask in the preaching moment: How is God's presence dynamically or newly shown now? How is God calling us to listen this day?

- Father Thomas Keating writes in his book *Open Mind, Open Heart*, "When we say, at the liturgy, 'Let us pray,' we mean, 'Let us enter into a relationship with God'; or, 'Let us deepen the relationship we have'; or, 'Let us exercise our relationship with God'" ([New York: Continuum, 1986], 133). Prayer is intentional time set apart to be with God. Mountaintop experiences do not have to be dynamic, but Jesus' transfiguration was spectacular! It happened because Jesus and the disciples took intentional time to go up the mountain. Invite worshipers to name on sticky notes how they will set aside time to go up the mountain to deepen their relationship with God. As the assembly departs, invite them to place the sticky notes on the doors leading out of the worship space or to take them home and place them where they will be a daily reminder.

- Jesus' brilliant light is reflected on us even when we do not immediately recognize what God is doing. Use a video clip of liturgical artist Stephanie Burke, who paints a portrait of Jesus upside down and then flips it over (https://www.youtube.com/watch?v=Mel2kiPZsU8). It is amazing to watch this artist scamper around, creating something seemingly abstract yet beautiful. The surprise for the observer is when the rendering is flipped: Jesus is clearly seen. This mirrors the transfiguration of Jesus from teacher to Son of God. The rotation of the image helps the congregation move from seeing itself as abstract, separate parts to a cohesive reflection of the transfigured Jesus.

Connections with the Liturgy

At baptism the candidate is signed with the cross, to which Jesus walks, and the minister calls each of the baptized "child of God." So each baptism recalls the transfiguration.

Let the Children Come

Today this season culminates in a dazzling bright light. The time after Epiphany begins and ends with baptismal imagery, light, and the declaration, "This is my Son, the Beloved; with him I am well pleased." Help children bookend this time by remembering the baptism of Jesus and their own baptism. (This could be the call for baptismal preparation during Lent, culminating at the Easter Vigil.) Anoint their foreheads with the cross of Christ in oil. You know the ashes that follow, but for today we want to linger up on the mountain in the dazzling light of God's Son, just like the disciples long to do.

Assembly Song
Gathering

How good, Lord, to be here! ELW 315, LBW 89

O Morning Star, how fair and bright! ELW 308, LBW 76

Christ, whose glory fills the skies ELW 553, LBW 265

Psalmody and Acclamations

Goreham, Norman J. "Why This Dark Conspiracy" (Christ ist erstanden) from LUYH.

Jennings, Carolyn. "Psalm 2" from PSCY.

Mathis, William H. Refrain for "Psalm 99" from *After the Prelude: Year A*. U/cant, hb. CG CGB658 (digital version), CGB659 (printed version). Use with ELW psalm tone 6 or 10 (in C).

ᴾ (GA) Schwandt, Daniel. "This Is My Chosen" from MSB2 S570.

Hymn of the Day

Oh, wondrous image, vision fair ELW 316, LLC 322, LBW 80
DEO GRACIAS

Jesus on the mountain peak ELW 317, WOV 53 *BETHOLD*

Come, beloved of the Maker ELW 306 *JILL*

Offering

Drawn to the Light ELW 593

We are marching in the light ELW 866, WOV 650, TFF 63

Communion

Love divine, all loves excelling ELW 631, LBW 315

Beautiful Savior ELW 838, LBW 518

Shine, Jesus, shine ELW 671, WOV 651, TFF 64

Sending

Alleluia, song of gladness ELW 318, WOV 654

Immortal, invisible, God only wise ELW 834, LBW 526

Farewell to Alleluia MSB2 S571

Additional Assembly Songs

Lumière de Dieu SP 26, MSB2 S568

And have the bright immensities LBW 391

⊕ Kortekangas, Olli. "Iloitse, maa!/Halleluja-laulu" from *Agape: Songs of Hope and Reconciliation*. U. Lutheran World Federation. Out of print. Available on Amazon.com.

⊕ Syrian, traditional. "Halle, Hallelujah" from *Pave the Way: Global Songs 3*. U. AFP 9780800676896.

☼ Assad, Audrey. "Breaking Through" from CCLI.

☼ Blakesley, Josh/Ed Cash. "You Are the Light" from CCLI.

☼ Bryson, Jim, et al. "Shine On" from CCLI.

☼ Evans, Darrel/Mike Weaver. "Light of the World" from CCLI.

☼ Smith, Michael W./Deborah D. Smith. "Shine on Us" from CCLI.

☼ Tomlin, Chris/Ed Cash/Matt Armstrong. "Countless Wonders" from CCLI.

Music for the Day
Choral

ᴾ ♫ Cherwien, David. "Come, Beloved of the Maker." SATB, org, fl, opt assembly. AFP 9780800675158.

♫ Eggert, John. "Jesus on the Mountain Peak." SATB, org, tpt, opt assembly. CPH 984108.

Farlee, Robert Buckley. "Farewell to Alleluia." U, opt tpt, opt assembly. AFP 9780800649487.

ᴾ Helgen, John. "Beautiful Savior." U or 2 pt, kybd. AFP 9780800638368.

Children's Choir

ᴾ Helgen, John. "Beautiful Savior." U, pno, opt desc. AFP 9780800638368.

Olsen, Alice. "Faith Will Light the Way" from *Sing Out! Rejoice!* U, Orff inst. Alice Olsen Publishing AC-400.

Schalk, Carl. "Fairest Lord Jesus." U/2 pt, hb, cong, org. CG CGA974.

Keyboard / Instrumental

ᴾ ♫ Biery, Marilyn. "Jesus on the Mountain Peak" (Bethold) from *An American Perspective: Settings of Old and New Tunes for Organ*. Org. AFP 9781451401820.

ᴾ Howarth, Mary, and Hiram Titus. "We Are Marching in the Light" (Siyahamba) from *Glorify! Hymn Settings for Piano*. Pno. AFP 9781451424218.

ᴾ ♫ Miller, Aaron David. "Oh, Wondrous Image, Vision Fair" (Deo gracias) from *Hymns in Jazz Style*. Pno. AFP 9780800678531.

ᴾ ♫ Sedio, Mark. "Jesus on the Mountain Peak" (Bethold) from *Come and Praise*, vol. 2. Org. AFP 9780806696928.

Handbell

Kellermeyer, David. "God of the Mountains." 3 or 5 oct hb, opt 3 oct hc, opt fl, L2. FLG HB722.

ᴾ McChesney, Kevin. "Transformation." 3-7 oct, L2+. CG CGB794.

♫ Tucker, Sondra. "Festival Prelude on 'Deo Gracias.'" 3-6 oct hb, opt 3-6 oct hc, L4. BP HB325.

⊕ = global song   ♫ = relates to hymn of the day
☼ = praise song   ᴾ = available in Prelude Music Planner

Lent

Preparing for Lent

Lectionary

Lent in year A is Lent at its best, Lent at its most basic, Lent closest to its origin, Lent at its core. The lectionary readings that shape Lent in year A are the primary readings (one could almost say the original readings) that shaped this season. They make the most sense when set in relationship to baptism.

For a church that wants to be evangelical, a missionary outpost, a baptizing community, a place of transformation and new life, catechetical and catechumenal, welcoming and renewing, Lent in year A is foundational. Lent in year A is a season of baptismal preparation, baptismal renewal, and baptismal discovery.

Baptismal Preparation

These readings were used by early Christian communities that were accompanying inquirers and candidates for baptism. This group of new followers of Jesus had been assembled over several years, attracted by the message of the gospel, the witness of other Christians, the mercy and service of the congregation, and the working of the Spirit. In the last year or so, they had expressed desire to become public followers of Jesus, that is, to be baptized. Now, after months of formation, only five or six weeks remained until baptism at Easter. These five gospel stories, with their Old Testament partners, moved these candidates (and the whole congregation) through Lent to baptism at Easter. They have been preserved and carried forward to us as the year A Lenten texts.

If holy baptism will ever be the focus of the Lenten journey in your congregation, then this is the lectionary year to do it. If you have ever considered a process of welcoming newcomers patterned on the catechumenate (called in some places Welcome to Christ, Faith Forming Faith, The Way, or Welcome to Baptism), this is the year to explore it more deeply. The chart just below presents one way to understand the lectionary readings as a journey to baptism, with suggestions for a preaching series.

If you have adult candidates for baptism at the Easter Vigil, introduce them to the assembly at the beginning of Lent. Welcome to Baptism (*ELW*, pp. 232–233; Leaders Edition, pp. 30, 592–595) may be used as part of this welcome. Walk with this group on a journey to baptism as a congregation through Lent. For more on this pattern of baptismal preparation, see *Go Make Disciples: An Invitation to Baptismal Living* (Augsburg Fortress, 2012), especially pages 108–123. Provisional Lutheran rites are suggested in *Welcome to Christ: Lutheran Rites for the Catechumenate* (Augsburg Fortress, 1997) and are available in electronic format on the *Go Make Disciples* CD-ROM (separate resource).

	Gospel *First reading*	Baptismal activity in the readings	Image of baptism	Preaching using the symbols and actions of Holy Baptism
Lent 1	Temptation of Jesus *Adam and Eve are tempted*	In the wilderness for (Lent's) forty days	Renouncing evil	Preach about the three renunciations and Jesus' three temptations: Whom do we serve?
Lent 2	Nicodemus *Abraham gets a blessing*	Born again to travel the way of the cross—Christ lifted up	Seeking new birth	Preach about the three affirmations (articles of the Apostles' Creed) and the candidate's request for baptism.
Lent 3	Woman at the well *Water from the rock*	Receiving living water	Living water that lasts	Preach about the symbol of water in baptism and the action of filling the font with water, Luther's Flood Prayer, and saving water stories.
Lent 4	Man born blind *David is anointed*	Receiving new sight	Light and new sight; anointing	Preach about the anointing and presentation of the light (candle).
Lent 5	Raising of Lazarus *Dry bones*	Receiving new life from death	Dying and rising	Preach about the water bath—going down into the water with Christ, drowning the old self.

Baptismal Renewal

If your congregation is not ready to begin a process of walking with candidates to Easter baptisms, you still have an opportunity to take the baptized assembly on a journey of renewal and deepening appreciation of their own baptisms. "Becoming the Story We Tell: Renewing Our Engagement with Christ Crucified and Risen" is a great downloadable resource for that journey developed by the Anglican Church in Canada (www .anglican.ca/primate/tfc/becoming/).

For Lenten midweek worship, shape a Service of Word and Prayer around the Old Testament readings, or create a service of Prayer around the Font. If the size or placement of your font doesn't allow for a community to gather around it physically, find another suitable place to gather and an appropriately large container or vessel filled with water around which to gather.

Fasting, prayer, and acts of love are the disciplines of Lent described on Ash Wednesday. Organize congregational activities or midweek prayer around these disciplines to reinforce this pattern of Lenten living. For example:

- Consider a Lenten fast from extra committee meetings or other events that could be postponed to give greater time for prayer and worship.
- If your midweek practice includes a meal, be intentional about providing a truly simple meal—soup and bread or soup and salad.
- Expand offerings by the prayer ministry team and opportunities for individual or corporate confession and forgiveness.
- Provide Lenten devotional resources for the assembly to deepen their prayer.
- Organize a Lenten service project that benefits an organization in your neighborhood.
- Surround candidates for baptism and affirmation of baptism with loving gestures of welcome: provide a weekly care packages of cookies, embroider a large baptismal towel, or make a quilt as a baptismal gift.
- Lent's forty days are roughly one-tenth of the year—a biblical tithe of time for fasting, prayer, and acts of love. Pointing out this built-in tithe in the assembly's life can be a way to begin a discussion of Christian stewardship in the season of Lent.

Alternatively, lift up the ministry-in-daily-life vocations of those already baptized by including the occupations of lay worship ministers along with their names in the worship folder. Use this season to discuss the vocations that flow from our baptism. Midweek services may include a series of blessing of vocations: teaching professions, healing professions, legal/justice professions, and so on. Be sure that all have been included by the end of the season.

Baptismal Discovery

As a way to discover the depths of baptism's images and symbols this season, consider a preaching series that uses the year A readings to unpack the symbols in the rite of Holy Baptism (see the table just above for one possible progression). Such a series might be expanded with experiential activities each week. For example:

- Tracing the sign of the cross on one another's eyes, ears, hands, heart, and feet accompanied with a blessing for service or a reminder of Christ's claim on us at baptism (any week/all weeks).
- Interacting with sand, representing the wilderness (Jesus' temptation in the wilderness; baptismal renunciations).
- Anointing and/or blessing hands for ministry (Nicodemus).
- Receiving and drinking cool water (woman at the well).
- Receiving a candle (man born blind).
- Interacting with a funeral pall or gauze fabric (Lazarus's grave clothes).

Such experiential activities could potentially be carried from midweek worship into daily prayer in the home. Send worshipers home with a wilderness stone, anointing (olive) oil, a small vessel of water, a candle, a piece of fabric.

Visual Environment

- Enhance the space around the baptismal font. Consider rugs, additional plants near a box of sand (forming an oasis in our wilderness), a mobile, additional accent lighting (spots or blue LED uplights). If you can, create more space around your baptismal font so the assembly can gather there.
- If your water vessel is small, temporarily replace it with a larger one. A large, clear bowl—which allows the water, the primary symbol, to be seen—may be placed over a smaller bowl. A small, movable font could be replaced with a larger vessel. For advice on constructing a large, temporary font, see *Go Make Disciples*, page 173.
- Preach from the baptismal space, especially if Lenten preaching picks up baptismal themes. A portable ambo or music stand can make this more comfortable for some preachers. Move the regular chancel candles to frame this space.
- Create a "river" over the course of the season, either through the worship space or church building, or as a backdrop to the baptismal space. Consider assorted blue fabrics (quilt scraps?) or tablecloth rolls, or even collected recycled blue paper.
- Create a mobile with blue paper water drops over the course of the season. Hang them over the font and then over the entire assembly so that by Holy Week worshipers experience themselves under the sea, deep in the font, ready to emerge at Easter.

- If you typically add a rough-hewn cross at Lent, add it to the baptismal space, or consider letting the baptismal font take pride of place this year and introduce the cross to the environment on Passion Sunday or Good Friday.
- If you physically "bury" the alleluia for Lent, hide it at the font.

Structure, Liturgical Music, Assembly Song

In Lent, simplified service orders, hymns, and musical settings of Holy Communion help create both anticipation and meditative space. Shape a simplified rite for holy communion. Conclude any gathering rites in the first ten minutes of the service. If worship begins at the entrance to the worship space or at the baptismal space, consider a processional Kyrie to move from the font to the place of the word. Fresh, sparse, seasonal texts can lift up Lenten themes and draw the assembly's attention anew. Generous silences invite reflection. Short, easily memorized sung responses can invite the assembly into prayer (consider sources like Taizé or the Iona Community). Avoid scheduling baptisms during Lent; instead, plan for these any Sunday during the fifty days of Easter. Let Lent be a time to anticipate and prepare.

Use Lent to learn service music and hymnody that can accompany Holy Baptism. This way, future baptismal observances will be surrounded by robust congregational song. Learn a couple of musical acclamations by heart so that the assembly may be ready to respond to each baptism in the congregation. The Service Music section of *Evangelical Lutheran Worship* contains several baptismal acclamations (#209–215).

Reformation 500

It is now six months until the observance of the 500th anniversary of the Reformation. If your congregation intends to observe this anniversary but has not yet begun planning, now is the time. Many resources to assist your planning are available, including those mentioned in the other general and seasonal introductions in this volume.

Teach or experience a new model for scripture reflection during midweek worship. Several methods are outlined in *Go Make Disciples* (pp. 140–143), including one called "Martin Luther's Four-Stranded Garland." This method, while initially presented by Luther as an individual form of meditation in "A Simple Way to Pray," has been adapted for use in groups. A period of preparation in which a passage of scripture is selected is followed by four strands: instruction, thanksgiving, wholeness, and presence.

A Reformation-themed possibility for your midweek services is to spend some time with Luther's Small Catechism. A midweek plan in the seasonal rites section (pp. 110–113) suggests one way to organize worship around this Reformation treasure that has ongoing significance and usefulness for Lutherans. Another possibility would be to explore Luther's Flood Prayer (patterned on a eucharistic great thanksgiving and unique to Lutherans) and Luther's baptismal theology, which would flow into the year A lectionary's stream of water stories leading to Easter baptism and renewal.

Seasonal Checklist

- Plan for a congregational catechumenal process. In addition to *Go Make Disciples: An Invitation to Baptismal Living* (Augsburg Fortress, 2012), two books by Lutheran pastor Paul E. Hoffman will aid your planning: *Faith Forming Faith* and *Faith Shaping Ministry* (Eugene, OR: Wipf and Stock, 2012 and 2013).
- Confirm any plans for Easter baptisms.
- Select seasonal texts and outline the shape of a simplified Sunday liturgy for the season.
- Consider especially Thanksgiving at the Table IV in *Evangelical Lutheran Worship*.
- Shape the worship environment for Lent. Accent the place of baptism.
- Review the liturgies for Ash Wednesday and the Sunday of the Passion in *Evangelical Lutheran Worship*.
- Gather or order worship participation leaflets and seasonal supplies, such as ashes, palm branches, and baptism candles.
- Determine the procession with palms route for Passion Sunday. Prepare signs or recruit volunteers to help direct people. Determine how those with physical disabilities will participate in the procession or be seated ahead of time.
- Schedule a rehearsal of readers in preparation for the passion reading on Passion Sunday.

Worship Texts for Lent

Confession and Forgiveness

This confession provides extended silence for listening, pondering, and self-reflection.
All may make the sign of the cross, the sign marked at baptism, as the presiding minister begins.

In the name of the Father,
and of the ☩ Son, and of the Holy Spirit.
Amen.

God of heaven and earth,
you come in close and make us yours.
Equip us by your Spirit to confess our sin,
embrace your forgiveness,
and seek the way you set before us in your Son,
Jesus Christ our Lord.
Amen.

With honesty of heart, let us confess our sin.

The assembly may kneel or stand.
An extended silence may be kept.

Merciful God,
forgive us.
Our will is handcuffed to sin, and we cannot break free.
We have spoken when we should have kept quiet.
Silence.
We were silent when we should have said something.
Silence.
We acted when we knew better.
Silence.
We were still when we know we should have moved.
Silence.
For the wrong we have done,
for the good we have failed to do,
have mercy on us,
through Jesus Christ, our Savior and Lord.
Amen.

People of God, look to the ☩ Son,
given to heal you and set you free
because God loved the world so much.
Take hold of life—eternal life!
Amen.

OR

During the season of Lent we are called to return to the Lord with all our heart. Let us confess our sin and seek reconciliation with God and neighbor.

Silence for reflection and self-examination.

Merciful God,
you sent Jesus Christ to save the lost.
We confess that we have strayed from you
and turned aside from your way.
We fail in love, neglect justice,
and ignore your truth.
Have mercy on us and wash away our sin.
Create in us clean hearts
for the sake of Jesus Christ our Savior. Amen.

Behold, now is the acceptable time;
now is the day of salvation.
Almighty God have mercy on us,
forgive us all our sins,
and bring us to everlasting life.
Amen.

OR

In the words of a reformation hymn,
let us confess our sin before God.

Silence for reflection and self-examination.

Out of the depths I cry to you;
O Lord God, hear me calling.
Incline your ear to my distress
in spite of my rebelling.
Do not regard my sinful deeds.
Send me the grace my spirit needs.
Without it I am nothing. Amen.

In God alone, in God we hope,
and not in our own merit.
We hope as Israel in the Lord,
who sends redemption through the ☩ Word.
Praise God for grace and mercy!
Amen.

Offering Prayer

Merciful God,
receive the sacrifice of our praise and thanksgiving
and the offering of our lives,
that following in the way of the cross,
we may know the joy of the resurrection;
through Christ our Lord.
Amen.

Invitation to Communion

Return to God with all your heart.
Receive bread for the journey, drink for the desert.

Prayer after Communion

Compassionate God,
you have fed us with the bread of heaven.
Sustain us in our Lenten pilgrimage:
may our fasting be hunger for justice,
our alms, a making of peace,
and our prayer, the song of grateful hearts;
through Christ our Lord.
Amen.

Blessing

May God who has called us forth from the dust of the earth,
and claimed us as children of the light,
strengthen you on your journey into life renewed.
The Lord bless you and keep you.
The Lord's face shine upon you with grace and mercy.
The Lord look upon you with favor
and give you ☩ peace.
Amen.

Dismissal

Marked with the cross of Christ,
go forth to love and serve the Lord.
Thanks be to God.

Seasonal Rites for Lent

With Awe and Love
A Midweek Lenten Series Based on Luther's Small Catechism

Introduction

The year 2017 marks the international observance of the 500th anniversary of the Reformation. In honor of that anniversary, this midweek Lenten series is built around Luther's Small Catechism. The Small Catechism was designed as a teaching tool of the faith, not just within the church but in the home. Luther intended for the home to be the place where faith was first shared and taught. To that end he created the Small Catechism: a simple explanation of the Ten Commandments, the Creed, the Lord's Prayer, and the Sacraments. He included basic prayers for morning and evening, and suggested ways to worship, praise, and revere God during each part of our day.

This series uses scripture readings from the daily lectionary (usually those appointed for the Wednesdays of each week in Lent) or passages referred to in the Small Catechism itself. The daily lectionary readings for year A are listed in *Evangelical Lutheran Worship*, pages 1121–1125; the Small Catechism is printed on pages 1160–1167. The first week of this series sets the stage with the handing down of the Ten Commandments in Exodus. The following weeks look at each major section of the Small Catechism in turn: the Creed, the Lord's Prayer, Baptism, and Holy Communion. Studying the Small Catechism offers a way of growing closer to God by thinking on God's word and the basics of our faith. If desired, congregations could supplement this series with a weekly study of that portion of the catechism, or use each portion in turn as part of the reflection.

For the Reflections

Various forms of reflection may follow the scripture reading, such as brief commentary, teaching, or personal witness; non-biblical readings; interpretation through music or other art forms; or guided conversation among those present. Commentary or teaching could connect scripture with the portion of the Small Catechism being featured each week. Or the congregation could experience some kind of hands-on project together that follows the theme of the week. For example:

- Creating posters, either for the worship space or as family groups to take home, that match each week's portion of the Small Catechism. For example, the first week the poster could be as simple as copying the Ten Commandments (or Luther's explanations) or having each group paraphrase the commandments and put Luther's explanation into their own words. At the end of the five weeks, the community, or each group, would have posters on the entire Small Catechism.
- If there are longtime Lutherans in your congregation/community, ask them to bring in copies of the Small Catechism in different languages or earlier editions. Comparing them can spark intergenerational discussion.
- How would the different sections of the Small Catechism work as blog posts, on social media sites, or as brief video skits? Groups could create tweets, one-minute videos, raps, or whatever fits your local context.

Overview

Week of Lent 1 - Ten Commandments
In Exodus God gives Moses the Law so that the people of Israel would know how to fulfill their part of God's covenant as God's people.

Link to Lent 1
The reading for this week comes from the daily lectionary, Wednesday of Lent 1, year A (*ELW*, p. 1123). If desired, the reflection can also link to the psalm for the first Sunday in Lent, Psalm 32.

Week of Lent 2 - Creed
How do we express belief? How do we share our faith? The Creed, crafted in the early days of the church, gives us a simple but firm foundation for sharing and professing.

Link to Lent 2
In Ezekiel, God promises Israel: "I will put my spirit within you, and make you follow my statutes and be careful to observe my ordinances" (36:27). The Creed reminds us of those ordinances, and how and why we are given the precious gifts of faith and belief by our loving God.

Week of Lent 3 - Lord's Prayer
Lent and Lenten worship call us to repent, to make a new beginning. One of the best ways to begin again with God is through conversation, also known as prayer. And what better prayer than the one that Jesus taught us?

Link to Lent 3
In Psalm 81 God yearns for Israel to turn from their ways and follow God. When the disciples asked Jesus how to pray, he gave

them, and us, the Lord's Prayer in Luke 11:1-4 (see also Matthew 6:9-13). In Luther's explanation of this prayer, he beautifully tells us not only what not to do, but expands on how to live in the way God desires.

Week of Lent 4 - Baptism

Dying to our old, sinful self in baptism, we rise from the waters as beloved children of God. We are walking wet throughout the forty days of Lent, reminded daily that we are dead to sin.

Link to Lent 4

In Psalm 23 the psalmist claims the promise to live in God's house forever. We too are given that promise in baptism, as Paul reminds us in Romans 6:3-5. Martin Luther uses this passage in the Small Catechism to tell us that we are "drowned" so that a new person may rise every day in God's service.

Week of Lent 5 - Holy Communion

As we approach Holy Week, we remember Jesus' sacrifice for us. We gather around the table to remind ourselves and one another of that sacrifice and how it shapes our lives.

Link to Lent 5

In Psalm 143 the psalmist thirsts for God, asking to be revived. In holy communion we are revived and renewed with God's gifts of life and salvation. Luther reminds us that all we need is faith to make us worthy and well prepared to receive that gift.

Opening Dialogue

Week 1

We begin in the name of the Lord, whom we are to fear and love.

Fear God? Are we to be afraid of our Creator?

Not afraid, but filled with reverent awe.

How shall we do this?

By trusting God above all things, and calling upon God's name.

In every time of need, in prayer, praise, and thanks.

And because we fear and love God, we love and respect all God's creation.

People and animals, plants and water, mountains and deserts.

Week 2

We begin in the name of God,

Father, Son, and Holy Spirit.

What does this mean, this belief?

I believe that God has created me together with all that exists. God daily and abundantly provides for me.

We confess that Jesus is Lord.

He has redeemed and freed us so that we may belong to him.

How is this possible when we are who we are?

We believe because the Holy Spirit calls us.

Called, gathered, enlightened, and made holy, we praise God.

This is most certainly true!

Week 3

Behold, Lord, an empty vessel that needs to be filled.

My Lord, fill it.

I am weak in the faith;

strengthen me.

I am cold in love;

warm me and make me fervent,
that my love may go out to my neighbor.

I do not have a strong and firm faith;

at times I doubt and am unable to trust you altogether.

O Lord, help me.

Strengthen my faith and trust in you.

Week 4

We begin in the name of the Father,
and of the ✝ Son, and of the Holy Spirit.

The name in which we baptize.

What is baptism?

It is water used according to God's command
and connected with God's word.

What gifts does baptism grant?

It brings about forgiveness of sins, redeems from
death, and gives eternal salvation to all who believe.

How can water do such great things?

The water does not do this alone, but the word of God
with and alongside of the water, and faith.

This is a grace-filled water of life.

A bath of new birth in the Holy Spirit.

Week 5

Bless the Lord, who forgives all our sins.

God's mercy endures forever.

Blessed be God, who gives us life and salvation.

A gift we can never deserve or earn.

Given for you, for me, for all for the forgiveness of sins

in bread and wine, body and blood, words and presence.

Given in grace, received by faith.

Give us truly believing hearts, O God,

so that we might receive this great gift.

Gathering Song

Week 1

The glory of these forty days   ELW 320, WOV 657

I'm going on a journey   ELW 446, TFF 115

Week 2

Holy God, we praise your name   ELW 414, LBW 535

Come, join the dance of Trinity   ELW 412

Week 3

Our Father, God in heaven above   ELW 746/747

Lord, listen to your children praying   ELW 752, TFF 247,
   WOV 775, W&P 92

Week 4

As the deer runs to the river   ELW 331

Jesus is a rock in a weary land   ELW 333

Week 5

Jesus, still lead on   ELW 624, LBW 341

My song is love unknown   ELW 343, WOV 661, LBW 94

Reading

Week 1 - Exodus 34:1-9, 27-28

Week 2 - Ezekiel 36:22-32

Week 3 - Matthew 9:6-15

Week 4 - Romans 6:1-14

Week 5 - Matthew 26:26-29 *or* Luke 22:14-20

Reflection

The reading of scripture is followed by silence for reflection. Other forms of reflection may also follow, such as brief commentary, teaching, or personal witness; non-biblical readings; interpretation through music or other art forms; or guided conversation among those present.

Song

Week 1

If you but trust in God to guide you   ELW 769, LBW 453

Week 2

I bind unto myself today   ELW 450, LBW 188

Week 3

Oh, love, how deep   ELW 322, LBW 88

Week 4

The King of love, my shepherd is   ELW 502, LBW 456

Week 5

In the cross of Christ I glory   ELW 324, LBW 104

Luther's Evening Blessing

I give thanks to you, heavenly Father,

through Jesus Christ your dear Son, that you have graciously protected me today. I ask you to forgive me all my sins, where I have done wrong, and graciously to protect me tonight. Into your hands I commend myself: my body, my soul, and all that is mine. Let your holy angel be with me, so that the wicked foe may have no power over me. Amen.

Lord's Prayer

Blessing

God the Father, ☩ Son, and Holy Spirit watch over us all.

Amen.

Sending Song

Week 1

Bless now, O God, the journey   ELW 326

Week 2

Restore in us, O God ELW 328, WOV 662

Week 3

All praise to thee, my God, this night ELW 565, LBW 278

Week 4

Christ, the life of all the living ELW 339, LBW 97

Week 5

Jesus, keep me near the cross ELW 335, TFF 73

Acknowledgments

The opening dialogues for weeks 2, 4, and 5 include adaptations
or paraphrases of the text of the Small Catechism as presented
in *Evangelical Lutheran Worship*, pages 1160–1167. The opening dialogue for week 3 is a prayer of Martin Luther, *Evangelical Lutheran Worship*, page 87. Luther's Evening Blessing is
from the Small Catechism.

March 1, 2017

Ash Wednesday

Lent begins with a solemn call to fasting and repentance as we begin our journey to the baptismal waters of Easter. As we hear in today's readings, now is the acceptable time to return to the Lord. During Lent the people of God will reflect on the meaning of their baptism into Christ's death and resurrection. The sign of ashes suggests our human mortality and frailty. What seems like an ending is really an invitation to make each day a new beginning, in which we are washed in God's mercy and forgiveness. With the cross on our brow, we long for the spiritual renewal that flows from the springtime Easter feast to come.

Prayer of the Day

Almighty and ever-living God, you hate nothing you have made, and you forgive the sins of all who are penitent. Create in us new and honest hearts, so that, truly repenting of our sins, we may receive from you, the God of all mercy, full pardon and forgiveness through your Son, Jesus Christ, our Savior and Lord, who lives and reigns with you and the Holy Spirit, one God, now and forever.

or

Gracious God, out of your love and mercy you breathed into dust the breath of life, creating us to serve you and our neighbors. Call forth our prayers and acts of kindness, and strengthen us to face our mortality with confidence in the mercy of your Son, Jesus Christ, our Savior and Lord, who lives and reigns with you and the Holy Spirit, one God, now and forever.

Gospel Acclamation

Return to the ⏐ Lord, your God,* who is gracious and merciful, slow to anger, and abounding in ⏐ steadfast love. (Joel 2:13)

Readings and Psalm

Joel 2:1-2, 12-17

Because of the coming Day of the Lord, the prophet Joel calls the people to a community lament. The repentant community reminds God of his gracious character and asks God to spare the people, lest the nations doubt God's power to save.

or Isaiah 58:1-12

Shortly after the return of Israel from exile in Babylon, the people were troubled by the ineffectiveness of their fasts. God reminds them that outward observance is no substitute for genuine fasting that results in acts of justice, such as feeding the hungry, sheltering the homeless, and clothing the naked. Sincere repentance will lead to a dramatic improvement of their condition.

Psalm 51:1-17

Have mercy on me, O God, according to your steadfast love. (Ps. 51:1)

2 Corinthians 5:20b—6:10

The ministry of the gospel endures many challenges and hardships. Through this ministry, God's reconciling activity in the death of Christ reaches into the depths of our lives to bring us into a right relationship with God. In this way, God accepts us into the reality of divine salvation.

Matthew 6:1-6, 16-21

In the Sermon on the Mount, Jesus commends almsgiving, prayer, and fasting, but emphasizes that spiritual devotion must not be done for show.

Preface   Lent

Color   Purple

Prayers of Intercession

The prayers are prepared locally for each occasion. The following examples may be adapted or used as appropriate.

Lifting our voices and turning toward God, let us pray for the church, the earth, and all who are in need.

A brief silence.

We pray for the church. Turn it toward you, loving God, and unite it in a desire to live for you alone. Hear us, O God.

Your mercy is great.

Sustain in us a willing spirit to care for the earth and all that lives on it, knowing that we are stewards of your creation. Hear us, O God.

Your mercy is great.

We pray for the nations (*especially*). Let no leader put an obstacle in the way of those seeking your justice, peace, and love. Hear us, O God.

Your mercy is great.

Let your light break forth and shine on those who suffer in body, mind, or spirit. Let your healing spring up quickly. (*We pray especially for . . .*) Hear us, O God.

Your mercy is great.

Guide this assembly constantly back to your word, your holy meal, and the unfailing waters of baptism. Hear us, O God.

Your mercy is great.

Here other intercessions may be offered.

We give thanks for the lives of the faithful departed who have returned to the dust and thus to you (*especially the hymnwriter George Herbert*). Inspire us by their examples of holy living. Hear us, O God.
Your mercy is great.

Into your hands, merciful God, we commend all for whom we pray, trusting in your steadfast love; through Christ our Lord. **Amen.**

Images in the Readings

Although cited only in the reading from Isaiah 58, **ashes** are the primary image for the day. Since the eleventh century, the ashes, made by burning last year's palms, cycle around from the triumphant celebration of Jesus' entry into Jerusalem to the humiliation of sinners covering their heads with the burnt greens. Ashes also bring to mind the fire of the Easter Vigil. Honesty is always good, if sometimes painful: this day we are honest about sin and death. The ash cross marks one's forehead as if it is the brand of one's owner. We journey forward wearing the sign of the cross.

The gospel reading is the source for the three **disciplines of Lent** that have proved useful for many of Christ's disciples. To increase one's giving to the poor, to intensify one's rituals of prayer, and to decrease one's focus on the self: the idea is that such disciplines open up the self to God and to the neighbor.

The **acceptable time**, the day of salvation, are ways Paul describes the here and now of the life of the baptized. Ash Wednesday calls us each day into life in Christ.

Several beloved hymns call Christ our **treasure**. The treasure described in both Matthew and Paul—"poor, yet making many rich"—is the countercultural value of the baptized life.

Ideas for the Day

- *Trending* on social media has become a popular way to gauge what has the public's attention. Clicking on a story link and using hashtags are two ways topics or movements become recognized as trending. The use of hashtags and the practice of replacing or altering a profile picture both identify supporters of or participants in a particular movement, cause, event, or issue. Lent calls us to rely on God. Have your congregation commit to "purpling" for Lent by tinting their social media profile pictures purple or replacing them with a purple block and explaining why in the caption. You could also propose a social media project in which worshipers post about ways God sustains them and tag the posts with *#40relyongod*.

- Marking our foreheads with ashes seems to contradict Jesus' words in the gospel text. Jesus seems to be instructing a modest and hidden acknowledgment of our sinfulness. How then has the practice evolved so that Christians worldwide leave worship marked with black smudged crosses for all the world to see? Jesus was speaking of seeking glory for one's feigned humility by drawing attention to oneself. The Christian ritual of being reminded that we are dust with the marking of the forehead signals a communal awareness of our dependence on God. The use of ashes may or may not resonate with today's assemblies. You might additionally consider inviting members of the congregation to wear black or purple armbands or bracelets throughout the forty days to mark their observance of Lent. If asked about the significance of the armband or bracelet by friends or colleagues, wearers have an opportunity to witness to the powerful nature of this season and our journey to the cross.

- There is joy, relief, and release in confessing our sins. Ash Wednesday's focus on introspection and confession makes us mindful of our own failings and gives us an opportunity to unburden ourselves of the guilt that accompanies them. The joy of Lent is in the liberation from sin and the intense focus on God.

Connections with the Liturgy

Ash Wednesday is an intensification of our regular rite of confession and forgiveness, a rare time in our culture during which we acknowledge our sin and beg for renewal. The Kyrie also recalls Ash Wednesday: "Lord, have mercy," "Lord, have mercy," over and over. At communion we sing, "Lamb of God, you take away the sin of the world, have mercy on us." There is always more and more need for mercy.

Let the Children Come

Ash Wednesday provides the liturgical safe place to remember our own mortality and brokenness in sin. All people wrestle with and wonder about death, regardless of their age—even children. And yet when we see children wrestling with existential issues, the wonders come to the surface through play. They don't have long conversations over coffee, but instead dress up or act out what they are wrestling with. Today the whole church joins children in their play, marked by ashes, remembering our sin and death. Be confident God has equipped children to enter this kind of liturgical play with the whole church.

Assembly Song and Music for the Day

Because of the nature of this day, music suggestions are listed by place in the service and categorized by type of leadership (in brackets): Ch=Choral; CC=Children's Choir; KI=Keyboard/ Instrumental; HB=Handbell. Many suggestions require assembly participation.

Gathering

Psalm 51 (see Psalmody and Acclamations)
Kyrie   ELW 151–158 or from communion settings
Now is the time of grace   MSB1 S403

☼ Cooney, Rory/Gary Daigle. "Hold Us in Your Mercy: Penitential Litany." GIA G-4760.

Bach, J. S. "Ich ruf zu dir, Herr Jesu Christ," BWV 639, from *Orgelbüchlein*. Org. Various editions. [KI]

Psalmody and Acclamations

Cherwien, David. "Psalm 51" from PSCY.

P Raabe, Nancy. "Have Mercy on Me, O God (Psalm 51:1-17)." MSB1 S402.

Schalk, Carl, or May Schwarz. "Psalm 51:1-17" from PWA.

P (GA) Organ, Anne Krentz. "Return to the Lord" with proper verse for Ash Wednesday. MSB1 S419.

☼ Angrisano, Steve. "Be Merciful, O Lord" from *Spirit and Song*, vol. 1. OCP.

P Patterson, Mark. "Psalm 51" from *ChildrenSing Psalms*. U, kybd, assembly. AFP 9780800663872. [CC]

Hymn of the Day

Out of the depths I cry to you ELW 600, LBW 295 *AUS TIEFER NOT*

Eternal Lord of love, behold your church ELW 321 *OLD 124TH*

Restore in us, O God ELW 328 *BAYLOR* WOV 662 *CATECHUMEN*

Confession of Sin

Music Sourcebook for Lent and the Three Days (MSB1) includes four musical settings of texts for corporate confession of sin, one using the text in the Ash Wednesday service (S408) and others using the text from Corporate Confession and Forgiveness, Evangelical Lutheran Worship Leaders Edition, p. 603 (S409–S411).

Imposition of Ashes

P Remember that you are dust MSB1 S413

Savior, when in dust to you ELW 601, LBW 91

⊕ Lockwood, Jorge. "Forgive Us, Lord/*Perdon, Señor*" from *Glory to God*. SATB. WJK 0664238971.

☼ Fox, Kipp. "This Dust" from CCLI.

P Ferguson, John. "All Things of Dust to Dust Return." SATB, org. AFP 9780800677916.

P♫ Uehlein, Christopher. "Restore in Us, O God" (Baylor) from *A Blue Cloud Abbey Organ Book for Lent*. Org. AFP 9781451401134. [KI]

P Bettcher, Peggy. "How Deep the Father's Love for Us." 2-3 oct, L3+, HOP 2630. 3-5 oct, L3+, HOP 3588. [HB]

Setting the Table

Music Sourcebook for Lent and the Three Days (MSB1) includes an appendix with hymn stanzas appropriate for use during the setting of the table on this and other days. These stanzas are also included on the CD-ROM that accompanies the volume.

☼ Dummer, Elias/Eric Fusilier/Aaron Powell/Josh Vanderlaan. "Yours" from CCLI.

⊕ = global song ♫ = relates to hymn of the day
☼ = praise song P = available in Prelude Music Planner

P Benson, Robert A. "Out of the Depths." SATB, org, alto sax. AFP 9781451479430. [Ch]

Bedford, Michael. "Grant, O God, Your Blessing" from *Seven Songs for the Church Year*. U, kybd, hb. CG CGA693. [CC]

♫ Dupré, Marcel. "Out of the Depths I Cry to You" (Aus tiefer Not) from *Seventy-Nine Chorales for the Organ, Op. 28*. Org. ALF 9780769241951. [KI]

♫ Kuhnau, Johann. "Out of the Depths I Cry to You" (Aus tiefer Not) from *Two Lenten Chorale Preludes*. Org. MSM 10-321. [KI]

♫ Ingram, Bill. "Draw Near and Take the Body of the Lord" from *Communion Hymns for Handbells*. 2-3 oct, L2-. CPH 97-7136. [HB]

Communion

Our Father, we have wandered ELW 606, WOV 733

Softly and tenderly Jesus is calling ELW 608, WOV 734, TFF 155

Once we sang and danced ELW 701

⊕ Wu, Mabel. "O Lamb of God." U. ELW 198.

☼ Hart, Sarah/Kevin B. Hipp. "Fill Me, O God" from *Spirit and Song*, vol. 2. OCP.

☼ Lee, Russ/Eddie Carswell. "Rock of Ages" from CCLI.

P♫ Ferguson, John. "Psalm 130: Out of the Depths." SATB, org. AFP 9780800656072. [Ch]

P Scott, K. Lee. "Out of the Depths I Cry to Thee." 2 pt mxd, kybd. AFP 9780800647322. [Ch]

Reeves, Jeff. "Create in Me a Clean Heart." U/2 pt, pno. CG CGA870. [CC]

P Cherwien, David. "By the Babylonian River" (Kas dziedaja) from *Good Friday Reflections: Organ Meditations on Stations of the Cross*. Org. MSM 10-365. [KI]

P Cherwien, David. "Softly and Tenderly Jesus Is Calling" (Thompson) from *In Heaven Above: Piano Music for Funerals and Memorials*. Pno. AFP 9781451401912. [KI]

P Geschke, Susan. "What Wondrous Love Is This?" from *Ring Praises!* 2-3 oct, L1+, CG CGB767. 3-5 oct, L1+, CG CGB768. [HB]

Sending

The glory of these forty days ELW 320, WOV 657

On my heart imprint your image ELW 811, LBW 102

Wednesday, March 1
George Herbert, hymnwriter, died 1633

As a student at Trinity College, Cambridge, England, George Herbert excelled in languages and music. He went to college with the intention of becoming a priest, but his scholarship attracted the attention of King James I. Herbert served in parliament for two years. After the death of King James and at the urging of a friend, Herbert's interest in ordained ministry was renewed. He was ordained a priest in 1630 and served the little parish of St. Andrew Bremerton until his death. He was noted for unfailing care for his parishioners, bringing the sacraments to them when they were ill, and providing food and clothing for those in need. Herbert is best remembered, however, as a writer of poems and hymns such as "Come, My Way, My Truth, My Life" (ELW 816).

Thursday, March 2
John Wesley, died 1791; Charles Wesley, died 1788; renewers of the church

The Wesleys were leaders of a revival in the Church of England. Their spiritual discipline (or method) of frequent communion, fasting, and advocacy for the poor earned them the name "Methodists." The Wesleys were missionaries in the American colony of Georgia for a time, but returned to England discouraged. Following a conversion experience while reading Luther's *Preface to the Epistle to the Romans*, John was perhaps the greatest force in eighteenth-century revival. The brothers' desire was that the Methodist Societies would be a movement for renewal in the Church of England, but after their deaths the societies developed a separate status.

Charles wrote more than six hundred hymns, including "Hark! The Herald Angels Sing" (ELW 270), "Christ, Whose Glory Fills the Skies" (ELW 553), and "Love Divine, All Loves Excelling" (ELW 631).

March 5, 2017
First Sunday in Lent

Today's gospel tells of Jesus' temptation in the desert. His forty-day fast becomes the basis of our Lenten pilgrimage. In the early church Lent was a time of intense preparation for those to be baptized at the Easter Vigil. This catechetical focus on the meaning of faith is at the heart of our Lenten journey to the baptismal waters of Easter. Hungry for God's mercy, we receive the bread of life to nourish us for the days ahead.

Prayer of the Day

Lord God, our strength, the struggle between good and evil rages within and around us, and the devil and all the forces that defy you tempt us with empty promises. Keep us steadfast in your word, and when we fall, raise us again and restore us through your Son, Jesus Christ, our Savior and Lord, who lives and reigns with you and the Holy Spirit, one God, now and forever.

Gospel Acclamation

One does not live by ' bread alone,* but by every word that comes from the ' mouth of God. (Matt. 4:4)

Readings and Psalm
Genesis 2:15-17; 3:1-7

Human beings were formed with great care, to be in relationship with the creator, creation, and one another. The serpent's promise to the first couple that their eyes would be opened led, ironically, to the discovery only that they were naked.

Psalm 32

Mercy embraces those who trust in the LORD. (Ps. 32:10)

Romans 5:12-19

Through Adam's disobedience, humanity came under bondage to sin and death, from which we cannot free ourselves. In Christ's obedient death, God graciously showers on us the free gift of liberation and life.

Matthew 4:1-11

Jesus experiences anew the temptations that Israel faced in the wilderness. As the Son of God, he endures the testing of the evil one.

Preface   Lent

Color   Purple

Prayers of Intercession

The prayers are prepared locally for each occasion. The following examples may be adapted or used as appropriate.
Lifting our voices and turning toward God, let us pray for the church, the earth, and all who are in need.
A brief silence.

Holy God, lead your church on earth to do your will and strive for your kingdom. Teach us your ways and increase our understanding. Hear us, O God.
Your mercy is great.

Show us how to care for your creation and to treasure the fruits of your creating. Guide our actions and increase our commitment. Hear us, O God.
Your mercy is great.

Give knowledge and wisdom to all leaders throughout your world. Turn hardened hearts of stone toward your nourishing word and let the powerful become providers of daily bread. Hear us, O God.
Your mercy is great.

Rush to the aid of your people in times of distress. Send your peace and healing to those in need. (*We pray especially for . . .*) Hear us, O God.
Your mercy is great.

Guide those preparing for baptism, sponsors, and this whole assembly toward living into the promises made in baptism. Lead us to scripture, the holy supper, and toward your will for all creation. Hear us, O God.
Your mercy is great.

Here other intercessions may be offered.

Accompany us on our Lenten journeys and inspire us by the witness of the saints who walked faithfully with you. Hear us, O God.
Your mercy is great.

Into your hands, merciful God, we commend all for whom we pray, trusting in your steadfast love; through Christ our Lord.
Amen.

Images in the Readings

Matthew writes that Jesus fasted for **forty days and forty nights**. In the Bible, forty is always the time between, the necessary span before the gracious conclusion. It is forty, days or years, that numbers the rain of Noah's flood, Moses on Mount Sinai, Israel in the wilderness, the spies scouting out Canaan, Israel in the hands of the Philistines, the taunting by Goliath, the reigns of Saul, David, and Solomon, Ezekiel lying on his right side, Nineveh's repentance, and Jesus' appearance after Easter. For us, it is forty days until the celebration of the resurrection.

The **tree of knowledge of good and evil**—a stark contrast with the wondrous tree of life that appears again in Revelation 22—is a fascinating, ambiguous symbol, perhaps signifying the human tendency to replace God's way with one's own way, God's word with human knowledge. It is a mystery tree that according to the story represents all that is wrong in human life.

Who initiated sin? In Genesis it is **the woman**, in Paul it is **Adam**—characters whom we recognize as being essentially ourselves. The storyteller of Genesis 3 joined with many others in antiquity by blaming the woman for all the troubles of humanity. In accord with a Christian theological interpretation of this story, all people are Adam, creatures of earth, and all people are Eve, bearers of life.

The gospel describes the **devil** as the tempter, the power that seeks to lure us away from God. It is this devil that much Christian tradition has used to explain the talking serpent of Genesis 3. The tradition of art has not given us profound enough depictions of this primordial evil, but in the usual image of a creature part human, part monster, we can see another picture of ourselves.

Ideas for the Day

- You could argue that by the end of his ministry Jesus has turned all the devil's temptations on their heads. He feeds thousands with a few loaves of bread. He trusts God to protect him all the way to the cross. He is King of kings and Lord of lords. Yet he does these things on God's terms and is faithful. We might start with the best of intentions, but too often the quick and easy way to success becomes appealing.

- First, the Holy Spirit descends on Jesus at his baptism, then the same Spirit leads Jesus into the wilderness to be tempted by the devil. It would be different if the devil pursued Jesus, but it seems that the Spirit of God *led* Jesus to this place of temptation. Maybe part of the reality is this: being baptized does not make life easier. Instead, it complicates life. Baptism leads you to care about people on the far side of the world, people you will never meet or know. Baptism calls you to work for justice and peace. Daily we are tempted to ignore the needs of the world in favor of our own comfort. Caring can start with a cup of coffee. Is this too much of a stretch? Read about Lutheran World Relief's involvement with the fair trade movement at http://lwr .org/getinvolved/fairtrade. The Good Gifts section of the ELCA's website has resources for congregations that wish to host a Good Gifts fair (look under "Congregational resources").

- Traditionally, Lent is a time for giving up something. People quit eating chocolate or drinking coffee or alcohol. Lent becomes a time to fast from all sorts of things that are not good for our physical or spiritual health. What if people were instead invited to *take on* a practice during Lent: daily prayer, daily scripture reading, meditative walks, acts of kindness and generosity. What might forty days of taking on such practice yield?

Connections with the Liturgy

Following Jesus, we respond to evil with the power of the word. Each Sunday we acknowledge the readings as "the word of the Lord," "Word of God, word of life." For the gospel, we stand, singing "Glory" to Christ, whom we laud in this word. In each baptismal liturgy, we recall this Sunday's gospel as we join with the candidates for baptism to renounce the devil, all the forces that defy God, and all the powers of this world that rebel against God. As God's Spirit enters us, we reject the spirit of evil that is both within and outside ourselves.

Let the Children Come

If you look at children's artwork, you may notice that both human and nonhuman creatures get equal attention: the ground, the sun, the birds, the mountain, the person. As our Lenten texts unfold, the whole cosmos is caught up in the brokenness of death and sin and being moved toward new life. During Lent the church moves from death to new life in the stories we hear and actions we live out. Today is a day for curious opposites, two ideas next to each other to give us new meaning: the old Adam in the living garden and the new Adam in the parched desert.

Assembly Song
Gathering

Great Litany ELW 238, LBW pp. 168–173
Eternal Lord of love, behold your church ELW 321
Bless now, O God, the journey ELW 326

Psalmody and Acclamations

Anderson, Mark. "Psalm 32," Refrain 2, from PSCY.
Bruxvoort Colligan, Richard. "Unfailing Love (Psalm 32:3, 5)" from *Sharing the Road*. AFP 9780800678630.
Helgen, John. "Psalm 32 from *ChildrenSing Psalm*s. U, assembly, kybd. AFP 9780800663872.
P (GA) Organ, Anne Krentz. "Return to the Lord" with proper verse for Lent 1. MSB1 S419.

Hymn of the Day

A mighty fortress is our God ELW 503–505, LBW 228/229, LLC 403 *EIN FESTE BURG*
I want Jesus to walk with me ELW 325, TFF 66, WOV 660 *SOJOURNER*
The glory of these forty days ELW 320, WOV 657 *ERHALT UNS, HERR*

Offering

Tree of Life and awesome mystery ELW 334, sts. 1, 2, 3, Lent 1
As the sun with longer journey ELW 329, WOV 655

Communion

Lord Jesus, you shall be my song ELW 808
Oh, love, how deep ELW 322, LBW 88
If God my Lord be for me ELW 788, LBW 454

Sending

Jesus, still lead on ELW 624, LBW 341
Guide me ever, great Redeemer ELW 618, LBW 343

Additional Assembly Songs

Let this season be ASG 19
Esto cuarenta días hoy LLC 323
O God, with hope I enter in CBM 98
⊕ Bell, John, arr. "The Courage to Say No" from *The Courage to Say No: 23 Songs for Lent and Easter*. U. GIA G-4244.
⊕ Cassina, Miguel. "I Depend upon Your Faithfulness" from *Glory to God*. U. WJK 0664238971.
☼ Cotrell, Travis/David Moffitt/Susan C. Smith. "My Passion" from CCLI.
☼ Ligertwood, Brooke. "Lead Me to the Cross" from CCLI.
☼ Maher, Matt. "40 Days" from *Spirit and Song*, vol. 2. OCP.
☼ Redman, Matt. "The Heart of Worship" from CCLI.
☼ Tomlin, Chris, et al. "The Name of Jesus" from CCLI.
☼ Walker, Tommy. "Your Word Will Be the Last Word" from CCLI.

Music for the Day
Choral

P ♫ Highben, Zebulon M. "Walk with Me." SATB or SAB. AFP 9780806698342.
P ♫ Miller, Aaron David. "I Want Jesus to Walk with Me." U or 2 pt, pno. AFP 9780800678418.
P Pelz, Walter. "O Lord, throughout These Forty Days." SATB or SAB, org, ob. AFP 9780800637538.
P ♫ Raabe, Nancy M. "A Mighty Fortress." SATB, assembly, org, tpt, opt tamb. AFP 9781451423914.

Children's Choir

Bedford, Michael. "Forty Days and Nights" from *Seasonal Songs for Young Singers*. U, kybd, opt hb or hc. CG CGA1160.
♫ Miller, Aaron David. "I Want Jesus to Walk with Me." U, pno, opt desc. AFP 9780800678418.
P Patterson, Mark. "Show Me Thy Ways" from *ChildrenSing: Seven Anthems for Elementary Age Singers*. U, opt 2 pt, pno. AFP 9780800677695.

Keyboard / Instrumental

♫ Hassell, Michael. "I Want Jesus to Walk with Me" (Sojourner) from *Traveling Tunes: Hymn Arrangements for Solo Instrument and Piano*. Inst, pno. AFP 9780800656195.
P Kim, Marianne. "Through the Night of Doubt and Sorrow" (Ebenezer) from *My Soul Proclaims: Piano Meditations for Worship*. Pno. AFP 9781451499131.
♫ Petersen, Lynn. "I Want Jesus to Walk with Me" (Sojourner) from *Spiritual Sounds for Trombone and Organ*. Inst (tbn, B flat tpt, or C inst), org. CPH 97-6887.

⊕ = global song   ♫ = relates to hymn of the day
☼ = praise song   P = available in Prelude Music Planner

P ♫ Sowash, Bradley. "A Mighty Fortress Is Our God" (Ein feste Burg) from *Great German Hymns Arranged in Contemporary Styles*. Pno. AFP 9780800637446.

Handbell

♫ Garee, Betty. "A Mighty Fortress Is Our God." 4-5 oct, L4+. ALF 23163.

♫ Stephenson, Valerie. "The Glory of These Forty Days." 2-3 oct, L4+. LOR 20/1127L.

♫ Tucker, Benjamin. "I Want Jesus to Walk with Me." 2-3 oct, L2. ALF 44243.

Tuesday, March 7

Perpetua and Felicity and companions, martyrs at Carthage, died 202

In the year 202 the emperor Septimius Severus forbade conversions to Christianity. Perpetua, a noblewoman, Felicity, a slave, and other companions were all catechumens at Carthage in North Africa. They were imprisoned and sentenced to death. Perpetua's father, who was not a Christian, visited her in prison and begged her to lay aside her Christian convictions in order to spare her life and spare the family from scorn. Perpetua responded and told her father, "We know that we are not placed in our own power but in that of God."

Friday, March 10

Harriet Tubman, died 1913; Sojourner Truth, died 1883; renewers of society

Harriet Tubman was born into slavery in Maryland and remained a slave until about age thirty when, fearing she would be sold and moved farther south, she escaped with the help of the Underground Railroad. After that, she helped about three hundred others to escape until slavery was abolished. After the Civil War, her home in Auburn, New York, became a center for women's rights and served the aged and poor.

Sojourner Truth, too, was born a slave, in New York state. Her birth name was Isabella. After slavery was abolished in New York in 1827, she was freed and, while working as a housekeeper, became deeply involved in Christianity. A number of years later, she discerned a call to become a preacher. Taking the name Sojourner Truth, she set out on an evangelistic journey, where people found her testimony to be deeply moving. In later life, she also became a popular speaker against slavery and for women's rights.

⊕ = global song   ♫ = relates to hymn of the day
☼ = praise song   P = available in Prelude Music Planner
120

March 12, 2017
Second Sunday in Lent

During Lent we journey with all those around the world who will be baptized at the Easter Vigil. In today's gospel Jesus tells Nicodemus that he must be born of water and Spirit. At the font we are given a new birth as daughters and sons of God. As God made a covenant with Abraham, in baptism God promises to raise us up with Christ to new life. From worship we are sent forth to proclaim God's love for all the world.

Prayer of the Day

O God, our leader and guide, in the waters of baptism you bring us to new birth to live as your children. Strengthen our faith in your promises, that by your Spirit we may lift up your life to all the world through your Son, Jesus Christ, our Savior and Lord, who lives and reigns with you and the Holy Spirit, one God, now and forever.

Gospel Acclamation

The Son of Man must be ˈ lifted up,* that whoever believes in him may have e- ˈ ternal life. (John 3:14-15)

Readings and Psalm

Genesis 12:1-4a

God's call of Abram and Sarai has a clear purpose—that through them all the families of the earth would gain a blessing. As they set out on their journey they are accompanied by promises of land, nation, and a great reputation.

Psalm 121

I lift up my eyes to the hills; my help comes from the LORD. (Ps. 121:1, 2)

Romans 4:1-5, 13-17

In the person and example of Abraham we discover that a right relationship with God does not involve earning a reward from God but entails trusting God's promises. Abraham is the forebear and model for both Jews and Gentiles, because we too trust that ours is a God who gives life to the dead.

John 3:1-17

A curious Pharisee visits Jesus by night to learn from the teacher his friends reject. Jesus speaks to him about life in the Spirit and the kingdom of God.

Preface   Lent

Color   Purple

Prayers of Intercession

The prayers are prepared locally for each occasion. The following examples may be adapted or used as appropriate.

Lifting our voices and turning toward God, let us pray for the church, the earth, and all who are in need.
A brief silence.

God of Abraham and Sarah, God of all earth's families, bless your church to be a blessing and bestow your grace to a hurting world. Hear us, O God.
Your mercy is great.

O God, you love the entire cosmos. Help us to love all of the creatures and life within it. Hear us, O God.
Your mercy is great.

O God, our help is in you. Keep the nations, their governments, and their people from all evil (*especially*). Hear us, O God.
Your mercy is great.

O God, your promises ease our pain and sorrow. Grant comfort, healing, and joy to all who are in need. (*We pray especially for . . .*) Hear us, O God.
Your mercy is great.

O God, lead this assembly in its Lenten journey toward faith, works of love, and prayer. Let those gathered here be fed and nourished by your word. Hear us, O God.
Your mercy is great.

Here other intercessions may be offered.

O God, we give thanks for the faithful departed who have joined your saints in light (*especially the bishop Gregory the Great*). Let their lives be guides to our own. Hear us, O God.
Your mercy is great.

Into your hands, merciful God, we commend all for whom we pray, trusting in your steadfast love; through Christ our Lord.
Amen.

Images in the Readings

John's language of "being born again" suggests the image of the **mother**. Historically, the church described itself as this mother and the font as the womb from which birth in God arises. Recently, God has also been described as the mother who births a new creation. But birth is not easy, and Lent allows us forty days to reenvision that birth.

Abram's immigration to the land of promise offers the image of the **journey**. Lent provides forty days for the annual journey back to the mystery of the resurrection and the new life to which we are called.

Paul's language of justification assumes that God is a **judge** who requires of us a life of righteousness. That justification comes via faith does not eliminate the necessity for such a radical reorientation of the self before God. It is instructive to hold the image of judge next to that of the mother: each image nuances the other.

Ideas for the Day

- Often the focus of John 3:16 seems to be on the words "everyone who believes ... may have." What if the focus was placed on the first part of the verse: "For God so loved the world that he gave"? God's love gives. Think of the beautiful list that sentence could produce. Inspire people to imagine all that God's love has already given them. How does that love inspire them to give to others?
- Nicodemus comes under the cover of darkness to visit Jesus. In the northern hemisphere, Lent begins in the darkness of winter, but each day closer to Easter means a few more minutes of daylight. Could Lent be seen as a season during which our eyes are gradually opened until at last we behold the full, glorious light of the resurrection? Much the same could be said of the journey of our lives. Through interactions with parents, siblings, family, friends, Jesus, and the church, we discover the joys and sorrows of being human. As we move through our lives, we grow in faith and love, discovering each day the gift of living in the presence of Jesus.
- If John 3:16 is the gospel in miniature, could John 3:17 be Lutheran theology in miniature?
- God commands Abram, "Go from your country," and Abram goes (Gen. 12:1). "Go in peace. Serve the Lord." This is the command the assembly hears as worship ends. The gift of faith has never been a gift for the sake of the one who receives it. Faith sends people out. Faith leads to serving, to generosity, and more. You might say worship is an event that has no ending, for even as the people of God leave the gathering place, they worship with their lives every moment of every day.

Connections with the Liturgy

In the rite called Welcome to Baptism, we pray that the catechumen, whether an infant or an adult, be brought "in peace and joy to fullness of life in Christ" through the waters of baptism. In baptism we are, like Abram and Nicodemus, called to the fullness of new life.

Let the Children Come

The curious opposites continue this Sunday! In today's gospel, John invites us to hold them tightly together for a brand-new thing: being born of water and Spirit brings new life. The baptismal imagery in all the Lenten texts draws us to the font. Gather the children with you during the thanksgiving for baptism and let them carry the bowl as the pastor sprinkles the assembly. Let them grow unbelievable earthly things in pots of soil near the font. How is the movement from death to new life continuing for children in your liturgy? As they leave the liturgy?

Assembly Song
Gathering

Lift high the cross ELW 660, LBW 377
All who believe and are baptized ELW 442, LBW 194
We are baptized in Christ Jesus ELW 451, WOV 698

Psalmody and Acclamations

Cotter, Jeanne. "Our Help Is from the Lord" from PCY, vol. 3.
O'Brien, Frances Patrick. "Our Help Is from the Lord." SAB, cant, assembly, kybd, opt gtr, fl, vc. GIA G-5449.
Roberts, Leon C. "My Help Shall Come from the Lord (Psalm 121)." TFF 16.
P (GA) Organ, Anne Krentz. "Return to the Lord" with proper verse for Lent 2. MSB1 S419.

Hymn of the Day

God loved the world ELW 323 *ROCKINGHAM OLD* LBW 292 *DIE HELLE SONN LEUCHT*
Waterlife ELW 457, W&P 145 *SPIRIT LIFE*
O living Breath of God/*Soplo de Dios viviente* ELW 407, LLC 368 *VÅRVINDAR FRISKA*

Offering

For by grace you have been saved ELW 598, W&P 38
Tree of Life and awesome mystery ELW 334, sts. 1, 2, 3, Lent 2

Communion

My faith looks up to thee ELW 759, LBW 479
Mothering God, you gave me birth ELW 735, WOV 769
Loving Spirit ELW 397, WOV 683

Sending

Eternal Lord of love, behold your church ELW 321
Lord, thee I love with all my heart ELW 750, LBW 325

Additional Assembly Songs

For God so loved the world ASG 10, LS 45
Kyrie eleison SP 21
I shall not be moved TFF 147

⊕ Guarani, traditional. "Oré poriajú verekó/Lord, Have Mercy" from *Agape: Songs of Hope and Reconciliation*. U, gtr. Lutheran World Federation. AFP. Out of print. Available on Amazon.com.

⊕ Lee, Song. "To the Hills I Lift My Eyes" from *Glory to God*. U. WJK 0664238971.

☼ Consiglio, Cyprian. "I Will Lift Up My Eyes" from *Spirit and Song*, vol. 1. OCP.

☼ Fox, Kipp. "Redemption" from CCLI.

☼ Mooring, Leeland. "Be Lifted High" from CCLI.

☼ Scott, Kathryn. "Hungry" from CCLI.

☼ Story, Laura. "You Gave Your Life" from CCLI.

☼ Zschesch, Darlene. "All Things Are Possible" from CCLI.

Music for the Day
Choral

Busarow, Donald. "God So Loved the World." SATB, org. GIA G-7509.

P Davis, Taylor. "Hope of the World." SAB, pno. AFP 9781451401004.

P Goss, John. "God So Loved the World" from *Augsburg Motet Book*. SATB, opt kybd. AFP 9781451423709.

P ♫ Helgen, John. "O Living Breath of God." SAB, pno. AFP 9780800621506.

Children's Choir

Edwards, Rusty. "For God So Loved the World" from *LifeSongs*. U, kybd. AFP 9780806642703.

P Horman, John. "God So Loved the World." U/2 pt, pno, opt fl or vln. CG CGA447.

Kemp, Helen. "A Mountain Psalm, A Meditation on Psalm 121." 2 pt, pno, opt assembly. CG CGA1061.

Keyboard / Instrumental

Alain, Jehan (1911–1940). "Choral Dorien" from *Augsburg Organ Library: Lent*. Org. AFP 9780800658977.

♫ Bender, Jan. "God Loved the World" (Die helle Sonn leucht) from *The Master Organ Works of Jan Bender, vol. 1: Chorale Preludes for Organ or Piano*. Org or pno. CPH 97-7098.

P ♫ Diemer, Emma Lou. "O Living Breath of God" (Vårvindar friska) from *Glory, Laud, and Honor: Organ Settings*. Org. AFP 9781451494068.

P ♫ Uehlein, Christopher. "God Loved the World" (Rockingham Old) from *A Blue Cloud Abbey Organ Book for Lent*. Org. AFP 9781451401134.

Handbell

♫ Glasgow, Michael J. "Contemplation on the Cross." 3-6 oct hb, opt 3-6 oct hc, L4-. LOR 20/1700L.

P Moats, William. "In the Shadow of the Cross." 3-5 oct hb, opt 3 or 5 oct hc, L2+. CG CGB821.

P Moklebust, Cathy. "I Will Lift Mine Eyes unto the Hills (Psalm 121)." 3-5 oct hb, L2, CG CGB529. Opt full score (org), CG CGB528.

Sunday, March 12
Gregory the Great, Bishop of Rome, died 604

Gregory was born into a politically influential family. At one time he held political office and at another time he lived as a monk, all before he was elected to the papacy. Gregory's work was extensive. He influenced public worship through the establishment of a lectionary and prayers to correlate with the readings. He established a school to train church musicians. Gregorian chant is named in his honor. He wrote a treatise underscoring what is required of a pastor serving a congregation. He sent missionaries to preach to the Anglo-Saxons who had invaded England. And at one time he organized distribution of grain during a shortage of food in Rome.

Friday, March 17
Patrick, bishop, missionary to Ireland, died 461

At sixteen, Patrick was kidnapped by Irish pirates and sold into slavery in Ireland. He himself admitted that up to this point he cared little for God. He escaped after six years, returned to his family in southwest Britain, and began to prepare for ordained ministry. He later returned to Ireland, this time to serve as a bishop and missionary. He made his base in the north of Ireland and from there made many missionary journeys, with much success. In his autobiography he denounced the slave trade, perhaps from his own experience as a slave. Patrick's famous baptismal hymn to the Trinity, "I Bind unto Myself Today" (ELW 450), can be used as a meditation on Lent's call to return to our baptism.

⊕ = global song   ♫ = relates to hymn of the day
☼ = praise song   P = available in Prelude Music Planner

March 19, 2017
Third Sunday in Lent

In today's gospel the Samaritan woman asks Jesus for water, an image of our thirst for God. Jesus offers living water, a sign of God's grace flowing from the waters of baptism. The early church used this gospel and those of the next two Sundays to deepen baptismal reflection during the final days of preparation before baptism at Easter. As we journey to the resurrection feast, Christ comes among us in word, bath, and meal—offering us the life-giving water of God's mercy and forgiveness.

Prayer of the Day

Merciful God, the fountain of living water, you quench our thirst and wash away our sin. Give us this water always. Bring us to drink from the well that flows with the beauty of your truth through Jesus Christ, our Savior and Lord, who lives and reigns with you and the Holy Spirit, one God, now and forever.

Gospel Acclamation

Lord, you are truly the Savior of the world;* give me this living water that I may never thirst again. (John 4:42, 15)

Readings and Psalm

Exodus 17:1-7

Because the thirsty Israelites quarreled with Moses and put the Lord to the test, Moses cried out in desperation to the Lord. The Lord commanded Moses to strike the rock to provide water for the people. The doubt-filled question—"Is the Lord among us or not?"—received a very positive answer.

Psalm 95

Let us shout for joy to the rock of our salvation. (Ps. 95:1)

Romans 5:1-11

Though we often hear that God helps those who help themselves, here Paul tells us that through Jesus' death God helps utterly helpless sinners. Since we who had been enemies are reconciled to God in the cross, we now live in hope for our final salvation.

John 4:5-42

Jesus defies convention to engage a Samaritan woman in conversation. Her testimony, in turn, leads many others to faith.

Preface   Lent

Color   Purple

Prayers of Intercession

The prayers are prepared locally for each occasion. The following examples may be adapted or used as appropriate.

Lifting our voices and turning toward God, let us pray for the church, the earth, and all who are in need.

A brief silence.

O God, let your church on earth, justified and reconciled through Jesus Christ, be bold in its proclamation of the gospel. Hear us, O God.

Your mercy is great.

In your hands are the depths of the earth and the sea which you made. Make us faithful inhabitants of this earth, caring for the waterways and their creatures. (*Local water sources may be named.*) Hear us, O God.

Your mercy is great.

Lead the nations of the world away from the wilderness of sin and evil, and toward the light of love and peace. Hear us, O God.

Your mercy is great.

To those who are thirsty for love, for justice, for peace, for belonging, give the water of life. For those who are suffering or in pain, bring healing balm and peace. (*We pray especially for . . .*) Hear us, O God.

Your mercy is great.

Lead this congregation in service to others. Embolden the faithful here with your promise and your presence. Hear us, O God.

Your mercy is great.

Here other intercessions may be offered.

We give thanks for the witness and testimony of the saints who have gone before us into eternal life (*especially Joseph, guardian of Jesus*). Let us boast in the hope they have shared, a hope that does not disappoint us. Hear us, O God.

Your mercy is great.

Into your hands, merciful God, we commend all for whom we pray, trusting in your steadfast love; through Christ our Lord. **Amen.**

Images in the Readings

The primary image for this Sunday is **water**. That life as we know it on earth requires water is perhaps the reason that water figures in countless stories in all cultures, stories of rivers and seas, wells and rain. The Bible is overflowing with water stories, some of which we will hear at the Easter Vigil. In our time, daily showers, public fountains, swimming pools, and water parks provide society with the refreshment of water. Yet we are told that the next world wars will be over water, and current Christian ecologists urge care for the waters of the earth. In medieval Christian art, a picture of Moses striking the rock so that water could flow was set next to a depiction of Christ on the cross being pierced with the sword, as the water of life flowed from his side.

Another image for the day is the **rock**. In the Psalms, God is called "Rock" twenty-two times. That water can flow from rock provides us with a double image for God.

Ideas for the Day

- Put today's gospel in conversation with our current ecological state. Consider the droughts and the wildfires that have adversely affected life in the western United States. Consider the stagnant water that is pooled in communities devastated by hurricanes and floods. Now consider what it means that Jesus has and is living water. Consider the fact that March 22, Wednesday of this week, is World Water Day. This year's theme is "Wastewater." Check out www.unwater.org to get the facts on the worldwide water crisis. Consider using this Sunday to take a special offering for a water project that will provide fresh, living water to those who thirst. ELCA World Hunger's Walk for Water page (elca.org/walk4water) also provides lots of great ideas.
- "Come and see" is a popular Johannine phrase used to call people to discipleship. It was the invitation Jesus used to call the first disciples. Then Philip used this invitation to draw Nathanael into a life of discipleship. And now this outsider woman is inviting other Samaritan outsiders to "come and see!" (John 4:29). It's worth noticing what the named disciples are doing in this text and what the unnamed woman is doing. One is evangelizing while others are looking for food. Who's the disciple worth emulating here?
- For a poetic take on the story of the woman at the well, read the poem "Aquavit" by Michael Coffey, posted on his blog: www.ocotillopub.org/2014/03/aquavit.html.
- Consider the setting: a well. A well in those days was the equivalent of today's Match.com. Many great biblical couples met by way of a well: Rebekah and Isaac, Rachel and Jacob, and Zipporah and Moses. It was the place people went to find a mate. What if you saw your baptismal font as the well: the place Christ comes to meet his mate, the church? Play with your space this week. If possible, situate your font in a central place or preach from beside the font. This is the well. We are the woman. Christ comes here to meet us.

Connections with the Liturgy

In *Evangelical Lutheran Worship* Thanksgiving at the Font V (p. 71) are the words, "Praise to you for your saving waters.... The Israelites ... drink from your gushing rock ... and the Samaritan woman will never be thirsty again." When using this thanksgiving, names of specific local waters—rivers, lakes, the sea—can be inserted into the second paragraph: "Glory to you for oceans and lakes, for rivers and streams, for..."

Let the Children Come

If you were to ask the children of your congregation, "Where have you seen living water?" what would they say? Granted, it is a few metaphorical leaps to get to baptism and the life-giving presence of God at work in our lives. But how does the imagery in your worship space convey living water? Is the font off to the side, the small bowl empty most weeks, or does it have a central focus in the space? Is it always full of clean, maybe even moving water? Can children see the water and touch it if they choose to?

Assembly Song
Gathering

O Jesus, joy of loving hearts ELW 658, LBW 356
Guide me ever, great Redeemer ELW 618, LBW 343
Jesus, keep me near the cross ELW 335, TFF 73

Psalmody and Acclamations

"Listen! Listen! Open Your Hearts!" *Psallite* A-36. Cant or SATB, assembly, kybd.
Gelineau, Joseph. "Psalm 95" from ACYG.
Houge, Ben. "Oh, Come, Let Us Sing." W&P 107.
P (GA) Organ, Anne Krentz. "Return to the Lord" with proper verse for Lent 3. MSB1 S419.

Hymn of the Day

As the deer runs to the river ELW 331 *JULION*
I heard the voice of Jesus say ELW 332, LBW 497 *THIRD MODE MELODY* ELW 611 *KINGSFOLD*
O blessed spring ELW 447, WOV 695 *BERGLUND*

Offering

Tree of Life and awesome mystery ELW 334, sts. 1, 2, 3, Lent 3
For all the faithful women ELW 419, sts. 1, 8, last; TFF 219, sts. 1, 11, 4

Communion

Rock of Ages, cleft for me ELW 623, LBW 327
Come to me, all pilgrims thirsty ELW 777
As the sun with longer journey ELW 329, WOV 655

Sending

Glorious things of you are spoken ELW 647, LBW 358
Come, thou Fount of every blessing ELW 807, LBW 499

Additional Assembly Songs

My soul thirst for God SP 28

Aquí del pan partido tomaré LLC 384

Surely it is God who saves me WOV 635

⊕ Lim, Swee Hong. "Kyrie." ELW 158.

⊕ Loh, I-to. "Lord, Have Mercy/*Ch'iu chu Lienmin Women*" from *Sent by the Lord: Songs of the World Church*, vol. 2. U. GIA G-3740.

☼ Baloche, Paul/Lincoln Brewster/Jason Ingram. "Shout for Joy" from CCLI.

☼ Brown, Brenton/Glenn Roberts. "All Who Are Thirsty" from CCLI.

☼ Hall, Mark/Matthew West. "The Well" from CCLI.

☼ Harris, Lauren/Chris Lawson Jones/Nick Herbert. "Come to the Waters" from CCLI.

☼ Ortega, Fernando. "Give Me Jesus" from CCLI.

☼ Stanfill, Kristian/Brett Younker. "Come to the Water" from CCLI.

Music for the Day
Choral

P♫ Cherwien, David. "O Blessed Spring." SATB or 2 pt, assembly, org, opt C inst. AFP 9781451420753.

P Childs, David N. "As the Hart Longs for the Water Brooks." SATB, pno. AFP 9781451401035.

P Goudimel, Claude. "As the Deer for Water Yearning" from *Chantry Choirbook*. SATB. AFP 9780800657772.

P Highben, Zebulon M. "Come to Me, All Pilgrims Thirsty." SATB, assembly, org, C inst. AFP 9780800621414.

Children's Choir

P Crunk, Kris/Cox, Randy. "Dance on the Water." U, pno. CG CGA1328.

Kerrick, Mary Ellen. "It Is Good to Sing Praise (Es gozoso alabar)." 2 pt, kybd. CG CGA829.

Lindh, Jody W. "Come, Let Us Sing." U, kybd. CG CGA 478.

Keyboard / Instrumental

Alain, Jehan. "Choral Phrygien." Org. Various editions.

♫ Cherwien, David. "O Blessed Spring" (Berglund) from *Rejoice in God's Saints: Organ Improvisations*. Org. AFP 9780800655362.

P♫ Howarth, Mary. "I Heard the Voice of Jesus Say" (Kingsfold) from *Glorify! Hymn Settings for Piano*. Pno. AFP 9781451424218.

P♫ Wahl, Carol. "As the Deer Runs to the River" (Julion) from *Cry of the Dove: Piano Settings*. Pno. AFP 9781451479614.

Handbell

P Bettcher, Peggy. "How He Loves" from *Easy to Ring Praise & Worship VII*. 2-3 oct, L2, HOP 2687. 3-5 oct, L2, HOP 2670.

P McKlveen, Paul. "Take My Life and Let It Be." 3-5 oct hb, opt 3 oct hc, L3. CG CGB539.

♫ Wagner, H. Dean. "Fantasy on 'Kingsfold.'" 3-6 oct hb, opt 3 oct hc, L2+, HOP 2134. Opt orch (fl, ob, hrn, tpt, perc, hp, str, synth str), HOP 2134O.

Monday, March 20
Joseph, Guardian of Jesus (transferred)

The gospels are silent about much of Joseph's life. We know that he was a carpenter or builder by trade. The Gospel of Luke shows him acting in accordance with both civil and religious law by returning to Bethlehem for the census and by presenting the child Jesus in the temple on the fortieth day after his birth. The Gospel of Matthew tells of Joseph's trust in God, who led him through visionary dreams. Because Joseph is not mentioned after the story of a young Jesus teaching in the temple, it is assumed that he died before Jesus reached adulthood.

Tuesday, March 21
Thomas Cranmer, Bishop of Canterbury, martyr, died 1556

Cranmer was serving as bishop of Taunton in England when he was chosen by King Henry VIII to become archbishop of Canterbury, largely because Cranmer would agree to the king's divorce from Catherine of Aragon. Cranmer's lasting achievement is contributing to and overseeing the creation of the Book of Common Prayer, which in revised form remains the worship book of the Anglican Communion. He was burned at the stake under Queen Mary for his support of the Protestant Reformation.

Wednesday, March 22
Jonathan Edwards, teacher, missionary to American Indians, died 1758

Edwards was a minister in Connecticut and described as the greatest of the New England Puritan preachers. One of Edwards's most notable sermons found its way into contemporary anthologies of literature. In this sermon, "Sinners in the Hands of an Angry God," he spoke at length about hell. However, throughout the rest of his works and his preaching he had more to say about God's love than God's wrath. His personal experience of conversion came when he felt overwhelmed with

⊕ = global song   ♫ = relates to hymn of the day
☼ = praise song   P = available in Prelude Music Planner

a sense of God's majesty and grandeur, rather than a fear of hell. Edwards served a Puritan congregation, where he believed that only those who had been fully converted ought to receive communion; his congregation thought otherwise. Edwards left that congregation and carried out mission work among the Housatonic Indians of Massachusetts. He became president of the College of New Jersey, later to be known as Princeton University.

Friday, March 24

Oscar Arnulfo Romero, Bishop of El Salvador, martyr, died 1980

Romero is remembered for his advocacy on behalf of the poor in El Salvador, though it was not a characteristic of his early priesthood. After being appointed as archbishop of San Salvador, he preached against the political repression in his country. He and other priests and church workers were considered traitors for their bold stand for justice, especially defending the rights of the poor. After several years of threats to his life, Romero was assassinated while presiding at the eucharist. During the 1980s thousands died in El Salvador during political unrest.

Saturday, March 25

Annunciation of Our Lord

Nine months before Christmas the church celebrates the annunciation. In Luke the angel Gabriel announces to Mary that she will give birth to the Son of God, and she responds, "Here am I, the servant of the Lord." Ancient scholars believed that March 25 was also the day on which creation began and was the date of Jesus' death on the cross. Thus, from the sixth to eighth centuries, March 25 was observed as New Year's Day in much of Christian Europe.

March 26, 2017
Fourth Sunday in Lent

Baptism is sometimes called enlightenment. The gospel for this Sunday is the story of the man born blind healed by Christ. I was blind, but now I see, declares the man. In baptism God opens our eyes to see the truth of who we are: God's beloved sons and daughters. As David was anointed king of Israel, in baptism God anoints our head with oil, and calls us to bear witness to the light of Christ in our daily lives.

Prayer of the Day

Bend your ear to our prayers, Lord Christ, and come among us. By your gracious life and death for us, bring light into the darkness of our hearts, and anoint us with your Spirit, for you live and reign with the Father and the Holy Spirit, one God, now and forever.

Gospel Acclamation

Jesus says, I am the light of the world;* whoever follows me will have the light of life. (John 8:12)

Readings and Psalm

1 Samuel 16:1-13

Samuel anointed David even though he was the eighth-oldest son of Jesse and did not match his brothers in height or other physical characteristics. With the anointing came endowment with the Spirit of the Lord, designating David as the Lord's chosen successor to Saul.

Psalm 23

You anoint my head with oil. (Ps. 23:5)

Ephesians 5:8-14

Because we now live in the divine light that is Jesus Christ, we conduct our lives in ways that reflect the light of Christ, so that our activity is truly pleasing to God.

John 9:1-41

Jesus heals a man born blind, provoking a hostile reaction that he regards as spiritual blindness to the things of God.

Preface   Lent

Color   Purple

Prayers of Intercession

The prayers are prepared locally for each occasion. The following examples may be adapted or used as appropriate.
Lifting our voices and turning toward God, let us pray for the church, the earth, and all who are in need.
A brief silence.

God of the ages, as your church prepares your table for all to celebrate in one holy meal, restore the unity of those who gather in your name. Hear us, O God.
Your mercy is great.

You shed light on your creation. Let the changing of the seasons bring forth growth and new life from what was dormant and fallow. Hear us, O God.
Your mercy is great.

Shine your light on the people of every nation. Reveal your reconciling love in places where fear and conflict thrive (*especially*). Hear us, O God.
Your mercy is great.

God of wholeness, bring clarity to those in confusing times, bring healing to those in painful times, bring peace to those in trying times. (*We pray especially for . . .*) Hear us, O God.
Your mercy is great.

Restore, renew, and enliven the ministry and work of this congregation. Help us to see your purpose clearly. Hear us, O God.
Your mercy is great.

Here other intercessions may be offered.

We remember and give thanks for those who have joined you in eternal light. Let their lives of faith shine in our hearts and guide our paths. Hear us, O God.
Your mercy is great.

Into your hands, merciful God, we commend all for whom we pray, trusting in your steadfast love; through Christ our Lord.
Amen.

Images in the Readings

The primary image for the day is **light**. According to Genesis 1, light is the first creation of God. In John, Christ not only brings light: he is the very light of God. And so the synoptics describe the crucifixion as effecting an eclipse, and when Judas leaves the company for the betrayal, the author of John writes, "And it was night." The Ephesians reading emphasizes that the light that is Christ is now the light within each believer.

Another image for the day is the **anointing**. In ancient times, and still today in the British monarchy, consecrated oil is poured on the head of the one chosen to lead. In some Christian churches, an anointing is a necessary part of the baptismal ritual. What was dry and brittle is now limber with life.

David was a **shepherd**. According to Israelite memory, the people were nomadic herders before becoming urban dwellers. So David embodies the good old tradition, a more innocent time. Other ancient Near Eastern cultures also used the metaphor of the shepherd to describe their king. The sheep are the source of the people's life, and the shepherd ensures that livelihood.

Ideas for the Day

- On Ash Wednesday we put dust on one another's foreheads and say, "Remember that you are dust, and to dust you shall return." Today Jesus makes something new using dust and spit. Dust hearkens back to the creation story when God first breathed life into the dust, creating Adam. In the life of the man born blind, God is continuing the work of creation. Dust seems to be God's medium of choice. Use an Internet search to find the song "Beautiful Things" by Gungor (*Beautiful Things*, Brash Music, 2010). This refrain could easily have come from the mouth of the man born blind.
- The reading from 1 Samuel speaks of anointing with oil. Anointing is a sign of being chosen by God. Consider the places where the church carries its horn of oil. Who do we anoint but the newly baptized, those in need of healing, and the dying? God seems to choose those who are most broken, vulnerable, and dead.
- Whereas last week it made sense to move your font to the center of the worship space, just as the well was at the center of town for the Samaritans, this week, if possible, consider moving your font to the door of the worship space. The pool of water at Siloam is a sending pool. It was the launchpad into a new life for the man born blind. How can you create a space that conveys the sending nature of the baptismal pool?
- Notice that John doesn't call him the "blind man" but rather "the man born blind." John identifies him by his humanity before his blindness. Everyone is concerned with who sinned, but Jesus is concerned with the way God's glory will be revealed through this man. One place in today's world where people with disabilities receive this same dignity and are met with this same expectation (that in them, God's glory will be revealed) is in the L'Arche community. Read their stories at www.larcheusa.org.

Connections with the Liturgy

Here are a few of the many connections between today's readings and worship throughout the year. (1) In the baptismal liturgy, the candidate is infused with the Spirit of God, as was David; the candidate may be anointed with oil and so "sealed by the Holy Spirit"; and a lighted candle is presented as a symbol of the light who is Christ now enlightening the newly baptized. (2) In more churches now, the candidate is fully immersed in a pool. (3) At the Easter Vigil, we gather around the candle, which symbolizes the risen Christ who is dispelling the darkness of our hearts and minds. This risen Christ "faithfully sheds light on all the human race." (4) For the blessing at the conclusion of the Sunday service, Luther preferred the Aaronic blessing. In the phrase "The Lord's face shine on you with grace and mercy," we hear again the call in Ephesians to rise into Christ's shining light. (5) And in evening prayer, the assembly gathers around a candle to praise Jesus Christ as the light of the world. It is as if each evening we are the man born blind, acknowledging Christ as the light of our life.

Let the Children Come

Today Jesus makes a miracle out of the most ordinary things: dirt and spit and sending the man off to wash in the pool. Isn't Jesus always doing something like this and we just skim right past the humor? Children will want to stop and linger, and now is a great time to point out all the ways Jesus makes ordinary things holy. Ordinary water becomes the life-giving water of baptism. Ordinary bread and wine become a feast for the whole world. We people, made of ash and flesh, become Christ's body. Death to new life, indeed.

Assembly Song
Gathering

God, whose almighty word ELW 673, LBW 400
Dearest Jesus, at your word ELW 520, LBW 248
Christ, the life of all the living ELW 339, LBW 97

Psalmody and Acclamations

Bruxvoort Colligan, Richard. "My Love Is My Shepherd (Psalm 23)" from *Sharing the Road*. AFP 9780800678630.
Cherwien, David. "Psalm 23: The Lord Is My Shepherd." U, assembly, org. MSM 80-840.
Farlee, Robert Buckley. "Psalm 23," Refrain 3, from PSCY.
P (GA) Organ, Anne Krentz. "Return to the Lord" with proper verse for Lent 4. MSB1 S419.

Hymn of the Day

Amazing grace, how sweet the sound ELW 779, LBW 448
NEW BRITAIN
Lead me, guide me ELW 768, TFF 70 *LEAD ME, GUIDE ME*
You, dear Lord ELW 702, LLC 429 *TÙ SEÑOR*

Offering

Tree of Life and awesome mystery ELW 334, sts. 1, 2, 3, Lent 4
I want to walk as a child of the light ELW 815, WOV 649

Communion

I heard the voice of Jesus say ELW 332, ELW 611, LBW 497
Drawn to the Light ELW 593
You Are Mine ELW 581, W&P 158

P = available in Prelude Music Planner

Sending

What God ordains is good indeed   ELW 776, LBW 446
Awake, O sleeper, rise from death   ELW 452, WOV 745

Additional Assembly Songs

My good shepherd is the Lord   ASG 23
Open our eyes, Lord   W&P 113, TFF 98
Your hand, O Lord, in days of old   LBW 431

⊕ Brazilian, traditional. "Ouve, Senhor, eu estour clamando/Hear Me, O Lord" from *Agape: Songs of Hope and Reconciliation*. U, gtr. Lutheran World Federation. Out of print. Available on Amazon.com.

⊕ Watts, Trisha. "I Will Live for You Alone" from *Agape: Songs of Hope and Reconciliation*. U, gtr. Lutheran World Federation. Out of print. Available on Amazon.com.

☼ Eichelberger, Brian/Zach Bolen. "Made Alive" from CCLI.

☼ Fox, Kipp. "Let There Be Light" from CCLI.

☼ Jobe, Kari/Ed Cash/Mia Fieldes. "Joyfully" from CCLI.

☼ Leonard, David/Leslie Jordan/Don Chaffer. "Wake Up" from CCLI.

☼ Martin, Joseph/Robert Sterling. "Shepherd of the Stars" from CCLI.

☼ Williams, Hank, Sr. "I Saw the Light" from CCLI.

Music for the Day
Choral

P ♫ Bertalot, John. "Amazing Grace." SATB, org. AFP 9780800649142.

P ♫ Bertalot, John. "Amazing Grace" from *The Augsburg Choirbook*. SATB, org. AFP 9780800656782.

Carter, John. "Amazing Grace." SAB, pno. AFP 9780800621377.

Pote, Allen. "The Lord Is My Shepherd." SATB or 3 pt mxd, pno. CG CGA551.

Scott, K. Lee. "Open My Eyes." SATB, org. CPH 982904.

Children's Choir

P Comer, Marilyn. "Psalm 23" from *ChildrenSing Psalms*. U, kybd. AFP 9780800663872.

♫ Eithun, Sandra. "Amazing Grace." U, pno. CG CGA1269.

P Page, Anna Laura. "Little Lamb, the Shepherd Loves You." U, pno, opt fl. CG CGA1110.

Keyboard / Instrumental

P ♫ Dahl, David P. "Amazing Grace, How Sweet the Sound" (New Britain) from *An American Suite for Organ*. Org. AFP 9781451401110.

P Evanovich, Joshua. "Be Thou My Vision" (Slane) from *String Reflections for Solo Violin and Piano*. Vln, pno. HOP 8578.

♫ Hassell, Michael. "Amazing Grace, How Sweet the Sound" (New Britain) from *Traveling Tunes: Hymn Arrangements for Solo Instrument and Piano*. Inst, pno. AFP 9780800656195.

P Wahl, Carol. "You Are Mine" (You Are Mine) from *Cry of the Dove: Piano Settings*. Pno. AFP 9781451479614.

Handbell

Ingram, Bill. "Guide Me, O Thou Great Jehovah." 3-5 oct hb, L3; kybd or 2-3 oct hb, L2. Ring Out! Press RO3285.

Lamb, Linda. "Open the Eyes of My Heart." 3-5 oct hb, opt 3 oct hc, L3. LOR 20/1751L.

P ♫ Waldrop, Tammy. "Amazing Grace" from *Spring Ring!* 2-3 oct, L2-, CG CGB829. 3-5 oct, L2-, CG CGB830.

Wednesday, March 29
Hans Nielsen Hauge, renewer of the church, died 1824

Hans Nielsen Hauge was a layperson who began preaching about "the living faith" in Norway and Denmark after a mystical experience that he believed called him to share the assurance of salvation with others. At the time, itinerant preaching and religious gatherings held without the supervision of a pastor were illegal, and Hauge was arrested several times. He also faced great personal suffering: his first wife died, and three of his four children died in infancy.

Friday, March 31
John Donne, poet, died 1631

This priest of the Church of England is commemorated for his poetry and spiritual writing. Most of his poetry was written before his ordination and is sacred and secular, intellectual and sensuous. He saw in his wife, Anne, glimpses of the glory of God and a human revelation of divine love. In 1615 he was ordained and seven years later he was named dean of St. Paul's Cathedral in London. By that time his reputation as a preacher was firmly in place. In his poem "Good Friday, 1613. Riding westward," he speaks of Jesus' death on the cross: "Who sees God's face, that is self life, must die; What a death were it then to see God die?"

⊕ = global song   ♫ = relates to hymn of the day
☼ = praise song   P = available in Prelude Music Planner

April 2, 2017
Fifth Sunday in Lent

In today's gospel Jesus reveals his power over death by raising Lazarus from the dead. The prophet Ezekiel prophesies God breathing new life into dry bones. To those in exile or living in the shadows of death, these stories proclaim God's promise of resurrection. In baptism we die with Christ that we might also be raised with him to new life. At the Easter Vigil we will welcome new sisters and brothers at the baptismal font, as we renew our baptismal promises.

Prayer of the Day

Almighty God, your Son came into the world to free us all from sin and death. Breathe upon us the power of your Spirit, that we may be raised to new life in Christ and serve you in righteousness all our days, through Jesus Christ, our Savior and Lord, who lives and reigns with you and the Holy Spirit, one God, now and forever.

Gospel Acclamation

I am the resurrection ' and the life;* whoever believes in me will ' never die. (John 11:25, 26)

Readings and Psalm

Ezekiel 37:1-14

Ezekiel's vision of the valley of dry bones is a promise that Israel as a nation, though dead in exile, will live again in their land through God's life-giving spirit. Three times Israel is assured that through this vision they will know that "I am the Lord."

Psalm 130

I wait for you, O LORD; in your word is my hope. (Ps. 130:5)

Romans 8:6-11

For Paul, Christian spirituality entails living in the reality of the Holy Spirit. The driving force behind our actions and values is not our sinful desire for self-satisfaction but the very Spirit by which God raised Jesus from the dead and will also raise us from the dead.

John 11:1-45

Jesus is moved to sorrow when his friend Lazarus falls ill and dies. Then, in a dramatic scene, he calls his friend out of the tomb and restores him to life.

Preface   Lent

Color   Purple

Prayers of Intercession

The prayers are prepared locally for each occasion. The following examples may be adapted or used as appropriate.

Lifting our voices and turning toward God, let us pray for the church, the earth, and all who are in need.
A brief silence.

God, our sure strength, set the mind of your church on the Spirit of love and kinship. Bring healing where there is division and hope where there is worry. Hear us, O God.
Your mercy is great.

You bring life where there was despair and death. Bring new hope and new growth to barren lands and water to parched earth. Hear us, O God.
Your mercy is great.

Listen to the voices of the weak and oppressed. Guard people in all lands from danger and injustice (*especially*). Hear us, O God.
Your mercy is great.

Martha and Mary pleaded for healing. Hear the cries of your people who call out in need and pain. Grant healing and comfort to those who are ill. (*We pray especially for . . .*) Hear us, O God.
Your mercy is great.

Bring life to dry bones in our community. Breathe your life-giving Spirit into the corners of our ministry that need renewal. Hear us, O God.
Your mercy is great.

Here other intercessions may be offered.

We give thanks for the faithful departed (*especially*) and for the assurance that we will join with them in the heavenly banquet. Hear us, O God.
Your mercy is great.

Into your hands, merciful God, we commend all for whom we pray, trusting in your steadfast love; through Christ our Lord.
Amen.

Images in the Readings

Many medieval churches house burials and even contain glass-encased skeletons, but most contemporary churches avoid picturing bones that are left after the flesh has rotted away. Our culture avoids dealing directly and honestly with death: many people are even replacing the verb *died* with the term *passed*, as if with everyone going off to heaven, there really is no death. In contrast, this Sunday presents us with the images of the **grave**, the **stink** of bodily decomposition, and the pile of **bones**. Furthermore, Paul's use of the term *flesh* as a metaphor for the misused human life intensifies this Sunday's honesty about human mortality. These texts represent the Bible's stark attention to the reality of death, both the "death" that is sin and the finality of death when our bodies die. For this Sunday, you might borrow a skeleton from a science classroom to hang prominently in the sanctuary. When we fully acknowledge the natural fact of death, we are ready to praise God's life as gift.

Ideas for the Day

- Today's passage from John offers rich opportunities for storytelling. Consider presenting the gospel from multiple perspectives: one of the disciples, confused by Jesus' words; Mary or Martha, approaching Jesus with a mixture of grief, disappointment, and hope; one of the mourners accompanying the sisters; Jesus, revealing his identity and God's power in this sign; and Lazarus, called forth from the grave. How might listeners find it easy or difficult to identify with various characters in the story?
- Ezekiel's powerful, hopeful imagery could be enhanced in proclamation with sound effects that evoke the sound of breath enlivening the bones. Try a rain stick or a recording of wind. You can find various recordings online by searching "pure wind sounds."
- Both Martha and Mary say to Jesus, "If you had been here, my brother would not have died." Like them, many faithful people in our time struggle to find Jesus' presence in times of death, loss, or difficulty. The classic "Footprints" poem suggests that Jesus does not abandon us in such times; in fact, he carries us through them. Cartoonist Kris Straub offers a humorous and provocative follow-up in a comic called "Footprints in the Sand, Part 1." Search for the cartoon online by that title and the name of the comic, "Chainsawsuit."
- Inspired by Lazarus brought back to life and Paul's promise of "life to your mortal bodies also through his Spirit" (Rom. 8:11), invite a testimony of life after a death-dealing experience. Recovering from addiction, finding a way forward after loss, and "coming out" after hiding an aspect of one's identity all can be experiences of new life and freedom. What does Jesus' call to come out of the grave sound like, and how does a community or church "unbind" us and set us free?

Connections with the Liturgy

In the words of the baptismal liturgy, "By water and the word God delivers us from sin and death and raises us to new life in Jesus Christ" (*ELW*, p. 227). Our creeds affirm not some immortality of the soul, but rather "the resurrection of the body, and the life everlasting," "the life of the world to come."

Christians trust that God enlivens not only this natural existence but also a life other than and beyond this world, a new creation after this entire created universe has come to its end. Our life in Christ begins at baptism and extends, by the mystery of God, beyond time and space.

Let the Children Come

The story of Lazarus is a direct telling of Jesus moving one from death to life. Today's story, and the coming death of Jesus, may leave children who have experienced the death of a loved one with the same feelings as Mary: indignant and expecting Jesus to prevent physical death. Indeed, adults struggle with this too! Setting this story so deeply into Lent, and foreshadowing Jesus' death, helps our conversations around death and new life expand. Children will ask for (demand) concrete answers. The mysterious and concrete thing is that time and time again, Jesus brings new life out of death.

Assembly Song
Gathering

Oh, for a thousand tongues to sing ELW 886, LBW 559
Jesus lives, my sure defense ELW 621, LBW 340
Through the night of doubt and sorrow ELW 327, LBW 355

Psalmody and Acclamations

Grotenhuis, Dale. "Out of the Depths I Cry to You." SATB, opt assembly, org. MSM 50-3015.
Pelz, Walter L. "Psalm 130." U, assembly, org. CG CGA980.
Arnatt, Ronald. "Psalm 130 (Waiting and Watching)." SATB, bar solo, assembly, kybd. ECS 5459.
ᴾ (GA) Organ, Anne Krentz. "Return to the Lord" with proper verse for Lent 5. MSB1 S419.

Hymn of the Day

Lord, thee I love with all my heart ELW 750, LBW 325
HERZLICH LIEB
The Word of God is source and seed ELW 506, WOV 658
GAUDEAMUS DOMINO
Jesus is a rock in a weary land ELW 333 *WEARY LAND*

Offering

Tree of Life and awesome mystery ELW 334, sts. 1, 2, 3, Lent 5
Out of the depths I cry to you ELW 600, LBW 295

Communion

Seed that in earth is dying ELW 330
I am the Bread of life ELW 485, WOV 702
Restore in us, O God ELW 328, WOV 662

Sending

What wondrous love is this ELW 666, LBW 385
Abide with me ELW 629, LBW 272

Additional Assembly Songs

Rich in promise OBS 75

Let this season be ASG 19

In the bulb there is a flower LS 56

⊕ Bell, John. "Behold the Lamb of God 1" from *Come, All You People: Shorter Songs for Worship*. SAB. GIA G-4391.

⊕ Liberius, R. F. "Khudaya, rahem kar" from *Agape: Songs of Hope and Reconciliation*. U, gtr. Lutheran World Federation. Out of print. Available on Amazon.com.

☼ Assad, Audrey/Sarah Hart. "Show Me" from CCLI.

☼ Brumley, Albert E. "I'll Fly Away" from CCLI.

☼ Cottrell, Travis/Carl Cartee. "Faithful God" from CCLI.

☼ Houston, Joel/Jill McCloghry. "Bones" from CCLI.

☼ Pederson-Groeneveld, Nancy/Vince Wilcox. "The Savior Who Weeps" from CCLI.

☼ Tomlin, Chris/Shawn Craig/Jesse Reeves. "Mighty Is the Power of the Cross" from CCLI.

Music for the Day
Choral

P ♫ Bach, J. S. "Lord, Thee I Love with All My Heart" from *Bach for All Seasons*. SATB, opt kybd. AFP 9780800658540.

♫ Johnson, Kyle. "Jesus Is a Rock in a Weary Land." SATB, pno. MSM 50-6104.

P ♫ Keesecker, Thomas. "Jesus Is a Rock in a Weary Land." U or 2 pt or 3 pt, pno. AFP 9780800679187.

Schalk, Carl. "Out of the Depths." SAB, org. MSM 50-3410.

Children's Choir

Cropper, Margaret. "Jesus' Hands Were Kind Hands" from *LifeSongs*. AFP 9780806642703.

Mayo, Beck Slagle/Lynn Shaw Bailey. "Dry Bones." U, pno. CG CGA1112.

Pelz, Walter L. "Psalm 130." U, org, opt assembly. CG CGA980.

Keyboard / Instrumental

Alain, Jehan. "Le Jardin Suspendu" from *Trois Pièces pour Grand Orgue*. Org. PRE 51300001.

P ♫ Carter, John. "Jesus Is a Rock in a Weary Land" (Weary Land) from *Spirituals for Piano*. Pno. AFP 9780800621698.

P ♫ Childs, Edwin T. "Jesus Is a Rock in a Weary Land" (Weary Land) from *Spirituals for Organ: For Manuals Only*. Org. AFP 9781451401141.

♫ Krebs, Johann Ludwig. "Lord, Thee I Love with All My Heart" (Herzlich lieb) from *Eight Chorale Preludes for Organ with Trumpet (or Oboe)*. Tpt or ob, org. PRE 453001070.

Handbell

♫ Eithun, Sandra. "Lord, Thee I Love with All My Heart." 3-6 oct hb, opt 3-6 oct hc, opt tpt, L2+. CPH 97-7677.

P Geschke, Susan. "Oh, How I Love Jesus" from *Ring Praises!* 2-3 oct, L1+, CG CGB767. 3-5 oct, L1+, CG CGB768.

Morris, Hart. "Dry Bones." 3-5 oct, opt perc, L2. HOP 2083.

Tuesday, April 4
Benedict the African, confessor, died 1589

Born a slave on the island of Sicily, Benedict first lived as a hermit and labored as a plowman after he was freed. When the bishop of Rome ordered all hermits to attach themselves to a religious community, Benedict joined the Franciscans, where he served as a cook. Although he was illiterate, his fame as a confessor brought many visitors to the humble and holy cook, and he was eventually named superior of the community. A patron saint of African Americans, Benedict is remembered for his patience and understanding when confronted with racial prejudice and taunts.

Thursday, April 6
Albrecht Dürer, died 1528;
Matthias Grünewald, died 1529;
Lucas Cranach, died 1553; artists

These great German artists revealed through their work the mystery of salvation and the wonder of creation. Dürer's work reflected the apocalyptic spirit of his time. Though he remained a Roman Catholic, he was sympathetic to Martin Luther's reforming work. Grünewald's paintings are known for their dramatic forms, vivid colors, and depiction of light. Cranach's work includes many fine religious examples and several portraits of Martin Luther. Cranach was also widely known for his woodcuts.

⊕ = global song   ♫ = relates to hymn of the day

☼ = praise song   P = available in Prelude Music Planner

April 9, 2017
Sunday of the Passion
Palm Sunday

Today's liturgy begins with a palm procession, commemorating Jesus' triumphal entry into Jerusalem. Quickly the tone of the service changes as we meditate upon Jesus' passion and death. Because this story is so central to our faith, we hear Matthew's account of the passion today and John's version on Good Friday. Though Jesus is obedient even unto death on the cross, he is exalted by God. We gather to remember his offering for the life of the world, and to be fed by his life-giving mercy. This holy week will culminate in the celebration of the Three Days of Jesus' suffering, death, and resurrection.

Prayer of the Day

Everlasting God, in your endless love for the human race you sent our Lord Jesus Christ to take on our nature and to suffer death on the cross. In your mercy enable us to share in his obedience to your will and in the glorious victory of his resurrection, who lives and reigns with you and the Holy Spirit, one God, now and forever.

or

Sovereign God, you have established your rule in the human heart through the servanthood of Jesus Christ. By your Spirit, keep us in the joyful procession of those who with their tongues confess Jesus as Lord and with their lives praise him as Savior, who lives and reigns with you and the Holy Spirit, one God, now and forever.

or

O God of mercy and might, in the mystery of the passion of your Son you offer your infinite life to the world. Gather us around the cross of Christ, and preserve us until the resurrection, through Jesus Christ, our Savior and Lord, who lives and reigns with you and the Holy Spirit, one God, now and forever.

Gospel Acclamation

Christ humbled himself and became obedient to the point of death—even death ' on a cross.* Therefore God also highly exalted him and gave him the name that is above ' every name. (Phil. 2:8-9)

Readings and Psalm

Procession with Palms: Matthew 21:1-11
Isaiah 50:4-9a

The servant of the Lord expresses absolute confidence in his final vindication, despite the fact that he has been struck and spit upon. This characteristic of the servant played an important role in the early church's understanding of the suffering, death, and resurrection of Jesus.

Psalm 31:9-16

Into your hands, O Lord, I commend my spirit. (Ps. 31:5)

Philippians 2:5-11

Paul uses an early Christian hymn to help us comprehend Jesus' obedient selflessness on the cross and how God has made Christ lord over all reality. The perspective of the cross becomes the way we rightly understand God, Christ, our own lives, and fellowship within the community of Christ.

Matthew 26:14—27:66 *or* Matthew 27:11-54

In fulfillment of scripture and obedience to God's will, Jesus goes to the cross so that a new covenant in his blood may bring forgiveness of sins. Even the soldiers who crucify him recognize him to be the Son of God.

Preface   Sunday of the Passion

Color   Scarlet *or* Purple

Prayers of Intercession

The prayers are prepared locally for each occasion. The following examples may be adapted or used as appropriate.

Lifting our voices and turning toward God, let us pray for the church, the earth, and all who are in need.
A brief silence.

Redeeming God, your church proclaims your gospel of truth and courage. Gather your children together to share in the promise of Christ. Hear us, O God.
Your mercy is great.

Hosanna, Son of David. Lead your children to care for your good creation and all its inhabitants: lands, waters, plants, and all living creatures. Hear us, O God.
Your mercy is great.

Soften the hearts of political leaders who ignore or deny suffering, struggle, and injustice. Lift up leaders who seek your will for the sake of their people. Hear us, O God.
Your mercy is great.

Bring companionship to those who feel abandoned, comfort to those in pain, hope to those in despair, and healing to all in need (*especially*). Hear us, O God.
Your mercy is great.

Walk with this community as we remember your life-giving passion and death. Send us forth burning with desire to share your word with a hurting world. Hear us, O God.
Your mercy is great.
Here other intercessions may be offered.
We remember those who were imprisoned or martyred for their faith (*especially the theologian Dietrich Bonhoeffer*) and give thanks for their bold confession and witness. Hear us, O God.
Your mercy is great.
Into your hands, merciful God, we commend all for whom we pray, trusting in your steadfast love; through Christ our Lord.
Amen.

Images in the Readings

Two opposite images of Christ come in the readings. First, Christ is **king**. In Matthew's passion narrative, he is acclaimed as the Son of David; he is the apocalyptic Son of Man, who will judge the world at the end of time; he is accused of falsely presenting himself as Messiah yet is affirmed by believers as the Christ; he is mocked as the "king of the Jews"; and ironically, even when dead, his body is attended by Roman guards. Much in American culture resists "king" as a positive image. Yet the hope that someone has ultimate power, absolute justice, and endless mercy persists in human imagination.

In an image that derives from the first and second readings, Christ is **servant**. God will vindicate the servant, even though he is now suffering. We are to adopt the mind of Christ Jesus, who became a servant, indeed a slave, for us. Once again, much in American culture resists "servant" as a positive image. Martin Luther's essay "The Freedom of the Christian" can help us here: through our baptism, we are both free, slaves to none, and simultaneously servants to all.

Ideas for the Day

- Among the four gospels, only Matthew focuses on the "earthshaking" aspect of Jesus' entry into Jerusalem and his death. Jesus' entrance causes "turmoil" in the city (the Greek word is "shaken," 21:10). At his death, the earth quakes strongly enough to split rocks and open graves (27:51-52), and it shakes again to open his tomb at the resurrection (28:2). How does Jesus' life, death, and resurrection "shake up" our communities and lives?
- Matthew emphasizes the fulfillment of scripture as a driving force in how the story of Jesus' life and death unfolds. If you present Matthew's passion as a dramatic reading with multiple characters' voices, consider including the "voice" of scripture as one of the characters (see 26:24, 56, 64; 27:9-10). Connections between the crucifixion (27:32-46) and Psalm 22 could also be highlighted (as they will be when the psalm is heard on Good Friday).
- During the reading of Matthew's passion story, provide a rough stone for each worshiper to hold. As you pause to guide reflection at key moments, the stones can help

listeners place themselves in the story by imagining tangible items: the weight of Judas's pieces of silver, the ground on which Jesus prays at Gethsemane, stones in the courtyard catching Peter's tears after his denial of Jesus, the rocks split at Jesus' death, and finally, the stone that closed the tomb. In Luke's version of the Palm Sunday story, some Pharisees told Jesus to silence his shouting disciples. Jesus answered, "I tell you, if these were silent, the stones would shout out" (Luke 19:40). Make sure you provide stones large enough not to be a choking hazard for young children.
- When we celebrate communion, our sung "Hosanna" accompanies Jesus' entry into our midst. Highlight the connection on Palm Sunday by inviting people to once again wave their palms as the communion elements are brought forward or when "Hosanna" is sung during the "Holy, holy, holy."

Connections with the Liturgy

Each Sunday at the eucharistic table, we sing the Hosanna: just as Jesus processed before the people on the first Palm Sunday, so we acclaim Jesus before us in bread and wine: "Hosanna: save us, Lord." As well, each Sunday's thanksgiving at the eucharistic table, like the song in Philippians, retells the Christian gospel. Jesus Christ is God for us, his death a living reality that gives us salvation.

Let the Children Come

Lent began with curious opposites, and now they return in the culminating Sunday, the Sunday of the Passion and Palm Sunday. The gospel readings today show us Jesus as both a triumphal king and a suffering servant. These are two concepts most children know only through books and movies. Caregivers have been telling children to sit down and not to wave stuff around in church for fifty-one Sundays. Imagine their delight when the whole assembly stands, processes, waves palm branches, and shouts, "Hosanna in the highest, blessed is the one who comes in the name of the Lord!"

Assembly Song
Gathering

All glory, laud, and honor ELW 344, LBW 108
Prepare the royal highway ELW 264, LBW 26
Ride on, ride on in majesty! ELW 346, LBW 121

Psalmody and Acclamations

Alonso, Tony. "Into Your Hands (Psalm 31)." SAB, cant, assembly, gtr, kybd, opt C inst, vc. WLP 006317.
Cooney, Rory. "I Place My Life" from PCY, vol. 4.
Sedio, Mark. "Psalm 31," Refrain 1, from PSCY.
P (GA) Organ, Anne Krentz. "Return to the Lord" with proper verse for Sunday of the Passion. MSB1 S419.

P = available in Prelude Music Planner

Hymn of the Day

O sacred head, now wounded ELW 351/352, LBW 116/117, LLC
342 *HERZLICH TUT MICH VERLANGEN*

Jesus, keep me near the cross ELW 335, TFF 73 *NEAR THE CROSS*

My song is love unknown ELW 343, WOV 661 *LOVE UNKNOWN*
LBW 94 *RHOSYMEDRE*

Offering

Come to the table ELW 481, W&P 33

Christ, the life of all the living ELW 339, LBW 97

Communion

Ah, holy Jesus ELW 349, LBW 123

Calvary ELW 453, TFF 85

Were you there ELW 353, LLC 344, TFF 81, LBW 92

Sending

A lamb goes uncomplaining forth ELW 340, LBW 105

There in God's garden ELW 342, WOV 668

Additional Assembly Songs

🌐 Chinula, Charles. "Behold the Holy Lamb of God" from *The Courage to Say No: 23 Songs for Lent and Easter*. SATB with cantor. GIA G-4244.

🌐 South African traditional. "Holy, Most Holy Lord" from *Glory to God*. SATB. WJK 0664238971.

☼ Boyd, Aaron, et al. "God of This City" from CCLI.

☼ Brown, Brenton/Paul Baloche. "Hosanna (Praise Is Rising)" from CCLI.

☼ Getty, Keith/Stuart Townend. "In God Alone" from CCLI.

☼ Morgan, Reuben/Ben Fielding. "Mighty to Save" from CCLI.

☼ Townend, Stuart. "How Deep the Father's Love for Us" from CCLI.

☼ Watts, Isaac/Lowell Mason/Chris Tomlin/Jesse Reeves. "The Wonderful Cross" from CCLI.

Music for the Day
Choral

P ♫ Larkin, Michael. "O Sacred Head, Now Wounded." SATB, pno. AFP 9780806697345.

P ♫ Leaf, Robert. "O Sacred Head, Now Wounded." SATB, cl, org. AFP 9780800652739.

P Schubert, Franz. "Hosanna to the Son of David" from *Augsburg Motet Book*. SATB, opt kybd. AFP 9781451423709.

P ♫ Strommen Campbell, Jonathan. "Jesus, Keep Me Near the Cross." SAB or SATB, pno, C inst. AFP 9781451492521.

Children's Choir

Bedford, Michael. "Meditation for Lent." 2 pt, kybd. AFP 9780800638399.

P Patterson, Mark. "The Triumphal Entry" from *ChildrenSing with Instruments*. U, kybd, opt C inst. AFP 9780800620349.

Ruiz, Rubén. "Filled with Excitement" from *LifeSongs*. U/2 pt, kybd, opt perc. AFP 9780806642703.

Keyboard / Instrumental

♫ Albrecht, Mark. "Jesus, Keep Me Near the Cross" (Near the Cross) from *Timeless Tunes for Piano and Solo Instrument*, vol. 2. Inst, pno. AFP 9780800659851.

P ♫ Culli, Benjamin. "My Song Is Love Unknown" (Love Unknown) from *New Songs of Celebration: Ten Settings for Organ*. Org. AFP 9781451494082.

P ♫ Diemer, Emma Lou. "O Sacred Head, Now Wounded" (Herzlich tut mich verlangen) from *Glory, Laud, and Honor: Organ Settings*. Org. AFP 9781451494068.

♫ Hassell, Michael. "My Song Is Love Unknown" (Love Unknown) from *Jazz Lenten Journey for Piano*. Pno. AFP 9780800659493.

Handbell

♫ Glasgow, Michael J. "Dies Irae." 3-7 oct hb, opt 2 oct hc, L3-, CG CGB682. Opt full score (ob, vc), CG CGB681.

♫ Glasgow, Michael J. "Rest at the Cross." 3-7 oct hb, opt 3-6 oct hc, opt vln, L3. LOR 20/1657L.

♫ Stults, Tyleen. "My Song Is Love Unknown." 3 oct, L2. CPH 97-7679.

Sunday, April 9
Dietrich Bonhoeffer, theologian, died 1945

Bonhoeffer (BON-heh-fer) was a German theologian who, at the age of twenty-five, became a lecturer in systematic theology at the University of Berlin. In 1933, and with Hitler's rise to power, Bonhoeffer became a leading spokesman for the Confessing Church, a resistance movement against the Nazis. He was arrested in 1943. He was linked to a failed attempt on Hitler's life and sent to Buchenwald, then to Schönberg prison. After leading a worship service on April 8, 1945, at Schönberg prison, he was taken away to be hanged the next day. His last words as he left were, "This is the end, but for me the beginning of life." *Evangelical Lutheran Worship* includes a hymn (626) by Bonhoeffer, "By Gracious Powers."

🌐 = global song   ♫ = relates to hymn of the day
☼ = praise song   P = available in Prelude Music Planner

April 10, 2017
Monday in Holy Week

During Holy Week some communities gather each day to meditate on Jesus' final days before his death on the cross. Today's gospel commemorates the anointing of Jesus by Mary, a foreshadowing of his death and burial. Isaiah speaks of the suffering servant who is a light for the nations and who faithfully brings forth justice. For Christians, Jesus' suffering is the path to resurrection and new life. We eagerly await the celebration of the great Three Days later this week.

Prayer of the Day

O God, your Son chose the path that led to pain before joy and to the cross before glory. Plant his cross in our hearts, so that in its power and love we may come at last to joy and glory, through Jesus Christ, our Savior and Lord, who lives and reigns with you and the Holy Spirit, one God, now and forever.

Gospel Acclamation

May I never boast of | anything* except the cross of our Lord | Jesus Christ. (Gal. 6:14)

Readings and Psalm

Isaiah 42:1-9

God's servant Israel is endowed with the Spirit in order to bring justice to the nations. The servant will not exercise authority boisterously or with violence, nor will weariness ever keep it from fulfilling its task. God's old promises have been fulfilled; the new assignment of the servant is to bring light to the nations.

Psalm 36:5-11

All people take refuge under the shadow of your wings. (Ps. 36:7)

Hebrews 9:11-15

Prior to Christ, forgiveness was mediated through animal sacrifice. Christ came as the great high priest to establish a new covenant. Through his blood we are liberated from our sins and promised eternal life.

John 12:1-11

A few days after raising Lazarus from the dead, Jesus visits the man's home. Lazarus's sister Mary is criticized when she anoints the feet of Jesus with costly perfume.

Preface   Sunday of the Passion

Color   Scarlet *or* Purple

Monday, April 10
Mikael Agricola, Bishop of Turku, died 1557

Agricola was consecrated as the bishop of Turku in 1554, without papal approval. As a result, he began a reform of the Finnish church along Lutheran lines. He translated the New Testament, the prayerbook, hymns, and the mass into Finnish, and through this work set the rules of orthography that are the basis of modern Finnish spelling. His thoroughgoing work is particularly remarkable in that he accomplished it in only three years. He died suddenly on a return trip from negotiating a peace treaty with the Russians.

April 11, 2017
Tuesday in Holy Week

As the great Three Days draw near, some communities gather each day of Holy Week for worship. Paul proclaims Christ crucified as the wisdom and power of God. Jesus speaks of the grain of wheat that falls into the earth and dies in order that it may bear fruit. We die with Christ in baptism that we may be raised with him to new life. We will celebrate this great mystery of death and resurrection at the Easter Vigil later this week.

Prayer of the Day

Lord Jesus, you have called us to follow you. Grant that our love may not grow cold in your service, and that we may not fail or deny you in the time of trial, for you live and reign with the Father and the Holy Spirit, one God, now and forever.

Gospel Acclamation

May I never boast of ¹ anything* except the cross of our Lord ¹ Jesus Christ. (Gal. 6:14)

Readings and Psalm

Isaiah 49:1-7

Here the servant Israel speaks for herself and acknowledges herself as God's secret weapon. Called like Jeremiah and John the Baptist before her birth, the servant is not only to restore Israel itself, but the servant's ultimate assignment is to bring news of God's victory to the ends of the earth. God in faithfulness has chosen Israel for this task.

Psalm 71:1-14

From my mother's womb you have been my strength. (Ps. 71:6)

1 Corinthians 1:18-31

To the world, the word of the cross is silly, because it claims God's power is most fully revealed in complete, utter weakness. For those who are being saved, however, the word of the cross unveils God's true wisdom, power, and source of true life.

John 12:20-36

Knowing that his hour has come, Jesus announces that his death will be an exaltation. God's name will be glorified when his death draws people to new life.

Preface   Sunday of the Passion

Color   Scarlet *or* Purple

April 12, 2017
Wednesday in Holy Week

This day was formerly called "Spy Wednesday," an allusion to the gospel accounts in which Judas is identified as the betrayer of Jesus. As Jesus endured the suffering of the cross, we are called to run the race of life with perseverance, confident of the joy to come. In the Three Days, which begin tomorrow evening, we will journey with Christ from darkness to light, from captivity to freedom, from death to life.

Prayer of the Day

Almighty God, your Son our Savior suffered at human hands and endured the shame of the cross. Grant that we may walk in the way of his cross and find it the way of life and peace, through Jesus Christ, our Savior and Lord, who lives and reigns with you and the Holy Spirit, one God, now and forever.

Gospel Acclamation

May I never boast of ¹ anything* except the cross of our Lord ¹ Jesus Christ. (Gal. 6:14)

Readings and Psalm

Isaiah 50:4-9a

The servant of the Lord expresses absolute confidence in his final vindication, despite the fact that he has been struck and spit upon. This characteristic of the servant played an important role in the early church for understanding the suffering, death, and resurrection of Jesus.

Psalm 70

Be pleased, O God, to deliver me. (Ps. 70:1)

Hebrews 12:1-3

In the way of the cross, Jesus has blazed the trail for our salvation. With faithful perseverance, we follow in his footsteps.

John 13:21-32

At the last supper, Jesus identifies Judas Iscariot as the one who will betray him, and sends him on his way.

Preface   Sunday of the Passion

Color   Scarlet *or* Purple

The Three Days

Preparing for the Three Days

If you are reading this essay, you have either (a) never prepared for the Three Days rites as proposed in *Evangelical Lutheran Worship* or (b) done so before, once or many times. If you are in the former category, be encouraged to enter for the first time into this ancient tradition always being made new. If you are in the latter, be inspired to deepen and strengthen your congregation's participation in the Three Days. The details are many, but the rewards of the Three Days of worship are numerous. The Three Days have become for countless Christians the center, the root, the anchor, the heart of the rest of the year's worship and daily life.

Collaboration is essential

The Three Days do not just fall together; preparations will take time. Clergy and musicians cannot succeed in shouldering the Three Days' planning on their own, in last-minute fashion. Collaboration is essential, starting with lay members of your congregation. January is not too early to gather a group interested in learning more about the Three Days, potential volunteers to attend to the days' details: Who will help strip the altar? Who will organize the reading of the passion from John? Who will verify fire safety codes, collect wood, and tend the Easter fire?

Small congregations or those new to the Three Days may invite a neighboring congregation—or group of congregations—into a creative planning process. Many of our full-communion partners have their own denominational Three Days resources, similar to *Evangelical Lutheran Worship*. Reap the gift of ecumenical assembly during the week Christians call holy.

Re-membered by the mystery

Every Sunday, we bring our little joys, our profound sorrows, our recurrent anxieties, and our unanswered questions to worship. Every Sunday, we try to make meaning of our messy or messed-up lives in the death and resurrection of Christ. Every Sunday, God gathers us, speaks to us, feeds us, and sends us forth to be what God has made us: the baptized body of Christ. "We have been buried with [Christ] . . . so we too might walk in newness of life" (Rom. 6:4, Easter Vigil).

But on ordinary Sundays, we sometimes forget that God is at work, putting to death our old selves and raising us up daily to new life in the Risen One. We forget that God's action in Christ's death and resurrection marks the center, the root,

the anchor, the heart of our life and faith. We forget to touch the font, sign the cross on our foreheads. Instead, we are distracted—by too little sleep, or an energetic toddler, or a recent success, or a medical diagnosis, or a community scandal. We are all over the place and no place at all, uncertain of Jesus' place.

In the face of distraction and dislocation, the Three Days are a yearly gift: They refocus us, re-member us, and re-turn our eyes and ears, our hands and feet, our mouths and minds, toward the mystery of Christ's death and resurrection. The Three Days reorient us, and the whole church, to our Christian "magnetic north"—the cross and the empty tomb—from which we can set a course.

Welcome everyone to every service, to any service

Think of the Three Days as a song we get to sing only once a year. The song tells us again who God is and who we are in God. The church anticipates it, relearns the familiar parts, and discovers new harmonies to add this year. In this song, there are four distinct stanzas—Maundy Thursday, Good Friday, Vigil of Easter, Easter Day. Yet the four stanzas form one song.

Encourage the members of your assembly to embrace all four stanzas of the song that is the Three Days. The Three Days is the church's March (or April) Madness, for it seems like madness to come together for so much worship. Yet is it madness, or is it indeed right, our duty, and our joy, that for one week each year we should worship in assembly more than any other time? In Holy Week, we gather again and again: we need to remember and be re-membered by Christ crucified and risen.

But worship leaders must be realistic. Many worshipers will pick and choose, attending one or two or three but not all four services. Visitors will also drop in, so that likely the Three Days worship will draw four distinct assemblies. Receive these varied assemblies with grace, knowing that however small or large, known or unknown to you, God has drawn each particular assembly together.

Preparing for all the services
Prayers of the day

If it is not your practice as presider to pray through the appointed prayer of the day multiple times before Sunday worship, this year's Three Days offers you the opportunity.

Sometime before Holy Week, examine the two options for the prayer of the day offered for each of the four services (*ELW*, pp. 30–32). If you are a sundaysandseasons.com subscriber, the lectionary notes that are part of the day resources (accessed via the home page) provide historical background for each prayer. Choose between the rich, traditional language of the older prayers and the vibrant, image-filled newer prayers.

Then pray the prayers of the day you have chosen so that you know them well, even by heart. By the time you lead these prayers at worship, they will have become part of you; you will be able to actually *pray* them on behalf of your assembly and in communion with many Christian assemblies around the world.

Space

Your worship space may provide adequate physical space for the Three Days worship. However, alternative spaces are worth trying. Perhaps your fellowship hall offers better space to try a footwashing rite for the first (or the fifth) time. In whatever space you use, is a new seating configuration possible? How will you adorn the space—with branches or candles or swaths of fabric? How can your space be truly bare on Good Friday?

The Easter Vigil requires some movement—it is like a communal procession through its four parts—but offers opportunity for even more. Some or all of the readings can take place in different parts of the worship space or church building. The litany of the saints can be sung in procession around the church building, moving then to the font. Such movement takes time but can enliven and energize the assembly until the service's end.

Time

The question of time is worth mentioning. It may well be futile to invite families with small children or older members who dislike driving at night to evening worship if these services take place too late. What in your congregation is considered "too late"? Is consistency of time for three evening services important?

Additionally, be honest with newcomers to these services about their actual length. None of these services can be done according to *Evangelical Lutheran Worship* rubrics in less than one hour. And a Vigil may last two or three. There is no need to apologize for the time they require. If people are willing to go to a two-hour party or a three-hour sporting event, they can be convinced to attend—and embrace—the Three Days worship, provided worship time is well stewarded by leaders.

Music

The Three Days worship happens only once a year. Assembly music cannot be too elaborate, for there is no time for the congregation to learn it. Additionally, if all choral energy is put into one service, the others will feel the imbalance.

In addition to song lists in *Sundays and Seasons* and *Indexes to Evangelical Lutheran Worship*, make use of the treasures in *Music Sourcebook for Lent and the Three Days* (Augsburg Fortress, 2009). Sing Sturm's "I Give You a New Commandment" as the gospel acclamation for Maundy Thursday, and Farlee's "Look to Jesus" on Good Friday. Or choose from other wonderful, recent compositions.

Some congregations sing one or more of the Three Days services without instrumental accompaniment. Music That Makes Community (www.musicthatmakescommunity.org) offers a growing list of online resources of "paperless" music to explore. Such paperless music is neither "traditional" nor "contemporary" but tries to bridge these often unhelpful categories. The simple melody, round, call and response, or echo forms of communal song are ideal for Three Days consideration.

Preparing for each service
Maundy Thursday

Eat, drink, wash, love. Hands, feet, body, blood. The vocabulary of Maundy Thursday is sensory, corporeal. *This day shall be a day of remembrance for you* (Exod. 12:14) and a day that our bodies are re-membered, tangibly. On Maundy Thursday, love is not an empty sentiment but grace enacted with washbasin and towel.

The readings are not squeamish about bodies: our feet need washing; our flesh is mortal; we will die like the sheep and goats and Jesus. But facing that reality, we wash and eat and live, that we might love one another as Christ has loved us.

There are three opportunities for the assembly's bodies to get up and move. Invite those who wish to come forward for individual laying on of hands and forgiveness; and again, to join in the washing of feet; and again, to gather at the table and be filled with Christ's body.

As you prepare to preach, keep in mind the bodies of your assembly. So many are ashamed or dissatisfied with their bodies. How might you speak a word of mercy to all the bodies present, however little or large, abused or betrayed, hurting or dirty they may be?

Good Friday

Tonight we look to Jesus and see our High Priest, the Suffering Servant, the great I AM, dying on the cross. At the cross, we lay our prayers. We pray and pray for everyone, trusting the Wounded One with all our wounds.

Invite your assemblies to the cross. Some congregations are accustomed to reverencing the cross—kissing it, kneeling or lying prostrate before it. Other assemblies may be helped by the opportunity to light candles around the cross. Certainly, children will eagerly do this and become their parents' teachers.

Vigil of Easter

This is the night that most fully proclaims the mystery of Christ—through fire and water, story and meal. Invite assembly members to decide how many of the twelve appointed readings (see *ELW*, p. 269) you will use this year. How creative will you invite your readers to be? In one assembly, two blind members faithfully read Genesis 1 in tandem, in Braille. In another congregation, an eleven-year-old break-dancer responds in dance to his mother's reading of Exodus 14, to his father's accompaniment on double bass. In another assembly, Daniel 3 is read outside by the still-smoking Easter fire, set ablaze again with last year's dried Christmas tree branches.

The Easter Vigil is always crowned by a baptism (or multiple baptisms), but whether or not any have undergone catechesis this year, the whole assembly gets to affirm their baptisms. Your preaching on this night may point listeners to the font, which is both cross and empty tomb for Christians.

Easter Day

Sunday morning will bring forgotten and new faces. Welcome them wholeheartedly, with trumpets and flowers and alleluias. But as worship leader, you are responsible for carrying the previous three nights of worship into Easter morning. Bring the bodies, the cross, and the newly lit paschal candle into Easter Day to help show forth Christ's death and resurrection—the center, the root, the anchor, the heart of our life in faith.

Seasonal Checklist

- Review the liturgies for Maundy Thursday, Good Friday, and the Vigil of Easter in *Evangelical Lutheran Worship* (Assembly Edition, pp. 258–270; Leaders Edition, including the Notes on the Services, pp. 628–653 and 36–42).
- Find extensive background and practical help in *Worship Guidebook for Lent and the Three Days*, and musical resources in *Music Sourcebook for Lent and the Three Days* (Augsburg Fortress, 2009).
- Prepare a detailed leaders book for worship leaders for all the Three Days liturgies, including all texts and music. Place them in three-ring binders (ceremonial binders are available from Augsburg Fortress). Highlight speaking parts and instructions for each worship leader in individual copies.
- Arrange rehearsals for all the liturgies of the Three Days. These unique services must be remembered and practiced each year, even by seasoned worship leaders.
- Equip and inform (and thank!) altar guild members for their work in these busy days.
- Order worship participation leaflets if used on Good Friday.
- Create worship folders for these services, or a single booklet-style worship folder for Maundy Thursday, Good Friday and the Easter Vigil. One booklet will illustrate that these services are one. Order preprinted covers as needed.
- Publicize Holy Week and Easter services in local newspapers, on your church's website and Facebook page, and through other social media. Consider designing and ordering an eye-catching banner to display curbside.
- Arrange for a thorough cleaning of the worship space between Maundy Thursday and the Easter Vigil.
- Consider silencing bells or chimes from the beginning of Maundy Thursday until the canticle of praise or the first "alleluias" are sung at the Easter Vigil.
- Purchase a new paschal candle and new congregational handheld candles.
- Prepare extra communion elements and communionware needed for larger numbers of communicants during Holy Week and Easter.
- If there will be baptisms of children and/or adults at the Easter Vigil (or on Easter Sunday), see the many suggestions in *Washed and Welcome: A Baptismal Sourcebook* and *Go Make Disciples: An Invitation to Baptismal Living* (Augsburg Fortress, 2010 and 2012).

Worship Texts for the Three Days

MAUNDY THURSDAY

Confession and Forgiveness

Friends in Christ, in this Lenten season we have heard our Lord's call to struggle against sin, death, and the devil—all that keeps us from loving God and each other. This is the struggle to which we were called at baptism. [We have shared this discipline of Lent with new brothers and sisters in Christ who will be baptized at the Easter Vigil.]

Within the community of the church, God never wearies of forgiving sin and giving the peace of reconciliation. On this night let us confess our sin against God and our neighbor, and enter the celebration of the great Three Days reconciled with God and with one another.

Silence is kept for reflection and self-examination.

Most merciful God,
**we confess that we are captive to sin
and cannot free ourselves.
We have sinned against you in thought, word, and deed,
by what we have done and by what we have left undone.
We have not loved you with our whole heart;
we have not loved our neighbors as ourselves.
For the sake of your Son, Jesus Christ,
have mercy on us.
Forgive us, renew us, and lead us,
so that we may delight in your will
and walk in your ways,
to the glory of your holy name. Amen.**

God, who is rich in mercy, loved us
even when we were dead in sin,
and made us alive together with Christ.
By grace you have been saved.
In the name of ✝ Jesus Christ, your sins are forgiven.
Almighty God strengthen you with power
through the Holy Spirit,
that Christ may live in your hearts through faith.
Amen.

Offering Prayer

God of glory,
receive these gifts and the offering of our lives.
As Jesus was lifted up from the earth,
draw us to your heart in the midst of this world,
that all creation may be brought from bondage to freedom,
from darkness to light, and from death to life;
through Jesus Christ, our Savior and Lord.
Amen.

Invitation to Communion

Come to Jesus, our host and our meal.

Prayer after Communion

Lord Jesus, in a wonderful sacrament
you strengthen us with the saving power
of your suffering, death, and resurrection.
May this sacrament of your body and blood
so work in us that the fruits of your redemption
will show forth in the way we live,
for you live and reign with the Father and the Holy Spirit,
one God, now and forever.
Amen.

VIGIL OF EASTER

Greeting

The grace of our Lord Jesus Christ, the love of God,
and the communion of the Holy Spirit be with you all.
And also with you.

Sisters and brothers in Christ, on this most holy night when our
Savior Jesus Christ passed from death to life, we gather with
the church throughout the world in vigil and prayer. This is the
passover of Jesus Christ. Through light and the word, through
water and oil, bread and wine, we proclaim Christ's death and
resurrection, share Christ's triumph over sin and death, and
await Christ's coming again in glory.

Offering Prayer

God of glory,
receive these gifts and the offering of our lives.
As Jesus was lifted up from the earth,
draw us to your heart in the midst of this world.
Bring all creation from bondage to freedom,
from darkness to light, and from death to life;
through Jesus Christ, our Savior and Lord.
Amen.

Invitation to Communion

Now let us feast this Easter day
on Christ, the bread of heaven. Hallelujah!

Prayer after Communion

Life-giving God,
in the mystery of Christ's death and resurrection
you send light to conquer darkness,
water to give new life,
and the bread of heaven to nourish your people.
Send us forth as witnesses to Jesus' resurrection
that we may show your glory to all the world;
through the same Jesus Christ, our risen Lord.
Amen.

Blessing

May God who has brought us from death to life
fill you with great joy.
Almighty God, Father, + Son, and Holy Spirit,
bless you now and forever.
Amen.

Dismissal

Alleluia! Christ is risen.
Christ is risen indeed. Alleluia!
You are the body of Christ raised up for the world.
Go in peace. Share the good news.
Thanks be to God.

Worship texts for Easter Day and Easter Evening begin on page 168.

Seasonal Rites for the Three Days

Resurrection of Our Lord
Vigil of Easter *or* Easter Day
John 20:1-18

Preparation

You will need four readers: two narrators, Mary, and Jesus (who also voices the angels at the tomb). One good rehearsal is probably sufficient. The two narrators stand together at the place where the gospel is normally read. Mary and Jesus stand within the assembly, on opposite sides, facing each other.

Script

Narrators 1 and 2: The holy gospel according to John.

Narrator 1: Early on the first day of the week, while it was still dark, Mary Magdalene came to the tomb and saw that the stone had been removed from the tomb.

Narrator 2: So she ran and went to Simon Peter and the other disciple, the one whom Jesus loved, and said to them,

Mary: They have taken the Lord out of the tomb! They have taken the Lord out of the tomb, and we do not know where they have laid him.

Narrator 1: Peter and the other disciple set out and went toward the tomb. The two were running together, but the other disciple outran Peter and reached the tomb first.

Narrator 2: He bent down to look in and saw the linen wrappings lying there, but he did not go in.

Narrator 1: Simon Peter came, following him, and went into the tomb. He saw the linen wrappings lying there, and the cloth that had been on Jesus' head, not lying with the linen wrappings but rolled up in a place by itself.

Narrator 2: Then the other disciple, who reached the tomb first, also went in, and he saw and believed; for as yet they did not understand the scripture, that he must rise from the dead.

Narrator 1: Then the disciples returned to their homes.
A brief pause.

But Mary stood weeping outside the tomb. As she wept, she bent over to look into the tomb.

Narrator 2: She saw two angels in white, sitting where the body of Jesus had been lying, one at the head and the other at the feet.

Jesus: Woman, why are you weeping?

Mary: They have taken away my Lord, and I do not know where they have laid him.

Narrator 1: When she had said this, she turned around and saw Jesus standing there, but she did not know that it was Jesus.

Jesus: Woman, why are you weeping? Whom are you looking for?

Narrator 2: Supposing him to be the gardener, she said to him,

Mary: Sir, if you have carried him away, tell me where you have laid him, and I will take him away.

Jesus: Mary!

Mary: Rabbouni!

Narrator 1: Which means "Teacher" in Hebrew.

Jesus: Do not hold on to me, because I have not yet ascended to the Father. But go to my brothers and say to them, "I am ascending to my Father and your Father, to my God and your God."

Narrator 2: Mary Magdalene went and announced to the disciples,

Mary: I have seen the Lord! I have seen the Lord.

Narrator 1: And she told them that he had said these things to her.

Narrators 1 and 2: The gospel of the Lord.

April 13, 2017
Maundy Thursday

With nightfall our Lenten observance comes to an end, and we gather with Christians around the world to celebrate the Three Days of Jesus' death and resurrection. At the heart of the Maundy Thursday liturgy is Jesus' commandment to love one another. As Jesus washed the feet of his disciples, we are called to follow his example as we humbly care for one another, especially the poor and the unloved. At the Lord's table we remember Jesus' sacrifice of his life, even as we are called to offer ourselves in love for the life of the world.

Prayer of the Day

Holy God, source of all love, on the night of his betrayal, Jesus gave us a new commandment, to love one another as he loves us. Write this commandment in our hearts, and give us the will to serve others as he was the servant of all, your Son, Jesus Christ, our Savior and Lord, who lives and reigns with you and the Holy Spirit, one God, now and forever.

or

Eternal God, in the sharing of a meal your Son established a new covenant for all people, and in the washing of feet he showed us the dignity of service. Grant that by the power of your Holy Spirit these signs of our life in faith may speak again to our hearts, feed our spirits, and refresh our bodies, through Jesus Christ, our Savior and Lord, who lives and reigns with you and the Holy Spirit, one God, now and forever.

Gospel Acclamation

I give you a ˈ new commandment,* that you love one another just as I ˈ have loved you. (John 13:34)

Readings and Psalm

Exodus 12:1-4 [5-10] 11-14

Israel remembered its deliverance from slavery in Egypt by celebrating the festival of Passover. This festival featured the Passover lamb, whose blood was used as a sign to protect God's people from the threat of death. The early church described the Lord's supper using imagery from the Passover, especially in portraying Jesus as the lamb who delivers God's people from sin and death.

Psalm 116:1-2, 12-19

I will lift the cup of salvation and call on the name of the LORD. (Ps. 116:13)

1 Corinthians 11:23-26

In the bread and cup of the Lord's supper, we experience intimate fellowship with Christ and with one another, because it involves his body given for us and the new covenant in his blood. Faithful participation in this meal is a living proclamation of Christ's death until he comes in the future.

John 13:1-17, 31b-35

The story of the last supper in John's gospel recalls a remarkable event not mentioned elsewhere: Jesus performs the duty of a slave, washing the feet of his disciples and urging them to do the same for one another.

Preface   Maundy Thursday

Color   Scarlet *or* White

Prayers of Intercession

The prayers are prepared locally for each occasion. The following examples may be adapted or used as appropriate.

As Jesus calls us to love one another, let us pray for the church, the world, and all who are in need.

A brief silence.

We pray for the church: Gather us together through your love. Heal the divisions holding us apart, especially at your table. Unite us in our common mission to be your servants in the world. Lord, in your mercy,

hear our prayer.

For the earth: Sustain all living creatures with seasonable weather and suitable environments. Protect fragile habitats from harm. Bless farmers, ranchers, and gardeners whose labors bring food to our tables. Lord, in your mercy,

hear our prayer.

For the nations: Lead all in authority to work for peace and justice. Bring an end to oppression. Heal nations and communities torn apart by violence and fear (*especially*). Lord, in your mercy,

hear our prayer.

For those in need: Fill the tables of the hungry. Comfort those who know the pain of betrayal, and all who suffer from grief or illness (*especially*). Lord, in your mercy,

hear our prayer.

For this assembly: Bless those who guide us in worship and those who lead us into the world to serve in your name. Lord, in your mercy,

hear our prayer.

Here other intercessions may be offered.

With thanksgiving, we remember those who have died (*especially*). Bring us to the fullness of your promise of resurrection and eternal life in you. Lord, in your mercy,
hear our prayer.
Into your hands, gracious God, we commend all for whom we pray, in the name of the one who gave himself for us, Jesus Christ our Lord.
Amen.

Images in the Readings

A primary image for Maundy Thursday is the **servant**. We recall from Passion Sunday's Servant Song that the image of the servant is not a readily accessible symbol in today's society. Even the waitstaff in many restaurants now present themselves not as servants but as personal friends. John's gospel offers us a lowly, even dirty, task as appropriate for a true servant.

The readings are filled with **body**: the body of the dead lamb, cooked and eaten; the body of Christ, shared in the bread; the body of the neighbor's actual feet. For people who like to keep their individual space, it is countercultural to share in one another's body in this public way.

The first reading says that it is the lamb's **blood** that reminds God not to punish the Israelites, and Paul says that the wine is a new covenant in Jesus' blood. In the ancient world, life was seen as residing in the blood. Thus the pouring out of blood is the giving up of life. Isn't it interesting that small children lick a bleeding wound in hopes of keeping their blood inside their body?

In all three readings, the people of God experience themselves as a **meal** community. Humans must eat to live, and humans eat together to become and maintain community. The Israelites are to keep the Passover meal "as a perpetual ordinance"; Paul assumes and corrects the meal practice of the Corinthians; John describes the last loving meal Jesus had with his disciples before his arrest. So it is that over the centuries most Christian assemblies have shared a meal at their weekly meeting. The liturgy of the Three Days begins with this meal.

Ideas for the Day

- Jesus' washing of his disciples' feet is the sacramental act in John's account of the last supper. Consider including footwashing during worship, either by invitation to the entire assembly or symbolically by having a few worshipers wash one another's feet. Footwashing is a compelling preaching topic even if you don't perform the act during worship, and especially if you hope to add it to your practice next year. That Jesus washed the feet of his disciples has many possible meanings. Footwashing was a purifying ritual in ancient Jewish and Roman culture. It might have been done as a way for Jesus to show honor or friendship to his disciples, in which case, the act would have elevated the status of the disciples in relationship with God.

Footwashing could also have been a sign of Jesus' sacrificial love, which was going to become more tangible in the days to come (see Jaime Clark-Soles, "John 13: Of Footwashing and History," in *John, Jesus and History, Volume 2: Aspects of Historicity in the Fourth Gospel*, ed. Paul N. Anderson, Felix Just, and Tom Thatcher [Atlanta: Society of Biblical Literature, 2009], 261–267).

- Paul's account of the words of institution in 1 Corinthians is the earliest record of the celebration of communion in Christian communities. This sacrament connects us to the first communities of believers, reminding us that Christianity is much broader and more inclusive than any single worshiping community.

- The new commandment (in Latin, *mandatum*) of John 13:34 is the origin of the name for Maundy Thursday. How does your community take seriously the command to love one another as Jesus has loved us? This passage provides an opportunity to highlight the serving ministries of your congregation. The command to love one another is also a reminder of the mission of the church universal. On his last night with them before his execution, Jesus didn't command the disciples to attend worship, serve on church council, or tithe. Jesus commanded them to love one another. How can we embody that command today?

Connections with the Liturgy

In *Evangelical Lutheran Worship*'s Thanksgiving at the Table I, adapted from the 1958 *Service Book and Hymnal*'s compilation from ancient Christian sources, we cite this day's words of Paul: "For as often as we eat of this bread and drink from this cup, we proclaim the Lord's death until he comes."

Let the Children Come

The great Three Days are the most liturgically, theologically, and spiritually dramatic of our faith. When liturgy is engaging, beautiful, and intentional, it will be meaning making for all ages. Maundy Thursday is a celebration of love and Jesus' command to us to love. Children will want to wash and have their feet washed, and their ease will make the others assembled more comfortable. Holy communion is shared by all, some children not remembering a time they weren't welcomed at the table, some experiencing perhaps their first communion. And then we leave the bare church in silence. Liturgy is memory making and faith growing.

Assembly Song and Music for the Day

Because of the nature of this day, music suggestions are listed by place in the service and categorized by type of leadership (in brackets): Ch=Choral; CC=Children's Choir; KI=Keyboard/ Instrumental; HB=Handbell. Many suggestions require assembly participation.

Laying On of Hands

Our Father, we have wandered   ELW 606, WOV 733

Come, let us return   MSB1 S435

⊕ Guarani traditional. "Oré poriajú verekó/Lord, Have Mercy" from *Agape: Songs of Hope and Reconciliation*. U, inst. Lutheran World Federation. Out of print. Available on Amazon.com.

☼ Doerken, Brian/Josh Fox. "Broken and Beautiful" from CCLI.

☼ Morgan, Reuben. "This Is Our God" from CCLI.

Kemp, Helen. "A Lenten Love Song." U, kybd. CG CGA486. [Ch]

Patterson, Mark. "A Prayer for Humility." U, pno. CG CGA989. [CC]

Bach, J. S. "Sarabande" from *Cello Suite No. 3 in C Major*, BWV 1009. Vc. Various editions. [KI]

ᴾ Raney, Joel. "Amazing Grace (My Chains Are Gone)." 3-5 oct hb, opt hc, L3-, HOP 2683. Opt SATB vcs, HOP C5644. Opt SAB vcs, HOP C5807. Opt 2 pt vcs, HOP C5886. [HB]

Psalmody and Acclamations

Alonso, Tony. "Our Blessing Cup (Psalm 116)." SAB, cant, assembly, gtr, kybd, opt C inst, vc. WLP 006254.

Bell, John L. "I Love the Lord." SATB, assembly, kybd, vc. GIA G-8013.

McRae, Shirley W. "Psalm 116" from *ChildrenSing Psalms*. U, assembly, kybd, 5 hb. AFP 9780800663872.

ᴾ (GA) Organ, Anne Krentz. "Return to the Lord" with proper verse for Maundy Thursday. MSB1 S419.

Hymn of the Day

Great God, your love has called us   ELW 358, WOV 666   *RYBURN*

Jesu, Jesu, fill us with your love   ELW 708, WOV 765, TFF 83   *CHEREPONI*

Love consecrates the humblest act   ELW 360, LBW 122   *TWENTY-FOURTH*

Footwashing

Ubi caritas et amor   ELW 642, WOV 665

Where true charity and love abide   ELW 653

☼ Baloche, Paul/Robin Mark. "Heaven's Gates" from CCLI.

ᴾ Organ, Anne Krentz. "Love One Another." SATB. AFP 9780800659646. Also in *Augsburg Motet Book*. SATB. AFP 9781451423709. [Ch]

Demessieux, Jeanne. "Where True Charity and Love Abide" (Ubi caritas) from *Twelve Choral Preludes on Gregorian Chant Themes, Op. 8*. Org. ALF 9780874876031. [KI]

Setting the Table

Music Sourcebook for Lent and the Three Days (MSB1) includes an appendix with hymn stanzas appropriate for use during the setting of the table on this and other days. These stanzas are also included on the CD-ROM that accompanies the volume.

⊕ Sedio, Mark. "¿Cómo podré pagar al Señor? (How Can I Repay the Lord)" from *Global Choral Sounds*. SATB. CPH 98-3610.

☼ Romanacce, George/Alex Couch/Dave Fournier. "We Hunger and Thirst" from CCLI.

☼ Getty, Keith/Kristyn Getty/Stuart Townend. "Behold the Lamb" from CCLI.

Nelson, Ronald A. "If You Love One Another." U or 2 pt, kybd. SEL 422-841. [Ch or CC]

Kemp, Helen. "A Lenten Love Song." U, kybd. CG CGA486. [CC]

ᴾ♫ Kerr, J. Wayne. "Jesu, Jesu, Fill Us with Your Love" (Chereponi) from *Amen: World Hymns for Organ*. Org. AFP 9781451486018. [KI]

♫ Helman, Michael. "Jesu, Jesu, Fill Us with Your Love." 3-5 oct hb, opt 3 oct hc, L3. AFP 1111025. [HB]

Communion

Lord, who the night you were betrayed   ELW 463, LBW 206

When twilight comes   ELW 566, WOV 663

Lamb of God, pure and sinless   ELW 357, LBW 111

☼ Powell, Mac/Brad Avery/David Carr/Tai Anderson/Mark D. Lee. "Communion" from CCLI.

☼ Sterling, Robert, J./Paul Williams. "A Communion Contemplation (In Remembrance of Our Lord)" from CCLI.

Martin, Joseph M. "A Shadow Fell on Sharon's Rose." SATB, kybd. HL 35000088. [Ch]

Willard, Kelly. "Make Me a Servant" from *LifeSongs*. U, kybd. AFP 9780806642703. [CC]

ᴾ♫ Raabe, Nancy. "Jesu, Jesu, Fill Us with Your Love" (Chereponi) from *Grace and Peace, vol. 3: Hymn Portraits for Piano*. Pno. AFP 9780806696959. [KI]

ᴾ Stephenson, Valerie. "Abide with Me." 3-5 oct, L1+. CG CGB547. [HB]

Stripping of the Altar

Gelineau, Joseph. "Psalm 22" from ACYG.

Harbor, Rawn. "My God, My God (Psalm 22)." TFF 2.

ᴾ Highben, Zebulon. "Lord, I Cry to You (Psalm 88)." MSB1 S446.

Sending

None

⊕ = global song   ♫ = relates to hymn of the day
☼ = praise song   ᴾ = available in Prelude Music Planner

April 14, 2017
Good Friday

At the heart of the Good Friday liturgy is the passion according to John, which proclaims Jesus as a triumphant king who reigns from the cross. The ancient title for this day—the triumph of the cross—reminds us that the church gathers not to mourn this day but to celebrate Christ's life-giving passion and to find strength and hope in the tree of life. In the ancient bidding prayer we offer petitions for all the world for whom Christ died. Today's liturgy culminates in the Easter Vigil tomorrow evening.

Prayer of the Day

Almighty God, look with loving mercy on your family, for whom our Lord Jesus Christ was willing to be betrayed, to be given over to the hands of sinners, and to suffer death on the cross; who now lives and reigns with you and the Holy Spirit, one God, forever and ever.

or

Merciful God, your Son was lifted up on the cross to draw all people to himself. Grant that we who have been born out of his wounded side may at all times find mercy in him, Jesus Christ, our Savior and Lord, who lives and reigns with you and the Holy Spirit, one God, now and forever.

Gospel Acclamation

Look to Jesus, who for the sake of the joy that was set before him endured the cross, disregard-ˡing its shame,* and has taken his seat at the right hand of the ˡ throne of God. (Heb. 12:2)

Readings and Psalm

Isaiah 52:13—53:12

The fourth servant poem promises ultimate vindication for the servant, who made his life an offering for sin. The early church saw in the servant's pouring himself out to death and being numbered with the transgressors important keys for under-standing the death of Jesus.

Psalm 22

My God, my God, why have you forsaken me? (Ps. 22:1)

Hebrews 10:16-25

In the death of Jesus, forgiveness of sins is worked and access to God is established. Hence, when we gather together for wor-ship and when we love others we experience anew the benefits of Jesus' death.

or Hebrews 4:14-16; 5:7-9

In his death Jesus functions as great high priest who experi-ences temptation and suffering in order that we would receive mercy and find grace, because he is the source of true salvation.

John 18:1—19:42

On Good Friday, the story of Jesus' passion—from his arrest to his burial—is read in its entirety from the Gospel of John.

Holy communion is normally not celebrated on Good Friday; accordingly, no preface is provided. The worship space having been stripped on the preceding evening, no paraments are used today.

Prayers of Intercession

On Good Friday, the church's ancient Bidding Prayer is said or sung. See Evangelical Lutheran Worship Leaders Edition, *pp. 636-638.*

Images in the Readings

The **cross** was the electric chair of the Roman Empire, the means of execution for low-class criminals. Some cultures have used the shape of the cross as a sign of the four corners of the earth. Christians mark the newly baptized with this sign, God coming through suffering and death, aligned with all who are rejected, and surprisingly in this way bringing life to the whole earth. In the suggested sixth-century hymn "Sing, my tongue," the cross is paradoxically likened to the archetypal tree of life.

In John's passion narrative, Jesus of Nazareth is called King of the Jews, the Son of God, and most significantly, I AM, the very **name** of God. Christians see in the man dying on the cross the mystery of God's self-giving love. Along with the wit-nesses in John's passion, we can sing with the hymnwriter Car-oline Noel, "At the name of Jesus every knee shall bow, every tongue confess him king of glory now."

In the Israelite sacrificial system, the **lamb** represented the life of the nomadic herders, and killing the lamb symbol-ized a plea that God would receive the animal's death as a gift that would prompt divine mercy. The New Testament often uses the image of the lamb as one way to understand the mean-ing of Jesus' death. The book of Revelation recalls Good Friday and Easter in its paradoxical vision of a lamb seated on a throne and standing as if slaughtered.

But any single image—such as the lamb—is not suf-ficient. Thus we are given the opposite image, Christ as the **high priest** who does the slaughtering. According to Israelite religion, the people needed an intermediary to approach God. Christ then is the mediator who prays to God for us. Yet for John, Christ is the God whom our prayers address. Good Friday lays each image next to another one, for no single metaphor can fully explain the mystery of Christ.

Ideas for the Day

- Today's first reading is the last of four "servant songs" in Isaiah 40–55 (Second or Deutero-Isaiah). This section of Isaiah provides the earliest example of Hebrew prophecy focusing on comfort and consolation, rather than warning of disaster (John J. Collins, *An Introduction to the Hebrew Bible* [Fortress Press, 2004], 380–381). Today's verses reference resurrection and could imply that suffering in this life will lead to rewards in life eternal. In the original context, the servant may have signified the nation of Israel, with a promise for Israel's restoration after a period of exile. In the context of Good Friday worship, Jesus is naturally assumed to be the suffering servant. The Isaiah reading allows for this interpretation while opening up the door to an even broader understanding of sacrificial love.

- The passion narrative in John has Jesus crucified on Thursday, with the body removed from the cross before the Passover begins that day at sundown. The other gospels have Jesus crucified on Friday, the first full day of Passover. Consider the other differences between John and the synoptic gospels. On high holy days, it can be tempting to harmonize the gospel accounts of Jesus' life. Resist that impulse today, and tell the story wholly from the point of view of the fourth evangelist and the community for which he wrote.

- In the Gospel of John, as Jesus faces his impending death, he says, "I, when I am lifted up from the earth, will draw all people to myself" (John 12:32). The intercessions on Good Friday are unfolded in faith that as Jesus is lifted up on the cross, his compassion does indeed extend to all people and the whole cosmos. The Good Friday intercessions—the practice of which can be traced to the fifth century—invite the congregation to intercessory prayer that is as wide as the embrace of the cross. There may be no other liturgical occasion during the year in which the intercessory prayers extend so intentionally and fully to all of humanity and all of creation (*Worship Guidebook for Lent and the Three Days* [Augsburg Fortress, 2009], 120).

Connections with the Liturgy

The Sunday liturgy opens "in the name" of the triune God; we are baptized into this triune name of God. Christians say that it is because of the exaltation of Christ on the cross that we can call upon and be sheltered within the power of God's saving name. Each time Christians assemble, it is the mystery of the life-giving cross around which we gather. For Christians, no

meeting can be so totally celebrative that it does have at its core our faith in the salvific death of Christ.

For each day's morning and evening prayer, Martin Luther wrote, "you are to make the sign of the holy cross and say . . ." (*ELW*, pp. 1166, 1167). Many Christians choose, whenever they hear the name of God, the Father, the Son, and the Holy Spirit, to make the sign of the cross. With this hand gesture, we place the cross of Good Friday on our very bodies.

Let the Children Come

Truthfully, many adults would have the children skip the hard part of this epic story and go straight to Easter Sunday with the pastel dresses and candy, right? And by doing so, children miss out on the majesty of how Christ is still at work, even through weakness, suffering, and death. Perhaps the most powerful liturgical "tool" for children on this day is prayer. Introduce children to Psalm 22, the ancient words that Jesus turned to as he cried out from the cross. Find ways for the assembled children to move during the liturgical action, staying close to the safety of their parents.

Assembly Song and Music for the Day

Because of the nature of the Good Friday liturgy, music suggestions are listed by place in the service. Many suggestions require assembly participation. For services other than the liturgy of Good Friday, see "Additional Music Suggestions" below.

Gathering

None

Psalmody and Acclamations

Farlee, Robert Buckley. "Psalm 22" from PWA.

P St. Gregory of Nyssa Episcopal Church. "My God, My God (Psalm 22)." MSB1 S447.

P Pavlechko, Thomas. "Look to Jesus (Gospel Acclamation)." MSB1 S452.

Hymn of the Day

There in God's garden ELW 342, WOV 668 *SHADES MOUNTAIN*
Tree of Life and awesome mystery ELW 334 *THOMAS*
Sing, my tongue ELW 355 *PANGE LINGUA* ELW 356, LBW 118 *FORTUNATUS NEW*

Procession of the Cross: Dialogue

Alonso, Tony. "Behold the Wood of the Cross" from *Music for the Adoration of the Holy Cross*. SAB, cant, assembly, gtr, kybd. WLP 005292.

P Organ, Anne Krentz. "Behold the Life-Giving Cross" and "We Adore You, O Christ." MSB1 S459.

P = available in Prelude Music Planner

McGoff, Kevin G. "This Is the Wood of the Cross." SATB, assembly. Use with refrain or verses only. GIA G-7794.

P Pavlechko, Thomas. "Behold the Life-Giving Cross" and "We Adore You, O Christ." MSB1 S458.

Procession of the Cross: Solemn Reproaches

Iona Community. "Contemporary Reproaches" from *Enemy of Apathy*. Cant, assembly. GIA G-3647.

P Mummert, Mark. "Solemn Reproaches." MSB1 S462.

P Pavlechko, Thomas. "Solemn Reproaches." MSB1 S464.

de Victoria, Tomás/arr. Geoffrey Cox. "The Reproaches." SATB, cant, a cap. OCP 4525.

Procession of the Cross: We Glory in Your Cross

P Organ, Anne Krentz. "We Glory in Your Cross." MSB1 S466.

P Pavlechko, Thomas. "We Glory in Your Cross." MSB1 S467.

Pearson, Donald. "We Glory in Your Cross, O Lord." SAB, a cap. OCP 4537.

Procession of the Cross: Other Choral Music

Alonso, Tony. "Faithful Cross" from *Music for the Adoration of the Holy Cross*. SAB, cant, assembly, gtr, kybd. WLP 005292.

P Jennings, Carolyn. "Ah, Holy Jesus." 2 pt trbl, vc. AFP 9780800645151.

P Shaw, Timothy. "Ah, Holy Jesus." SATB. AFP 9781451451535.

Hymn of Triumph

Holy God, holy and glorious ELW 637

Adoramus te Christe MSB1 S469

What wondrous love is this ELW 666, LBW 385

♫ Haugen, Marty. "Tree of Life." SATB, assembly, org, C inst. GIA G-2944.

P♫ Scott, K. Lee. "The Tree of Life" (There in God's Garden). SATB, assembly, org, opt br qt, opt hb. MSM 50-3000.

Additional Music Suggestions

The suggestions listed below may also be appropriate, especially for services other than the liturgy of Good Friday.

Assembly Songs

⊕ Bell, John L. "Lo, I Am with You" from *There Is One Among Us*. SAB. GIA G-5111.

⊕ Hontiveros, Eduardo P. "Behold the Man We Nailed on the Cross" from *Sound the Bamboo*. U. GIA G-6830.

☼ Baloche, Paul/Kathryn Scott. "You Gave Your Life Away" from CCLI.

☼ Blakesley, Josh/Mia Fieldes/Sarah Hart/Sarah Kroger. "Run to the Cross" from CCLI.

☼ Dearman, Kirk/Jessie Brown Pounds. "The Way of the Cross Leads Home" from CCLI.

☼ Getty, Keith/Stuart Townend. "Gethsemane" from CCLI.

☼ Redman, Matt. "The Way of the Cross" from CCLI.

☼ Smith, Timothy R. "Wondrous Loss" from *Spirit and Song*, vol. 2. OCP.

Choral

See above under "Procession of the Cross: Other Choral Music" and "Hymn of Triumph."

Children's Choir

African American spiritual. "Were You There" from *LifeSongs*. U, kybd. AFP 9780806642703.

Burrows, Mark. "Love Can Never End" from *Again, I Say Rejoice!* U, pno. CG CGC56.

Simon, Julia. "Why the Cross?" U, opt 2 or 3 pt, pno. AFP 9780800679163.

Keyboard / Instrumental

P♫ Farlee, Robert Buckley. "There in God's Garden" (Shades Mountain) from *Treasures Old and New: Hymn Preludes for Organ*. Org. AFP 9781451499094.

Kuhnau, Johann (1660–1722). "O Sacred Head, Now Wounded" (Herzlich tut mich verlangen) from *Two Lenten Chorale Preludes*. Org. MSM 10-321.

♫ Organ, Anne Krentz. "There in God's Garden" (Shades Mountain) from *Woven Together: Reflections and Intonations for Piano and Solo Instrument*. B flat or C inst, pno. AFP 9780800658168.

P♫ Wahl, Carol. "Tree of Life and Awesome Mystery" (Thomas) from *Cry of the Dove: Piano Settings*. Pno. AFP 9781451479614.

Handbell

P Bettcher, Peggy. "Alas! And Did My Savior Bleed." 3-5 oct hb, opt 2 oct hc, L2+. HOP 2677.

♫ Kerr, J. Wayne. "There in God's Garden." 3-5 oct, fl, L2. MSM 30-820.

♫ Nelson, Susan. "A Plainchant Meditation." 3 oct, L3. AFP 1110696.

⊕ = global song   ♫ = relates to hymn of the day
☼ = praise song   P = available in Prelude Music Planner

April 15, 2017
Resurrection of Our Lord
Vigil of Easter

This is the night! This is our Passover with Christ from darkness to light, from bondage to freedom, from death to life. Tonight is the heart of our celebration of the Three Days and the pinnacle of the church's year. The resurrection of Christ is proclaimed in word and sign, and we gather around a pillar of fire, hear ancient stories of our faith, welcome new sisters and brothers at the font, and share the food and drink of the promised land. Raised with Christ, we go forth into the world, aflame with the good news of the resurrection.

Prayer of the Day

Eternal giver of life and light, this holy night shines with the radiance of the risen Christ. Renew your church with the Spirit given us in baptism, that we may worship you in sincerity and truth and may shine as a light in the world, through your Son, Jesus Christ our Lord, who lives and reigns with you and the Holy Spirit, one God, now and forever.

or

O God, you are the creator of the world, the liberator of your people, and the wisdom of the earth. By the resurrection of your Son free us from our fears, restore us in your image, and ignite us with your light, through Jesus Christ, our Savior and Lord, who lives and reigns with you and the Holy Spirit, one God, now and forever.

Gospel Acclamation

Alleluia. Let us sing to the Lord, who has ˈ triumphed gloriously;* our strength and our might, who has become ˈ our salvation. *Alleluia.* (Exod. 15:1-2)

Vigil Readings and Responses

Readings marked with an asterisk are not omitted.

*1 Genesis 1:1—2:4a

Creation

Response: Psalm 136:1-9, 23-26

God's mercy endures forever. (Ps. 136:1)

2 Genesis 7:1-5, 11-18; 8:6-18; 9:8-13

Flood

Response: Psalm 46

The Lord of hosts is with us; the God of Jacob is our stronghold. (Ps. 46:7)

3 Genesis 22:1-18

Testing of Abraham

Response: Psalm 16

You will show me the path of life. (Ps. 16:11)

*4 Exodus 14:10-31; 15:20-21

Deliverance at the Red Sea

Response: Exodus 15:1b-13, 17-18

I will sing to the Lord, who has triumphed gloriously. (Exod. 15:1)

*5 Isaiah 55:1-11

Salvation freely offered to all

Response: Isaiah 12:2-6

With joy you will draw water from the wells of salvation. (Isa. 12:3)

6 Proverbs 8:1-8, 19-21; 9:4b-6
or **Baruch 3:9-15, 32—4:4**

The wisdom of God

Response: Psalm 19

The statutes of the Lord are just and rejoice the heart. (Ps. 19:8)

7 Ezekiel 36:24-28

A new heart and a new spirit

Response: Psalms 42 and 43

I thirst for God, for the living God. (Ps. 42:2)

8 Ezekiel 37:1-14

Valley of the dry bones

Response: Psalm 143

Revive me, O Lord, for your name's sake. (Ps. 143:11)

9 Zephaniah 3:14-20

The gathering of God's people

Response: Psalm 98

Lift up your voice, rejoice, and sing. (Ps. 98:4)

10 Jonah 1:1—2:1

The deliverance of Jonah

Response: Jonah 2:2-3 [4-6] 7-9

Deliverance belongs to the Lord. (Jonah 2:9)

11 Isaiah 61:1-4, 9-11

Clothed in the garments of salvation

Response: Deuteronomy 32:1-4, 7, 36a, 43a

Great is our God, the Rock, whose ways are just. (Deut. 32:3-4)

*12 Daniel 3:1-29

Deliverance from the fiery furnace

Response: Song of the Three 35-65

Praise and magnify the Lord forever. (Song of Thr. 35)

New Testament Reading and Gospel

Romans 6:3-11

We were incorporated into the death of Jesus Christ in baptism and so were liberated from the dominion of sin. We also anticipate that we will be incorporated into the resurrection of Christ and so will be liberated from the hold death has over our mortal bodies.

John 20:1-18

John's gospel describes the confusion and excitement of the first Easter: the stone is moved, disciples race back and forth, and angels speak to a weeping woman. Then, Jesus himself appears.

Preface   Easter

Color   White *or* Gold

Prayers of Intercession

The prayers are prepared locally for each occasion. The following examples may be adapted or used as appropriate.

Rejoicing in the risen life of Christ, let us pray for the church, the world, and all who are in need.

A brief silence.

We pray for the church. Renew it and unite your people in mission. Heal the wounds caused by division and empower the ministry of all women and men who proclaim the gospel. Lord, in your mercy,

hear our prayer.

For the earth. For oceans and woodlands, prairies and mountains, lakes and rivers. For creatures who move upon the land, in the waters, and through the air. Make us good stewards of creation. Lord, in your mercy,

hear our prayer.

For the nations. For those we name as friends and those we call our enemies. For all who govern. For those who work for peace and those who protect the weak and vulnerable. Lord, in your mercy,

hear our prayer.

For those in need. For those affected by flooding, earthquake, windstorm, fire, or drought. For refugees and those who are persecuted for their faith. For the grieving and those who are sick (*especially*). Lord, in your mercy,

hear our prayer.

For this assembly. For the newly baptized (*those baptized this night may be named*) and for those who affirm their faith. For pastors, teachers, and spiritual mentors. For those who seek a deeper relationship with you and with the church. Lord, in your mercy,

hear our prayer.

Here other intercessions may be offered.

Trusting in the promise of resurrection and life, we remember those who have died (*especially*). Bring us all to the fullness of your glory where your saints sing alleluias without end. Lord, in your mercy,

hear our prayer.

Joining our voices with your faithful ones in every time and place, we offer our prayers in the name of the Risen One, Jesus Christ our Lord.

Amen.

Images in the Readings

At the beginning of the Vigil, Christ is symbolized by the candle, which gives **light** to our darkness, and whose light remains bright even when we all share in its flame. The early church called baptism enlightenment. Sharing this light outdoors in darkness makes the image emotionally effective.

Each reading offers an image with which to picture salvation: the earth is God's perfect creation; we are saved in the ark during the flood; we are granted a reprieve from sacrifice; we escape the enemy army; we are enlivened by spring rains; we are instructed by Woman Wisdom; we are given a new heart; our bones are brought back to life; we enjoy a homeland; swallowed by the fish, we do not drown but are coughed up on dry ground; we wear party clothes; thrown into a furnace, we emerge untouched by the fire; we are risen with Christ; and although we do mistake Christ for the gardener, he appears to us and enlivens our faith.

Ideas for the Day

- The Vigil of Easter is an immersion into the paschal mystery. The twelve Old Testament readings tell this story with texts that almost beg for illustration. This is an excellent opportunity to use artwork to deepen the encounter with the word. The use of projection can allow for a series of art images to correspond with the readings. Use of art from a wide variety of eras and cultures speaks to the universal message of the gospel. Consider some of these contemporary biblical artists as a resource: He Qi, Sadao Watanabe, Jim Janknegt, and Martin Erspamer. The website christianmodernart.com lists many artists. Be sure to obtain permission where required.

- Creating art can be a meaningful way to prepare for the Vigil, especially if baptism or affirmation of baptism is planned. A vibrant catechumenate ministry could include a Lenten project of creating visual representations of the Vigil readings. Even those who don't think of themselves as artistic can make use of color, words, and shapes or create a collage. In a twist on the fourteen stations of the cross, the twelve Old Testament readings, plus the readings from Romans and the gospel, could be the fourteen stations of the resurrection. These images could be carried in procession for the readings portion of the service, and then they could be gathered around the font for baptism/affirmation of baptism, giving witness to the story into which we are baptized.

- Everything about the Vigil of Easter relates to baptism and the paschal mystery. Making generous use of water on this night helps make this connection palpable and celebratory. Even in congregations that don't normally sprinkle, you can do so on this night. A generous and splashy use of water during the Litany of the Saints or Apostles' Creed adds playful delight. If your font is not large or the water not easily accessible by the assembly, consider having a large container of water, such as a galvanized tub or tank, to allow everyone to participate in the baptismal connections of this night with joyful exuberance. A small recirculating pump can create the sound of flowing water throughout the liturgy.

Connections with the Liturgy

Since the first century, the primary day for Christians to assemble around word and sacrament has been Sunday, because every Sunday is understood as the day of resurrection. The preface to the eucharistic prayer for standard Sundays says of Jesus Christ, he "on this day overcame death and the grave, and by his glorious resurrection opened to us the way of everlasting life."

Let the Children Come

The Easter Vigil, our most sacred, central worship, borrows the language of children: story. Woven into the story are the wild elements of the universe: fire, water, song, and light. It may be tempting to concede that this worship is too long or too late for little ones, but the assembly is not complete on this holiest of dawns without them. This might be the time for pajamas in the pew, as well as your most attentive planning. The fire, the procession, the baptisms, and most of all, the telling of the stories, must be engaging and accessible for all ages.

Assembly Song and Music for the Day

Because of the nature of this day, music suggestions are listed by place in the service and categorized by type of leadership (in brackets): Ch=Choral; CC=Children's Choir; KI=Keyboard/Instrumental; HB=Handbell. Many suggestions require assembly participation.

Fire and Procession

Alonso, Tony. "This Is the Night: Procession of the Paschal Candle and Exsultet." SATB, cant, assembly, kybd, gtr, opt fl, ob, vc. WLP 005314.

P Highben, Zebulon. "Processional Refrains (Stanza 1)." MSB1 S471.

Easter Proclamation

Alonso, Tony. "This Is the Night: Procession of the Paschal Candle and Exsultet." SATB, cant, assembly, kybd, gtr, opt fl, ob, vc. WLP 005314.

Farrell, Bernadette. "Christ, Be Our Light (Easter Vigil Text)." Assembly, opt cant, kybd, gtr, fl, tpt. OCP 11502.

Hillebrand, Paul. "Exsultet." Cant, SATB, assembly, kybd, gtr. OCP 30113062.

P Plainsong. "Easter Proclamation (Exsultet)." MSB1 S473.

Vigil Readings and Responses

Responses to each reading are included in Music Sourcebook for Lent and the Three Days *(MSB1) and* Psalter for Worship Year A. *Related hymns are listed in* Indexes to Evangelical Lutheran Worship. *The responses listed below are from other resources.*

1 Creation

Many and great, O God ELW 837, WOV 794

Cooney, Rory. "Genesis Reading for the Great Vigil." SATB, cant, assembly, kybd, gtr, fl. GIA G-5018.

P Horman, John. "It's Good" from *Sing the Stories of God's People*. U, kybd. AFP 9781451460438. [CC]

Lisicky, Paul. "God's Love Is Everlasting." SATB, cant, assembly, kybd, fl, gtr. WLP 007743.

2 Flood

"A River Flows." *Psallite* A-238. Cant or SATB, assembly, kybd.

Moore, James E., Jr. "Be Still." SATB, assembly, kybd, gtr. GIA G-5731.

Summers, Roger. "It Wasn't Even Raining!" U or 2 pt, pno. LOR 10/2664K. [CC]

3 Testing of Abraham

Haas, David. "The Easter Vigil in the Holy Night: After the Second Reading" from COJ:S.

Lawton, Liam. "Evermore I'll Sing Your Praise." Cant, assembly, kybd, gtr. GIA G-5294.

P = available in Prelude Music Planner

Stachowski, Zack. "Keep Me Safe." U or 2 pt choir, assembly, kybd, gtr, opt ob, str qrt. GIA G-8324.

4 Deliverance at the Red Sea

Cooney, Rory. "Exodus Reading for the Great Vigil." SATB, cant, assembly, kybd, gtr, opt fl. GIA G-4117.

Duncan, Norah IV. "Easter Vigil III" from LP:LG.

P Schulz-Widmar, Russell. "Miriam Dances at the Red Sea." SATB, kybd or br, opt perc. AFP 9780800621476. [Ch]

5 Salvation freely offered to all

Haas, David. "The Easter Vigil in the Holy Night: After the Fifth Reading" from COJ:S.

Haugen, Marty. "With Joy You Shall Draw Water" from PCY, vol. 2.

6 The wisdom of God

"Your Word Is Life, Lord." *Psallite* A-58. Cant or SATB, assembly, kybd.

Alonso, Tony. "Lord, You Have the Words of Everlasting Life" from TLP:S.

7 A new heart and a new spirit

"Like a Deer That Longs for Running Streams." *Psallite* A-59. Cant or SATB, assembly, kybd.

Kean, Daniel. "Psalm 42." SATB, cant, assembly, pno, ob. GIA G-4895 and G-4895INST.

☼ Ligertwood, Brooke/Scoot Ligertwood. "Beneath the Waters (I Will Rise)" from CCLI.

True, Lori. "The Easter Vigil in the Holy Night: After the Seventh Reading" from COJ:S.

8 Valley of the dry bones

Daw, Carl P. Jr. "Hear My Prayer, O God" (Hymn Chant) from PAS 143A.

Hopson, Hal. "Psalm 143" from TPP.

9 The gathering of God's people

Bruxvoort Colligan, Richard. "Shout for Joy (Psalm 98)" from *Shout for Joy*. AFP 9780806698632.

Christopherson, Dorothy. "Psalm 98" from *ChildrenSing Psalms*. U, assembly, kybd, fc, tamb. AFP 9780800663872.

10 The deliverance of Jonah

Guimont, Michel. "Easter Vigil X" from PRCL.

Horman, John D. "Jonah" from *Sing the Stories of God's People*. U, kybd. AFP 9780806698397. [CC]

Pavlechko, Thomas. "Jonah 2:2-3 [4-6] 7-9" from PSCY.

11 Clothed in the garments of salvation

Guimont, Michel. "Easter Vigil XI" from PRCL.

Mummert, Mark. "Deuteronomy 32:1-4, 7, 36a, 43a" from PSCY.

12 Deliverance from the fiery furnace

P Jennings, Kenneth. "All You Works of the Lord, Bless the Lord." SATB, org. AFP 9780800645311. [Ch]

Joncas, Jan Michael. "Canticle of the Three Young Men." SATB, assembly, 2 cant, org. GIA G-8441.

MacKenzie, Valerie. "Cool under Fire." U, pno. Canadian International Music, dist. LOR. CIM 1051. [CC]

Proulx, Richard. "Song of the Three Children." U, 2 pt, assembly, org, tamb, tri, fc, drm. GIA G-1863. [Ch or CC]

Gospel Acclamation

French, Paul M. " Alleluia and Psalm 118." SATB, assembly, cant, org. MSM 80-319. [Ch]

⊕ Halle, halle, hallelujah ELW 172, WOV 612, TFF 25

Procession to the Font

Springs of water, bless the Lord ELW 214

I bind unto myself today ELW 450, LBW 188

Litany of the Saints ELW 237

P Highben, Zebulon. "Processional Refrains (Stanza 2)." MSB1 S471.

⊕ Neto Rodolfo Gaede. "For the Troubles and the Sufferings/ *Pelas dores destem undo*" from *Glory to God*. U. WJK 0664238971.

Setting the Table

Music Sourcebook for Lent and the Three Days includes an appendix with hymn stanzas appropriate for use during the setting of the table on this and other days. These stanzas are also included on the CD-ROM that accompanies the volume.

Our Paschal Lamb, that sets us free MSB1 S499, WOV 679

Now the green blade rises ELW 379, LBW 148, LLC 357

At the Lamb's high feast we sing ELW 362, LBW 210

☼ Fike, Richie/Travis Ryan/Brandon Collins/Jennie Lee Riddle. "God, You Reign (You Are Holy)" from CCLI.

☼ Maher, Matt/Marc Byrd. "On the Third Day" from CCLI.

Brighton, James. "The Heavens Declare the Glory of God." U, assembly, hb, opt hc, ob. CG CGA1172. [CC]

P Kerr, J. Wayne. "All You Works of God, Bless the Lord" (Linstead) from *Amen: World Hymns for Organ*. Org. AFP 9781451486018. [KI]

Blair, Dallas. "At the Lamb's High Feast We Sing" (Sonne der Gerechtigkeit) from *Hymn Introductions and Descants for Trumpet and Organ, Set 1*. Tpt, org. MSM 20-400. [KI]

Afdahl, Lee. "At the Lamb's High Feast." 3-5 oct hb, opt 2 oct hc, L2+. CPH 97-7309. [HB]

⊕ = global song   ♫ = relates to hymn of the day

☼ = praise song   P = available in Prelude Music Planner

Communion

At the Lamb's high feast we sing ELW 362, LBW 210

Oh, Mary, don't you weep TFF 88

We who once were dead ELW 495, LBW 207

☼ Getty, Keith/Kristyn Getty/Stuart Townend. "Come People of the Risen King" from CCLI.

☼ Hughes, Tim/Ben Cantelon. "Happy Day" from CCLI.

Busarow, Donald. "Good Christian Friends, Rejoice and Sing." SAB, C inst, kybd. MSM 50-4406. [Ch]

P Patterson, Mark. "Alleluia, Christ Is Risen" from *ChildrenSing: Seven Anthems for Elementary Age Singers*. U, pno. AFP 9780800677695. [CC]

P Carter, John. "Wade in the Water" (Wade in the Water) from *Spirituals for Piano*. Pno. AFP 9780800621698. [KI]

Wissinger, Kathleen. "Broken for You." 3-5 oct, L3. AGEHR AG35179. [HB]

Sending

Christ has arisen, alleluia ELW 364, TFF 96, WOV 678, LLC 349

The strife is o'er, the battle done ELW 366, LBW 135, LLC 352

The day of resurrection! ELW 361, LBW 141

Bach, J. S. "Heut triumphieret Gottes Sohn," BWV 630, from *Orgelbüchlein*. Org. Various editions. [KI]

Blair, Dallas. "This Joyful Eastertide" (Vruechten) from *Hymn Introductions and Descants for Trumpet and Organ, Set 1*. Tpt, org. MSM 20-400. [KI]

Gramann, Fred. "Alleluia! The Strife Is O'er." 3-6 oct hb, L2+. LOR 20/1377L. Full score with opt org. LOR 20/1378L. [HB]

April 16, 2017
Resurrection of Our Lord
Easter Day

On this day the Lord has acted! On the first day of the week God began creation, transforming darkness into light. On this, the "eighth day" of the week, Jesus Christ was raised from the dead. We celebrate this new creation in the waters of baptism and in the feast of victory. With great joy we celebrate this day of days, even as we begin the great fifty days of Easter. Filled with hope, we go forth to share the news that Christ is risen!

Prayer of the Day

O God, you gave your only Son to suffer death on the cross for our redemption, and by his glorious resurrection you delivered us from the power of death. Make us die every day to sin, that we may live with him forever in the joy of the resurrection, through your Son, Jesus Christ our Lord, who lives and reigns with you and the Holy Spirit, one God, now and forever.
or
God of mercy, we no longer look for Jesus among the dead, for he is alive and has become the Lord of life. Increase in our minds and hearts the risen life we share with Christ, and help us to grow as your people toward the fullness of eternal life with you, through Jesus Christ, our Savior and Lord, who lives and reigns with you and the Holy Spirit, one God, now and forever.

Gospel Acclamation

Alleluia. Christ, our paschal lamb, | has been sacrificed.* Therefore, let us | keep the feast. *Alleluia.* (1 Cor. 5:7, 8)

Readings and Psalm
Acts 10:34-43

Peter's sermon, delivered at the home of Cornelius, a Roman army officer, is a summary of the essential message of Christianity: Everyone who believes in Jesus, whose life, death, and resurrection fulfilled the words of the prophets, "receives forgiveness of sins through his name."

or Jeremiah 31:1-6

This passage makes clear that God's final word is always "Yes." Because God's love is everlasting, God always remains faithful. Ancient Israel is assured that it will be rebuilt and have plentiful crops. The people of God too will ultimately be reunited.

Psalm 118:1-2, 14-24

This is the day that the LORD has made; let us rejoice and be glad in it. (Ps. 118:24)

Colossians 3:1-4

Easter means new life for us as it first meant new life for Christ. His resurrection reshapes the entire focus and motivation for our lives, since we are now hidden with the risen Christ in God.

☼ = praise song   P = available in Prelude Music Planner

or **Acts 10:34-43**

See above.

Matthew 28:1-10

Sorrow gives way to "fear and great joy" when two women are sent by an angel to proclaim the good news: Jesus is risen!

or **John 20:1-18**

John's gospel describes the confusion and excitement of the first Easter: the stone is moved, disciples race back and forth, and angels speak to a weeping woman. Then, Jesus himself appears.

Preface Easter

Color White *or* Gold

Prayers of Intercession

The prayers are prepared locally for each occasion. The following examples may be adapted or used as appropriate.

Rejoicing in the resurrection of Christ, let us pray for the church, the world, and all who are in need.

A brief silence.

We pray for the church. Unite all Christians in our shared calling to proclaim the gospel. Raise up women and men to serve as faithful leaders. Make us bold witnesses to the resurrection. Lord, in your mercy,

hear our prayer.

For the earth. Renew your creation with seasonable weather and growth. Protect plants and animals from the damage of excessive heat or cold, drought or flooding, windstorm or hail. Lord, in your mercy,

hear our prayer.

For the nations. Bring peace to communities torn apart by warfare (*especially*). Guide all refugees to safety. Bolster the courage of those who put themselves in danger to preserve the lives of others. Lord, in your mercy,

hear our prayer.

For those in need. Shelter the homeless. Protect those who suffer abuse or neglect. Befriend the lonely. Give peace to the dying, comfort the bereaved, and heal the sick (*especially*). Lord, in your mercy,

hear our prayer.

For this assembly. Free us from fear, and renew us in faith. Bless the newly baptized, those who seek to know your love, and all who come to your holy table. Lord, in your mercy,

hear our prayer.

Here other intercessions may be offered.

With thanksgiving, we remember those who have died (*especially*) and all who yearn for the fulfillment of your Easter promise of resurrection and life. Lord, in your mercy,

hear our prayer.

Joining our voices with your faithful ones in every time and place, we offer our prayers in the name of the Risen One, Jesus Christ our Lord.

Amen.

Images in the Readings

Matthew's accounts of the crucifixion (27:51) and the resurrection (28:2) include **earthquakes**. The eastern Mediterranean area is prone to earthquakes. Although we explain earthquakes in geological terms, often at theophanies or in apocalyptic material in the Hebrew Scriptures earthquakes are interpreted as manifestations of God's power. Matthew means to say that the entire world was shaken by the actions of God at the tomb.

In biblical symbolism, **angels** are messengers of God, extensions of the power of God. The description of angels attending God suggests that heaven resembles an ancient royal court in which the monarch has servants who carry out the sovereign's will. Like the Elohist source of the Old Testament, Matthew has people seeing an angel, rather than seeing the being of God. Luther's morning and evening prayers ask for God's presence in the form of "your holy angel."

The language of being **raised** from death relies on the commonplace human idea, evident in speech and story, that up is good and down is bad. The ancient three-tier universe placed divine powers on the top level, humans in the middle—between life and death—and the dead below the earth. In today's readings, God raised Jesus (Acts), we go up to Zion (Jeremiah), Christ is above at the right hand of God (Colossians), and the angel descends like lightning. Current scientific understandings of the universe teach us that there is no "up." Thus this language must function for us symbolically: up is life, down is death.

Ideas for the Day

- The Gospel of Matthew places the death and resurrection of Jesus in the context of the Roman Empire of death resisting God's empire of life enacted in Jesus. In the resurrection story, Pilate and the religious leaders send guards to make sure the tomb is secure. When the heavenly messenger appears and rolls back the stone to announce the good news, the guards shake with fear and are like dead men. This turnaround shows the ironic character of the good news. The guards are now dead men. Jesus is alive. The empire of death is dead. The empire of God's life-giving power rules. How can irony in the Easter sermon show forth all the powers of death and oppression today so their power is seen to be dead? How can the power of God's reign of life be shown to be alive?

- The Acts reading includes the suggestive verse: "They put him to death by hanging him on a tree" (Acts 10:39). In his book *The Cross and the Lynching Tree* (Maryknoll, NY: Orbis, 2011), James Cone details the powerful connections between the crucifixion of Jesus and the lynching of African Americans and others. Easter can be a time to proclaim the hope of God's power to overcome injustice and death. This hope empowers Christians who face oppression to rise above any empire or system of injustice and proclaim liberation and maintain identity. The history of African American churches is a witness to the power of faith in the gospel in the face of the cross and the lynching tree.

- Colossians proclaims the strange news that "you have died, and your life is hidden with Christ in God" (Col. 3:3). The message is that we are halfway to resurrection, and the hard part, death, has already taken place. We might not feel it to be true, but baptism unites us with Christ in death. The hardest part of the paschal mystery has already taken place. We are halfway to the fullness of resurrection with Christ. When have you experienced being halfway on a journey and realized the hardest part was already behind you?

Connections with the Liturgy

Every Sunday is a celebration of the resurrection. Thus each Sunday's worship includes references to today's readings. "On the third day he rose again," we affirm in the Nicene Creed. "He descended to the dead. On the third day he rose again," says the Apostles' Creed. "Christ has died, Christ is risen," we may call out during the eucharistic prayer. When we receive the dismissal, it is as if we are the women seeing the risen Christ: "Go in peace. Share the good news."

Let the Children Come

Let the whole cosmos proclaim, Hallelujah! The Easter story in the Gospel of Matthew seems to reflect that the earth itself is rumbling and rejoicing at Jesus' resurrection from the dead. Our Lent began with recognizing our bondage to death and sin, with all of creation; ash, snake, tree, garden, humankind. Throughout Lent we received clues that God promises to bring life out of death for all creatures. And this is the morning we hear that even the earth shakes with joy! How do your Easter celebrations model for children how we are to care for all creatures in our shared new life?

Assembly Song
Gathering

We know that Christ is raised   ELW 449, LBW 189
Now all the vault of heaven resounds   ELW 367, LBW 143
Jesus Christ is risen today   ELW 365, LBW 151, LLC 355

Psalmody and Acclamations

Rennick, Charles. "This Is the Day the Lord Has Made." SATB, cant, assembly, org, hb, br qrt, timp. GIA G-4804 and G-4804INST.

Shields, Valerie. "Psalm for Easter." SATB, cant, assembly, org, opt tpt, hb, perc. MSM 80-405.

Shute, Linda Cable. "This Is the Day." SATB, assembly, kybd, opt hb, C inst. AFP 9780800659745.

(GA) Ferguson, John. "Gospel Processional." SATB, org, tpt, assembly. AFP 9780800677084.

(GA) Haas, David. "Alleluia: Our God Is Speaking." SATB, cant, assembly, kybd, gtr, 2 C inst. GIA G-7727.

Hymn of the Day

Christ Jesus lay in death's strong bands   ELW 370, LBW 134
CHRIST LAG IN TODESBANDEN
The strife is o'er, the battle done   ELW 366, LBW 135, LLC 352
VICTORY
Christ has arisen, alleluia   ELW 364, TFF 96, WOV 678, LLC 349   *MFURAHINI, HALELUYA*

Offering

Christ is arisen   ELW 372, LBW 136, LLC 356
Be not afraid   ELW 388

Communion

Hail thee, festival day!   ELW 394, LBW 142
Awake, my heart, with gladness   ELW 378, LBW 129
Now the green blade rises   ELW 379, LBW 148, LLC 357

Sending

Christ is alive! Let Christians sing   ELW 389, LBW 363
Good Christian friends, rejoice and sing!   ELW 385, LBW 144

Additional Assembly Songs

Low in the grave he lay   TFF 94
In the fair morning   OBS 68
God's Paschal Lamb is sacrificed for us   MSB1 S498
⊕ Sosa, Pablo. "Éste es el Día/This Is the Day" from *Éste es el Día*. U. GIA G-7021.
⊕ Toppenberg, Edouard. "Hallelu, Let the People All Sing" from *Let the Peoples Sing*. SATB. AFP 9780800675394.
☼ Claude, Ely. "Ain't No Grave (Gonna Hold This Body Down)" from *American IV: Ain't No Grave*.
☼ Cottrell, Travis/David Moffitt/Sue C. Smith. "Alive Forever Amen" from CCLI.
☼ Cottrell, Travis/David Moffitt/Sue C. Smith. "The Lamb Has Overcome" from CCLI.
☼ Crocker, Matt/Brooke Ligertwood. "Man of Sorrows" from CCLI.
☼ Johnson, Jenn/Ian McIntosh/Gabriel Wilson. "For the Cross" from CCLI.
☼ Marino, Paul/James McGranahan/Jeremy Johnson. "Hallelujah for the Cross" from CCLI.

⊕ = global song   ♫ = relates to hymn of the day
☼ = praise song   P = available in Prelude Music Planner

Music for the Day
Choral

P ♫ Bach, J. S. "Christ Jesus Lay in Death's Strong Bands" from *Bach for All Seasons*. SATB, kybd. AFP 9780800658540.

P Ellingboe, Bradley. "The Chief Cornerstone." 2 pt mxd, kybd, opt tpt. AFP 9780800676391.

P Larter, Evelyn. "I Know That My Redeemer Lives (Shout On)." SATB, pno, fl. AFP 9781451492507.

P ♫ Norris, Bradley R. "Easter Anthem in Celtic Style: Christ Jesus Lay in Death's Strong Bands." SATB, pno, opt fc, opt cym. AFP 9781451492453.

Children's Choir

McRae, Shirley. "Now the Green Blade Rises." U/2 pt, fl, hb, tamb. CG CGA795.

P Schram, Ruth Elaine. "Now All the Vault of Heaven Resounds." U/2 pt, kybd, opt C instr. AFP 9780800678388.

P Young, Carolton. "When Christ Arose" from *ChildrenSing in Worship*. U, kybd, opt hb. AFP 9781451401806.

Keyboard / Instrumental

P ♫ Biery, James. "Christ Has Arisen, Alleluia" (Mfurahini, haleluya) from *The Paschal Lamb: Easter Settings for Organ*. Org. AFP 9781451494099.

P ♫ Linneweber, Edie. "Alleluia! Jesus Is Risen" (Earth and All Stars) from *Christ Is Near: Hymn Settings for the Church Pianist*. Pno. AFP 9781451401158.

P Powell, Robert J. *Easter Carillon*. Br qrt, timp, org. MSM 20-449.

P ♫ Raabe, Nancy. "Christ Has Arisen, Alleluia" (Mfurahini, haleluya) from *Grace and Peace, vol. 2: Hymn Portraits for Piano*. Pno. AFP 9780800679019.

Verhaalen, S. Marion. *Outburst for Trumpet and Organ*. Tpt, org. AFP 11-7633.

Handbell

♫ Gramann, Fred. "Alleluia! The Strife Is O'er." 3-6 oct hb, L2+, LOR 20/1377L. Opt full score (org), LOR 20/1378L.

♫ Lohr, Alan. "Christ lag in Todesbanden." 5 oct, L4. SF 118349.

♫ Moats, William. "Haleluya." 3 oct, L2. Genesis Press GP2040.

♫ = relates to hymn of the day
P = available in Prelude Music Planner

April 16, 2017
Resurrection of Our Lord
Easter Evening

Isaiah proclaims the great feast to come, when God will swallow up death forever. Paul invites us to celebrate the paschal feast with the unleavened bread of sincerity and truth. The Easter evening gospel tells of the risen Christ being made known to the disciples in the breaking of the bread. Our hearts burn within us as the hope of the resurrection is proclaimed in our midst, and as Jesus appears to us at the holy table.

Prayer of the Day

O God, whose blessed Son made himself known to his disciples in the breaking of bread, open the eyes of our faith, that we may behold him in all his redeeming work, Jesus Christ, our Savior and Lord, who lives and reigns with you and the Holy Spirit, one God, now and forever.

Gospel Acclamation

Alleluia. Our hearts ˈ burn within us* while you open to ˈ us the scriptures. *Alleluia.* (Luke 24:32)

Readings and Psalm

Isaiah 25:6-9

The prophet portrays a wonderful victory banquet at which death, which in ancient Canaan was depicted as a monster swallowing everyone up, will be swallowed up forever. The prophet urges celebration of this victory, which is salvation.

Psalm 114

Tremble, O earth, at the presence of the LORD. (Ps. 114:7)

1 Corinthians 5:6b-8

In preparation to celebrate Passover, God's people cleaned out all the old leaven from their homes. Paul draws on this practice to portray Christ as our Passover lamb whose sacrifice means that we now clean out the old leaven of malice and wickedness from our lives and replace it with sincerity and truth.

Luke 24:13-49

On the day of his resurrection, Jesus joins two disciples on the road to Emmaus and makes himself known to them in the breaking of bread.

Preface   Easter

Color   White *or* Gold

Wednesday, April 19
Olavus Petri, priest, died 1552; Laurentius Petri, Bishop of Uppsala, died 1573; renewers of the church

These two brothers are commemorated for their introduction of the Lutheran movement to the Church of Sweden after studying at the University of Wittenberg. They returned home and, through the support of King Gustavus Vasa, began their work. Olavus published a catechism, hymnal, and a Swedish version of the mass. He resisted attempts by the king to gain royal control of the church. Laurentius was a professor at the university in Uppsala. When the king wanted to abolish the ministry of bishops, Laurentius persuaded him otherwise. The historic episcopate continues in Sweden to this day. Together the brothers published a complete Bible in Swedish and a revised liturgy in 1541.

Friday, April 21
Anselm, Bishop of Canterbury, died 1109

This eleventh- and twelfth-century Benedictine monk stands out as one of the greatest theologians between Augustine and Thomas Aquinas. He is counted among the medieval mystics who emphasized the maternal aspects of God. Of Jesus Anselm says, "In sickness you nurse us and with pure milk you feed us." Anselm is perhaps best known for his "satisfaction" theory of atonement. He argued that human rebellion against God demands a payment, but because humanity is fallen it is incapable of making that satisfaction. But God takes on human nature in Jesus Christ, Anselm proposed, in order to make the perfect payment for sin.

Easter

Preparing for Easter

Christ Is with Us

Following the traumatic events of the crucifixion and a terrifying resurrection, the disciples in their confusion and grief had to be wondering, *What's next?* The lectionary readings for the Easter season provide the road map ahead as the disciples discover a new postresurrection life and reality: Christ is with us. Behind closed doors, in our doubt, on our journey, in water, bread, and wine, the Good Shepherd calls us to follow, going before us to prepare the way, bringing peace, breathing the Spirit on us, so that we may tell this story to people of every land and nation. Jesus' promise to be with us always is the game changer.

Today, how do we acknowledge Christ's presence with us in our Sunday assemblies? What does it mean for us that this is the true body and blood of our Lord Jesus Christ? Do we worship as if we believe Christ is truly present with us? If not, what could we do differently? How can we make known Christ's presence with us in our worship through our words and actions, art and music? Here are some ways assemblies can visibly and physically reveal Christ's presence with God's people today.

Processional Cross

The processional cross has a long history of use in Western and Eastern Christianity and is often a significant work of art. While many congregations have a cross on a pole standing near the altar table, this cross might be used rarely as intended. When the cross is carried into the midst of the assembly, it becomes a powerful sign of Christ's presence with us. The celebration of the Easter season is particularly suited to using the cross in procession. During the gathering song, the cross may be carried into the church by the crucifer. It might be flanked by two candle torches and followed by the lector carrying a Bible or lectionary book, the assisting and presiding ministers, and processional banners. A tradition is for the assembly to face the cross as it enters and to bow as a sign of reverence, acknowledging Christ's presence, as it passes. If a gospel procession is included, the cross may lead the procession of a Bible or lectionary book and ministers to the center of the assembly for the reading of the gospel when we hear Jesus' voice alive and present with us again. As the sending song is sung, the cross leads the assembly to the entrance doors for the dismissal as a sign we carry the presence of Christ with us into the world.

Thanksgiving for Baptism

The thanksgiving for baptism, with its images of new life in the risen Christ, is a fitting alternative to confession and forgiveness during the Easter season (see page 168 for a newly written example). The ministers gather at the baptismal font for the thanksgiving. Water may be poured into the font as the prayer is said. As a reminder of the gift of baptism, the assembly may be sprinkled with water as a song is sung. A small glass bowl of water and an evergreen branch work well for the sprinkling. This sprinkling of the assembly is a reminder that "by water and the Holy Spirit we are reborn children of God and made members of the church, the body of Christ" (*ELW*, p. 227). In addition to "This is the feast" or an Easter hymn, songs for Holy Baptism are especially appropriate when accompanied by sprinkling. If your baptismal font and paschal candle do not occupy a prominent place in your worship space, consider creating such an area with ample space to accommodate baptismal groups.

Sign of the Cross

The Easter season is the perfect time to teach children and adults to remember their baptism by introducing the sign of the cross to the assembly. In his Small Catechism, Martin Luther instructs us to make the sign of the holy cross and say, "God the Father, Son, and Holy Spirit watch over me. Amen," as soon as we get out of bed in the morning and before going to bed in the evening (*ELW*, pp. 1166–1167). We are encouraged also to make the sign of the cross each time we begin and end worship. Notice in *Evangelical Lutheran Worship* the red crosses in the texts for confession and forgiveness, thanksgiving for baptism, and the blessing. These crosses are not just cues for the presiding minister to make the sign of the cross but are there so that *all* may make the sign of the cross, the sign that is marked at baptism. Invite everyone to make the sign of the cross with the presiding minister at these times. The sign of the cross is made by touching your hand to your forehead, then to your lower chest, then to each shoulder. Additionally, people may be encouraged to dip their fingers into the water of the baptismal font and trace the sign of the cross on their foreheads as they enter church or come to the table for communion. This is another reminder of our baptism: "Child of God, you have been sealed by the Holy Spirit and marked with the cross of Christ forever" (*ELW*, p. 231). Engaging with the means of grace regularly is essential to our faith formation.

Bible or Lectionary Book

A significant Bible or lectionary book placed on the ambo or pulpit is a visible sign of the centrality of the word of God in Christian worship. Rather than reading from a sheet of paper that will be discarded later, we demonstrate how important scripture is to us by reading from a permanent book. When carried to the center of the assembly for the reading of the gospel, the Bible or lectionary book is a symbol of the life-giving word of God and the proclamation of the gospel—Jesus alive and active in the world today.

The Feast of Victory

The Use of the Means of Grace (1997) reminds us that holy communion is known by many names, each emphasizing a certain aspect of the sacrament (Principle 36). Easter calls us to see the meal as a great thanksgiving for creation's redemption in Jesus Christ and to share with the risen Lord a foretaste of the feast to come. During the Easter season, make your celebration of the meal a feast of victory. Consider using a delicious loaf of fresh-baked leavened bread and a good wine you would enjoy drinking with a fine meal. Stand instead of kneel to receive the sacrament. Train your communion ministers to boldly proclaim to each person the good news: "The body of Christ, given for you." "The blood of Christ, shed for you." Sing lively music fitting for a celebration. Finally, and very importantly, consider how you can physically and visibly send the sacrament from the table with communion ministers for distribution to those who are sick, homebound, imprisoned, or absent from the assembly for any reason. Like Jesus bursting forth from the tomb, the walls of the church can no longer contain the Easter feast of victory.

Music

The seasonal liturgical music and song you choose play a vital role in creating a unified Easter cycle (Ash Wednesday through the Day of Pentecost). Sing a strong Easter hymn as the gathering song each week to remind people we continue to celebrate the resurrection every Sunday. The music from Lent should feel as if it is transformed in the Easter season. If you sang a Kyrie during Lent, sing the same Kyrie during the Easter season followed by a complementary setting of "This is the feast." The Lenten gospel acclamation is replaced with the return of the alleluia. Consider using a setting of the gospel acclamation that complements the "Holy, holy, holy" of the great thanksgiving. This will help connect two climactic elements of the liturgy, the proclamation of the gospel and the thanksgiving at the table. If you choose to include a gospel procession (carrying a Bible or lectionary book to the center of the assembly to read the gospel), sing the alleluias with the appointed verse before the reading and repeat the alleluias alone as the procession returns. Retain the musical setting of the great thanksgiving used during Lent but now with sung acclamations and amen. The "Lamb of God" may be retained, or you may replace it with "The Disciples Knew the Lord Jesus" from *Music Sourcebook for Lent and the Three Days* (Augsburg Fortress, 2010), S496, S497.

As much as possible, continue to include instrumental parts and choral descants used on Easter Day throughout the season. A joyous celebration of the entire Easter season can reverberate through every Sunday of the church year, transforming our worship with the new life of the risen Christ who is present with us at every gathering of the assembly.

Reformation 500

One way your congregation can observe the 500th anniversary of the Reformation during the Easter season is to sing hymns with texts attributed to Martin Luther and those with important historic roots in Lutheran church history. The hymn of the day for Easter Day could be Luther's classic "Christ Jesus lay in death's strong bands" (ELW 370). It is rich in Luther's theology and paired with a tune of its own significance derived from plainsong. Sing "Come, Holy Ghost, God and Lord" (ELW 395), one of the finest hymns from the Lutheran heritage, on the Day of Pentecost. The gospel acclamation for the season could be "Christ is arisen" (ELW 372). If you include a gospel procession, an alleluia with the appointed verse could precede the reading and this hymn could be sung following the gospel. In the spirit of the Reformation composers, write your own gospel acclamation based on well-known tunes. As an example, use the refrain from "The strife is o'er, the battle done" (ELW 366) combined with psalm tone 1 or tone 4 (transposed to D) and the proper verse (see *Evangelical Lutheran Worship Accompaniment Edition: Liturgies*, pp. 215, 220). Selected stanzas of "At the Lamb's high feast we sing" (ELW 362) can be the assembly's song at the setting of the table. For more information on these hymns, see *Hymnal Companion to Evangelical Lutheran Worship* (Augsburg Fortress, 2010).

Seasonal Checklist

- Visually extend the festive celebration of Easter Day throughout the season by refreshing lilies or other flowers and retaining art and decorations through the Day of Pentecost. In addition to adorning the table and ambo, consider ornamenting the cross, paschal candle, and baptismal font as well.
- It is particularly appropriate during the Easter season to use thanksgiving for baptism as an alternative to confession and forgiveness.
- Sing the canticle of praise "This is the feast" either following the thanksgiving for baptism (with the option of sprinkling with water) or as the table is set for the meal.
- Use the Nicene Creed.
- Appropriate options for the thanksgiving at the table include prayers IV, VII, or X in *Evangelical Lutheran Worship* (pp. 111, 67, 69) and those for the season of Easter (E) and the Day of Pentecost (F) in *With One Voice Leaders Edition* (pp. 69, 70).

- Publicize Ascension and Pentecost services, helping the community understand the importance of these festivals. Since Ascension of Our Lord falls on a Thursday, it may provide an opportunity for local congregations and full communion partners to worship together in a joint Ascension Day service.
- Consider observing the Day of Pentecost as the next baptismal festival following the Vigil of Easter.
- Determine ways to emphasize the Day of Pentecost, such as using red flowers or balloons, inviting people to wear red, or using a diversity of languages in scripture readings, prayers, or music. If you will use a diversity of languages for the Day of Pentecost, make preparations in advance with musicians and readers.
- On Pentecost, seven votive candles in red glass holders may be lighted near the altar table to recall the gifts of the Spirit identified in the rites of Holy Baptism and Affirmation of Baptism (Isa. 11:2).
- If your congregation celebrates affirmation of baptism (confirmation) during this season, review the rite in *Evangelical Lutheran Worship*.

Worship Texts for Easter

Thanksgiving for Baptism

*All may make the sign of the cross, the sign marked at baptism,
as the presiding minister begins.*

Alleluia! Christ is risen.

Christ is risen indeed. Alleluia!

*As an alternative to the assembly's spoken response, a sung
refrain may be used.*

Just as God's work of creation never ends,
so the gifts received in baptism are renewed every day.
Let us give thanks together for the life given in baptism.

We give you thanks, O God, for the waters of life:
for water to bathe in, water to drink,
for waters to play in and waters that inspire wonder,
for water that gives life to our planet.

We give you thanks, O God, for the waters of life.

We give you thanks, O God, for the waters of this place:
for water from our tap, for rain [and snow],
for [*local water sources may be named*].

We give you thanks, O God, for the waters of this place.

We give you thanks for your salvation through water:
for delivering Noah and his family through the floodwaters,
for leading your people Israel through the sea into freedom,
for preserving your prophet Elijah through the time of drought,
for guiding your people across the Jordan into a new land,
for quenching the Samaritan woman's thirst with living water.

We give you thanks for your salvation through water.

We give you thanks for the life of all the baptized,
and for all who gather here;
for godparents and baptismal sponsors,
for children and grandchildren,
[for those newly baptized *at the Easter Vigil/in this holy season;*] for our brothers and sisters in Christ
whom we have never seen but to whom we are bound.

We give you thanks for the life of all the baptized.

We give you thanks for life in Christ through your Holy Spirit:
for our entry into Jesus' death through these waters,
for our new birth into a life of freedom and service,
for our calling to be your people,
sent out for the life of the world.

**We give you thanks, blessed and holy Trinity,
now and forever. Amen.**

Offering Prayer

Be known to us, O Lord, in the breaking of the bread,
as you were made known to the disciples.
Receive these gifts, and the offering of our lives,
that we may be your risen body in the world.

Amen.

Invitation to Communion

Now let us feast this Easter day
on Christ, the bread of heaven. Hallelujah!

Prayer after Communion

Life-giving God,
in the mystery of Christ's death and resurrection
you send light to conquer darkness,
water to give new life,
and the bread of heaven to nourish your people.
Send us forth as witnesses to Jesus' resurrection
that we may show your glory to all the world;
through the same Jesus Christ, our risen Lord.

Amen.

Blessing

May God who has brought us from death to life
fill you with great joy.
Almighty God, Father, + Son, and Holy Spirit,
bless you now and forever.
Amen.

Dismissal

Alleluia! Christ is risen.
Christ is risen indeed. Alleluia!
You are the body of Christ raised up for the world.
Go in peace. Share the good news.
Thanks be to God.

Especially on the Day of Pentecost
Go in peace. The Spirit sends us forth to serve.
Thanks be to God.

Seasonal Rites for Easter

Volunteer Recognition Litany

The following litany may be adapted as needed to reflect the congregation's volunteer ministries.

The body of Christ is made up of many members.
Not all have the same function.
We are blessed with many members who care for the functioning of the body of Christ at *name of congregation*.
We thank God for them.

They give of their time and talents.
Without their efforts and gifts we could not be all God calls us to be.
Paul writes of the Macedonian Christians who wanted to share in ministry: "They gave themselves first to the Lord and, by the will of God, to us." (2 Cor. 8:5)
Ministry flows from a commitment to serve the Lord.
By the will of God our volunteers are committed to the Lord and to us. God has worked mightily through them to bless us.
We thank God for them.

Our volunteers put flesh and bone on our call to be the body of Christ in the world.
They add muscle to our calling to be Christ to one another.
Sunday school and vacation Bible school teachers, confirmation and youth leaders, mentors and nursery helpers;
musicians, readers, assisting ministers, ushers, leaders of prayer, communion assistants, acolytes;
mission-project organizers, stewardship coordinators, offering counters, special event planners;
quilters, gardeners, artists, bakers, cooks;
prayer chain participants, visitors to the hospitalized and homebound, those who prepare funeral lunches;
ministers of hospitality of every kind;
cleaners, bulletin assemblers, envelope stuffers, office helpers, and so many more:
We thank God for you!

An acclamation may be sung (for example, ELW #171–175, 682, 846, 875, 884/885).

Blessing of Fields and Gardens

Let us bless God, the creator of all things. God has given us the earth to cultivate, so that we might receive the bounty of its fruits. Just as the rain falls from heaven and waters the earth, bringing forth vegetation, so God's word will flourish and will not return empty.

Reading

Genesis 1:1, 11-12, 29-31

Prayer

Abundant God, we give you thanks for the fruitful earth, which produces what is needed for life. Bless those who work in the fields; grant favorable weather to all engaged in agriculture; and help us to ensure that all people share the fruits of the earth, rejoicing in your goodness; through your Son, Jesus Christ our Lord.
Amen.

Hymn

For the fruit of all creation   ELW 679, WOV 760, LBW 563
We plow the fields and scatter   ELW 680/681, LLC 492, LBW 362
Praise and thanksgiving   ELW 689, LBW 409
God, whose farm is all creation   ELW 734

April 23, 2017
Second Sunday of Easter

In today's gospel the risen Christ appears to the disciples and offers them the gift of peace. Even amid doubts and questions, we experience the resurrection in our Sunday gathering around word and meal, and in our everyday lives. Throughout the coming Sundays of Easter the first two readings will be from the Acts of the Apostles and the first letter of Peter. Even as the early Christians proclaimed the resurrection, we rejoice in the new birth and living hope we receive in baptism.

Prayer of the Day

Almighty and eternal God, the strength of those who believe and the hope of those who doubt, may we, who have not seen, have faith in you and receive the fullness of Christ's blessing, who lives and reigns with you and the Holy Spirit, one God, now and forever.

Gospel Acclamation

Alleluia. Blessed are those who ǀ have not seen* and yet have come ǀ to believe. *Alleluia.* (John 20:29)

Readings and Psalm

Acts 2:14a, 22-32

After the Holy Spirit came to the apostles on Pentecost, Peter preaches the gospel to the gathered crowd. He tells them that Jesus, who obediently went to his death according to God's plan, was raised from the dead by God. Finally, he appeals to scripture, quoting Psalm 16:8-11, to show that Jesus is the Messiah: though crucified, the risen Jesus is now enthroned.

Psalm 16

In your presence there is fullness of joy. (Ps. 16:11)

1 Peter 1:3-9

This epistle was written to encourage Christians experiencing hardships and suffering because of their faith in Christ. The letter opens by blessing God for the living hope we have through Christ's resurrection even in the midst of difficult circumstances and surroundings.

John 20:19-31

The risen Jesus appears to his disciples, offering them a benediction, a commission, and the gift of the Holy Spirit. But one of their number is missing, and his unbelief prompts another visit from the Lord.

Preface   Easter

Color   White

Prayers of Intercession

The prayers are prepared locally for each occasion. The following examples may be adapted or used as appropriate.

Rejoicing in the risen life of Christ, let us pray for the church, the world, and all who are in need.

A brief silence.

We pray for the church. Breathe your Spirit into us. Renew us with your power. Unite us in mission and send us into the world with your love. Lord, in your mercy,

hear our prayer.

For the earth. For fields and forests, gardens and vineyards, and all newly planted crops. Sustain our world with clean water and favorable weather. Lord, in your mercy,

hear our prayer.

For the nations. Empower leaders to work for the well-being of all. Send peace into every place where people live in the shadow of violence and displacement (*especially*). Free all who are isolated behind walls of fear. Lord, in your mercy,

hear our prayer.

For those in need. Look with compassion toward those who bear hidden wounds. Draw near to those who seek you. Comfort the dying, console the grieving, and heal the sick (*especially*). Lord, in your mercy,

hear our prayer.

For this assembly. Give us courage to welcome newcomers graciously. Walk with those who are inquiring, those who harbor doubts and questions, and those who are absent from us. Lord, in your mercy,

hear our prayer.

Here other intercessions may be offered.

With thanksgiving, we remember those who have died in faith (*especially Toyohiko Kagawa, renewer of society*). Inspire us by their witness. Bring us with them to the heavenly feast. Lord, in your mercy,

hear our prayer.

Joining our voices with your faithful ones in every time and place, we offer our prayers in the name of the Risen One, Jesus Christ our Lord.

Amen.

Images in the Readings

Usually depictions of the crucified Christ include the marks on his **hands and side**. Our archaeological knowledge that for crucifixions nails were driven through the wrist ought not negate the symbolism of the palm, which is central to a person's hand. Neither need we get fascinated by the accounts of the stigmata, for we all carry the mark of the crucified and risen Christ on our palm each time we receive the body of Christ at communion. In John 19:34, blood and water flow from the wound on Jesus' side, and church tradition has seen in this detail not an erroneous description of human anatomy but rather the proclamation that baptism and eucharist flow from the death of Christ.

Each year on the second Sunday of Easter we meet **doubting Thomas**. He is all of us, and we doubters are glad to share with all other doubters the peace of the risen Christ.

That Christ is **king** is an image behind the reading from Acts: King David testifies to this power; Jesus is now on David's throne; Christ is the anointed one, the messiah.

God is the Father of our Lord Jesus Christ, and in baptism we have been given a new **birth**, to live as children of this heavenly father. The imagery continues: only children receive the full inheritance.

Ideas for the Day

- This perennial Easter season gospel is both rich narrative and profound theology. Careful readers note Thomas doesn't demand proof; he demands a first-person encounter. Jesus returns to stand in the middle of things not once but twice; the second time, *just* for Thomas. Jesus, even in resurrection glory, retains his scars, and he prefers the skeptic, the seeker, the one who is late. Is this why Peter enacts the style of first-person testimony in Acts 2? Is this why Peter stands *with* the Eleven? Worship today can embody openness, testimony, solidarity: preachers in pulpits may wish to come out. Readers can be encouraged to speak with deep conviction. Chancel or nave doors, normally closed, could be set open.

- The church celebrates the coming of the Holy Spirit on the fiftieth day of Easter, at Pentecost. This year Pentecost falls on June 4 and may be overlooked among a secular calendar of graduations and summer travel. Yet in John "Pentecost" comes Easter evening: The Holy Spirit is given (John 20:22) and the commission/sending is *now*. The second Sunday of Easter may be an ideal time for congregations to celebrate a faith milestone, recognize the anniversary of a ministry, commission a particular set of volunteers, or affirm baptismal promises in the familiar phrasing of 1 Peter 1:3.

- *Inside Out* (Disney Pixar, 2015) is an animated fantasy film. The protagonist is eleven-year-old Riley, and much of the film is spent inside Riley's mind, a control center occupied by five personified emotions: Joy, Sadness, Fear, Anger, and Disgust. Sketched as a raw nerve and voiced by actor Bill Hader, Fear's job is "to protect Riley and keep her safe. He is constantly on the lookout for potential disasters. . . . There are very few activities and events that Fear does not find to be dangerous and possibly fatal" (http://movies.disney.com/inside-out). The film has won praise from scientists as a realistic depiction of human emotion. But the movie left out the widely accepted sixth universal emotion: *surprise*. A relatable sermon could be composed on the topic of how all six emotions are at play in today's readings.

Connections with the Liturgy

Each Sunday Christians exchange with one another the peace of the risen Christ. In some assemblies, the Peace has become a kind of seventh-inning stretch during which everyone chats with everyone else about the week's news. However, the liturgical intention of this greeting is that we are enacting John 20, receiving from one another the peace that Christ gave to the disciples. We fill the room with the life of the Holy Spirit, breathing to one another the meaning of Christ's death and resurrection.

Let the Children Come

Have you ever thought of this as a "low attendance Sunday"? Perhaps everyone is like Thomas, out in the city looking for Jesus. Children cannot usually get themselves to church on their own. Children's sense of time and relationships may make them especially sensitive to feeling as if they have been away a very long time, even when they only missed one Sunday. Leaders should be especially attentive to welcome children warmly and not make a big deal out of their absence. How do you celebrate in your liturgy the work of God's people out in the world when they are away from the church building?

Assembly Song
Gathering

Come, you faithful, raise the strain ELW 363, LBW 132
That Easter day with joy was bright ELW 384, LBW 154
With high delight let us unite ELW 368, LBW 140

Psalmody and Acclamations

Inwood, Paul. "Centre of My Life" from *Psalm Songs 2*. AFP 0800657713.
Miller, Aaron David. "Psalm 16," Refrain 3, from PSCY.
Sedio, Mark. "Psalm 16" from PWA.
(GA) Haas, David. "Alleluia: Our God Is Speaking." SATB, cant, assembly, kybd, gtr, 2 C inst. GIA G-7727.

Hymn of the Day

O sons and daughters, let us sing ELW 386, LBW 139 *O FILII ET FILIAE*

We walk by faith ELW 635 *SHANTI* WOV 675 *DUNLAP'S CREEK*

Alleluia! Christ is arisen/*¡Aleluya! Cristo resucitó* ELW 375, LLC 361 *SANTO DOMINGO*

Offering

The peace of the Lord ELW 646, LLC 471

We who once were dead ELW 495, sts. 1, 3, 5, 6; LBW 207, sts. 1, 3, 5, 6

Communion

Now the green blade rises ELW 379, LBW 148, LLC 357

The risen Christ ELW 390

We have seen the Lord ELW 869

Sending

Thine is the glory ELW 376, LBW 145

Rise, O church, like Christ arisen ELW 548

Additional Assembly Songs

May you look beyond seeing ASG 22

Up from the earth in bright array CBM 106

Make songs of joy LBW 150

⊕ Colligan, Richard Bruxvoort. "Peace of God Be with You/*Assalaamu lakum*" from *Glory to God*. U. WJK 0664238971.

⊕ Yoruba, traditional. "Aleluya Y'in Louwa/Alleluia, Praise the Lord" from *Agape: Songs of Hope and Reconciliation*. SATB. Lutheran World Federation. Out of print. Available on Amazon.com.

☼ Baloche, Paul/Matt Redman. "I Cling to the Cross" from CCLI.

☼ Good, Linnea. "Doubters" from OCP.

☼ Hall, Mark/Michael Bleecker. "Glorious Day (Living He Loved Me)" from CCLI.

☼ Hughes, Tim/Nick Herbert. "Plans" from CCLI.

☼ Ryan, Travis/Richie Fike/Matt Hooper. "We Believe" from CCLI.

☼ Stockstill, Jonathan. "He Rose" from CCLI.

Music for the Day
Choral

ᴾ♫ Helman, Michael. "We Walk by Faith." SATB, pno, opt hb, opt fl. AFP 9780800659752.

ᴾ♫ Organ, Anne Krentz. "We Walk by Faith." 2 pt mxd, pno. AFP 9781451492637.

ᴾ♫ Organ, Anne Krentz. "O Sons and Daughters, Let us Sing." 2 pt mxd, org, opt tamb. MSM 50-9936.

Schalk, Carl. "I Have Set the Lord Always before Me." SATB, MSM 50-9019.

Children's Choir

ᴾ Albrecht, Mark. "Christ Is Alive, Alleluia." U, opt C inst, perc. AFP 9780800677466.

ᴾ Biery, Marilyn. "This Joyful Eastertide" from *ChildrenSing in Worship*. U, org. AFP 9781451401806.

Purifoy, John. "We Welcome Glad Easter." U/2 pt, SATB, kybd. LOR 10/1228T.

Keyboard / Instrumental

ᴾ♫ Biery, James. "Alleluia! Christ Is Arisen" or "¡Aleluya! Cristo resucitó" (Santo Domingo) from *The Paschal Lamb: Easter Settings for Organ*. Org. AFP 9781451494099.

Dandrieu, Jean-François. "O Sons and Daughters, Let Us Sing" (O filii et filiae) from *French Noëls for Organ*. Org. DOV 0486296962.

♫ Hassell, Michael. "We Walk by Faith" (Dunlap's Creek) from *Traveling Tunes: Hymn Arrangements for Solo Instrument and Piano*. Inst, pno. AFP 9780800656195.

ᴾ♫ Stevens, Wendy Lynn. "We Walk by Faith" (Dunlap's Creek) from *How Sweet the Sound: Piano Arrangements for Worship*. Pno. AFP 9780806696966.

Handbell

♫ Frizzel, J.D. "Easter Triumph." 3-6 oct, L2+. LOR 20/1562L.

Glasgow, Michael J. "Celebration on 'Lancashire'" from *Easter and Beyond*. 3-5 oct hb, opt 2 oct hc, L2+. LOR 20/1885L.

Krug, Jason W. "Come, O Spirit, Dwell among Us" from *Easter and Beyond*. 3-6 oct hb, opt 2 oct hc, L2+. LOR 20/1885L.

Sunday, April 23
Toyohiko Kagawa, renewer of society, died 1960

Toyohiko Kagawa (toy-oh-hee-koh ka-ga-wah) was born in 1888 in Kobe, Japan. Orphaned early, he was disowned by his remaining extended family when he became a Christian. Kagawa wrote, spoke, and worked at length on ways to employ Christian principles in the ordering of society. His vocation to help the poor led him to live among them. He established schools, hospitals, and churches. He also worked for peace and established the Anti-War League. He was arrested for his efforts to reconcile Japan and China after the Japanese attack of 1940.

Tuesday, April 25
Mark, Evangelist

Though Mark himself was not an apostle, it is likely that he was a member of one of the early Christian communities. It is possible that he is the John Mark of Acts 12 whose mother owned

⊕ = global song   ♫ = relates to hymn of the day

☼ = praise song   ᴾ = available in Prelude Music Planner

the house where the apostles gathered. The gospel attributed to him is brief and direct. It is considered by many to be the earliest gospel. Tradition has it that Mark went to preach in Alexandria, Egypt, became the first bishop there, and was martyred.

Saturday, April 29

Catherine of Siena, theologian, died 1380

Catherine of Siena was a member of the Order of Preachers (Dominicans), and among Roman Catholics she was the first woman to receive the title Doctor of the Church. She was a contemplative and is known for her mystical visions of Jesus. This gift of mysticism apparently extended back into her childhood, much to the dismay of her parents, who wanted her to be like other children. Catherine was a humanitarian who worked to alleviate the suffering of the poor and imprisoned. She was also a renewer of church and society and advised both popes and any persons who told her their problems. Catherine's contemplative life was linked to her concern for the poor and suffering. She is a reminder that prayer and activism belong together.

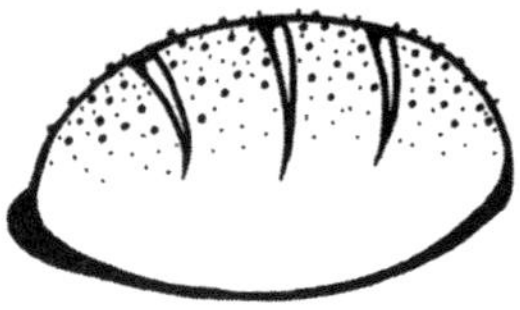

April 30, 2017

Third Sunday of Easter

Today's gospel begins with two disciples walking to Emmaus, overcome with sadness, loss, and disappointment. They had hoped Jesus, who was crucified, would be the one to redeem Israel! Yet the risen Christ walks with them, and then opens their eyes in the breaking of the bread. Each Sunday our hearts burn within us as the scriptures are proclaimed and Christ appears to us as bread is broken and wine is poured. The story of Emmaus becomes the pattern of our worship each Lord's day.

Prayer of the Day

O God, your Son makes himself known to all his disciples in the breaking of bread. Open the eyes of our faith, that we may see him in his redeeming work, who lives and reigns with you and the Holy Spirit, one God, now and forever.

Gospel Acclamation

Alleluia. Our hearts | burn within us* while you open to | us the scriptures. *Alleluia.* (Luke 24:32)

Readings and Psalm

Acts 2:14a, 36-41

Today's reading is the conclusion of Peter's sermon preached following the giving of the Holy Spirit to the apostles on the day of Pentecost. The center of his preaching is the bold declaration that God has made the crucified Jesus both Lord and Christ.

Psalm 116:1-4, 12-19

I will call on the name of the LORD. (Ps. 116:13)

1 Peter 1:17-23

The imagery of exile is used to help the readers of this letter understand that they are strangers in a strange land. Christians no longer belong to this age. Through the death of Christ we belong to God, so that our focus, faith, and hope are no longer on such things as silver or gold.

Luke 24:13-35

The colorful story of Jesus' appearance to two disciples on the road to Emmaus answers the question of how Jesus is to be recognized among us. Here, he is revealed through the scriptures and in the breaking of bread.

Preface
Easter

Color
White

Prayers of Intercession

The prayers are prepared locally for each occasion. The following examples may be adapted or used as appropriate.

Rejoicing in the risen life of Christ, let us pray for the church, the world, and all who are in need.

A brief silence.

We pray for the church. Remove all that hinders us from sharing your love. Raise up faithful preachers and teachers to lead your people. Heal our divisions. Unite us at your table. Lord, in your mercy,

hear our prayer.

For the earth. Protect animals whose environments are endangered. Bring bountiful sunshine and sufficient rainfall for fields, pastures, and orchards. Bless those whose labors bring food to our tables. Lord, in your mercy,

hear our prayer.

For the nations. Give all leaders wisdom and courage to work for the common good. Strengthen disaster relief workers, peacemakers, and all whose contributions to society go unnoticed. Lord, in your mercy,

hear our prayer.

For those in need. Draw near to those who have lost hope. Provide food for the hungry and shelter for those who need safe housing. Comfort the grieving and heal the sick (*especially*). Lord, in your mercy,

hear our prayer.

For this assembly. Empower our ministries of outreach and hospitality. Strengthen the newly baptized and those who mentor them. Bless those who set the table for the holy meal. Lord, in your mercy,

hear our prayer.

Here other intercessions may be offered.

With thanksgiving, we remember those who have died in faith (*especially*). Bring us with them to the fullness of your glory with all your saints. Lord, in your mercy,

hear our prayer.

Joining our voices with your faithful ones in every time and place, we offer our prayers in the name of the Risen One, Jesus Christ our Lord.

Amen.

Images in the Readings

The **meal** of Emmaus is one of the many Lukan accounts of eating with Jesus, and Luke's accounts follow the biblical theme that God feeds the people. To be true to the biblical image of the life shared with Christ, the bread we break, the wine we share, and our methods of distribution ought to make clear that holy communion is a meal. A loaf of bread or a large circular flatbread, home baked or purchased from a local store and broken for all to see, presents a quite different image of salvation than do medieval quarter-sized tasteless hosts bought from an ecclesiastical supply company. Think about the image presented by your eating and drinking.

The **preaching** of Peter and the teaching of Christ along the road are images of our receiving the "living and enduring" saving word.

The passage from 1 Peter presents an array of images, one rushing along after another. A significant image for the book of 1 Peter is **exile**: the baptized are living in an alien land. When Christians become too comfortable in what Acts calls "this corrupt generation," we are called to be ransomed out of it and purified by obedience to the truth.

Ideas for the Day

- The term *pundit* was first used in the English language in 1672. Originally a Sanskrit term for a learned person, pundits were well-versed conductors of religious ceremonies and counselors to royalty. In 2011 a Hamilton College paper summarized a humorous truth: few American media pundits were above average in having their predictions come true; many did no better than a coin toss, and several were substantially worse than a coin toss at predicting future events (http://www.hamilton.edu/news/polls/pundit). But this is not a new phenomenon. In both Luke 24 and Acts 2, speculative conversation becomes conversion. And pundits become humble learners, disciples *once more*, because a risen Lord Jesus shows up.

- Years ago in a Baptist congregation in Minneapolis the ushers dressed in suits and took the offering. But these ushers were charged with *another* solemn task: carrying tissues. When worshipers sniffled, wept, or wailed, the usher strode down the aisle to attend to them. This dedication to worshipers' emotions may not make our congregation's list of usher duties, but perhaps our congregations can expect and even publicly embrace the truth that Jesus' resurrection *will* turn hearts inside out, make feet move, make witnesses out of those who a few hours prior were shuffling away in disappointment.

- Hearts figure prominently in today's readings. The disciples on the Emmaus road are "slow of heart" (Luke 24:25), and their hearts burn within them (Luke 24:32). First Peter urges early Christian communities to "love one another deeply from the heart" (1:22). *Heart: A Natural History of the Heart-Filled Life* by Gail Godwin is part survey, part memoir, and part meditation. Godwin muses, "Could it be that our utmost experiences of darkness *always engage the heart*? If my heart, if the inmost sanctuary of my being, the taproot of its love and will . . . has not been touched, or broken, or altered, or shaken to the core . . . hasn't it been just another head trip, a barren intellectual undertaking that bears no fruit? ([New York: HarperCollins, 2001], 197). How is the experience Godwin describes necessary to transformation? How do today's readings bring wholehearted living to our attention?

Connections with the Liturgy

Every eucharistic service repeats the story of Emmaus: we are walking together, we welcome a stranger, we hear the word, we share the meal, we recognize at our table the risen Christ, and we go to tell others. The frontispiece for the Holy Communion section of *Evangelical Lutheran Worship* (p. 89) depicts the couple of Emmaus at table with the risen Christ. The art was drawn by the contemporary Chinese artist He Qi.

The gospel acclamation for Setting Ten of Holy Communion (*ELW*, p. 205) specifically quotes the Emmaus account when we sing, "Open now your saving word. Let it burn like fire within us." It is as if hearing the gospel reading, we are the disciples running back to Jerusalem, telling the others about meeting Jesus on the road.

Let the Children Come

God is up to the old fun of peek-a-boo again. The road to Emmaus story is about the resurrected Jesus' hiddenness and revelation to his followers. The details play out through a walking path and at a table—and notice we still have them in our worship together! How is Christ hidden and revealed for children during the procession? Are they able to walk along? Do those in the assembly turn their bodies toward the cross and bow? How is Christ hidden and revealed for children during the holy meal? How are children treated differently at the table than other worshiping people?

Assembly Song
Gathering

This joyful Eastertide ELW 391, LBW 149
With high delight let us unite ELW 368, LBW 140
Christ the Lord is risen today! ELW 373, LBW 130

Psalmody and Acclamations

Glynn, John. "Lord, How Can I Repay" from *Psalm Songs 2*. AFP 0800657713.
McRae, Shirley W. "Psalm 116" from *ChildrenSing Psalms*. U, assembly, kybd, 5 hb. AFP 9780800663872.
Roberts, Leon C. "I Will Call upon the Name of the Lord (Psalm 116)." TFF 14.
(GA) Haas, David. "Alleluia: Our God Is Speaking." SATB, cant, assembly, kybd, gtr, 2 C inst. GIA G-7727.

Hymn of the Day

Day of arising ELW 374 *RAABE*
We who once were dead ELW 495, LBW 207 *MIDDEN IN DE DOOD*
Alleluia! Jesus is risen! ELW 377, WOV 674, TFF 91 *EARTH AND ALL STARS*

Offering

Bread of life, our host and meal ELW 464
Draw us in the Spirit's tether ELW 470, WOV 703

Communion

Let us talents and tongues employ ELW 674, WOV 754, TFF 232
Christ Jesus lay in death's strong bands ELW 370, LBW 134
You satisfy the hungry heart ELW 484, WOV 711

Sending

The risen Christ ELW 390
Hallelujah! Jesus lives! ELW 380, LBW 147

Additional Assembly Songs

¿Qué venías conversando? LLC 362
Open our eyes, Lord TFF 98, LS 31, WP 113
Stay with us WOV 743
⊕ Farlee, Robert Buckley, arr. "Cristo vive/Christ Is Risen." SATB, assembly, perc. AFP 9780800658830.
⊕ Nyberg, Anders, arr. "Hamba Nathi/Come, Walk with Us" from *Global Songs 2*. SATB, cant. AFP 9780800656744.
☼ Alonzo, Tony. "Emmaus" from *Gather*, 3rd ed. GIA.
☼ Carwell, Eddie/Michel O'Brian. "Emmaus Love" from Musicnotes.
☼ Critchley, Robert. "God of the Breakthrough" from CCLI.
☼ Fielding, Ben/Dean Ussher. "All Things New" from CCLI.
☼ Muglia, Chris. "Our God Is Here" from *Spirit and Song*, vol. 2. OCP.
☼ Tomlin, Chris/Stephan Conley Sharp/Ed Cash. "Made to Worship" from CCLI.

Music for the Day
Choral

Alonso, Tony. "Emmaus." 2 pt trbl or mxd, kybd, vln or C inst. GIA G-7099.
Ferguson, John. "On Emmaus' Journey." SATB, fl, cl, perc. GIA G-5680.
P Highben, Zebulon M. "In the Breaking of the Bread." 2 pt mxd, org. MSM 50-9937.
P ♫ Schalk, Carl. "Day of Arising." SATB, org. AFP 9780800658670.

Children's Choir

Cull, Bob. "Open Our Eyes, Lord" from *LifeSongs*. U, kybd. AFP 9780806642703.
P McRae, Shirley. "Psalm 116" from *ChildrenSing Psalms*. U, kybd, hb. AFP 9780800663872.
Sosa, Pablo. "Heaven Is Singing" from *Halle, Halle: We Sing the World Round*. U, kybd, perc. CG CGC41.

Keyboard / Instrumental

♫ Albrecht, Mark. "Alleluia! Jesus Is Risen" (Earth and All Stars) from *Timeless Tunes for Flute and Piano*. B flat or C inst, pno. AFP 9780800659073.
♫ Kosche, Kenneth T. "We Who Once Were Dead" (Midden in de dood) from *Augsburg Organ Library: Baptism and Holy Communion*. Org. AFP 9780800623555.
P ♫ Miller, Aaron David. "Day of Arising" (Raabe) from *Chorale Preludes for Piano in Traditional Styles*. Pno. AFP 9780800679033.
P ♫ Raabe, Nancy. "Day of Arising" (Raabe) from *Day of Arising: A Tapestry of Musical Traditions*. Pno. AFP 9780800637460.

⊕ = global song ♫ = relates to hymn of the day
☼ = praise song P = available in Prelude Music Planner

Handbell

ℙ Dobrinski, Cynthia. "Glorious Celebration." 3-6 oct, L2+. HOP 2678.

♫ Eithun, Sandra. "Earth and All Stars." 3-6 oct hb, opt 3-7 oct hc, L2+. CPH 97-7675.

Page, Anna Laura. "This Joyful Eastertide" from *Easter and Beyond*. 3-5 oct hb, opt 3 oct hc, L2. LOR 20/1885L.

Monday, May 1
Philip and James, Apostles

Philip was one of the first disciples of Jesus, who after following Jesus invited Nathanael to "come and see." According to tradition, Philip preached in Asia Minor and died as a martyr in Phrygia. James, the son of Alphaeus, is called "the Less" (meaning "short" or "younger") to distinguish him from another apostle named James who is commemorated July 25. Philip and James are commemorated together because the remains of these two saints were placed in the Church of the Apostles in Rome on this day in 561.

Tuesday, May 2
Athanasius, Bishop of Alexandria, died 373

Athanasius (ath-an-AY-shus) attended the Council of Nicaea in 325 as a deacon and secretary to the bishop of Alexandria. At the council, and when he himself served as bishop of Alexandria, he defended the full divinity of Christ against the Arian position held by emperors, magistrates, and theologians. Because of his defense of the divinity of Christ, he was considered a troublemaker and was banished from Alexandria on five occasions. As bishop, one of his paschal letters to surrounding bishops gives a list for books that should be considered canonical scripture. He lists the twenty-seven New Testament books that are recognized today.

Thursday, May 4
Monica, mother of Augustine, died 387

Monica was married to a pagan husband who was ill-tempered and unfaithful. She rejoiced greatly when both her husband and his mother became Christian. But it is because she is the mother of Augustine that she is best known. Monica had been a disciple of Ambrose, and eventually Augustine came under his influence. Almost everything we know about Monica comes from Augustine's *Confessions*, his autobiography. She died far from her home but said to her son, "Do not fret because I am buried far from our home in Africa. Nothing is far from God, and I have no fear that God will not know where to find me, when Christ comes to raise me to life at the end of the world." Her dying wish was that her son remember her at the altar of the Lord, wherever he was.

May 7, 2017
Fourth Sunday of Easter

Today is sometimes called "Good Shepherd Sunday." Jesus is called the "gate" of the sheep in today's gospel. The risen Christ opens the way to abundant life. He anoints our heads with oil and guides us beside the still waters of our baptism. Each Sunday he spreads a feast before us in the midst of the world's violence and war. We go forth to be signs of the resurrection and extend God's tender care to all creation.

Prayer of the Day

O God our shepherd, you know your sheep by name and lead us to safety through the valleys of death. Guide us by your voice, that we may walk in certainty and security to the joyous feast prepared in your house, through Jesus Christ, our Savior and Lord, who lives and reigns with you and the Holy Spirit, one God, now and forever.

Gospel Acclamation

Alleluia. Jesus says, I am ˈ the good shepherd.* I know my own and my ˈ own know me. *Alleluia.* (John 10:14)

Readings and Psalm

Acts 2:42-47

Today's reading is a description of life in the community following Peter's sermon on the day of Pentecost, when the Spirit was outpoured on God's people. This new community is founded on the teachings of the apostles and sustained in the breaking of the bread.

Psalm 23

The LORD is my shepherd; I shall not be in want. (Ps. 23:1)

1 Peter 2:19-25

Doing the right things does not guarantee that one will not experience difficulties, hardships, rejection, or even suffering. Here Christ is presented as the model for our path of endurance and loyalty to God, particularly in the midst of adversity.

John 10:1-10

Jesus uses an image familiar to the people of his day to make a point about spiritual leadership. Good shepherds bring people to life through Jesus, but those who avoid Jesus are dangerous to the flock.

Preface Easter

Color White

Prayers of Intercession

The prayers are prepared locally for each occasion. The following examples may be adapted or used as appropriate.

Rejoicing in the risen life of Christ, let us pray for the church, the world, and all who are in need.

A brief silence.

We pray for the church. Strengthen ministers of word, sacrament, and service who are called to shepherd your people. Renew your church and unite us through your Spirit. Send us out to serve our neighbors and to receive their care with gratitude. Lord, in your mercy,

hear our prayer.

For the earth. For pastures and prairies, rivers and streams, oceans and mountains. For those who care for livestock and pets. For all animals, wild and domestic, with whom we share this world. Lord, in your mercy,

hear our prayer.

For the nations. Guide leaders into the path of peace. Uphold all who govern. Bring an end to injustice, warfare, and violence. Protect those who risk their lives to shield others from danger. Lord, in your mercy,

hear our prayer.

For those in need. For those who lack safe housing and adequate food. For workers whose pay is insufficient to meet their daily needs. Comfort the grieving and heal the sick (*especially*). Lord, in your mercy,

hear our prayer.

For this assembly. For ushers, acolytes, and greeters. For those who clean and prepare this space for worship. Give wisdom to our councils, committees, and all who guide this congregation's ministry. Lord, in your mercy,

hear our prayer.

Here other intercessions may be offered.

With thanksgiving, we remember those who have died in faith (*especially*). In your goodness and mercy, bring us to the fulfillment of your promise to dwell in your house forever. Lord, in your mercy,

hear our prayer.

Joining our voices with your faithful ones in every time and place, we offer our prayers in the name of the Risen One, Jesus Christ our Lord.

Amen.

Images in the Readings

To deepen our contemplation of the metaphor of Christ as **shepherd**, it is good to review the positive use that the Bible makes of the image of **sheep**. The Jewish scriptures remembered their people as having been sheep- and goatherders. Sheep signified the communal life of the people, constituted a source of food and clothing, and functioned as the primary sacrificial gifts to God. The single wandering lamb from the parable of the lost sheep is not the image in John 10. Nor is a barefoot, white-robed man a realistic depiction of the shepherd, who by the first century was thought of as lower class and religiously unclean. In Genesis 29 Rachel is a shepherd.

Still today some herders in Iran, after gathering the sheep into an enclosure at night, lie down to sleep at the opening of the pen. The wolf cannot enter through the opening because the body of the herder has become the **gate**. In some medieval churches, the main doorway was elaborately decorated with biblical scenes, sometimes also surrounded with the signs of the zodiac, as if the door was a symbol of Christ, proclaimed in the Bible and encompassing the universe. The body of our Lord, taken in holy communion, is a gate to eternal life.

The image in Acts 2 of the Christian **commune** connects with the church's actual history and present situation, in that the baptized, living with generous hearts, contribute to all who have need. It is appropriate that at every meeting of Christians for worship there be a collection of money, goods, or services for the needy.

Ideas for the Day

- John 9—the gospel for the fourth Sunday in Lent this year—almost seems to end with a cliffhanger. Jesus heals a man blind from birth, and a series of conversations centered on how the man received his sight ensue. At the end of the story, the religious leaders are the ones who don't "see." John 10 begins without addressing chapter 9's cliffhanger. Jesus again speaks to the religious leaders but now employs a "figure of speech" focused on another sense: hearing. He uses the relationship of sheep and shepherd to describe an audible connection of the believer to God. In this season of Easter, how are our senses revealing God's truth?

- Sheep or shepherds are referenced more than five hundred times in scripture. Lynn Anderson, in his book *They Smell Like Sheep: Spiritual Leadership for the 21st Century* (West Monroe, LA: Howard, 1997), infers that this shepherd/sheep metaphor would have been quickly understood. It would have been appreciated in the biblical world where on a typical day one expected to observe at least one flock of sheep trailing behind its shepherd. In Jesus' day, shepherds and sheep were as common as smartphones are today. What would be an appropriate, quickly understood metaphor for the church during this Easter season?

- One busy school day, two classrooms of students were in the cafeteria just prior to the morning bell, awaiting the arrival of their homeroom teachers. The children were chatting and moving about the room. The first bell rang. The students became antsy and began to wander. A staff person appeared and informed the students that a teachers' meeting went long. She then tried to get the students to line up by classes, but the children refused to adhere to the stranger's instructions. Finally, the teachers appeared and called out, "Line up, please." Immediately the students became quiet and lined up. How do you respond when you hear the Good Shepherd's call?

Connections with the Liturgy

The commendation spoken at the close of Christian burial (*ELW*, p. 283) asks the Savior to receive "a sheep of your own fold, a lamb of your own flock"; and the final blessing (p. 285) refers to our Lord Jesus as "the great shepherd of the sheep."

Let the Children Come

Have you ever thought of Good Shepherd Sunday as being particularly ecological? Today we imagine Jesus' sacrificial love for us through the metaphor of the sheep and shepherd, and also the expectation of sacrifice in caring for all of creation. Jesus is the model sacrificial caregiver; how do we follow this shepherd? Children are drawn to stories about animals and naturally want to be helpful. How does your community support children in nurturing all of creation? Frequently the "blessing of the animals" happens in the fall, and yet does today seem like a good day for a mutual blessing with our fellow creatures?

Assembly Song
Gathering

Christ the Lord is risen today; Alleluia! ELW 369, LBW 128

All people that on earth do dwell ELW 883, LBW 245

Rise, O Sun of righteousness ELW 657

Psalmody and Acclamations

Gelineau, Joseph. "Psalm 23" from ACYG.

Pishner, Stephen. "Fourth Sunday of Easter (A)" from COJ:A.

Pavlechko, Thomas. "Psalm 23" from SMP.

(GA) Haas, David. "Alleluia: Our God Is Speaking." SATB, cant, assembly, kybd, gtr, 2 C inst. GIA G-7727.

Hymn of the Day

The King of love my shepherd is ELW 502, LBW 456
   ST. COLUMBA

Savior, like a shepherd lead us ELW 789, TFF 254 *BRADBURY*
   LBW 481 *HER VIL TIES*

My Shepherd, you supply my need ELW 782 *RESIGNATION*

Offering

Have no fear, little flock   ELW 764, LBW 476

The Lord's my shepherd   ELW 778, LBW 451

Communion

Shepherd me, O God   ELW 780

You satisfy the hungry heart   ELW 484, WOV 711

At the Lamb's high feast we sing   ELW 362, LBW 210

Sending

Praise the Lord, rise up rejoicing   ELW 544, LBW 196

I know that my Redeemer lives!   ELW 619, LBW 352

Additional Assembly Songs

Our Paschal Lamb, that sets us free   MSB1 S499, WOV 679

My good shepherd is the Lord   ASG 23

O God of Jacob, by whose hand   LBW 477

⊕ Dexter, Noel. "The Lord Is My Shepherd" from *Let the Peoples Sing*. SATB. AFP 9780800675394.

⊕ Mahamba, Deogratias. "Blessed Be the Name/*Heri ni jina*." SATB. ELW 797.

☼ Assad, Audrey/Matt Maher. "Restless" from CCLI.

☼ Blakesley, Joshua. "The Lord Is My Shepherd" from *Spirit and Song*, vol. 2. OCP.

☼ Grant, Natalie/Christa Wells. "Our Hope Endures" from CCLI.

☼ Hart, Sarah/Matt Maher. "Praying with a Broken Heart" from OCP.

☼ Miller, Tony. "Shepherd of My Soul" from CCLI.

☼ Myrin, Jonas/Chris Tomlin/Tim Wanstall/Matt Redman. "Endless Hallelujah" from CCLI.

Music for the Day
Choral

♫ Highben, Zebulon M. "The Good Shepherd." SAB, pno, fl. GIA G-7483.

♫ Pelz, Walter L. "The King of Love My Shepherd Is." SATB, assembly, kybd, opt fl. AFP 9780800646011.

P ♫ Roberts, William Bradley. "Savior, like a Shepherd Lead Us." U, opt fl. AFP 9780800646981.

P ♫ Wetzler, Robert. "Shepherd, Lead Us." SATB, pno. AFP 9780806697178.

Children's Choir

Bartha, Daniel. "I'm the Good Shepherd." U/2 pt. CG CGA861.

Lord, Suzanne. "Do You Know Your Shepherd's Voice?" 2 pt, kybd. CG CGA673.

Pote, Allen. "The Lord Is My Shepherd." U/2 pt, pno. CG CGA930.

Keyboard / Instrumental

Berthier, Jacques. *Pastorale for Oboe and Organ*. Ob, org. GIA G-3123.

P Miller, Aaron David. "Have No Fear, Little Flock" (Little Flock) from *Hymns in Jazz Style*. Pno. AFP 9780800678531.

P ♫ Titus, Hiram. "The King of Love My Shepherd Is" (St. Columba) from *Glorify! Hymn Settings for Piano*. Pno. AFP 9781451424218.

P Wright, M. Searle. "The Lord's My Shepherd" (Brother James' Air) from *Augsburg Organ Library: Marriage*. Org. AFP 9781451486025.

Handbell

♫ Childers, Brian. "The Shepherd." 3-4 oct hb solo, pno. FTT 1047.

♫ Edwards, Dan. "My Shepherd Will Supply My Need." 3 oct, L2. CPH 97-7432.

♫ Evanovich, Joshua. "My Shepherd, the King of Love." 3-6 oct hb, opt 2 oct hc, L2+, GIA G-8325. Opt B flat or C inst, GIA G-8325INST.

Monday, May 8
Julian of Norwich, renewer of the church, died around 1416

Julian (or Juliana) was most likely a Benedictine nun living in an isolated cell attached to the Carrow Priory in Norwich (NOR-rich), England. Definite facts about her life are sparse. However, when she was about thirty years old, she reported visions that she later compiled into a book, *Sixteen Revelations of Divine Love*, a classic of medieval mysticism. The visions declared that love was the meaning of religious experience, provided by Christ who is love, for the purpose of love. A prayer and a hymn attributed to Julian are included in *Evangelical Lutheran Worship* (p. 87, #735).

Tuesday, May 9
Nicolaus Ludwig von Zinzendorf, renewer of the church, hymnwriter, died 1760

Count Zinzendorf was born into an aristocratic family and after the death of his father was raised by his Pietistic grandmother. This influence was a lasting one, and he moved away from what he felt was an overly intellectual Lutheranism. When he was twenty-two, a group of Moravians asked permission to live on his lands. He agreed, and they established a settlement they called Herrnhut, or "the Lord's watch." Eventually worldwide Moravian missions emanated from this community. Zinzendorf participated in these missions and is also remembered for writing hymns characteristic of his Pietistic faith, including "Jesus, Still Lead On" (ELW 624).

⊕ = global song   ♫ = relates to hymn of the day

☼ = praise song   P = available in Prelude Music Planner

May 14, 2017
Fifth Sunday of Easter

As we continue to celebrate the fifty days of Easter, today's gospel includes Jesus' promise that he goes to prepare a place for his followers in his Father's house. Our baptism commissions us to share Jesus' mission in the world. As First Peter reminds us, we are a holy people, called to proclaim the one who called us out of darkness into light. In words and deeds we bear witness to the risen Christ—our way, our truth, our life.

Prayer of the Day

Almighty God, your Son Jesus Christ is the way, the truth, and the life. Give us grace to love one another, to follow in the way of his commandments, and to share his risen life with all the world, for he lives and reigns with you and the Holy Spirit, one God, now and forever.

Gospel Acclamation

Alleluia. I am the way, the truth, | and the life.* No one comes to the Father ex- | cept through me. *Alleluia.* (John 14:6)

Readings and Psalm

Acts 7:55-60

Stephen was one of the seven men chosen by the apostles to serve tables so that the apostles could be free to serve the word (Acts 6:1-6). Stephen does more than distribute food, however. For his preaching of God's word, he becomes the first martyr of the faith.

Psalm 31:1-5, 15-16

Into your hands, O Lord, I commend my spirit. (Ps. 31:5)

1 Peter 2:2-10

Christ is the cornerstone of God's saving work and the foundation of our lives. We are God's chosen, holy people who continuously celebrate and declare the mercy of God we experience through Jesus Christ.

John 14:1-14

On the night that he is to be arrested, Jesus shares final words with his disciples. As the one through whom God is known, he promises to go before them and act on their behalf.

Preface   Easter

Color   White

Prayers of Intercession

The prayers are prepared locally for each occasion. The following examples may be adapted or used as appropriate.
Rejoicing in the risen life of Christ, let us pray for the church, the world, and all who are in need.

A brief silence.
We pray for the church. Show us your ways. Teach us your truth. Enliven us in mission. Keep us from discord. Lead us to unity for the sake of the gospel. Lord, in your mercy,
hear our prayer.
For the earth. Turn us away from impulses to pollute this world. Protect fragile habitats. Nurture our planet to be a life-sustaining home for generations yet to be born. Lord, in your mercy,
hear our prayer.
For the nations. Fill all leaders with a spirit of compassion for the poor and oppressed. Give courage to those who work for justice and equality. Bring an end to conflict and violence. Lord, in your mercy,
hear our prayer.
For those in need. Draw near to those who struggle with depression. Comfort those for whom this day evokes heartache or sorrow. Console those who grieve, and heal those who are ill (*especially*). Lord, in your mercy,
hear our prayer.
For this assembly. Bless mothers and all who offer motherly care. Strengthen child care workers, nursery attendants, and those who teach our youth. Uphold our elders and those who care for aging parents. Lord, in your mercy,
hear our prayer.
Here other intercessions may be offered.
With thanksgiving, we remember those who have died in faith and those who have borne witness to your love (*especially the apostle Matthias*). Bring us with them to dwell with you forever. Lord, in your mercy,
hear our prayer.
Joining our voices with your faithful ones in every time and place, we offer our prayers in the name of the Risen One, Jesus Christ our Lord.
Amen.

Images in the Readings

For some Christians and pieties, the image of Christ as the **way** has been used to condemn most other people. John's community did indeed think of itself as enjoying the greatest **truth** and **life** eternal. However, we are called to recognize the Way as the good news that God loves the whole world, as the wideness of God's mercy.

John's metaphor of the Father's **house** and its many dwelling places has been literalized for many Christians, as if heaven were a king's mansion with outbuildings provided for the lesser inhabitants. In a different application of this image, the house is the room in which we weekly gather: Here God dwells. Here God serves up our meals. First Peter uses the image of house to be a metaphor for the believing community.

First Peter is filled with images. Several medieval mystics used the image of the eucharist being **milk**. The central image of this passage is Christ as the **cornerstone**, the living stone, of the house that is the church. Many cornerstones are engraved with the date of construction. For Christians, this date is the year of our baptism. Perhaps those congregations that publish members' birthdays could replace these dates with their baptismal anniversary.

Ideas for the Day

- If a lion and a tiger were on the same path, approaching each other in the jungle, which animal do you think would step aside to avoid defeat? In Rudyard Kipling's 1894 classic *The Jungle Book*, a conversation takes place between Mowgli, the man cub, and the other animals. They are discussing what the most feared thing is in the jungle. The best answer is given by the Owl: that the most feared thing in the jungle is death, because when death is on the path it moves for no one. In John 14 Jesus is trying to explain to his disciples that he is on a road face-to-face with death for their sake. Jesus is not afraid and will not step aside. He is the Way to defeat death. On Easter we realize that it was death who stepped aside.

- The "I am" statements in the Gospel of John remind us of the connection between Yahweh and Christ. Jesus' words, "I am the way, the truth, and the life" (John 14:6), are preceded by Thomas's protest that "we do not know where you are going. How can we know the way?" How often do we feel compelled to confess what we are not or what we do not know when confronted with difficult circumstances? I am not a teacher; I cannot help you understand the Bible. I am not a pastor; I cannot pray for you. Easter gives us permission to say "I can" because *Jesus is.* To answer my baptismal call, and because of who God is, *I can* ask for anything in Jesus' name—"I AM"—and it will be done.

- A blacksmith was observed using fire to design a sword. The blacksmith would leave the metal in the fire pit for a long time while the fire raged. Not only was the metal in the fire, but there was also fire in the metal. The relationship between the fire and the metal is similar to the relationship between Jesus and the Father. Jesus says, "I am in the Father and the Father is in me" (John 14:11). Like the fire and metal, the two are separate yet are one.

Connections with the Liturgy

As we are dismissed from worship, we go in peace, since Christ is with us. Christ is with us on the way: Christ is our Way.

Cited from *Daily Prayer*, a 1941 publication by Eric Milner-White and George Wallace Briggs, in both Morning Prayer (p. 304) and Evening Prayer (p. 317) in *Evangelical Lutheran Worship* is a beloved prayer that asks God to be with us as we journey on the way. "You have called your servants to ventures of which we cannot see the ending . . . knowing that your hand is leading us and your love supporting us." We can think of Thomas's question to Jesus as we pray this prayer.

Let the Children Come

The Montessori method of education with children includes the principle of a "prepared environment." The idea is that the place itself is a key part of learning because it has been carefully prepared ahead of time to have everything the learner needs and no extraneous clutter that is not helpful. Our worship places are similar. While you may have rooms especially prepared for children, the worship space is shared by many people. What obstacles do children have in your worship space? What might be distracting? What might be especially engaging for children? Take a tour of your worship environment from a child's vantage point.

Assembly Song
Gathering

Now all the vault of heaven resounds ELW 367, LBW 143
Alleluia! Jesus is risen! ELW 377, WOV 674, TFF 91
Awake, my heart, with gladness ELW 378, LBW 129

Psalmody and Acclamations

Bruxvoort Colligan, Richard. "Into Your Hands (Psalm 31:5, 15)" from *Sharing the Road*. AFP 9780800678630.
Haugen, Marty. "I Put My Life in Your Hands" from PCY, vol. l.
Sedio, Mark. "Psalm 31:1-5, 15-16" from PWA.
(GA) Haas, David. "Alleluia: Our God Is Speaking." SATB, cant, assembly, kybd, gtr, 2 C inst. GIA G-7727.

Hymn of the Day

Here, O Lord, your servants gather ELW 530 *TŌKYŌ*
Come, my way, my truth, my life ELW 816, LBW 513 *THE CALL*
Sing with all the saints in glory ELW 426, WOV 691 *MISSISSIPPI*

Offering

Blessing, Honor, and Glory ELW 433, W&P 21
As the grains of wheat ELW 465, WOV 705

Communion

I received the living God ELW 477, WOV 700
You are the way ELW 758, LBW 464
Now We Remain ELW 500, W&P 106

Sending

Christ is alive! Let Christians sing ELW 389, LBW 363

Evening and morning ELW 761, LBW 465

Additional Assembly Songs

I will trust in the Lord TFF 256

Alleluia, alleluia, give thanks WOV 671

Go in peace and serve the Lord W&P 46

⊕ Bell, John. "Who Am I?" from *Heaven Shall Not Wait*. U. GIA G-3646.

⊕ Hehe tune, arr. Austin Lovelace. "Christ Is the Way" from *Set Free: A Collection of African Hymns*. SATB, cantor. AFP 9780806600451.

☼ Douglass, Jonathon/Joel Houston. "One Way" from CCLI.

☼ Evans, Darrell. "I Lay Me Down" from CCLI.

☼ Ferguson, James/Rich Thompson. "The Love of the Father" from CCLI.

☼ Moore, David. "Forever Yours" from CCLI.

☼ Mooring, Jack/Leeland Mooring/Steve Wilson. "The Door" from CCLI.

☼ Smith, Christi/Patrick Smith/Steve Angrisano/Tom Tomaszek. "You Are the Way" from *Spirit and Song*, vol. 1. OCP.

Music for the Day
Choral

P ♫ Costello, Michael D. "Sing with All the Saints in Glory." SATB, assembly, org, fl. AFP 9780806698311.

P ♫ Larkin, Michael. "Come, My Way, My Truth, My Life." SATB, kybd. AFP 9781451492446.

P Patterson, Mark. "Sing This Day with Joy!" SATB, kybd, opt 2 tpts. AFP 9781451401080.

♫ Vaughan Williams, Ralph/arr. Jonathan Barnhart. "The Call." 2 pt trbl, kybd. ECS 15259.

Children's Choir

Gay, Sandra T. "Sing Thankful Songs (Cantad cancion de gratitude)." U/2 pt, kybd, opt fl, opt hb/hc. CG CGA828.

Hopson, Hal H. "Lord, Lead Us Day by Day." U, kybd. HOP HH 3908.

Marshall, Jane. "Dear Lord, Lead Me Day by Day." U, kybd, opt fl. CG CGA637.

Keyboard / Instrumental

♫ Hassell, Michael. "Sing with All the Saints in Glory" (Mississippi) from *More Folkways: Hymn Arrangements for Solo Instrument and Piano*. Inst, pno. AFP 9780800657307.

P ♫ Kerr, J. Wayne. "Here, O Lord, Your Servants Gather" (Tōkyō) from *Organ Celebrations*. Org. AFP 9781451451740.

P Organ, Anne Krentz. "I Know That My Redeemer Lives" (Duke Street) from *Piano Reflections on Hymns of the Faith*. Pno. AFP 9780806698069.

P ♫ Raabe, Nancy. "Sing with All the Saints in Glory" (Mississippi) from *Grace and Peace, vol. 6: Songs of Heaven*. Pno. AFP 9781451479621.

Handbell

P Glasgow, Michael J. "No Dark Valley." 3-7 oct hb, opt 3-6 oct hc, L3+. HOP 2665. Opt vln, opt DB, opt gtr/banjo/mandolin, HOP 2665P. Opt acc CD, HOP A514.

♫ McChesney, Kevin. "Come My Way, My Truth, My Life." 2-3 oct, L2. LOR 20/1554L.

Payn, William A. "Commemoration of the Spirit." 5 oct, L5. AGEHR AG5031J.

Monday, May 15
Matthias, Apostle (transferred)

After Christ's ascension, the apostles met in Jerusalem to choose a replacement for Judas. Matthias was chosen over Joseph Justus by the casting of lots. Little is known about Matthias, and little is reported about him in the account of his election in Acts 1:15-26. Matthias traveled among the disciples from the beginning of Jesus' ministry until his ascension. His task, after he was enrolled among the eleven remaining disciples, was to bear witness to the resurrection.

Thursday, May 18
Erik, King of Sweden, martyr, died 1160

Erik, long considered the patron saint of Sweden, ruled from 1150 to 1160. He is honored for efforts to bring peace to the nearby pagan kingdoms and for his crusades to spread the Christian faith in Nordic lands. He established a protected Christian mission in Finland that was led by Henry of Uppsala. As king, Erik was noted for his desire to establish fair laws and courts and for his concern for the poor and sick. Erik was killed by a Danish army that approached him at worship on the day after the Ascension. He is reported to have said, "Let us at least finish the sacrifice. The rest of the feast I shall keep elsewhere." As he left worship he was killed.

⊕ = global song   ♫ = relates to hymn of the day

☼ = praise song   P = available in Prelude Music Planner

May 21, 2017
Sixth Sunday of Easter

Jesus does not leave his followers orphaned. Through the Holy Spirit Jesus comes to abide with his disciples of every generation. As Pentecost draws near, we are reminded that the risen Christ dwells in us as the Spirit of truth. We receive this Spirit in baptism and pray that in our gathering around the Lord's table the Spirit will transform us to be the body of the risen Christ in the world.

Prayer of the Day

Almighty and ever-living God, you hold together all things in heaven and on earth. In your great mercy receive the prayers of all your children, and give to all the world the Spirit of your truth and peace, through Jesus Christ, our Savior and Lord, who lives and reigns with you and the Holy Spirit, one God, now and forever.

Gospel Acclamation

Alleluia. Those who love me will keep my word, and my Fa-
ꞁ ther will love them,* and we will come to them and make our
ꞁ home with them. *Alleluia.* (John 14:23)

Readings and Psalm

Acts 17:22-31

In Athens, Paul faces the challenge of proclaiming the gospel to Greeks who know nothing of either Jewish or Christian tradition. He proclaims that the "unknown god" whom they worship is the true Lord of heaven and earth who will judge the world with justice through Jesus, whom God has raised from the dead.

Psalm 66:8-20

Bless our God, you peoples; let the sound of praise be heard. (Ps. 66:8)

1 Peter 3:13-22

Christians have a zeal for doing what is right in God's eyes no matter what the circumstances because in baptism we are saved and made alive. Thus our Christian beliefs and behavior are to be a matter of public record just as our baptism is.

John 14:15-21

In final words to his disciples on the night of his arrest, Jesus encourages obedience to his commandments and speaks of the Spirit, who will be with them forever.

Preface   Easter

Color   White

Prayers of Intercession

The prayers are prepared locally for each occasion. The following examples may be adapted or used as appropriate.

Rejoicing in the risen life of Christ, let us pray for the church, the world, and all who are in need.
A brief silence.

We pray for the church. Draw your whole church together as one. Bring an end to division. Send your Spirit into your people and rouse us to greater love and mission. Lord, in your mercy,
hear our prayer.

For the earth. For scientists, photographers, and explorers. For scholars, poets, musicians, artists, and all who lead us to greater knowledge and appreciation of beauty. For lakes and rivers, watersheds and wetlands, ponds and oceans. Lord, in your mercy,
hear our prayer.

For the nations. Give wisdom to those who govern. Strengthen all who work for peace. Protect those who have been displaced or have left their homes in search of safety and freedom. Lord, in your mercy,
hear our prayer.

For those in need. For those who suffer abuse or neglect. For those who suffer post-traumatic stress. For those who struggle with addiction. For those who grieve and all who are ill (*especially*). Lord, in your mercy,
hear our prayer.

For this assembly. Bless those preparing for baptism and affirmation of baptism. Strengthen our ministries of evangelism, outreach, and pastoral care. Deepen our faith and knowledge of you. Lord, in your mercy,
hear our prayer.

Here other intercessions may be offered.

With thanksgiving, we remember those who have died (*especially Helena, the mother of Constantine*). Inspire us by their witness to your love. Bring us into your eternal presence to live with you forever. Lord, in your mercy,
hear our prayer.

Joining our voices with your faithful ones in every time and place, we offer our prayers in the name of the Risen One, Jesus Christ our Lord.
Amen.

Images in the Readings

John calls the Spirit of truth our **Advocate**. This image implies a trial and the probability of judgment. Standing before God, we need someone to speak on our behalf. The reading from 1 Peter also includes the image of a trial in which we must defend our stance.

In John 14, Jesus uses adoption imagery for those who receive the Spirit of truth. Yet Paul's sermon at the Areopagus calls all his pagan hearers God's **offspring**. For centuries, Jewish and Christian theologians have discussed how humans are both like and unlike God, how we enact our relationship to the Divine. A dominant teaching has been that just as God cares for creation, so as God's offspring we are to be dedicated to that care.

The church is the **ark**, floating above the chaos of the seas, brought in safety to the harbor. One early Christian bishop directed his clergy to hold the baptismal candidates down under the water three times until they rose up gasping for air. The water of baptism not only gently washes the infant; it also joins the candidate to the death and resurrection of Christ. The eighteenth-century Welsh Methodist poet Ann Griffiths wrote, "We'll yet escape the drowning / because God is our ark."

Ideas for the Day

- The whole church plays in the baptismal font during Easter. Today is an especially good day to pay attention to what kind of font you have. What is its shape? If it's a traditional font, perhaps it has eight sides. This octagonal star shape has many meanings in the Christian tradition, one being that it symbolizes the eight persons saved on the ark in the great flood of Genesis 6. Today's second reading alludes to this story and is an opportunity to invite the congregation to study your font's particular style (and a great opportunity to do some research yourself). If your font has a deep bowl, great connections can be made to the shape of the bowl and the ark that held all life for forty days and forty nights.
- The Religious Society of Friends tradition speaks of "inner light" in ways similar to how Jesus speaks of the Spirit abiding with and in his followers. And in the second part of this gospel reading, Jesus even proclaims that he makes a dwelling (abides) in his disciples. Nineteenth-century Quaker Lucretia Mott wrote in a sermon, "The likeness we bear to Jesus is more essential than our notions of him" (Anna Davis Hallowell, ed., *James and Lucretia Mott: Life and Letters* [Boston: Houghton Mifflin, 1884]). What does it mean to imagine Christ as actually abiding in us and all humanity, rather than just imagining ideas about Christ?
- Today's gospel reading sets the stage for Jesus' ascension. Jesus tells his disciples that he will not leave them alone or "orphaned" (John 14:18). He will reveal himself to those who "keep his commandments," perhaps a reference to the previous chapter where Jesus commands his followers to "love one another" as a sign of discipleship (13:34-35). How does love, and specifically God's love, keep us from feeling alone in this world? Lift up stories of love within your congregation or stories of feeling alone and then being found.

Connections with the Liturgy

In the liturgy for Holy Baptism (*ELW*, p. 230), the thanksgiving over the font likens the water in the font to the waters of the flood, through which God delivered Noah and his family. The additional thanksgivings at the font, II, IV, and V (pp. 70–71), also use Noah's flood as a metaphor for baptism.

Let the Children Come

Language acquisition is an amazing thing. If we relied only on the gospel for our understanding of the word *commandment*, we might find *love* as its synonym. And yet somehow the word *commandment* takes on a different hue than love in our wider vocabulary. Children come to understand God's love through the context of family and then community. How does your church community model for children the command to love one another? How does the grace-filled command to love one another overflow from Maundy Thursday to all of these abundant Sundays of Easter?

Assembly Song
Gathering

Alleluia! Sing to Jesus   ELW 392, LBW 158

We know that Christ is raised   ELW 449, LBW 189

Come, thou almighty King   ELW 408, LBW 522

Psalmody and Acclamations

Organ, Anne Krentz. "Psalm 66:8-20" from PWA.

Smith, Alan. "Shout with Joy" from *Psalm Songs 2*. AFP 0800657713.

Tate, Paul. "Sixth Sunday of Easter (A)" from COJ:A.

(GA) Haas, David. "Alleluia: Our God Is Speaking." SATB, cant, assembly, kybd, gtr, 2 C inst. GIA G-7727.

Hymn of the Day

Dear Christians, one and all, rejoice   ELW 594, LBW 299
NUN FREUT EUCH

Come down, O Love divine   ELW 804, LBW 508   *DOWN AMPNEY*

Loving Spirit   ELW 397   *RESTORATION*

Offering

Now thank we all our God   ELW 839/840, LBW 533/534

Waterlife   ELW 457, W&P 145

Communion

Bread of life from heaven ELW 474

Children of the heavenly Father ELW 781, LBW 474

Like the murmur of the dove's song ELW 403, WOV 685

Sending

Go, my children, with my blessing ELW 543, TFF 161, WOV 721

Rise, O church, like Christ arisen ELW 548

Additional Assembly Songs

Shout for joy loud and long WOV 793

Seigneur, rassemble-nous SP 35

Come, O Holy Spirit, come WOV 681

⊕ Haya tune, arr. Joas Kijugo. "The Love of God Almighty" from *Set Free: A Collection of African Hymns*. SATB, cantor. AFP 9780806600451.

⊕ Sedio, Mark. "Alleluia Verse in African Style" from *Global Choral Sounds*. SATB, cantor. perc. CPH 98-3610.

☼ Angrisano, Steve/Tom Tomaszek. "Come to the Lord" from *Spirit and Song*, vol. 1. OCP.

☼ Dean, Dan/Don Poythress/Tony Wood. "I Choose to Believe" from CCLI.

☼ Foote, Billy J./Cindy Foote. "You Are God Alone" from CCLI.

☼ Lee, Kyle Wayne/Randy Phillips. "These Bones" from CCLI.

☼ Maher, Matt/Mia Fieldes/Jason Ingram. "Everything Is Grace" from CCLI.

☼ Millard, Bart/Jim Bryson/Nathan Cochran/Mike Scheuchzer/Robby Shaffer/Barry Graul. "The Hurt and the Healer" from CCLI.

Music for the Day
Choral

♫ Dake, Kenneth. "I Will Arise." SATB. MSM 50-2850.

Gumpeltzhaimer, Adam. "O Praise the Lord." SAB. GIA G-2294.

Tallis, Thomas. "If Ye Love Me." SATB. Various editions.

♫ Wolff, S. Drummond. "Come Down, O Love Divine." SAB, org, tpt. MSM 50-5500.

Children's Choir

Cherwien, David. "In Thee Is Gladness." U or SATB, org, opt rec, tamb. CG CGA873.

Peterson, Dale. "Sing a Jubilant Song." 2 pt, kybd. CG CGA498.

Sleeth, Natalie. "If You Love Me" from *LifeSongs*. U, kybd, opt Orff instr. AFP 9780806642703.

Keyboard / Instrumental

P♫ Childs, Edwin T. "Loving Spirit" (Restoration) from *American Folk Hymns for Organ*. Org. AFP 9781451494051.

P Hansen, Sherri. "Waterlife" (Spirit Life) from *Piano Weavings*. Pno. AFP 9781451497861.

P♫ Organ, Anne Krentz. "Loving Spirit" (Restoration) from *Piano Reflections on Pentecost Tunes*. Pno. AFP 9781451499148.

P Wahl, Carol. "Holy, Holy, Holy" (Argentine Santo) from *Cry of the Dove: Piano Settings*. Pno. AFP 9781451479614.

Handbell

P Bettcher, Peggy. "Our God" from *Easy to Ring Praise & Worship VII*. 2-3 oct, L2, HOP 2687. 3-5 oct, L2, HOP 2670.

♫ Stewart, Kevin. "Come, Ye Sinners, Poor and Needy." 2-3 oct, L3. GIA G-7588.

♫ Tucker, Sondra. "Come Down, O Love Divine" from *Easter and Beyond*. 3-5 oct hb, opt 2 oct hc, L2+. LOR 20/1885L.

Sunday, May 21
Helena, mother of Constantine, died around 330

Wife of the co-regent of the West, Helena (or Helen) was mother of Constantine, who later became Roman emperor. After he was converted to Christianity, he influenced her also to become Christian. From that point she lived an exemplary life of faith, particularly through acts of generosity toward the poor. She is also remembered for traveling through Palestine and building churches on the sites she believed to be where Jesus was born, where he was buried, and from which he ascended.

Wednesday, May 24
Nicolaus Copernicus, died 1543; Leonhard Euler, died 1783; scientists

Remembering scientists such as Copernicus and Euler offers an opportunity to ponder the mysteries of the universe and the grandeur of God's creation. Copernicus is an example of a renaissance person. He formally studied astronomy, mathematics, Greek, Plato, law, medicine, and canon law. He also had interests in theology, poetry, and the natural and social sciences. Copernicus is chiefly remembered for his work as an astronomer and his idea that the sun, not the earth, is the center of the solar system.

Euler (OY-ler) is regarded as one of the founders of the science of pure mathematics and made important contributions to mechanics, hydrodynamics, astronomy, optics, and acoustics.

⊕ = global song   ♫ = relates to hymn of the day
☼ = praise song   P = available in Prelude Music Planner

May 25, 2017
Ascension of Our Lord

In today's gospel the risen Christ ascends into heaven and his followers are assured that the Spirit will empower them to be witnesses throughout the earth. The disciples were told to not gaze up into heaven to look for Jesus; we find his presence among us as we proclaim the word and share the Easter feast. We too long for the Spirit to enliven our faith and invigorate our mission.

Prayer of the Day

Almighty God, your only Son was taken into the heavens and in your presence intercedes for us. Receive us and our prayers for all the world, and in the end bring everything into your glory, through Jesus Christ, our Sovereign and Lord, who lives and reigns with you and the Holy Spirit, one God, now and forever.
or
Almighty God, your blessed Son, our Savior Jesus Christ, ascended far above all heavens that he might fill all things. Mercifully give us faith to trust that, as he promised, he abides with us on earth to the end of time, who lives and reigns with you and the Holy Spirit, one God, now and forever.

Gospel Acclamation

Alleluia. Go and make disciples of all nations, ǀ says the Lord;*
I am with you always, to the end ǀ of the age. *Alleluia.* (Matt. 28:19, 20)

Readings and Psalm

Acts 1:1-11

Before he is lifted into heaven, Jesus promises that the missionary work of the disciples will spread out from Jerusalem to all the world. His words provide an outline of the book of Acts.

Psalm 47

God has gone up with a shout. (Ps. 47:5)

or Psalm 93

Ever since the world began, your throne has been established. (Ps. 93:2)

Ephesians 1:15-23

The risen and exalted Christ reigns over the entire universe. The author of Ephesians prays that we would be given the wisdom to comprehend this and display it through love toward others.

Luke 24:44-53

On the day of his ascension, Jesus leaves his disciples with a commission, a blessing, and a promise of the Holy Spirit.

Preface   Ascension

Color   White

Prayers of Intercession

The prayers are prepared locally for each occasion. The following examples may be adapted or used as appropriate.
Rejoicing in the risen life of Christ, let us pray for the church, the world, and all who are in need.
A brief silence.
We pray for the church. Clothe us with your power. Uphold all preachers and teachers of the gospel. Unite us through the Spirit and lead us out in mission. Lord, in your mercy,
hear our prayer.
For the earth. For hills and valleys, prairies and pastures. For deserts and mountains, tundra and bogs. Nurture all plants and animals, and sustain those whose labor produces our food. Lord, in your mercy,
hear our prayer.
For the nations. Guide all local, national, and international leaders. Build up safe communities. Bring an end to violence in families as well as between nations. Liberate those who live under oppression. Strengthen those who work for equality. Lord, in your mercy,
hear our prayer.
For those in need. For those who travel. For those who are abused or neglected. For all refugees and immigrants. For students approaching a graduation. For those who are ill (*especially*). Lord, in your mercy,
hear our prayer.
For this assembly. Bless those who are preparing for baptism or affirmation of baptism. Strengthen our ministries of education and outreach. Uphold those who lead us in prayer and song. Lord, in your mercy,
hear our prayer.
Here other intercessions may be offered.
With thanksgiving, we remember those who have died (*especially*). Inspire us by their witness and bring us to receive our inheritance with all the saints in your glory. Lord, in your mercy,
hear our prayer.

Joining our voices with your faithful ones in every time and place, we offer our prayers in the name of the Risen One, Jesus Christ our Lord.
Amen.

Images in the Readings

Ascension Day plays with the ancient cosmological picture of the three-tier universe, the highest level of which is **heaven**, or "the heavens." Over the centuries, Christians have speculated in quite different ways about what this heaven is. By the nineteenth century, heaven came to be described as a kind of family summer camp, perfection in populist human terms. However, in the Bible, "heaven" is often a synonym for God, a way to speak about divine majesty and mercy. In Acts, the ascending Jesus is covered with a cloud, which in the Hebrew Scriptures usually refers to the elusive presence yet cosmic power of God. It is important that today's references to heaven not suggest that it is a place that is far away. The risen Christ is here in the assembly of believers.

Luke has two men in **white robes** speaking with the disciples. The Christian church has regularized the wearing of white robes as the sign of baptism. We all can speak of the power of the ascended Christ.

In Ephesians, the **body of Christ** is the church imagined like Atlas, a giant standing on earth holding up the skies, the head being Christ, and the body being the church that fills the world. Today we blend this understanding of "body of Christ" with the bread we eat and the assembly gathered to worship.

Ideas for the Day

- Develop the images and meanings of *open*, *opened*, and *openness* today. Luke mentions that Jesus "opened their minds" (24:45). Likewise, Jesus blessed the disciples while lifting up his open hands (24:50). Echoing the baptism of Jesus, we can visualize the heavens being opened to receive the ascending Christ. What does it mean to have a newly opened mind in light of the open tomb at Easter? How is Christ received in the open hands at the table? How are we called to be open to Christ's larger presence in the world now that the historical Jesus is physically no longer here?
- In the Acts text we hear the charge to be witnesses through the Holy Spirit, who is present even as Christ is not physically present. There are many vulnerable persons in our world who would benefit from signs of God's presence, even when physical presence is difficult. Today is a good Sunday to lift up those who are separated from communities but who still need to feel presence. The Rocky Mountain Synod of the ELCA has a prison ministry called New Beginnings Worshiping Community. Check out their community at http://www.newbeginningswc.org. This ministry is attempting to be a godly presence for those in prison, locked away from the presence of their loved ones. Consider ways your community is or can be a presence for those who need to feel Christ's embrace.
- Ascension Day sparks the imagination and has over the centuries. Do a quick online search for images of today's texts to spark your imagination (try "ascension," "ascending Christ," "Jesus' ascension" and "ascension, Bethany." Secure any required permission before using images in worship, and let the wonderful images of these texts inspire wonder in you.

Connections with the Liturgy

"He ascended into heaven and is seated at the right hand of the Father," says the Nicene Creed. "He ascended into heaven, he is seated at the right hand of the Father," says the Apostles' Creed.

Let the Children Come

"You are witnesses to these things." Those words convey so much! What has been seen is awe inspiring. What has been seen is worthy of being retold. What has been seen might be hard for some to believe. Witnesses have the important job of carrying the story into the future. To be a witness, one must have a first-hand account of the action. Will the children in your community have a firsthand account of God's story, or are they at the periphery of the action? What are children witnessing about how the grace of God is shared in community?

Assembly Song
Gathering

A hymn of glory let us sing! ELW 393, LBW 157
Crown him with many crowns ELW 855, LBW 170
Rejoice, for Christ is king! ELW 430, LBW 171

Psalmody and Acclamations

Haugen, Marty. "God Mounts His Throne" from PCY, vol. 1.
Inwood, Paul. "A Blare of Trumpets" from *Psalm Songs 2*. AFP 0800657713.
Gelineau, Joseph. "Psalm 93" from ACYG.
(GA) Haas, David. "Alleluia: Our God Is Speaking." SATB, cant, assembly, kybd, gtr, 2 C inst. GIA G-7727.

Hymn of the Day

Alleluia! Sing to Jesus ELW 392, LBW 158 *HYFRYDOL*
Hail thee, festival day! ELW 394, LBW 142 *SALVE FESTA DIES*
Christ is alive! Let Christians sing ELW 389, LBW 363 *TRURO*

Offering

My Lord of light ELW 832, WOV 796
Praise, praise! You are my rock ELW 862

Communion

Lord, enthroned in heavenly splendor ELW 475, LBW 172
Beautiful Savior ELW 838, LBW 518
The head that once was crowned ELW 432, LBW 173

Sending

Go, make disciples ELW 540, W&P 47
O Christ, our hope ELW 604, LBW 300

Additional Assembly Songs

Canten, canten himnos a Dios LLC 363
Up through endless ranks of angels LBW 159
Laudate omnes gentes SP 22

⊕ Olson, Howard S., arr. "He's Ascended into Heaven" from *Set Free: A Collection of African Hymns*. SATB, cantor. AFP 9780806600451.

⊕ Yoruba folk melody, "Open Your Mouth and Praise the Lord!" from *Glory to God*. SATB, cant. WJK 0664238971.

☼ Arndt, John/David Gungor/Michael Gungor/Lisa Gungor. "Breathe" from CCLI.

☼ Bryant, Ben/Luke Hellebronth/Myles Dhillon/Tim Hughes. "Spirit Break Out" from CCLI.

☼ Fee, Steve. "Rise and Sing" from CCLI.

☼ Morgan, Reuben/Jason Ingram. "Alive in Us" from CCLI.

☼ Smith, Timothy R. "Alleluia! Alleluia! Let the Holy Anthem Rise" from *Spirit and Song*, vol. 1. OCP.

☼ Tomlin, Chris/Ben Fielding/Matt Maher/Marty Sampson. "The Saving One" from CCLI.

Music for the Day
Choral

P Albrecht, Mark. "Christ Is Alive, Alleluia!" U, pno, opt C inst, opt perc. AFP 9780800677466.

P♫ Highben, Zebulon M. "Christ Is Alive! Let Christians Sing." SATB, assembly, org, br qrt. AFP 9781451451580.

P Larter, Evelyn. "I Know That My Redeemer Lives (Shout On)." SATB, pno, fl. AFP 9781451492507.

P Cherwien, David. "Up through Endless Ranks of Angels." SAB, assembly, org, opt tpt. AFP 9780800658816.

Children's Choir

P Cherwien, Susan Palo. "Day of Arising" from *O Blessed Spring: Hymns of Susan Palo Cherwien*. U or 2 pt, kybd. AFP 9781451423242.

Peacock, David/Owens, Jimmy. "Clap Your Hands, All You People" from *LifeSongs*. U, kybd. AFP 9780806642703.

Sleeth, Natalie. "Go Now in Peace" from *LifeSongs*. U, or 2/3 pt, opt Orff inst. AFP 9780806642703.

Keyboard / Instrumental

Bach, J. S./arr. Michael Helman. "Qui sedes" from *Five Trios from Bach's Mass in B Minor*. Org. ALF 9780757994517.

Burkhardt, Michael. "A Hymn of Glory Let Us Sing!" (Lasst uns erfreuen) from *Five Hymn Accompaniments for Brass Quartet and Organ, Set 1*. Br qrt, Org. MSM 20-842.

P♫ Mackie, Dave. "Hail Thee, Festival Day!" (Salve festa dies) from *By Day and By Night: Piano Settings*. Pno. AFP 9781451420890.

Vaughan Williams, Ralph. "Lord, Enthroned in Heavenly Splendor" (Bryn Calfaria) from *Augsburg Organ Library: Summer*. Org. AFP 9780800676872.

Handbell

♫ Krug, Jason W. "Christ Is Alive!" 3-6 oct, L3-. BP HB366.

♫ Moklebust, Cathy. "Alleluia! Sing to Jesus!" 3-6 oct, L3, CG CGB413. Opt org, CG CGB414. Opt SATB vcs and assembly, CG CGA1047. Opt br qrt or qnt, opt timp, CG CGRP12. Opt full score, CG CGB412.

♫ Wagner, Douglas. "Hail Thee, Festival Day." 3-5 oct, L3+. LOR HB354.

Saturday, May 27
John Calvin, renewer of the church, died 1564

John Calvin began his studies in theology at the University of Paris when he was fourteen. In his mid-twenties he experienced a conversion that led him to embrace the views of the Reformation. His theological ideas are systematically laid out in his *Institutes of the Christian Religion*. He is also well known for his commentaries on scripture. He was a preacher in Geneva, was banished once, and then later returned to reform the city under a theocratic constitution.

⊕ = global song ♫ = relates to hymn of the day
☼ = praise song P = available in Prelude Music Planner

May 28, 2017
Seventh Sunday of Easter

In these days between Ascension and Pentecost, we gather with the disciples in the upper room, waiting for the Spirit to transform the church around the world. In today's gospel Jesus prays for his followers and for their mission in his name. Amid religious, social, and economic divisions, we seek the unity that Jesus had with his Father. Made one in baptism, we go forth to live our faith in the world, eager for the unity that God intends for the whole human family.

Prayer of the Day

O God of glory, your Son Jesus Christ suffered for us and ascended to your right hand. Unite us with Christ and each other in suffering and in joy, that all the world may be drawn into your bountiful presence, through Jesus Christ, our Savior and Lord, who lives and reigns with you and the Holy Spirit, one God, now and forever.

Gospel Acclamation

Alleluia. I will not leave you orphaned, ' says the Lord.* I am com-'ing to you. *Alleluia.* (John 14:18)

Readings and Psalm

Acts 1:6-14

Today's reading is part of the introduction to the narrative of the outpouring of the Spirit on Pentecost. These verses tell of the risen Lord's conversation with his disciples on the eve of his ascension.

Psalm 68:1-10, 32-35

Sing to God, who rides upon the clouds. (Ps. 68:4)

1 Peter 4:12-14; 5:6-11

Our faith in Christ does not make us immune from the scorn of others. Nevertheless, we are to resist the designs of evil when we experience disparagement from others, because we trust God's grace will strengthen and guide us.

John 17:1-11

On the night before his crucifixion, Jesus prays to his heavenly Father, asking that those who continue his work in this world will live in unity.

Preface   Ascension

Color   White

Prayers of Intercession

The prayers are prepared locally for each occasion. The following examples may be adapted or used as appropriate.

Rejoicing in the risen life of Christ, let us pray for the church, the world, and all who are in need.

A brief silence.

We pray for the church. Keep us steadfast in your word. Shape us according to your will. Heal our divisions. Protect us from discord. Unite us in your love. Empower us for mission. Lord, in your mercy,

hear our prayer.

For the earth. For forests and vineyards, marshes and springs. For grasslands and pastures, farmlands and orchards. Protect your creation from damage by earthquake, flood, wind, drought, fire, or hail. Lord, in your mercy,

hear our prayer.

For the nations. For those who govern and all who hold authority. For those who have been displaced by warfare, economic hardship, or disaster (*especially*). Bring freedom, justice, and stability to areas of conflict. Lord, in your mercy,

hear our prayer.

For those in need. For those who are anxious. For those who suffer abuse or neglect. For those who are hungry or homeless. For those who grieve and all who are sick (*especially*). Lord, in your mercy,

hear our prayer.

For this assembly. Deepen our lives of prayer. Open us to the guiding of your Spirit. Fill us with compassion. Nourish us at your holy table. Strengthen us in service to our community. Lord, in your mercy,

hear our prayer.

Here other intercessions may be offered.

With thanksgiving we remember those who have died, especially our loved ones and those who have given their lives in service. Inspire us by their example and bring us to your eternal home. Lord, in your mercy,

hear our prayer.

Joining our voices with your faithful ones in every time and place, we offer our prayers in the name of the Risen One, Jesus Christ our Lord.

Amen.

Images in the Readings

John writes about the **name** of God. When we say, "Stop in the name of the law," we mean that our very invoking of "the law" brings with it the powerful authority behind the law. So the name of God conveys divine mercy and might. Jews still today, careful not to misuse God's name, invoke *Hashem*, "the Name," as a circumlocution for God. Christians can call on the name of the Lord by invoking Jesus Christ.

Eternal life, John writes in this chapter, is knowing God now.

As did the gospel of the first Sunday of Lent, 1 Peter speaks in a literal way about the **devil**. One of the primary questions raised by the world's religions is why there is evil in the world and within the human heart. Borrowed from dualistic religions, the image of the devil personifies the power of evil into a kind of perpetually troublesome anti-God. Christians trust in the mighty hand of God to protect them against this adversary.

Ideas for the Day

- Jesus' prayer for the protection of his disciples is not a petition that they be shielded from all harm, but that their faith be guarded so that they remain obedient and true through times of evil and suffering, regardless of how their trust in God may be challenged. The faith that remains constant in spite of suffering is often countercultural and has a vital role in the world. A startling and dramatic example of this expression can be found in the statements made by family members of victims of the June 17, 2015, mass shooting at Emanuel AME Church in Charleston, South Carolina. See Elahe Izadi, "The Powerful Words of Forgiveness Delivered to Dylann Roof by Victims' Relatives," *Washington Post*, June 19, 2015.

- The 2009 ELCA Churchwide Assembly was notable for its adoption of the social statement *Human Sexuality: Gift and Trust* and its accompanying "Recommendations for Ministry Policies." Also of note, however, was the prayer that marked the difficult and impassioned debate; presiding bishop Mark Hanson halted the proceedings every twenty minutes to lead the voting members of the assembly in prayer. Often members who were arguing on opposing sides would lay hands on and pray for each other in a demonstration of mutual respect and Christian love. While there is still disagreement over the outcome of the debate, the witness of prayer across differences is needed and still relevant. Especially as social media such as Facebook and Twitter increasingly polarize controversial conversations, this example can illuminate a different approach.

- The remembrance of Jesus' High Priestly Prayer is a good time to remind worshipers of the benefit of carrying this prayer forward as the body of Christ. While making allowance for those who may be uncomfortable with the action, members of the worshiping assembly may be invited to place their hands on one another's shoulders for prayers of unity in Christ, healing of divisions, and strengthening of witness together even across differences. This could be especially powerful with the community gathered, insofar as possible, around the baptismal font.

Connections with the Liturgy

In the profession of faith in Holy Baptism (*ELW*, p. 229), the candidates are asked to "renounce the devil and all the forces that defy God." Christians are asked to take seriously the power of that "roaring lion" about which 1 Peter warns us.

Let the Children Come

The paschal candle was lighted from the Easter Vigil fire, and it burns for each Sunday of Easter. It is also lit whenever someone is baptized and at a funeral. Where does the light go when the candle is not lit? How does the season of Easter give way to the light burning in new ways out in the world? As the assembly gathers in a thanksgiving for baptism, children can remember their baptism with candles at the font and paschal candle as we get ready for the Day of Pentecost.

Assembly Song
Gathering

Oh, love, how deep ELW 322, LBW 88

Alleluia! Sing to Jesus ELW 392, LBW 158

A hymn of glory let us sing! ELW 393, LBW 157

Psalmody and Acclamations

Cooney, Rory. "You Have Made a Home for the Poor" from PCY, vol. 4.

Messner, Sally. "Psalm 68:1-10, 32-35" from PWA.

Pavlechko, Thomas. "Psalm 68:1-10, 32-35" from PSCY.

(GA) Haas, David. "Alleluia: Our God Is Speaking." SATB, cant, assembly, kybd, gtr, 2 C inst. GIA G-7727.

Hymn of the Day

Rise, O Sun of righteousness ELW 657 *SONNE DER GERECHTIGKEIT*

Lord, who the night you were betrayed ELW 463, LBW 206 *SONG 1*

I come with joy ELW 482 *DOVE OF PEACE*

Offering

As the grains of wheat ELW 465, WOV 705

Like the murmur of the dove's song ELW 403, WOV 685

Communion

Christ is the king! ELW 662, LBW 386

Thine the amen ELW 826, WOV 801

Father, we thank you ELW 478, WOV 704

Sending

Crown him with many crowns ELW 855, LBW 170

The head that once was crowned ELW 432, LBW 173

Additional Assembly Songs

You are the seed WOV 753, TFF 226, LLC 486

Grains of wheat/*Una espiga* WOV 708, LLC 392

Alleluia Canon WOV 677

⊕ Dexter, Noel, arr. "Peace and Love" from *Let the Peoples Sing.* SATB. AFP 9780800675394

⊕ Sosa, Pablo. "Heaven Is Singing for Joy/*El cielo canta alegría.*" U. ELW 664.

☼ Crist, Ben. "Hear Our Prayers" from CCLI.

☼ Hall, Mark/ Bernie Herms. "If We've Ever Needed You" from CCLI.

☼ Keyes, Aaron/Ben Smith/Joseph Barrett/Matt Redman. "I Am Not the Same" from CCLI.

☼ Maher, Matt/Jason Ingram. "Sing Over Your Children" from CCLI.

☼ Reeves, Sarah/Ed Cash. "Let Us Rise" from CCLI.

☼ Townend, Stuart/Keith Getty. "Across the Lands" from CCLI.

Music for the Day
Choral

Biery, James. "Sing Praises to God." SATB, org, opt tpt. MSM 50-2603.

P Cherwien, David. "Up through Endless Ranks of Angels." SAB, assembly, org, opt tpt. AFP 9780800658816.

♫ Dake, Kenneth. "I Come with Joy." SATB. MSM 50-2825.

P Fleming, Larry L. "Lord of the Dance." SATB. AFP 9780800655358.

Children's Choir

Anon. "We Are All One in Christ" from *LifeSongs.* U, kybd, opt perc. AFP 9780806642703.

P Patterson, Mark. "Sing Alleluia" from *The Joy of Part Singing.* U or 2/3 pt, opt hb, hc, Orff inst. CG CGBK67.

Ziegenhals, Harriet. "Oh, Sing to the Lord/Cantad al Señor." U/2 pt, kybd. CG CGA640.

Keyboard / Instrumental

P ♫ Childs, Edwin T. "I Come with Joy" (Dove of Peace) from *American Folk Hymns for Organ.* Org. AFP 9781451494051.

♫ Powell, Robert J. "Rise, O Sun of Righteousness" (Sonne der Gerechtigkeit) from *Instruments for All Seasons,* vol. 2. Cl, org. CPH 97-7255.

P Sowash, Bradley. "A Hymn of Glory Let Us Sing!" (Lasst uns erfreuen) from *Great German Hymns Arranged in Contemporary Styles.* Pno. AFP 9780800637446.

P Sullivan, Christine. "A Hymn of Glory Let Us Sing!" (Lasst uns erfreuen) from *All Good Gifts Around Us: Piano Settings of Creation Hymns.* Pno. AFP 9781451401899.

Handbell

♫ Afdahl, Lee J. "At the Lamb's High Feast." 3-5 oct hb, opt 2 oct hc, L2+. CPH 97-7309.

P Geschke, Susan. "Thine Is the Glory." 2 oct, L2. HOP 2583.

♫ Phillips, Judy. "Dove of Peace." 3-6 oct, L3+. GIA G-7292.

Monday, May 29
Jiří Tranovský, hymnwriter, died 1637

Jiří Tranovský (YEAR-zhee truh-NOF-skee) is considered the "Luther of the Slavs" and the father of Slovak hymnody. Trained at the University of Wittenberg in the early seventeenth century, Tranovský was ordained in 1616 and spent his life preaching and teaching in Prague, Silesia, and finally Slovakia. He produced a translation of the Augsburg Confession and published his hymn collection *Cithara Sanctorum* (Lyre of the Saints), the foundation of Slovak Lutheran hymnody.

Wednesday, May 31
Visit of Mary to Elizabeth

Sometime after the Annunciation, Mary visited her cousin Elizabeth. This occasion is sometimes referred to simply as "The Visitation." Elizabeth greeted Mary with the words "Blessed are you among women," and Mary responded with her famous song, the Magnificat. Luke's gospel tells that even John the Baptist rejoiced and leapt in his mother's womb when Elizabeth heard Mary's greeting. On this festival two women are seen: one, seemingly too old to have a child, bears the last prophet of the old covenant, and the other, quite young, bears the incarnate Word and the new covenant.

Thursday, June 1
Justin, martyr at Rome, died around 165

Justin was born of pagan parents. At Ephesus he was moved by stories of early Christian martyrs and came under the influence of an elderly Christian man he met there. Justin described his conversion by saying, "Straightway a flame was kindled in my soul and a love of the prophets and those who are friends of Christ possessed me." Justin was a teacher of philosophy and engaged in debates about the truth of Christian faith. He was arrested and jailed for practicing an unauthorized religion. He refused to renounce his faith, and he and six of his students, one a woman, were beheaded.

Justin's description of early Christian worship around the year 150 is one of the foundations of the church's pattern of worship, East and West.

⊕ = global song   ♫ = relates to hymn of the day
☼ = praise song   P = available in Prelude Music Planner

June 3, 2017
Vigil of Pentecost

At this liturgy we gather in vigilant prayer as the disciples did in the days preceding Pentecost. Our world waits for an end to war and violence. The whole creation waits for an end to suffering. With undying hope we pray for the crowning gift of Easter—the Spirit of the risen Christ among us.

Prayer of the Day

Almighty and ever-living God, you fulfilled the promise of Easter by sending the gift of your Holy Spirit. Look upon your people gathered in prayer, open to receive the Spirit's flame. May it come to rest in our hearts and heal the divisions of word and tongue, that with one voice and one song we may praise your name in joy and thanksgiving; through Jesus Christ, our Savior and Lord, who lives and reigns with you and the Holy Spirit, one God, now and forever.

Gospel Acclamation

Alleluia. Come, Holy Spirit, fill the hearts ' of your faithful,* and kindle in us the fire ' of your love. *Alleluia.*

Readings and Psalm

Exodus 19:1-9

At Sinai God assured Israel that they were God's prized possession and commissioned them to serve as mediating priests for the nations. God's word spoken to Moses is the basis of the people's trust.

or Acts 2:1-11

Believers are filled with the Spirit to tell God's deeds.

Psalm 33:12-22

The LORD is our helper and our shield. (Ps. 33:20)

or Psalm 130

There is forgiveness with you. (Ps. 130:4)

Romans 8:14-17, 22-27

The Holy Spirit has made us God's children who eagerly await the glorious future God has prepared for all of creation. While we cannot fully see what God has in store for us and creation, we eagerly anticipate it in hope. Even when we are unable to pray, the same Spirit prays for us.

John 7:37-39

Jesus describes the Holy Spirit as living water, quenching the thirst of all who come to him and filling the hearts of believers till they overflow.

Preface   Vigil and Day of Pentecost

Color   Red

Saturday, June 3
The Martyrs of Uganda, died 1886

Christianity had been introduced to Uganda after 1877, but was made available primarily to those in the court of King Mutesa. His successor, King Mwanga, was angered by these Christian members of the court whose first allegiance was not to him but to Christ. On June 3, 1886, thirty-two young men were burned to death for refusing to renounce Christianity. Other martyrs followed. But many were impressed by the confident manner in which these Christians went to their deaths, and the persecution led to a much stronger Christian presence in the country.

Saturday, June 3
John XXIII, Bishop of Rome, died 1963

In his ministry as a bishop of Venice, John (then Archbishop Roncalli) was loved by his people. He visited parishes and established new ones. He had warm affection for the working class—he himself was the child of Italian peasants—and he worked at developing social-action ministries. At age seventy-seven he was elected bishop of Rome. Despite the expectation that he would be a transitional pope, he had great energy and spirit. He convened the Second Vatican Council to open the windows of the church and "let in the fresh air of the modern world." The council brought about great changes in Roman Catholic worship, changes that have influenced Lutherans and many other Protestant churches as well.

June 4, 2017
Day of Pentecost

Today's festival derives its name from the Jewish festival of Pentecost, observed fifty days after Passover. On the fiftieth day of Easter we celebrate the Holy Spirit as the power of God among us that heals, forgives, inspires, and unites. In the reading from Acts, images of wind and fire describe the Spirit poured out on disciples of all nations. In John's gospel the risen Christ breathes the Spirit on his followers on Easter evening. In the one Spirit we are baptized into one body, and at the Lord's table the Spirit unites us for witness in the world.

Prayer of the Day

O God, on this day you open the hearts of your faithful people by sending into us your Holy Spirit. Direct us by the light of that Spirit, that we may have a right judgment in all things and rejoice at all times in your peace, through Jesus Christ, your Son and our Lord, who lives and reigns with you and the Holy Spirit, one God, now and forever.

Gospel Acclamation

Alleluia. Come, Holy Spirit, fill the hearts ˈ of your faithful,* and kindle in us the fire ˈ of your love. *Alleluia.*

Readings and Psalm
Acts 2:1-21

Pentecost was a Jewish harvest festival that marked the fiftieth day after Passover. Luke portrays the Holy Spirit being poured out upon the disciples before the gathered and astonished people assembled in Jerusalem for the festival. Filled with the Spirit, the disciples were able to witness to the power of Christ's resurrection.

or Numbers 11:24-30

The Spirit of God rested upon seventy elders in Israel who had been chosen to share the burden of leadership with Moses. When some became jealous that two others also had the spirit and could prophesy, Moses said that he hoped that all of God's people would be prophets.

Psalm 104:24-34, 35b

Send forth your Spirit and renew the face of the earth. (Ps. 104:30)

1 Corinthians 12:3b-13

Paul is helping the Corinthians understand the relationship between our God-given unity and Spirit-created diversity. The Spirit creates the unity of faith and gives all Christians diverse gifts for the common benefit of all. We need one another's diverse spiritual gifts, because the same Spirit has given them to each person for the common good.

or Acts 2:1-21

See above.

John 20:19-23

The risen Jesus appears to his disciples, offering them a benediction, a commission, and the gift of the Holy Spirit.

or John 7:37-39

Jesus describes the Holy Spirit as living water, quenching the thirst of all who come to him and filling the hearts of believers till they overflow.

Preface   Vigil and Day of Pentecost

Color   Red

Prayers of Intercession

The prayers are prepared locally for each occasion. The following examples may be adapted or used as appropriate.

Rejoicing in the risen life of Christ, let us pray for the church, the world, and all who are in need.

A brief silence.

We pray for the church. Inspire us with your Spirit. Unite us in your love. Raise up faithful leaders from among our youth and our elders to guide your church throughout the world. Lord, in your mercy,

hear our prayer.

For the earth. For city parks and wildlife refuges. For community gardens, farms, and ranches. For agricultural workers, seafood harvesters, and subsistence farmers. Nourish the earth with seasonable weather and adequate rainfall. Lord, in your mercy,

hear our prayer.

For the nations. For people of every land and language. End violence, warfare, and ethnic strife. Lead us from fear to friendship, from injustice to equality, from oppression to freedom. Lord, in your mercy,

hear our prayer.

For those in need. For those who are neglected or abused. For the unemployed. For those who struggle with addiction. For those nearing death, those who grieve, and all who are ill (*especially*). Lord, in your mercy,

hear our prayer.

For this assembly. For those who work with children. For those discerning a call to ministry. For all the baptized and those who have newly affirmed their baptism. For visitors, new members, and those who are absent from us today. Lord, in your mercy,

hear our prayer.

Here other intercessions may be offered.

With thanksgiving, we remember those who have died (*especially*). Inspire us by their witness and bring us to the fullness of your promise of resurrection and eternal life. Lord, in your mercy,

hear our prayer.

Joining our voices with your faithful ones in every time and place, we offer our prayers in the name of the Risen One, Jesus Christ our Lord.

Amen.

Images in the Readings

Anthropologists describe **fire** as one of the markers of the human species. For tens of thousands of years, humans gathered around fire for light, warmth, protection, community, and better food. Many passages in the Bible liken God to fire. The Holy Spirit of God appeared on Sinai in flames of fire, which on Pentecost appeared on the forehead of each believer. Moses experienced God in fire; through fire the Israelites presented offerings to God; God led the people through the wilderness with a pillar of fire. Seraphim are fire spirits, extensions of the Divine. Yet fire is also a sign of divine judgment: the angel in Eden hides the tree of life from humanity with a sword of fire, and John the Baptist predicts that fire will consume the chaff. Fire both occasions human life and has the power to destroy. Think fire, think God.

The Hebrew noun *ruah* can be translated into English as **spirit**, breath, or wind. Spirit is the most amorphous of these words. In Christian theology, the Spirit we experience is the Spirit of the risen Christ, a spirit of service, a spirit of love, a spirit of resurrection beyond death.

In the narrative in Numbers, **seventy** elders receive the Spirit. In the Bible, seventy is a number that connotes totality, seven times ten. In Genesis 10, there are seventy nations in Israel's world; Jacob moves to Egypt with seventy family members; and there are many more seventies. Luke says that seventy were sent out to preach the word.

Ideas for the Day

- Neil Douglas-Klotz's book *Prayers of the Cosmos: Meditations on the Aramaic Words of Jesus* (New York: Harper-Collins, 1990) beautifully unpacks the etymological roots of the Aramaic words of Jesus in the Lord's Prayer and the Beatitudes. His poem/exploration of the Lord's Prayer includes a section on "The Creative Fire" that can inform the imagery of fire and Spirit for this day.

- In "Little Gidding" from T. S. Eliot's *Four Quartets* (Orlando: Harcourt, 1943, renewed 1971), the fire of Pentecost is described this way:

  "The only hope, or else despair
  Lies in the choice of pyre or pyre—
  To be redeemed from fire by fire."

  These lines can speak powerfully of the work of the Holy Spirit in difficult but necessary contemporary national conversations about racism and injustice. The full excerpt can be found on patheos.com by searching "7 essential poems for Pentecost."

- While many worshipers are familiar with the idea that the festival of Pentecost is "the birthday of the church," they may resist a deep connection with the experience of the power of the Spirit that marked the disciples on this day. Lacking a personal experience of feeling the Spirit, they may question their own baptismal calling to, and capacity for, proclamation. Many people are simply hesitant about speaking the good news, fearing they lack sufficient understanding of the faith to speak clearly. The Spirit removed barriers to understanding in Luke's narrative so that everyone could understand the message of the disciples. What "barriers to understanding" do disciples in the contemporary congregation fear? What words or concepts common to faith do they still find confusing or ambiguous? Time could be provided to allow people to identify "faith jargon" for which they desire clarification; back-and-forth conversation between preacher and hearers can offer both proclamation and education, and encourage worshipers to believe that they too are baptized with Pentecost power.

Connections with the Liturgy

In Thanksgiving at the Table X (*ELW*, p. 69), we praise God with these words: "O God, you are Breath: send your Spirit on this meal. O God, you are Fire: transform us with hope."

In the Presentation for Holy Baptism (*ELW*, p. 227), the baptized community is described in phrases recalling this Sunday's readings in 1 Corinthians and Acts: "We are united with all the baptized in the one body of Christ, anointed with the gift of the Holy Spirit, and joined in God's mission for the life of the world."

If John 20 is chosen for this day, see the second Sunday of Easter for a discussion of the greeting of peace.

Let the Children Come

Red! Today we are seeing red! This festive day points us to the birthday of the church and the excitement of God's work among us in the world. The worship space, the leaders, even the assembly wears red. Make sure you have some backup red ribbons or cloth for the child who didn't remember so that everyone feels a part of the fun. Children will understand what a festive day this is. The red banners, red-hot candies, red velvet cake, and many songs and languages are all memorable in children's minds of this very festive day.

Assembly Song
Gathering

O day full of grace ELW 627, LBW 161

Hail thee, festival day! ELW 394, LBW 142

Creator Spirit, heavenly dove ELW 577/578, LBW 284

Psalmody and Acclamations

Alonso, Tony. "Lord, Send Out Your Spirit/*Señor, Envía tu Espíritu*." SAB, cant, assembly, pno, gtr. GIA G-7241.

Joncas, Michael. "Lord, Send Out Your Spirit (Psalm 104)." SATB, cant, assembly, org or str qrt, hp. GIA G-7141.

Makeever, Ray. "When You Send Forth Your Spirit (Psalm 104)" from DH.

(GA) Ferguson, John. "Gospel Processional." SATB, org, tpt, assembly. AFP 9780800677084.

(GA) Haas, David. "Alleluia: Our God Is Speaking." SATB, cant, assembly, kybd, gtr, 2 C inst. GIA G-7727.

Hymn of the Day

Come, Holy Ghost, God and Lord ELW 395, LBW 163 *KOMM, HEILIGER GEIST, HERRE GOTT*

God of tempest, God of whirlwind ELW 400 *CWM RHONDDA*

O living Breath of God/*Soplo de Dios viviente* ELW 407, LLC 368 *VÅRVINDAR FRISKA*

Offering

Spirit of Gentleness ELW 396, WOV 684

Like the murmur of the dove's song ELW 403, WOV 685

Communion

Loving Spirit ELW 397, WOV 683

Now to the Holy Spirit let us pray ELW 743, LBW 317

Gracious Spirit, heed our pleading ELW 401, WOV 687, TFF 103

Sending

Holy Spirit, ever dwelling ELW 582, LBW 523

Lord, you give the great commission ELW 579, WOV 756

Additional Assembly Songs

Send forth your Spirit SP 36

Spirit of the living God TFF 101

Santo Espíritu, plenitud pascual LLC 370

⊕ Ghanian melody. "When Our Savior Yesu Went Away" from *Glory to God*. U. WJK 0664238971.

⊕ Nigerian melody. "Come, O Holy Spirit, Come/Wa wa wa Emimimo" from *Glory to God*. 2 pt, cant. WJK 0664238971.

☼ Booth, Tom/Tammy Booth. "We Wait for You" from *Spirit and Song*, vol. 2. OCP.

☼ Hall, Mark/Jason Hoard. "Spirit Wind" from CCLI.

☼ Jobe, Kari/Ed Cash. "Breathe on Us" from CCLI.

☼ Jobe, Kari/Jason Ingram/Bryan Brown/Tofer Brown. "Hands to the Heavens" from CCLI.

☼ Pridham, BJ/Ed Cash. "Spirit of God" from CCLI.

☼ Younker, Brett/Matt Maher/Jesse Reeves/Daniel Carson. "Burning in My Soul" from CCLI.

Music for the Day
Choral

P ♫ Bach, J. S. "Come, Holy Ghost, God and Lord" from *Bach for All Seasons*. SATB, opt kybd. AFP 9780800658540.

P ♫ Helgen, John. "O Living Breath of God." SAB, pno. AFP 9780800621506.

Highben, Zebulon M. "Come, O Holy Spirit, Come (Pentecost Sequence)." 2 pt trbl or mxd, opt assembly, pno, opt org, opt fl or cl. GIA G-8866.

P ♫ Jennings, Carolyn. "God of Tempest, God of Whirlwind." SATB, org. AFP 9781451420685.

Children's Choir

Kemp, Helen. "Alleluia! Loving Spirit." U, kybd, opt hb. CG CGA862.

P Patterson, Mark. "Spirit, Come Down" from *ChildrenSing with Instruments*. U, pno, opt C inst. AFP 9781451461121.

P Taylor, Terry D. "I'm Gonna Sing with Over My Head." 2 pt, pno. CG CGA1326

Keyboard / Instrumental

Berthier, Jacques. "Come, Creator Spirit" from *Liturgical Meditations: Fourteen Pieces for Flute and Organ*. Fl, org. GIA G-3133.

Demessieux, Jeanne. "Toccata" (Veni Creator Spiritus) from *Twelve Choral Preludes on Gregorian Chant Themes, Op. 8*. Org. ALF 9780874876031.

Kohrs, Jonathan. "Spirit of Gentleness" (Spirit) from *Four Tunes for Piano and Two Instruments*. 2 inst (C or B flat), pno. AFP 9780800658786.

P ♫ Maxwell, David. "O Living Breath of God" (Vårvindar friska) from *We Walk By Faith: Organ Settings*. Org. AFP 9781451479584.

Handbell

Glasgow, Michael J. "A Disciple's Prayer." 2-3 oct hb, opt 2-3 oct hc, opt vln, L2+. LOR 20/1887L. 3-6 oct hb, opt 3-7 oct hc, opt vln, L2+. LOR 20/1886L.

Honore, Jeffrey. "Come, Holy Ghost." 3-5 oct hb, opt narr, L3-. WLP 3413.

♫ Krug, Jason W. "Grace." 2-6 oct hb, opt 2-6 oct hc, L2+. Ring Out! Press RO3326.

⊕ = global song   ♫ = relates to hymn of the day
☼ = praise song   P = available in Prelude Music Planner

Monday, June 5
Boniface, Bishop of Mainz, missionary to Germany, martyr, died 754

Boniface (his name means "good deeds") was born Wynfrith in Devonshire, England. He was a Benedictine monk who at the age of thirty was called to missionary work among the Vandal tribes in Germany. His first missionary attempt was unsuccessful, but he returned two years later and was able to plant the gospel in an area filled with superstitious and violent practices. He led large numbers of Benedictine monks and nuns in establishing churches, schools, and seminaries. Boniface was also a reformer. He persuaded two rulers to call synods to put an end to the practice of selling church offices to the highest bidder. Boniface was preparing a group for confirmation on the eve of Pentecost when he and they were killed by a band of pagans.

Wednesday, June 7
Seattle, chief of the Duwamish Confederacy, died 1866

Noah Seattle was chief of the Suquamish tribe and later became chief of the Duwamish Confederacy, a tribal alliance. When the tribes were faced with an increasing number of white settlers, Seattle chose to live and work peacefully with them rather than engage in wars. After Seattle became a Roman Catholic, he began the practice of morning and evening prayer in the tribe, a practice that continued after his death. On the centennial of his birth, the city of Seattle—named for him against his wishes—erected a monument over his grave.

Friday, June 9
Columba, died 597; Aidan, died 651; Bede, died 735; renewers of the church

These three monks from the British Isles were pillars among those who kept alive the light of learning and devotion during the Middle Ages. Columba founded three monasteries, including one on the island of Iona, off the coast of Scotland. That monastery was left in ruins after the Reformation but today is home to an ecumenical religious community. Aidan, who helped bring Christianity to the Northumbria area of England, was known for his pastoral style and ability to stir people to charity and good works. Bede was a Bible translator and scripture scholar. He wrote a history of the English church and was the first historian to date events *anno Domini* (A.D.), "year of our Lord." Bede is also known for his hymns, including "A Hymn of Glory Let Us Sing!" (ELW 393).

Summer

Preparing for Summer

Summer may be when students and teachers are not interacting on a daily basis in classrooms throughout schools, colleges, and universities, but that doesn't stop the lectionary from spending time teaching us and sharing stories of Jesus teaching others. Summer during Matthew's gospel year may well be summer school for all of us, teaching us how to be disciples and about the nature of the kingdom of heaven.

Teaching Discipleship

The lectionary readings in the summer months begin with Jesus giving the great commission to make disciples of all nations, baptizing them and teaching them (Matt. 28:19-20)—and then go on for several weeks to explain what discipleship means. Matthew and our worshiping communities might be at odds when it comes to what discipleship means, so this summer might be a good time to wrestle with that in preaching and teaching. In the gospel appointed for June 18 (Lectionary 11), Jesus tells his disciples to go only to lost sheep, not to Gentiles or Samaritans, to proclaim that the kingdom of heaven has drawn near; and then he tells them that he is sending them out like sheep into the midst of wolves (Matt. 10:5-6, 16). The next week Jesus tells us that disciples should love him more than their families. Being a disciple, Jesus says, means taking up the cross and following him (Matt. 10:37-38). This is discipleship according to Jesus in Matthew's gospel—losing our lives for the sake of the kingdom.

Yet Jesus does not leave us with death; we too will be raised to new life with him in the kingdom that has drawn near. Dietrich Bonhoeffer reminds us in *The Cost of Discipleship* (1937) that "[grace] is costly because it compels a man to submit to the yoke of Christ and follow him; it is grace because Jesus says: 'My yoke is easy and my burden is light.'" After all the warnings about what discipleship is and the cost it has, Jesus reminds us that discipleship is meant neither to be a chore nor to drain our life. Discipleship is not burning out by being the only one to plan worship or chair the funeral luncheon committee or grudgingly teach Sunday school year after year. Discipleship is following Jesus and teaching the nations. Jesus tells us that even if we follow him to the cross, we will be filled with life, not drained of it.

Our worship life together this summer might remind people of this through a thanksgiving for baptism instead of confession and forgiveness. If the thanksgiving for baptism provided in *Evangelical Lutheran Worship* is beginning to feel overly familiar, try crafting your own local version. The book *In These or Similar Words: Crafting Language for Worship* (Augsburg Fortress, 2015) is a great resource for preparing to craft liturgical language that runs deep with tradition and is also contextualized for a local worshiping community. This resource would be a great help in crafting a thanksgiving for baptism that helps the assembly recall how God has joined us to Christ through baptism and so clothes us with mercy and forgiveness. The importance and beauty of this thanksgiving might be one of the things that could awaken the calling in unbaptized people to explore Christian faith and life. A locally crafted thanksgiving for baptism might include naming the realities of a life of discipleship—both daily dying and continuous resurrection. Holding these in tension in liturgical language (and preaching) is a great and important task.

Growing Season

The second half of the summer (Lectionary 15–21) is devoted primarily to Jesus' teaching crowds of people with parables. Jesus does perform miracles, but these seem in the lectionary's wide arc to be more about revealing Jesus as the Son of Man than about the act of healing itself. (However, on those Sundays when the gospel contains a prominent healing story, it may be appropriate to add the order for healing to the worship service [*ELW*, pp. 276–278].) Particularly these parables lead us to wonder about the growth not just of seeds, but of faith. Growth in faith is a good thing to spend the second half of the summer talking about, especially because in many parts of the country the summer is quite literally a growing season. In other places, seeds and agriculture are foreign concepts, due to heat, lack of accessible green space, or other factors. These parables may need to be contextualized during preaching so that they make sense in your ministry setting.

Jesus' final words to his disciples in these summer lectionary texts are a warning not to tell anyone that he is the Messiah (Lectionary 21). It is interesting that the year A lectionary in the time after Pentecost begins with the great commission; continues with teachings on discipleship, faith, and Jesus' identity; and then brings the summer to a close with the order to tell no one. It may be appropriate on the last Sunday in August to spend part of the sermon teaching about the Revised Common Lectionary: that it can contain long arcs and narratives that take several weeks to cover (teachings about discipleship, parables), and that each Sunday can also stand on its own with integrity. Maybe this warning not to tell anyone that Jesus is the Messiah is one of those days, or maybe you will find a way to connect it to the rest of the summer.

Reformation 500

This summer brings us closer to the 500th commemoration of the Reformation in October. Some communities will have been making this anniversary observance part of their worship for the past year in some way or another. Summer is a great time in the liturgical calendar to reform parts of our worship life. Crafting a thanksgiving for baptism locally is one place to start. A healing prayer station during communion distribution may be another reform to introduce to our congregational life. Singing music that is less familiar, singing global music to connect our communities to those around the globe, and writing our own simple chants to sing together are other ways to reform our worship life. Because the summer months tend to be a more relaxed and experimental time in congregational life, especially those who find changes in worship anxiety provoking can be encouraged to live with the changes for a season and then reflect on the experience along with the whole community.

Inviting participation in these experiments is a great way to foster a collaborative culture and give our communities ownership over what happens in worship. When people are cocreators of liturgy rather than passive consumers, they become stakeholders in reformed practice because they experience the breath of the Spirit in that work. A helpful outline for encouraging a collaborative process of creating liturgical media art is found in Eileen Crowley's *A Moving Word: Media Art in Worship* (Augsburg, 2006). This process can also be used for other aspects of liturgical life.

Reformation need not always become the law of the land in our liturgies. The things we introduce during the summer months may become part of our liturgical repertoire—or not—and that is okay. What is important is to help the people of God move away from the mind-set of "We've always done it this way" and move toward a mind-set of "How will we worship that will better equip us to be the body of Christ here and now?" Ultimately, reforms we choose to keep beyond the summer months will help expand and enrich our worship life at other times of the year. Reformation should not be treated as law, something we are required to do because of our theological heritage. Rather, we would do well to treat the opportunity for ongoing reformation as gospel, something that frees us to see beyond patterns we cling to without accompanying reflection.

Summer Music

Music might be part of our summer reformation project as well. A majority of Christians now live in the southern hemisphere, so summer would be a great time to begin using songs from our sisters and brothers from that part of the world in addition to our old favorites. Because summer is a long stretch of ordinary time unbroken by principal festivals, new music is important to introduce so that our worship does not become rote and monotonous. Adding global music, praise music, traditional hymns, or whatever is not common to your assembly's worship style is important so that your worship reflects the always-creating, always-renewing God we worship. One option would be to use "Send me, Lord" (ELW 809) as the dismissal instead of the usual "Go in peace. Serve the Lord," so that people can become familiar with a song week after week and begin to bring it into regular use during other times of the year. During the second half of the summer when we learn what God's kingdom looks like, "When we are living" (ELW 639) might be the hymn of the day for a few weeks so we can sing about the kingdom we all belong to. Another summer option especially for English-speaking assemblies is to try using Holy Communion Setting Seven (*ELW*, pp. 175–183), which presents the liturgical songs in both Spanish and English.

Visual Environment

When we worship, "the visual arts and the spaces for worship assist the congregation to participate in worship, to focus on the essentials, and to embody the Gospel" (*The Use of the Means of Grace*, Application 11B). Lutherans have a rich musical tradition, but like many denominations they have not always supported or encouraged worship through all the senses. Certainly beautiful music brings worshipers to moments of transcendence, but it is critical for us to find other ways for people to experience God breaking into their lives in our worship spaces.

Enhancing the visual worship space need not be relegated only to a few artists or people with expertise, but can be a communal process. Even if people believe they have no artistic ability, encourage them to participate in generating the ideas, sourcing the supplies, and installing the art. Creating something together will help build community, and the more people are involved, the more they will feel ownership of their worship environment.

The first half of the summer, when Jesus is teaching us what it means to be disciples, this team might find ways to explore what discipleship means in visual or interactive ways. Perhaps a wall could be painted in a public space with chalkboard paint with prompts each week that echo the lectionary's theme for what it means to be a disciple. Let people write their answers to "Who are the lost sheep we are called to go to?"

so that everyone can see everyone else's answers. If painting isn't possible, covering a wall with brown Kraft paper is a great alternative.

Discipleship is not just evangelizing; it involves service to the neighbor as well. Perhaps a school supply drive throughout the summer would be appropriate. Contact a local school to see what students and teachers need most throughout the year. Create a prominent collection center in the worship space. By the end of the summer, with a huge pile of supplies, not only will you see the impact you are making on the world directly outside your doors, but you will see the abundance of God's kingdom.

The second half of the summer, when the focus becomes more agrarian, a new team may form or re-form to plan and prepare the late summer environment. Plant pots of seedlings and place them along the aisle, in front of the altar table, or near the font. Just watching them grow week after week is a way for people to understand growing in faith (just don't forget to water them!). Lush plants could create a natural backdrop behind the table or could surround the assembly to celebrate the goodness of creation. The gathered community will be able to come up with other ideas as well that will be specific to each local worship space. When it comes to worship environments, the possibilities are literally endless as you cocreate places where you experience and participate in God's kingdom among you.

Seasonal Checklist

- If the summer worship schedule changes, update your website (especially so summer visitors can consider worshiping with you), and change listings on exterior signs and church voice mail.
- Encourage people to visit a local church if they are traveling this summer. Create a printed Service of the Word booklet with a short liturgy and some favorite hymns to give people to use when they can't be at worship.
- Create a hashtag for people to use on social media and ask them to share images of where they see God when they are traveling.
- Bless people's bikes, hiking gear, camping equipment, fishing poles, and the like early in the summer to connect recreational life to faith life.
- Use Farewell and Godspeed (*ELW*, p. 75) when people leave the congregation to move to a new community or to bid farewell to graduates leaving for college, other study, or other opportunities.

Worship Texts for Summer

Confession and Forgiveness

*All may make the sign of the cross, the sign marked at baptism,
as the presiding minister begins.*
Blessed be the holy Trinity, ✛ one God,
full of compassion and mercy,
abounding in steadfast love.
Amen.

Trusting God's promise of forgiveness,
let us confess our sin against God and one another.

Silence for reflection and self-examination.

Eternal God our creator,
in you we live and move and have our being.
Look upon us, your children,
the work of your hands.
Forgive us all our offenses,
and cleanse us from proud thoughts and empty desires.
By your grace draw us near to you,
our refuge and our strength;
through Jesus Christ our Lord. Amen.

Since we are justified by faith,
we have peace with God through our Lord Jesus Christ.
God's love has been poured into our hearts
through the Holy Spirit given to us.
In the mercy of almighty God,
Christ died for us while we still were sinners;
and for his sake, God ✛ forgives you all your sins.
Amen.

Offering Prayer

Merciful God,
you open wide your hand
and satisfy the need of every living thing.
You have set this feast before us.
Open our hands to receive it.
Open our hearts to embrace it.
Open our lives to live it.
We pray this through Christ our Lord.
Amen.

Invitation to Communion

Come, let us eat, for now the feast is spread.
Our Lord's body let us take together.

Prayer after Communion

Jesus Christ, host of this meal,
you have given us not only this bread and cup,
but your very self, that we may feast on your great love.
Filled again by these signs of your grace,
may we hunger for your reign of justice,
may we thirst for your way of peace,
for you are Lord forevermore.
Amen.

Blessing

May God, whose power working in us
can do infinitely more than we can ask or imagine,
grant you the gifts of faith and hope.
Almighty God, Father, ✛ Son, and Holy Spirit,
bless you now and forever.
Amen.

Dismissal

Go in peace. The Spirit sends us forth to serve.
Thanks be to God.

Seasonal Rites for Summer

Blessings for Travelers

O God, whose glory fills the whole creation,
and whose presence we find wherever we go:
Preserve *us/those* who travel:
surround *us/them* with your loving care;
protect *us/them* from every danger;
and bring *us/them* in safety to *our/their* journey's end;
through Jesus Christ our Lord.
Amen.

Adapted from the prayer for travelers in Prayers and Thanksgivings, *The Book of Common Prayer* (1979 edition).

O God,
our beginning and our end,
you kept Abraham and Sarah in safety
throughout the days of their pilgrimage,
you led the children of Israel through the midst of the sea,
and by a star you led the magi to the infant Jesus.
Protect and guide us now as we *[or substitute the names of travelers]* set out to travel.
Make our ways safe and our homecomings joyful,
and bring us at last to our heavenly home,
where you dwell in glory with our Lord Jesus Christ
and the life-giving Holy Spirit,
one God, now and forever.
Amen.

Adapted from *Evangelical Lutheran Worship*, p. 331.

June 11, 2017
The Holy Trinity
First Sunday after Pentecost

Though the word *trinity* is not found in the scriptures, today's second reading includes the apostolic greeting that begins the liturgy: The grace of our Lord Jesus Christ, the love of God, and the communion of the Holy Spirit be with you all. In the gospel Jesus sends his disciples forth to baptize in the name of the Father, and the Son, and the Holy Spirit. More than a doctrine, the Trinity expresses the heart of our faith: we have experienced the God of creation made known in Jesus Christ and with us always through the Holy Spirit. We celebrate the mystery of the Holy Trinity in word and sacrament, as we profess the creed, and as we are sent into the world to bear witness to our faith.

Prayer of the Day

Almighty Creator and ever-living God: we worship your glory, eternal Three-in-One, and we praise your power, majestic One-in-Three. Keep us steadfast in this faith, defend us in all adversity, and bring us at last into your presence, where you live in endless joy and love, Father, Son, and Holy Spirit, one God, now and forever.

or

God of heaven and earth, before the foundation of the universe and the beginning of time you are the triune God: Author of creation, eternal Word of salvation, life-giving Spirit of wisdom. Guide us to all truth by your Spirit, that we may proclaim all that Christ has revealed and rejoice in the glory he shares with us. Glory and praise to you, Father, Son, and Holy Spirit, now and forever.

Gospel Acclamation

Alleluia. Holy, holy, holy is the ¹ Lord of hosts;* God's glory fills ¹ the whole earth. *Alleluia.* (Isa. 6:3)

Readings and Psalm

Genesis 1:1—2:4a

This first creation story reached its current form during the crisis of the Babylonian exile of the people of Israel. God, not their captors' god Marduk, was responsible for their existence. God created women and men as rulers over creation, to preserve and protect it. God also rested on the seventh day, hallowing that day forever as the Sabbath.

Psalm 8

How majestic is your name in all the earth! (Ps. 8:1)

2 Corinthians 13:11-13

Paul closes a challenging letter to the Corinthians with an appeal to Christian fellowship grounded in the triune harmony of Christ's grace, God's love, the Spirit's partnership.

Matthew 28:16-20

After his resurrection, Jesus summons his remaining disciples and commissions them to baptize and teach all nations in the name of Father, Son, and Holy Spirit.

Preface   Holy Trinity

Color   White

Prayers of Intercession

The prayers are prepared locally for each occasion. The following examples may be adapted or used as appropriate.

Called together in the Spirit's embrace, let us pray for the mending of God's world.

A brief silence.

Holy Mystery, you call us to be your church. Keep calling your people to faithful reform. Give us vision and courage to share your new life with all the world. Lord, in your mercy,

hear our prayer.

Joyful Creator, you made a wondrous universe and call us to be partners in its care. Inspire delight in the furry, scaly, watery, breezy, sandy stuff you love. Inspire us to bring about creation's healing. Lord, in your mercy,

hear our prayer.

Merciful God, you love our enemies and bless all people. Make our hearts yearn to be joyful and share your generosity. Help leaders and citizens use political power in service of your peace. Lord, in your mercy,

hear our prayer.

Compassionate One, you bring about the fullness of life. When sorrow wounds faith, send wise ones to comfort and encourage those who suffer. Heal your people in body, mind, and spirit (*especially*). Lord, in your mercy,

hear our prayer.

Holy Trinity, you call us together to bless your world. Guide all who are preparing for baptism into the joy of new life in your name. Lord, in your mercy,

hear our prayer.

Here other intercessions may be offered.

Holy God, you bring life out of death at every turn. We give you thanks for all the saints (*especially the apostle Barnabas*) and for dear ones whom we mourn (*especially*). Lord, in your mercy, **hear our prayer.**

All these things, and whatever else you see that we need, we entrust to your care through Christ our Lord. **Amen.**

Images in the Readings

If by Matthew's language of **Father, Son, and Holy Spirit** we imagine two males and a mist, the biblical imagery is failing us. God is beyond all things, alive in Jesus Christ, and experienced in the assembly. Many contemporary hymns add other imagery to the doctrinal language in hopes of opening up the mystery of God. In Genesis 1, God is creator, word, and breath. In Paul, God is love, grace, and communion.

The rhetorically magnificent story of **creation** in Genesis 1 poetically describes the entire universe as originally perfect and formed by God to focus on human need. According to biblical scholars, Genesis 1 was written as praise of the God of Israel, rather than as revealed science, and according to Christian theology, God's creating continues throughout time, rather than being a single prehistoric event. Creation by God through the Word in the Spirit happens today. The postexilic authors sought also to ground the Jewish Sabbath in God's resting on the seventh day. Christians have moved their holy day from Saturday rest to Sunday assembly so as to meet the risen Christ on the day of the resurrection.

Ideas for the Day

- Creation care themes are front and center with the grand poetic account of creation from Genesis 1. The Creator who is acknowledged as triune has a will for creation; creation exists only because of that will. It would be particularly appropriate for the confession and the prayers of intercession on this Sunday to include references to creation care in the context of the local environment.

- In the northern hemisphere, this creation story will be heard at a time when creation bursts into color. Invite the gardeners in your congregation to adorn the worship space with cut flowers from their own gardens, a practice that recognizes the gifts of those persons and is also a much greener practice than using flowers flown in from continents away. Also, in the weeks prior to Trinity Sunday, invite people to bring in their own photographs of the natural world and provide an area for their display.

- Although Jesus is about to leave his disciples, he does not permit them—or us—to stand gazing into the clouds. Instead, our eyes are directed to communities and nations, to creation, to all that is broken and in need of healing, all to which the church is called to bring good news. As a way

to orient our bodies to that need, try a "points of the compass" orientation in the prayers of intercession. When writing the prayers, include petitions for people, institutions, communities, and needs of creation that stand to the north, east, south, and west of your church. During the petitions for needs in each direction, ask worshipers to face that direction as the assembly prays.

- The exact manner in which the persons of the Trinity interact is a mystery to us. Likewise, though we have gained extraordinary knowledge of the created order, the complexities of exactly how creation is woven together still remain a mystery. The response of the human and nonhuman creation both to the Trinity and to the mysteries of the natural world is to be "lost in wonder, love, and praise" (ELW 631).

Connections with the Liturgy

The standard greeting with which to begin the Sunday liturgy (*ELW*, p. 98) quotes 2 Corinthians: "The grace of our Lord Jesus Christ, the love of God, and the communion of the Holy Spirit be with you all." Christian worship begins not with the usual social hello of "Good morning." To some grieving and troubled worshipers and in times of great communal sorrow, it is not a good morning. Rather, we are privileged to use the uniquely Christian greeting: we give to one another the grace, love, and communion of the triune God.

The "holy kiss" that Paul speaks of is the earliest version in the worshiping assembly of our greeting of peace.

Let the Children Come

The Trinity is such a mystery that explanation, especially with children, is sure to end in some kind of unintended heresy. And yet the majesty of the first creation story followed by Psalm 8, paired with the apostolic challenge to go and baptize in the name of the Trinity throughout the world, leaves the assembly in awe. Children will feel the same awe as adults. Many times when adults encounter challenging theological concepts, we "word wrestle" until we are satisfied (or the ecumenical council ends). Children are much more comfortable with holding the mystery gently, without explanation. Let us learn from them.

Assembly Song
Gathering

Holy, holy, holy, Lord God Almighty! ELW 413, LBW 165, LLC 371

Kyrie! God, Father ELW 409, LBW 168

Come, all you people ELW 819, WOV 717, TFF 138

Psalmody and Acclamations

Cherwien, David and Susan. "Two Psalm Settings (Psalm 8)." U/2-pt, kybd, assembly, opt tr, 3 hb or hc. CG CGA1077.

Helgen, John. "Psalm 8" from *ChildrenSing Psalms*. U, kybd, 2 hb, fc. AFP 9780800663872.

Valentine, Timothy, SJ. "How Majestic Your Name." SAB, cant, assembly, gtr, kybd, opt inst. GIA G-4833.

(GA) ELW 173 with proper verse for Holy Trinity.

Hymn of the Day

We all believe in one true God   ELW 411, LBW 374
WIR GLAUBEN ALL

Come, join the dance of Trinity   ELW 412   KINGSFOLD

Mothering God, you gave me birth   ELW 735, WOV 769
NORWICH

Offering

Listen, God is calling   ELW 513, WOV 712, TFF 130

Now the silence   ELW 460, LBW 205

Communion

When long before time   ELW 861, WOV 799

O living Breath of God/*Soplo de Dios viviente*   ELW 407, LLC 368

Creating God, your fingers trace   ELW 684, WOV 757

Sending

Thy strong word   ELW 511, LBW 233

Holy God, we praise your name   ELW 414, LBW 535

Additional Assembly Songs

Enter, Holy Spirit!   ASG 31

Come, let us sing the holiness of God   CBM 68

Praise the Spirit in creation   WOV 682

⊕ Korean melody. "While the Earth Remains" from *One Is the Body: Songs of Unity and Diversity*. U. GIA G-5790.

⊕ Loh, I-to, arr. "For the Beauty of the Earth" from *Sound the Bamboo*. U. GIA G-6830.

☼ Crocker, Matt/Ben Fielding. "This I Believe (The Creed)" from CCLI.

☼ Getty, Keith/Kristyn Getty/Stuart Townend. "Creation Sings the Father's Song" from CCLI.

☼ Hall, Mark/Chad Cates/David Hunt. "Father Spirit Jesus" from CCLI.

☼ Modlin, Rick. "Holy, Holy, Holy Cry" from *Spirit and Song*, vol. 2. OCP.

☼ Tomlin, Chris/Ed Cash. "Praise the Father, Praise the Son" from CCLI.

☼ Wiens, Laura/Johnny Markin. "Creation Speaks" from CCLI.

Music for the Day
Choral

P ♫ Highben, Zebulon M. "Mothering God, You Gave Me Birth." SAB, gtr or pno. AFP 9781451424249.

P ♫ Hopp, Roy. "Come, Join the Dance of Trinity." SATB, kybd, fl or C inst. AFP 9780800678296.

Sleeth, Natalie. "Go into the World." 2 pt or 3 pt trbl or mxd, pno. CG CGA209.

P ♫ Trenney, Tom. "Mothering God, You Gave Me Birth." SATB, pno. AFP 9781451492545.

Children's Choir

P Horman, John D. "It's Good" from *Sing the Stories of God's People*. U, kybd. AFP 9781451460438.

P Rose, Audrey. "Now We Worship" from *ChildrenSing*. U, kybd. AFP 9781451461251.

Sleeth, Natalie. "Go into the World" from *LifeSongs*. U, kybd, opt descant. AFP 9780806642703.

Keyboard / Instrumental

Bach, J. S. "Largo" from *Trio Sonata No. 2 in C Minor, BWV 526*. Org. Various editions.

♫ Cherwien, David. "Mothering God, You Gave Me Birth" (Norwich) from *O God, beyond All Praising*. Org. AFP 9780800657246.

P Evanovich, Joshua. "Holy, Holy, Holy, Lord God Almighty!" (Nicaea) from *String Reflections for Solo Violin and Piano*. Vln, pno. HOP 8578.

P ♫ Harbach, Barbara. "Come Join the Dance of Trinity" (Kingsfold) from *Come, Join the Dance: Folktunes and Spirituals for Organ*. Org, fl, ob. AFP 9781451432510.

Handbell

♫ McChesney, Kevin. "Kingsfold." 3-5 oct, L2+. RW RW8212.

P Stephenson, Valerie. "Spirit of God, Descend upon My Heart." 3-5 oct hb, opt 3-5 oct hc, L2+. CG CGB329.

P Tucker, Sondra. "Morning Hymn (Father, We Praise Thee)." 3-5 oct, L1. CG CGB787.

Monday, June 12
Barnabas, Apostle (transferred)

The Eastern church commemorates Barnabas as one of the Seventy commissioned by Jesus. Though he was not among the Twelve mentioned in the gospels, the book of Acts gives him the title of apostle. His name means "son of encouragement." When Paul came to Jerusalem after his conversion, Barnabas took him in over the fears of the other apostles, who doubted Paul's discipleship. Later, Paul and Barnabas traveled together on missions. At the Council of Jerusalem, Barnabas defended the claims of Gentile Christians in relation to the Mosaic law.

⊕ = global song   ♫ = relates to hymn of the day   + = semicontinuous psalm
☼ = praise song   P = available in Prelude Music Planner

Wednesday, June 14

Basil the Great, Bishop of Caesarea, died 379; Gregory, Bishop of Nyssa, died around 385; Gregory of Nazianzus, Bishop of Constantinople, died around 389; Macrina, teacher, died around 379

The three men in this group are known as the Cappadocian fathers; all three explored the mystery of the Holy Trinity. Basil was influenced by his sister Macrina to live a monastic life, and he settled near the family estate in Caesarea. Basil's Longer Rule and Shorter Rule for monastic life are the basis for Eastern monasticism to this day, and express a preference for communal monastic life over that of hermits. Gregory of Nazianzus

(nah-zee-AN-zus) was sent to preach on behalf of the Orthodox faith against the Arians in Constantinople, though the Orthodox did not have a church there at the time. He defended Orthodox trinitarian and Christological doctrine, and his preaching won over the city. Gregory of Nyssa (NISS-uh) was the younger brother of Basil the Great. He is remembered as a writer on spiritual life and the contemplation of God in worship and sacraments.

Macrina (muh-CREE-nuh) was the older sister of Basil and Gregory of Nyssa. She received an excellent education centered on the Bible, and when her fiancé died she devoted herself to the pursuit of Christian perfection. She was a leader of a community, based at the family estate, dedicated to asceticism, meditation, and prayer. Macrina's teaching was influential within the early church.

June 18, 2017

Time after Pentecost — Lectionary 11

Moses tells the Israelites that they are called to be a priestly kingdom and a holy people. Jesus sends out the disciples as laborers into the harvest. In baptism we too are anointed for ministry, sharing God's compassion with our needy world. From the Lord's table, we go forth to proclaim the good news, to heal the sick, and to share our bread with the hungry.

Prayer of the Day

God of compassion, you have opened the way for us and brought us to yourself. Pour your love into our hearts, that, overflowing with joy, we may freely share the blessings of your realm and faithfully proclaim the good news of your Son, Jesus Christ, our Savior and Lord.

Gospel Acclamation

Alleluia. The kingdom of God ¹ has come near;* repent, and believe in ¹ the good news. *Alleluia.* (Mark 1:15)

Readings and Psalm

Exodus 19:2-8a

At Sinai God assured Israel, "You shall be my treasured possession," and commissioned them to serve as mediating priests for the nations. The people commit themselves completely to God's will.

Psalm 100

We are God's people and the sheep of God's pasture. (Ps. 100:3)

Romans 5:1-8

We are no longer God's enemies but have peace with God, because we were brought into a right relationship with God through Christ's death. A tested character has been forged for

us which empowers endurance in the midst of suffering and hope for final salvation.

Matthew 9:35—10:8 [9-23]

The mission of Jesus' followers is to continue the mission of Jesus himself. Here, he instructs his first disciples how they might proclaim the gospel through their words and deeds.

Semicontinuous reading and psalm
Genesis 18:1-15 [21:1-7]

God, in the form of three messengers, announces to Sarah and Abraham that they will have a child. Sarah, because of her advanced age, laughs at this seeming impossibility. But nothing is impossible for God, and in due course Isaac is born (Gen. 21:1-7). Now, Sarah confesses, everyone will share in her joyous laughter.

Psalm 116:1-2, 12-19

I will call on the name of the Lord. (Ps. 116:13)

Preface   Sundays

Color   Green

Prayers of Intercession

The prayers are prepared locally for each occasion. The following examples may be adapted or used as appropriate.

Called together in the Spirit's embrace, let us pray for the mending of God's world.

A brief silence.

Steadfast God, you send your church as laborers into your harvest. Heal our divisions and unite us in mission. Make us one at your table. Hear us, O God.

Your mercy is great.

Faithful Creator, protect your earth and breathe life into its future. Stir our hearts to compassion, that we become healers for the sake of your whole creation as it is made new. Hear us, O God.

Your mercy is great.

Holy One, you desire peace for all nations. Give rulers and citizens wisdom in the use of power, that wars may cease and all who suffer exile, hunger, and terror find safe haven. Hear us, O God.

Your mercy is great.

Compassionate One, you have brought us to yourself. Stay near to all who suffer broken hearts, fearful spirits, and disruptive illness (*especially*). Bring healing and hope to your people. Hear us, O God.

Your mercy is great.

Abba, Father, your love for your children is boundless. Bless all who father among us and all who yearn for a protective father. Grant wisdom, patience, and good humor. Thank you for those who have shown us fatherly care. Hear us, O God.

Your mercy is great.

Here other intercessions may be offered.

Living Lord, all who live and all who die belong to you. Thank you for all whose lives have witnessed to your glory (*especially*). Comfort all who mourn. Hear us, O God.

Your mercy is great.

All these things, and whatever else you see that we need, we entrust to your care through Christ our Lord.

Amen.

Images in the Readings

Once the Israelites were settled in Canaan, nomads became famers, and many biblical passages use the image of the **harvest** to connote fulfillment. Some of the Jewish religious festivals that commemorated their past memories were actually reinterpretations of more ancient harvest festivals, Passover at the barley harvest, and Pentecost at the end of the wheat harvest and beginning of the grape harvest. Because God is given credit for all growth of life, harvest is an occasion for thanksgiving. Yet God calls us to work the harvest, a task seen in our culture as far too much hard work for its meager pay, a job for other poor people to fill.

The **mother eagle** swoops under the fledglings, her wings outspread to catch them if they falter.

Twelve is the number of completion, from the twelve sons of Jacob to the twelve gates in the city of Jerusalem at the end of time. The two lists of the Twelve cited in the synoptics are not identical. The point is not historical accuracy, but rather the perfection of Jesus' ministry and the church's mission. The apostles replace the twelve tribes of Israel and begin the completion of all things.

Ideas for the Day

- Jesus' mission happened as he was walking. So also the mission of the church is dynamic and on the move. Ask a few people to give testimony to how they are in mission in their daily work. Then commission the entire assembly for their mission in the world, using the affirmation of Christian vocation (*ELW*, p. 84).

- In Graham Greene's novel *The Power and the Glory*, a morally flawed and nameless Roman Catholic priest walks from town to town in an area of Mexico where the church has been outlawed. Finding deep human need wherever he goes, he determines to act with compassion and to be true to his calling despite his flaws, even when it means walking into a fatal trap set by the story's antagonist. In the gospel reading the call is wonderfully specific. Jesus calls specific people with names, flaws, and gifts for ministry. So does God call us.

- The gospel reading makes reference to the disciples being called to the ministry of healing, work that in our culture has largely been turned over to the health care industry. Remind the assembly of God's care for the sick and of the church's call to heal by incorporating a ritual around anointing and prayers for the sick (*ELW*, p. 276). One option is to offer laying on of hands and anointing during communion at a station separate from where the bread and wine are distributed.

- In the reading from Exodus, God tells Moses, "The whole earth is mine, but you shall be for me a priestly kingdom and a holy nation" (Exod. 19:5-6). These words remind us of our own relationship to creation, that it all belongs to God. It's a further reminder to God's people to be priests on behalf of all creation, offering loving care and intercession not only on behalf of the human order but also on behalf of the animals, plants, lands, seas, and skies.

Connections with the Liturgy

The final section of the service of Holy Communion is the Sending. With the Twelve, we are blessed and dismissed in the peace of Christ to "share the good news."

Let the Children Come

This Sunday begins the long, green time after Pentecost. The image of a green, growing plant in the warmth of the sun helps us to envision how God is working among us. The festivals have come to a close until, just before Advent, our year will begin to "reform" with festivals again. How does your worshiping assembly help children embrace the rhythm of the church year? Does the rhythm of Sunday morning change to feel more like growth? Does the schedule of Sunday morning change to allow a slower pace for families in the percolating time of summer?

Assembly Song
Gathering

In Christ called to baptize ELW 575

Rise up, O saints of God! ELW 669, LBW 383

All people that on earth do dwell ELW 883, LBW 245

Psalmody and Acclamations

Pelz, Walter L. "Psalm 100" from PWA.

Roberts, William Bradley. "Psalm 100" from PSCY.

+ Haugen, Marty. "Our Blessing Cup" from PCY, vol. 1. (GA) ELW 169 with proper verse for Lectionary 11.

Hymn of the Day

Hallelujah! We sing your praises ELW 535, TFF 158, WOV 722
  HALELUYA! PELO TSA RONA

Lord, you give the great commission ELW 579, WOV 756
  ABBOT'S LEIGH

O Christ, your heart, compassionate ELW 722 ELLACOMBE

Offering

God, who stretched the spangled heavens ELW 771, LBW 463

Let the vineyards be fruitful ELW 181

Communion

Where cross the crowded ways of life ELW 719, LBW 429

This is my Father's world ELW 824, LBW 554

United at the table/*Unidos en la fiesta* ELW 498, LLC 408

Sending

I love to tell the story ELW 661, LBW 390, TFF 228

Praise to the Lord, the Almighty ELW 858/859, LBW 543

Additional Assembly Songs

For the healing of the nations SP 12a

Christ of the sending CBM 65

You are the seed WOV 753, TFF 226, LLC 486

⊕ Democratic Republic of Congo. "Know That God Is Good/ Mungu ni mwema" from *One Is the Body: Songs of Unity and Diversity*. U. GIA G-5790.

⊕ Punjabi melody, arr. I-to Loh. "Blest Be God, Praised Forever/ Rab ki hove Sanaa hameshaa" from *Glory to God*. U. WJK 0664238971.

☼ Darnell, Casey/Ian Eskelin/Tony Wood. "What Will You Do" from CCLI.

☼ Guglielmucci, Mike. "Healer" from CCLI.

☼ Hart, Sarah. "Able" from CCLI.

☼ Heath, Brandon/Thad Cockrell. "Hands of the Healer" from CCLI.

☼ Jobe, Kari/Ed Cash/Chris Tomlin. "Everyone Needs a Little" from CCLI.

☼ Miller, Tyler/Jonathan Smith/Eddie Hoagland/Jason Ingram. "Come Ye Sinners" from CCLI.

Music for the Day
Choral

Gerike, Henry V. "Psalm 100." U or solo, opt assembly, org, opt str qrt. MSM 80-860.

P Organ, Anne Krentz. "Give Thanks." SAB, opt assembly, pno. AFP 9781451498813.

Rutter, John. "O Be Joyful in the Lord." SATB, org. OXF 9780193503878.

Shields, Valerie. "Psalm 100." U or 2 pt trbl, kybd, opt insts. ECS 5782.

Children's Choir

P Horman, John D. "Sarah Laughed" from *Sing the Stories of God's People*. U/2 pt, kybd. AFP 9781451460544.

P Kerrick, Mary Ellen. "From the Ends of the Earth We Hear Singing." U/2 pt, pno. CG CGA1351.

P Shaw, Timothy. "A Psalm of Thanksgiving." U/2 pt, kybd, opt C inst. CG CGA1321.

Keyboard / Instrumental

P ♫ Koch, Lynn Arthur. "O Christ, Your Heart, Compassionate" (Ellacombe) from *Churchworks*. Org. AFP 9780800637477.

P ♫ Miller, Aaron David. "Lord, You Give the Great Commission" (Abbot's Leigh) from *Hymns in Jazz Style*. Pno. AFP 9780800678531.

P ♫ Raabe, Nancy. "Hallelujah! We Sing Your Praises" (Haleluya! Pelo tsa rona) from *Grace and Peace, vol. 4: Hymn Portraits for Piano*. Pno. AFP 9781451443561.

P ♫ Sedio, Mark. "Lord, You Give the Great Commission" (Abbot's Leigh) from *Come and Praise*. Org. AFP 9780800678500.

Handbell

♫ Afdahl, Lee J. "Abbot's Leigh." 3-5 oct, L2+. HOP 2103.

♫ Geschke, Susan. "Songs of Praise." 2-3 oct, opt wch, L2. CG CGB327.

P Waldrop, Tammy. "Sweet Hosannas Ring!" from *Spring Ring!* 2-3 oct, L2-, CG CGB829. 3-5 oct, L2-, CG CGB830.

⊕ = global song   ♫ = relates to hymn of the day   + = semicontinuous psalm
☼ = praise song   P = available in Prelude Music Planner

Wednesday, June 21

Onesimos Nesib, translator, evangelist, died 1931

Onesimos (oh-NESS-ee-mus neh-SEEB) was born into the Oromo people of Ethiopia. He was captured by slave traders and taken from his homeland to Eritrea, where he was bought, freed, and educated by Swedish missionaries. He translated the Bible into Oromo and returned to his homeland to preach the gospel. His tombstone includes a verse from Jeremiah 22:29, "O land, land, land, hear the word of the Lord!"

Saturday, June 24

John the Baptist

The birth and life of John the Baptist is celebrated exactly six months before Christmas Eve. For Christians in the Northern Hemisphere, these two dates are deeply symbolic. John said that he must decrease as Jesus increased. According to tradition, John was born as the days are longest and then steadily decrease, while Jesus was born as the days are shortest and then steadily increase. In many countries this day is celebrated with customs associated with the summer solstice.

June 25, 2017

Time after Pentecost — Lectionary 12

Jeremiah knew the frustration of having his words rejected. Jesus declares that his words may not bring peace, but division. In baptism we are buried with Christ that we may walk in newness of life. As we take stands for the sake of justice and lose our lives for the sake of others, we need not be afraid. The hairs of our head are counted. In baptism we are marked with the cross of Christ forever.

Prayer of the Day

Teach us, good Lord God, to serve you as you deserve, to give and not to count the cost, to fight and not to heed the wounds, to toil and not to seek for rest, to labor and not to ask for reward, except that of knowing that we do your will, through Jesus Christ, our Savior and Lord.

Gospel Acclamation

Alleluia. Jesus says, The Spirit of the Lord will testify on ' my behalf,* and you also ' are to testify. *Alleluia.* (John 15:26, 27)

Readings and Psalm

Jeremiah 20:7-13

Jeremiah accuses God of forcing him into a ministry that brings him only contempt and persecution. Yet Jeremiah is confident that God will be a strong protector against his enemies and commits his life into God's hands.

Psalm 69:7-10 [11-15] 16-18

Answer me, O LORD, for your love is kind. (Ps. 69:16)

Romans 6:1b-11

In baptism we were incorporated into the reality of Christ's death. Our lives in the present are marked and shaped by his crucifixion, just as our lives in the future will be marked and shaped by his resurrection.

Matthew 10:24-39

Jesus warns his disciples that their ministry in his name will meet with opposition, requiring absolute trust in God and an unswerving commitment to their Lord.

Semicontinuous reading and psalm

Genesis 21:8-21

Unable to conceive a child, Sarah selected Hagar, her Egyptian maid, to be a surrogate mother. Though Hagar gave birth to Ishmael, Sarah subsequently gave birth to a son named Isaac, which led to Sarah's sending away of Hagar and Ishmael. God, however, heard Ishmael's cry and promised to make of him a great nation.

Psalm 86:1-10, 16-17

Have mercy on me; give your strength to your servant. (Ps. 86:16)

Preface   Sundays

Color   Green

Prayers of Intercession

The prayers are prepared locally for each occasion. The following examples may be adapted or used as appropriate.
Called together in the Spirit's embrace, let us pray for the mending of God's world.
A brief silence.

God of grace, we give you thanks for renewing the church in every age (*especially through Philipp Melanchthon and the witness of the Augsburg Confession*). Bless missionaries who boldly proclaim your mercy throughout the world. Lord, in your mercy,
hear our prayer.

Generous God, you love the sparrows and shower your whole creation with abundance. Guide our stewardship by your wisdom so that all life flourishes as you intend. Lord, in your mercy,
hear our prayer.

God of peace, change the hearts of leaders who go to war. Enlighten their minds with your holy imagination, opening new paths to peace and renewed life. Lord, in your mercy,
hear our prayer.

Compassionate God, you tell us not to fear, but we do. Give courage to everyone who faces oppression and bigotry, hunger and homelessness. Bring healing and hope to all your people (*especially*). Lord, in your mercy,
hear our prayer.

God of community, thank you for the gift of this congregation. Bless all who are new here. Teach us how to welcome one another. Unite us as we proclaim your love. Shine through our common life. Lord, in your mercy,
hear our prayer.

Here other intercessions may be offered.

We give thanks for all who have been baptized into Christ Jesus and now rest in the fullness of Christ's resurrection (*especially*). Lord, in your mercy,
hear our prayer.

All these things, and whatever else you see that we need, we entrust to your care through Christ our Lord.
Amen.

Images in the Readings

God's care for **sparrows** calls us to trust in God, since Matthew states here and in chapter 7 (see Lectionary 8) that humans have more value than birds. Sparrows were among the cheapest birds sold in the markets of Matthew's time. Unfortunately, such biblical passages have been used to devalue God's creation, as if humans are the only creatures to receive divine blessing. Here Matthew states that God does indeed care for the sparrow.

Of course Matthew's description of the natural and married **family** experiencing hatred is disturbing. Matthew even assumes that discipleship will bring about such dissension. Pacifist Christians assert that Matthew's word about the **sword** is only metaphoric, but even as metaphor, it is a harsh word about the difficulties of the Christian life. In Paul's imagery, the Christian life requires our old self to be crucified, as if baptism aims the sword at oneself.

Matthew's words about a reversal of **slave and master** may sound benign to Americans who believe in equality, but such words would have sounded bizarre—like losing one's life to live—to citizens of a slave culture. Matthew is saying that cultural patterns may be totally inappropriate for those who follow Christ.

Ideas for the Day

- Jeremiah and Matthew each give a vivid description of the difficulty—and potential consequences—of naming hard truths. Fear of shame or conflict can stifle truth even when it is "like a burning fire" in us (Jer. 20:9). In her book *Fierce Conversations* (New York: Berkley, 2002), Susan Scott challenges readers to stop evasive talk and engage in the conversations we need the most. Likewise, today's scriptures call us to proclaim truth even in hostile situations with faith in God's abounding grace. What conversation is your congregation putting off? What hard truths go unsaid among you? Empowered by God's grace, seek ways to model the transformative power of truthful speech in your assembly.

- Leo Tolstoy opens *Anna Karenina* with the words, "All happy families are alike; each unhappy family is unhappy in its own way." Jesus' words in Matthew about divisions within families will likely resonate with unique hurts and broken relationships among the individuals gathered for worship. Consider ways to acknowledge these complex hurts. Invite a social worker or family therapist from your congregation to speak about work with hurting families. At the same time, look for ways to affirm people's unconditional inclusion in God's family. Celebrate the font and table as places of belonging, and generously invite people to find God's grace in them. Begin the Lord's Prayer with the words, "Make us one family and teach us to pray . . ."

- In the context of this Sunday's readings, the theme of death and resurrection in Romans provides the opportunity to highlight confession and forgiveness as part of the daily dying and rising that continues our baptism. God's grace enables people gathered together to "confess publicly in everyone's presence, no one being afraid of anyone else" (*The Book of Concord* [Augsburg Fortress, 2000], 477). To strengthen the connection with baptism, consider leading confession and forgiveness from the font during the gathering—with the assembly gathered closely around, if possible. Use Romans 6:3-5 as a congregational dialogue to begin.

Connections with the Liturgy

In the confession and forgiveness of the Sunday liturgy (*ELW*, pp. 94–96), one of the texts by which the presiding minister announces God's forgiveness cites today's second reading: "God, who is rich in mercy, loved us even when we were dead in sin, and made us alive together with Christ."

Many of the psalms we sing resemble the reading from Jeremiah: we lament our situation before God, and then we praise God, even if our terrible situation remains. God is praised because God is God, not because we have been relieved of our troubles.

Let the Children Come

Keeping secrets is often hurtful. Children should never be asked to keep a secret, even in jest. Today's gospel reading speaks of "nothing secret that will not become known," so that we might know of the fullness and security of God's love. The church is God's hands and feet at work in the world. Adult leaders working with children in the church are seen as God's special helpers. Does your congregation have a policy and plan for screening and training adults working with children and youth? How can such policies alleviate fears and convey value?

Assembly Song
Gathering

How firm a foundation ELW 796, LBW 507
Give to our God immortal praise! ELW 848, LBW 520
We are baptized in Christ Jesus ELW 451, WOV 698

Psalmody and Acclamations

Harmon, Kathleen. "Twelfth Sunday in Ordinary Time (A)" from COJ:A.
Kogut, Malcolm. "Lord, in Your Great Love." SATB, cant, assembly, kybd, gtr. GIA G-5001.
+ Pavlechko, Thomas. "Psalm 86:1-10, 16-17" from SMP. (GA) ELW 169 with proper verse for Lectionary 12.

Hymn of the Day

By gracious powers ELW 626 *TELOS* WOV 736 *BERLIN*
Will you come and follow me ELW 798, W&P 137 *KELVINGROVE*
O God, my faithful God ELW 806, LBW 504 *WAS FRAG ICH NACH DER WELT*

Offering

Have no fear, little flock ELW 764, LBW 476
Let the vineyards be fruitful ELW 182

Communion

Take up your cross, the Savior said ELW 667, LBW 398
Children of the heavenly Father ELW 781, LBW 474
Borning Cry ELW 732, WOV 770

Sending

O God, my faithful God ELW 806, LBW 504
Let us ever walk with Jesus ELW 802, LBW 487

Additional Assembly Songs

By grace God calls us into life CBM 64
Weary of all trumpeting WOV 785
For the healing of creation SP 12b
⊕ Caribbean traditional. "Now Go in Peace" from *One Is the Body: Songs of Unity and Diversity*. U. GIA G-5790.
⊕ Kenyan hymn. "Here on Jesus Christ I Will Stand/Kwake Yesu Nasimama" from *Glory to God*. U. WJK 0664238971.
☼ Fieldes, Mia/Jonathan Smith/Maggie Eckford. "Fearless" from CCLI.
☼ Helser, Jonathan David/Melissa Helser. "No Longer Slaves" from CCLI.
☼ Moen, Don/Tom Lane/Mia Fieldes. "No Fear" from CCLI.
☼ Neufeld, Tim/Jon Neufeld/Allen Salmon. "I Will Go" from CCLI.
☼ Rend Collective. "Build Your Kingdom Here" from CCLI.
☼ Smith, Martin/Stuart Garrard/Jon Thatcher/Matt Redman. "Now Is the Time" from CCLI.

Music for the Day
Choral

♫ Bell, John A./arr. Gary A. Daigle. "The Summons (Will You Come and Follow Me)." 2 pt trbl or mxd, pno, opt fl, opt gtr, opt assembly. GIA G-5410.
P Helgen, John. "Spirit of God, Descend upon my Heart." SATB, kybd, opt vc. AFP 9780800676377.
P ♫ Roberts, William Bradley. "By Gracious Powers." U or SATB, org. AFP 9780800678210.
P ♫ Schulz-Widmar, Russell. "By Gracious Powers." SAB or SATB, kybd, opt ob or vln. AFP 9781451451573.

Children's Choir

Burkhardt, Michael. "Sing unto the Lord" from *Part Singing Global Style: 15 Songs from Around the World for Children's Voices*. U/2 pt, opt solo, kybd. MSM 50-9811.
Gay, Sandra T. "Sing Thankful Songs (Cantad cancion de gratitude)." U/2 pt, kybd, opt fl, opt 3 oct hb or hc. CG CGA828.
P Helgen, John. "Oh, Sing to the Lord" from *ChildrenSing Around the World*. U/2 pt, pno, opt desc, opt perc. AFP 9781451492132.

Keyboard / Instrumental

♫ Bach, J. S. (arr. S. Taylor from Cantata 129). "Was frag ich nach der Welt" from *Three Extended Chorales from Church Cantatas*. Org. Hinrichsen Edition H353.
♫ Bender, Jan. "O God, My Faithful God" (Was frag ich nach der Welt) from *The Master Organ Works of Jan Bender, vol.*

⊕ = global song   ♫ = relates to hymn of the day   + = semicontinuous psalm
☼ = praise song   P = available in Prelude Music Planner

1: Chorale Preludes for Organ or Piano. Org or pno. CPH 97-7098.

℗ Kosche, Kenneth T. "Children of the Heavenly Father" (Tryggare kan ingen vara) from *Oh, Sing Jubilee: Organ Trios on Nordic Hymns.* Org. AFP 9781451401882.

℗♫ Titus, Hiram. "Will You Come and Follow Me?" (Kelvingrove) from *Glorify! Hymn Settings for Piano.* Pno. AFP 9781451424218.

Handbell

℗ Lamb, Linda. "Glorify Thy Name." 3-5 oct hb, opt 3 oct hc, L3-. HOP 2661.

♫ Thompson, Martha Lynn. "O God, Our Faithful God." 3-5 oct hb, opt 2 oct hc, opt trbl C inst, opt solo voice. MSM 30-827

♫ Wilson, Malcolm. "Reflection on 'Kelvingrove.'" 2-3 oct, L1. LOR 20/1130L.

Sunday, June 25
Presentation of the Augsburg Confession, 1530

On this day in 1530 the German and Latin editions of the Augsburg Confession were presented to Emperor Charles of the Holy Roman Empire. The Augsburg Confession was written by Philipp Melanchthon and endorsed by Martin Luther and consists of a brief summary of points in which the reformers saw their teaching as either agreeing with or differing from that of the Roman Catholic Church of the time. In 1580 when the *Book of Concord* was drawn up, the unaltered Augsburg Confession was included as the principal Lutheran confession.

Sunday, June 25
Philipp Melanchthon, renewer of the church, died 1560

Though he died on April 19, Philipp Melanchthon (meh-LAHNK-ton) is commemorated today because of his connection with the Augsburg Confession. Colleague and co-reformer with Martin Luther, Melanchthon was a brilliant scholar, known as "the teacher of Germany." The University of Wittenberg hired him as its first professor of Greek, and there he became a friend of Luther. Melanchthon was a popular professor—even his classes at six in the morning had as many as six hundred students. As a reformer he was known for his conciliatory spirit and for finding areas of agreement with fellow Christians. He was never ordained.

Tuesday, June 27
Cyril, Bishop of Alexandria, died 444

Remembered as an outstanding theologian as well as a contentious personality, Cyril defended the orthodox teachings about the person of Christ against Nestorius, bishop of Constantinople. Nestorius taught that the divine and human natures of Christ were entirely distinct, and therefore Mary could not be referred to as the *theotokos*, or bearer of God. This conflict, which also had roots in a rivalry for preeminence between Alexandria and Constantinople, involved all of the major Christian leaders of the time, including the patriarchs of Rome, Antioch, and Jerusalem, and finally also the emperor. In the end it was decided that Cyril's interpretation, that Christ's person included both divine and human natures, was correct.

Wednesday, June 28
Irenaeus, Bishop of Lyons, died around 202

Irenaeus (ee-ren-AY-us) believed that the way to remain steadfast to the truth was to hold fast to the faith handed down from the apostles. He believed that only Matthew, Mark, Luke, and John were trustworthy gospels. Irenaeus was an opponent of gnosticism and its emphasis on dualism. As a result of his battles with the gnostics, he was one of the first to speak of the church as "catholic." By catholic he meant that local congregations did not exist by themselves but were linked to one another in the whole church. He also maintained that this church was not contained within any national boundaries. He argued that the church's message was for all people, in contrast to the gnostics and their emphasis on "secret knowledge."

Thursday, June 29
Peter and Paul, Apostles

These two are an odd couple of biblical witnesses to be brought together in one commemoration. It appears that Peter would have gladly served as the editor of Paul's letters: in a letter attributed to him, Peter says that some things in Paul's letters are hard to understand. Paul's criticism of Peter is more blunt. In Galatians he points out ways that Peter was wrong. One of the things that unites Peter and Paul is the tradition that says they were martyred together on this date in 67 or 68. What unites them more closely is their common confession of Jesus Christ. Together Peter and Paul lay a foundation and build the framework for our lives of faith through their proclamation of Jesus Christ.

Saturday, July 1

Catherine Winkworth, died 1878; John Mason Neale, died 1866; hymn translators

Neale was an English priest associated with the movement for church renewal at Cambridge. Winkworth lived most of her life in Manchester, where she was involved in promoting women's rights. These two hymn writers translated many hymn texts into English. Catherine Winkworth devoted herself to the translation of German hymns, nineteen of which are included in *Evangelical Lutheran Worship*; the fourteen hymn translations of John Mason Neale in the collection represent his specialization in ancient Latin and Greek hymns.

July 2, 2017

Time after Pentecost — Lectionary 13

The welcome of baptism is for all God's children. This baptismal gift sets us free from the power of sin and death. In today's gospel, Christ promises that the disciple who gives a cup of cold water to the little ones serves Christ himself. From worship we are sent on our baptismal mission: to serve the little ones of this world and to be a sign of God's merciful welcome.

Prayer of the Day

O God, you direct our lives by your grace, and your words of justice and mercy reshape the world. Mold us into a people who welcome your word and serve one another, through Jesus Christ, our Savior and Lord.

Gospel Acclamation

Alleluia. You are a chosen race, a royal priesthood, a | holy nation,* in order that you may proclaim the mighty acts of the one who called you out of darkness into his | marvelous light. *Alleluia.* (1 Peter 2:9)

Readings and Psalm

Jeremiah 28:5-9

Through a symbolic action, Jeremiah insisted that Judah and all the surrounding nations should submit to the king of Babylon. Hananiah contradicted Jeremiah, who in reply insisted that Hananiah's rosy prediction should not be believed until it came true. God confirmed the word of Jeremiah and sentenced the false prophet Hananiah to death (vv. 16-17).

Psalm 89:1-4, 15-18

Your love, O LORD, forever will I sing. (Ps. 89:1)

Romans 6:12-23

Sin is an enslaving power that motivates us to live self-serving, disobedient lives. Sin's final payoff is death. We, however, have been set free from sin's slavery to live obediently under God's grace, whose end is the free gift of eternal life.

Matthew 10:40-42

When Jesus sends his disciples out as missionaries, he warns them of persecution and hardships they will face. He also promises to reward any who aid his followers and support their ministry.

Semicontinuous reading and psalm

Genesis 22:1-14

Abraham was prepared to obey God's command in the midst of extreme contradiction: the child to be sacrificed is the very child through whom Abraham is to receive descendants. God acknowledged Abraham's obedient faith, and Abraham offered a ram in the place of his son Isaac.

Psalm 13

I trust in your unfailing love, O LORD. (Ps. 13:5)

Preface   Sundays

Color   Green

Prayers of Intercession

The prayers are prepared locally for each occasion. The following examples may be adapted or used as appropriate.

Called together in the Spirit's embrace, let us pray for the mending of God's world.

A brief silence.

We pray for the church. For exiled Christians, oppressed churches, and all who suffer persecution because of faith in you: deliver freedom, courage, and partners in peacemaking. Hear us, O God.

Your mercy is great.

We pray for the earth and its creatures. For sage grouse, wolverines, and all vulnerable species; for humans and the choices we face: sustain life and guide our stewardship of all that you have made. Hear us, O God.
Your mercy is great.

We pray for the United States and Canada as we celebrate the founding of our nations. For the president and prime minister (*these leaders may be prayed for by name*); for the congress and parliament: grant wisdom and hearts for justice, that all our people flourish. Hear us, O God.
Your mercy is great.

We pray for those in need. For those who seek jobs, shelter, food, health, and love; for dear ones known to us (*especially*): meet their need by your bountiful compassion and our community's action. Hear us, O God.
Your mercy is great.

We pray for all who worship you today. For wise elders and curious seekers, joyful spirits and burdened souls: give holy welcome, share tender mercies, and deepen trust in your goodness. Hear us, O God.
Your mercy is great.

Here other intercessions may be offered.

We give thanks for all who have died in the faith and received the reward of the righteous (*especially*). Bless their memory among us and their life with you. Hear us, O God.
Your mercy is great.

All these things, and whatever else you see that we need, we entrust to your care through Christ our Lord.
Amen.

Images in the Readings

Both of the two primary images in today's readings are somewhat alien to us. In the Bible, a true **prophet** is not a fortune-teller or a court appointee, but rather the mouthpiece of God, proclaiming not what will be but what is. For Christians, the preeminent prophet is Christ, whose words of God are spoken through the Scriptures and in the bread and wine. The words are always double-sided, attending to both human sin and divine mercy—what Lutherans have called "law and gospel."

The idea in a **slave** economy is that everyone is born into a lifelong place in a hierarchy in which each obeys those who are above and cares for those who are below. Persons could not choose or alter their place in the hierarchy, and many Christians taught that God was responsible for who was placed where in this ordering of obedience. Despite our resistance to this idea, Paul writes that we are all born slaves of sin. The freedom of our will comes only through baptism, administered in many denominations even to infants, transferring our allegiance over to God and the neighbor. We are enslaved to God—in our culture, not an attractive suggestion.

Ideas for the Day

- Matthew reminds us that even a small cup of water can be a means of communicating God's love. Consider the ways that your community of faith communicates love by serving people's basic physical needs. Incorporate a tangible service project into your worship. Create an "assembly line" to put together care kits with basic necessities as people exit your worship space, or organize a service project immediately following the service that addresses the basic needs of people marginalized in your context.

- Another theme in today's readings is hospitality. Some congregations will have more guests in worship this Sunday because of the proximity of a national holiday. Allowing people to feel seen and known in a worship space can be transformative—yet in many contexts both big and small, we often fail to take the time to deepen our relationships with the people around us. Consider providing space during the gathering time for individuals—both guests and members—to introduce themselves and say something about who they are. Have the assembly affirm each introduction with the words "You are welcome here." Reflect on the diversity of the body of Christ, the ways that we mutually support one another, and the opportunity we have to be Christ to one another.

- Jeremiah and Matthew each speak of the difficulty of receiving prophets sent by God. Many people still have questions about whether there are prophets today and how to recognize them. While the exact social role of the prophet as known in ancient Israel has disappeared, Abraham Heschel and others point to a tradition of prophetic ways of seeing and speaking that continues to this day—see *The Prophets* (New York: Perennial Classics, 2001). Brother Robert Lentz has made a similar claim through his icons of such modern-day prophets as Martin Luther King Jr., Oscar Romero, and Dorothy Day (available through trinitystores.com). Consider ways to help those in your context better receive the prophets in their midst by pointing to some of these contemporary examples.

Connections with the Liturgy

Each Sunday, after the first and second readings, the lector calls out, "The word of the Lord," or "Word of God, word of life." We all respond, "Thanks be to God," even when the word has been a hard one to hear. Jeremiah and Matthew invite us to welcome the true words proclaimed by a prophet sent by God, and in the liturgy the church acclaims that the Bible is this true word and the lector has indeed been sent by God to proclaim the word of life.

Let the Children Come

Jesus speaks of children quite a lot in the gospels; more than many other topics we think of as being especially Christian in nature. The gospel text in Matthew is similar to others in the synoptic gospels. Joyce Ann Mercer, in her book *Welcoming Children: A Practical Theology of Childhood* (St. Louis: Chalice, 2005), points out the equation of welcome: those who welcome children, welcome God, thus becoming "God-welcomers." Imagine how different our congregations (indeed the world) would be if we were committed to welcoming children, thus becoming God-welcomers? And if we can welcome children, who else might we welcome?

Assembly Song
Gathering

Where cross the crowded ways of life   ELW 719, LBW 429
As we gather at your table   ELW 522
Let us go now to the banquet   ELW 523, LLC 410

Psalmody and Acclamations

Duncan, Norah, IV. "Thirteenth Sunday in Ordinary Time (A)" from LP:LG.
Martinson, Joel. "Psalm 89." Cant, opt SATB, assembly, org, ob. MSM 80-006.
+   Krentz, Michael. "Psalm 89:1-4, 15-18" and "Psalm 13" from PWA.
(GA) ELW 169 with proper verse for Lectionary 13.

Hymn of the Day

Let us ever walk with Jesus   ELW 802, LBW 487   *LASSET UNS MIT JESU ZIEHEN*

All Are Welcome   ELW 641   *TWO OAKS*

Oh, praise the gracious power   ELW 651, WOV 750   *CHRISTPRAISE RAY*

Offering

We give thee but thine own   ELW 686, LBW 410
Let the vineyards be fruitful   ELW 184, LBW p. 86

Communion

All who love and serve your city   ELW 724, LBW 436
Strengthen for service, Lord   ELW 497, LBW 218
Just as I am, without one plea   ELW 592, LBW 296

Sending

The church of Christ, in every age   ELW 729, LBW 433
This is my song   ELW 887

Additional Assembly Songs

Comes a new song   SP 6
New things, O God, you now declare   CBM 92
Al Dios creador damos gracias   LLC 502

⊕   Bell, John, arr. "The Love of God Comes Close" from *Love and Anger: Songs of Lively Faith and Social Justice*. U. GIA G-4947.

⊕   Martinez, Salvador T. "Let Heaven Your Wonders Proclaim" from *Sent by the Lord: Songs of the World Church*, vol. 2. U. GIA G-3740.

☼   Booth, Tom. "I Will Choose Christ" from *Spirit and Song*, vol. 1. OCP.

☼   Cowart, Benji/Josh Wilson/Jeff Pardo. "No More" from CCLI.

☼   Getty, Keith/Kristyn Getty/Stuart Townend. "Hear the Call of the Kingdom" from CCLI.

☼   Maher, Matt. "Your Grace Is Enough" from *Spirit and Song*, vol. 2. OCP.

☼   Smith, Michael W./Whitney Smith/Deborah D. Smith/Ryan Smith/Leeland Mooring. "Come See" from CCLI.

☼   Wilbur, Paul/Lee Black/Steve Merkel. "Salvation Belongs to Our God" from CCLI.

Music for the Day
Choral

Beethoven, Ludwig Van. "Prayer" from *Rejoice Now, My Spirit*. MH solo, kybd. AFP 9780800651084.

♫   Cherwien, David. "Let Us Ever Walk with Jesus." SATB a cap, solo inst. MSM 50-7077.

♫   Manz, Paul. "Let Us Ever Walk with Jesus." U, org. MSM 50-9405.

Scott, K. Lee. "It Is a Thing Most Wonderful" from *Treasures in Heaven*. 2 pt mxd, org. AFP 9780800679477.

Children's Choir

Gallina, Jill. "Funga Alafia (Song of Welcome)." 2 pt, kybd, opt perc. SHW HL 35027604.

P   Miller, Aaron David. "Blessing" from *ChildrenSing in Worship*, vol. 3. U/2 pt, pno. AFP 9781451462548.

P   Patterson, Mark. "Sing unto God (Round)" from *The Joy of Part Singing*. U/2 pt, opt pno. CG CGBK67.

Keyboard / Instrumental

Albrecht, Mark. "When in Our Music God Is Glorified" (Engelberg) from *Timeless Tunes for Piano and Solo Instrument*, vol. 2. Inst, pno. AFP 9780800659851.

P   Hassell, Michael. "Just As I Am, without One Plea" (Woodworth) from *Jazz Old Time Favorites*. Pno. AFP 9781451434507.

P ♫   Manz, Paul O. "Let Us Ever Walk with Jesus" (Lasset uns mit Jesu ziehen) from *Augsburg Organ Library: Marriage*. Org. AFP 9781451486025.

P   Petersen, Lynn. "As We Gather at Your Table" (In Babilone) from *Thankfulness and Praise: Ten Organ Settings*. Org. AFP 9781451424188.

⊕ = global song   ♫ = relates to hymn of the day   + = semicontinuous psalm
☼ = praise song   P = available in Prelude Music Planner

Handbell

♫ Behnke, John. "Let Us Ever Walk with Jesus." 3 oct, L2. CPH 97-7106.

℗ Joy, Michael. "Clarion Call." 3-5 oct, L2+. CG CGB864.

♫ McAninch, Diane. "Prelude on 'All Are Welcome.'" 3-5 oct hb, opt 3 oct hc, opt fl, L3. GIA G-7083.

Monday, July 3
Thomas, Apostle

Thomas is perhaps best remembered as "Doubting Thomas." But alongside this doubt, the Gospel of John shows Thomas as fiercely loyal: "Let us also go, that we may die with him" (John 11:16). And John's gospel shows Thomas moving from doubt to deep faith. Thomas makes one of the strongest confessions of faith in the New Testament, "My Lord and my God!" (John 20:28). From this confession of faith, ancient stories tell of Thomas's missionary work to India, where Christian communities were flourishing a thousand years before the arrival of sixteenth-century missionaries.

Thursday, July 6
Jan Hus, martyr, died 1415

Jan Hus was a Bohemian priest who spoke against abuses in the church of his day in many of the same ways Luther would a century later. He spoke against the withholding of the cup at the eucharist and because of this stance was excommunicated, not for heresy but for insubordination toward his archbishop. He preached against the selling of indulgences and was particularly mortified by the indulgence trade of two rival claimants to the papacy who were raising money for war against each other. He was found guilty of heresy by the Council of Constance and burned at the stake. The followers of Jan Hus became known as the Czech Brethren and eventually continued as the Moravian Church.

July 9, 2017
Time after Pentecost — Lectionary 14

The mystery of God's ways is sometimes hidden from the wise and intelligent. Jesus associates with the lowly and outcast. Like Paul, we struggle with our own selfish desires and seek God's mercy and forgiveness. We gather to be refreshed by Christ's invitation: "Come to me, all you that are weary." Gathered around word, water, and meal, we find rest for our souls.

Prayer of the Day

You are great, O God, and greatly to be praised. You have made us for yourself, and our hearts are restless until they rest in you. Grant that we may believe in you, call upon you, know you, and serve you, through your Son, Jesus Christ, our Savior and Lord.

Gospel Acclamation

Alleluia. Blessed are you, Lord of ˈ heav'n and earth;* you have revealed these ˈ things to infants. *Alleluia.* (Matt. 11:25)

Readings and Psalm
Zechariah 9:9-12

The coming messianic king will inaugurate an era of disarmament and prosperity. Because of God's covenant with Israel, they are designated as "prisoners of hope."

Psalm 145:8-14

The LORD is gracious and full of compassion. (Ps. 145:8)

Romans 7:15-25a

Life enslaved under sin is a catch-22 existence in which we know good but do not do it and do things we know to be bad. Through Jesus Christ, God has set us free from such a futile existence.

Matthew 11:16-19, 25-30

Jesus chides people who find fault with both his ministry and that of John the Baptist. He thanks God that wisdom and intelligence are not needed to receive what God has to offer.

Semicontinuous reading and psalm
Genesis 24:34-38, 42-49, 58-67

The marriage of Isaac and Rebekah helped to fulfill God's promise that Abraham and Sarah would become the ancestors of many nations. While her family urged delay, Rebekah eagerly set out to meet Isaac.

Psalm 45:10-17

God has anointed you with the oil of gladness. (Ps. 45:7)

or **Song of Solomon 2:8-13**

Arise, my love, my fair one, and come away. (Song of Sol. 2:10)

Preface   Sundays

Color   Green

Prayers of Intercession

The prayers are prepared locally for each occasion. The following examples may be adapted or used as appropriate.

Called together in the Spirit's embrace, let us pray for the mending of God's world.

A brief silence.

Humble God, lead your church in the way of service. Prosper the work of campus ministries and Young Adults in Global Mission as they raise up leaders to serve the world. Lord, in your mercy,

hear our prayer.

Cultivating God, bless and encourage all who work the land to feed your people. Give them joy in their vocation. Shower rain on crops and health on livestock. Lord, in your mercy,

hear our prayer.

Holy One, you command peace to the nations. Give peaceful hearts and discerning minds to world leaders and citizens alike, that all who suffer violence and hunger come to know the fullness of life. Lord, in your mercy,

hear our prayer.

Gracious God, you bid the weary come to you for rest. Renew energy for bone-tired people. Support our brothers and sisters who are burdened by grief, loneliness, and illness (*especially*). Lord, in your mercy,

hear our prayer.

God of everything, you have compassion for all that you have made. Show our congregation what mercy looks like in our own community, that we become faithful partners in your ministry. Lord, in your mercy,

hear our prayer.

Here other intercessions may be offered.

God of life, we give you thanks and praise for all the people who have blessed our lives, for saints among us whose steadfast faith has strengthened ours (*especially*). Lord, in your mercy,

hear our prayer.

All these things, and whatever else you see that we need, we entrust to your care through Christ our Lord.

Amen.

Images in the Readings

The **yoke** ties together two beasts of burden. According to this image, Christians do not walk alone but are tied to Christ and to one another.

In the several centuries before Christ, Jewish poetry developed the image of **wisdom**. Borrowing from neighboring polytheistic religions the picture of the divine consort, the great goddess who personified wisdom, Jews adapted this divine female figure into a way to speak of God's law, a beautiful and powerful aspect of the Almighty, who guided the people into truth. Christians altered the image once again, seeing Christ as this wisdom, whose words sound like foolishness to the world. In the eighth-century "O" antiphons preceding Christmas and versified in the hymn "O come, O come, Emmanuel," Christ is our Wisdom, coming in strength and beauty.

Ideas for the Day

- Frederick Dale Bruner writes, "A yoke is not a sitting instrument. . . . Jesus does not say, 'Take my chair and learn from me'; he says, 'Take my yoke and learn from me.'" Bruner explains how followers of Jesus are "not left with a mattress or a vacation, but rather given . . . a fresh way to bear responsibilities" (*Matthew: A Commentary*, vol. 1 [Grand Rapids: Eerdmans, 2004], 538–539). How might a faith community translate the ancient connotations of a yoke? A proclaimer who brings modern rest and work items into the worship space sets a memorable contrast. Preaching from a recliner, and then a treadmill? In house slippers, then running shoes? Use familiar objects to enliven Jesus' invitation.

- Call forth a blessing on all worshipers' work lives. *Evangelical Lutheran Worship Pastoral Care* (Augsburg Fortress, 2008) offers prayers in a category called "Difficulty in Vocational Life, Unemployment." For example: "We pray for . . . all who face any difficulty in their lives of labor. Surround them with your never-failing love; free them from restlessness and anxiety; keep them in every perplexity and distress; and renew them in facing the opportunities and challenges." Other pertinent prayers are under "Vocation in Daily Life" and "Entering Retirement" (pp. 375–378).

- Perhaps Jesus is not pointing fingers so much as beckoning a sideways welcome in Matthew 11:16-19. *It does not have to be this way,* Jesus seems to be saying. A vital preaching path is to make these invitations specific and personal: What will one do with one's freedoms? What qualities make toil worthwhile, even meaningful? And how does partnership with God bring genuine rest, a lightening of burdens? These are the questions Jesus raises. Individual responses, however, are unique. Invite one or more persons with a compelling story to recount his or her particular expression of faithful living. Give careful thought to gender, sexual identity, class, race, education level, and/or stage of life. There are infinite ways to respond to Jesus' prayerful summons.

Connections with the Liturgy

The oracle from Zechariah provides the background for the palm procession at the outset of Holy Week, since Christians have seen the figure of a triumphant king, paradoxically riding a donkey, to be Jesus Christ.

The prayer of Catherine of Siena (*ELW*, p. 87) uses Matthew's image of wisdom as her address to Christ.

Let the Children Come

Throughout this year, a focus for Let the Children Come has been to move leaders to think about children as full members of the body of Christ, offering and receiving, teaching and learning. The readings today home in on this theology of childhood. So often we expect children to "behave" a certain way during worship, and we react with surprise when they do not meet our expectations. How is God moving your assembly to make a welcoming place for children while still celebrating authentic Christian liturgy? How is liturgy naturally engaging and inviting for people of all ages?

Assembly Song
Gathering

Lord of all hopefulness ELW 765, LBW 469

Rejoice, ye pure in heart! ELW 873/874, LBW 553

Give Me Jesus ELW 770, WOV 777, TFF 165

Psalmody and Acclamations

Trapp, Lynn. "Four Psalm Settings." U or cant, assembly, org, opt SATB. MSM 80-701.

Whitney, Rae E. "O My God and King and Savior" (Holy Manna) from PAS 145F.

+ Pelz, Walter E. "Psalm 45:10-17" or "Song of Solomon 2:8-13" from PWA.

(GA) ELW 169 with proper verse for Lectionary 14.

Hymn of the Day

I heard the voice of Jesus say ELW 332, LBW 497 *THIRD MODE MELODY* ELW 611 *KINGSFOLD*

Light dawns on a weary world ELW 726 *TEMPLE OF PEACE*

Softly and tenderly Jesus is calling ELW 608, WOV 734, TFF 155 *THOMPSON*

Offering

What a friend we have in Jesus ELW 742, LBW 439

Let the vineyards be fruitful ELW 182

Communion

Come to me, all pilgrims thirsty ELW 777

Day by day ELW 790, WOV 746

Just a closer walk with thee ELW 697, TFF 253

Sending

How sweet the name of Jesus sounds ELW 620, LBW 345

If you but trust in God to guide you ELW 769, LBW 453

Additional Assembly Songs

This is the day TFF 262

Each morning brings us WOV 800

My soul finds rest in God alone ASG 26

⊕ South African traditional. "Your Will Be Done/*Mayenziwe*." SATB. ELW 741.

⊕ Pantou, Rudolf R. "Soft the Master's Love Song" from *Sound the Bamboo*. U. GIA G-6830.

☼ Borthwick, Jean Laurie/Jason Ingram/Jean Sibelius/Kari Jobe/Kathrina Amalia von Schlegel. "Be Still My Soul (In You I Rest)" from CCLI.

☼ Clark, Elizabeth/Jennie Lee Riddle. "Water" from CCLI.

☼ Ord, Gramham. "The Lord Is Gracious and Compassionate" from CCLI.

☼ Powell, Mac/David Nasser. "Restore in Me" from CCLI.

☼ Tomlin, Chris/Ed Cash/Wayne Jolley. "The Table" from CCLI.

☼ Walther, Ben. "Come Make Your Home in Me" from CCLI.

Music for the Day
Choral

♫ Cherwien, David. "Softly and Tenderly Jesus Is Calling." SATB, solo. MSM 50-6304.

P Fleming, Larry L. "Come unto Me" from *Augsburg Motet Book*. SATB, solo. AFP 9781451423709.

♫ Horn, Richard. "I Heard the Voice of Jesus Say." SAB, hp or org. MSM 50-6203.

P Leaf, Robert. "Come with Rejoicing." U, kybd. AFP 9780800645755.

Children's Choir

Burkhardt, Michael. "Yo Soy la Luz del Mundo" from *Part Singing Global Style: 15 Songs from Around the World for Children's Voices*. 2 pt, pno, opt perc. MSM 50-9811.

P Burrows, Mark. "Cooperate" from *Again, I Say Rejoice!* U, kybd. CG CGC56.

P Scroggins, Debra. "An Instrument of Thy Peace." U/2 pt, kybd. CG CG1330.

Keyboard / Instrumental

P ♫ Cherwien, David. "I Heard the Voice of Jesus Say" (Kingsfold) from *Organ Plus, vol. 2: Hymn Preludes for Organ and Instruments*. Org, fl, ob. AFP 9780800678548.

P ♫ Hobby, Robert A. "Softly and Tenderly Jesus Is Calling" (Thompson) from *For All the Saints*, vol. 2. Org. AFP 9780800679101.

⊕ = global song   ♫ = relates to hymn of the day   + = semicontinuous psalm
☼ = praise song   P = available in Prelude Music Planner

♫ Miller, Aaron David. "Light Dawns on a Weary World" (Temple of Peace) from *Chorale Preludes for Piano in Traditional Styles*. Pno. AFP 9780800679033.

P♫ Raabe, Nancy. "Softly and Tenderly Jesus Is Calling" (Thompson) from *Day of Arising: A Tapestry of Musical Traditions*. Pno. AFP 9780800637460.

Handbell

♫ Hopson, Hal H. "Variations on 'Kingsfold.'" 3 or 5 oct hb, L2+. AFP 1110703.

♫ Rogers, Sharon Elery. "A Medley of Faith." 2-3 oct, L1. ALF 12381.

Tucker, Sondra. "Make Me a Channel of Your Peace." 3-5 oct, L3. AFP 08000659864.

Tuesday, July 11
Benedict of Nursia, Abbot of Monte Cassino, died around 540

Benedict is known as the father of Western monasticism. He was educated in Rome but was appalled by the decline of life around him. He went to live as a hermit, and a community of monks came to gather around him. In the prologue of his rule for monasteries he wrote that his intent in drawing up his regulations was "to set down nothing harsh, nothing burdensome." It is that moderate spirit that characterizes his rule and the monastic communities that are formed by it. Benedict encourages a generous spirit of hospitality, saying that visitors to Benedictine communities are to be welcomed as Christ himself.

Wednesday, July 12
Nathan Söderblom, Bishop of Uppsala, died 1931

In 1930, this Swedish theologian, ecumenist, and social activist received the Nobel Prize for peace. Söderblom (ZAY-der-blom) saw the value of the ancient worship of the church catholic and encouraged the liturgical movement. He also valued the work of liberal Protestant scholars and believed social action was a first step on the path toward a united Christianity. He organized the Universal Christian Council on Life and Work, one of the organizations that in 1948 came together to form the World Council of Churches.

July 16, 2017
Time after Pentecost — Lectionary 15

God's word is like the rain that waters the earth and brings forth vegetation. It is also like the sower who scatters seed indiscriminately. Our lives are like seeds sown in the earth. Even from what appears to be little, dormant, or dead, God promises a harvest. At the Lord's table we are fed with the bread of life, that we may bear fruit in the world.

Prayer of the Day

Almighty God, we thank you for planting in us the seed of your word. By your Holy Spirit help us to receive it with joy, live according to it, and grow in faith and hope and love, through Jesus Christ, our Savior and Lord.

Gospel Acclamation

Alleluia. The word is very ⁞ near to you;* it is in your mouth and ⁞ in your heart. *Alleluia.* (Deut. 30:14)

Readings and Psalm

Isaiah 55:10-13

God's word to Israel's exiles is as sure and effective as never-failing precipitation. Their return to the Holy Land in a new exodus is cheered on by singing mountains and by trees that clap their hands.

Psalm 65:[1-8] 9-13

Your paths overflow with plenty. (Ps. 65:11)

Romans 8:1-11

There is no condemnation for those who live in Christ. God sent Christ to accomplish what the law was unable to do: condemn sin and free us from its slavery. The Spirit now empowers proper actions and values in our lives and gives us the promise of resurrected life.

Matthew 13:1-9, 18-23

In Matthew's gospel, both Jesus and his disciples "sow the seed" of God's word by proclaiming the good news that "the kingdom of heaven is near." Now, in a memorable parable, Jesus explains why this good news produces different results in those who hear.

Semicontinuous reading and psalm

Genesis 25:19-34

Although Jacob was younger than his twin, Esau, he eventually gets the birthright away from his brother. Jacob is portrayed in the Bible as deceptive, gripping his brother when he came out of the womb and driving a hard bargain by buying the birthright for a bowl of lentils.

Psalm 119:105-112

Your word is a lamp to my feet and a light upon my path. (Ps. 119:105)

Preface Sundays

Color Green

Prayers of Intercession

The prayers are prepared locally for each occasion. The following examples may be adapted or used as appropriate.

Called together in the Spirit's embrace, let us pray for the mending of God's world.

A brief silence.

Gracious God, we give thanks for your living word that goes out and does not return empty. Make your church a partner in accomplishing what you desire. Unite us in faith, witness, and mission. Hear us, O God.

Your mercy is great.

For land, creatures, and people suffering from drought, that gentle rain bring life and hope. For mountains, hills, and the trees of the field, that all creation clap for joy. Hear us, O God.

Your mercy is great.

For nations suffering the violence and hunger of war (*especially*). For exiles and refugees. Lead them home in peace and bless them with your fullness. Hear us, O God.

Your mercy is great.

For victims and perpetrators of race-based crime. For all who suffer sorrow, illness, or injury (*especially*). Bring them justice, healing, and new life by the power of your Spirit. Hear us, O God.

Your mercy is great.

For this congregation and its leaders; through our shared work, let your word prosper among us and bring life to the community beyond our doors. Hear us, O God.

Your mercy is great.

Here other intercessions may be offered.

In thanksgiving for all who have died recently, for strangers and dear ones who have blessed our lives and sparked our hope (*especially*). Give comfort and confidence to all who mourn. Hear us, O God.

Your mercy is great.

All these things, and whatever else you see that we need, we entrust to your care through Christ our Lord.
Amen.

Images in the Readings

Although seed was valuable, the **sower** cast the seed widely. In Christian imagination, the sower is Christ, and also the preacher, and also every Christian spreading the good news to others.

Those who live in the Spirit bear good **fruit**, says Matthew. The imagery of plentiful growth recurs throughout the Bible and can alert us to the beauteous variety of plants and trees we humans can enjoy. In the vision of the heavenly city in the book of Revelation, the tree of life can by itself produce twelve different fruits.

The **trees** are clapping their hands. The troublesome thorn is replaced by the medicinally useful evergreen cypress, identified as a tree used in the building of the temple. The briar has been replaced with myrtle, an aromatic evergreen used in the rituals of Sukkoth.

Ideas for the Day

- Two truths held in tension in this parable may be: seed is precious, *and* seed is meant to be used. Consider the myriad congregational ministries your worshipers are familiar with, and choose one or more story to lift up this Sunday as an example of abundance and/or the fruitfulness of God's word. Working against the assumption that preciousness is determined by *scarcity*, an engaging worship service will highlight unending resources, transformations, seasonality, and taking the long view.
- Scattering expectations or routines can bring growth. With preparation time and support, shuffle age- or gender-segregated volunteer roles on this day. Perhaps adolescents usher or greet while retirees acolyte. Invite a young reader (and parent-partner) to proclaim scripture. A men's group serves as altar guild while preschoolers collect communion cups. Invite Facebook fans to craft the prayers of intercession. This exercise could extend far beyond worship too. Plan ample reflection time with all participants; this is key. Celebrate what takes root.
- The act of sowing seed is foreign to many in North America. Furthermore, the word is confused by prereaders with its homophone, *sewing*. Invite a sower to bring simple equipment to worship; explain tools, gestures, and materials; and demonstrate the action. This can be done in a dedicated location or thoughtfully pantomimed among the aisles as the gospel is read, for example. Take care to highlight what is seen, heard, smelled, and touched in the process of sowing. What conditions cannot be prepared or controlled? Many insights and emotions become accessible when a gospel parable is enacted.

- Farmers markets are in full swing in most parts of North America in mid-July. If your congregation has a community garden or partners with an agency that collects fresh produce, consider this Sunday as the kickoff to collecting the harvest. Invite worshipers to bring their own garden produce, and include neighborhood grocers, who are often eager to participate. The visual power of an in-kind offering, a communion table overflowing with fruits, vegetables, and flowers, highlights the hundred-, sixty-, and thirty-fold harvest Jesus celebrates (Matt. 13:23) and echoes the accomplishment of purpose (Isa. 55:11).

Connections with the Liturgy

In each thanksgiving at the table, we pray with Paul that the Spirit of God would come to dwell among us: with your Word and Holy Spirit to bless us; Holy God, we long for your Spirit; Come, Holy Spirit; pour out upon us the Spirit of your love; send now, we pray, your Holy Spirit, whose breath revives us for life; Come, Spirit of freedom!; we pray for the gift of your Spirit, in our gathering, within this meal, among your people; the life of the Spirit of our risen Savior, to establish our faith in truth; Come, Holy Spirit.

Let the Children Come

The whole cosmos takes part in God's creative and redeeming work. Yes, this is a parable of parables and how faith grows, but it is also Jesus inviting us into a story about the earth. We hear how all the creatures work together to feed one another with God's overflowing abundance. Some children among you will be experienced gardeners; some will not know where their food really comes from. Invite children to join the offering procession of wine, bread, and money with food from the garden. Help children connect their table at home with the table at church and with the abundance of the earth.

Assembly Song
Gathering

What is this place ELW 524
Open now thy gates of beauty ELW 533, LBW 250
Almighty God, your word is cast ELW 516, LBW 234

Psalmody and Acclamations

Alonso, Tony. "The Seed That Falls on Good Ground" from TLP:A.
Long, Larry J. "Psalm 65," Refrain 1, from PSCY.
+ Mummert, Mark. "Psalm 119:105-112" from PSCY.
(GA) ELW 169 with proper verse for Lectionary 15.

Hymn of the Day

As rain from the clouds ELW 508 *AFTON WATER*
The Word of God is source and seed ELW 506, WOV 658
  GAUDEAUMUS DOMINO
God, whose farm is all creation ELW 734 *HARVEST GIFTS*

Offering

Lord, let my heart be good soil   ELW 512, WOV 713
We plow the fields and scatter   ELW 680/681, LBW 362, LLC 492

Communion

Lord, your hands have formed   ELW 554, WOV 727
For the fruit of all creation   ELW 679, WOV 760, LBW 563
As the grains of wheat   ELW 465, WOV 705

Sending

The Spirit sends us forth to serve   ELW 551, LBW 723
Sent forth by God's blessing   ELW 547, LBW 221

Additional Assembly Songs

Bring Forth the Kingdom   LS 35, W&P 22
When seed falls on good soil   LBW 236
As sunshine to a garden   ASG 1

⊕ Caribbean Pentecostal chorus. "If You Only Had Faith/Si tuvieras fe" from *Glory to God*. U. WJK 0664238971.

⊕ Zimbabwean traditional. "Listen Now for the Gospel/Yakanaka Vhangeri" from *One Is the Body: Songs of Unity and Diversity*. SATB, cant. GIA G-5790.

☼ Brading, Simon/Kate Simmonds/Ben Hall. "Let the Rain Come" from CCLI.

☼ Doerksen, Brian/ Phillip Janz. "No Condemnation" from CCLI.

☼ Huerta, Joe/ Leila Huerta. "Go Out with You" from CCLI.

☼ Keyes, Aaron/Andy Lehman. "Not Guilty Anymore" from CCLI.

☼ Rend Collective. "Build Your Kingdom Here" from CCLI.

☼ Spence, Kate. "Isaiah 55" from CCLI.

Music for the Day
Choral

Ferguson, John. "Word of God Come Down on Earth." SATB, org. GIA G-3764.

P Greene, Maurice. "You Visit the Earth" from *Sing Forth God's Praise*. MH solo, kybd. AFP 9780800675264.

Jennings, Carolyn. "Blessed Are They." SATB, org, opt fl. CG CGA896.

Mendelssohn, Felix. "I Will Sing of Thy Great Mercies" from *Sing a Song of Joy*. ML solo, kybd. AFP 9780800652821.

Children's Choir

Bolt, Conway A., Jr. "The Kingdom of God." 2 pt. CG CGA677.

P Burrows, Mark. "Change" from *Again, I Say Rejoice!* U, kybd. CG CGC56.

Mathia, Catherine/Audrey Sillick. "The Tiny Seed" from *LifeSongs*. U. AFP 9780806642703.

Keyboard / Instrumental

P ♫ Hamilton, Gregory. "As Rain from the Clouds" (Afton Water) from *Piano Blessings*. Pno. AFP 9781451443103.

P Hansen, Sherri. "Lord, Let My Heart Be Good Soil" (Good Soil) from *Piano Weavings*. Pno. AFP 9781451497861.

♫ Miller, Aaron David. "As Rain from the Clouds" (Afton Water) from *Augsburg Organ Library: Baptism and Holy Communion*. Org. AFP 9780800623555.

P ♫ Sedio, Mark. "God, Whose Farm Is All Creation" (Harvest Gifts) from *Come and Praise*, vol. 2. Org. AFP 9780806696928.

Handbell

P Linker, Janet/Jane McFadden. "Hymn of Promise." 3-5 oct hb, opt 3 oct hc, L2+, HOP 2708. Pno (not opt), HOP 2708D.

Waugh, Timothy. "Rondo Borincano." 3 or 5 oct, L3+. FTT 20143.

Wissinger, Kathleen. "The Sower." 3-5 oct, L3. GIA G-6149.

Monday, July 17
Bartolomé de Las Casas, missionary to the Indies, died 1566

Bartolomé de Las Casas was a Spanish priest and a missionary in the Western Hemisphere. He first came to the West while serving in the military, and he was granted a large estate that included a number of indigenous slaves. When he was ordained in 1513, he granted freedom to his servants. This act characterized much of the rest of Las Casas's ministry. Throughout the Caribbean and Central America, he worked to stop the enslavement of native people, to halt the brutal treatment of women by military forces, and to promote laws that humanized the process of colonization.

Saturday, July 22
Mary Magdalene, Apostle

The gospels report Mary Magdalene was one of the women of Galilee who followed Jesus. She was present at Jesus' crucifixion and his burial. When she went to the tomb on the first day of the week to anoint Jesus' body, she was the first person to whom the risen Lord appeared. She returned to the disciples with the news and has been called "the apostle to the apostles" for her proclamation of the resurrection. Because John's gospel describes Mary as weeping at the tomb, she is often portrayed in art with red eyes. Icons depict her standing by the tomb and holding a bright red egg, symbol of the resurrection.

⊕ = global song   ♫ = relates to hymn of the day   + = semicontinuous psalm
☼ = praise song   P = available in Prelude Music Planner

July 23, 2017
Time after Pentecost — Lectionary 16

It is an age-old question: why is there evil in the world? In the parable of the wheat and the weeds Jesus suggests that both grow together until the harvest. With Paul, we long for the day that all creation will be set free from bondage and suffering. Having both weeds and wheat within us, we humbly place our hope in the promises of God, and from the Lord's table we go forth to bear the fruit of justice and mercy.

Prayer of the Day

Faithful God, most merciful judge, you care for your children with firmness and compassion. By your Spirit nurture us who live in your kingdom, that we may be rooted in the way of your Son, Jesus Christ, our Savior and Lord.

Gospel Acclamation

Alleluia. My word shall accomplish that ' which I purpose,* and succeed in the thing for ' which I sent it. *Alleluia.* (Isa. 55:11)

Readings and Psalm

Isaiah 44:6-8

God claims the right to sole rule, because God announces things that actually do happen, while supposed divine opponents remain silent. God is Israel's redeemer, that is, the best brother or sister they ever had.

or Wisdom 12:13, 16-19

God's deeds of forgiveness and gift of hope indicate that God's faithful people must also show kindness. No other god cares for all people.

Psalm 86:11-17

Teach me your way, O LORD, and I will walk in your truth. (Ps. 86:11)

Romans 8:12-25

For Paul, true spirituality means that we experience the reality of the Spirit, which enables us to pray as God's children, keeps us in solidarity with creation, and gives us unseen hope that God will liberate us and creation from bondage to death and decay.

Matthew 13:24-30, 36-43

Jesus tells a parable about the co-existence of good and evil in this world. God's judgment will remove all evildoers and causes of sin, but not until the end of human history.

Semicontinuous reading and psalm

Genesis 28:10-19a

God's graciousness to Jacob is shown in God's revelation of the divine self to the patriarch, who is running for his life after cheating his brother Esau out of the family inheritance. Jacob promises that if God brings him back to the land, he will be loyal to God and give God a tenth of everything.

Psalm 139:1-12, 23-24

You have searched me out and known me. (Ps. 139:1)

Preface   Sundays

Color   Green

Prayers of Intercession

The prayers are prepared locally for each occasion. The following examples may be adapted or used as appropriate.

Called together in the Spirit's embrace, let us pray for the mending of God's world.

A brief silence.

Enliven your church with love for your world, O God. Give undivided hearts to Christians from Africa and the Americas, Asia and Europe. Make us one in faithful witness to your will. Lord, in your mercy,

hear our prayer.

Renew the life of this earth, O God, even as it groans because of misuse and decay. Cultivate in us an eager longing for a healthy and life-giving earth. Lord, in your mercy,

hear our prayer.

Bridge the chasms that divide the nations, O God. Inspire a reconciling vision among the world's leaders, and bring together people of differing commitments for the sake of the world's most vulnerable people. Lord, in your mercy,

hear our prayer.

Embrace those who suffer, O God. Give peace to all who are near death, hope to those who are depressed, shelter to the homeless, and healing to the sick (*especially*). Lord, in your mercy,

hear our prayer.

Embolden our witness to your love, O God. Send us out into the world with courageous hearts, persistence, and holy wisdom. Inspire us to tend to and delight in our children's faith. Lord, in your mercy,

hear our prayer.

Here other intercessions may be offered.

Raise up your saints, O God. Inspire us by the lives of all reformers and renewers of your church (*especially Birgitta of Sweden*). Receive our thanks for the saints among us who have recently died (*especially*). Lord, in your mercy,
hear our prayer.
All these things, and whatever else you see that we need, we entrust to your care through Christ our Lord.
Amen.

Images in the Readings

Contemporary English-language Bibles cleverly translate this parable with nouns that sound nearly identical: wheat and **weeds**. It is easy to think of the other as a weed. Christian theology reminds us that each one of us is both wheat and weed. In Martin Luther's language, we are always both saint and sinner.

Once again this Sunday's readings give us the images of the seed and the harvest. In explicating the allegory, Matthew writes about the furnace of **fire**, where there will be weeping and gnashing of teeth. Scholars suggest that the image of eternal separation from God as fire, Gehenna, recalled the perpetually burning refuse dump that was outside the city walls. Thus God's judgmental fire was about expulsion from the community and destruction of what is worthless. That this fire is an image is made clear in that people are gnashing their teeth; thus they still have bodies that are, however, not being burned up.

We are **children** of God: not natural offspring but instead adopted, beloved, dependent, obedient.

That the entire universe is **in labor** is a striking image of God's creation that rejects a commonplace Christian notion that God cares only for human beings. According to biblical theology, all God's creation is good; all creation has fallen; all is groaning in pain until God brings about new birth. As in the natural world, so in the human part of it: countless mothers die in childbirth, for new birth is a painful, even dangerous event. The image of all the earth in labor fits well with our scientific knowledge of the earth and its creatures, all of which must continually struggle for life. The natural world is not a benign zoo but rather billions of life forms created by God that all are headed toward decay.

God is **the first and the last**. Revelation casts this as Alpha and Omega, A and Z. So Christian theology has taught that God was before all things, and when all things come to their end, what will remain is God.

Ideas for the Day

- This is the second of three weeks in which the gospel reading focuses on seeds and growing. Today's parable describes the plants themselves, their heartiness, and the weeds that might grow up among otherwise healthy crops. Consider what plants people may have growing in their gardens or fields in your community. What weeds might be inhibiting the growth of desired plants? Some weeds can

be useful in their own right—dandelions, for example, are good in salads or for making tea. What would you lose if you let your garden or field run wild in the way that Jesus suggests the kingdom of heaven might do?

- Today's gospel reading describes God's final judgment of humanity. One primary message of the parable is that "the church [is] a mixed body . . . made up of good and bad, a situation that will be resolved only at the final judgment" (Arland J. Hultgren, *The Parables of Jesus: A Commentary* [Grand Rapids: Eerdmans, 2000], 294). Though the parable suggests judgment, it also affirms that judgment does not belong to humanity but to God, who will separate the wheat from the weeds at the end of time. It is easy for communities to identify those who are not like "us." This parable may remind worshipers that it is not our job to judge one another. That responsibility lies with God alone—and we might find ourselves surprised at God's judgment.

- The readings from Matthew and Romans both emphasize patience. If you do not like what is growing in your field, wait patiently until the time of harvest. With patience we hope for what we cannot now see. Perhaps your community is patiently awaiting some change—a plan for a new building or the recommendation of a call committee for a new pastor. Perhaps a beloved member is patiently awaiting graduation or employment, marriage, or death. Consider inviting your community into the spiritual practice of patience. Being able to embody patience can be extraordinarily difficult but also rewarding.

Connections with the Liturgy

Already in the mid AD 50s, Paul indicated that Christians addressed God as their loving Father. For Paul, God's being *Abba* to human "children" is no natural situation but results only because of the sufferings of Jesus Christ. The most common Christian prayer throughout the centuries opens by calling God our Father.

Let the Children Come

What do you want to be when you grow up? This is a question adults seem to delight in asking and children seem to delight in pondering. The answers could be endless, right? Children could be anything when they grow up; we'll have to wait and see. A handful of various seeds might all look the same in the beginning but grow into a varied, diverse garden. Even in this story, God's creation seems to celebrate and embrace diversity. In the wider gospel story, how does God confound the binary of good and bad? How can our language help children hold both good and bad within ourselves and others in tension?

Assembly Song
Gathering

O Holy Spirit, root of life   ELW 399, WOV 688

Sing to the Lord of harvest   ELW 694, LBW 412

Almighty God, your word is cast   ELW 516, LBW 234

Psalmody and Acclamations

Dean, Stephen. "Lord, You Are Good and Forgiving" from *Psalm Songs 3*. AFP 0800657721.

Trapp, Lynn. "Four Psalm Settings." U or cant, assembly, org, opt SATB. MSM 80-701.

+ Sedio, Mark. "Psalm 86:11-17" and "Psalm 139:1-12, 23-24" from PWA.

(GA) Gospel acclamation from ELW setting seven (S179a). Use psalm tone 1, 6, 7, or 10 in E major with proper verse for Lectionary 16.

Hymn of the Day

O Holy Spirit, enter in   ELW 786, LBW 459   *WIE SCHÖN LEUCHTET*

We plow the fields and scatter   ELW 680, LLC 492
SAN FERNANDO

Come, ye thankful people, come   ELW 693, LBW 407
ST. GEORGE'S, WINDSOR

Offering

As the grains of wheat   ELW 465, WOV 705

Praise and thanksgiving   ELW 689, LBW 409

Communion

Neither death nor life   ELW 622

Great is thy faithfulness   ELW 733, TFF 283, WOV 771

Father, we thank you   ELW 478, WOV 704

Sending

On what has now been sown   ELW 550, LBW 261

Spread, oh, spread, almighty Word   ELW 663, LBW 379

Additional Assembly Songs

Don't be worried   TFF 212

In peace, in peace, through Christ   CBM 83

Beauty for brokenness   W&P 17

⊕ Loh, I-to. "Search Me, O God" from *Glory to God*. U. WJK 0664238971.

⊕ Olson, A. Louise Anderson, arr. "Praised Be the Rock" from *Set Free: A Collection of African Hymns*. SATB. AFP 9780806600451.

☼ Baker, Bob. "Until" from CCLI.

☼ Chisum, John/Lynn DeShazo. "Lord of the Harvest" from CCLI.

☼ Gaither, William J./Gloria Gaither. "Should the Harvest Never Come" from CCLI.

☼ Getty, Keith/Kristyn Getty/Stuart Townend. "By Faith" from CCLI.

☼ Nockels, Nathan/Christy Nockels. "Holy Roar" from CCLI.

☼ Weins, Laura/Johnny Markin. "Show Me Your Ways" from CCLI.

Music for the Day
Choral

♫ Berg, Ken. "Come, Ye Thankful People, Come." SATB, opt assembly, pno, org. MSM 20-706-E.

Marcello, Benedetto/arr. Dale Grotenhuis. "Teach Me Now, O Lord." 2 pt trbl or mxd, kybd. MSM 50-9418.

P Scott, K. Lee. "The Call" from *Sing a Song of Joy*. MH solo, kybd. AFP 9780800647889.

♫ Ward, Robert. "Sweet Freedom's Song No. 3: Come, Ye Thankful People, Come." SATB, opt pno. ECS 7.0629.

Children's Choir

Avery, Richard/Donald Marsh. "We Are the Church" from *Life-Songs*. U, kybd. AFP 9780806642703.

P Horman, John D. "Jacob and the Ladder of Angels" from *Sing the Stories of God's People*. U, kybd. AFP 9780806698397.

P Messick, Pat. "God's Wondrous World" from *ChildrenSing in Worship*. U, kybd, opt Orff inst. AFP 9781451401806.

Keyboard / Instrumental

♫ Distler, Hugo. "O Holy Spirit, Enter In" (Wie schön leuchten) from *Short Chorale Arrangements for Organ, Op. 8.3*. Org. MMP 1466. Various editions.

P♫ Kerr, J. Wayne. "We Plow the Fields and Scatter" (San Fernando) from *Amen: World Hymns for Organ*. Org. AFP 9781451486018.

P♫ Organ, Anne Krentz. "Come, Ye Thankful People, Come" (St. George's, Windsor) from *Reflections on Hymn Tunes for the Fall Festivals*. Pno. AFP 9780800663834.

P Sowash, Bradley. "We Plow the Fields and Scatter" (Wir pflügen) from *Great German Hymns Arranged in Contemporary Styles*. Pno. AFP 9780800637446.

Handbell

♫ Gramann, Fred. "Everlasting Light." 3-5 oct, L4. CG CGB361.

P Morris, Hart. "Down by the Riverside." 3-5 oct hb, L3+, HOP 2684. Opt full score (cl, DB, drms), HOP 2684P.

♫ Prins, Matthew. "Come, Ye Thankful People, Come." 2-5 oct hb, L2+, GIA G-7941. Opt C inst, GIA G-7941INST.

⊕ = global song   ♫ = relates to hymn of the day   + = semicontinuous psalm

☼ = praise song   P = available in Prelude Music Planner

Sunday, July 23
Birgitta of Sweden, renewer of the church, died 1373

Birgitta (beer-GEE-tuh) was married at age thirteen and had four daughters with her husband. She was a woman of some standing who, in her early thirties, served as the chief lady-in-waiting to the queen of Sweden. She was widowed at the age of thirty-eight, shortly after she and her husband had made a religious pilgrimage. Following the death of her husband the religious dreams and visions that had begun in her youth occurred more regularly. Her devotional commitments led her to give to the poor and needy all that she owned, and she began to live a more ascetic life. She founded an order of monks and nuns, the Order of the Holy Savior (Brigittines), whose superior was a woman. Today the Society of St. Birgitta is a laypersons' society that continues her work of prayer and charity.

Tuesday, July 25
James, Apostle

James is one of the sons of Zebedee and is counted as one of the twelve disciples. Together with his brother John they had the nickname "sons of thunder." One of the stories in the New Testament tells of their request for Jesus to grant them places of honor in the kingdom. They are also reported to have asked Jesus for permission to send down fire on a Samaritan village that had not welcomed them. James was the first of the Twelve to suffer martyrdom and is the only apostle whose martyrdom is recorded in scripture. He is sometimes called James the Elder to distinguish him from James the Less, commemorated with Philip on May 1, and James of Jerusalem, commemorated on October 23.

Friday, July 28
Johann Sebastian Bach, died 1750; Heinrich Schütz, died 1672; George Frederick Handel, died 1759; musicians

These three composers have done much to enrich the worship life of the church. Johann Sebastian Bach drew on the Lutheran tradition of hymnody and wrote about two hundred cantatas, including at least two for each Sunday and festival day in the Lutheran calendar of his day. He has been called "the fifth evangelist" for the ways he proclaimed the gospel through his music. George Frederick Handel was not primarily a church musician, but his great work *Messiah* is a musical proclamation of the scriptures. Heinrich Schütz wrote choral settings of biblical texts and paid special attention to ways his composition would underscore the meaning of the words.

Saturday, July 29
Mary, Martha, and Lazarus of Bethany

Mary and Martha are remembered for the hospitality and refreshment they offered Jesus in their home. Following the characterization drawn by Luke, Martha represents the active life, Mary the contemplative. Mary is identified in the fourth gospel as the one who anointed Jesus before his passion and who was criticized for her act of devotion. Lazarus, Mary's and Martha's brother, was raised from the dead by Jesus as a sign of the eternal life offered to all believers. It was over Lazarus's tomb that Jesus wept for love of his friend.

Saturday, July 29
Olaf, King of Norway, martyr, died 1030

Olaf is considered the patron saint of Norway. In his early career he engaged in war and piracy in the Baltic and in Normandy. In Rouen, though, he was baptized and became a Christian. He returned to Norway, succeeded his father as king, and from then on Christianity was the dominant religion of the realm. He revised the laws of the nation and enforced them with strict impartiality, eliminating the possibility of bribes. He thereby alienated much of the aristocracy. The harshness that he sometimes resorted to in order to establish Christianity and his own law led to a rebellion. After being driven from the country and into exile, he enlisted support from Sweden to try to regain his kingdom, but he died in battle.

July 30, 2017
Time after Pentecost — Lectionary 17

As Solomon prays for wisdom, we seek to more deeply know the treasures of faith. In today's gospel Jesus offers everyday images that reveal to us the reign of God: a tree that becomes a sheltering home, yeast that penetrates and expands, a treasured pearl, a net that gains a great catch. Even as we seek the riches of God's reign, the great surprise is that God's grace finds us first!

Prayer of the Day

Beloved and sovereign God, through the death and resurrection of your Son you bring us into your kingdom of justice and mercy. By your Spirit, give us your wisdom, that we may treasure the life that comes from Jesus Christ, our Savior and Lord.

Gospel Acclamation

Alleluia. Many will come from ^ˈ east and west* and will eat in the king- ^ˈ dom of heaven. *Alleluia.* (Matt. 8:11)

Readings and Psalm

1 Kings 3:5-12

Because Solomon did not ask for long life, riches, or the defeat of his enemies, God gave him what he asked for: wisdom to govern the people well. In verse 13 God gives him additional honor and riches beyond compare.

Psalm 119:129-136

When your word is opened, it gives light and understanding. (Ps. 119:130)

Romans 8:26-39

These words celebrate the depth of God's actions for us. Through Christ's death for us and the activity of the Spirit praying for us, we are fused to God's love poured out in Jesus Christ. Nothing, not even death itself, is able to separate us from such incredible divine love.

Matthew 13:31-33, 44-52

Throughout Matthew's gospel, Jesus and his disciples proclaim the good news that "the kingdom of heaven is near!" Here, Jesus offers several brief parables that explore the implications of this announcement for people's lives.

Semicontinuous reading and psalm

Genesis 29:15-28

The young shepherd Jacob met his match in the old shepherd, Laban, his father-in-law. Laban gave Jacob his older daughter, Leah, when he had promised to give him Rachel. Jacob worked fourteen years to earn his favorite wife, Rachel, but the years seemed like a few days because of his love for her.

Psalm 105:1-11, 45b

Make known the deeds of the LORD among the peoples. Hallelujah! (Ps. 105:1, 45)

or Psalm 128

Happy are they who follow in the ways of God. (Ps. 128:1)

Preface   Sundays

Color   Green

Prayers of Intercession

The prayers are prepared locally for each occasion. The following examples may be adapted or used as appropriate.

Generous, compassionate God, we gather before you to pray for the church, the world, and all in need.

A brief silence.

Shine the light of understanding on your church on earth. Bind us together in the word to share your love with the world. Lord, in your mercy,

hear our prayer.

Protect birds and their nests, fields full of crops, the seas and the fish that swim in them. Inspire us to care for the creation you love. Lord, in your mercy,

hear our prayer.

Raise up just and wise advocates and judges from small-town courts to international tribunals. Enlighten all leaders to discern what is right and do what is good. Lord, in your mercy,

hear our prayer.

Nurture faith in those who doubt. Lift up those who are weak in body, mind, or spirit. Heal the sick, comfort the grieving, and surround with love those facing their last days (*especially*). Lord, in your mercy,

hear our prayer.

Expand the understanding of this assembly to see our neighbors as you see them. Let the yeast of your word grow beyond us to expand your boundless love to those around us. Lord, in your mercy,

hear our prayer.

Here other intercessions may be offered.

Sustain us by the intercession of your Holy Spirit. Let the Spirit's sighs, too deep for words, comfort us until we rejoice with those already united with you (*especially*). Lord, in your mercy,

hear our prayer.

Into your hands we place all our prayers, spoken and unspoken, trusting in the mercy of Christ Jesus.

Amen.

Images in the Readings

The parables are full of images that raise many questions. The **mustard seed** actually grows into a straggly annual bush, not the monumental tree of life (see, for example, Ezekiel 31:2-9) that is paradoxically evoked in the opening parable. In Jewish religious symbolism, the preferred sex is the man, the holy minister is a priest, and the holy bread is unleavened; yet in the parable the woman adds **leaven** to three measures of flour. The man sells "all that he has" to gain a **treasure**, and we think of Solomon, for whom the preferred treasure was wisdom that comes only from God. The **net** that catches all kinds of fish is a commonplace symbol for the church. Yet by "the kingdom of heaven," Matthew does not mean merely "the church."

The first reading is one of several biblical tales about the **wisdom of Solomon**, a phrase come into our language to signify immense and deep understanding. According to the monarchical myths of the ancient Near East, the king was anointed by God, next in power to God, God's servant, even God's son. Yet the later stories in 2 Kings describe Solomon as having been as prone to foolishness and error as any other king, as having given in to many temptations that separated him from the love of God. For Christians, Christ himself is wisdom.

Ideas for the Day

- Jesus offers various descriptions of the kingdom of God. Just as the kingdom of God does not have a single interpretation, so also the ways in which God relates to humankind are varied. Each person encounters God in a different way. A preacher could share his or her own story about encountering God and also invite worshipers to consider where they meet God. The congregation might write their own parables to add to those in Matthew 13 as part of a Bible study or as an interactive worship activity.
- The last three parables in this passage (13:44-50) are unique to Matthew's gospel. It is possible that Jesus addressed them to his disciples only, since in 13:36 he entered a house with the disciples and began explaining the parables to them, and there is no indication of a change of scene. If these parables were intended for his closest followers, perhaps they were meant to describe how the disciples will encounter God's kingdom. The value of the objects in these last parables is more apparent than in the first two, which could indicate the importance of Jesus' relationship with the disciples as compared to the crowds.

For more on this topic, see John R. Donahue, *The Gospel in Parable* (Fortress Press, 1988), 66–69.

- Today's reading from Romans is a favorite at funerals. It could be good for your congregation to hear a sermon on this passage outside of that context, but do be aware of possible connections for worshipers who have recently experienced loss. In the context of life and death, this passage is comforting because it reminds those who grieve that their loved ones are not lost forever but remain in the love of God. In daily life, other interpretations are possible. Many things can keep us from being aware of God's love for us. Busy schedules, family obligations, health concerns, and countless other distractions keep us from focusing on our faith. The assurance of this reading is that even when we are distracted or burdened with worry, God's love is with us.

Connections with the Liturgy

At each service of Holy Communion, we read from the ancient scriptures, and the sermon explicates a meaning of these texts for contemporary life: thus we are the householder who brings out of the treasury what is new and what is old.

Both the first and second reading speak about prayer. Whenever the church gathers for worship, the assembly prays for the church, the world of nature, the human community, all who are sick or suffering, and the specific needs of that congregation. Our intercessions, recalling Romans 8:26, are always "not as we ought but as we are able" (*ELW*, p. 109). We pray along with the risen Christ, who Paul writes is interceding for us.

Let the Children Come

Today the parables are like popcorn! So many wonderful images; five rapid-fire descriptions of what this kingdom of heaven is like. Each one, on its own, could be a divine rabbit trail to explore, and yet how do all five together become a parable of absurd abundance? This inexhaustible way of describing what it is to be in God's kingdom is a lesson on its own. How might a "procession of the parables" convey the abundant diversity of living in God's community? In the midst of summer and the green, growing time of year, can we invite whimsy into our midst to celebrate God's absurd abundance?

Assembly Song
Gathering

God of grace and God of glory   ELW 705, LBW 415

Gather Us In   ELW 532, WOV 718

Let us go now to the banquet   ELW 523, LLC 410

Psalmody and Acclamations

Walker, Christopher. "Teach Me, O God" from *Psalm Songs 3*. AFP 0800657721.

Kallman, Daniel. "Psalm 119:129-136" from PWA.

+ Arnatt, Ronald. "Psalm 128." Cant, assembly, kybd. ECS 5417.

(GA) Gospel acclamation from ELW setting seven (S179a). Use psalm tone 1, 6, 7, or 10 in E major with proper verse for Lectionary 17.

Hymn of the Day

Jesus, priceless treasure ELW 775, LBW 457 *JESU, MEINE FREUDE*
ELW 458 *GUD SKAL, ALTING MAGE*

Soul, adorn yourself with gladness ELW 488, LBW 224
SCHMÜCKE DICH ELW 489, LLC 388 *CANTO AL BORINQUEN*

We eat the bread of teaching ELW 518 *WISDOM'S FEAST*

Offering

Accept, O Lord, the gifts we bring ELW 691, WOV 759

We Are Called ELW 720, W&P 147

Communion

Neither death nor life ELW 622

Be thou my vision ELW 793, WOV 776

Build us up, Lord ELW 670

Sending

All my hope on God is founded ELW 757, WOV 782

Sent forth by God's blessing ELW 547, LBW 221

Additional Assembly Songs

You are the seed WOV 753, TFF 226, LLC 486

Seek ye first WOV 783, W&P 122, TFF 149

Where two or more are gathered ASG 45

⊕ Mahamba, Deogratias. "Blessed Be the Name/Heri ni jina." SATB. ELW 797.

⊕ Scots traditional. "The Treasure" from *I Will Not Sing Alone*. U. GIA G-6512.

☼ Corum, Casey/Angie Corum/Anabeth Morgan/Abigail Corum. "Heaven Come Down" from CCLI.

☼ Evans, Sam/Jonathan Hunt. "Wonderful Savior" from CCLI.

☼ Frye, Jordan. "Kingdom" from CCLI.

☼ Houghton, Israel/Micah Massey. "Your Presence Is Heaven" from CCLI.

☼ Rainey, Mildred/Kathryn Scott. "Everything Changes" from CCLI.

☼ Torwalt, Bryan/ Katie Torwalt. "Let the Sound of Heaven" from CCLI.

Music for the Day
Choral

P ♫ Bach, J. S. "Jesus, My Sweet Pleasure" from *Bach for All Seasons*. SATB, kybd. AFP 9780800658540.

Handel, G. F. "If God Is for Us, Who Is Against Us?" from *Messiah*. Sop solo, kybd. Various editions.

Hopson, Hal. "Song of the Mustard Seed." U, pno. GIA G-2239.

P Pooler, Marie. "Be Thou My Vision" from *Augsburg Easy Choirbook*. U, kybd, opt desc. AFP 9780800676025.

Children's Choir

P Horman, John. "Teach Us to Pray" from *Sing the Stories of Jesus*. U, kybd. AFP 9780800679453.

Lowe, Helenclair. "We Will Sing for Joy." U, kybd. CG CGA202.

Wold, Wayne L. "To the Banquet, Come" from *LifeSongs*. U, kybd. AFP 9780806642703.

Keyboard / Instrumental

P Cherwien, David. "God of Tempest, God of Whirlwind" (Cwm Rhondda) from *Organ Plus, vol. 2: Hymn Preludes for Organ and Instruments*. Org, tpt. AFP 9780800678548.

P ♫ Hamilton, Gregory. "Soul, Adorn Yourself with Gladness" (Canto a Borinquen) from *Piano Blessings*. Pno. AFP 9781451443103.

P Raabe, Nancy. "Be Thou My Vision" (Slane) from *Day of Arising: A Tapestry of Musical Traditions*. Pno. AFP 9780800637460.

P ♫ Rübsam, Wolfgang. "Soul, Adorn Yourself with Gladness" (Schmücke dich) from *Fourteen Chorale Preludes: A Guide to Liturgical Improvisation*. Org. AFP 9780806698038.

Handbell

P Morris, Hart. "Contemplation and Dance on 'Kingsfold.'" 3-5 oct hb, opt 3 oct hc, L3+, HOP 2705. Opt full score (fl, drm), HOP 2705P.

Sherman, Arnold. "O Sacred Head, Now Wounded." 3-5 oct, L2+. HOP 1732.

♫ Wagner, Douglas. "Communion Meditation." 3-5 oct, L2. LOR 20/1446L.

⊕ = global song ♫ = relates to hymn of the day + = semicontinuous psalm

☼ = praise song P = available in Prelude Music Planner

August 6, 2017
Time after Pentecost — Lectionary 18

In today's first reading God invites all who are hungry or thirsty to receive food and drink without cost. Jesus feeds the hungry multitude and reveals the abundance of God. At the eucharistic table we remember all who are hungry or poor in our world today. As we share the bread of life, we are sent forth to give ourselves away as bread for the hungry.

Prayer of the Day

Glorious God, your generosity waters the world with goodness, and you cover creation with abundance. Awaken in us a hunger for the food that satisfies both body and spirit, and with this food fill all the starving world; through your Son, Jesus Christ, our Savior and Lord.

Gospel Acclamation

Alleluia. One does not live by ˡ bread alone,* but by every word that comes from the ˡ mouth of God. *Alleluia.* (Matt. 4:4)

Readings and Psalm

Isaiah 55:1-5

God invites Israel to a great feast at which both food and drink are free. God also promises to make an everlasting covenant with all the people, with promises that previously had been limited to the line of kings. As David was a witness to the nations, these nations shall now acknowledge the ways in which God has glorified Israel.

Psalm 145:8-9, 14-21

You open wide your hand and satisfy the desire of every living thing. (Ps. 145:16)

Romans 9:1-5

This begins a new section in Paul's letter in which he will deal with the place of Israel in God's saving plan. He opens by highlighting how Israel's heritage and legacy include being God's children, having God's covenants, being given God's law, participating in worship of God, and receiving divine promises.

Matthew 14:13-21

After John the Baptist is murdered, Jesus desires a time of solitude. Still, his compassion for others will not allow him to dismiss those who need him, and he is moved to perform one of his greatest miracles.

Semicontinuous reading and psalm

Genesis 32:22-31

Jacob wrestled all night with God, and when God wanted to get away as dawn was breaking, Jacob would not let God go until God had blessed him. Jacob's name is changed to Israel to mark his new relationship with God as he enters the land. Jacob is astonished that he remains alive after seeing God face to face.

Psalm 17:1-7, 15

I shall see your face; when I awake, I shall be satisfied. (Ps. 17:15)

Preface   Sundays

Color   Green

Prayers of Intercession

The prayers are prepared locally for each occasion. The following examples may be adapted or used as appropriate.

Generous, compassionate God, we gather before you to pray for the church, the world, and all in need.

A brief silence.

God of the covenant, call your church on earth to worship together to glorify your name in every language and in every land. Lord, in your mercy,

hear our prayer.

God of abundance who provides fields of wheat and vineyards of grapes, bless farmers and growers who furnish bread and wine for tables of abundance. Lord, in your mercy,

hear our prayer.

God of all compassion, raise up just leaders who care for the poor and hungry. Let nations share your bounty across the world and assure that no one goes without food. Lord, in your mercy,

hear our prayer.

God of all, fill those who are starving whether they long for food or companionship. Comfort the lonely and grieving; heal those who are sick in body, mind, or spirit (*especially*). Lord, in your mercy,

hear our prayer.

God who satisfies, bless the feeding programs of this congregation and community. Be with sandwich makers and cookie bakers, with those who stock food pantry shelves and those who point out need whether in our neighborhood or half a world away. Lord, in your mercy,

hear our prayer.

Here other intercessions may be offered.

Bless us as we remember the saints at your everlasting feast until we join them at your bountiful table. Lord, in your mercy, **hear our prayer.**
Into your hands we place all our prayers, spoken and unspoken, trusting in the mercy of Christ Jesus.
Amen.

Images in the Readings

The most common biblical image for divine mercy is **food**. In Genesis 1 the plants and trees that God created are given to humans as food. Ancient narratives told of God providing food during famine. The Israelites' memories of their nomadic years recalled a miraculous food, manna, which God sent to keep them alive in the wilderness. Religious rules commanded the faithful to share their food with the hungry and to abstain from eating with the wicked. Disobedience was met with the punishment of deprivation of food. The people of Israel themselves were likened to food that God has planted. Food or no food was central to all the primary religious festivals of the Old Testament. Poems described the law of God as if it were nourishing food. Christ was born in Bethlehem, which means "house of bread." In John's metaphoric theology, Christ says, "I am the bread of life." We need food to live, and Christians have each week served out the word and the sacrament as the food that Christ continues to distribute to those of us who are hungry.

The oracle from Isaiah includes **wine** as one of the foodstuffs that God gives away freely. Wine was not only the safest drink in the ancient world, but it signifies communal celebration, as if the alcohol symbolizes the Spirit who alters the human body into unity with others around the table. However, the church has often been stingy with its wine: only the smallest sip is granted, or none at all, and since 1869, when Thomas Welch invented pasteurized grape juice, wine has sometimes been replaced with a tamer drink. Each congregation may want to think through how the image of wine is conveyed in its communion practice.

Ideas for the Day

- Visit www.bread.org and learn about Bread for the World, an organization that is continuing Jesus' work of ensuring that everyone is fed. Encourage worshipers to email their elected officials urging them to take action on behalf of the hungry. Or organize an offering of letters. Templates are provided on the site.
- This is a great Sunday for a potluck or picnic after worship. Gather a team of people ahead of time, read the Isaiah passage together, and use it for inspiration as you prepare a space where people might "delight [them]selves in rich food" (Isa. 55:2). Get creative! Open it up to the community and invite others outside your congregation to come "without money and without price" (Isa. 55:1).

- Some churches today are in a financial predicament where they must fund-raise in order to pay the bills, rather than rely solely on tithes and offerings. This can take up a lot of the leadership's time and energy that might otherwise be spent developing the true mission of proclaiming the gospel of Jesus Christ. The focus can easily shift from proclaiming the gospel to bringing in money to pay the bills. Today's scripture offers a helpful corrective to this problem. Everything in today's readings is free, from the meal described by Isaiah to the meal hosted by Christ in the wilderness. This week's texts beg the question: What are we giving away for free? Raise this question to provoke a more missional mind-set.
- Every community faces issues such as homelessness and hunger. Individuals looking for food or assistance frequently make their way to churches. Consider Jesus' words: "You give them something to eat" (Matt. 14:16). Host an adult forum to discuss and discern how your church might respond to hungry individuals. Do you provide grocery gift cards? Bag lunches? Do you support a local food pantry or run a food pantry? Consider using the documentary *A Place at the Table* (Magnolia Pictures, 2012) to start the conversation about your community's response to Jesus' command that we feed those who are hungry.

Connections with the Liturgy

The description of Jesus feeding the multitude says, "Taking the loaves, he blessed and broke the loaves and gave them to his disciples." These words are echoed in the synoptic gospels' accounts of Jesus' meal on the night he was betrayed and so included in every great thanksgiving (for example, *ELW*, p. 109). What Jesus did during his ministry—thanking God for bread and distributing it to those around him—he continues to do through us in holy communion.

Let the Children Come

How often have you heard someone implore a child to share something they really like, perhaps a toy or a cookie? Children do not share naturally, and sharing is a learned skill that takes a very long time to develop. Today's gospel is not a story about sharing. It is about how Jesus takes a meager supply and transforms it into abundance. How is Jesus doing this among your assembly? How is Jesus feeding children in your community or far-off places through (the perhaps meager supply of) your community? How are the offering and the table connected in your liturgy?

Assembly Song
Gathering

All who hunger, gather gladly ELW 461
God extends an invitation ELW 486, LLC 397
O Jesus, joy of loving hearts ELW 658, LBW 356

Psalmody and Acclamations

Harmon, Kathleen. "Eighteenth Sunday in Ordinary Time (A)" from COJ:A.

Makeever, Ray. "Psalm 145:8-9, 14-21" from PWA.

+ Marshall, Jane. "Psalm 17." U, kybd. CG CGA891.

(GA) Gospel acclamation from ELW setting seven (S179a). Use psalm tone 1, 6, 7, or 10 in E major with proper verse for Lectionary 18.

Hymn of the Day

We come to the hungry feast ELW 479, WOV 766 *HUNGRY FEAST*

United at the table/*Unidos en la fiesta* ELW 498, LLC 408
   UNIDOS EN LA FIESTA

Break now the bread of life ELW 515, LBW 235 *BREAD OF LIFE*

Offering

When the poor ones/*Cuando el pobre* ELW 725, LLC 508

Come, let us eat ELW 491, LBW 214, TFF 119

Communion

Praise and thanksgiving ELW 689, LBW 409

Lord, whose love in humble service ELW 712, LBW 423

O living Bread from heaven ELW 542, LBW 197

Sending

Let us talents and tongues employ ELW 674, WOV 754, TFF 232

Hallelujah! We sing your praises ELW 535, TFF 158, WOV 722

Additional Assembly Songs

Hope of the world LBW 493

My soul thirsts for God SP 28

Now we offer WOV 761, TFF 129

⊕ Catena, Osvaldo. "Bendice, Señor, nuestro pan/God Bless to Us Our Bread" from *Sing with the World: Global Songs for Children*. U. GIA G-7339.

⊕ Prescod, Patrick, arr. "Communion Hymn" from *Let the Peoples Sing*. SATB. AFP 9780800675394.

❀ Andrews, Meredith/Paul Mabury/Paul Duncan. "Start with Me" from CCLI.

❀ Brown, Brenton/ Travis Ryan/Brandon Collins. "Jesus, My Victory" from CCLI.

❀ Craven, Avon. "Jesus Can" from CCLI.

❀ Egan, John/Paul Mabury/Mia Fieldes. "Take Me to the River" from CCLI.

❀ Kendrick, Graham. "Banquet" from CCLI.

❀ Smith, Dustin/Michael Farren. "Rushing Waters" from CCLI.

Music for the Day
Choral

P Berger, Jean. "The Eyes of All Wait upon Thee" from *Augsburg Motet Book*. SATB. AFP 9781451423709. Also as an octavo. AFP 9780800645595.

P Franck, Cesár. "O Bread of Life/Panis Angelicus" from *To God Will I Sing*. MH solo, kybd. AFP 9780800674342.

Hayes, Mark. "Give Me Jesus" from *10 Spirituals for Solo Voice*. MH solo, pno. ALF 17954 Book.

Nelson, Ronald A. "You Hear the Hungry Crying." SATB, opt assembly, kybd. AFP 9781451401790.

Children's Choir

P Burrows, Mark. "What's in the Box/When We See" from *Again, I Say Rejoice!* U, kybd. CG CGC56.

Edwards, Dan R. "Hevenu Shalom Aleichem (May Peace Be upon You)." U/2 pt, pno, opt cl and perc. CG CGA1402.

Schulz, Johann A. P. "All Good Gifts around Us" from *Life-Songs*. U, pno. AFP 9780806642703.

Keyboard / Instrumental

P♫ Biery, Marilyn. "Break Now the Bread of Life" (Bread of Life) from *An American Perspective: Settings of Old and New Tunes for Organ*. Org. AFP 9781451401820.

P Carter, John. "Let Us Break Bread Together" (Break Bread Together) from *Spirituals for Piano*. Pno. AFP 9780800621698.

♫ Cherwien, David. "We Come to the Hungry Feast" (Hungry Feast) from *O God, Beyond All Praising*. Org. AFP 9780800657246.

Hassell, Michael. "All Who Hunger, Gather Gladly" (Holy Manna) from *Jazz Pastorale*. Pno. AFP 9780800658052.

Handbell

P Moklebust, Cathy. "When You Do This, Remember Me." 3-5 oct hb, opt 3 oct hc, L2, CG CGB866. Opt full score (org), CG CGB865.

P Page, Anna Laura. "His Eye Is on the Sparrow." 3-5 oct, L3. CG CGB827.

♫ Prins, Matthew. "Break Thou the Bread of Life." 2-3 oct, L2+. FTT 20322.

Tuesday, August 8

Dominic, founder of the Order of Preachers (Dominicans), died 1221

Dominic was a Spanish priest who preached against the Albigensians, a heretical sect that held gnostic and dualistic beliefs. Dominic believed that a stumbling block to restoring heretics to the church was the wealth of clergy, so he formed an itinerant religious order, the Order of Preachers (Dominicans), who

⊕ = global song   ♫ = relates to hymn of the day   + = semicontinuous psalm

❀ = praise song   P = available in Prelude Music Planner

lived in poverty, studied philosophy and theology, and preached against heresy. The method of this order was to use kindness and gentle argument, rather than harsh judgment, to bring unorthodox Christians back to the fold. Dominic was opposed to burning Christians at the stake. Three times Dominic was offered the office of bishop, which he refused so that he could continue in his work of preaching.

Thursday, August 10
Lawrence, deacon, martyr, died 258

Lawrence was one of seven deacons of the congregation at Rome and, like the deacons appointed in Acts, was responsible for financial matters in the church and for the care of the poor. Lawrence lived during a time of persecution under the emperor Valerian. The emperor demanded that Lawrence surrender the treasures of the church. Lawrence gathered lepers, orphans, the blind and lame. He brought them to the emperor and said, "Here is the treasure of the church." This act enraged the emperor, and Lawrence was sentenced to death. Lawrence's martyrdom was one of the first to be observed by the church.

Friday, August 11
Clare, Abbess of San Damiano, died 1253

At age eighteen, Clare of Assisi heard Francis preach a sermon in a church in town. From that time, she determined to follow in his example of Christian living. With Francis's help (and against the wishes of her father) she and a growing number of companions established a women's Franciscan community, called the Order of Poor Ladies, or Poor Clares. She became a confidante and advisor to Francis, and in standing up against the wishes of popes for the sake of maintaining complete poverty, she helped inspire other women to pursue spiritual goals.

August 13, 2017
Time after Pentecost — Lectionary 19

Elijah finds the presence of God not in earthquake, wind, or fire, but in the sound of sheer silence. When the disciples face a great storm on the sea, they cry out with fear. Jesus says: "Take heart, it is I; do not be afraid." Amid the storms of life, we gather to seek the calm presence of Christ that soothes our fears. In comforting words of scripture and in the refreshing bread and cup of the eucharist, God grants us peace and sends us forth to be a sign of God's presence to others.

Prayer of the Day

O God our defender, storms rage around and within us and cause us to be afraid. Rescue your people from despair, deliver your sons and daughters from fear, and preserve us in the faith of your Son, Jesus Christ, our Savior and Lord.

Gospel Acclamation

Alleluia. I wait for ' you, O LORD;* in your word ' is my hope. *Alleluia.* (Ps. 130:5)

Readings and Psalm
1 Kings 19:9-18

On Mount Horeb, where God had appeared to Moses with typical signs of God's presence—earthquake, wind, and fire—Elijah now experienced God in "sheer silence." God assured Elijah that he is not the only faithful believer. Seven thousand Israelites are still loyal. God instructed Elisha to anoint two men as kings and to anoint Elisha as his own successor.

Psalm 85:8-13

I will listen to what the LORD God is saying. (Ps. 85:8)

Romans 10:5-15

A right relationship with God is not something we achieve by heroic efforts. It is a gift received in the proclamation whose content is Jesus Christ. This proclaimed word creates our faith in the Lord Jesus Christ. Hence Christian proclamation is an indispensable component of God's saving actions.

Matthew 14:22-33

Matthew's gospel typically portrays Jesus' disciples as people of "little faith" who fail despite their best intentions. In this story, Matthew shows how Jesus comes to the disciples when they are in trouble and sustains them in their time of fear and doubt.

Semicontinuous reading and psalm

Genesis 37:1-4, 12-28

Though Joseph was Jacob's favorite son, his jealous brothers sold him into slavery. Judah, who protected Joseph's life, later gives a moving speech before Joseph in Egypt, indicating that the brothers had changed their ways (44:18-34).

Psalm 105:1-6, 16-22, 45b

Make known the deeds of the Lord among the peoples. Hallelujah! (Ps. 105:1, 45)

Preface   Sundays

Color   Green

Prayers of Intercession

The prayers are prepared locally for each occasion. The following examples may be adapted or used as appropriate.

Generous, compassionate God, we gather before you to pray for the church, the world, and all in need.
A brief silence.

O God our ruler, continue to send out your church on earth to be light and salt to the world. Keep giving us the heart to do your work. Lord, in your mercy,
hear our prayer.

O God our creator, you quiet the seas and silence the wind. Restore your creation to the perfection and beauty you spoke into being. Lord, in your mercy,
hear our prayer.

O God our redeemer, inspire leaders with the righteousness that comes from faith, so that your justice thrives throughout the world. Lord, in your mercy,
hear our prayer.

O God our sustainer, comfort those who are lonely, fearful, or burdened by doubt. Give meaningful work to those who seek employment. Walk with those who are grieving or ill, and with all who face the last days of their lives (*especially*). Lord, in your mercy,
hear our prayer.

O God our encourager, empower this assembly to boldly proclaim and live out your love to all who long to hear a word of hope and kindness. Equip us to use our hands, feet, voices, and minds to share the bounty you have given us. Lord, in your mercy,
hear our prayer.

Here other intercessions may be offered.

O God our savior, we rejoice in the example of the saints who have gone before us (*especially the nurses Florence Nightingale and Clara Maass, renewers of society*) until we join them around your throne. Lord, in your mercy,
hear our prayer.

Into your hands we place all our prayers, spoken and unspoken, trusting in the mercy of Christ Jesus.
Amen.

Images in the Readings

The disciples are nearly drowned by the storm of **wind and waves**. Many poetic passages in the Bible speak of wind and waves as though they are harbingers of death and of a sea monster as embodying chaos. Watch once again the film *Titanic*. In the tale of Jonah, God both sends the storm and calms it. The theophany in Job 38 credits God with having control over the sea, and the authors of Genesis 1, in praising God's creative power, report that God created the sea monsters.

Mount Horeb, where Elijah meets God, is Mount Sinai. According to Exodus, God had appeared in earthquake, wind, and fire, but Elijah encounters only **silence**. This story comforts many of the faithful, for whom there seems to be more sheer silence than powerful wind from the Spirit.

Much Christian iconography has drawn the church as the **boat** from which Jesus, the I AM who is God, brings calm to the waters experienced by the faithful. We assemble weekly in the nave—think "navy"—to receive the peace of Christ.

Ideas for the Day

- The New Revised Standard Version translates Jesus' words to the frightened disciples as "Take heart." The New International Version translates these words as "Take courage" (Matt. 14:27). *Heart* and *courage* come from the same root word. To better understand this connection, watch Brené Brown's TED Talk "The Power of Vulnerability," which you can find at brenebrown.com/videos. Around 0:08 she says, "The original definition of courage . . . from the Latin word *cour*, meaning 'heart' . . . is to tell the story of who you are with your whole heart." Notice Peter's actions through this lens. At what point in the story does Peter speak wholeheartedly? Is it when he tests Jesus (14:28), or the moment when he cries out, "Lord, save me"? Where have you heard people sharing their story with their whole heart? These are the people who are embodying the courage Jesus offers!

- Jesus enters the storm his disciples are facing. One way that Christ is still penetrating storm-tossed communities is through the work of Camp Noah, a ministry of Lutheran Social Service of Minnesota. This camp travels to communities that have been struck by disaster—including storms—to give voice to the children who have been affected. Read their story at www.campnoah.org and lift up this ministry in worship or education hour.

- Elijah meets God in the sheer silence. Every Sunday the assembly benefits from times of silence, and this Sunday it would be particularly appropriate to use silence in worship intentionally. You can use a bell or a singing bowl to begin and close the times of silence. Particularly good times to enter into silence include at the beginning of the service, during the confession, and after the sermon. You might also prepare intercessions that consist of three petitions that are rich yet concise. Close each petition with "Speak to us in the silence, O God," and then use the bell to hold a substantive moment of silence between each petition.

Connections with the Liturgy

Paul wrote to the Romans that if you confess with your lips that Jesus is Lord and believe in your heart that God raised him from the dead, you will be saved, and in today's gospel story, the disciples confess Jesus as the Son of God. So whenever we confess the creed, on each Sunday, at every baptism, we join with Paul and with the disciples in the boat to call Jesus Christ the Son of God, our Lord, and we believe that he rose again on the third day.

Paul's citation of Isaiah 52:7, "How beautiful . . . are the feet of the messenger," applies not only to called ministers but to all believers: at the dismissal of holy communion, one option is, "Go in peace. Share the good news." We all are to spread the gospel.

Let the Children Come

Silence isn't a word that pops into your head when imagining children, right? And yet babies are the masters of silence, and acquire, from the adults around them, language. Too often our worship, prayer time, and Sunday school hours are filled with words, and silence is nudged out. In our readings today, both Elijah and Jesus find peace in the silence. Even amid the wind, fire, earthquake, and battering waves, they take time to listen for God in the silence. Do you invite children into times of silence during worship? Is your assembly comfortable with times of silence, or does the silence fill up fast?

Assembly Song
Gathering

Jesus, Savior, pilot me ELW 755, LBW 334
Shout to the Lord ELW 821, W&P 124
O God, our help in ages past ELW 632, LBW 320

Psalmody and Acclamations

Balhoff, Mike/Gary Daigle/Darryl Ducote. "Lord, Let Us See Your Kindness." SATB, cant, assembly, kybd, gtr. GIA G-5397.

Makeever, Ray. "Psalm 85:8-13" from PWA.

+ Woehr, Roland. "Psalm 105" from PSCY, vol.2.

(GA) Gospel acclamation from ELW setting seven (S179a). Use psalm tone 1, 6, 7, or 10 in E major with proper verse for Lectionary 19.

Hymn of the Day

Evening and morning ELW 761, LBW 465 *DIE GÜLDNE SONNE*
Praise, praise! You are my rock ELW 862 *ZACHARY WOODS ROCK*
Eternal Father, strong to save ELW 756, LBW 467 *MELITA*

Offering

Now the silence ELW 460, LBW 205
When peace like a river ELW 785, LBW 346, TFF 194

Communion

Calm to the waves ELW 794
Precious Lord, take my hand ELW 773, WOV 731, TFF 193
What a fellowship, what a joy divine ELW 774, WOV 780, TFF 220

Sending

My life flows on in endless song ELW 763, WOV 781
God, my Lord, my strength ELW 795, LBW 484

Additional Assembly Songs

Though the earth shall change SP 42
For the healing of creation SP 12b
When the storms of life are raging TFF 198

⊕ Lee, Dong Hoon. "Lonely the Boat" from *Sound the Bamboo*. U. GIA G-6830.

⊕ Thangaraj, M. Thomas. "Ocean of Love" from *Pave the Way: Global Songs 3*. U. AFP 9780800676896.

☼ Bryson, Jim, et al. "You Are I Am" from CCLI.

☼ DiMarco, Kristene. "Song of Your Love" from CCLI.

☼ Gill, Randy. "Deep Calls to Deep" from CCLI.

☼ Hoagland, Eddie/Tyler Miller. "Strong to Save" from CCLI.

☼ Miller, Mary Elizabeth/Thomas Miller. "Save Me" from CCLI.

☼ Tomlin, Chris/Ed Cash. "Fear Not" from CCLI.

Music for the Day
Choral

P Cherwien, David. "How Can I Keep from Singing?" U, pno. AFP 9780800658335.

Davis, Taylor. "How Can I Keep from Singing?" SATB, pno, vln, ob. MSM 50-2545.

♫ Hildebrand, Kevin. "Eternal Father, Strong to Save." U or SATB, opt assembly, 2 tpts, org. MSM 60-8710.

P♫ Miller, Aaron David. "Praise, Praise! You Are My Rock." SAB, pno. AFP 9781451492583.

Children's Choir

P Burrows, Mark. "Reach Up, Reach In, Reach Out" from *Again, I Say Rejoice!* U, kybd. CG CGC56.

Lord, Suzanne. "Faith That's Sure." U, pno, opt banjo or autoharp. CG CGA695.

P Miller, Aaron David. "I Want Jesus to Walk with Me." U, pno, opt desc. AFP 9781451421606.

⊕ = global song ♫ = relates to hymn of the day + = semicontinuous psalm
☼ = praise song P = available in Prelude Music Planner

Keyboard / Instrumental

♪♫ Hansen, Sherri. "Praise, Praise! You Are My Rock" (Zachary Woods Rock) from *Piano Weavings*. Pno. AFP 9781451497861.

Hassell, Michael. "Jesus, Savior, Pilot Me" (Pilot) from *Traveling Tunes: Hymn Arrangements for Solo Instrument and Piano*. Inst, pno. AFP 9780800656195.

♫ Manz, Paul O. "Evening and Morning" (Die güldne Sonne) from *Three Hymns for Flute, Oboe, and Organ*. Fl, ob, org. MSM 20-871.

♪♫ Raabe, Nancy. "Evening and Morning" (Die güldne Sonne) from *Grace and Peace, vol. 6: Songs of Heaven*. Pno. AFP 9781451479621.

Handbell

♫ Behnke, John. "Eternal Father, Strong to Save." 3-6 oct hb, opt 3-5 oct hc, L2. CPH 97-7434.

℗ Krug, Jason W. "Praise to the Lord, the Almighty." 3-6 oct hb, opt 3 oct hc, L3. HOP 2657.

℗ Page, Anna Laura. "Stand by Me." 3-5 oct hb, opt 3 oct hc, L3. CG CGB780.

Sunday, August 13

Florence Nightingale, died 1910; Clara Maass, died 1901; renewers of society

When Florence Nightingale decided she would be a nurse, her family was horrified. In the early 1800s nursing was done by people with no training and no other way to earn a living. Florence trained at Kaiserswerth, Germany, with a Lutheran order of deaconesses. She returned home and worked to reform hospitals in England. Nightingale led a group of thirty-eight nurses to serve in the Crimean War, where they worked in appalling conditions. She returned to London as a hero and resumed her work there for hospital reform.

Clara Maass was born in New Jersey and served as a nurse in the Spanish-American War, where she encountered the horrors of yellow fever. She later responded to a call for subjects in research on yellow fever. During the experiments, which included receiving bites from mosquitoes, she contracted the disease and died. The commemoration of these women invites the church to give thanks for all who practice the arts of healing.

Monday, August 14

Maximilian Kolbe, died 1941; Kaj Munk, died 1944; martyrs

Father Kolbe was a Franciscan priest, born Raymond Kolbe. After spending some time working in Asia, he returned in 1936 to his native Poland, where he supervised a friary that came to house thousands of Polish war refugees, mostly Jews. The Nazis were watching, however, and he was arrested. Confined in Auschwitz, Kolbe gave generously of his meager resources and finally volunteered to be starved to death in place of another man who was a husband and father. After two weeks, he was executed by a lethal injection.

Kaj (pronounced KYE) Munk, a Danish Lutheran pastor and playwright, was an outspoken critic of the Nazis, who occupied Denmark during the Second World War. His plays frequently highlighted the eventual victory of the Christian faith despite the church's weak and ineffective witness. The Nazis feared Munk because his sermons and articles helped to strengthen the Danish resistance movement. He was executed by the Gestapo on January 5, 1944.

Tuesday, August 15

Mary, Mother of Our Lord

The church honors Mary with the Greek title *theotokos*, meaning God-bearer. Origen first used this title in the early church, and the councils of Ephesus and Chalcedon upheld it. Luther upheld this same title in his writings. The honor paid to Mary as *theotokos* and mother of our Lord goes back to biblical times, when Mary herself sang, "from now on all generations will call me blessed" (Luke 1:48). Mary's life revealed the presence of God incarnate, and it revealed God's presence among the humble and poor. Mary's song, the Magnificat, speaks of reversals in the reign of God: the mighty are cast down, the lowly are lifted up, the hungry are fed, and the rich are sent away empty-handed.

August 20, 2017
Time after Pentecost — Lectionary 20

In Isaiah we hear that God's house shall be a house of prayer for all people and that God will gather the outcasts of Israel. The Canaanite woman in today's gospel is a Gentile, an outsider, who is unflinching in her request that Jesus heal her daughter. As Jesus commends her bold faith, how might our church extend its mission to those on the margins of society? In our gathering around word and meal we receive strength to be signs of comfort, healing, and justice for those in need.

Prayer of the Day

God of all peoples, your arms reach out to embrace all those who call upon you. Teach us as disciples of your Son to love the world with compassion and constancy, that your name may be known throughout the earth, through Jesus Christ, our Savior and Lord.

Gospel Acclamation

Alleluia. Jesus preached the good news ׀ of the kingdom* and cured every sickness a- ׀ mong the people. *Alleluia.* (Matt. 4:23)

Readings and Psalm

Isaiah 56:1, 6-8

The prophet calls upon Israel to do justice in view of God's imminent intervention to save. Righteousness and obedience define who belongs to the Israelite community—not race, nationality, or any other category.

Psalm 67

Let all the peoples praise you, O God. (Ps. 67:3)

Romans 11:1-2a, 29-32

God has not rejected Israel. Rather, the call and gifts of God are irrevocable, so that while all have been disobedient, God has mercy upon all.

Matthew 15:[10-20] 21-28

Jesus teaches his disciples that true purity is a matter of the heart rather than outward religious observances. Almost immediately, this teaching is tested when a woman considered to be pagan and unclean approaches him for help.

Semicontinuous reading and psalm

Genesis 45:1-15

Moved to tears by Judah's plea on behalf of Benjamin, Joseph declares, "I am Joseph!" and asks, "Is my father still alive?" The evil intent of the brothers had been trumped by God's using Joseph to preserve many lives at a time of famine.

Psalm 133

How good and pleasant it is to live together in unity. (Ps. 133:1)

Preface   Sundays

Color   Green

Prayers of Intercession

The prayers are prepared locally for each occasion. The following examples may be adapted or used as appropriate.

Generous, compassionate God, we gather before you to pray for the church, the world, and all in need.

A brief silence.

Unite us, O God, so that all who worship receive assurance and nourishment by faith. Rescue those who suffer from religious persecution. Lord, in your mercy,

hear our prayer.

Teach us, O God, so that the holy mountains and peaceful valleys of your good creation can be restored to the health you intend. Lord, in your mercy,

hear our prayer.

Empower us, O God, to advocate for those on the margins. Open the hearts of leaders in every nation to serve those who are most vulnerable. Lord, in your mercy,

hear our prayer.

Equip us, O God, with your love for our brothers and sisters. Heal the sick, comfort the grieving, feed the hungry, and calm those in distress (*especially*). Lord, in your mercy,

hear our prayer.

Rouse us, O God, to praise you with gladness. We give thanks for musicians, worship leaders, intercessors, those who prepare the communion table, and all who make our worship express our joy. Lord, in your mercy,

hear our prayer.

Here other intercessions may be offered.

We give you thanks, O God, for the saints who have deepened our lives of prayer (*especially Bernard, abbot of Clairvaux*). Gather us with them in endless praise of you. Lord, in your mercy,

hear our prayer.

Into your hands we place all our prayers, spoken and unspoken, trusting in the mercy of Christ Jesus.

Amen.

Order Now
Year B 2018

Sundays and Seasons Year B 2018

978-1-4514-9605-5 .... $39.00
(2 or more $32.00 ea.)

Sundays and Seasons: Preaching Year B 2018

Features new commentary and ideas for proclamation, contributed by practicing preachers as well as scholars, together with succinct notes on each day and its readings.

978-1-4514-9609-3 .... $29.00

Planning Guide and Preaching Combo Pack

Purchase *Sundays and Seasons* and *Sundays and Seasons: Preaching* together, and save!

978-1-5064-1831-5 .... $55.00
($68.00 if purchased separately)

Worship Planning Calendar Year B 2018

The perfect complement to *Sundays and Seasons*. Spiral-bound, this is both an appointment calendar and a workbook for preparing worship. Contains daily lectionary reading citations.

978-1-4514-9606-2 .... $22.00

Planning Guide and Calendar Combo Pack

Sundays and Seasons and *Worship Planning Calendar* work together to save you time and provide all you need to prepare engaging worship.

978-1-5064-1830-8 .... $51.00
($61.00 if purchased separately)

sundaysandseasons.com

A rich and reliable resource for worship planning, Sundays and Seasons online worship planner follows the three-year lectionary cycle and provides everything you need to support your worship ministry in one convenient location, always accessible online. Learn more at sundaysandseasons.com

---

Worship Planning Resources
Year B 2018 Order Form

To order by mail, detach, fold, and seal your completed card. Please be sure to attach postage. You can also order by calling 1-800-328-4648, faxing 1-800-722-7766, or visiting our online store at augsburgfortress.org.

SHIP TO _____

Address _____

City _____

State_____ ZIP _____

Phone _____

Email _____

BILL TO _____

Address _____

City _____

State_____ ZIP _____

Phone _____

METHOD OF PAYMENT *(select one)*

AF Account #_____

Credit Card #_____

Exp. Date_____ *Card must be valid through Oct. 2017. Products ship by Sept. 2017.*

Signature_____
Signature required on all credit card orders.

Sundays and Seasons 2018
QTY: _____ 978-1-4514-9605-5 .... $39.00*
QTY: _____ SUNSEASONS .... Standing Order

Sundays and Seasons: Preaching 2018
QTY: _____ 978-1-4514-9609-3 .... $29.00*
QTY: _____ SUNSEPREAC .... Standing Order

Planning Guide and Preaching Combo Pack 2018
QTY: _____ 978-1-5064-1831-5 .... $55.00*
QTY: _____ SUNSEAPPC .... Standing Order

Worship Planning Calendar 2018
QTY: _____ 978-1-4514-9606-2 .... $22.00*
QTY: _____ WRSHPPLNCL .... Standing Order

Planning Guide and Calendar Combo Pack 2018
QTY: _____ 978-1-5064-1830-8 .... $51.00*
QTY: _____ SUNSEAWPC .... Standing Order

Calendar of Word and Season 2018
QTY: _____ 978-1-4514-9610-9 .... $10.95*
QTY: _____ CALWRDSESN .... Standing Order

Church Year Calendar 2018
QTY: _____ 978-1-4514-9607-9 .... $1.95*

Church Year Calendar 2018 PDF
ONLINE 978-1-4514-9608-6 .... $9.96

Bread for the Day 2018
QTY: _____ 978-1-4514-9611-6 .... $8.95*

Ritual Lectionary, Year B
QTY: _____ 978-0-8066-5611-3 .... $115.00*

Study Edition Lectionary, Year B
QTY: _____ 978-0-8066-5612-0 .... $27.50*

The RCL: 20th Anniversary Annotated Edition
QTY: _____ 978-1-4514-3603-7 .... $30.00*

AUGSBURG FORTRESS

Prices do not include shipping. Prices valid through April 1, 2017.

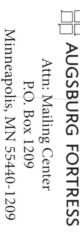

sundays and seasons

Detach this card, fold it in half here, and seal the edges.

sundays
and
seasons

Order Now
for Year B 2018

Great gifts and useful resources for living the church's year!

Bread for the Day 2018

Bible readings and prayers for the full year. Follows the daily lectionary. Quantity discounts available.

978-1-4514-9611-6

Quantity	1–9	10–99	100–299	300–499	500–999	1,000+
Price	$8.95	$7.16	$6.71	$6.27	$5.37	$4.48

Calendar of Word and Season Year B 2018

Full-color wall calendar with room for adding family and church activities. Features beautiful art each month and identifies church festivals, national holidays, the color of the day, and Revised Common Lectionary citations. 8³/₈" x 10⁷/₈". Spiral-bound and punched for hanging.

978-1-4514-9610-9

Quantity	1–11	12–49	50–99	100–499	500+
Price	$10.95	$4.50	$3.50	$3.00	$2.50

Church Year Calendar Year B 2018

Provides dates, lectionary readings, hymn of the day, and the liturgical color for each Sunday and festival. The ideal time-saver for all who live by the liturgical year. Two-sided. 11" x 8½".

978-1-4514-9607-9

Quantity	1–11	12–99	100+
Price	$1.95	$0.83	$0.75

Lectionary for Worship, Ritual Edition Year B
978-0-8066-5611-3 .... *$115.00*

Lectionary for Worship, Study Edition Year B
978-0-8066-5612-0 .... *$27.50*

The Revised Common Lectionary: 20th Anniversary Annotated Edition
978-1-4514-3603-7 .... *$30.00*

Shipping and Handling

Prices and Product Availability are subject to change without notice.

Sales Tax: Exempt customers must provide Augsburg Fortress with a copy of their state-issued exemption certificate prior to purchase. Customers without tax-exempt status must add applicable state/province and local sales tax for their area. Canadian customers will be charged GST.

Shipping Charges are additional on all orders. U.S. and Canadian orders (except U.S. cash orders) are assessed actual shipping charges based on standard group rates. Additional shipping charges are assessed for expedited service requests and international shipments.

Return Policy: With proof of purchase, non-dated, in print product in saleable condition may be returned for credit. Please call Sales and Service at 1-800-328-4648 (U.S.) or 1-800-265-6397 (Canada) for assistance if you receive items that are damaged, defective, or were shipped in error. Specific return restrictions apply to some product lines. Please contact us prior to returning a special order item or item shipped directly from the manufacturer. Send U.S. order returns by a secure, prepaid, traceable method to the Augsburg Fortress Distribution Center, PBD Worldwide, c/o AF Distribution, 905 Carlow Dr., Unit B, Bolingbrook, IL 60490. Canadian orders may be returned to Augsburg Fortress Canadian Distribution Center, 500 Trillium Drive, Box 9940, Kitchener, Ontario N2G 4Y4.

Images in the Readings

That Jesus obliquely refers to the Canaanite woman as a **dog** has inspired much creative interpretation over the centuries. Traditionally the sentence was explained away as the technique Jesus employed to test the woman's faith. Some contemporary exegesis reads the exchange seriously and thus credits the woman with instructing Jesus about the breadth of God's mercy. Both of these explanations assume that the story is accurate historical reporting. The story also suggests that if our faith is strong enough, our wishes will be granted. Like the Jesus of Matthew's narrative, we too think of the other as a dog. Like the storyteller, we hope that our faith will bring us instant healing. It is a difficult story to proclaim and expound.

Despite our knowledge of anatomy, the **heart** continues over the millennia to be an image for the source and center of human intention.

Ancient temples were understood to be **houses of the deity**. Architecturally similar to the Lincoln Memorial, an open structure housed a statue of the god or goddess, and sacrifices were offered before the image of the divine. After the exile, strict traditionalists urged hierarchical regulations about how close to the presence of God each type of person could come. But Third Isaiah rejects this understanding of worship, saying the house of God will welcome all peoples. Christians have thought about their churches as in some way houses of God for all peoples. Yet for Christians, God dwells in the community and in word and sacrament, not in a house, and church buildings are less like temples and more like meeting places for the communal prayer of all peoples.

Ideas for the Day

- The Canaanite woman's confrontation of Jesus demonstrates great faith. It's not quiet piety or habit learned over years; it's a chance inspired by the Holy Spirit and seized in a moment. Her sudden appearance and disappearance are a signal in this gospel that God's grace in Jesus is not limited to a certain inside race or group. Boldness, bravery, stubbornness, and open vulnerability can be faith assets, not liabilities. Lift up recent stories, locally, nationally, and internationally, that point to everyday kinds of faithfulness. If projection or other visuals are possible, use clippings from magazines or newspapers or screenshots from Internet sources. Look for parents intervening for children, children working together, a community uniting for a project, or a wide variety of people joining over an issue.
- Most homes have a "junk drawer"—a place where odds and ends get put for all kinds of reasons. The foreigners mentioned in Isaiah have ended up as religious odds and ends in the shadow of a rebuilt temple. God urges the Israelites to recognize the value of these people and to heed the call to perceive their usefulness. God has not relegated the foreigners to a spiritual "junk drawer" but has reestablished

them in a place where they can be useful tools for the kingdom.
- The Canaanite woman would have been considered unclean to the practicing Jews around her. Who knew what she ate or what she had touched? Everything about her was suspect. We often see this same attitude about certain types of foods and restaurants in our own time. Yet regular greed, gossip, slander, sarcasm, and stress are all much harder on our bodies than the occasional sweet treat or fried delicacy. Most diet plans ultimately point to the importance of whole foods—nutrition sources with minimal processing. What would whole [soul] food spirituality look like? How would putting scripture, prayer, and holy community directly into our faith diet affect our spiritual fitness and well-being?

Connections with the Liturgy

Each Sunday that we sing the Kyrie, we join with the Canaanite woman pleading for the Lord's mercy. In the Bible "Lord" is a complex title. In its most common usage, it is an address to a distinguished male; in early Christian confession, it affirmed the resurrection of Jesus the Messiah; and in Jewish theological language, it substituted for pronouncing the Hebrew name of God. Christian invocation of the Lord is a trinitarian title: God as Lord, Christ as Lord, the Spirit as "the Lord and giver of life."

Let the Children Come

Systemic racism is a learned behavior and also a sin intrinsic within humankind. How we communicate with children about people unlike ourselves, in both spoken and unspoken ways, has a lasting impact on individuals and society. It is a sin of which we can repent. Today's gospel text portrays Jesus as excluding the Canaanite woman and then recognizing her full inclusion in the life-giving kingdom. What conversations does your community have about systemic racism? How do you engage children and youth in conversations about power, privilege, and the social construct of race?

Assembly Song
Gathering

Oh, praise the gracious power ELW 651, WOV 750
Oh, for a thousand tongues to sing ELW 886, LBW 559
Jesus shall reign ELW 434, LBW 530

Psalmody and Acclamations

Chepponis, James. "Let Nations Sing Your Praise." Cant, assembly, opt SATB, kybd, gtr, hb, B flat or C inst. GIA G-4226.
Folkening, John. "Six Psalm Settings with Antiphons." SATB, U or cant, assembly, opt kybd. MSM 80-700.

+ Alonso, Tony. "How Good It Is." SATB, pno, opt assembly, str qrt, horn in F. GIA G-7242.

(GA) Gospel acclamation from ELW setting seven (S179a). Use psalm tone 1, 6, 7, or 10 in E major with proper verse for Lectionary 20.

Hymn of the Day

There's a wideness in God's mercy ELW 587 ST. HELENA
ELW 588, LBW 290 LORD, REVIVE US
Creating God, your fingers trace ELW 684 PROSPECT
WOV 757 DUNEDIN
Gather Us In ELW 532, WOV 718 GATHER US IN

Offering

Healer of our every ill ELW 612, WOV 738
Lord of all nations, grant me grace ELW 716, LBW 419

Communion

One bread, one body ELW 496, TFF 122, WOV 710
Let us go now to the banquet ELW 523, LLC 410
O Christ, the healer, we have come ELW 610, LBW 360

Sending

In Christ there is no east or west ELW 650, LBW 359, TFF 214
Soli Deo Gloria ELW 878

Additional Assembly Songs

When in the hour of deepest need LBW 303
Seigneur, rassemble-nous SP 35
Revealed in Christ, the word of God CBM 104

⊕ Prescod, Patrick, arr. "Let All the Peoples Praise You/Todos los pueblos canten" from *Let the Peoples Sing*. SATB. AFP 9780800675394.

⊕ Traditional Greek melody. "Kyrie eleison" from *Sent by the Lord: Songs of the World Church*, vol. 2. U. GIA G-3740.

☼ Becker, Margaret/David M. Edwards. "Create in Me" from CCLI.

☼ Blanc, Anna/ Susanna Erwin/Nate Hunt. "For I Was Far" from CCLI.

☼ Crocker, Matt. "I Surrender" from CCLI.

☼ Fellowship Church. "Name of Jesus" from CCLI.

☼ Knott, Richard/Sam de Jong. "In Your Name" from CCLI.

☼ Scott, Kathryn. "Deliverance" from CCLI.

Music for the Day
Choral

P ♫ Ellingboe, Bradley. "There's a Wideness in God's Mercy." SATB, pno. AFP 9780800676544.

P Hellerman, Fred/Fran Minkoff/arr. David Cherwien. "O Healing River" from *To God Will I Sing*. MH solo, kybd. AFP 9780800674342.

♫ Johnson, Ralph M. "Creating God, Your Fingers Trace." 2 pt mxd, pno. KJO 6366.

P ♫ Kidwell, Sally. "There's a Wideness in God's Mercy." SATB, pno. AFP 9781451451696.

Children's Choir

Bedford, Michael. "Let All the Peoples Praise You, O God." 2 pt, pno, fl. CG CGA933.

Butler, Donna. "Prayer for Mothers." U/2 pt, pno. CG CGA1154.

P Patterson, Mark. "Come into God's Presence (Echo Song)" from *The Joy of Part Singing*. 2 pt, pno, opt metallophone and xyl. CG CGBK67.

Keyboard / Instrumental

P ♫ Childs, Edwin T. "Creating God, Your Fingers Trace" (Prospect) from *American Folk Hymns for Organ*. Org. AFP 9781451494051.

Linker, Janet. "Lord, Whose Love in Humble Service" (Beach Spring) from *Augsburg Organ Library: Baptism and Holy Communion*. Org. AFP 9780800623555.

P ♫ Miller, Aaron David. "There's a Wideness in God's Mercy" (Lord, Revive Us) from *Chorale Preludes for Piano in Traditional Styles*. Pno. AFP 9780800679033.

♫ Stover, Harold. "There's a Wideness in God's Mercy" (St. Helena) from *Carillon: Organ Hymn Preludes*. Org. AFP 9780806698144.

Handbell

♫ Nelson, Susan. "The Hills Are Bare in Bethlehem" (Prospect). 3-5 oct hb, opt vln or trbl C inst, L2. SF 279034.

♫ Roberts, Philip. "Gather Us In." 3-5 oct hb, opt trbl C inst, L4. GIA G-6704.

♫ Tucker, Sondra. "There's a Wideness in God's Mercy." 3-5 oct, L3. AFP 08000674901.

Sunday, August 20
Bernard, Abbot of Clairvaux, died 1153

Bernard was a Cistercian monk who became an abbot of great spiritual depth. He was a mystical writer deeply devoted to the humanity of Christ who emphasized the inner human experience of prayer and contemplation. He was critical of one of the foremost theologians of the day, Peter Abelard, because he believed Abelard's approach to faith was too rational and did not provide sufficient room for mystery. Bernard's devotional writings are still read today. His sermon on the Song of Solomon treats that Old Testament book as an allegory of Christ's love for humanity. Bernard wrote several hymns that are still sung today in translation, including "Jesus, the Very Thought of You" (ELW 754).

⊕ = global song   ♫ = relates to hymn of the day   + = semicontinuous psalm
☼ = praise song   P = available in Prelude Music Planner

Thursday, August 24
Bartholomew, Apostle

Bartholomew is mentioned as one of Jesus' disciples in Matthew, Mark, and Luke. The list in John does not include him but rather Nathanael. These two are therefore often assumed to be the same person. Except for his name on these lists of the Twelve, little is known. Some traditions say Bartholomew preached in India or Armenia following the resurrection. In art, Bartholomew is pictured holding a flaying knife to indicate the manner in which he was killed.

August 27, 2017
Time after Pentecost — Lectionary 21

In Isaiah the people are bid to look to their spiritual ancestors as the rock from which they were hewn. Jesus declares that the church will be built on the rock of Peter's bold confession of faith. God's word of reconciliation and mercy are keys to the church's mission. Paul urges us to not be conformed to this world, but to offer our bodies as a living sacrifice, using our individual gifts to build up the body of Christ. From the table we go forth to offer our spiritual worship through word and deed.

Prayer of the Day

O God, with all your faithful followers of every age, we praise you, the rock of our life. Be our strong foundation and form us into the body of your Son, that we may gladly minister to all the world, through Jesus Christ, our Savior and Lord.

Gospel Acclamation

Alleluia. You are ˈ the Messiah,* the Son of the ˈ living God. *Alleluia*. (Matt. 16:16)

Readings and Psalm
Isaiah 51:1-6

Just as God had called Abraham and Sarah and given them many descendants, so now God offers comfort to Zion. God's deliverance will come soon and will never end.

Psalm 138

O Lᴏʀᴅ, your steadfast love endures forever. (Ps. 138:8)

Romans 12:1-8

In response to God's merciful activity, we are to worship by living holistic, God-pleasing lives. Our values and viewpoints are not molded by this age, but are transformed by the Spirit's renewing work. God's grace empowers different forms of service among Christians, but all forms of ministry function to build up the body of Christ.

Matthew 16:13-20

At a climactic point in Jesus' ministry, God reveals to Peter that Jesus is "the Messiah, the Son of the living God," and Jesus responds with the promise of a church that will overcome the very gates of Hades.

Semicontinuous reading and psalm
Exodus 1:8—2:10

The brave Hebrew midwives defied Pharaoh to save many infants from death. When the mother of Moses placed him in a basket in the Nile, the daughter of Pharaoh found him, adopted him, and brought him up. But the sister of Moses and his mother played crucial roles in this drama.

Psalm 124

We have escaped like a bird from the snare of the fowler. (Ps. 124:7)

Preface   Sundays

Color   Green

Prayers of Intercession

The prayers are prepared locally for each occasion. The following examples may be adapted or used as appropriate.

Generous, compassionate God, we gather before you to pray for the church, the world, and all in need.

A brief silence.

God our rock, provide a strong foundation for your church on earth. Unite it in joyful praise, service, and mission. Lord, in your mercy,

hear our prayer.

You make deserts into gardens and the wilderness into Eden. Restore the clean and pleasant beauty of your creation. Lord, in your mercy,

hear our prayer.

You shine the light of justice on the nations. Deliver us quickly from evil, protect the defenseless, and bring peace to warring lands (*especially*). Lord, in your mercy,

hear our prayer.

You renew our minds and transform our bodies. Wait with all who seek a cure or long for relief from chronic pain. Bring comfort and healing to all who suffer illness in spirit, mind, or body (*especially*). Lord, in your mercy,

hear our prayer.

You give gifts to all. Build up this assembly. Increase our generosity, compassion, and cheerfulness. Lift up from among us prophets, ministers, teachers, and diligent leaders. Lord, in your mercy,

hear our prayer.

Here other intercessions may be offered.

Your salvation lasts forever. Console us here on earth until we join all who praise you without end. Lord, in your mercy,

hear our prayer.

Into your hands we place all our prayers, spoken and unspoken, trusting in the mercy of Christ Jesus.

Amen.

Images in the Readings

Rock is an image for the day. The psalms speak of the safety accorded by the rock; the prophet likens his religious heritage to a rock; Simon gets the name Peter, "Rocky." The Sermon on the Mount speaks of Jesus' teaching as a rock on which we are to build, and Paul writes in 1 Corinthians 4 that the rock from which water flowed was Christ. According to Jewish legend, the miraculous rock followed the Israelites throughout their nomadic decades, perpetually providing water. For Christians, the water of baptism follows the body of Christ, watering us throughout our journey.

According to the worldview of the New Testament, **Hades**, the lowest of the three levels of the universe, housed the dead. Matthew uses the category Hades to indicate the challenge that confronts the Christian community: to fight against the power of death. Especially Eastern Orthodox Christians recall this worldview in their beloved icon of the resurrection, in which Christ is standing on the broken doors of Hades and is raising from death into his arms both Adam and Eve.

The Isaiah reading includes the image of the **arm of the LORD**. In the Old Testament, God is described in terms humans know: God has ears, eyes, a mouth, fingers, hands, and strong arms. In the story of Noah's flood, God even smells the pleasant odor of the animal sacrifices. Our task is to ensure that these bodily images do not demote the divine into merely a superman. Christians can apply these very images to **the body** of Christ.

Ideas for the Day

- Peter's rock-solid faith can seem intimidating to those of us who are still wrestling with questions or living faithfully with our doubts. Rocks are often more pesky than helpful. Ask anyone who is trying to till a field, dig a hole, run or walk at dusk, or bring a boat into shallower water. Rocks can get in the way. The rocks we remove during these tasks often become decorations (no longer necessary), supports (helpful in a different way), or boundaries (giving structure and shape). What are the bedrock elements of faith that are critical to your community? What are those issues that are now getting in the way of living and dying together in Christ and need to be moved?

- The apostle Peter is often painted or drawn with keys in his hand. These are imagined as the keys for binding and loosing things on earth, with a reciprocal action in heaven. Binding and loosing are most often connected with forgiveness and the letting go of wrongs and wrongdoing. Modern disciples, the present church, inherited this role from Peter. We often think of the heavenly work of forgiveness as being contingent on our having forgiven others first. With Christ as our solid rock, though, we are always standing on the reality of having been loved and forgiven out of grace itself. Our loosing does not create the space for the same in heaven. Our practice of forgiveness and mercy mirrors heaven's action now and throughout all time.

- Isaiah reminds the Israelites that they are "a chip off the old block." As children of God shaped in God's image, they are called into being coworkers with God. They must be drawn, in faith, to the vision that God has for them and all creation. When they need a guide for their actions, the prophet calls them to consider God's actions in history. To their ancestors, as well as to strangers in their midst, God has always been kind and merciful. They are called to the same behavior, imitating God.

Connections with the Liturgy

In the creed the church joins Peter to name Jesus "Christ"—the Messiah. In pronouncing the forgiveness of sin, the minister takes up the authority to "loose on earth" what we trust will be loosed "in heaven," that is, with God.

Let the Children Come

How often have you heard or said, "Say you're sorry"? So often we want to wrap up conflict with the nice, neat bow of a half-hearted "I'm sorry." Even as we are compelling children to apologize, we know that forgiveness is not that easy. How do we encourage children in ways of authentically expressing feelings of hurt, betrayal, jealousy, or anger? How do we encourage children to ask for forgiveness? How do we encourage children to think about a disagreement awhile and return with a cooler head and repentant heart? How do parents and other adults model this with their children?

Assembly Song
Gathering

Christ is made the sure foundation ELW 645, WOV 747, LBW 367

The church's one foundation ELW 654, LBW 369

Lord Jesus Christ, be present now ELW 527, LBW 253

Psalmody and Acclamations

Cooney, Rory. "Psalm 138: On the Day I Called." Cant, SAB, assembly, kybd, gtr, fl. OCP 10474.

Inwood, Paul. "In the Presence of the Angels" from *Psalm Songs 3*. AFP 0800657721.

+ Weber, Paul D. "Psalm 124," Refrain 1, from PSCY. (GA) ELW 169 with proper verse for Lectionary 21.

Hymn of the Day

Built on a rock ELW 652, LBW 365 KIRKEN DEN ER ET GAMMELT HUS

My hope is built on nothing less ELW 596, TFF 192, LBW 293 THE SOLID ROCK ELW 597, LBW 294 MELITA

We sing to you, O God ELW 791 LOVE UNKNOWN

Offering

Alleluia! Voices raise ELW 828

Yours, Lord, is the glory ELW 849, LLC 605

Communion

O Savior, precious Savior ELW 820, LBW 514

Take my life, that I may be ELW 583/685, LLC 570, LBW 406

Holy God, holy and glorious ELW 637

Sending

We all are one in mission ELW 576, WOV 755

My life flows on in endless song ELW 763, WOV 781

⊕ = global song   ♫ = relates to hymn of the day   + = semicontinuous psalm
☼ = praise song   P = available in Prelude Music Planner

Additional Assembly Songs

Seek ye first WOV 783, W&P 122, TFF 149

Only you, O God SP 31

Praised be the rock TFF 290

⊕ African American spiritual. "Jesus Is a Rock in a Weary Land." U. ELW 333.

⊕ Nyanga, Zambia, traditional. "Chimwemwe mwa Yesu/Rejoice in Jesus" from *Agape: Songs of Hope and Reconciliation*. U, gtr. Lutheran World Federation. Out of print. Available on Amazon.com.

☼ Eskelin, Ian/Glenn Packiam. "Our Messiah Reigns" from CCLI.

☼ Jobe, Kari/Cody Carnes. "Savior's Here" from CCLI.

☼ Neufeld, Tim/Jon Neufeld. "No Other Savior" from CCLI.

☼ Smith, Sue C./David Moffit. "For Who You Really Are" from CCLI.

☼ Strumpel, Aaron/ Latifah Phillips. "Mightier" from CCLI.

☼ Zschech, Darlene/Israel Houghton/Kari Jobe. "Victor's Crown" from CCLI.

Music for the Day
Choral

P ♫ Highben, Zebulon M. "My Hope Is Built." SATB, perc. AFP 9781451462395.

Hillert, Richard. "The Lord Is My Light and My Salvation." U, kybd, B flat or C inst. GIA G-4951.

P Mendelssohn, Felix. "On God Alone My Hope I Build" from *Chantry Choirbook*. SATB. AFP 9780800657772.

Scott, K. Lee. "King of Glory, King of Peace" from *Rejoice Now, My Spirit*. MH solo, kybd. AFP 9780800651084.

Children's Choir

Burrows, Mark. "Make a Joyful Noise" from *Again, I Say Rejoice!* U, pno. CG CGC56.

Patterson, Mark. "I Will Praise You, O Lord." U/2 pt, kybd. CG CGA867.

Pooler, Marie. "You Made Every Part of Me" from *LifeSongs*. U, pno. AFP 9780806642703.

Keyboard / Instrumental

P ♫ Carlson, J. Bert. "We Sing to You, O God" (Love Unknown) from *Drawn to the Light: Hymn Preludes for Organ*. Org. AFP 9781451475920.

♫ Hassell, Michael. "Built on a Rock" (Kirken den er et Gammelt Hus) from *Jazz Pastorale*. Pno. AFP 9780800658052.

P Howarth, Mary. "My Life Flows On in Endless Song" (How Can I Keep from Singing) from *Glorify! Hymn Settings for Piano*. Pno. AFP 9781451424218.

P Titus, Hiram. "Take My Life, That I May Be" (Toma mi voluntad) from *Glorify! Hymn Settings for Piano*. Pno. AFP 9781451424218.

Handbell

♫ Helman, Michael. "Built on a Rock." 3-5 oct hb, opt 3 oct hc, opt assembly, L3. ALF 19006.

♫ Lamb, Linda. "The Solid Rock." 3-5 oct, L2. ALF 25336.

♫ Stults, Tyleen. "My Song Is Love Unknown." 3-5 oct, L2+. CPH 97-7679.

Monday, August 28

Augustine, Bishop of Hippo, died 430

Augustine was one of the greatest theologians of the Western church. Born in North Africa, he was a philosophy student in Carthage, where he later became a teacher of rhetoric. Much of his young life was a debauched one. As an adult he came under the influence of Ambrose, the bishop of Milan, and through him came to see Christianity as a religion appropriate for a philosopher. Augustine was baptized by Ambrose at the Easter Vigil in 387. He was ordained four years later and made bishop of Hippo in 396. Augustine was a defender of the Christian faith and argued, against the Donatists, that the holiness of the church did not depend on the holiness of its members, particularly the clergy, but that holiness comes from Christ, the head of the church. Augustine's autobiography, *Confessions*, tells of his slow movement toward faith and includes the line "Late have I loved thee."

Monday, August 28

Moses the Black, monk, martyr, died around 400

A man of great strength and rough character, Moses the Black was converted to Christian faith toward the close of the fourth century. Prior to his conversion he had been a thief and a leader of a gang of robbers. The story of his conversion is unknown, but eventually he became a desert monk at Skete. The change in his heart and life had a profound impact on his native Ethiopia. He was murdered when Berber bandits attacked his monastery.

Saturday, September 2

Nikolai Frederik Severin Grundtvig, bishop, renewer of the church, died 1872

Grundtvig was one of two principal Danish theologians of the nineteenth century; the other was Søren Kierkegaard. Grundtvig's ministry as a parish pastor had a difficult start. He was officially censured after his first sermon, though he did receive approval a year later to be ordained. He served with his father for two years but was unable to receive a call for seven years after that. In 1826 he was forced to resign after he attacked the notion that Christianity was merely a philosophical idea rather than God's revelation made known to us in Christ and through word and sacrament. This belief would be a hallmark of Grundtvig's writing. He spent his last thirty-three years as a chaplain at a home for elderly women. From his university days he was convinced that poetry spoke to the human spirit better than prose. He wrote more than a thousand hymns, including "God's Word Is Our Great Heritage" (ELW 509).

Autumn

TIME AFTER PENTECOST

SUMMER

AUTUMN

NOVEMBER

Preparing for Autumn

Neither autumn nor Reformation is a liturgical season, but in many congregations the months of September and October 2017 will likely include a variety of emphases that highlight both of these calendar considerations. Is there anything that ties together the resumption of fall patterns and schedules, the beginning of the academic year, stewardship, lectionary themes for these months, and the 500th anniversary of the Reformation? Without a particular liturgical season, color, and symbols to give framework, this chunk of the long time after Pentecost may be overtaken by a list of special topics. As always, what links these weeks together is the centrality of worship in the life of our assemblies and its role in forming us as a people of gratitude, generosity, and service.

Reformation Celebrations

Whether individual worshiping communities observe the Reformation anniversary throughout 2017, during the month of October, or with greater intensity on Sunday, October 29, consider framing the observance as re-formation. In other words, rather than merely marking a past historical event, this unique observance enables Lutherans and others both to give thanks for our heritage and to look to the future, centered in the weekly assembly, a spiritual formation through word and sacrament. The prefix *re* suggests repetition. Again and again we return to God's grace and mercy poured out in baptism. Sunday after Sunday we gather as the people of God and then depart for service in Christ's name. Simply reflecting on a number of *re* words provides much grist for these months: reformation, repentance, reconciliation, renewal, reevaluation, reorientation, and so many more.

A wonderful variety of materials is available to assist in planning a congregation's observance of Reformation 2017. In particular, look at this resource: *Reformation 500 Sourcebook: Anniversary Resources for Congregations* (Augsburg Fortress, 2016). The additional liturgical resources and planning checklist are particularly helpful.

Not too long ago, Reformation Sunday for Lutherans was the most important festival between Easter and Christmas. Congregations not only decked themselves in red but often brought out brass music and all the festive elements they could muster. Yet due to centuries of conflict, the subtext was that Lutherans were celebrating the gospel that sets us free,

in contrast to the trappings of the Roman Catholic Church. Gradually, the observance reflected a tone of continued reformation and reconciliation. Yet, to a large extent, Lutherans are the only denomination that celebrates Reformation as a yearly liturgical festival. With this ecumenical awareness, it is important that our celebrations hold a balance between gratitude for the gospel and gratitude for our unique heritage, while being mindful of our place within the body of Christ. When we also consider decreased religious participation among many people today, this anniversary might be an opportunity to speak of the future, especially the gift of community and our common witness to the gospel amid changing times.

The Lectionary and Fall Observances

The autumn lectionary texts do not suggest one unifying theme, as the appointed gospels are semicontinuous readings from Matthew. The texts for September 10, when many congregations observe Rally Day or at least resume fall schedules, focus on themes of forgiveness, judgment, and reconciliation. Amid religious pluralism and division, worship re-forms us to be in relationship with those whom we have harmed and to forgive those who have sinned against us. This might be a day to mention a number of mutual condemnations that have been lifted as part of the ecumenical spirit of recent decades.

Some congregations bless animals on the first Sunday in October, occurring near the observance of St. Francis on October 4. Though several denominations appoint particular texts for the feast of St. Francis, *Evangelical Lutheran Worship* designates it a commemoration and not a lesser festival; thus it might be wise to remain with the Sunday lectionary on October 1, providing continuity with the semicontinuous readings of Philippians and Matthew. Perhaps a preacher can link the image of vineyard or the parable of the man with two sons to our call to imitate Francis in caring for the earth and embracing a life of simplicity and generosity.

The autumn months often include a stewardship emphasis in many congregations. For a fresh approach, you might consider using the word *generosity* to help people approach the topic in new ways. Worship re-forms us for lives of generosity, gratitude, service, and living our baptismal vocation in the world. The texts for October 15 use the image of feast in a variety of ways, calling us to invite others to the bountiful wedding banquet. The gospel on October 22 is the well-known passage in which Jesus invites us to give to the emperor the things that are the emperor's and to God the things that are God's. How can this text help us to consider stewardship as a way of life, not simply the means to support a church's budget? How does a reformation emphasis color the interpretation of all of these texts in 2017?

Finally, October 29, Reformation Sunday, offers two sets of lectionary texts. Many congregations move the pericopes for Reformation Day (October 31) to the last Sunday in October. The readings clearly hold up the theological emphases of the Reformation. Another interesting option is to use the texts for Sunday (Lectionary 30), in this case a gospel that includes the two great commandments, love of God and neighbor. In a spirit of repentance, reconciliation, and reorientation, this text invites congregations to consider our celebration from a wider angle than our own particular history.

Environment

There are no clear and obvious choices for the worship environment during autumn. Green continues to be the dominant liturgical color for the Sundays in September and October. Some congregations use leaves, pumpkins, gourds, and other autumnal décor to accent what is happening in nature in many places in North America during these weeks.

It may be tempting to turn this whole season into a mini Reformation festival in 2017 and use the color red for multiple Sundays. Though red catches our attention, partly because there are few festivals that call for it and many of our red vestments are quite handsome, overusing it could call attention to the wrong message. Certainly red is used at Pentecost to represent the fiery colors of the Holy Spirit, and therefore for festivals of the church, such as ordinations, dedications, and anniversaries. Yet to make red dominant for multiple weeks puts us out of step with the catholic and ecumenical church. Whatever our choices, let the Reformation anniversary be an opportunity for us to celebrate with a sense of humility and longing for greater unity among Christians.

Music: Hymns for Re-formation

Lutherans are proud of their musical heritage. Many treasures of hymnody, organ and choral music, and texts were written by Martin Luther, J. S. Bach, and many other fine Reformation-era composers. All assemblies will likely sing "A mighty fortress" on Reformation Sunday or other special occasions. The suggestions below, all from *Evangelical Lutheran Worship*, are an eclectic mix with themes of unity, reconciliation, and common ministry and could provide nuance to other emphases, such as grace and justification.

247 Come now, O Prince of peace: *Though often sung in Advent, this powerful text prays that God make us one body with the repeated phrase "reconcile your people."*

463 Lord, who the night you were betrayed: *At the eucharist we pray for unity and ask God to heal our divisions.*

575 In Christ called to baptize: *United in baptism and eucharist, we are called to witness through teaching, compassion, and service.*

576 We are all one in mission: *Though our gifts and ministries are different, our purpose is the same.*

645 Christ is made the sure foundation: *Christ binds the church in one.*

649 Behold, how pleasant: *Psalm 133 invites God's people to live together in unity.*

650 In Christ there is no east or west: *A classic text inviting Christian unity in diverse ways.*

651 Oh, praise the gracious power: *Themes of grace, reconciliation, and unity are heard in relation to both church and world.*

654 The church's one foundation: *Despite schisms, the people of God are one and united in the triune God.*

662 Christ is the King!: *The scattered people of God all the world over are invited to sing with one voice.*

Music: Chorale Service

Some congregations may consider following the tradition of Luther's German Mass and using a chorale service of Holy Communion sometime during these weeks. In this service, hymn paraphrases are used for the fixed liturgical texts.

Evangelical Lutheran Worship Occasional Services for the Assembly outlines a possible chorale service on pages 50–51. The principal chorales are included in *Evangelical Lutheran Worship*:

409 Kyrie! God, Father (Kyrie)

410 All glory be to God on high (Canticle of praise: Glory to God)

411 We all believe in one true God (Creed)

868 Isaiah in a vision did of old (Holy, holy, holy)

357 Lamb of God, pure and sinless (Communion song)

As Lutheran liturgical scholar Ben Stewart observes, even in Luther's recommendations for the German Mass and Formulae Missae, together these two proposals use not only German, his primary language, but Greek (Kyrie), Hebrew (Hallelujah), and Latin (Formula Missae). In this sense there is commitment not only to the vernacular but to the catholic and cosmopolitan dimension of the liturgy. *With One Voice* takes this concept further with its Holy Communion Setting Six, titled "All Times and Places" (pp. 42–45). The order includes a creative list of service music from a variety of countries, styles, and time periods. Much of this music is also included in *Evangelical Lutheran Worship*. One option for a Reformation observance is to develop a liturgy that not only uses some of the specific materials from the German Mass, but also makes use of other musical pieces from the global church.

Unity

Consider this title of an article written by Anthony Ruff, a monk at St. John's Abbey in Collegeville, Minnesota: "After Vatican II: Are We All Protestants Now? Or Are We All Catholics Now?" (*The Hymn* 64:1 [winter 2013], 6–12). Ruff describes the amazing convergence in Catholic and Protestant worship during the past fifty years. He mentions how one of his theology professors, a Benedictine monk, suggested that Martin Luther had been a "silent father" at the Second Vatican Council.

The Roman Catholic–Lutheran *Joint Declaration on the Doctrine of Justification* (1999), considered one of the most significant ecumenical achievements of the past fifty years, is an important document to study, lift up, and celebrate during the anniversary observance. The booklet *From Conflict to Communion* (Lutheran–Roman Catholic Commission on Unity) presents a compelling overview of Lutheran–Roman Catholic relations in the twenty-first century and guidelines for how to interpret similarities and differences.

Another helpful document, prepared by Lutherans and Roman Catholics in the USA, is *Declaration on the Way* (Augsbug Fortress, 2016). It summarizes 32 areas of convergence while noting ways in which the dialogue continues.

Because the Reformation caused a division between Lutherans and Roman Catholics, an ecumenical emphasis on unity, healing, and reconciliation involving these denominations seems particularly appropriate in 2017. The *Reformation 500 Sourcebook* provides a variety of litanies, prayers, and service outlines for ecumenical occasions.

Christian unity need not be the endpoint, however. A number of Lutherans are proposing eco-justice as an important emphasis for the occasion (http://www.lutheransrestoring creation.org/500th-anniversary-of-the-reformation), and this occasion is an opportunity to highlight the importance of interfaith dialogue as well.

Seasonal Checklist

- Make sure your outside signs, website, and social media posts reflect worship schedule changes and special Reformation services or events.
- Consider whether your congregation will participate in the ELCA's "God's work. Our hands." Sunday. How will the theme be integrated into worship on that day?
- How are young people preparing for affirmation of baptism encountering the Reformation? How might people of all ages engage with Luther's catechisms during this time?
- If a blessing of teachers and students will be held, see possible forms in the seasonal rites section.
- If Bibles will be distributed to young readers, consider having their parents or baptismal sponsors involved in physically distributing the Bibles as a way to honor the promises made at baptism. Words to accompany this action are provided in the seasonal rites section.
- If a blessing of animals service is held within worship or at another time, consider publicizing it as an outreach opportunity.
- Use the resource *Reformation 500 Sourcebook* (Augsburg Fortress, 2016) to generate creative ideas for worship during these weeks.
- Invite a Roman Catholic preacher or someone from another denomination to preach on Reformation Sunday or during these months.
- In preparing worship, sermons, and the Reformation 2017 celebration, determine how you can communicate effectively to people in your congregation and community the answer to the question, "Who are the Lutherans?"
- Consider using harvest decorations through Thanksgiving.
- Though red is the color appointed for Reformation Sunday, think carefully about the use of festive decorations during this season to accentuate the green of the season after Pentecost, autumn colors, and the red of the actual Reformation festival. Perhaps deep hues of yellow, orange, red, and brown could be overlaid on the green as the season progresses.
- Plan how music from the Lutheran heritage as well as from diverse cultures and styles could deepen your Reformation celebration.

Worship Texts for Autumn

Confession and Forgiveness

All may make the sign of the cross, the sign marked at baptism,
as the presiding minister begins.

Blessed be the ✝ holy Trinity,
the one who fashions us,
the one who heals us,
the one who reforms us again and again.
Amen.

Let us confess our sin, calling for God's transforming power.

Silence for reflection and self-examination.

Source of all life,
we confess that we have not allowed
your grace to set us free.
We fear that we are not good enough.
We hear your word of love freely given to us,
yet we expect others to earn it.
We turn the church inward,
rather than moving it outward.
Forgive us. Stir us.
Reform us to be a church powered by love,
willing to speak for what is right,
act for what is just,
and seek the healing of your whole creation.
Amen.

God hears our cry and sends the Spirit to change us
and to empower our lives in the world.
Our sins are forgiven,
✝ God's love is unconditional,
and we are raised up as God's people
who will always be made new,
in the name of Jesus Christ.
Amen.

Offering Prayer

God of life,
you give us these gifts of the earth,
these resources of our life and our labor.
Take them, offered in great thanksgiving,
and use them to set a table that will heal the whole creation;
through Jesus Christ, our Savior and Light.
Amen.

Invitation to Communion

Speak to us, O Lord, in the breaking of the bread,
and make us one with you.

Prayer after Communion

Holy and compassionate God,
in bread and wine you give us gifts
that form us to be humble and courageous.
May your words come to life
in our serving and in our witness,
that we might speak a living voice
of healing and justice to all the world,
through Jesus Christ, our rock and our redeemer.
Amen.

Blessing

God, creator of all things, speaking reformation into being;
Jesus Christ, savior of the world, raising the dead;
Holy Spirit, living voice, calling and enlightening the church:
Almighty God, Father, ✝ Son, and Holy Spirit,
bless you now and forever.
Amen.

Dismissal

Go in peace. Sound the good news.
Thanks be to God.

Seasonal Rites for Autumn

Blessings for Teachers and Students

For the marvels of your creation,
we praise you, O God.
For the opportunity to explore and study,
we praise you, O God.
For those who guide us, teachers and mentors,
we praise you, O God.
Teach us your ways and guide us in your path,
for you are the creator of all that is, seen and unseen.
Amen.

or

Let us pray for all who are beginning a new school year,
that both students and teachers
will be blessed in their academic endeavors.

Almighty God, you give wisdom and knowledge.
Grant teachers the gift of joy and insight,
and students the gift of diligence and openness,
that all may grow in what is good and honest and true.
Support all who teach and all who learn,
that together we may know and follow your ways;
through Jesus Christ our Lord.
Amen.

Presentation of the Bible

A representative of the congregation may present a Bible to each person. These or similar words may be spoken:
Receive this Bible.
Hear God's word with us.
Learn and tell its stories.
Discover its mysteries.
Honor its commandments.
Rejoice in its good news.
May God's life-giving word
inspire you and make you wise.

Reformation 500

The Lutheran church is diverse, and it is decentralized—meaning that no one will be giving congregations a blueprint for how they should observe the 500th anniversary of the Reformation. Those choices will vary, depending on your context. Through several avenues, the Evangelical Lutheran Church in America and Augsburg Fortress have been highlighting a wide range of ideas and possibilities from various sources. For example:

- The seasonal resources in this volume.
- *Reformation 500 Sourcebook: Anniversary Resources for Congregations* (Augsburg Fortress, 2016). Gathered in this sourcebook are a variety of helps for worship, education, song, service, connection with other Christians, and more.
- *500 Years: Lutherans from the Reformation through Today* (Augsburg Fortress, 2016). Suitable for adult group study not only in connection with this anniversary but as an ongoing resource for introducing people to the Lutheran church, with an accompanying leader guide.
- *Papa Luther* (Augsburg Fortress, 2016). A graphic novel for middle-elementary learners. Accompanied by a leader guide, it will open up a basic understanding of the way God's good news frees us to live, and how Martin Luther and his friends lifted up that good news for us all.
- www.elca500.org. This site highlights the Evangelical Lutheran Church in America's Reformation observances and facilitates connections among ELCA partners, networks, and expressions. Find news and resources, explore upcoming events, and share your own ideas and activities.
- *From Conflict to Communion.* The Lutheran–Roman Catholic Commission on Unity invites all Christians to study its report and to walk along the path toward the full, visible unity of the church. Free, downloadable document and study guide available at elca500.org.
- https://2017.lutheranworld.org. Connect with Lutherans around the globe at the Lutheran World Federation's Reformation anniversary site under the theme "Liberated by God's Grace."

How will Lutherans observe this anniversary in ways that are forward-looking, outward-directed, and focused on the amazing mercy of God in Jesus Christ? Blessings to you as you seek to answer that question in the places where you live and serve.

Thanksgiving at the Table
Anniversary of the Reformation
A Variable Prayer Form

This prayer is based on the readings appointed for Reformation Day: Jeremiah 31:31-34; Romans 3:19-28; and John 8:31-36. For an abbreviated prayer, use only the first line of each unit (A lines), placing a period where needed. For use on Sundays, use the first and the second line of each unit (A and B lines). For use on festivals, add an appropriate third line. Here the third lines printed in italics (C lines) are especially appropriate for the 500th anniversary of the Reformation.

A   We praise you, all-holy God,
B   our maker, our lover, our keeper,
C   *our Covenant Lord, our Redeemer, the Strength of Truth,*

A   for the universe beyond our knowing,
B   for seas and forests and fields,
C   *for the waters of Wittenberg and for flowers in this place,*

A   for creatures seen and unseen,
B   for animals both wild and tame,
C   *for our ancestors and godparents from around the globe,*

A   and for the places we humans call home,
B   for cities and churches and schools,
C   *for seminaries and missions and fellowship halls.*

A   We praise you for your covenant people,
B   for Moses and Miriam and Aaron,
C   *for Jeremiah and the psalmists,*

A   and for centuries of faithful Christians,
B   for Mary Magdalene, Peter and Paul,
C   *for Luther, Melanchthon, Muhlenberg, and Fedde,*
     for Katie Luther and Cranach, Bach and Nicolai,
     Nommensen and Kierkegaard,
     Bonhoeffer and Hammarskjöld,
     for all servants of the Reformation.

A   We praise you, O God, for Jesus Christ,
B   who saves us from sin and from evil,
C   *embodying forgiveness, granting us grace, setting us free,*

A   who on the night before he died,
     took bread, and gave thanks; broke it,
     and gave it to his disciples, saying:
     Take and eat; this is my body, given for you.
     Do this for the remembrance of me.

Again, after supper, he took the cup, gave thanks,
and gave it for all to drink, saying:
This cup is the new covenant in my blood,
shed for you and for all people for the forgiveness of sin.
Do this for the remembrance of me.

A   And so we remember your Word,
B   his life, his death, and his glorious resurrection,
C   *his presence in this meal around the world,*

A   and we proclaim the mystery of our faith:

Christ has died.
Christ is risen.
Christ will come again.

A   We pray, O God, for your Spirit,
B   your breath, your fire, your wisdom,
C   *your law, your grace, your freedom.*

A   Bless this meal and all those who share it;
B   inspire your people for service;
C   *continue the reformation of your churches;*

A   and renew the world with your mercy,
B   with your healing, your justice, and your peace,
C   *with the joy of life in your household.*

A   We praise you, all-holy God,
B   the Father, the Son, the Holy Spirit,
C   *mighty Fortress, victorious Champion, powerful Shield,*

A   today, tomorrow, and forever.
Amen!

Thanksgiving at the Table
A Prayer for Church Anniversaries

This prayer is based on the readings appointed for Reformation Day: Jeremiah 31:31-34; Romans 3:19-28; and John 8:31-36. Passages in italics are especially appropriate for giving thanks at the Reformation. These may be adapted for other church anniversary occasions.

O God before time, O God at the end,
we delight in the splendor of your universe.
Daily we laud your continuing creation,
and we give thanks
for all the homelands of your Reformation people.
We glorify you, now and forever.
We glorify you, now and forever.

O God of the covenant, O God of the church,
we hear you speaking to centuries of your people.
We come as your children to this table,
and we give thanks for your presence
among Lutheran congregations around the world.
We praise you, now and forever.
We praise you, now and forever.

You gave us Mary and Magdalene, Peter and Paul,
Luther and Melanchthon, Henry Muhlenberg, and
Elizabeth Fedde
—let us call out more names—
Katharina Luther the homemaker, Cranach the artist,
Bach the musician, Nicolai the hymnwriter,
Nommensen the missionary, Kierkegaard the philosopher,
Bonhoeffer the martyr, Hammarskjöld the statesman,
countless other servants of the Reformation.
We bless you, now and forever.
We bless you, now and forever.

You came as Jesus, our wisdom, our guide,
embodying forgiveness, granting us grace, setting us free,
dying for sin, and alive for the life of the world.
We worship you, now and forever.
We worship you, now and forever.

In the night in which he was betrayed,
our Lord Jesus took bread, and gave thanks;
broke it, and gave it to his disciples, saying:
Take and eat; this is my body, given for you.
Do this for the remembrance of me.

Again, after supper, he took the cup, gave thanks,
and gave it for all to drink, saying:
This cup is the new covenant in my blood,
shed for you and for all people for the forgiveness of sin.
Do this for the remembrance of me.

Remembering his death, we cry out Amen.
Amen.
Celebrating his resurrection, we shout Amen.
Amen.
Trusting his presence in every time and place, we plead Amen.
Amen.

Come, Holy Spirit, and make here the body of Christ.
Breathe onto this food, that it bring us your life.
Empower your Reformation people throughout the world
to preach and teach, baptize and feed,
pray and sing, comfort and heal.
By your Spirit,
preserve what is faithful;
reform what we treasure;
create in us what is vital and new.
We honor you, now and forever.
We honor you, now and forever.

O God before time, O God at the end,
Father, Son, and Spirit,
we laud you,
Covenant Lord, our Redeemer, the Strength of truth.
Glory and praise, blessing and worship,
honor and power and might be to you, our God,
forever and ever.
Amen.

Blessing of Animals

This service may be used entirely on its own, perhaps for an observance on or near the commemoration of Francis of Assisi, renewer of the church, died 1226 (October 4). Various elements of this order may also be incorporated into another worship service, though this material is not intended to replace the customary Sunday worship of the congregation. For practical reasons this service may be conducted outdoors or in a facility other than a congregation's primary worship space.

Greeting and Prayer

The grace of our Lord Jesus Christ, the love of God,
and the communion of the Holy Spirit be with you all.
And also with you.

Let us pray.
Sovereign of the universe, your first covenant of mercy was with every living creature. When your beloved Son came among us, the waters of the river welcomed him, the heavens opened to greet his arrival, the animals of the wilderness drew near as his companions. With all the world's people, may we who are washed into new life through baptism seek the way of your new creation, the way of justice and care, mercy and peace; through Jesus Christ, our Savior and Lord.
Amen.
or
Source and sustainer of life, we cherish the myriad works of your hands. Water, earth, and sky are yours, as are all their inhabitants, wild and tame. We thank you for creatures that nourish and serve us, befriend, enrich, entertain, and protect us. May we, who are made in your image, care for them well. And may your groaning yet wondrous creation rally and thrive, revealing to all who come after us your wise, redemptive, transfiguring love; through Jesus Christ, our Savior and Lord.
Amen.

Readings

Genesis 1:1, 20-28
Genesis 6:17-22
Psalm 8
Psalm 84:1-4
Psalm 148

The reading of scripture is followed by silence for reflection. Other forms of reflection may also follow, such as brief commentary, teaching, or personal witness; non-biblical readings; interpretation through music or other art forms; or guided conversation among those present.

Song

God of the sparrow ELW 740
Oh, that I had a thousand voices ELW 833
All creatures, worship God most high! ELW 835
All things bright and beautiful WOV 767
This is my Father's world ELW 824

Blessing of Animals

The leader may ask all who have brought pets or animals to the celebration to come forward for the following prayer.

The Lord be with you.
And also with you.

Let us pray.
Gracious God, in your love you created us in your image and made us stewards of the animals that live in the skies, the earth, and the sea. Bless us in our care for our pets and animals *(names of pets may be added here)*. Help us recognize your power and wisdom in the variety of creatures that live in our world, and hear our prayer for all that suffer overwork, hunger, and ill-treatment. Protect your creatures, and guard them from all evil, now and forever.
Amen.

Lord's Prayer

Blessing

Almighty God bless us,
and direct our days and our deeds in peace.
Amen.

September 3, 2017
Time after Pentecost — Lectionary 22

The prophet Jeremiah speaks of the incurable wound of his suffering, yet finds in God's words the delight of his heart. When Peter doesn't grasp Jesus' words about suffering, Jesus tells the disciples they will find their lives in losing them. Such sacrificial love is described by Paul when he urges us to associate with the lowly and not repay evil with evil. In worship we gather as a community that we might offer ourselves for the sake of our suffering world.

Prayer of the Day

O God, we thank you for your Son, who chose the path of suffering for the sake of the world. Humble us by his example, point us to the path of obedience, and give us strength to follow your commands, through Jesus Christ, our Savior and Lord.

Gospel Acclamation

Alleluia. May the God of our Lord Jesus Christ enlighten the eyes ¹ of our hearts,* so that we may know the hope to which ¹ God has called us. *Alleluia.* (Eph. 1:17, 18)

Readings and Psalm

Jeremiah 15:15-21

Jeremiah's delight in the word of the Lord is contradicted by the heaviness of God's hand upon him and God's seeming unfaithfulness. God's tough love to Jeremiah says that if he repents, he will be allowed to continue in his strenuous ministry. Jeremiah is strengthened by the simple words: "I am with you."

Psalm 26:1-8

Your love is before my eyes; I have walked faithfully with you. (Ps. 26:3)

Romans 12:9-21

Paul presents benchmarks for faithful relationships with Christians and non-Christians. Love is the unflagging standard of our behavior. When we encounter evil, we do not resort to its tactics but seek to overcome it with good. While Christians cannot control the actions and attitudes of others, we seek to live at peace with all people.

Matthew 16:21-28

After Peter confesses that Jesus is "the Messiah, the Son of the living God" (16:16), Jesus reveals the ultimate purpose of his ministry. These words prove hard to accept, even for a disciple whom Jesus has called a "rock."

Semicontinuous reading and psalm

Exodus 3:1-15

Moses experienced the call of God when God appeared to him in a bush that burned but was not consumed. When Moses expressed his unworthiness, God promised to be with him. When Moses objected that people would demand to know God's name, God revealed his personal name, Yahweh (I AM WHO I AM), or the Lord. Israel discovered God's true identity when God took them out of Egypt.

Psalm 105:1-6, 23-26, 45b

Make known the deeds of the LORD among the peoples. Hallelujah! (Ps. 105:1, 45)

Preface   Sundays

Color   Green

Prayers of Intercession

The prayers are prepared locally for each occasion. The following examples may be adapted or used as appropriate.

Open to the gifts of the Holy Spirit, we pray for the church, the world, and all of God's creation.

A brief silence.

We pray for the church and its mission. Make your church ready to lose its life for your sake. Unite it in service, sustain it in suffering, and let its love for others be genuine. Lord, in your mercy,

hear our prayer.

We pray for the earth and its well-being. Make us mindful of the gifts you have labored to give us, and inspire us to commit ourselves to their care. Lord, in your mercy,

hear our prayer.

We pray for the nations and their leaders. Overcome evil with good. Show us how to live peaceably with all. Teach us how to love our enemies. Lord, in your mercy,

hear our prayer.

We pray for those in any need. Provide for the hungry. Rescue the persecuted. Bless those who advocate for fair and safe working conditions and for just and livable wages. Lord, in your mercy,

hear our prayer.

We pray for this community and its ministry. Move us to persevere in prayer, to extend hospitality to strangers, to rejoice with those who rejoice, and to weep with those who weep (*especially*). Lord, in your mercy,
hear our prayer.
Here other intercessions may be offered.
Alpha and Omega, we give thanks for all the saints who now rest from their labors (*especially*). Keep us in union with them until we are joined around your throne. Lord, in your mercy,
hear our prayer.
Into your hands, gracious God, we commend all for whom we pray, trusting the power of Christ and the gifts of the Spirit.
Amen.

Images in the Readings

That believers are to deny themselves, take up their **cross**, and follow Jesus has been a commonplace message throughout Christian centuries. Care must be taken that more privileged persons do not mouth these words to the less privileged, to those with minimal power to affect their own situation, as if what Jesus meant was to suffer in silence. All the baptized have been marked by the cross, and in the mystery of the resurrection, this cross is the way to life. Perhaps the cross we are called to carry is someone else's, which we willingly help to carry. One possibility is that Matthew was referring to the Tau, the sign of the end time for those who await the return of Christ.

Jesus calls Peter **Satan**, the one who opposes God. Ancient Israel knew no supernatural power of evil. In the book of Job, Satan is in God's throne room, goading God and accusing the righteous. By the time of Jesus, largely through influence of their Zoroastrian neighbors, Jews had come to believe in a supernatural being who personified evil and who, like the medieval devil, tempted persons to immoral behavior. Yet Christian theology has always resisted the popular dualist idea that there is a good god and a bad god and that human life is the battlefield between God and the devil. According to the New Testament, evil, although still present, has already been conquered in Christ's resurrection. Satan is behind us. Watch the remarkable film *The Apostle*, in which during the final sermon the Holiness preacher calls out to the devil, "Get behind me! Get behind me!"

The **burning coals** are an image for the shame that evildoers will experience when they encounter Christian forgiveness and generosity. In Romans 12:20, Paul is quoting Proverbs 25:21-22, an example of the degree to which Christian ethics repeats the teachings of the Hebrew Scriptures.

Ideas for the Day

- James Cone declares in his book *The Cross and the Lynching Tree*, "*Every time a white mob lynched a black person, they lynched Jesus. The lynching tree is the cross in America.* When American Christians realize that they can meet Jesus only in the crucified bodies in our midst, they will encounter the real scandal of the cross" ([Maryknoll, NY: Orbis, 2011], 158, italics in original). The image of the cross has been mainstreamed in such a way that it is not associated with the suffering it imposed. Perhaps by relating the cross to the lynching tree, the suffering of Jesus can be experienced in the suffering of African Americans in the United States. Racism is still a part of the current reality, and the cross is a symbol that speaks of both undeserved suffering and resurrection. How does the church respond to racism, and how does it ensure it is not complicit in it?

- Paul exhorts his hearers to "rejoice in hope, be patient in suffering, persevere in prayer. . . . Weep with those who weep" (Rom. 12:12, 15). Praying for others who suffer and who carry crosses known and unknown can be part of our work this week. Provide a slip of paper to each worshiper, and invite all to write down, anonymously, a burden or cross each is bearing right now. Have worshipers place these folded slips of paper in a large basket or other container. Invite worshipers to draw a slip of paper from the basket and commit to praying for that individual every day this week.

- These readings fall on Labor/Labour Day weekend. Jesus' work is to suffer, die, and be raised. Our labor, he says, is to deny ourselves, take up our cross, and follow him. That is not as far removed as it might seem from the office, assembly line floor, store, schoolroom, and home where we labor. How often in the course of the week do we say and hear others say, "This is killing me"? A sermon on this Sunday might help hearers explore how in our everyday struggle we take up the cross and follow. The power of Jesus' death and resurrection enables us to function in our daily lives as a part of God's redeemed new creation.

Connections with the Liturgy

The authors of the New Testament maintained a strong belief in the eschaton, the end of the world coming sooner or later and the judgment to which today's gospel refers. In the language of the creeds, "he will come to judge the living and the dead," "he will come again in glory to judge the living and the dead." Paul's words, "Bless those who persecute you," have been a reminder to Christians to include prayer for their enemies in the weekly intercessions.

Recalling Paul's message to the Romans, one option in *Evangelical Lutheran Worship* for the final blessing calls on God to grant us "to live in harmony with one another" and to fill us "with all joy and peace in believing" (p. 115).

Let the Children Come

Our church sees Jesus' suffering on the cross as God's solidarity with humankind in suffering. Where we see suffering, we know God and God's church are there too. As Christians, we follow the cross. Liturgically, the processional cross is a way for the assembly to move their bodies to follow the cross. Invite children into the gesture of following the processional cross with their bodies and bowing as it passes. If the assembly already moves this way, children will already know how to do this. If it is new for all, children can help the whole assembly open up to this new way of being together.

Assembly Song
Gathering

Son of God, eternal Savior ELW 655, LBW 364
For the beauty of the earth ELW 879, LBW 561
Come, follow me, the Savior spake ELW 799, LBW 455

Psalmody and Acclamations

Messner, Sally. "Psalm 26:1-8" from PWA.
Warner, Steven C. "Harbor of My Heart" from PAS 16B.
+ Makeever, Ray. "Tell What God Has Done for Us (Psalm 105)" from DH.
(GA) ELW 169 with proper verse for Lectionary 22.

Hymn of the Day

Lord Jesus, you shall be my song ELW 808 *LES PETITES SOEURS*
Take up your cross, the Savior said ELW 667 *BOURBON*
   LBW 398 *NUN LASST UNS DEN LEIB BEGRABEN*
Lift high the cross ELW 660, LBW 377 *CRUCIFER*

Offering

Day by day ELW 790, WOV 746
By gracious powers ELW 626, WOV 736

Communion

Will you come and follow me ELW 798, W&P 137
Blest be the tie that binds ELW 656, LBW 370
Let us ever walk with Jesus ELW 802, LBW 487

Sending

Jesus, still lead on ELW 624, LBW 341
Rise, O church, like Christ arisen ELW 548

Additional Assembly Songs

Step by Step W&P 132
I can hear my Savior calling TFF 146
By grace God calls us into life CBM 64
⊕ Dexter, Noel. "I Come to the Cross" from *Let the Peoples Sing*. SATB. AFP 9780800675394.
⊕ Loh, I-to. "Christ Is Our Peace" from *Sound the Bamboo*. U. GIA G-6830.

☼ Cowart, Benji/Michael Weaver. "Redeemed" from CCLI.
☼ Faircloff, Scott/Michael Merritt. "Uprising" from CCLI.
☼ Mann, Robin. "Love One Another" from CCLI.
☼ Phelps, David/Regie Hamm. "Satisfaction" from CCLI.
☼ Smith, Rob. "Undivided" from CCLI.
☼ Stanfill, Kristian/Jason Ingram/Brett Younker/Daniel Carson. "My Heart Is Yours" from CCLI.

Music for the Day
Choral

♫ Busarow, Donald. "Lift High the Cross." 2 pt mxd or SATB, assembly, org, opt tpt. AFP 9780800645892.
P ♫ Carlson, J. Bert. "Lift High the Cross." SATB, org. AFP 9781451479393.
P ♫ Giamanco, Anthony. "Take Up Your Cross." 2 pt mxd, kybd. AFP 9780800678968.
♫ Hopson, Hal. "Take Up Your Cross." 2 pt mxd, kybd. AFP 9780800654504.

Children's Choir

Helms, Judith A. "Let Me Be Your Servant, Jesus" from *Life-Songs*. U, pno. AFP 9780806642703.
Page, Sue Ellen. "Sing Alleluia" from *LifeSongs*. U, pno, opt perc and Orff inst. AFP 9780806642703.
Reeves, Jeff. "Oh, How Good Is Christ the Lord" from *Can't Wait to Sing! Anthems and Fun Songs to Sing All Year*. U, pno, opt perc. CG CGC50.

Keyboard / Instrumental

P Mackie, Dave. "Day by Day" (Blott en dag) from *By Day and By Night: Piano Settings*. Pno. AFP 9781451420890.
P Nelson, Ronald A. "Rise, O Church, like Christ Arisen" (Surge ecclesia) from *Easy Hymn Settings for Organ*, vol. 4. Org. AFP 9781451486049.
P Raabe, Nancy. "Jesus, Still Lead On" (Seelenbräutigam) from *Day of Arising: A Tapestry of Musical Traditions*. Pno. AFP 9780800637460.
P ♫ Stevens, Wendy Lynn. "Take Up Your Cross, the Savior Said" (Bourbon) from *How Sweet the Sound: Piano Arrangements for Worship*. Pno. AFP 9780806696966.

Handbell

P Dobrinski, Cynthia. "Song of Hope." 3-6 oct, L2. HOP 2716.
P Moklebust, Cathy. "The King of Love My Shepherd Is." 3-5 oct hb, opt 3-5 oct hc, L3+. CG CGB825.
♫ Tucker, Sondra. "Lift High the Cross." 3-5 oct hb, opt 2 oct hc, L3-, LOR 20/1714L. Opt org, opt br qnt, LOR 30/3098L.

⊕ = global song   ♫ = relates to hymn of the day   + = semicontinuous psalm
☼ = praise song   P = available in Prelude Music Planner

Saturday, September 9
Peter Claver, priest, missionary to Colombia, died 1654

Peter Claver was born into Spanish nobility and was persuaded to become a Jesuit missionary. He served in Cartagena (in what is now Colombia) by teaching and caring for the slaves. The slaves arrived in ships, where they had been confined in dehumanizing conditions. Claver met and supplied them with medicine, food, clothing, and brandy. He learned their dialects and taught them Christianity. He called himself "the slave of the slaves forever." Claver also ministered to the locals of Cartagena who were in prison and facing death.

September 10, 2017
Time after Pentecost — Lectionary 23

Conflict is a part of relationships and life in community. Jesus' words in today's gospel are often used in situations having to do with church discipline. The prophet Ezekiel tells of warning the wicked to turn from their ways, and Paul reminds us that love is the fulfilling of the law. We gather in the name of Christ, assured that he is present among us with gifts of peace and reconciliation.

Prayer of the Day

O Lord God, enliven and preserve your church with your perpetual mercy. Without your help, we mortals will fail; remove far from us everything that is harmful, and lead us toward all that gives life and salvation, through Jesus Christ, our Savior and Lord.

Gospel Acclamation

Alleluia. In Christ God was reconciling the world ׀ to himself,* entrusting the message of reconcilia- ׀ tion to us. *Alleluia.* (2 Cor. 5:19)

Readings and Psalm
Ezekiel 33:7-11

God appointed Ezekiel as a sentinel for the house of Israel. Ezekiel must faithfully convey God's warnings to the people. Remarkably, God—who is about to attack Jerusalem—gives a warning with the hope that repentance will make the attack unnecessary.

Psalm 119:33-40

I desire the path of your commandments. (Ps. 119:35)

Romans 13:8-14

The obligation of Christians is to love one another and so fulfill the heart and goal of the law. Clothes make the person as we "put on the Lord Jesus Christ" and live today in light of the future God has in store for us.

Matthew 18:15-20

Jesus offers practical advice to his disciples on how individuals—and the church as a whole—should show wrongdoers their need for repentance.

Semicontinuous reading and psalm
Exodus 12:1-14

Israel remembered its deliverance from slavery in Egypt by celebrating the festival of Passover. This festival featured the Passover lamb, whose blood was used as a sign to protect God's people from the threat of death. The early church described the Lord's supper using imagery from the Passover, especially in portraying Jesus as the lamb who delivers God's people from sin and death.

Psalm 149

Sing the LORD's praise in the assembly of the faithful. (Ps. 149:1)

Preface   Sundays

Color   Green

Prayers of Intercession

The prayers are prepared locally for each occasion. The following examples may be adapted or used as appropriate.

Open to the gifts of the Holy Spirit, we pray for the church, the world, and all of God's creation.
A brief silence.

We pray for the church universal. Reconcile our differences. Forgive our divisions. Unite us at your table. Hear us, O God.
Your mercy is great.

For your creation. Increase our stewardship of all that you have given to us. Let the earth flourish for those who come after us. Hear us, O God.
Your mercy is great.

For peace in the world. End conflicts among nations (*especially*). Help leaders and citizens truly to listen to one another and to act for the good of all. Teach us by your example. Hear us, O God.

Your mercy is great.

For all those in need. Bind up our hurts. Heal divisions in our families, friendships, and neighborhoods. Comfort those who need your special care (*especially*). Hear us, O God.

Your mercy is great.

For this congregation. Make us signs of your love and forgiveness in this community and in the world. Help us to grow in our love for one another. Hear us, O God.

Your mercy is great.

Here other intercessions may be offered.

In thanksgiving for all the faithful witnesses who put on the Lord Jesus Christ (*especially*). Keep us faithful until the day we rejoice in your majesty with them. Hear us, O God.

Your mercy is great.

Into your hands, gracious God, we commend all for whom we pray, trusting the power of Christ and the gifts of the Spirit.

Amen.

Images in the Readings

We are **bound**, we are **loosed**: these are strong images describing the powers that hold us captive and the gift of God's Spirit that frees us for a life of love. The responsibility for correction, discipline, and forgiveness belongs to the community.

Tax collectors were despised collaborators who were infamous for cheating. Mercifully, Jesus is described as eating with tax collectors. This is good news for all of us.

Ezekiel calls us to be **sentinels**, those assigned to watch from the city walls for both any approaching dangers and any welcome visitors. The life of the Christian is an active life, watching in the world for the bad and the good and reporting to the community what we see.

Paul calls us to wake up; the **day** has come; get dressed, wearing Christ; for today there might be a battle.

In his mixing of metaphors, Paul blends the robe of baptism with the **armor** of a warrior. It's a dangerous world out there, everywhere affected by human sin.

Ideas for the Day

- An odd business is spelled out in the gospel reading. It is the Christian business, the ministry of reconciliation. We live in a culture that is both litigious and conflict avoidant, and members of the church reflect that culture. This is not to be the model for the Christian community. We will not walk away, from either a congregation, a group, or an individual, because our feelings are hurt. We will not nurse a grudge. We will not engage in scorekeeping and paybacks. Jesus died and rose to reconcile us to God. We are adopted into the family by baptism. Reconciliation is the family business.

- Sometimes this gospel reading has been used as the basis of a bureaucratic program to expel unwanted people from the church. That procedure might seem like it ought to work—until we get to the punch line: "Let such a one be to you as a Gentile and a tax collector" (Matt. 18:17). How did Jesus treat Gentiles and tax collectors? He ate dinner with them, ministered to them, and called them to be disciples.

- In the Olympics, athletes can be disqualified for a variety of reasons, including the use of performance-enhancing drugs. Use an image of a disgraced athlete who received medals that were later stripped. The gospel reading is not instructing Christians to look for reasons to exclude. In fact, it is the opposite. God wants to give everyone a chance to be an active member of the team. God uses the community to help keep us on the Way.

Connections with the Liturgy

It is almost as if the gospel reading provides an outline for much Sunday worship: we confess our sins, we are loosed from sin's bonds, we intercede for all the world, and we gather around the table to meet the risen Christ. As well, Paul alludes to baptism, our putting on Jesus Christ. This is what it means to be the church of Christ.

Let the Children Come

The gospel today describes how Christian people are to interact with one another in times of conflict, disagreement, or even ordinary conversation, in a way that honors God's presence among us. The method of direct communication described in today's text is easily taught to and practiced with children. We speak directly to one another, not about or over one another. Adults should be especially mindful to speak directly to children and not about them to others. Even preverbal babies can be spoken to directly, and we should pause to listen for an answer. No one appreciates being talked about behind their back, including children!

Assembly Song
Gathering

Joyful, joyful we adore thee   ELW 836, LBW 551

Lord of all nations, grant me grace   ELW 716, LBW 419

Praise, my soul, the God of heaven   ELW 865/864, LBW 549

Psalmody and Acclamations

"Change Your Heart and Mind." *Psallite* A-171. Cant or SATB, assembly, kybd.

Becker, John W. "Psalm 119:33-40" from PWA.

+   Pavlechko, Thomas. "Psalm 149" from SMP.

(GA) ELW 169 with proper verse for Lectionary 23.

+ = semicontinuous psalm

Hymn of the Day

In all our grief ELW 615, WOV 739 *FREDERICKTOWN*

God, when human bonds are broken ELW 603, WOV 735 *MERTON*

Beloved, God's chosen ELW 648 *ANDREW'S SONG*

Offering

When we are living ELW 639, LLC 462

Blessed be the name ELW 797

Communion

Draw us in the Spirit's tether ELW 470, WOV 703

Where charity and love prevail ELW 359, LBW 126, TFF 84

Blest be the tie that binds ELW 656, LBW 370

Sending

Awake, O sleeper, rise from death ELW 452, WOV 745

Earth and all stars! ELW 731, LBW 558

Additional Assembly Songs

Bind us together WOV 748, TFF 217

To you all hearts are open SP 43

O God, with hope I enter in CBM 98

⊕ Hesla, Bret. "Let Us Put On the Clothes of Christ" from *Global Songs 2*. SATB. AFP 9780800656744.

⊕ Mxadana, George. "Alleluia" from *Sent by the Lord: Songs of the World Church*, vol. 2. U. GIA G-3740.

☼ Brown, Bryan/Chad Bohi. "Jesus Is Here" from CCLI.

☼ Crocker, Matt/Brooke Ligertwood. "To Be like You" from CCLI.

☼ Houston, Joel/Michael Guy Chislett. "Here Now (Madness)" from CCLI.

☼ Peacock, Charlie. "In the Light" from CCLI.

☼ Schweitzer, Winnie. "House of Love" from CCLI.

☼ Torwalt, Bryan/Katie Torwalt. "Holy Spirit" from CCLI.

Music for the Day
Choral

P Attwood, Thomas. "Teach Me, O Lord" from *Augsburg Motet Book*. SATB, opt kybd. AFP 9781451423709.

P♫ Keesecker, Thomas. "In All Our Grief and Fear We Turn to You." 2 pt mxd, pno. AFP 9780806697352.

Marcello, Benedetto/arr. Dale Grotenhuis. "Teach Me Now, O Lord." 2 pt trbl or mxd, kybd. MSM 50-9418.

Hurd, David. "Teach Me, O Lord." SATB. GIA G-2715.

Children's Choir

Brokering, Lois and Herbert F. "Love, Love, Love!" from *LifeSongs*. U, pno, opt perc. AFP 9780806642703.

P Patterson, Mark. "Let All God's Children Sing" from *Child renSing with Instruments*. U, pno, opt perc. AFP 9780800620349.

Shaw, Timothy. "Teach Me Your Way, O Lord." U/2 pt, pno, opt C inst. CG CGA1081.

Keyboard / Instrumental

Diemer, Emma Lou. "When We Are Living" (Somos del Señor) from *Augsburg Organ Library: Summer*. Org. AFP 9780800676872.

P Roberts, Al. "When We Are Living" (Somos del Señor) from *We Belong to God: Piano Settings of Folk Tunes*. Pno. AFP 9781451451801.

P♫ Weber, Jacob B. "Beloved, God's Chosen" (Andrew's Song) from *With High Delight: Organ Hymn Preludes*. Org. AFP 9781451479591.

P Wold, Wayne L. "Praise, My Soul, the God of Heaven" (Lauda anima) from *Light On Your Feet, vol. 3: A Collection for Organ with Minimal Pedal*. Org. AFP 9780806698021.

Handbell

P Eithun, Sandra. "Steal Away." 3-6 oct hb, opt 3-5 oct hc, L2+. CG CGB775.

P Glasgow, Michael J. "Reminiscence." 3-7 oct hb, opt 3-7 oct hc, L3+. CG CGB814.

P Page, Anna Laura. "God Is Our Refuge and Strength." 3-6 oct hb, opt fl, opt tpt, L3, CG CGB846. Opt SATB vcs, opt pno, opt children's vcs, CG CGA1381. Opt full score, CG CGB845.

Wednesday, September 13
John Chrysostom, Bishop of Constantinople, died 407

John was a priest in Antioch and an outstanding preacher. His eloquence earned him the nickname "Chrysostom" ("golden mouth"), but it also got him into trouble. As bishop of Constantinople he preached against corruption among the royal court. The empress, who had been his supporter, sent him into exile. His preaching style emphasized the literal meaning of scripture and its practical application. This interpretation stood in contrast to the common style at the time, which emphasized the allegorical meaning of the text.

Thursday, September 14
Holy Cross Day

Helena, the mother of Constantine, made a pilgrimage to Israel to look for Christian holy sites. She found what she believed were the sites of the crucifixion and burial of Jesus, sites that modern archaeologists believe may be correct. Here Constantine built two churches. The celebration of Holy Cross Day originated with the dedication of the Church of the Resurrection in 335. Today the festival provides the church an opportunity to lift up the victory of the cross with a spirit of celebration that might be less suitable on Good Friday.

⊕ = global song ♫ = relates to hymn of the day + = semicontinuous psalm
☼ = praise song P = available in Prelude Music Planner

Saturday, September 16

Cyprian, Bishop of Carthage, martyr, died around 258

Cyprian worked for the unity of the church and cared for his flock in North Africa during a time of great persecution. During Cyprian's time as bishop many people had denied the faith under duress. In contrast to some who held the belief that the church should not receive these people back, Cyprian believed they should be welcomed into full communion after a period of penance. He insisted on the need for compassion in order to preserve the unity of the church. His essay *On the Unity of the Catholic Church* stressed the role of bishops in guaranteeing the visible, concrete unity of the church. Cyprian was also concerned for the physical well-being of the people under his care. He organized a program of medical care for the sick during a severe epidemic in Carthage.

September 17, 2017

Time after Pentecost — Lectionary 24

In today's second reading Paul questions why we judge one another, since we all stand before the judgment of God. Yet we do sin against one another, and Jesus' challenge that we forgive seventy-seven times reveals God's boundless mercy. When we hear the words of forgiveness in worship and sign ourselves with the cross, we are renewed in baptism to be signs of reconciliation in the world.

Prayer of the Day

O Lord God, merciful judge, you are the inexhaustible fountain of forgiveness. Replace our hearts of stone with hearts that love and adore you, that we may delight in doing your will, through Jesus Christ, our Savior and Lord.

Gospel Acclamation

Alleluia. We have an advocate, Jesus ˡ Christ the righteous;* your sins are forgiven on account ˡ of his name. *Alleluia.* (1 John 2:1, 12)

Readings and Psalm

Genesis 50:15-21

After Jacob's death, the brothers of Joseph begged for forgiveness for the crime they had done against him. You intended to do me harm, Joseph said, but God used this as an opportunity to do good and save many lives.

Psalm 103:[1-7] 8-13

LORD, you are full of compassion and mercy. (Ps. 103:8)

Romans 14:1-12

This Christian community has significant struggles with diversity. Here Paul helps us understand that despite different practices in worship and personal piety, we do not judge one another. All Christians belong to the Lord Jesus Christ who died for all of us and will judge each of us.

Matthew 18:21-35

When Peter asks about the limits of forgiveness, Jesus responds with a parable that suggests human forgiveness should mirror the unlimited mercy of God.

Semicontinuous reading and psalm

Exodus 14:19-31

Having decided to let the Israelites go from Egypt, Pharaoh had second thoughts and sent his army after them (14:5-8). Though the passage through the Red Sea became a sign of salvation for the people of Israel, Pharaoh's forces drowned in the waters. As a result the Israelites believed in the Lord and in the Lord's servant Moses.

Psalm 114

Tremble, O earth, at the presence of the LORD. (Ps. 114:7)

or Exodus 15:1b-11, 20-21

I will sing to the LORD, who has triumphed gloriously. (Exod. 15:1)

Preface   Sundays

Color   Green

Prayers of Intercession

The prayers are prepared locally for each occasion. The following examples may be adapted or used as appropriate.

Open to the gifts of the Holy Spirit, we pray for the church, the world, and all of God's creation.

A brief silence.

Good and gracious God, we pray for the church. Bless the ministries of congregations in our community (*here specific local congregations may be named*). Unite us in the proclamation of your life-giving gospel. Lord, in your mercy,

hear our prayer.

Creator God, you spoke light into being, you separated the waters, you formed the dry land. Protect and enliven the creation you so love, and make us willing partners in its care. Lord, in your mercy,

hear our prayer.

God of the nations, you love all tribes, peoples, and languages. We pray for all who govern. Give them wise and generous hearts for those they serve. Lord, in your mercy,

hear our prayer.

Divine Healer, calm the anxiety of those who are wrongly accused, who suffer under crushing debt, or who are in prison. Reassure those who are lonely, impatient, brokenhearted, homebound, hospitalized, or ill (*especially*). Lord, in your mercy,

hear our prayer.

We pray for this assembly; for our guests and visitors, for newcomers to this community, for those who are certain and those who doubt, and for all who seek you in this place. Lord, in your mercy,

hear our prayer.

Here other intercessions may be offered.

We remember and give thanks for the faithful of every age who did not live to themselves but lived to you (*especially Hildegard, Abbess of Bingen*). Raise us with them on the last day. Lord, in your mercy,

hear our prayer.

Into your hands, gracious God, we commend all for whom we pray, trusting the power of Christ and the gifts of the Spirit.

Amen.

Images in the Readings

Seventy-seven plays with the ancient idea that seven is the number of fullness and perfection, because seven combines three, a number that suggests divinity, and four, recalling the corners of the flat earth. So with seventy-seven, Jesus multiplies the number of total perfection.

Matthew's allegory utilizes imagery from the economic system of the first century: a **lord** was the owner of land and of all those who worked the land, and a **slave** was one perpetually in the service of another. In our English-language Bibles, "Lord" translates the Hebrew and the Greek words that denote such a masculine societal authority figure. Christian faith in Christ's resurrection occasions the claim that "Jesus is Lord." "Lord" is the usual circumlocution used in our Bibles to render YHWH, God's first name. That we are slaves of God is New Testament imagery, albeit not a currently popular metaphor.

By the mysterious design of God, **Joseph** brought life to his people. Early Christian preachers saw in the Joseph story a parallel to Jesus, who was first brought low but was then raised to power and authority so as to forgive everyone and to feed the world.

Ideas for the Day

- Things from the head can be counted, but things from the heart cannot be measured. Can you really remember every instance that someone offended you or you offended someone else? When Peter asked Jesus how often he should forgive, Jesus' response is not seven times but seventy-seven times; this speaks to an infinite amount of forgiveness. Forgiveness is not about scorekeeping. Under the jurisdiction of our Lord Jesus, forgiveness is the norm. It is the way we live together. Jesus teaches that forgiveness should be a heart thing, not a head thing.

- School debt looms over the heads of many recent (and not so recent) graduates. In a mainly for-profit higher education culture, it is not uncommon for students to complete their education and not have adequate income to cover both the cost of living and the cost of educational debt. Imagine complete debt forgiveness for a student loan. Or consider those who are underwater on their mortgages. What if that debt were completely forgiven? Would you share the gift of mercy? Would you forgive someone indebted to you? Jesus invites us to see forgiveness not as something to be received but as something to be shared. How are you sharing forgiveness?

- The families of the nine people killed in Charleston, South Carolina, on June 17, 2015, by Dylann Roof had an opportunity to speak at his bond hearing just days after the murders. They took the opportunity not only to forgive but to go further. They professed their love for him and their concern for his soul. The story in Matthew 18 about forgiveness goes that far. It is easy to forgive a family for a cross word or a significant other for a thoughtless act, but are we truly ready to forgive as Jesus does? What other contemporary stories exemplify God's mercy in undeserved forgiveness and restoration? How can we continue to wrestle with extending forgiveness in situations where it seems undeserved?

Connections with the Liturgy

The Lord's Prayer includes a petition that summarizes today's allegory: "Forgive us our sins, as we forgive those who sin against us." Matthew's version of this prayer uses the word *debt*, and Luke's both *debt* and *sin*. The 1975 English translation of the prayer uses *sin*, since *debt* now usually connotes finances, and *trespass*, begun in the third century, now usually refers to walking on another's private property.

"First be reconciled with your brother or sister," says Matthew 5:24. One of the meanings of the liturgy's greeting of peace enacts Joseph's forgiveness of his brothers: we are reconciled with one another before we join together at the table of the risen Christ. Not merely a morning greeting, the passing of the peace is a sign of forgiveness within the community.

Let the Children Come

A mother relates that when one of her daughters was about four, she was very afraid of Santa Claus. Finally, she verbalized that she was afraid Santa would come and take away some of her toys because she had so many and other children had few or none. Our sense of justice can be frightening. We have all been granted mercy on top of mercy. Just as God's abundance overflows in creation and at the table, God's mercy overflows for everyone. However, the math gets weird whenever we start keeping track. How can we help children to be assured that God's mercy doesn't need to be hoarded; there is enough to go around?

Assembly Song
Gathering

Awake, O sleeper, rise from death ELW 452, WOV 745
As we gather at your table ELW 522
All creatures, worship God most high! ELW 835, LBW 527

Psalmody and Acclamations

Alonso, Tony. "The Lord Is Kind and Merciful/El Señor es compasivo." SATB, pno, gtr, assembly. GIA G-7868.
Folkening, John. "Six Psalm Settings with Antiphons." SATB, U or cant, assembly, opt kybd. MSM 80-700.
+ Schwandt, Daniel E. "Psalm 114" from PSCY.
+ Sedio, Mark. "Exodus 15:1b-11, 20-21" from PWA.
(GA) ELW 169 with proper verse for Lectionary 24.

Hymn of the Day

Forgive our sins as we forgive ELW 605, LBW 307 *DETROIT*
Our Father, we have wandered ELW 606, WOV 733 *HERZLICH TUT MICH VERLANGEN*
Where true charity and love abide ELW 653 *UBI CARITAS*

Offering

Goodness is stronger than evil ELW 721
When we are living ELW 639, LLC 462

Communion

Where charity and love prevail ELW 359, LBW 126, TFF 84
I come with joy ELW 482
Ubi caritas et amor ELW 642, WOV 665

Sending

Praise the Lord, rise up rejoicing ELW 544, LBW 196
Go, my children, with my blessing ELW 543, TFF 161, WOV 721

Additional Assembly Songs

O God, empower us LBW 422
If we live SP 16
Si tú puedes, cántalo LLC 596
⊕ Shaha, Bart. "Lord, We Did Not Live Up to Your Teachings" from *Sound the Bamboo*. U. GIA G-6830.
⊕ South African traditional. "Sanna, sannanina" from *Global Songs 2*. SATB. AFP 9780800656744.
☼ Daugherty, Derri/Steve Hindalong/Andrew Peterson West. "The Gathering" from CCLI.
☼ Hall, Mark/Matthew West. "City on a Hill" from CCLI.
☼ Haseltine, Dan/Charlie Lowell/Stephen Mason/Matt Odmark. "Shelter" from CCLI.
☼ Percival, Philip. "Freedom" from CCLI.
☼ Rutledge, Brett/Brian Yakaboski. "Perfect Redemption" from CCLI.
☼ West, Matthew. "Forgiveness" from CCLI.

Music for the Day
Choral

Beck, John Ness. "Canticle of Praise." SATB div, kybd. PRE 312-40588.
Berthier, Jacques. "Ubi caritas." SATB, kybd, opt insts. GIA G-2586.
Cherubini, Luigi/arr. Austin Lovelace. "Like as a Father." U or 2 pt or SAB, pno. CG CGA156.
P ♫ Johnson, Ralph M. "Our Father, We Have Wandered." SATB, opt assembly, pno, ob or cl. AFP 9781451492576.

Children's Choir

Brokering, Lois. "What Does It Mean to Follow Jesus?" from *LifeSongs*. U, pno. AFP 9780806642703.
P Horman, John D. "Miriam's Song" from *Sing the Stories of God's People*. U, kybd. AFP 9781451460537.
Lindh, Jodi W. "Ready to Forgive." U/2 pt, pno, fl. CG CGA1145.

Keyboard / Instrumental

P ♫ Biery, Marilyn. "Where True Charity and Love Are Found" (Ubi caritas) from *Augsburg Organ Library: Lent*. Org. AFP 9780800658977.
Hassell, Michael. "Go, My Children, with My Blessing" (Ar hyd y nos) from *Folkways: Hymn Arrangements for Solo Instrument and Piano*. Inst, pno. AFP 9780800656904.

⊕ = global song   ♫ = relates to hymn of the day   + = semicontinuous psalm
☼ = praise song   P = available in Prelude Music Planner

P ♫ Sowash, Bradley. "Our Father, We Have Wandered" (Herzlich tut mich verlangen) from *Great German Hymns Arranged in Contemporary Styles*. Pno. AFP 9780800637446.

♫ Visser, Larry. "Where True Charity and Love Abide" (Ubi caritas) from *Paraphrases on Four Gregorian Themes for Organ*. Org. Wayne Leupold WL600091.

Handbell

P Larson, Lloyd. "I Then Shall Live." 3-5 oct, L2+, HOP 2631. Opt SATB vcs, opt pno, opt org, HOP C5342. Opt SAB vcs, opt pno, opt org, HOP C5800.

♫ McMichael, Catherine. "Contemplation on 'Ubi caritas.'" 3-6 oct hb, opt 3 oct hc, L3+. AGEHR AG36036.

♫ Roberts, Philip. "Sacred Harp Suite." 5 oct, L2+. GIA G-6448.

Sunday, September 17
Hildegard, Abbess of Bingen, died 1179

Hildegard lived virtually her entire life in convents, yet was widely influential within the church. After an uneventful time as a nun, she was chosen as abbess of her community. She reformed her community as well as other convents. Around the same time, she began having visions and compiled them, as instructed, in a book she called *Scivias*. Hildegard's importance went beyond mysticism. She advised and reproved kings and popes, wrote poems and hymns, and produced treatises in medicine, theology, and natural history. She was also a musician and an artist.

Monday, September 18
Dag Hammarskjöld, renewer of society, died 1961

Dag Hammarskjöld (HAH-mar-sheld) was a Swedish diplomat and humanitarian who served as secretary general of the United Nations. He was killed in a plane crash on this day in 1961, in what is now Zambia, while he was on his way to negotiate a cease-fire between the United Nations and the Katanga forces. For years Hammarskjöld had kept a private journal, and it was not until that journal was published as *Markings* that the depth of his Christian faith was known. The book revealed that his life was a combination of diplomatic service and personal spirituality, and of contemplation on the meaning of Christ in his life and action in the world.

Thursday, September 21
Matthew, Apostle and Evangelist

Matthew ("Levi" in the gospels of Mark and Luke) was a tax collector for the Roman government in Capernaum. Tax collectors were distrusted because they were dishonest and worked as agents for a foreign ruler, the occupying Romans. In the gospels, tax collectors are mentioned as sinful and despised outcasts, but it was these outcasts to whom Jesus showed his love. Matthew's name means "gift of the Lord." Since the second century, tradition has attributed the first gospel to him.

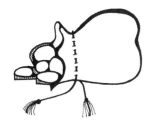

September 24, 2017
Time after Pentecost — Lectionary 25

Matthew narrates one of Jesus' controversial parables, in which Jesus says the reign of God is like workers who get paid the same no matter when they start. When God changes his mind about punishing Nineveh for their evil ways, Jonah is angry. Yet God is gracious and merciful, abounding in steadfast love. In baptism we receive the grace of God that is freely given to all. As Luther wrote, in the presence of God's mercy we are all beggars.

Prayer of the Day

Almighty and eternal God, you show perpetual lovingkindness to us your servants. Because we cannot rely on our own abilities, grant us your merciful judgment, and train us to embody the generosity of your Son, Jesus Christ, our Savior and Lord.

Gospel Acclamation

Alleluia. Open our ¹ hearts, O Lord,* to give heed to what is said ¹ by your Son. *Alleluia.*

Readings and Psalm
Jonah 3:10—4:11

After Jonah's short sermon in 3:4, the Ninevites all repented and God decided to spare the city. Jonah objected to this and became even more angry when God ordered a worm to destroy a plant that was providing shade. The book ends with a question that challenges any who are not ready to forgive: You, Jonah, are all worked up about a bush, but should not I be concerned about a hundred and twenty thousand Ninevites who do not know the difference between their right and left hands?

Psalm 145:1-8

The LORD is slow to anger and abounding in steadfast love. (Ps. 145:8)

Philippians 1:21-30

Paul writes to the Philippians from prison. Though he is uncertain about the outcome of his imprisonment, he is committed to the ministry of the gospel and calls on the Philippians to live lives that reflect and enhance the gospel mission.

Matthew 20:1-16

Jesus tells a parable about God's generosity, challenging the common assumption that God rewards people according to what they have earned or deserve.

Semicontinuous reading and psalm
Exodus 16:2-15

Faced with hunger in the wilderness, the Israelites longed for life back in Egypt and said they wished the exodus had never happened. Then God miraculously and graciously gave them quails and manna to eat.

Psalm 105:1-6, 37-45

Make known the deeds of the LORD among the peoples. Hallelujah! (Ps. 105:1, 45)

Preface   Sundays

Color   Green

Prayers of Intercession

The prayers are prepared locally for each occasion. The following examples may be adapted or used as appropriate.

Open to the gifts of the Holy Spirit, we pray for the church, the world, and all of God's creation.

A brief silence.

Let us pray for the church and its ministry. Unite us in one Spirit, striving side by side with one mind for the faith of the gospel. Lord, in your mercy,

hear our prayer.

God who stretched the spangled heavens, we thank and praise you for the gift of the sun, moon, stars, mountains, valleys, grasslands, and deserts. Lord, in your mercy,

hear our prayer.

God of great mercy and love, you show faithfulness and kindness to the world every day. Guard those who suffer because of dishonest policies, corrupt government, or unfair labor practices. Lord, in your mercy,

hear our prayer.

God, you provide for all our needs. We pray for those who are homeless, jobless, or hopeless. We pray for those who are forgotten, ignored, or isolated. We pray for all in any need (*especially*). Lord, in your mercy,

hear our prayer.

We pray for our congregation and our neighborhood. Accompany us wherever we are on our journey of faith. Give us joy in the present and hope for the future. Lord, in your mercy,

hear our prayer.

Here other intercessions may be offered.

God of endings and beginnings, we remember before you all the faithful departed (*especially*). Comfort those who mourn. Lord, in your mercy,

hear our prayer.

Into your hands, gracious God, we commend all for whom we pray, trusting the power of Christ and the gifts of the Spirit. **Amen.**

Images in the Readings

The **vineyard** is a common biblical metaphor that designates the religious community. In biblical times, wine was not only usually safer to drink than water, but it also symbolized the shared joy of the community. Its production relies on both the blessing of the Creator and the long-term joint efforts of growers and vintners, and its alcohol transforms our very bodies. Yet many congregations are quite stingy with the cup.

The Jonah story provides many allegorical images: **Nineveh** is the powerful enemy; **Tarshish** is for Jonah the farthest destination in the opposite direction from Nineveh, across the Mediterranean Sea; the **bush** suggests personal comfort; the **worm** suggests God's correction to our selfishness; the **wind** is the breath of God; **Jonah** himself is a comic depiction of our very selves and of the church when we live out of typical human emotions. We too often do not know our right from our left hand. It is a great story.

The **spirit** of the risen Christ will bring us into the unity expressive of a mutually forgiving community.

Ideas for the Day

- In the NFL, the last draft pick is referred to as "Mr. Irrelevant." The last pick is not expected to make a team. The day laborers in this text were lower on the socioeconomic scale, unskilled but willing to work. They had to wait to see if they would be chosen, like those in the NFL draft. The landowner in this text shows his compassion for the last hired; he allows them to be paid first and at the same rate as everyone else. Being last in this case was not bad at all.

- The cries of those who worked in the vineyard all day are sometimes echoed in our churches. We compare: "I have served or been a member longer, so my value is greater." We covet: "I want or deserve what someone else has." We complain: "They don't deserve that because I did more." We criticize: "They were chosen last, so they are not as good as me anyway." In God's vineyard, these cries are covered over by God's grace. God lavishes us with mercy, forgiveness, and eternal life. Why would we still want to compare, covet, complain, or criticize?

- Grace comes from God. We want grace for ourselves, but we do not always want to give it to others or see others get it at what we believe to be our expense. Grace is a gift that costs everything to the giver and nothing to the receiver. We should be willing to give grace as Jesus did. He flips the established order when he says: "So the last will be first, and the first will be last" (Matt. 20:16). Jesus is teaching that first and last do not matter in the kingdom of God. Finishing first is not a requirement or an advantage. Who

do we judge to be undeserving of God's grace based on where they finish in life? How can we learn to truly share God's grace freely?

Connections with the Liturgy

The last sentence of the book of Jonah indicates that God cares also for the animals. Following the outline of the intercessions in *Evangelical Lutheran Worship*, we pray every Sunday for the well-being of creation. Much of that well-being is our responsibility, but we pray also for God's continuing creative power over the earth, for divine mercy granted to "many animals."

Let the Children Come

Once again, our readings bring us to how we relate to one another in a fair and just way. Children, especially older elementary-aged children, are fascinated with fairness. Is the cake sliced equally? Who got to pick the last bedtime story? Today it seems we hear in both the reading from Jonah and the gospel, "Because I'm God, that's why." God chooses to shower abundant grace and mercy on all creation, and sometimes we don't like it. Since both of these readings have such an animated narrative, plan for attentive readers or storytellers to present these texts so that the words might really come alive in the assembly.

Assembly Song
Gathering

When morning gilds the skies ELW 853, LBW 545/546
Rise up, O saints of God! ELW 669, LBW 383
Great God, your love has called us ELW 358, WOV 666

Psalmody and Acclamations

Gelineau, Joseph. "Psalm 145" from ACYG.
Whitney, Rae E. "O My God and King and Savior" (Holy Manna) from PAS 145F.
+ Woehr, Roland. "Psalm 105" from PSCY.
(GA) Iona Community (Scotland). "Alleluia 1" from *Come, All You People: Shorter Songs for Worship*. U/SATB. GIA G-4391. Use ELW psalm tone 7 in F major with proper verse for Lectionary 25.

Hymn of the Day

Salvation unto us has come ELW 590, LBW 297 *ES IST DAS HEIL*
As saints of old ELW 695, LBW 404 *FOREST GREEN*
All who love and serve your city ELW 724 *NEW ORLEANS*
   LBW 436 *BIRABUS*

Offering

Give Me Jesus ELW 770, WOV 777, TFF 165
Will you let me be your servant ELW 659

⊕ = global song   ♫ = relates to hymn of the day   + = semicontinuous psalm
☼ = praise song   P = available in Prelude Music Planner

Communion

There's a wideness in God's mercy   ELW 587/588, LBW 290

Lord of all hopefulness   ELW 765, LBW 469

All who love and serve your city   ELW 724, LBW 436

Sending

Voices raised to you   ELW 845

Lord of light   ELW 688, LBW 405

Additional Assembly Songs

In the Lord I'll be ever thankful   SP 18

God recycles, reconciles us   ASG 13

Welcome Table   TFF 263

- Gibson, Colin A. "For the Man and for the Woman" from *Sound the Bamboo*. U. GIA G-6830.
- South African traditional. "Hamba nathi/Come, Walk with Us" from *Global Songs 2*. SATB. AFP 9780800656744.
- Carswell, Eddie/Sarah Hart/Russ Lee. "The Reason" from CCLI.
- Cook, Jay. "Rise" from CCLI.
- Kirkland, Eddie/Steve Fee. "Kings and Queens" from CCLI.
- Robinson, Noel. "Outrageous Love" from CCLI.
- Sczebel, Joel/Pat Sczebel. "Generous King" from CCLI.
- Story, Laura/Ian Morgan Cron/Cindy Morgan. "O Love of God" from CCLI.

Music for the Day
Choral

- Bach, J. S. "Salvation unto Us Has Come" from *Bach for All Seasons*. SATB, opt kybd. AFP 9780800658540.
- Distler, Hugo. "Salvation unto Us Has Come" from *Chantry Choirbook*. SATB. AFP 9780800657772.
- Hobby, Robert A. "Strengthen for Service." 2 pt mxd, opt assembly, org. AFP 9780800678265.
- Kidwell, Sally. "There's a Wideness in God's Mercy." SATB, pno. AFP 9781451451696.

Children's Choir

Dengler, Lee. "Sing Out with Gladness." U/2 pt, pno, opt perc. SHW HL 35029813.

- Horman, John D. "Jonah" from *Sing the Stories of God's People*. U, kybd. AFP 9781451460537.
- Patterson, Mark. "Sing for Joy, Sing Together." U/2 pt, pno, opt fl, fc. CG CGA1352.

Keyboard / Instrumental

- Carter, John. "Give Me Jesus" (Give Me Jesus) from *Shall We Gather: Settings for Four-Hand Piano*. Pno (4 hand). HOP 8569.
- Lenz, Charles L. "All Who Love and Serve Your City" (New Orleans) from *All Are Welcome: Hymn Variations for Organ*. Org. AFP 9781451424164.

- Raabe, Nancy. "There's a Wideness in God's Mercy" (St. Helena) from *Grace and Peace, vol. 6: Songs of Heaven*. Pno. AFP 9781451479621.
- Walcha, Helmut (1907–1991). "Salvation unto Us Has Come" (Es ist das Heil) from *Chorale Preludes*, vol. 1. Org. PET EP4850.

Handbell

- Bettcher, Peggy. "Wonderful, Merciful Savior" from *Easy to Ring Praise & Worship VII*. 2-3 oct, L2, HOP 2687. 3-5 oct, L2, HOP 2670.
- Krug, Jason W. "Steadfast Assurance." 3 or 5 oct hb, opt 2 oct hc, L3-. BP HB429.
- Waugh, Timothy. "Shades of 'Forest Green.'" 3-5 oct hb, opt fc, L3. Ring Out! Press RO2115.

Friday, September 29
Michael and All Angels

On this festival day the church ponders the richness and variety of God's created order and the limits of human knowledge of it. The scriptures speak of angels (the word means "messengers") who worship God in heaven, and in both testaments angels speak for God on earth. They are remembered most vividly as they appear to the shepherds and announce the birth of the Savior. Michael is an angel whose name appears in Daniel as the heavenly being who leads the faithful dead to God's throne on the day of resurrection. In Revelation, Michael fights in a cosmic battle against Satan.

Saturday, September 30
Jerome, translator, teacher, died 420

Jerome is remembered as a biblical scholar and translator. Rather than choosing classical Latin as the basis of his work, he translated the scriptures into the Latin that was spoken and written by the majority of the persons in his day. His translation is known as the Vulgate, from the Latin word for *common*. While Jerome is remembered as a saint, he could be anything but saintly. He was well known for his short temper and his arrogance, although he was also quick to admit to his personal faults. Thanks to the work of Jerome, many people received the word in their own language and lived lives of faith and service to those in need.

October 1, 2017
Time after Pentecost — Lectionary 26

Jesus' parable about two sons who don't do what they say reveals surprises in the reign of God, such as prostitutes and tax collectors going before others into God's kingdom. In the reading from Ezekiel the people question whether the ways of the Lord are unfair; instead they are to repent and turn to the Lord. Paul urges us to look to Christ as a model of humility, looking to the interests of others above our own. Nourished by the broken bread and shared cup, we offer our lives for the sake of our needy world.

Prayer of the Day

God of love, giver of life, you know our frailties and failings. Give us your grace to overcome them, keep us from those things that harm us, and guide us in the way of salvation, through Jesus Christ, our Savior and Lord.

Gospel Acclamation

Alleluia. My sheep hear my voice, | says the Lord;* I know them and they | follow me. *Alleluia.* (John 10:27)

Readings and Psalm

Ezekiel 18:1-4, 25-32

Ezekiel challenges those who think they cannot change because of what their parents were and did, or who think they cannot turn from their wicked ways. God insistently invites people to turn and live.

Psalm 25:1-9

Remember, O Lord, your compassion and love. (Ps. 25:6)

Philippians 2:1-13

As part of a call for harmony rather than self-seeking, Paul uses a very early Christian hymn that extols the selflessness of Christ in his obedient death on the cross. Christ's selfless perspective is to be the essential perspective we share as the foundation for Christian accord.

Matthew 21:23-32

After driving the moneychangers out of the temple (21:12), Jesus begins teaching there. His authority is questioned by the religious leaders, who are supposed to be in charge of the temple.

Semicontinuous reading and psalm

Exodus 17:1-7

Because the thirsty Israelites quarreled with Moses and put the Lord to the test, Moses cried out in desperation to the Lord. Nevertheless, the Lord commanded Moses to strike the rock to provide water for the people. The doubt-filled question—"Is the Lord among us or not?"—received a dramatic and positive answer.

Psalm 78:1-4, 12-16

We will recount to generations to come the power of the Lord. (Ps. 78:4)

Preface Sundays

Color Green

Prayers of Intercession

The prayers are prepared locally for each occasion. The following examples may be adapted or used as appropriate.

Open to the gifts of the Holy Spirit, we pray for the church, the world, and all of God's creation.

A brief silence.

We pray for the mission of the gospel. Unite your church in its proclamation and witness. Let the same mind be in us that is in Christ Jesus. Hear us, O God.

Your mercy is great.

Creator God, you provide daily for our nourishment. Bless fields and orchards, oceans and lakes, birds and animals, insects and fish. Sustain those who harvest your life-sustaining bounty. Help us share the gifts you have freely given. Hear us, O God.

Your mercy is great.

God of the nations, give all your people the mind of Christ. Guide national and international leaders to advocate for policies that look to the interests of the most vulnerable. Humble us when we question your mercy toward those who are different from us. Hear us, O God.

Your mercy is great.

Self-emptying God, stir up compassion for those in need. Send your Spirit to those who are in crisis, troubled, weary, or discouraged. (*We pray especially for . . .*) Hear us, O God.

Your mercy is great.

We pray for our congregation and community. Guide our deliberations over difficult decisions. Strengthen our commitment to our ministries (*here specific congregational ministries may be named*). Hear us, O God.

Your mercy is great.

Here other intercessions may be offered.

Gracious God, we give thanks for the saints whose tongues confessed Jesus Christ as Lord. Keep us confident in your promises until we join them in endless praise. Hear us, O God.
Your mercy is great.
Into your hands, gracious God, we commend all for whom we pray, trusting the power of Christ and the gifts of the Spirit.
Amen.

Images in the Readings

The parable speaks of a good and a bad **son**. Christianity lauds yet another son, the "only Son," who both answers yes and does the will of God. In the biblical worldview, a son is not understood as an independent agent but is an extension of the father, owing the father everything. As well, according to the biological understanding of the time, it was the sperm that conveyed full humanity to the fetus. This sense of the child's connection with the parent is evident also in the reading from Ezekiel. Our culture thinks differently.

We are very distant from the first century's horror at the image of the **cross**. The Roman government reserved this method of death by torture for the lowest criminals, and in Deuteronomy 21:22-23, even God is said to curse anyone executed by hanging on a tree. In the fourth century, the emperor Constantine outlawed crucifixion as a mode of execution, and since then jewels and gold, art and design have made of the cross an often beauteous sign of veneration. Some scholars suggest that "even death on a cross" is a Pauline interpolation into the hymn. The Good Friday liturgy invites people to come forward to a full-sized rough-hewn cross and bend the knee before it in praise of Jesus.

Ideas for the Day

- Today's gospel highlights questions: the religious leaders', Jesus', and ours. The Reformation tradition began with questions, propositions, and challenges. Begin the sermon with teaser questions, providing a framework for the reading. Print the questions in the worship folder or project them onto a screen or wall. Invite worshipers to silently ponder these questions following the sermon or during communion. In what ways has Christianity embraced questions? In what ways have we attempted to stop them from being asked?

- Jesus' question to the chief priests and elders as well as the subsequent parable invites us to consider how we participate in God's work in this world. What is "from heaven" (Matt. 21:25)? The ELCA's own tagline, "God's work. Our hands," makes a claim on our actions falling in line with God's will. Discussing how our words and actions are congruous or incongruous with God's desire for the world would be fruitful today. Does God need us for God's work to be done? Does God act without us or despite us in the world, and if so, how and what does that mean for our

work? Writer Ann Lamott offers this bit of wisdom: "If there is a God, and most days I do think there is, He or She does not need us to bring hope and new life back into our lives, but keeps letting us help" (*Stitches* [New York: Riverhead, 2013], 60-61).

- What makes something or someone trustworthy? Jesus' trustworthiness is brought into question by the religious leaders. In our world we have information flying at us constantly through television, internet, and social media. How do we learn what to trust or not to trust? Our own Reformation heritage of *sola scriptura*, *sola fide*, and *sola gratia* (scripture alone, faith alone, grace alone) provides a plumb line for discerning what is authoritative and trustworthy when it comes to faith. In the 500th anniversary year of the Reformation, resurrecting these terms and presenting them to the congregation to discuss and ponder would bring history, and the scriptures, alive and to the forefront. How is scripture authoritative in our tradition, and in our lives?

Connections with the Liturgy

Today's second reading includes the central Christian affirmation that Jesus is Lord. That is, we grant to Jesus the same title that originally referred to God. In greeting one another with the peace of "the Lord" and in the opening dialogue of Holy Communion—"The Lord be with you" —"the Lord" is the risen Christ, the one who suffered death on a cross and has been exalted in the resurrection. The classic hymn of praise concludes by referring to the Trinity, "Jesus Christ, with the Holy Spirit, in the glory of God the Father," as Lord.

Let the Children Come

There are no more pressing justice issues in a family than those between siblings—at least it seems to be so in the heat of the moment. Each person lays claim to their own authority: oldest, first, curly hair—the list goes on. The issues of justice and fairness will play out for children in a larger community too: who is sitting by the pastor, who gets there first, who most reliably shows up, who always has the "right" answers, whose parent heads that committee. How does living and being in your community model the kingdom of God? How is access granted freely?

Assembly Song
Gathering

God is here! ELW 526, WOV 719
Awake, my soul, and with the sun ELW 557, LBW 269
The trumpets sound, the angels sing ELW 531, W&P 139

Psalmody and Acclamations

Mathis, William H. Refrain for "Psalm 25" from *After the Prelude: Year A*. U/cant, hb. CG CGB658 (digital version), CGB659 (printed version). Use with ELW psalm tone 6 or 7 (in C).

Parker, Val. "Psalm 25: To You, O Lord, I Lift My Soul." SATB, assembly, kybd, gtr. OCP 21060.

+ Nicholson, Paul. "Psalm 78," Refrain 1, from PSCY.

(GA) Iona Community (Scotland). "Alleluia 1" from *Come, All You People: Shorter Songs for Worship*. U/SATB. GIA G-4391. Use ELW psalm tone 7 in F major with proper verse for Lectionary 26.

Hymn of the Day

Lord, keep us steadfast in your word ELW 517, LBW 230
ERHALT UNS, HERR

At the name of Jesus ELW 416, LBW 179 *KING'S WESTON*

Strengthen for service, Lord ELW 497 *BUCKHURST RUN*

Offering

O blessed spring ELW 447, WOV 695

Lord, whose love in humble service ELW 712, LBW 423

Communion

Take, oh, take me as I am ELW 814

In the singing ELW 466

O Master, let me walk with you ELW 818, LBW 492

Sending

The Lord now sends us forth ELW 538, LLC 415

What God ordains is good indeed ELW 776, LBW 446

Additional Assembly Songs

Now we offer WOV 761, TFF 129

Jesus, name above all names TFF 268

Who will set us free? SP 44

⊕ African American traditional. "Guide My Feet" from *Pave the Way: Global Songs 3*. U. AFP 9780800676896.

⊕ South African traditional. "Sizohamba naye/We Will Go with God" from *Global Songs 2*. SATB. AFP 9780800656744.

☼ Canedo, Ken. "Jesus Christ Is Lord" from *Spirit and Song*, vol. 2. OCP.

☼ Coleman Jeff/Joel Engle. "Lord of All" from CCLI.

☼ Egan, John. "Overcome" from CCLI.

☼ Evans, Sam/Henry Seeley. "Send Me" from CCLI.

☼ Ligertwood, Brooke. "None but Jesus" from CCLI.

☼ Riddle, Jeremy. "My Love for You" from CCLI.

Music for the Day
Choral

ᴾ♫ Hobby, Robert A. "Strengthen for Service." 2 pt mxd, opt assembly, org. AFP 9780800678265.

ᴾ Patterson, Mark. "Show Me Thy Ways." U or 2 pt, kybd. AFP 9780800676230.

ᴾ Pelz, Walter L. "Show Me Thy Ways." SATB, gtr, ob or fl. AFP 9780800645427.

ᴾ Pelz, Walter L. "Show Me Thy Ways" from *The Augsburg Choirbook*. SATB, gtr, ob or fl. AFP 9780800656782.

ᴾ Anerio, Giovanni Francesco. "Christ Humbled Himself" from *Augsburg Motet Book*. SATB, opt kybd. AFP 9781451423709.

Children's Choir

Barta, Daniel. "Lead Me in Your Truth." 2 pt, pno. CG CGA880.

Patterson, Mark. "Show Me Thy Ways." U, kybd. AFP 9780800676230.

Praetorius, Michael, adapt. "God Gave to Me a Life to Live" from *LifeSongs*. U, kybd. AFP 9780806642703.

Keyboard / Instrumental

Hassell, Michael. "O Master, Let Me Walk with You" (Maryton) from *Traveling Tunes: Hymn Arrangements for Solo Instrument and Piano*. Inst, pno. AFP 9780800656195.

ᴾ♫ Organ, Anne Krentz. "Lord, Keep Us Steadfast in Your Word" (Erhalt uns, Herr) from *Reflections on Hymn Tunes for the Fall Festivals*. Pno. AFP 9780800663834.

♫ Pelz, Walter L. "Lord, Keep Us Steadfast in Your Word" (Erhalt uns, Herr) from *Triptych on Lord, Keep Us Steadfast in Your Word*. Org. MSM 10-808.

ᴾ♫ Rübsam, Wolfgang. "Strengthen for Service, Lord" (Buckhurst Run) from *Fourteen Chorale Preludes: A Guide to Liturgical Improvisation*. Org. AFP 9780806698038.

Handbell

♫ Eithun, Sandra. "Lord, Keep Us Steadfast in Thy Word." 3-5 oct, L2+. CPH 97-7116.

ᴾ Geschke, Susan. "This Glorious Day." 2-3 oct, L2-. HOP 2623.

♫ Gramann, Fred. "Fantasy on 'King's Weston' (At the Name of Jesus)." 3-6 oct, L5. HOP 1671.

Wednesday, October 4

Francis of Assisi, renewer of the church, died 1226

Francis was the son of a wealthy cloth merchant. In a public confrontation with his father, he renounced his wealth and future inheritance and devoted himself to serving the poor. Francis described this act as being "wedded to Lady Poverty." Under his leadership the Order of Friars Minor (Franciscans)

⊕ = global song   ♫ = relates to hymn of the day   + = semicontinuous psalm
☼ = praise song   ᴾ = available in Prelude Music Planner

was formed, and they took literally Jesus' words to his disciples that they should take nothing on their journey and receive no payment for their work. Their task in preaching was to "use words if necessary." Francis had a spirit of gladness and gratitude for all of God's creation. This commemoration has been a traditional time to bless pets and animals, creatures Francis called his brothers and sisters. A prayer and a hymn attributed to St. Francis are included in *Evangelical Lutheran Worship* (p. 87, #835).

Wednesday, October 4
Theodor Fliedner, renewer of society, died 1864

Fliedner's (FLEED-ner) work was instrumental in the revival of the ministry of deaconesses among Lutherans. While a pastor in Kaiserswerth, Germany, he also ministered to prisoners in Düsseldorf. Through his ministry to prisoners, he came in contact with Moravian deaconesses, and it was through this Moravian influence that he was convinced that the ministry of deaconesses had a place among Lutherans. His work and writing encouraged women to care for those who were sick, poor, or imprisoned. Fliedner's deaconess motherhouse in Kaiserswerth inspired Lutherans all over the world to commission deaconesses to serve in parishes, schools, prisons, and hospitals.

Friday, October 6
William Tyndale, translator, martyr, died 1536

William Tyndale was ordained in 1521, and his life's desire was to translate the scriptures into English. When his plan met opposition from King Henry VIII, Tyndale fled to Germany, where he traveled from city to city, living in poverty and constant danger. He was able to produce a New Testament in 1525. Nine years later he revised it and began work on the Old Testament, which he was unable to complete. He was captured, tried for heresy, and burned at the stake. Miles Coverdale completed Tyndale's work, and the Tyndale-Coverdale version was published as the "Matthew Bible" in 1537. For nearly four centuries the style of this translation has influenced English versions of the Bible such as the King James (Authorized Version) and the New Revised Standard Version.

Saturday, October 7
Henry Melchior Muhlenberg, pastor in North America, died 1787

Muhlenberg (MYOO-len-berg) was prominent in setting the course for Lutheranism in North America. He helped Lutheran churches make the transition from the state churches of Europe to a new identity on American soil. Among other things, he established the first Lutheran synod in America and developed an American Lutheran liturgy. His liturgical principles became the basis for the Common Service of 1888, used in many North American service books for a majority of the past century. That Muhlenberg and his work are remembered today was anticipated at his death. The inscription on his grave reads, in Latin, "Who and what he was, future ages will know without a stone."

October 8, 2017
Time after Pentecost — Lectionary 27

In today's gospel reading, Jesus tells a parable of the vineyard, an image of Israel, the prophets' mission, and Christ's death. For Christians, the vineyard also speaks of God's love poured out in the blood of Christ, given to us for the forgiveness of sin. Grafted onto Christ the vine at baptism, we are nourished with wine and bread, that we may share Christ's sufferings and know the power of his resurrection.

Prayer of the Day

Beloved God, from you come all things that are good. Lead us by the inspiration of your Spirit to know those things that are right, and by your merciful guidance, help us to do them, through Jesus Christ, our Savior and Lord.

Gospel Acclamation

Alleluia. Jesus says, I chose you and ap- | pointed you* to go and bear fruit | that will last. *Alleluia.* (John 15:16)

Readings and Psalm

Isaiah 5:1-7

The prophet sings a sad, parable-like love song about the relationship between God and Israel. In this song Israel is compared to a promising vineyard. Despite God's loving care, the vineyard that is Israel has brought forth "wild grapes" of injustice and distress, when fine grapes of justice and righteousness were expected.

Psalm 80:7-15

Look down from heaven, O God; behold and tend this vine. (Ps. 80:14, 15)

Philippians 3:4b-14

Paul reviews some of his supposed credentials, which no longer have any bearing in comparison to the right relationship he has been given through the death of Christ. The power of Christ's resurrection motivates him to press on toward the ultimate goal, eternal life with Christ.

Matthew 21:33-46

Jesus tells a parable to the religious leaders who are plotting his death, revealing that their plans will, ironically, bring about the fulfillment of scripture.

Semicontinuous reading and psalm

Exodus 20:1-4, 7-9, 12-20

The God of the Exodus graciously gave Israel the Ten Commandments. Primarily stated as negative imperatives, the Ten Commandments forbid gross sins such as murder, adultery, theft, and perjury. In most of life they grant Israel freedom to live righteously, with maximum love for God and neighbor.

Psalm 19

The statutes of the LORD are just and rejoice the heart. (Ps. 19:8)

Preface   Sundays

Color   Green

Prayers of Intercession

The prayers are prepared locally for each occasion. The following examples may be adapted or used as appropriate.

Open to the gifts of the Holy Spirit, we pray for the church, the world, and all of God's creation.

A brief silence.

Restore what is broken in your church, loving God. Heal divisions among Christian communities, give courage to leaders facing hardship, and open our ears to the prophets' cries among us. Hear us, O God.

Your mercy is great.

Restore what is broken in creation, gracious God. Revive farmlands and vineyards, protect waters needed by all living things, and move us to care for this earthly home. Hear us, O God.

Your mercy is great.

Restore what is broken in our world, mighty God. Quell the rush to violence between peoples and nations. Break down dividing walls and promote growth for the sake of the common good. Hear us, O God.

Your mercy is great.

Restore our broken bodies, O God. We pray for those suffering any loss: the grieving, those who have lost homes or property, the imprisoned, those neglected or abandoned, and the sick (*especially*). Hear us, O God.

Your mercy is great.

Restore our faith in you, saving God. We pray for Bible study and small group leaders, Sunday school teachers, musicians, devotion writers, and for all whose work nurtures our faith. Hear us, O God.

Your mercy is great.

Here other intercessions may be offered.

We remember the saints whose devotion proclaimed your saving help. In company with them, root us firmly in your everlasting love. Hear us, O God.

Your mercy is great.
Into your hands, gracious God, we commend all for whom we pray, trusting the power of Christ and the gifts of the Spirit. **Amen.**

Images in the Readings

The importance of wine in the diet of biblical societies is evident in the Bible's continual use of the **vineyard** as an image of the people. Wine, suggesting the goodness of communal participation, serves as a corrective to more recent individualist interpretations of Christian faith. Vineyards grow from age-old roots and require dedicated tending. God owns the vineyard: we are only renters; we need to collaborate with one another to produce good wine.

The passage in the Psalms about the rejected stone becoming the **cornerstone** caught on in Christianity. In Ephesians 2:20 Paul calls Christ Jesus the cornerstone of the household of God; in Acts 4:11 Luke uses the cornerstone as a metaphor for Christ, as does the author of 1 Peter in 2:7. It is yet another biblical image about the reversal of values that God intends. The idea is that a huge stone at the foundation is not merely a decorative marker but actually supports the weight of the building above.

Ideas for the Day

- Wine and grape juice are elements of grace at God's table and aren't meant to be hoarded as the workers in the vineyard do in today's gospel. At the table we approach God's vineyard and are embraced, not rejected. Lift up the wine at today's eucharist, connecting it directly with the vineyard in the gospel and the Isaiah text. Perhaps surprise the congregation by using a different wine in color or origin, providing a different experience of God's grace in light of a difficult parable.
- Jesus' parable is tough news. The religious leaders understand Jesus to be referencing them and, upon hearing it, desire Jesus' arrest. How do we deal with revelatory news that may be difficult, especially news we'd rather not hear? Today's readings are ripe for inviting people to look honestly at themselves, systemic violence (the parable has plenty of violence), hard conversations, and the like. Invite honest responses somewhere in the service. For example, you might provide a large mirror somewhere in the worship space and invite people to write honest revelations about themselves directly onto the mirror with oil crayons. The point is not to "feel bad" but rather to "see honestly."
- The vineyards in Israel and Palestine are still scenes of violence even today. As Jewish and Palestinian farmers argue over land rights, questions loom large over who can make rightful claims to this land. An internet search for "West Bank grapes of wrath" will take you to an article from *The Telegraph* (March 24, 2013) that describes this

reality. The ELCA's work through its campaign Peace Not Walls and its partnership with the Evangelical Lutheran Church in Jordan and the Holy Land is attempting to put a face on the parts of the world many Westerners encounter only in scripture and through the news. Today is a good day to highlight the church's peace and justice efforts so that no more killing happens in the vineyards of Israel and Palestine, or anywhere.

Connections with the Liturgy

The poetic litany of Good Friday, called the Solemn Reproaches, newly adapted for our century, includes the refrain "What more could I have done for you?" echoing Isaiah 5:4, and in its fourth stanza, we refer to the church as the vineyard that brings forth bitter fruit.

Let the Children Come

There was a school that encouraged the children to learn many different ways. The children would grow wheat and grapes in their school garden. They would grind the wheat into flour and bake it into bread; they would ferment the grape juice into wine. They carried their produce through the nave to the altar and then celebrated their first communion. (This sounds idealized, but it was a custom of Italian Montessori schools in the early twentieth century!) How does our connection to the earth, garden, and harvest show up in worship? How can you invite children into that relationship?

Assembly Song
Gathering

Lord our God, with praise we come ELW 730
All creatures, worship God most high! ELW 835, LBW 527
Lord Christ, when first you came to earth ELW 727, LBW 421

Psalmody and Acclamations

Bruxvoort Colligan, Richard. "Turn and Restore Us" (Psalm 80)" from *Shout for Joy*. AFP 9780806698632.
Wold, Wayne L. "Psalm 80," Refrain 2, from PSCY.
+ Cool, Jayne Southwick. "Psalm 19" from *ChildrenSing Psalms*. U, kybd. AFP 9780800663872.
(GA) Iona Community (Scotland). "Alleluia 1" from *Come, All You People: Shorter Songs for Worship*. U/SATB. GIA G-4391. Use ELW psalm tone 7 in F major with proper verse for Lectionary 27.

Hymn of the Day

There in God's garden ELW 342, WOV 668 *SHADES MOUNTAIN*
God the sculptor of the mountains ELW 736, TFF 222 *JENNINGS-HOUSTON*
My song is love unknown ELW 343, WOV 661 *LOVE UNKNOWN* LBW 94 *RHOSYMEDRE*

+ = semicontinuous psalm

Offering

You are holy   ELW 525
Jesus loves me!   ELW 595, TFF 249

Communion

Thine the amen   ELW 826, WOV 801
My Lord of light   ELW 832, WOV 796
How clear is our vocation, Lord   ELW 580

Sending

When I survey the wondrous cross   ELW 803, LBW 482, TFF 79
If you but trust in God to guide you   ELW 769, LBW 453

Additional Assembly Songs

Make me a channel of your peace   W&P 95
Beloved and most loving source   CBM 61
Do not forsake me   SP 8

⊕ "I Truly Am the Vine" from *Aleluya* as found in *Set Free: A Collection of African Hymns*. SATB. AFP 9780806600451.

⊕ El Salvadorean. "O Great God and Lord of the Earth" from *One Is the Body: Songs of Unity and Diversity*. U. GIA G-5790.

☼ Carlson, Jeremiah/Ian Eskelin. "Rules and Reigns" from CCLI.

☼ Cash, Ed, et al. "Amen (Because He Lives)" from CCLI.

☼ Cottrell, Travis Alan/David Moffitt/Sue C. Smith. "To Our God" from CCLI.

☼ Curran, Sean/Justin Ebach. "Bring Us Back" from CCLI.

☼ Gray, Jason/Nicole Nordeman. "Nothing Is All I Need" from CCLI.

☼ Tedder, Mark/Matt Redman. "Lord Have Mercy" from CCLI.

Music for the Day
Choral

Ashdown, Franklin D. "As the Branch Is to the Vine." SATB, org, opt assembly. SMP 10/3071S.

P ♫ Cool, Jayne Southwick. "My Song Is Love Unknown." SATB, kybd. AFP 9781451401066.

Scott, K. Lee. "A Vineyard Grows." SAB, org, opt fl, opt ob. MSM 50-9106.

P ♫ Scott, K. Lee. "The Tree of Life (There in God's Garden)." SATB, assembly, org, opt br qt, opt hb. MSM 50-3000.

Children's Choir

P Burrows, Mark. "God Gave Me Feelings" from *Again, I Say Rejoice!* U, pno or gtr. CG CGC56.

P Horman, John. "Psalm 80" from *ChildrenSing Psalms*. U, assembly, kybd, opt tamb. AFP 9780800663872.

P Mayo, Becki Slagle/Bailey, Lynn Shaw. "The Lord God Made Them All." U/2 pt, pno, opt hb/hc. CG CGA1322.

Keyboard / Instrumental

P Hobby, Robert A. "Jesus Loves Me!" (Jesus Loves Me) from *For All the Saints*, vol. 2. Org. AFP 9780800679101.

P ♫ Nelson, Ronald A. "God the Sculptor of the Mountains" (Jennings-Houston) from *Easy Hymn Settings for Organ*, vol. 4. Org. AFP 9781451486049.

P ♫ Raabe, Nancy. "There in God's Garden" (Shades Mountain) from *Grace and Peace, vol. 6: Songs of Heaven*. Pno. AFP 9781451479621.

P ♫ Vaughan Williams, Ralph (1872–1958). "My Song Is Love Unknown" (Rhosymedre) from *Three Preludes Founded on Welsh Hymn Tunes*. Org. MMP 2536 or *Augsburg Organ Library: Lent*. Org. AFP 9780800658977.

Handbell

P Bettcher, Peggy. "Revelation Song" from *Easy to Ring Praise & Worship VII*. 2-3 oct, L2, HOP 2687. 3-5 oct, L2, HOP 2670.

♫ Kerr, J. Wayne. "There in God's Garden." 3-5 oct hb, fl, L2. MSM 30-820.

♫ Moklebust, Cathy. "My Song Is Love Unknown." 3-5 oct, L3. CG CGB203.

Monday, October 9, 2017
Day of Thanksgiving (Canada)

See Day of Thanksgiving (U.S.A.), pp. 310–312.

⊕ = global song   ♫ = relates to hymn of the day
☼ = praise song   P = available in Prelude Music Planner

October 15, 2017
Time after Pentecost — Lectionary 28

In Isaiah we are given a vision of the great feast to come, when God will wipe away death forever. In Jesus' parable about a great banquet, those invited do not come, so the invitation is extended to others. In our liturgy God spreads a table before us. Even amid anxiety and hardship we rejoice in the peace of God which surpasses all understanding. With great joy we feast at the table of the Lord, and we go forth to share the wonderful invitation with others hungering and thirsting for the abundant life of God.

Prayer of the Day

Lord of the feast, you have prepared a table before all peoples and poured out your life with abundance. Call us again to your banquet. Strengthen us by what is honorable, just, and pure, and transform us into a people of righteousness and peace, through Jesus Christ, our Savior and Lord.

Gospel Acclamation

Alleluia. This is the Lord for whom ¹ we have waited;* let us be glad and rejoice in ¹ God's salvation. *Alleluia.* (Isa. 25:9)

Readings and Psalm

Isaiah 25:1-9

After a hymn of praise acknowledging God as a shelter for the poor, the prophet portrays a wonderful victory banquet at which death—which in ancient Canaan was depicted as a monster swallowing everyone up—will be swallowed up forever. The prophet urges celebration of this victory of salvation.

Psalm 23

You prepare a table before me, and my cup is running over. (Ps. 23:5)

Philippians 4:1-9

Though writing from prison and facing an uncertain future, Paul calls on the Philippians to rejoice and give thanks to God no matter what the circumstance. God's peace is with us and binds together our hearts and minds in Jesus Christ, especially when things around us do not seem peaceful.

Matthew 22:1-14

Jesus tells a parable indicating that the blessings of God's kingdom are available to all, but the invitation is not to be taken lightly.

Semicontinuous reading and psalm

Exodus 32:1-14

After Israel sinned by worshiping the golden calf, Moses interceded with God to spare Israel, lest the Egyptians conclude that God had evil intents in the Exodus. Moses reminds God of the promises God made to Israel's matriarchs and patriarchs.

Psalm 106:1-6, 19-23

Remember, O Lord, the favor you have for your people. (Ps. 106:4)

Preface   Sundays

Color   Green

Prayers of Intercession

The prayers are prepared locally for each occasion. The following examples may be adapted or used as appropriate.

Open to the gifts of the Holy Spirit, we pray for the church, the world, and all of God's creation.

A brief silence.

You rejoice in your church, gracious God. Welcome your children to the table you have prepared and send us forth to share the saving mercy we meet in Jesus Christ. Hear us, O God.

Your mercy is great.

You rejoice in your good creation. Provide moisture for parched places, wind and sun for flooded lands, and shelter and sustenance for creatures of every kind. Hear us, O God.

Your mercy is great.

You rejoice in the people and places of the world. We pray for nations who cannot sit at table together, for leaders distracted by anxiety and fear, and for refugees unwelcome in their homelands. Hear us, O God.

Your mercy is great.

You bring peace that surpasses understanding. We pray for all who cannot worship with us this day: those who are homebound, hospitalized, imprisoned, or working (*especially*). Comfort their hearts and ours with your healing presence. Hear us, O God.

Your mercy is great.

You rejoice in this congregation. We pray for its ministries of hospitality: for ushers, greeters, wedding coordinators, and all who welcome guests in this place. Hear us, O God.

Your mercy is great.

Here other intercessions may be offered.

You promise an eternal feast. We give thanks for the saints of every time and place (*especially Teresa of Avila, whom we commemorate today*). Hold us in communion with them until all are united at your heavenly banquet. Hear us, O God. **Your mercy is great.**

Into your hands, gracious God, we commend all for whom we pray, trusting the power of Christ and the gifts of the Spirit. **Amen.**

Images in the Readings

Here is a listing of only some of this Sunday's images. Matthew's parable merges several biblical images that describe our life with God. The **wedding** suggests lifelong love, commitment to the other, and communal joy in the union as a description of God's choosing and caring for us. Especially in a culture in which food was not plentiful and cheap, the **feast** connotes communal participation and extraordinary fullness. God is likened to a **king**, to whom honor and service are due. We are **guests**: that is, the meal is God's, not ours. The **wedding robe** suggests the white garment of baptism. Since the Bible often describes God as light, **outer darkness** suggests life totally distant and apart from God. Paul calls the somewhat problematic Philippian assembly his **crown**. Another ten images fill the poem from Isaiah. God not only throws out the unprepared guest: God also **shelters** us from storm; removes the **shroud** that finally covers all humans; like some kind of monster **eats up death**; and like a lover or a parent, **wipes away our tears**.

Ideas for the Day

- In 1964 French philosopher Jean-Paul Sartre refused to accept the Nobel Prize. His reasons were primarily his unwillingness to accept official honors and his conviction that a writer should not be "transformed into an institution" (Jean-Paul Sartre, *New York Review of Books*, trans. Richard Howard, December 17, 1964. www.nybooks.com/articles/archives/1964/dec/17/sartre-on-the-nobel-prize/). The prize carries weight, and that matters. The parable in the gospel reading shows the importance of both the invitation and the response. What remains for discussion is what the invitation does to or for the invited.

- Even though a wedding banquet is the setting, Jesus' parable lacks a joyful or celebratory tone. The only hint of joy is from the king who announces the preparations are complete and eagerly awaits the guests. The guests who are initially invited fail to share in both the joy and urgency of the event. Both qualities may be valuable for an audience. New Testament scholar Klyne Snodgrass comments, "The witness of the church should be characterized by the joy of inviting people to the banquet God has prepared" (*Stories with Intent* [Grand Rapids: Eerdmans, 2008], 322). What parts of community life and worship clearly communicate the joy of sharing the invitation?

- The 1967 film *Guess Who's Coming to Dinner* features a family's encounter with an unexpected guest. When a daughter brings home her new fiancé of a different race,

the characters find their sense of commitment and preparedness challenged in terms of welcoming the new relationship. At the end of Jesus' parable, the guests who are not expected are the ones who show up to the banquet. But the punishment at the end suggests that showing up is not all that matters. The parable invites believers to explore ways in which the values of preparation and honest commitment are practiced corporately and individually.

Connections with the Liturgy

Again in *Evangelical Lutheran Worship*, one possible invitation to the table is "Come to the banquet." The thanksgivings at the table IV, VI, and VII refer to the feast. In Thanksgiving at the Table X, recalling Isaiah 25:6, we praise God as wine, who will "warm our hearts and make us one" (p. 69).

Let the Children Come

One year the four-year-old's birthday invitations were mailed and party preparations under way. The big day came, and yet one of her best friends did not show up. She was so sad. Come to find out, the invitation was lost in the mail. Her parents felt terrible that they didn't call when they didn't get a reply beforehand. Do you find yourselves expecting folks to arrive, only to find them not coming to the banquet? Hospitality takes an enormous amount of effort, but it is what the church does. How do you connect with families throughout the week so they are welcomed in worship?

Assembly Song
Gathering

Arise, my soul, arise! ELW 827, LBW 516

As we gather at your table ELW 522

Rejoice, ye pure in heart! ELW 873/874, LBW 553

Psalmody and Acclamations

Bruxvoort Colligan, Richard. "My Love Is My Shepherd (Psalm 23)" from *Sharing the Road*. AFP 9780800678630.

Pishner, Stephen. "Twenty-Eighth Sunday in Ordinary Time (A)" from COJ:A.

+ Pavlechko, Thomas. "Psalm 106:1-6, 19-23" from SMP.

(GA) Iona Community (Scotland). "Alleluia 1" from *Come, All You People: Shorter Songs for Worship*. U/SATB. GIA G-4391. Use ELW psalm tone 7 in F major with proper verse for Lectionary 28.

Hymn of the Day

At the Lamb's high feast we sing ELW 362, LBW 210 *SONNE DER GERECHTIGKEIT*

Let us go now to the banquet ELW 523, LLC 410 *VAMOS TODOS AL BANQUETE*

The trumpets sound, the angels sing ELW 531, W&P 139 *THE FEAST IS READY*

Offering

Bread of life, our host and meal   ELW 464

Come, let us eat   ELW 491, LBW 214, TFF 119

Communion

God extends an invitation   ELW 486, LLC 397

Thine the amen   ELW 826, WOV 801

Around you, O Lord Jesus   ELW 468, LBW 496

Sending

United at the table/*Unidos en la fiesta*   ELW 498, LLC 408

Sent forth by God's blessing   ELW 547, LBW 221

Additional Assembly Songs

A multitude comes from the east   LBW 313

To the banquet, come   LS 106

Grains of wheat/*Una espiga*   WOV 708, LLC 392

⊕ Cuéllar, Guillermo. "Come, the Banquet Hall Is Ready" from *Global Songs 2*. SATB. AFP 9780800656744.

⊕ Feliciano, Francisco F. "The Lord Is My Shepherd" from *Sound the Bamboo*. SATB. GIA G-6830.

☼ Anderson, Jared G. "Go Ye" from CCLI.

☼ Brenner, Scott/Cheryl Thomas. "Marriage of the Lamb" from CCLI.

☼ Getty, Keith/Kristyn Getty/Stuart Townend. "Behold the Lamb" from CCLI.

☼ Kendrick, Graham. "Banquet" from CCLI.

☼ Peterson, Mark. "Hallelujah to the King of Kings" from CCLI.

☼ Shelton, Eva. "The Feast of Life" from CCLI.

Music for the Day
Choral

P Ferguson, John. "The Lord's My Shepherd, I'll Not Want." SATB div, tamb. AFP 9781451401752.

Highben, Zebulon M. "St. Teresa's Blessing." SATB, fl. MSM 50-8918.

♫ Stoldt, Frank. "At the Lamb's High Feast." SATB, assembly, org, br qrt, opt hb. MSM 20-441.

P Zimmermann, Heinz Werner. "Psalm 23: The Lord Is My Shepherd." SATB, org, DB. AFP 9780800645380.

Children's Choir

P Pooler, Marie. "The Lord's My Shepherd" from *ChildrenSing in Worship*, vol. 3. 2 pt, kybd. AFP 9781451462548.

Pote, Allen. "Praise, Rejoice and Sing!" U/2 pt, kybd, opt fl. CG CGA392.

Traditional. "Rejoice in the Lord Always" from *LifeSongs*. U/2 or 3 pt, opt kybd. AFP 9780806642703.

Keyboard / Instrumental

♫ Burkhardt, Michael. "At the Lamb's High Feast We Sing" (Sonne der Gerechtigkeit) from *Five Hymn Accompaniments for Brass Quartet and Organ*, Set 1. Br qrt, Org. MSM 20-842.

P Farlee, Robert Buckley. "Around You, O Lord Jesus" (O Jesu, än de dina) from *Treasures Old and New: Hymn Preludes for Organ*. Org. AFP 9781451499094.

♫ Mackie, Dave. "Let Us Go Now to the Banquet" (Vamos todos al banquete) from *By Day and By Night: Piano Settings*. Pno. AFP 9781451420890.

Organ, Anne Krentz. "God Extends an Invitation" (Nuestro Padre nos invita) from *Reflections on Hymn Tunes for Holy Communion*, vol. 2. Pno. AFP 9780800679095.

Handbell

♫ Afdahl, Lee J. "At the Lamb's High Feast." 3-5 oct hb, opt 2 oct hc, L2+. CPH 97-7309.

Glasgow, Michael J. "Sempiternam." 5-7 oct hb, opt 5-7 oct hc, L4+. FTT20298HB. Opt tpt, FTT 20298BB. Opt alt hb solo, FTT 20298WC. Opt full score, FTT 20298M.

P Waldrop, Tammy. "The GatheRing" from *Spring Ring!* 2-3 oct, L2-, CG CGB829. 3-5 oct, L2-, CG CGB830.

Sunday, October 15
Teresa of Avila (Teresa de Jesús), teacher, renewer of the church, died 1582

Teresa of Avila (AH-vee-la) is also known as Teresa de Jesús. She chose the life of a Carmelite nun after reading the letters of Jerome. Frequently sick during her early years as a nun, she found that when she was sick her prayer life flowered, but when she was well it withered. Steadily her life of faith and prayer deepened, and she grew to have a lively sense of God's presence with her. She worked to reform her monastic community in Avila, which she believed had strayed from its original purpose. Her reforms asked nuns to maintain life in the monastic enclosure without leaving it and to identify with those who are poor by not wearing shoes. Teresa's writings on devotional life have enjoyed a wide readership.

Tuesday, October 17
Ignatius, Bishop of Antioch, martyr, died around 115

Ignatius was the second bishop of Antioch, in Syria. It was there that the name "Christian" was first used to describe the followers of Jesus. Ignatius is known to us through his letters. In them he encouraged Christians to live in unity sustained with love while standing firm on sound doctrine. Ignatius believed

⊕ = global song   ♫ = relates to hymn of the day   + = semicontinuous psalm
☼ = praise song   P = available in Prelude Music Planner

279

Christian martyrdom was a privilege. When his own martyr-dom approached, he wrote in one of his letters, "I prefer death in Christ Jesus to power over the farthest limits of the earth.... Do not stand in the way of my birth to real life." Ignatius and all martyrs are a reminder that even today Christians face death because of their faith in Jesus.

Wednesday, October 18
Luke, Evangelist

St. Luke is identified by tradition as the author of both Luke and Acts. Luke is careful to place the events of Jesus' life in both their social and religious contexts. Some of the most loved parables, including the good Samaritan and the prodigal son, are found only in this gospel. Luke's gospel has also given the church some of its most beautiful songs: the Benedictus sung at morning prayer, the Magnificat sung at evening prayer, and the Nunc dimittis sung at the close of the day. These songs are pow-erful witnesses to the message of Jesus Christ.

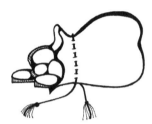

October 22, 2017
Time after Pentecost — Lectionary 29

In today's first reading God uses the Gentile ruler Cyrus to accomplish divine purposes. When the Pharisees try to trap Jesus, he tells them to give the emperor what belongs to him and to God what belongs to God. To gather for worship reminds us that our ultimate allegiance is to God rather than to any earthly authority. Created in the image of God, we offer our entire selves in the service of God and for the sake of the world.

Prayer of the Day

Sovereign God, raise your throne in our hearts. Created by you, let us live in your image; created for you, let us act for your glory; redeemed by you, let us give you what is yours, through Jesus Christ, our Savior and Lord.

Gospel Acclamation

Alleluia. Shine like stars ' in the world;* holding fast to the ' word of life. *Alleluia.* (Phil. 2:15, 16)

Readings and Psalm
Isaiah 45:1-7

The prophet announces that Cyrus the Persian emperor is the one the Lord has anointed to end Israel's exile. The Lord makes this choice so that the whole world will recognize this Lord as the only God. Persia had a god of light and a god of darkness; the Lord claims sovereignty over both light and darkness.

Psalm 96:1-9 [10-13]

Ascribe to the LORD honor and power. (Ps. 96:7)

1 Thessalonians 1:1-10

Most likely this letter is the first written by Paul. Paul is giving pastoral encouragement and reassurances to new Christians living in an antagonistic pagan environment. Their commit-ment of faith, love, and hope makes them a model for other new Christian communities.

Matthew 22:15-22

After Jesus begins teaching in the temple, religious leaders try to trap him with questions. First they ask if God's people should pay taxes to an earthly tyrant like Caesar.

Semicontinuous reading and psalm
Exodus 33:12-23

Moses successfully interceded with God to accompany Israel to the holy land after their sin with the golden calf. In response to a request to display his glory, God recites a sentence that appears frequently in the Old Testament: "I will be gracious to whom I will be gracious." Moses is not allowed to see God's face, but only God's back.

Psalm 99

Proclaim the greatness of the LORD our God. (Ps. 99:5)

Preface   Sundays

Color   Green

Prayers of Intercession

The prayers are prepared locally for each occasion. The following examples may be adapted or used as appropriate.
Open to the gifts of the Holy Spirit, we pray for the church, the world, and all of God's creation.
A brief silence.

Trusting in God, we pray for the church. Fill all worshipers with your Holy Spirit. Grant them generous hearts to share God's splendor revealed to them in Jesus Christ. Lord, in your mercy,
hear our prayer.

We pray for creation: for the power of sun, wind, and water, for the riches buried in rock and soil, for the magnificence of life in forms too many to number. Lord, in your mercy,
hear our prayer.

We pray for the nations: for leaders of governments, for fair commerce between nations, for treasurers, boards of directors, and all who justly distribute monetary resources. Lord, in your mercy,
hear our prayer.

We pray for the poor and outcast, for those who cannot afford food, medicine, clothing, and shelter, for the communities and agencies who serve the needy and advocate on their behalf (*especially*). Lord, in your mercy,
hear our prayer.

Trusting in God's healing power, we pray for this congregation: for the unemployed and overworked, for all who are burdened by debt, for the sick and those in particular need (*especially*). Lord, in your mercy,
hear our prayer.

Here other intercessions may be offered.

We give thanks for the saints of every time and place. By your Spirit, grant us sure confidence in the everlasting glory you promise. Lord, in your mercy,
hear our prayer.

Into your hands, gracious God, we commend all for whom we pray, trusting the power of Christ and the gifts of the Spirit.
Amen.

Images in the Readings

Typically, a **coin** is impressed with an image of the authority on which the coin relies. In the United States, coins and bills bear the image of presidents who function as representatives of the sovereign people. In baptism it is the cross of Christ that has been impressed on our bodies: he is the authority to whom we owe allegiance. As for taxes, Christians in different countries have widely ranging views about how much of our days' wages is rightly owed to the government.

The Isaiah reading plays with the idea of one's **name**. God calls Cyrus by name; God's personal name is YHWH, represented in most English-language Bibles as "the LORD." In his encouragement to the Thessalonians, Paul writes of God the Father, the Lord Jesus Christ, and the Holy Spirit. In baptism the candidates are first called by their secular name, after which this triune name of God is placed on them. Yet in the second century, Justin Martyr wrote that to imagine that we can know and speak the very name of the almighty God is madness.

Perhaps the name of God that we are given in the Bible is like a potholder, a way to hold on to something that is far too hot for bare human hands.

Ideas for the Day

- In his 2013 photo book *Happy End,* Dietmar Eckell photographs old airplane crash sites. The images challenge a sense of predictability because he only documents sites where everyone in the crash survived. It is striking that the remains of an airplane crash stand as a symbol of a happy ending. Similarly, today's reading from Isaiah tells of God's deliverance of Israel through Cyrus. Twice the prophet points out that this will take place even though Cyrus does not know the Lord, emphasizing the unpredictability of God's action. How might communities of faith seek and interpret God's action when it takes place in unexpected ways?

- In *The Merchant of Venice*, Shakespeare's character Shylock thinks he has Antonio trapped in a contract violation and demands justice. It takes Portia's clever thinking to find a way to save Antonio (act 4, scene 1). The second part of Matthew 22 features a series of challenges to Jesus' interpretation of religious practices. Apparently it is merely Jesus' clever thinking that amazes (Matt. 22:22) and astounds (Matt. 22:33) the leaders. But his answer challenges the audience to imagine a different type of economy than the one even the religious leaders seem to support.

- The trick question presented to Jesus concerns the issue of his interpretive abilities. In contemporary times, consensus on correct interpretation may be a frustrating endeavor. Still, faith communities face issues that require careful interpretation. How might interpreting theology be a good communal activity? What forums facilitate or inhibit such activities?

- In the semicontinuous first reading from Exodus, Moses is allowed to see the glory of God from a rock cleft. This is a safe place but not a comfortable one. Moses cannot remain here but must continue leading the people of Israel. What images come to mind when envisioning God's glory? What does seeing the glory of God mean for a sense of comfort or assurance, and what else might it prompt?

Connections with the Liturgy

That Paul writes of "remembering you in our prayers" models for us the Sunday intercessions. The prayer of the day and the thanksgiving at the table offer occasions for the assembly to pray for itself, while the primary purpose of the intercessions is to pray for everything and everybody else in the world. The petition for "the church universal" can focus each week on some community of believers other than our own, especially those experiencing persecution.

Let the Children Come

As soon as a child begins to ask about money, they are ready for an allowance. A helpful way of approaching allowance is in increments of three: a coin for spending, a coin for saving, and a coin for giving. An allowance is given by the parents with no strings attached, just the grace of being in the family. A child should do personal tasks (make bed, brush teeth, etc.) and chores, like helping with dinner, because they are responsibilities of living in community, not to get a reward. Chores, personal tasks, and allowance grow with age, and so do saving and giving.

Assembly Song
Gathering

Sing praise to God, the highest good   ELW 871, LBW 542

God is here!   ELW 526, WOV 719

O God beyond all praising   ELW 880, WOV 797

Psalmody and Acclamations

Haugen, Marty. "Give the Lord Glory and Honor" from TLP:A.

Shute, Linda Cable. "Psalm 96," Refrain 2, from PSCY.

+ Hopson, Hal. "Psalm 99" from TPP.

(GA) Iona Community (Scotland). "Alleluia 1" from *Come, All You People: Shorter Songs for Worship*. U/SATB. GIA G-4391. Use ELW psalm tone 7 in F major with proper verse for Lectionary 29.

Hymn of the Day

Lift every voice and sing   ELW 841, LBW 562, TFF 296   *LIFT EVERY VOICE AND SING*

All my hope on God is founded   ELW 757, WOV 782   *MICHAEL*

When our song says peace   ELW 709   *JENKINS*

Offering

We raise our hands to you, O Lord   ELW 690

God, whose giving knows no ending   ELW 678, LBW 408

Communion

Lord, Be Glorified   ELW 744, TFF 248, W&P 89

O God of every nation   ELW 713, LBW 416

Now the feast and celebration   ELW 167, WOV 410

Sending

We give thee but thine own   ELW 686, LBW 410

God of grace and God of glory   ELW 705, LBW 415

Additional Assembly Songs

Give thanks   TFF 292, W&P 41

O Lord, I worship you   ASG 30

In the Lord I'll be ever thankful   SP 18

⊕ Helsa, Bret. "Everything That We Have" from *Global Songs 2*. SATB. AFP 9780800656744.

⊕ Pangosban, Ben. "Sing a Song to the Lord" from *Sound the Bamboo*. U. GIA G-6830.

☼ Blakesley, Josh. "All of Me" from CCLI.

☼ Farren, Michael/Travis Ryan/Brandon Collins. "Until My Voice Is Gone" from CCLI.

☼ Ivey, Aaron/Jason Ingram/Chris McClarney. "Everything and Nothing Less" from CCLI.

☼ McDowell, William/Sam Hinn. "I Give Myself Away" from CCLI.

☼ Riddle, Jennie Lee/Crystal Yates. "I Surrender" from CCLI.

☼ Stanfill, Kristian/Jason Ingram/Brett Younker/Daniel Carson. "My Heart Is Yours" from CCLI.

Music for the Day
Choral

P Benson, Robert A. "Sing to the Lord a New Song." SATB, org. AFP 9780806698304.

P Kosche, Kenneth T. "Sing to the Lord a New Song." 2 pt mxd, pno. AFP 9781451498981.

P Schütz, Heinrich. "Sing to the Lord a New Song" from *Augsburg Motet Book*. SATB, cont. AFP 9781451423709.

P Sweelinck, Jan Pieterszoon. "Sing to the Lord, New Songs Be Raising" in *Chantry Choirbook*. SATB. AFP 9780800657772.

Children's Choir

P Benson, Robert A. "What Shall We Give to God?" from *ChildrenSing in Worship*, vol. 3. U, kybd, opt desc or C inst. AFP 9781451462548.

P Christopherson, Dorothy. "The Lord Is King: Go Tell It" from *ChildrenSing in Worship*, vol. 3. 2 pt, pno. AFP 9781451462548.

P Patterson, Mark. "Where You Need Me I Will Go." U/2 pt, pno. CG CGA893.

Keyboard / Instrumental

P ♫ Cherwien, David. "When Our Song Says Peace" (Jenkins) from *We Sing of God: Hymn Settings for Organ*. Org. AFP 9780806698052.

P ♫ Farlee, Robert Buckley. "All My Hope on God Is Founded" (Michael) from *Treasures Old and New: Hymn Preludes for Organ*. Org. AFP 9781451499094.

P Organ, Anne Krentz. "O God of Every Nation" (Llangloffan) from *Piano Reflections on Hymns of the Faith*. Pno. AFP 9780806698069.

P Wahl, Carol. "God, Whose Giving Knows No Ending" (Rustington) from *Cry of the Dove: Piano Settings*. Pno. AFP 9781451479614.

⊕ = global song   ♫ = relates to hymn of the day   + = semicontinuous psalm

☼ = praise song   P = available in Prelude Music Planner

Handbell

P   Helman, Michael. "Lord, Whose Love through Humble Service." 3-5 oct hb, opt 3 oct hc, L3. CG CGB586.

P   Raney, Joel. "Thine Is the Glory." 3-5 oct hb, L2, HOP 2713. Opt full score (pno), HOP 2713D.

♫   Smith, Vicki. "Lift Every Voice and Sing." 3-5 oct, L3. CPH 97-6943.

Monday, October 23
James of Jerusalem, martyr, died around 62

James became an early leader of the church in Jerusalem. He is described in the New Testament as the brother of Jesus, and secular historian Josephus calls James the brother of Jesus, "the so-called Christ." Little is known about James, but Josephus reported that the Pharisees respected James for his piety and observance of the law. His enemies had him put to death.

Thursday, October 26
Philipp Nicolai, died 1608; Johann Heermann, died 1647; Paul Gerhardt, died 1676; hymnwriters

These three outstanding hymnwriters all worked in Germany during times of war and plague. When Philipp Nicolai was a pastor in Westphalia, the plague killed thirteen hundred of his parishioners. One hundred seventy people died in one week. His hymns "Wake, Awake, for Night Is Flying" (ELW 436) and "O Morning Star, How Fair and Bright!" (ELW 308) were included in a series of meditations he wrote to comfort his parishioners during the plague. The style of Johann Heermann's hymns moved away from the more objective style of Reformation hymnody toward expressing the emotions of faith. Among his hymns is the plaintive text "Ah, Holy Jesus" (ELW 349). Paul Gerhardt lost a preaching position at St. Nicholas Church in Berlin because he refused to sign a document stating he would not make theological arguments in his sermons. The author of beloved hymns such as "O Sacred Head, Now Wounded" (ELW 351), some have called Gerhardt the greatest of Lutheran hymnwriters.

Saturday, October 28
Simon and Jude, Apostles

Little is known about Simon and Jude. In New Testament lists of the apostles, Simon the "zealot" or Cananaean is mentioned, but he is never mentioned apart from these lists. Jude, sometimes called Thaddeus, is also mentioned in lists of the Twelve. At the last supper Jude asked Jesus why he had chosen to reveal himself to the disciples but not to the world. A traditional story about Simon and Jude says that they traveled together on a missionary journey to Persia and were both martyred there.

October 29, 2017
Reformation Sunday

On this day we celebrate the heart of our faith: the gospel of Christ—the good news—that makes us free! We pray that the Holy Spirit would continue to unite the church today in its proclamation and witness to the world. In the waters of baptism we are made one body; we pray for the day that all Christians will also be one at the Lord's table.

Prayer of the Day

Almighty God, gracious Lord, we thank you that your Holy Spirit renews the church in every age. Pour out your Holy Spirit on your faithful people. Keep them steadfast in your word, protect and comfort them in times of trial, defend them against all enemies of the gospel, and bestow on the church your saving peace, through Jesus Christ, our Savior and Lord, who lives and reigns with you and the Holy Spirit, one God, now and forever.
or
Gracious Father, we pray for your holy catholic church. Fill it with all truth and peace. Where it is corrupt, purify it; where it is in error, direct it; where in anything it is amiss, reform it; where it is right, strengthen it; where it is in need, provide for it; where it is divided, reunite it; for the sake of your Son, Jesus Christ, our Savior, who lives and reigns with you and the Holy Spirit, one God, now and forever.

Gospel Acclamation

Alleluia. If you continue in my word, you are truly | my disciples,* and you will know the truth, and the truth will | make you free. *Alleluia.* (John 8:31-32)

Readings and Psalm

Jeremiah 31:31-34

The renewed covenant will not be breakable, but like the old covenant it will expect the people to live upright lives. To know the Lord means that one will defend the cause of the poor and needy (Jer. 22:16). The renewed covenant is possible only because the Lord will forgive iniquity and not remember sin. Our hope lies in a God who forgets.

Psalm 46

The LORD of hosts is with us; the God of Jacob is our stronghold. (Ps. 46:7)

Romans 3:19-28

Paul's words stand at the heart of the preaching of Martin Luther and the other Reformation leaders. No human beings make themselves right with God through works of the law. We are brought into a right relationship with God through the divine activity centered in Christ's death. This act is a gift of grace that liberates us from sin and empowers our faith in Jesus Christ.

John 8:31-36

Jesus speaks of truth and freedom as spiritual realities known through his word. He reveals the truth that sets people free from sin.

Preface   Sundays

Color   Red

Prayers of Intercession

The prayers are prepared locally for each occasion. The following examples may be adapted or used as appropriate.

Open to the gifts of the Holy Spirit, we pray for the church, the world, and all of God's creation.
A brief silence.

We pray for the unity of your church. Free us to be Christ's one body, graciously receiving his life and boldly offering it to a world in need. Lord, in your mercy,
hear our prayer.

We pray for the renewal of creation: for a shared, plentiful harvest, for lands unable to bear fruit, for what is neglected or destroyed by our hand, and for the earth's advocates. Lord, in your mercy,
hear our prayer.

We pray for all nations of the world: for leaders of villages, cities, states, and nations, for lawmakers and judges, for teachers and students, and for all who work for peace. Lord, in your mercy,
hear our prayer.

We pray for those who seek refuge and strength: refugees, the imprisoned, and those bound by addictions or burdened by guilt. We pray for the ill or injured (*especially*). Lord, in your mercy,
hear our prayer.

We pray for continual reformation in this and every assembly. In new beginnings, impart wisdom. In established traditions, inspire creativity. In all ministries, revive our hope in the one who makes all things new. Lord, in your mercy,
hear our prayer.

Here other intercessions may be offered.

We give thanks for your saints. United with them in the covenant of baptism, increase our faith in your promised life for all. Lord, in your mercy,

hear our prayer.
Into your hands, gracious God, we commend all for whom we pray, trusting the power of Christ and the gifts of the Spirit.
Amen.

Images in the Readings

The gospel's image of **freedom** presents a challenge to contemporary Americans, and perhaps to other Western societies as well, since popularly "freedom" is understood as the right of the individual to live out personal choices. John's gospel suggests instead that the freedom granted in Christ is the freedom of the son, who remains in the father's house and does the will of that father. Sixteenth-century Christians used this proclamation of freedom to leave behind church regulations of the medieval church, but even Martin Luther wrote detailed interpretations of the Ten Commandments, understood as "law" for Christian use. We are free to be obedient children.

A **covenant** was a legal agreement in which the master promised protection because the participants met certain obligations. Ancient Israelites adopted this cultural category for their understanding of the relationship that God had offered the chosen people. Christians continued to use this language in articulating the renewed relationship with God that was effected through Christ. Particularly Methodists have kept this language alive in referring to the baptismal covenant and in their annual covenant renewal ceremonies. Lutherans understand the covenant as God's continuing mercy given in word and sacrament.

Ideas for the Day

- The Reformation is a time to explore the meaning of freedom in the gospel. We know from Luther's treatise "On the Freedom of a Christian" that this freedom is total freedom from the law and total freedom to love and serve our neighbor. In Luther's words, "A Christian is a perfectly free lord of all, subject to none. A Christian is a perfectly dutiful servant of all, subject to all." How do Jesus' words that he makes us "free indeed" (John 8:36) find expression in the powerful words of Luther in the treatise? This is a day to explore honestly both of the ways we diminish the freedom of the gospel in our culture: being unable to let go of law, and being unable to freely love our neighbor.
- The Reformation begun by Luther did not abandon the theological, sacramental, and liturgical traditions of the church. It sought to reform them so that the gospel would shine through all the church does. Since the beginning of the Lutheran Reformation to this day, there have been twenty-six thousand Sundays to proclaim the gospel and share in the gracious presence of Christ in the communion meal. How many souls have heard the good news because of what happened in 1517? How many hearts have been transformed? Celebrate the impact of the Lutheran Reformation on real lives of ordinary people over time and place through word and sacrament.
- The reading from Romans reminds us that there is no room for pride, even on this day. Perhaps Lutherans and others can only fully celebrate the Reformation by first confessing when and where we have turned the gospel into law. And perhaps we can only fully celebrate by naming all the ways the church in its diversity proclaims and lives out the gospel. Today is a day to show humble gratitude and to give thanks for every part of the church where the gospel is shared as good news in Christ. Name the other churches in your community and in the world through preaching and prayer so the fullness of the gospel in the whole church is celebrated.

Connections with the Liturgy

In the opening confession and forgiveness in *Evangelical Lutheran Worship*'s Holy Communion (p. 95), we confess that "we are captive to sin." This language recalls Jesus' words in today's gospel that we are slaves to sin.

The rite of Holy Baptism within *Evangelical Lutheran Worship* (p. 231) announces that the newly baptized are now daughters and sons of God. We now have a place in God's house forever.

Baptismal sponsors promise to help the newly baptized live "in the covenant of baptism," recalling the imagery from Jeremiah. The new covenant is sealed by Christ's blood, poured out for us in the weekly meal of grace (*ELW*, pp. 108, 109).

Let the Children Come

For many birthdays in one family, the children would receive two envelopes: one announcing their new privilege and one announcing their new responsibility for their new age. Living in relationship with children, either in families or in community, is a celebration of privilege and responsibility. On this 500th anniversary of the Reformation, we give thanks for Martin Luther, who not only helped reform the church but also reformed the families in which children grow. He recognized the immense gift and privilege of living in familial relationships. He recognized the immense responsibility for families to nurture each other and God's gift of faith.

Assembly Song
Gathering

Built on a rock   ELW 652, LBW 365

A mighty fortress is our God   ELW 503–505, LBW 228/229, LLC 403

Lord, keep us steadfast in your word   ELW 517, LBW 230

Psalmody and Acclamations

Cherwien, David. "Psalm 46: God Is Our Refuge." U, assembly, org. MSM 80-800.

Erickson, Rick. "Psalm 46," Refrain 1, from PSCY.

Mummert, Mark. "Psalm 46." SATB, org, assembly. AFP 9781451462449.

(GA) Chepponis, James. "Festival Alleluia." Assembly, cant, org, opt SATB, br qrt/qnt, timp, suspended cymbal, fl, hb. MSM 80-847A.

Hymn of the Day

Salvation unto us has come ELW 590, LBW 297 *ES IST DAS HEIL*

That priceless grace ELW 591, TFF 68 *THAT PRICELESS GRACE*

The church of Christ, in every age ELW 729, LBW 433
WAREHAM

Offering

Rise, O Sun of righteousness ELW 657

God, my Lord, my strength ELW 795, LBW 484

Communion

I received the living God ELW 477, WOV 700

Listen, God is calling ELW 513, WOV 712, TFF 130

For by grace you have been saved ELW 598, W&P 38

Sending

Thy strong word ELW 511, LBW 233

The church's one foundation ELW 654, LBW 369

Additional Assembly Songs

O God, O Lord of heaven and earth LBW 396

Here and now God ASG 17

By grace we have been saved ASG 4

⊕ Garcia, Juan Luis. "God's Word Is Upright/La palabra del Señor" from *Glory to God*. U. WJK 0664238971.

⊕ Harbor, Rawn. "The Lord of Hosts Is with Us" (Psalm 46) from TFF. U.

☼ Andrews, Meredith/Benji Cowart/Paul Mabury. "The Gospel Changes Everything" from CCLI.

☼ Brewster, Lincoln/Colby Wedgeworth/Mia Fieldes. "Shout It Loud" from CCLI.

☼ Doerksen, Brian/Steve Mitchinson. "Fortress 144" from CCLI.

☼ Furtick, Steven/Mack Brock/Chris Brown/Wade Joye/Lauren Ramkissoon/London Gatch. "Fortress" from CCLI.

☼ Ingram, Jason/Bryan Brown/Tony Wood. "Jesus Firm Foundation" from CCLI.

☼ Nockels, Chisty/Nathan Nockels. "A Mighty Fortress Is Our God" from CCLI.

☼ Rend Collective. "Christ Has Set Me Free" from CCLI.

Music for the Day
Choral

P ♫ Bach, J. S. "Salvation unto Us Has Come" from *Bach for All Seasons*. SATB, opt kybd. AFP 9780800658540.

P ♫ Distler, Hugo. "Salvation unto Us Has Come" from *Chantry Choirbook*. SATB. AFP 9780800657772.

P Highben, Zebulon M. "Now to the Holy Spirit Let Us Pray." SATB, assembly, org, tpt. AFP 9781451492569.

P Raabe, Nancy M. "A Mighty Fortress." SATB, assembly, org, tpt, opt tamb. AFP 9781451423914.

Children's Choir

P Bedford, Michael. "Two Psalms for Young Singers." U, pno, opt hb/hc. CG CGA1140.

Lindh, Jodi W. "Praise the Lord Who Reigns Above." U, Orff inst, opt hb. CG CGA583.

P Powell, Susan. "I Praise the God of Grace." U/2 pt, pno. CG CGA1300.

Keyboard / Instrumental

Bender, Jan. *Missa pro organo, Op. 52* (contains settings of the tunes Kyrie, Gott Vater; Allein Gott in der Höh; Wir glauben all; Jesiah, dem Propheten; and Christe, du Lamm Gottes). Org. Edition Merseburger MERS 885.

P ♫ Miller, Aaron David. "The Church of Christ, in Every Age" (Wareham) from *Chorale Preludes for Piano in Traditional Styles*. Pno. AFP 9780800679033.

P Organ, Anne Krentz. "A Mighty Fortress Is Our God" (Ein feste Burg) from *Reflections on Hymn Tunes for the Fall Festivals*. Pno. AFP 9780800663834.

♫ Speed, Robert M. "Fanfares and Variations on 'Wareham'" from *Marilyn Mason Music Library*, vol. 2. Org. MSM 10-991.

Handbell

♫ Afdahl, Lee J. "The Church of Christ in Every Age." 3-5 oct hb, opt 3-5 oct hc, L2. AGEHR AG35306.

Moklebust, Cathy/David Moklebust. "A Mighty Fortress." 3-5 oct hb, L3, CG CGB650. Opt org, CG CGB651. Opt br, opt timp, CG CGRP22. Opt SATB vcs and assembly, CG CGA1202. Opt full score, CG CGB649.

Raney, Joel/Arnold Sherman. "A Mighty Fortress." 4-6 oct, L4. HOP 2112.

⊕ = global song ♫ = relates to hymn of the day
☼ = praise song P = available in Prelude Music Planner

October 29, 2017
Time after Pentecost — Lectionary 30

Jesus' summary of the law in today's gospel echoes our first reading from Leviticus. We are called not only to love God with heart, soul, and mind, but also to love our neighbor as ourselves. It is out of such deep care that Paul shares the gospel with the Thessalonian community. In the confession of sins, we acknowledge that we have not loved God, neighbor, and self; yet we gather to hear the word of forgiveness and to be strengthened by word and meal to be signs of God's love and mercy in the world.

Prayer of the Day

O Lord God, you are the holy lawgiver, you are the salvation of your people. By your Spirit renew us in your covenant of love, and train us to care tenderly for all our neighbors, through Jesus Christ, our Savior and Lord.

Gospel Acclamation

Alleluia. Beloved, since God loved ˈ us so much,* we also ought to love ˈ one another. *Alleluia*. (1 John 4:11)

Readings and Psalm

Leviticus 19:1-2, 15-18

The holiness code in Leviticus urges people to be holy because God is holy. Holiness is lived out in partiality for and consideration of the poor and the weak. We are to love our neighbors as ourselves. God's people exercise justice and love in their dealings with one another.

Psalm 1

Their delight is in the law of the LORD. (Ps. 1:2)

1 Thessalonians 2:1-8

Paul uses maternal imagery to depict the caring and nurturing relationship he shares with the Thessalonian Christians. When he first came to their city it was not to benefit himself but to share the gospel with them, which was his responsibility as an apostle of Christ.

Matthew 22:34-46

Put on the spot by the Pharisees, Jesus displays wisdom by summarizing the law of God in just two commandments and by demonstrating the Messiah must be more than the son of David.

Semicontinuous reading and psalm

Deuteronomy 34:1-12

Before his death, Moses, who was not allowed to enter the holy land, was granted the right to see the land from Mount Nebo. The statement that no prophet has arisen in Israel like Moses (34:10) stands in tension with Deuteronomy 18:15 (God will "raise up for you a prophet like me") and led to the expectation that another Moses would still come. In several New Testament passages Jesus is identified as that prophet.

Psalm 90:1-6, 13-17

Show your servants your works, and your splendor to their children. (Ps. 90:16)

Preface   Sundays

Color   Green

Prayers of Intercession

The prayers are prepared locally for each occasion. The following examples may be adapted or used as appropriate.

Open to the gifts of the Holy Spirit, we pray for the church, the world, and all of God's creation.

A brief silence.

Holy God, grant courage to your church. In all things and among all people of faith, prosper our Lord's call to love and serve in strength and humility. Hear us, O God.

Your mercy is great.

Holy Creator, protect this world so lovingly made. Align our stewardship with yours so that plants offer shelter and nourishment, water sources sustain life, habitats thrive, and all creation flourishes as you intend. Hear us, O God.

Your mercy is great.

Sovereign God, bring justice to the nations. Turn enemies from vengeance and warfare, direct leaders in fair and honest governance, and equip citizens to seek the needs of their neighbors. Hear us, O God.

Your mercy is great.

Holy Provider, you care for all your children. Heal those in need: the sick and their caregivers (*especially*), victims of family strife, and any who grieve this day. Hear us, O God.

Your mercy is great.

Gracious God, you bless this congregation and community. Reveal your servant-love through our ministries, that our work on behalf of our neighbors bears fruit that endures. Hear us, O God.

Your mercy is great.

Here other intercessions may be offered.

We give you thanks, Holy One, for those who served you in this earthly life (*especially*). Renew our hope until that day when all are nourished by your tree of life. Hear us, O God.
Your mercy is great.
Into your hands, gracious God, we commend all for whom we pray, trusting the power of Christ and the gifts of the Spirit.
Amen.

Images in the Readings

The term *law* is tricky for us. According to the covenant in the Old Testament, the law was graciously given by God to delineate the way toward communal happiness. However, Paul uses the term critically, teaching that keeping these 613 commands will not bring us to God. Luther uses the term far more broadly to refer to everything in the Bible that preaches our sin and announces our death. For many contemporary hearers, the term means governmental regulations. Our task is to make sure that the meaning of any particular use of the term is clear. Psychologists suggest, in accord with Luther, that confronting the truth of the human condition is, although sad, finally welcomed; but then as Christians we gladly take refuge in the gospel of God's love in Christ Jesus.

Probably in 1 Thessalonians 2:7 Paul is suggesting that evangelists are like a **nursing mother**, since the children are her own. So Paul offers a balance to Matthew's image of the late-first-century church leader as an exegetical authority. Both are helpful images.

Psalm 110, cited in Matthew 22, pictures the messiah sitting at the **right hand** of God. In ancient Near Eastern courts, the prince or a kind of prime minister sat on the right side of the monarch. From the psalm, the phrase made it all the way into our creeds. In the fifteenth century, the mystic Julian reminds us that the phrase is a metaphor: "But it is not meant that the Son sits on the right hand as one man sits by another in this life, for there is no such sitting, as to my sight, in the Trinity." She suggests that the metaphor means that the Son is "right in the highest nobility of the Father's joy."

Ideas for the Day

- These texts are assigned to the same Sunday as Reformation Sunday. For those who don't wish to use the same assigned Reformation texts as years past, these readings work well for a Reformation observance. The gospel's theme on which commandment is the greatest can be used to explore the right understanding of the law in a Lutheran Reformation context. Jesus' answer, that love of God is combined with love of neighbor, fits well with Luther's understanding of living out our gospel freedom by loving our neighbor. The key question to explore is: How does the good news of Jesus draw us into loving God, and how does this transform us to love our neighbor?

- The Matthew text begins with the Pharisees hearing that Jesus had "silenced the Sadducees." After the Pharisees question Jesus about the law, the text ends with more silence: "No one was able to give him an answer, nor from that day did anyone dare to ask him any more questions" (Matt. 22:46). All have been silenced by Jesus' authority and profound responses. If we are gathering before God in worship with many challenging questions, when do we need to become silent? How does the life, death, and resurrection of Jesus silence us with its profound authority and move us to pause and simply be in awe of him?

- The verses skipped over in the reading from Leviticus speak about the prohibition against harvesting to the edges of the field. The assumption was that travelers and the poor would need something to eat, so the produce of the earth near the edges belonged to those who were hungry. This is in stark contrast to most of our modern assumptions about property rights and maximizing profit. What sounds like theft to our ears is in the eyes of God the right of the hungry. What ways in our modern society do we "harvest to the edges" and leave little for those in need? Michael Coffey's poem "Edges" explores what it means to lose sight of God's holiness when we forget to leave the edges for those who are hungry (www.ocotillo pub.org/2014/02/edges.html).

Connections with the Liturgy

Each time we use *Evangelical Lutheran Worship*'s first option for an opening prayer of confession, we echo today's gospel: "We have not loved our neighbors as ourselves."

Let the Children Come

Children know the rules. They are surrounded by them on the school bulletin boards and signs around town. Children will be aware of the ten commandments through Sunday school, home conversations, or even wider cultural references, but they may not be aware of this greatest commandment. How are they related to one another? What do social order and love have in common? Many older churches have stained glass windows depicting the ten commandments divided into three on one tablet and seven on the other. How would we draw an image that could depict love for God and love for our neighbor?

Assembly Song
Gathering

Great God, your love has called us   ELW 358, WOV 666
Love divine, all loves excelling   ELW 631, LBW 315
O Christ, your heart, compassionate   ELW 722

Psalmody and Acclamations

Horman, John D. "Psalm 1" from *ChildrenSing Psalms*. U, kybd. AFP 9780800663872.

Organ, Anne Krentz. "Psalm 1" from PWA.

Wold, Wayne L. "Psalm 1," Refrain 2, from PSCY.

(GA) Chepponis, James. "Festival Alleluia." Assembly, cant, org, opt SATB, br qrt/qnt, timp, suspended cymbal, fl, hb. MSM 80-847A.

Hymn of the Day

Jesu, Jesu, fill us with your love ELW 708, WOV 765, TFF 83
CHEREPONI

To be your presence ELW 546 *ENGELBERG*

When the poor ones/*Cuando el pobre* ELW 725, LLC 508
EL CAMINO

Offering

We Are Called ELW 720, W&P 147

Come, my way, my truth, my life ELW 816, LBW 513

Communion

Lord, thee I love with all my heart ELW 750, LBW 325

Goodness is stronger than evil ELW 721

Let streams of living justice ELW 710

Sending

Lord of all nations, grant me grace ELW 716, LBW 419

The church of Christ, in every age ELW 729, LBW 433

Additional Assembly Songs

By grace God calls us into life CBM 64

For the healing of the nations SP 12a

Let me be yours forever LBW 490

⊕ Traditional. Thai melody. "Happy Is He Who Walks in God's Wise Way" from *Sound the Bamboo*. U. GIA G-6830.

⊕ Zata, Mr. "Musande mambo mwari" from *Agape: Songs of Hope and Reconciliation*. SATB, perc. Lutheran World Federation. Out of print. Available on Amazon.com.

☼ Brewster, Lincoln. "Love the Lord" from CCLI.

☼ Copeland, Roger. "Reach Out" from CCLI.

☼ Field, Paul/Henk Pool/Ralph Van Manem/Robert Riekert. "Testify to Love" from *Spirit and Song*, vol. 2. OCP.

☼ Houghton, Israel/Aaron Lindsey/Tommy Sims. "Love God, Love People" from CCLI.

☼ Maher, Matt. "I Love You Lord" from *Spirit and Song*, vol. 2. OCP.

☼ Martin, Jennifer. "Break My Heart (The Compassion Song)" from *Spirit and Song*, vol. 2. OCP.

Music for the Day
Choral

♫ Cherwien, David. "When the Poor Ones." SATB, pno or gtr. MSM 50-5425.

Marshall, Jane. "Blessed Is the Man." SATB, kybd. HIN HMC827.

♫ Nelson, Daniel. "To Be Your Presence." SAB, pno. GIA G-8831.

♫ Stanford, C. V. "To Be Your Presence." SATB, org, tpt. GIA G-5413.

Children's Choir

P Horman, John D. "Psalm 1" from *ChildrenSing Psalms*. U, kybd. AFP 9780800663872.

Leaf, Robert. "To the Glory of Our King." U, pno/org. CG CGA173.

Traditional. "Love God and Your Neighbor" from *LifeSongs*. U/2 or 3 pt, pno. AFP 9780806642703.

Keyboard / Instrumental

Albrecht, Mark. "Let Streams of Living Justice" (Thaxted) from *Timeless Tunes for Flute and Piano*. B flat or C inst, pno. AFP 9780800659073.

Bach, J. S. "Lord, Thee I Love with All My Heart" (Herzlich lieb), BWV 1115, from *Neumeister Chorales*. Org. BAR 5181.

P ♫ Nelson, Ronald A. "Jesu, Jesu, Fill Us with Your Love" (Chereponi) from *Easy Hymn Settings for Organ*, vol. 3. Org. AFP 9781451462562.

P ♫ Roberts, Al. "When the Poor Ones" (El camino) from *We Belong to God: Piano Settings of Folk Tunes*. Pno. AFP 9781451451801.

Handbell

P Eithun, Sandra. "Sweet Hour of Prayer" from *Ring Praises!* 2-3 oct, L1+, CG CGB767. 3-5 oct, L1+, CG CGB768.

♫ Larson, Lloyd. "Tribute to the Saints" (Engelberg). SATB vcs and assembly, LOR 10/4025L. Opt full score (3 oct hb, tpt), LOR 30/2613L. Opt acc CD, LOR 99/2714L.

♫ McChesney, Kevin. "Jesu, Jesu, Fill Us with Your Love." 2-3 oct, L2. AFP 1119085.

Tuesday, October 31
Reformation Day

By the end of the seventeenth century, many Lutheran churches celebrated a festival commemorating Martin Luther's posting of the Ninety-five Theses, a summary of the abuses in the church of his time. At the heart of the reform movement was the gospel, the good news that it is by grace through faith that we are justified and set free.

⊕ = global song   ♫ = relates to hymn of the day
☼ = praise song   P = available in Prelude Music Planner

Wednesday, November 1
All Saints Day

The custom of commemorating all of the saints of the church on a single day goes back at least to the third century. All Saints celebrates the baptized people of God, living and dead, who make up the body of Christ. We remember all who have died in the faith and now serve God around the heavenly throne.

Friday, November 3
Martín de Porres, renewer of society, died 1639

Martín was the son of a Spanish knight and Ana Velázquez, a freed black slave from Panama. Martín apprenticed himself to a barber-surgeon in Lima, Peru, and was known for his work as a healer. Martín was a lay brother in the Order of Preachers (Dominicans) and engaged in many charitable works. He was a gardener as well as a counselor to those who sought him out. He was noted for his care of all the poor, regardless of race. His own religious community described him as the "father of charity." His work included the founding of an orphanage, a hospital, and a clinic for dogs and cats. He is recognized as an advocate for Christian charity and interracial justice.

November

Preparing for November

We catch a glimpse of what the month of November might be about, liturgically, seasonally, and spiritually, by looking at the literary forms through which the gospel comes to us in these weeks. On November 5, All Saints Sunday, the gospel comes in eight "Beatitudes," or eight statements that proclaim commandingly—no holds barred—what life in the kingdom of God is and is to be like. "Blessed are . . . ," we hear: the poor in spirit, those who mourn, the meek, those who hunger and thirst for righteousness, the merciful, the pure in heart, the peacemakers, those who are persecuted for righteousness' sake. This is no "pie in the sky by and by" theology. Jesus doesn't say "Blessed were," "Blessed will be," or "Blessed should be." No, these almost hard-nosed blessings make no mistake about saying that blessing comes in the present moment, however complicated and compromised that moment might be.

In the other gospel readings for the month, Jesus speaks in parables, again, through them, giving pictures of the kingdom. The kingdom of God is like a bridesmaid (Lectionary 32). Some of the bridesmaids are prepared to wait for the groom even long through the night; others miss him altogether because they aren't prepared. We wait for Jesus, no doubt about it, but that waiting implies taking action now, in this day—this very day—even when our efforts seem futile, maybe misguided.

The kingdom of God, too, is like a man who gives out talents to his slaves (Lectionary 33), each according to their ability, in the promise that as they sow their gifts, their talents will prosper. The first two slaves make good on the money, investing it well. The third hides it in the sand, afraid of what might come of it, fearful of making any lasting decisions with it. The last one is judged, not the first two. God doesn't care about any sort of worry about justice coming our way, one commendation and then more for each talent used. God wants us to remain present in the day, giving whatever we have been given to give, unhindered by thoughts of where it's all going or what's going to come of it. Generosity with ourselves, not fear, is to be the word of the day, regardless of how it looks like things are shaping up around us.

And a last sort of parable, on Christ the King Sunday: Jesus tells a story about a king who separates the "sheep" from the "goats" on the last day. But it is not the last day that has the emphasis—only the present. Those who ignored the hungry, the thirsty, the stranger, the naked, the sick, and the imprisoned have missed the nature of the kingdom altogether, and even missed the king himself when he came in the present, through those who suffer. But those who tend to the hungry, thirsty, and sick now, in this day—without thought for any sort of future glory through their actions—are the ones who see the king now, right now, right before them. They don't even really need to wait for that future day when he comes to separate the flock. In their care for those who experience life as burden, who have nothing to offer to life but their pain, they have seen the king, truly, already, in all of his glory. Christ the king comes in the now, not so much when life is pulling together, one happy thread after another, as when it is unraveling.

It is November. As Guns N' Roses put it in a song, "It's hard to hold a candle / In the cold November rain." It's a challenge to keep hope going as the last leaf falls off the tree, as the first crunch of the ground swallows life beneath us—as nature moves this time of the year in many parts of the globe. It's a struggle to keep faithful as night takes over day, as it does now in the northern hemisphere. But the texts before us beckon us to hear, in no uncertain terms, that it is in just this time that the faithful are called to be what they are: faithful. We are to remember the dead in hope. We are to call forth faith from the baptized, even when they cannot remember ever having been chosen for it. We are to give thanks for all that is life in the very heart of November, just as the abundance of life passes from our hands. We are, as Søren Kierkegaard—a Danish saint and theologian commemorated on November 11—said, a people who know that "when one has once fully entered the realm of love, the world—no matter how imperfect—becomes rich and beautiful, it consists solely of opportunities for love." And hope. And joy. And trust. Even in November.

All Saints

The second reading for All Saints in year A, Revelation 7:9-17, paints a beautiful picture of the living relationship between Christ and those who have died in the faith. Christ tends to them, in the language of Psalm 23, as "their shepherd." The faithful walk with this shepherd, who guides them "to springs of the water of life." Every sorrow, every hurt they have known in life is taken up and restored by love: As beloved parent to beloved child, God wipes away "every tear from their eyes" (Rev. 7:17).

The prayer of the day affirms this image, speaking of the "inexpressible joys" prepared for the baptized. The kingdom ahead involves far more than walking streets of gold! In preparation for All Saints Sunday, take a survey asking the baptized to share what they think the kingdom to come might be like. Many people—even the baptized!—might have the more secular idea that heaven sounds a little boring, sitting around on a cloud playing a harp all day. How good would it be, as All Saints approaches, to get those thoughts out! Share the results of the survey in worship, during the sermon or perhaps as a kind of announcement into the day. As you process what people have to say, make connections between the kingdom to come and the sacraments. We are baptized not into endless time, but into ongoing relationship. We are given the promise of one who stands for us, stays with us. We are baptized into the promise that Christ is ours, and we are his, and nothing can separate us from his love. Encourage the baptized to think of the mood and movements at baptism. There is joy. There is song. Love is expressed, not just between Christ and the one being baptized, but between the child or adult at the font and the congregation itself. What might those images suggest about the great day to come?

Think also of the mood and movements of holy communion. Food is eaten. Wine is drunk. Song, again, is present. We eat a meal, with our Savior as host, and come as guests both individually and collectively. Joy and peace prevail. Again, what might such images suggest about the life to come?

The prayer of the day also gives thanks for those who have gone before us and asks that we may be led in their way: "Grant us grace to follow your blessed saints in lives of faith and commitment." In preparation for All Saints, you might construct, collaboratively, a large collage of saints. Include pictures of Luther, whose life we celebrate in a special way this fall, and Kierkegaard, the Danish theologian who strove to reform the church into a living relationship with a living God. Include images of the first disciples, like Mary Magdalene and Peter, as well as saints who have special significance in your local ministry context. Add pictures of the newly baptized in your own congregation and of those who have died during the past year. Include with each picture a sentence or two about what the person pictured did to live out her or his life in "faith and commitment." Display the collage in the worship space on All Saints Sunday. Perhaps during fellowship or an educational hour, ask people who their favorite saint is, and why.

Continue to connect All Saints with baptism during a remembrance of the saints in worship. Many congregations light a candle and/or ring a bell after naming those who have been recently baptized and those saints who have recently died. After each candle is lit and/or each bell is rung, pray this prayer or one like it: "We give you thanks for the witness [name] gave in daily life, letting *her/his* light so shine that we saw *her/his* good works and gave glory to you, O God." You might also connect the first reading to a remembrance of the saints. Again, after each candle is lit and/or each bell is rung, pray this prayer or one like it: "We give you thanks, shepherding God, that [name] now is with you in inexpressible joy, where you guide *her/him* to the springs of the water of life, wiping every tear from *her/his* eyes."

Thanksgiving Day

Connect your thanksgiving celebrations to what we do every time we gather for holy communion: in the midst of a real victory not yet fully realized, we give thanks for the surety of God's presence with us, and the "real and certain" hope that as we eat the meal, we know just a taste of what is coming at us: the full revelation of Christ's victory over sin, death, and the power of the devil.

Christ the King

We close the church year remembering that Christ is a king like no other—stooping to serve, and calling us to do the same. Sing "Will you let me be your servant" (ELW 659) or "Jesu, Jesu, fill us with your love" (ELW 708). If you project worship content on a screen, display pictures of the congregation engaging in acts of service—both inside and outside the church—while you sing. After singing, offer a prayer thanking God for the faith and commitment shown by the congregation, as well as for the faith and commitment God shows continually, in Christ, to all the baptized.

Environment

In November we acknowledge the reality of death and celebrate the promise of new life that is always ours in Christ. We give thanks for those who have witnessed to this new life by their faith and commitment. Ask artists in your congregation to create banners out of fall colors—dark greens, deep reds, browns, yellows. Encourage them to think of ways to create these banners not just out of cloth, but out of other mediums as well: paper, canvas, or even decoupaged leaves.

If your font is movable and your seating flexible, consider moving the baptismal font into the center of the assembly this month as you remember the promise of life that holds us even in the midst of death. Keep the candles you lit for All Saints in place through the end of the liturgical year. Light them, giving thanks each Sunday for all those who, in the midst of the November vicissitudes of life, live each present day in faith and commitment.

Reformation 500

This November, we are just barely on the other side of the worldwide and local observances of the 500th anniversary of the Reformation. There may be some residual enthusiasm to continue the observance into these last weeks of 2017. While the typical practice is to commemorate saints on their death dates, this year you might also consider lifting up Martin Luther's birth date (November 10, 1483) and giving thanks for his life. Plan an informal evening gathering with food and drink. Sing some Reformation-era hymns (see "Preparing for Autumn" on pages 249–251 for suggestions). Read excerpts from Luther's Large and Small Catechisms (the complete text of the latter is available in *Evangelical Lutheran Worship*) and his Letter to the Romans, Letter to the Galatians, The Babylonian Captivity of the Church, or the Smalcald Articles. Follow the readings with informal discussion about how the reformer's life and writings continue to shape the church. Close with prayers of thanksgiving for church reformers of every time and place.

Seasonal Checklist

- Consider using harvest decorations during November, from All Saints Sunday through the end of the church year.
- Publicize any special food collections and arrange for delivery to the appropriate agency after the collection.
- Provide a book of remembrance for All Saints Sunday and the month of November in which names of loved ones may be written and remembered aloud in prayer. If candles are lit, order these in advance and prepare to display them appropriately.
- Incorporate the names of those who have died into baptismal remembrance or into the prayers of intercession on All Saints Sunday. Or prepare a sung litany. See *Music*

Sourcebook for All Saints through Transfiguration (Augsburg Fortress, 2013) for guidance.

- Omit the Kyrie.
- Use the canticle of praise ("This is the feast").
- Use the Nicene Creed for the festivals of All Saints and Christ the King; use the Apostles' Creed for other Sundays in November.
- Continue planning for Advent 2017.
- Begin publicizing the schedule of Advent and Christmas worship services.

Worship Texts for November

Confession and Forgiveness

All may make the sign of the cross, the sign marked at baptism, as the presiding minister begins.

Blessed be the holy Trinity, ✢ one God,
who calls us into an everlasting hope,
who guides us to springs of the water of life,
who enlightens us with the spirit of wisdom.
Amen.

One with the communion of saints in all times and places,
let us confess our sin against God and one another.

Silence for reflection and self-examination.

O God, our merciful redeemer,
we confess the ways we live only for ourselves.
We fail to see you in our neighbor's face.
We turn our ears from voices that cry out.
We pass by the hungry and the oppressed.
In your great mercy, forgive our sin
and strengthen us for service to all in need;
through Jesus Christ our Lord. Amen.

In the mercy of almighty God,
Jesus Christ was given to die for you,
and for ✢ his sake,
God forgives you all your sin.
Blessed are you! Rejoice and be glad,
beloved people of God.
Amen.

Offering Prayer

Creator God,
you made everything, and you provide for every need.
The bread we break and the wine we pour come from you.
As we eat and drink with thanksgiving,
fill us with your love;
let that love flow through us to others;
and join us to the saints before us
in a holy and boundless communion;
through Jesus Christ our Lord.
Amen.

Invitation to Communion

Hunger no more. Thirst no more.
Come to the banquet of life.

Prayer after Communion

Sovereign God,
in this meal you give us a foretaste
of the great feast to come.
Keep us faithful to you,
that we, with all your saints,
may at length celebrate
the marriage feast of the Lamb,
Jesus Christ our Lord.
Amen.

Blessing

The love of God surround you;
the grace of ✢ Christ release you;
and the Holy Spirit be your guide and strength,
now and forevermore.
Amen.

Dismissal

Led on by the saints before us,
go in peace to serve the Lord.
Thanks be to God.

Seasonal Rites for November

Thanksgiving for Saints of the Congregation

A litany may be sung on All Saints Day or at other times when remembering and giving thanks for the lives of the saints, especially those from a particular congregation. This litany needs to be prepared well in advance by inviting congregational members to submit names and attributes of people they wish to include.

Music for this litany may be found in *Music Sourcebook for All Saints through Transfiguration* (Augsburg Fortress, 2013) #S507.

The cantor establishes a drone either hummed by all or carried by the organ, a shruti box, or another sustaining instrument. If the drone is carried by an instrument, the assembly may sing only the responses and not the drone.

Leader (*improvised chant, monotone, or spoken*):
O God of the pilgrim's way, we give thanks for those in generations past who have been examples for us of God's love at work in the world. As we pray, we know that we are surrounded by this great, rejoicing cloud of witnesses. Yet even as we name these holy ancestors, we thank God for others whose names we never knew or have forgotten, who showed us the meaning of life in Christ.

Cantor (*improvises the remembrances*):
For blessed *name*, compassionate teacher of children.
For blessed *name*, thoughtful companion.
For blessed *name*, artisan of simple beauty.

Assembly: We give thanks.

At the end of the litany, the leader intones the closing collect:
Leader (*improvised chant, monotone, or spoken*):
Holy God, we honor these, our ancestors in faith
and members of our family.
We, too, seek to do your will: guide us.
We, too, desire to be your servants: strengthen us.
We, too, long to know you clearly: teach us.
And in time, bring us to our eternal home of peace and joy.

Assembly: Amen.

Preparation
The following list may be helpful in constructing appropriate attributes, or other brief, poetic phrases may be created. The worship folder only needs to have the people's response printed and the list of names of those being remembered.

Teacher
Compassionate teacher of children
Teacher of your holy word
Learned bearer of knowledge

Doctor, nurse, psychologist, counselor, caregiver
Healer of mind and spirit
Skilled and helpful healer
Compassionate healer

Altar/Flower Guild member, sacristan
Preparer of holy vessels
Gifted arranger of God's natural beauty

Choir member, instrumentalist, organist
Singer of God's praise
Singer of beautiful song
Master/Mistress of music

Council, governing board, committee member
Steward of our earthly gifts
Trustee of God's beauty and our sacred space
Leader and wise counsel

Artists, writers, composers
Artisan of simple beauty
Gifted writer and poet
Creator in color and joy
Skilled composer of beautiful music

Other
Hospitable example
Generous and gracious provider
Caretaker of God's creation
Advocate of the world's needy
Home of quiet endurance
Tireless servant to the poor

Text by Marilyn Haskel from *Music Sourcebook for All Saints through Transfiguration*. © 2013 Augsburg Fortress.

November 5, 2017
All Saints Sunday

All Saints celebrates the baptized people of God, living and dead, who are the body of Christ. As November heralds the dying of the landscape in many northern regions, the readings and liturgy call us to remember all who have died in Christ and whose baptism is complete. At the Lord's table we gather with the faithful of every time and place, trusting that the promises of God will be fulfilled and that all tears will be wiped away in the new Jerusalem.

Prayer of the Day

Almighty God, you have knit your people together in one communion in the mystical body of your Son, Jesus Christ our Lord. Grant us grace to follow your blessed saints in lives of faith and commitment, and to know the inexpressible joys you have prepared for those who love you, through Jesus Christ, our Savior and Lord, who lives and reigns with you and the Holy Spirit, one God, now and forever.

Gospel Acclamation

Alleluia. They are before the ¹ throne of God,* and the one who is seated on the throne will ¹ shelter them. *Alleluia.* (Rev. 7:15)

Readings and Psalm

Revelation 7:9-17

The book of Revelation is written to seven churches in western Asia Minor during a time of great oppression. Today's reading is a response to the question asked in 6:17: "Who is able to stand?" The writer gives the faithful the assurance of God's protection and a vision of victory.

Psalm 34:1-10, 22

Fear the LORD, you saints of the LORD; for those who fear the LORD lack nothing. (Ps. 34:9)

1 John 3:1-3

A saint is one who has been set apart by God for God's purposes. God, out of divine love, set us apart to be the children of God. Our holy hope is that we shall see God as God really is.

Matthew 5:1-12

In the Beatitudes, Jesus provides a unique description of those who are blessed with God's favor. His teaching is surprising and shocking to those who seek wealth, fame, and control over others.

Preface   All Saints

Color   White

Prayers of Intercession

The prayers are prepared locally for each occasion. The following examples may be adapted or used as appropriate.

Welcoming God's reign of righteousness and mercy, let us pray with people of every time and place.

A brief silence.

Gather your church from every nation, tribe, people, and language to proclaim your salvation. Defend and preserve those who are persecuted because of their faith. Lord, in your mercy,

hear our prayer.

Reveal your will for your creation, mighty God. Renew waters, lands, and skies that are threatened by our carelessness. Teach us to honor and care for the works of your hands. Lord, in your mercy,

hear our prayer.

Move the hearts of all who participate in upcoming elections. Give courage, generosity, and vision to candidates and voters alike. Guide elected officials to answer the call of those who cry out for fair and just policies. Lord, in your mercy,

hear our prayer.

Soothe the pain of those who suffer (*especially*). Comfort those who mourn through the ministry of nurses, those who provide hospice care, visitation ministers, chaplains, and caregivers. Lord, in your mercy,

hear our prayer.

Seek the lost, those who hunger and thirst with questions of faith, and those absent from our worship today. Make us ready to receive newcomers you send to our congregation. Lord, in your mercy,

hear our prayer.

Here other intercessions may be offered.

We remember with thanksgiving the blessed saints whom you have received into your glory, especially (*those who have died during the past year may be named*). Guide us with them to the springs of the water of life. Lord, in your mercy,

hear our prayer.

Receive these prayers and the hopes and concerns of our hearts, O God, as we entrust into your loving care all for whom we pray, through Jesus Christ our Lord.

Amen.

Images in the Readings

The main image in the gospel reading is **the kingdom of heaven**. The image of kingdom stresses a communal and social reality, not an individual psychic experience. This image has been so narrowed by especially nineteenth-century artists into a kind of summer camp in the skies that it is not easy to see in the image God's transforming rule of righteousness. In Revelation the kingdom is imagined with all the angels and saints gathered around God's throne, a depiction common in medieval art but itself distant from our understanding of the universe.

The reading from Revelation resembles a concordance of biblical imagery, each of which connects with numerous biblical passages: **every nation**, **throne**, **Lamb**, **palm branches**, **angels**, **the four living creatures**, **washed**, **blood**, **hunger**, **thirst**, **the sun's heat**, **shepherd**, **springs of the water of life**. That the saints are **robed in white** suggests early Christian baptismal garb, and the word *alb* refers to these white robes that clothe the baptized. In true metaphoric fashion, in which words assert the opposite of a literal meaning, the robes are made white by being washed in blood.

Ideas for the Day

- In the movie *St. Vincent* starring Bill Murray (Weinstein Company, 2014), a young boy whose parents have just divorced finds a mentor in his neighbor who is a cantankerous, loud, irascible war veteran. The movie ends with the boy honoring the man by choosing to research him for a class project on saints. The movie demonstrates the complexities of how we hold the known and unknown together in tension as we think about whom we revere in society. *St. Vincent* highlights the concept that Lutherans consider all Christians simultaneously saint and sinner. Just as the young boy surprised the audience by naming Vincent a saint, God continually surprises us by calling each of us a saint through our baptism.
- The Sermon on the Mount could be seen as a protest of the values of this world. It is not uncommon to see lines of the Beatitudes painted on signs held up at protests or rallies by people of faith who are working for justice. Individuals and/or communities might consider what they would paint on their own protest signs today. See a sample image at religion.blogs.cnn.com/2011/10/07/my-take-occupy-wall-street-looks-like-church-to-me/.
- With over eight million followers on social media, Humans of New York (www.humansofnewyork.com) is a popular photoblog that attempts to be an exhaustive catalog of typical New York City inhabitants. The project has morphed over the years to include not only photographs but also quotes and stories of people whom Brandon Stanton, the site's creator, meets on the street. Invite your congregation to create their own "Saints of Our Congregation" photoblog. This could take place over social media or

even on a bulletin board. Often on All Saints Day stories of famous saints are told. How might the proclamation not only acknowledge but also be drawn from the often equally inspirational stories of all the unknown saints whose lives testify to a God of startling grace and forgiveness?

Connections with the Liturgy

"This is the feast," an optional canticle of praise in *Evangelical Lutheran Worship* (p. 101), quotes today's reading from Revelation: "blessing and honor, glory and might." An optional call to the table (p. 112) cites today's psalm: "Taste and see that the Lord is good."

Let the Children Come

Sometimes adults are reluctant to include children in conversations about death. For children to be included fully in the body of Christ, we must recognize that children wonder about death and grieve. It is an aspect of being human. Remembering the saints is one way we convey the value of human life and show love for one another. Make sure the rituals for the day are accessible for children. For example, if you have a table in the welcome area with photos of saints, is it low enough for children to see easily or add their own offerings of photographs or drawings?

Assembly Song
Gathering

For all your saints, O Lord ELW 427, LBW 176
O God, our help in ages past ELW 632, LBW 320
Rejoice in God's saints ELW 418, WOV 689

Psalmody and Acclamations

Chepponis, James. "Psalm 34." SATB, assembly, org, opt chamber ensemble, hb. MSM 80-848A.
Gelineau, Joseph. "Psalm 34" from ACYG.
Hobby, Robert A. "Psalm 34: I Will Bless the Lord." U, assembly, org. MSM 80-707.
P (GA) Haskel, Marilyn. "I Am Alpha and Omega." MSB2 S519.

Hymn of the Day

For all the saints ELW 422, LBW 174 *SINE NOMINE*
Shall we gather at the river ELW 423, WOV 690, TFF 179 *HANSON PLACE*
Blest are they ELW 728, WOV 764 *BLEST ARE THEY*

Offering

Sing with all the saints in glory ELW 426, WOV 691
Give Thanks for Saints ELW 428

Communion

Taste and see ELW 493, TFF 126
Behold the host arrayed in white ELW 425, LBW 314
Jerusalem, my happy home ELW 628, LBW 331

Sending

Holy God, we praise your name ELW 414, LBW 535
The church's one foundation ELW 654, LBW 369

Additional Assembly Songs

Oh, when the saints go marching in TFF 180
Out from your throne, O God CBM 102
If we live SP 16

⊕ Harbor, Rawn. "Taste and See the Goodness of the Lord" (Psalm 34) from TFF. U.

⊕ Scots traditional. "Hey, My Love" from *I Will Not Sing Alone.* U. GIA G-6512.

☼ Avery, Richard Kinsey/Donald Stuart Marsh. "O How Blessed Are the Poor in Spirit" from CCLI.

☼ Kendrick, Graham. "Blessed Are the Humble" from CCLI.

☼ Maher, Matt. "Unwavering" from CCLI.

☼ Powell, Mac/Tai Anderson/David Carr/Mark Lee. "Children of God" from CCLI.

☼ Townend, Stuart/Andrew Small. "Salvation's Song" from CCLI.

☼ Watson, Wayne. "Blessed Are" from CCLI.

Music for the Day
Choral

P Martinson, Joel. "By All Your Saints" from *Augsburg Easy Choirbook*, vol. 2. 2 pt mxd, org. AFP 9780800677510.

Nelson, Ronald A. "Jesus at the Door." 2 pt mxd, pno. GIA G-6764.

P ♫ Pelz, Walter. "For All the Saints." SATB, assembly, org, br qrt, opt timp. AFP 9780800664374.

P ♫ Schultz, Donna Gartman. "Shall We Gather at the River." SATB, kybd. AFP 9780800659370.

Children's Choir

Bedford, Michael. "Blessed Are They (The Beatitudes)." U/2 pt, org, fl. CG CGA1025.

Traditional. "Glory, Glory, Hallelujah" from *The Book of Church Songs and Spirituals.* U, kybd. GIA G-7816.

P Wold, Wayne L. "I Sing a Song of the Saints of God." U/2 pt, kybd, C inst, opt assembly, opt hb. AFP 9780800632045.

Keyboard / Instrumental

P ♫ Carter, John. "Shall We Gather at the River" (Hanson Place) from *Shall We Gather: Settings for Four-Hand Piano.* Pno (4 hand). HOP 8569.

Kohrs, Jonathan. "Sing with All the Saints in Glory" (Mississippi) from *Four Tunes for Piano and Two Instruments.* 2 insts (C or B flat), pno. AFP 9780800658786.

Lindberg, Oskar. "Gammal fäbodpsalm från Dalarna" from *Augsburg Organ Library: Epiphany.* Org. AFP 9780800659349.

Messiaen, Olivier. "Desseins Eternels" (Eternal Purposes) from *La Nativité du Seigneur.* Org. LED AL 19266.

Handbell

♫ Glasgow, Michael J. "Faith of the Saints." 3-7 oct hb, opt 2 oct hc, opt tpt, L2+. LOR 20/1614L.

♫ Helman, Michael. "Blest Are They." 3-6 oct hb, opt 3-5 oct hc, opt fl, L3-. GIA G-7043.

♫ Tucker, Margaret. "Shall We Gather at the River." 3-5 oct hb, opt 3-4 oct hc, L2. CG CGB298.

November 5, 2017
Time after Pentecost — Lectionary 31

Micah declares God's condemnation of those who abhor justice. Jesus warns against hypocrisy. Paul urges the Thessalonians to lead a life worthy of God. Called to be humble servants, we gather for worship, seeking justice and welcoming all people to share the banquet of life.

Prayer of the Day

O God, generous and supreme, your loving Son lived among us, instructing us in the ways of humility and justice. Continue to ease our burdens, and lead us to serve alongside of him, Jesus Christ, our Savior and Lord.

Gospel Acclamation

Alleluia. You have one instructor, ' the Messiah;* the greatest among you will ' be your servant. *Alleluia.* (Matt. 23:10, 11)

Readings and Psalm

Micah 3:5-12

The Lord announces judgment against prophets who can be bribed to give favorable oracles. Because rulers too can be bribed to practice injustice, Micah announces the coming destruction of Jerusalem. Later, Jeremiah escaped execution because of Micah's daring precedent (Jer. 26:18-19).

Psalm 43

Send out your light and truth, that they may lead me. (Ps. 43:3)

1 Thessalonians 2:9-13

Paul uses paternal imagery to depict the guidance and encouragement he provided to the Thessalonians. They received from Paul the word of God, which energizes their faith.

Matthew 23:1-12

Jesus encourages his disciples to obey the words of Moses they hear from their teachers, but to shun the hypocrisy and pretension of those who do not practice what they teach.

Semicontinuous reading and psalm

Joshua 3:7-17

The Lord promises to be with Joshua as the Lord was with Moses. The entry into the promised land was a liturgical procession in which the priests carried the ark of the covenant, the sign of the Lord's presence.

Psalm 107:1-7, 33-37

We give thanks to you, LORD, for your wonderful works. (Ps. 107:8)

Preface   Sundays

Color   Green

Prayers of Intercession

The prayers are prepared locally for each occasion. The following examples may be adapted or used as appropriate.

Welcoming God's reign of righteousness and mercy, let us pray with people of every time and place.

A brief silence.

Put your word to work within your church, O God. Give pastors and all who teach the faith the wisdom to listen and discern your truth. Lord, in your mercy,

hear our prayer.

Inspire us to establish sanctuaries for endangered species. Spark our passion and curiosity to discover new ways to care for and preserve your beautiful creation. Lord, in your mercy,

hear our prayer.

Move the hearts of all who participate in upcoming elections. Give courage, generosity, and vision to candidates and voters alike. Guide elected officials to answer the call of those who cry out for fair and just policies. Lord, in your mercy,

hear our prayer.

Relieve the burdens of all who suffer in mind, body, or spirit (*especially*). Ease the stress of those who are unemployed and those who are weary from their labors. Lord, in your mercy,

hear our prayer.

Call us all to be students of the Messiah. Give curiosity and insight to Sunday school students, Bible study and book groups, and all teachers and learners to enlarge our understanding of your ways. Lord, in your mercy,

hear our prayer.

Here other intercessions may be offered.

We remember with thanksgiving the blessed saints whom you have received into your glory, especially (*those who have died during the past year may be named*). Guide us with them to the springs of the water of life. Lord, in your mercy,

hear our prayer.

Receive these prayers and the hopes and concerns of our hearts, O God, as we entrust into your loving care all for whom we pray, through Jesus Christ our Lord.

Amen.

Images in the Readings

In the second reading and the gospel, God is likened to a **father**. First-century Jews did not address YHWH as father, but in Greco-Roman paganism, Jupiter was indeed "Father of fathers." The New Testament adopts this cultural title for God yet distinguishes the one who is father of Jesus from the father Jupiter who blasts humankind with lightning, alienates men from each other, and rapes women at will. Especially fourth-century theologians wrote about what Christians mean by calling God Father, explicitly denying that any male sexuality is intended. The psalm for the day illumines "father" by praising God who gives strength, light, truth, joy, gladness, help. Our address "Father" tries to contain these ideas, and far more.

Throughout Scripture, God talks. God's **word** is heard from the beginning of time, it is spoken through the mouths of prophets and preachers, and it is embodied in Jesus Christ himself. The power and authority vested in this Word challenge our culture's postmodern preference for relativism. The churches that take ordination with high seriousness hope that the authority of proclaiming the word is merged with a vocation of servanthood.

Yet again on this Sunday we are called to be **servants**. The extent to which this call is countercultural cannot be exaggerated.

Ideas for the Day

- A popular meme circulating around social media says in large bold letters: "The church is not full of hypocrites." In smaller letters below, it says, "There is always room for more." While it would be easy to read Jesus' words about the religious leaders and apply them to "other" people who are hypocrites, this meme pokes fun and points to the reality of the church's own capacity for hypocrisy.
- Word and servant are two images present in today's readings. It would be appropriate to highlight the significant ministries being carried out through leaders who are called to ministries of word and service. If your congregation is blessed to have one of these leaders present, he or she might be asked to share about his or her work. They are often especially gifted in identifying how God's word is at work in the world.
- Paul remembers with thanksgiving his work with the Thessalonians. He goes on to say, "As for us . . . when . . . we were made orphans by being separated from you—in person, not in heart—we longed with great eagerness to see you face to face" (1 Thess. 2:17). If this Sunday is kept in commemoration of All Saints, Paul's words tap into the great longing so many of us feel for the saints who have gone before us from whom we have been separated "in person, not in heart." Using Paul's imagery, encourage worshipers to spend a few minutes face-to-face engaging with one another around these questions: "Which saints do you long to meet again?" and "How do you see God's word at work in the lives of saints past or present?" Consider incorporating this time of sharing into the proclamation.
- Micah nudges the church to take a close look at its relationship with elected officials and others whom we consider to be modern-day prophets. In what ways might we speak out like Micah today? Are there faith-based community organizers already at work in your community addressing economic injustices? What is your church's relationship with them?

Connections with the Liturgy

"Our Father in heaven" remains the primary Christian address to God. It is good to attend to what Christian theology has meant by that title, as well as what meanings it has denied.

The "peace" that we call out to each other on Sunday is not a pleasant morning greeting, because, like the prophets Micah decries, we "have something to eat." Rather, the peace is the radically altered existence that comes from the Spirit of the risen Christ.

Let the Children Come

Children are attuned to the adult world of titles. We are given a title at baptism. If you look at the liturgy for Holy Baptism, notice how frequently you see a line with "*Name*" above it. We are all baptized into this body of Christ, with our title clarified as "child of God." If we all come into this family with equal status and access, just at different times along the journey, do other social constructs of titles serve a purpose in church? How are some titles helpful (for instance, denoting vocation), while others may widen the divide between children and adults?

Assembly Song
Gathering

Oh, praise the gracious power ELW 651, WOV 750

My soul does magnify the Lord ELW 882, TFF 168

Gather Us In ELW 532, WOV 718

Psalmody and Acclamations

Hopson, Hal. "Psalm 43" from TPP.

Hurd, Bob. "As the Deer Longs" from *Psalm Songs 2*. AFP 0800657713.

+ Pavlechko, Thomas. "Psalm 107:1-7, 33-37" from SMP.

P (GA) Haskel, Marilyn. "I Am Alpha and Omega." MSB2 S519.

Hymn of the Day

Canticle of the Turning ELW 723, W&P 26 *STAR OF COUNTY DOWN*

Praise the Almighty! ELW 877, LBW 539 *LOBE DEN HERREN, O MEINE SEELE*

Will you let me be your servant ELW 659 *THE SERVANT SONG*

⊕ = global song ♫ = relates to hymn of the day + = semicontinuous psalm
☼ = praise song P = available in Prelude Music Planner

Offering

Come to us, creative Spirit ELW 687, LBW 758

Praise to the Lord, all of you ELW 844

Communion

Love consecrates the humblest act ELW 360, LBW 122

Come to the table ELW 481, W&P 33

Lord, whose love in humble service ELW 712, LBW 423

Sending

Soli Deo Gloria ELW 878

Praise to you, O God of mercy ELW 208, WOV 790

Additional Assembly Songs

Shout for joy loud and long WOV 793

Camina, pueblo de Dios LLC 436

O God, we call SP 30

⊕ Botswanan traditional. "Reamo leboga/To God Our Thanks We Give" from *Global Songs 2*. SATB. AFP 9780800656744.

⊕ Mozambique traditional. "Nzamuranza" from *Pave the Way: Global Songs 3*. SATB, cantor. AFP 9780800676896.

✷ Baloche, Paul, et al. "You Have Shown Us" from CCLI.

✷ Hughes, Tim/Rob Hill. "May the Words of My Mouth" from CCLI.

✷ Leiweke, Stephen/John Hartley/Kelly Minter/Henk Pool. "We Will Not Go" from CCLI.

✷ Peterson, Mark. "Whatever Happens" from CCLI.

✷ Powell, Mac/Shawn Lewis/Laura Story. "Praise the Lord" from CCLI.

✷ Seay, Robbie/Ryan Owens/Dan Hamilton/Taylor Johnson. "Hallelujah God Is Near" from CCLI.

Music for the Day
Choral

Balakireff, M. A. "Send Out Thy Light." SATB. MSM 50-6035.

P♫ Costello, Michael D. "Canticle of the Turning: Magnificat." SATTBB, org, tbn, opt assembly. AFP 9781451401615.

P Fleming, Larry L. "Humble Service." SATB. AFP 9780800646226.

P♫ Organ, Anne Krentz. "Canticle of the Turning: My Soul Cries Out with a Joyful Shout." SATB, pno, fl, ob, vc, opt assembly. AFP 9781451498776.

Children's Choir

P Burrows, Mark. "God's Hands" from *Again, I Say Rejoice!* U, kybd. CG CGC56.

Haugen, Marty. "Thanks Be to God." U, SATB, kybd, gtr. GIA G-3994.

Patterson, Mark. "A Prayer for Humility." U, pno. CG CGA989.

Keyboard / Instrumental

Albrecht, Mark. "Gather Us In" (Gather Us In) from *Timeless Tunes for Flute and Piano*. B flat or C inst, pno. AFP 9780800659073.

P♫ Organ, Anne Krentz. "Canticle of the Turning" (Star of County Down) from *Piano Reflections on Advent Tunes*. Pno. AFP 9781451462647.

P♫ Powell, Robert J. "Praise the Almighty!" (Lobe den Herren, O meine Seele) from *Our Cheerful Songs, Hymn Preludes for Organ*. Org. AFP 9781451486070.

P Wilson, Terry D. "Come to Us, Creative Spirit" (Castlewood) from *Creative Spirit: Piano Settings*. Pno, opt C inst. AFP 9781451479607.

Handbell

P Geschke, Susan. "Resounding Joy." 3-5 oct, L2+. HOP 2682.

P Morris, Hart. "Praise to the Lord, the Almighty." 3-5 oct hb, opt hc, L3+, HOP 2703. Opt full score (org), HOP 2703D.

♫ Thompson, Karen. "Canticle of the Turning." 3-6 oct hb, opt 3 oct hc, L3. GIA G-8491.

Tuesday, November 7

John Christian Frederick Heyer, died 1873; Bartholomaeus Ziegenbalg, died 1719; Ludwig Nommensen, died 1918; missionaries

Three missionaries are commemorated on this date. Heyer was the first missionary sent out by American Lutherans. Ordained in 1820, he established Sunday schools and taught at Gettysburg College and Seminary. Heyer became a missionary in the Andhra region of India. During a break in his mission work he received the M.D. degree from what would later be Johns Hopkins University.

Bartholomaeus Ziegenbalg (ZEEG-en-balg) was a missionary to the Tamils of Tranquebar on the southeast coast of India. The first convert to Christianity was baptized about ten months after Ziegenbalg began preaching. His missionary work was opposed by the local Hindus and also by Danish authorities in that area. Ziegenbalg was imprisoned for his work on a charge of converting the natives. Today, the Tamil Evangelical Lutheran Church carries on his work.

Ludwig Ingwer Nommensen was born in Schleswig-Holstein, Germany. In the early 1860s he went to Sumatra to serve as a Lutheran missionary. His work was among the Batak people, who had previously not seen Christian missionaries. Though he encountered some initial difficulties, the missions began to succeed following the conversion of several tribal chiefs. Nommensen translated the Scriptures into Batak while honoring much of the native culture.

Saturday, November 11
Martin, Bishop of Tours, died 397

Martin's pagan father enlisted him in the army at age fifteen. One winter day, a beggar approached Martin for aid, and he cut his cloak in half and gave a portion to the beggar. Later, Martin understood that he had seen the presence of Christ in that beggar, and this ended his uncertainty about Christianity. He soon asked for his release from his military duties, but he was imprisoned instead. After his release from prison he began preaching, particularly against the Arians. In 371 he was elected bishop of Tours. As bishop he developed a reputation for intervening on behalf of prisoners and heretics who had been sentenced to death.

Saturday, November 11
Søren Aabye Kierkegaard, teacher, died 1855

Kierkegaard (KEER-keh-gore), a nineteenth-century Danish theologian whose writings reflect his Lutheran heritage, was the founder of modern existentialism. Though he was engaged to a woman he deeply loved, he ended the relationship because he believed he was called to search the hidden side of life. Many of his works were published under a variety of names, so that he could reply to arguments from his own previous works. Kierkegaard's work attacked the established church of his day—its complacency, its tendency to intellectualize faith, and its desire to be accepted by polite society.

November 12, 2017
Time after Pentecost — Lectionary 32

Today the prophet Amos calls for justice to roll down like waters. Paul urges us to encourage one another with the promised coming of the Lord. Jesus tells the parable of the wise and foolish bridesmaids. Surrounded by the faithful of every time and place, we celebrate Christ's coming in our midst in the word of life and the feast of victory—the marriage feast of the lamb.

Prayer of the Day

O God of justice and love, you illumine our way through life with the words of your Son. Give us the light we need, and awaken us to the needs of others, through Jesus Christ, our Savior and Lord.

Gospel Acclamation

Alleluia. Keep awake ¹ and be ready,* for you do not know on what day your ¹ Lord is coming. *Alleluia.* (Matt. 24:42, 44)

Readings and Psalm
Amos 5:18-24

In the days of Amos people thought that the day of the Lord would be a time of great victory, but Amos announced that it would be a day of darkness, not light. He said liturgy is no substitute for obedience. The Lord demands justice and righteousness in the community.

or Wisdom 6:12-16

Wisdom is part of the structure of the universe and is easily accessible to those who want to find her. Wisdom actually seeks people out. People who are wise are free from care.

Psalm 70

You are my helper and my deliverer; O LORD, do not tarry. (Ps. 70:5)

or Wisdom 6:17-20

The beginning of wisdom is the most sincere desire for instruction. (Wis. 6:17)

1 Thessalonians 4:13-18

Some of the Thessalonians are worried that dead Christians will be excluded from the resurrection to eternal life when Christ comes again. Paul reassures them with the word of hope that all Christians, living or dead, will be raised into everlasting life with Christ.

Matthew 25:1-13

Jesus tells a parable about his own second coming, emphasizing the need for readiness at all times.

Semicontinuous reading and psalm
Joshua 24:1-3a, 14-25

In this farewell speech, Joshua exhorts the people to serve only the Lord. Joshua erected a stone monument to serve as a witness to the solemn promise the people had made to serve the Lord.

Psalm 78:1-7

We will recount to generations to come the power of the LORD. (Ps. 78:4)

Preface   Sundays

Color   Green

Prayers of Intercession

The prayers are prepared locally for each occasion. The following examples may be adapted or used as appropriate.

Welcoming God's reign of righteousness and mercy, let us pray with people of every time and place.

A brief silence.

Awaken your church to be ready to respond when Christ meets us in the cries of those in need. We lift up the church's mission of care through Lutheran World Relief and other agencies (*especially*). Lord, in your mercy,

hear our prayer.

We give thanks for natural resources like oil, coal, trees, sun, water, and wind. Help us to use them wisely. Lord, in your mercy,

hear our prayer.

Answer the cries of your people in nations caught in war and destruction (*especially*). Hold in your care all veterans and their families. Ease the burden of tough memories and bring restoration and wholeness. Lord, in your mercy,

hear our prayer.

Shine your merciful and healing light on the despairing places of our minds and souls. Bring hope in the midst of danger, depression, and illness. (*We pray especially for . . .*) Lord, in your mercy,

hear our prayer.

Bless those who prepare for marriage or who have been married in this place. Strengthen all bonds of friendship and relationship in our community. Give us joy in life together. Lord, in your mercy,

hear our prayer.

Here other intercessions may be offered.

Keep us alert for Christ's coming, sustained by the promise that we will be reunited with all the faithful who have died (*especially*). Thank you for their lives of witness. Lord, in your mercy,

hear our prayer.

Receive these prayers and the hopes and concerns of our hearts, O God, as we entrust into your loving care all for whom we pray, through Jesus Christ our Lord.

Amen.

Images in the Readings

The **wedding feast** is a biblical image for our life with God, and Christians have used the image as one way to describe holy communion. Philipp Nicolai's hymn "Wake, awake, for night is flying" (ELW 436), honored by some Christians with the title the Queen of Chorales, is a fine example of the use of marriage imagery. In biblical times a wedding was not about personal choice and lavish expense but about the communal celebration of the promise of new life and commitment.

Christians have used the **lamp** as an image for the word of God, with which we see God's way. Many Christians use oil as part of the ritual of baptism.

When Amos writes of the **waters** and "ever-flowing stream," Christians think of the water of baptism, which means to carry us, in the ship of the church, into a life of justice and righteousness.

Many Christians have literalized Paul's eschatological imagery of Christ's **appearance** in the skies, an **archangel**, a **trumpet**, and **clouds**. Recall that for Paul, this picture fit scientifically with his understanding of the universe. For us it does not, and to be Christian does not mean to hide in archaic thinking. Thus we need to use care when citing this first-century picture of the end of all things. We repeat Martin Luther: "What is this? What does this mean?"

Ideas for the Day

- The images of Matthew and Amos call to mind the idiom "rude awakening," the shock of realizing that the truth in a situation is not what one had thought. Such moments can be harrowing, but the scriptures call us to take advantage of such moments to be transformed by God's grace. Consider exploring this theme by sharing stories of "rude awakenings." A classic and well-known one is Aesop's *The Tortoise and the Hare*, where the hare awakes to realize that his pride has lost him a race he easily could have won. Many versions of this story are available online and can be found through a quick search.

- In the parable of the ten bridesmaids, Matthew distinguishes between wise and foolish ways of waiting. John Mayer's 2006 song "Waiting on the World to Change" (from the album *Continuum* [Columbia Records, 2006]) explores a feeling of powerless waiting in the face of injustice. Yet Martin Luther says in his Small Catechism that God's kingdom is coming already—we just pray that we may be involved as we await its fulfillment. Explore the line between complacency or resignation and hopeful preparation as you look at wise and foolish ways of waiting in your context. Call on your assembly to name what they are waiting for or feel our world is waiting for. Ponder what they say as you begin preparing for Advent, the season of hopeful expectation.

- The reading from Amos draws a connection between true worship and work against injustice. The "Nairobi Statement on Worship and Culture" (Lutheran World Federation, 1996) similarly calls on all worship to contain countercultural components. God calls both Amos and us to hear the cry to stand in solidarity with those most marginalized and oppressed in our society. Use the opportunity of this moment in the lectionary to establish a relationship with an organization working for justice in your context. Invite guest speakers who have been affected by systemic injustices or who work in solidarity with those affected in your area. Let your worship be one in which cries for justice and songs of praise are lifted together.

Connections with the Liturgy

As part of Thanksgiving at the Table prayers I, III, IV, VI, VII, VIII, and IX in *Evangelical Lutheran Worship*, the assembly calls out the ecumenically popular credo "Christ has died. Christ is risen. Christ will come again." With Paul we place our faith in the death and resurrection of Christ, and we stand with Amos, Paul, and Matthew to anticipate the coming of God our Savior. Christians believe that Christ comes not only at the end of time but here this Sunday in word, bread, and wine.

Let the Children Come

Who can't sympathize with the eager bridesmaids—so eager they didn't take time to slow down and get ready? The practice of "getting ready" to enter sacred space, holy time, and worship is a skill. Children do not do this on their own but need the adults around them to teach them how to be ready. The Godly Play® method of faith nurture points out that "getting ready" is important to cross the threshold between the ordinary and the sacred. How does your welcome area help children begin to slow down? How does the gathering space help them get rid of figurative or literal baggage before worship?

Assembly Song
Gathering

Come, we that love the Lord ELW 625, WOV 742, TFF 135
Rejoice, rejoice, believers ELW 244, LBW 25
Through the night of doubt and sorrow ELW 327, LBW 355

Psalmody and Acclamations

Mathis, William H. Refrain for "Psalm 70" from *After the Prelude: Year A*. U/cant, hb. CG CGB658 (digital version), CGB659 (printed version). Use with ELW psalm tone 9 (in Dm).
Raabe, Nancy. "Psalm 70" from PSCY.
+ Nicholson, Paul. "Psalm 78," Refrain 1, from PSCY.
P (GA) Haskel, Marilyn. "I Am Alpha and Omega." MSB2 S519.

Hymn of the Day

Wake, awake, for night is flying ELW 436, LBW 31, LLC 276
   WACHET AUF
Blessed assurance ELW 638, TFF 118 *ASSURANCE*
Soul, adorn yourself with gladness ELW 488, LBW 224
   SCHMÜCKE DICH ELW 489, LLC 388 *CANTO A BORINQUEN*

Offering

When long before time ELW 861, WOV 799
Soon and very soon ELW 439, WOV 744, TFF 38

Communion

Wait for the Lord ELW 262
Arise, my soul, arise! ELW 827, LBW 516
For the bread which you have broken ELW 494, LBW 200

Sending

Let streams of living justice ELW 710
Let justice flow like streams ELW 717, WOV 763

Additional Assembly Songs

Let justice roll like a river W&P 85
Come, beloved of the Maker CBM 67, ELW 306
Who will set us free? SP 44
⊕ Bell, John. "Send Out Your Light" from *Come, All You People: Shorter Songs for Worship*. SAB. GIA G-4391.
⊕ South African traditional. "Sizohamba naye/We Will Go with God" from *Global Songs 2*. SATB. AFP 9780800656744.
☼ Carter, Sean/Brandon Collins/Magen Thurman/Crystal Yates. "Until That Day Comes" from CCLI.
☼ Christensen, Chris. "Let Justice Roll Down" from CCLI.
☼ Slater, Tom/Brenton Brown. "Let My Life Be Like a Love Song" from CCLI.
☼ Smith, Dustin/Michael Farren/Michael W. Smith/Seth Mosley. "He Is Alive" from CCLI.
☼ Tomlin, Chris/Matt Redman/Jesse Reeves. "Shout" from CCLI.
☼ Wesley, Charles/John Cennick/Rich Gundelock/Zack Sprowls. "See He Comes" from CCLI.

Music for the Day
Choral

P♫ Christiansen, F. Melius. "Wake, Awake." SSAATTBB. AFP 9780800645069.
P Helgen, John. "Keep Your Lamps Trimmed and Burning." U or 2 pt, pno. AFP 9780800677497.
P♫ Perkins, Scott. "Soul, Adorn Yourself with Gladness." SATB, org. AFP 9781451424041.
Thomas, André. "Keep Your Lamps." SATB, conga drm. HIN HMC-577.

Children's Choir

P Gilpin, Greg. "Little Innocent Lamb." U/2 pt, pno. CG CGA1359.
P Horman, John. "The Covenant" from *Sing the Stories of God's People*. U, kybd. AFP 9781451460537.
Wright, Vicki Hancock. "Give Me Oil in My Lamp" from *Can't Wait to Sing! Anthems and Fun Songs to Sing All Year*. U, pno, opt perc. CG CGC50.

⊕ = global song   ♫ = relates to hymn of the day   + = semicontinuous psalm
☼ = praise song   P = available in Prelude Music Planner

Keyboard / Instrumental

♫ Carter, John. "Blessed Assurance" (Assurance) from *Gospel Treats for Jazz Piano*. Pno. AFP 9780800677596.

♫ Manz, Paul O. "Wake, Awake, for Night Is Flying" (Wachet auf) from *Improvisations for the Christmas Season, Set 1*. Org. MSM 10-100.

P Maxwell, David. "When Long before Time" (The Singer and the Song) from *We Walk by Faith: Organ Settings*. Org. AFP 9781451479584.

P ♫ Raabe, Nancy. "Soul, Adorn Yourself with Gladness" (Canto a Borinquen) from *Grace and Peace, vol. 4: Hymn Portraits for Piano*. Pno. AFP 9781451443561.

Handbell

♫ Eithun, Sandra. "Jesus Is Mine." 3-6 oct hb, opt 3-5 oct hc, L3. ALF 38732.

♫ Eithun, Sandra. "Soul, Adorn Yourself with Gladness." 3-5 oct hb, opt fl, L2+. CPH 97-7385.

Glasgow, Michael J. "Keep Your Lamps (Trimmed and Burning)." 3-6 oct hb, opt 3 oct hc, L3. HOP 2586.

Friday, November 17

Elizabeth of Hungary, renewer of society, died 1231

This Hungarian princess lived her entire life in east-central Germany, and is often called Elizabeth of Thuringia. Married to a duke, she gave large sums of money, including her dowry, for relief of the poor and sick. She founded hospitals, cared for orphans, and used the royal food supplies to feed the hungry. Though she had the support of her husband, her generosity and charity did not earn her friends within the royal court. At the death of her husband, she was driven out. She joined a Franciscan order and continued her charitable work, though she suffered abuse at the hands of her confessor and spiritual guide. Her lifetime of charity is particularly remarkable when one remembers that she died at the age of twenty-four. She founded two hospitals, and many more are named for her.

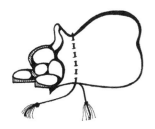

November 19, 2017

Time after Pentecost — Lectionary 33

Our readings during November speak of the end times. Zephaniah proclaims that the coming day of the Lord will be filled with wrath and distress. Paul says it will come like a thief in the night and urges us to be awake and sober. Jesus tells the parable of the talents, calling us to use our gifts, while we still have time, for the greater and common good. In a world filled with violence and despair, we gather around signs of hope—word, water, bread and wine—eager to welcome the good news of Christ's coming among us.

Prayer of the Day

Righteous God, our merciful master, you own the earth and all its peoples, and you give us all that we have. Inspire us to serve you with justice and wisdom, and prepare us for the joy of the day of your coming, through Jesus Christ, our Savior and Lord.

Gospel Acclamation

Alleluia. Abide in me as I a- ' bide in you;* those who abide in me ' bear much fruit. *Alleluia.* (John 15:4, 5)

Readings and Psalm

Zephaniah 1:7, 12-18

Zephaniah (like the prophet Amos in last week's first reading) presents the day of the Lord as one of judgment and wrath. Descriptions of the last day in the New Testament include details taken from Old Testament accounts of the day of the Lord.

Psalm 90:1-8 [9-11] 12

So teach us to number our days that we may apply our hearts to wisdom. (Ps. 90:12)

1 Thessalonians 5:1-11

Though we do not know and cannot calculate the day of Christ's return, we live faithfully in the here and now as we anticipate the day when we will be given eternal salvation through our Lord Jesus Christ.

Matthew 25:14-30

Jesus tells a parable about his second coming, indicating that it is not sufficient merely to maintain things as they are. Those who await his return should make good use of the gifts that God has provided them.

Semicontinuous reading and psalm

Judges 4:1-7

Deborah was a prophetess and judge who, with her general, Barak, led a victorious holy war against a stronger Canaanite force from the north.

Psalm 123

Our eyes look to you, O God, until you show us your mercy. (Ps. 123:2)

Preface   Sundays

Color   Green

Prayers of Intercession

The prayers are prepared locally for each occasion. The following examples may be adapted or used as appropriate.

Welcoming God's reign of righteousness and mercy, let us pray with people of every time and place.

A brief silence.

We pray for the church. Enliven its witness in ecumenical ministries, feeding programs, and new ventures. Open our hearts to friendships that share faith, and open our mouths to share your good news. Lord, in your mercy,

hear our prayer.

We pray for parks and open spaces, for clean air and clear water. Help us protect places where we are reminded of God's work in creation and find renewal. Lord, in your mercy,

hear our prayer.

We pray for those who have been and are still today enslaved, trafficked, or oppressed. Make clear the needs of those who are silenced by suffering, that we may listen and bring an end to exploitation. Lord, in your mercy,

hear our prayer.

We pray for those who cry out for healing, hope, or help, and for those for whom we have promised to pray (*especially*). Bring relief to caregivers and surround those who are lonely with your powerful presence. Lord, in your mercy,

hear our prayer.

We pray for this congregation and the talents and treasures each person brings. Bring new talents to blossom among us, as we encourage and build up one another. Lord, in your mercy,

hear our prayer.

Here other intercessions may be offered.

Lord, our dwelling place in all generations, we remember with thanksgiving all who have died in you (*especially*). Teach us to count our days as gifts from you. Lord, in your mercy,

hear our prayer.

Receive these prayers and the hopes and concerns of our hearts, O God, as we entrust into your loving care all for whom we pray, through Jesus Christ our Lord.

Amen.

Images in the Readings

It is interesting that our English word ***talent***, meaning "ability," comes from interpretations of this parable. Christians believe that God's creation is ongoing, that every human capability is a gift from the Creator, and that we are called to use all of God's creation wisely.

Zephaniah's litany describing **a day of wrath** continues in our time especially in popular disaster movies. Humans continue to be fearful of an unknown future. When Christians gather on Sunday before an image of the crucified Christ, we acknowledge our fears, and protecting ourselves with the breastplate and helmet of the faith, we join together hoping for God's mercy.

Paul likens the coming of the end to **labor pains**. With the pregnant woman, we hope that the pains will lead to life. The infant will come into the light.

Ideas for the Day

- The end-time scenarios we read today have an important place in the sacred story because they offer an unflinching view of God's attention to the consequences of evil, injustice, greed, and other personal and corporate sins. Today many people already live in "the outer darkness" of extreme poverty, terrorism, racism, and prejudice—and we cannot ignore their plight. If we are indeed children of light, destined not for wrath but for salvation, what good news do we offer the marginalized and oppressed? What ministries, global and local, best exemplify our faithful living as children of light who embrace others out of our abundance and offer tangible signs of God's grace and salvation?

- Luise Schottroff (*The Parables of Jesus*, Fortress, 2006) does not think that the parable of the talents is an example of God's unwavering justice. She reminds us that in Matthew's gospel Jesus always identifies with the poor, the hungry, and the outcasts. When the slave who was given one talent says that his master is a harsh man, he tells the truth. Jesus is an altogether different master and lord. He offers hope for those who can't find success in the dominant social systems. Consider again the people you see and read about every day who might be unfairly judged as worthless. In what appropriate ways can you share their stories and affirm their dignity as women, men, and children made in the image of God?

- Even though today's readings emphasize threats of destruction and divine retribution, we know of other biblical end-time teachings that promise great joy and peace. Some of us may doubt that there is a place of eternal damnation, but we cannot deny that the idea of a day of judgment helps guard against spiritual complacency. Frederick Buechner once said that "doubts are the ants in the pants of faith. They keep it awake and moving" (*Wishful*

Thinking: A Seeker's ABC, HarperOne, 1993). As the church year comes to a close, celebrate the things that keep us awake and moving, prayerful, careful, and yet bold in our proclamation of God's salvation through the grace of our Lord Jesus Christ.

Connections with the Liturgy

Paul's description of us as "children of light" is found in the rite of Holy Baptism: a candle, lit from the paschal candle of Easter, is presented to the newly baptized. Jesus, the light of life, gives light to the baptized, and we are to live so that others may see us shining with Christ.

Let the Children Come

While Paul writes to the community of Thessalonica not to worry about the times and seasons, indeed we feel the calendar of the church year coming to an end, getting ready for a new beginning. For those at the northernmost latitudes, you already feel the days getting shorter. While the wider culture is already clamoring with Christmas commercials, the church knows that we cannot speed up time; we pass through it in due course. Take time as a community to support children faithfully through the coming season, so that it may be full of meaning instead of empty with clutter.

Assembly Song
Gathering

O God, our help in ages past ELW 632, LBW 320

Christ is made the sure foundation ELW 645, WOV 747, LBW 367

Through the night of doubt and sorrow ELW 327, LBW 355

Psalmody and Acclamations

Mathis, William H. Refrain for "Psalm 90" from *After the Prelude: Year A*. U/cant, hb. CG CGB658 (digital version), CGB659 (printed version). Use with ELW psalm tone 1 or 6 (in C).

True, Lori. "You Have Been Our Dwelling Place." SATB, cant, assembly, kybd, gtr, C inst. GIA G-6067.

+ Gelineau, Joseph. "Psalm 123" from ACYG.

P (GA) Haskel, Marilyn. "I Am Alpha and Omega." MSB2 S519.

Hymn of the Day

Lord of light ELW 688, LBW 405 *ABBOT'S LEIGH*

As saints of old ELW 695, LBW 404 *FOREST GREEN*

Lord of glory, you have bought us ELW 707, LBW 424 *HYFRYDOL*

Offering

O Christ the same ELW 760, WOV 778

Let us talents and tongues employ ELW 674, WOV 754, TFF 232

Communion

Christ, Be Our Light ELW 715

When peace like a river ELW 785, LBW 346, TFF 194

Sending

Go, my children, with my blessing ELW 543, TFF 161, WOV 721

Oh, happy day when we shall stand ELW 441, LBW 351

Additional Assembly Songs

Herald, sound the note of judgment LBW 556

Heal us, Lord SP 14

I've just come from the fountain WOV 696, TFF 11

⊕ Chen-Chang, Yang. "In All the Seasons Seeking God" from *Sound the Bamboo*. U. GIA G-6830.

⊕ Dexter, Noel. "The Right Hand of God." SATB. ELW 889.

☼ Getty, Keith/Stuart Townend. "O Church Arise" from CCLI.

☼ Hopson, Hal. "Take My Gifts (Gifts)" from CCLI.

☼ Mohr, John. "Find Us Faithful" from CCLI.

☼ Peterson, Mark. "The Day Will Come" from CCLI.

☼ Smith, Todd/Jennie Lee Riddle/Jordan Merritt. "People of the Cross" from CCLI.

☼ Story, Laura/Jason Ingram. "There Is a Kingdom" from CCLI.

Music for the Day
Choral

Bouman, Paul. "Rejoice, Rejoice, Believers." SATB, org. MSM 50-0004.

P Haydn, Franz Joseph. "Through Every Age, Eternal God" from *Augsburg Motet Book*. 3 pt mxd, opt kybd. AFP 9781451423709.

P Highben, Zebulon M. "O God of Light." SATB, assembly, org, tpt. AFP 9781451462425.

Parker, Alice. "Through Every Age, Eternal God." SATB. GIA G-5090.

Children's Choir

Bell, John L. "Over My Head" from *Sing with the World: Global Songs for Children*. U, kybd, opt descant. GIA G-7339.

Widestrand, Olle. "Many Are the Lightbeams" from *LifeSongs*. U, kybd. AFP 9780806642703.

P Patterson, Mark. "When in Our Music God Is Glorified" from *ChildrenSing with Instruments!* U, pno, opt hb/hc. AFP 9781451461145.

Keyboard / Instrumental

Kohrs, Jonathan. "Let Us Talents and Tongues Employ" (Linstead) from *Four Tunes for Piano and Two Instruments*. 2 insts (C or B flat), pno. AFP 9780800658786.

P Organ, Anne Krentz. "O Christ the Same" (Red Hill Road) from *Reflections on Hymn Tunes for the Fall Festivals*. Pno. AFP 9780800663834.

⊕ = global song ♫ = relates to hymn of the day + = semicontinuous psalm
☼ = praise song P = available in Prelude Music Planner

P ♫ Sedio, Mark. "As Saints of Old" (Forest Green) from *Come and Praise*, vol. 2. Org. AFP 9780806696928.

♫ Vaughan Williams, Ralph (1872–1958). "Lord of Glory, You Have Bought Us" (Hyfrydol) from *Three Preludes Founded on Welsh Hymn Tunes*. Org. MMP 2536.

Handbell

♫ Afdahl, Lee J. "Abbot's Leigh." 3-5 oct, L2+. HOP 2103.

♫ Geschke, Susan. "Lord of Glory." 2-3 oct, L1. ALF 19640.

♫ Kerr, J. Wayne. "I Sing the Mighty Power of God (Forest Green)." 3-5 oct, L2+. MSM 30-829.

November 23, 2017
Day of Thanksgiving (U.S.A.)

At harvest time we join the psalmist in offering thanksgiving to God: "You crown the year with your goodness, and your paths overflow with plenty." We are grateful for the abundance of the good things of God's creation. Paul reminds us that our thanksgiving overflows into generosity. As the body of Christ in the world, we give ourselves away as bread for the hungry.

Prayer of the Day

Almighty God our Father, your generous goodness comes to us new every day. By the work of your Spirit lead us to acknowledge your goodness, give thanks for your benefits, and serve you in willing obedience, through Jesus Christ, our Savior and Lord.

Gospel Acclamation

Alleluia. God is able to provide you with every blessing | in abundance,* so that by always having enough of everything, you may share abundantly in ev- | 'ry good work. *Alleluia.* (2 Cor. 9:8)

Readings and Psalm

Deuteronomy 8:7-18

Times of abundance tempt us to forget the Lord and rely on our own power and resources. But the Lord is the one who took Israel out of Egypt, led and fed them in the wilderness, brought them into the land, and gave them power to be productive. To thank this God is to remember and proclaim God's deeds.

Psalm 65

You crown the year with your goodness, and your paths overflow with plenty. (Ps. 65:11)

2 Corinthians 9:6-15

Christian fellowship involves sharing with those in need. Here Paul is gathering a collection for the church in Jerusalem from all the Gentile churches he helped found. We can be extravagant in our giving because God is extravagant, not stingy, in providing for our lives.

Luke 17:11-19

A Samaritan leper becomes a model for thanksgiving. He does not take for granted the kindness shown to him, but takes time to thank Jesus and glorify God.

Preface   Weekdays

Color   of the season

Prayers of Intercession

The prayers are prepared locally for each occasion. The following examples may be adapted or used as appropriate.

Welcoming God's reign of righteousness and mercy, let us pray with people of every time and place.

A brief silence.

Holy God, you invite us to share abundantly in every good work. As congregations join together in worship, make us bold in our generosity so that all may be fed. Lord, in your mercy,
hear our prayer.

On this Day of Thanksgiving, you crown the year with your goodness in creation. Supply seed to the sower, bread for food, and a shared harvest for all. Lord, in your mercy,
hear our prayer.

Lift up First Nations, native peoples, and indigenous tribes who live in many places all across the world (*especially*). Support those who teach and preserve our many cultures that they may be understood as reflections of your diverse creation. Lord, in your mercy,
hear our prayer.

Put an end to poverty, homelessness, and hunger. Fill our tables with healthy food. We pray for those who are lonely, stressed, and sick (*especially*). Surround them with your presence and care. Lord, in your mercy,
hear our prayer.

♫ = relates to hymn of the day

P = available in Prelude Music Planner

Open our hearts to be cheerful givers, sharing abundantly in your good work. Teach us to give thanks to you for every blessing and work of healing in our lives. Lord, in your mercy,
hear our prayer.

Here other intercessions may be offered.

Comfort all who grieve with the assurance of hope that all who have died will be raised with Christ. We remember and honor those whose witness of the faith echoes beyond the grave (*especially Clement, bishop of Rome, and Miguel Agustín Pro*). Lord, in your mercy,
hear our prayer.

Receive these prayers and the hopes and concerns of our hearts, O God, as we entrust into your loving care all for whom we pray, through Jesus Christ our Lord.
Amen.

Images in the Readings

We are **lepers**, this is true: our very bodies are dying, little by little. Most of us are also **Samaritans**, this is true: we are seen by at least some others as not religiously pure enough. So in this worship service and with our entire lives, we are to praise God with a loud voice.

Paul's use here of the image of the **seed** can be applied to the New Testament's metaphor of the word of God as seed. God provides the seed in the hearts of the baptized, and that seed grows in order for its fruit to be shared with others.

The **good land**, as the Deuteronomy passage calls the Promised Land, has been interpreted in the church as our life together in the faith. The land with the flowing streams, vines, and wheat—these not only can have literal reference to a contemporary life of plenty but also can refer to the gifts of God that are realized in faith. But millions of people in the world, many Christians, and perhaps some worshipers present are not "eating their fill."

Ideas for the Day

- Though strictly speaking, Thanksgiving is a secular holiday, consider its potential as an intersection between the life of the church and the wider culture. It provides a tremendous opportunity for worship to cut through a sometimes perfunctory cultural ritual to transform people's understanding of and appreciation for a day set aside for giving thanks. Thoughtfulness in a Thanksgiving service demonstrates the way Christian faith deepens every aspect of our lives. For more thinking on how thoughtful Christian speech can transform our culture, check out the chapter "Talking Ourselves into Being Christian" in Thomas G. Long's *Testimony* (San Francisco: Jossey-Bass, 2009).
- Luke's story of the lepers should encourage us to be like the one man who returned with thanks. Often as communities, we fail to give proper thanks to one another for the gift that we are to one another—through hard work, talents and gifts, financial support, and presence through difficult times. We also often forget to take time to reflect on where God has brought us over the past year and on the transformations God has seen us through as communities of faith. Consider ways to thank the people of your community in general and specific ways to thank individuals for their contributions to your common life. Think about providing some space in your service for people to share thanks for ways they have seen God active in your community through one another.
- Paul calls the church at Corinth and us to respond to God's generosity by passing that generosity on to our neighbors. Yet unfortunately Thanksgiving often becomes a moment of conspicuous consumption in our culture. Consider ways that your community could be countercultural in this regard within your context. If possible, consider organizing a Thanksgiving dinner at your church where all share a common table. As a congregation or entity, think about making a special Thanksgiving gift of financial support to another church or organization that is struggling to model giving as a godly manifestation of your gratitude.

Connections with the Liturgy

The Greek name for holy communion is *eucharist*, "thanksgiving." Heeding Paul's admonition, assemblies continue to take up a collection for the poor at every gathering. Recent patterns of direct withdrawal from the bank accounts of members ought not confuse this essential Christian calling with a kind of dues owed to the parent organization.

Let the Children Come

God's abundant harvest is always enough, and we give thanks. The church pauses to give thanks on this civic holiday while the wheels of commerce are engrossed in commercializing and capitalizing on the church's upcoming holy days. The buying and selling frenzy comes at the expense of children. The church is implored to decommercialize holy days, and one part of that is being thankful for what we have. How can the church support families in a life of thankfulness? How does the eucharist every Sunday subvert a wider culture of excess and consumption?

Assembly Song
Gathering

Come, ye thankful people, come   ELW 693, LBW 407
For the beauty of the earth   ELW 879, LBW 561
Sing to the Lord of harvest   ELW 694, LBW 412

Psalmody and Acclamations

Dudley-Smith, Timothy. "Every Heart Its Tribute Pays" (St. George's, Windsor) from PAS 65E.
Long, Larry J. "Psalm 65," Refrain 2, from PSCY.

Schutte, Daniel L. "Glory and Praise to Our God" from PAS 65D.

(GA) Gospel acclamation from ELW setting seven (S179a). Use psalm tone 1, 6, 7, or 10 in E major with proper verse for the Day of Thanksgiving.

Hymn of the Day

Great is thy faithfulness ELW 733, TFF 283, WOV 771
FAITHFULNESS

We praise you, O God ELW 870, LBW 241 *KREMSER*
For the fruit of all creation ELW 679, WOV 760 *AR HYD Y NOS*
LBW 563 *SANTA BARBARA*

Offering

God of the sparrow ELW 740
Have you thanked the Lord? ELW 829, TFF 270

Communion

The numberless gifts of God's mercies ELW 683
Praise and thanksgiving ELW 689, LBW 409
O God beyond all praising ELW 880, WOV 797

Sending

Now thank we all our God ELW 839/840, LBW 533/534
Let all things now living ELW 881, LBW 557

Additional Assembly Songs

Give thanks TFF 292, W&P 41
All things bright and beautiful WOV 767
A Dios gloria, alabanza LLC 577
⊕ Kim, Seung Nam. "Soft Rains of Spring Flow" from *Glory to God*. U. WJK 0664238971.
⊕ Solis, Melchizedek M. "In Great Thanksgiving" from *Sound the Bamboo*. 2 pt. GIA G-6830.
☼ Altrogge, Mark. "Greater than We Can Imagine" from CCLI.
☼ Cottrell, Travis/David Moffitt/Sue C. Smith. "Thanks Be to Our God" from CCLI.
☼ Jordan, Leslie/David Leonard/Jason Ingram. "We Give You Thanks" from CCLI.
☼ Moen, Don/Tony Wood. "With a Thankful Heart" from CCLI.
☼ Morgan Reuben/Brooke Ligertwood. "You Crown the Year" from CCLI.
☼ Tomlin, Chris/Phil Wickham. "Thank You God for Saving Me" from CCLI.

Music for the Day
Choral

P Bach, J. S. "Now Thank We All Our God" from *Bach for All Seasons*. SATB, kybld. AFP 9780800658540.
P♫ Helgen, John. "Great Is Thy Faithfulness." SATB, pno. AFP 9780800620226.

P Patterson, Mark. "When in Our Music God Is Glorified." U or 2 pt, pno, opt hb. AFP 9780800638108.
Willan, Healey. "Sing to the Lord of Harvest." SATB, opt children's choir, opt assembly, org. CPH 982013.

Children's Choir

P Miller, Aaron David. "I Will Bless the Lord at All Times." U, kybld. AFP 9780800677503.
P Patterson, Mark. "Now We Give Thanks" from *Young ChildrenSing*. U, kybld. AFP 9780800676803
Wilson, Terry D. "As a Child I Give Thanks." 2 pt, pno. AFP 9780800620332.

Keyboard / Instrumental

P Carter, John. "How Great Thou Art" (O store Gud) from *Shall We Gather: Settings for Four-Hand Piano*. Pno (4-hand). HOP 8569.
♫ Powell, Robert J. "We Praise You, O God" (Kremser) from *Three for Thanksgiving: Three-Part Instrumental Settings*. Various (vln, hrn, vc, fl, cl, bsn, vla), opt kybld. CPH 97-5976.
P Sedio, Mark. "Let All Things Now Living" (The Ash Grove) from *Come and Praise*, vol. 2. Org. AFP 9780806696928.
P♫ Stoldt, Frank. "For the Fruit of All Creation" (Ar hyd y nos) from *Augsburg Organ Library: November*. Org. AFP 9780800658960.

Handbell

P♫ Moklebust, Cathy. "Great Is Thy Faithfulness." 3-5 oct, L3-. HOP 2671.
P♫ Raney, Joel. "We Gather Together." 3-5 oct hb, opt 3-5 oct hc, L3. HOP 2656.
♫ Thompson, Karen. "For the Fruit of All Creation (All Through the Night)." 3-5 oct hb, opt 3-6 oct hc, L3. SF 20/1780SF.

Thursday, November 23
Clement, Bishop of Rome, died around 100

Clement was the third bishop of Rome and served at the end of the first century. He is best remembered for a letter he wrote to the Corinthian congregation, still having difficulty with divisions in spite of Paul's canonical letters. Clement's writing echoes Paul's. "Love . . . has no limits to its endurance, bears everything patiently. Love is neither servile nor arrogant. It does not provoke schisms or form cliques, but always acts in harmony with others." Clement's letter is also a witness to early understandings of church government and the way each office in the church works for the good of the whole.

⊕ = global song   ♫ = relates to hymn of the day
☼ = praise song   P = available in Prelude Music Planner

Thursday, November 23
Miguel Agustín Pro, martyr, died 1927

Miguel Agustín Pro grew up among oppression in Mexico, where revolutionaries accused the church of siding with the rich. He was a Jesuit priest who served during a time of intense anticlericalism, and therefore he carried out much of his ministry in private settings. He worked on behalf of the poor and homeless. Miguel and his two brothers were arrested, falsely accused of throwing a bomb at the car of a government official, and executed by a firing squad. Just before the guns fired, he yelled, "¡Viva Cristo Rey!" which means "Long live Christ the king!"

Friday, November 24
Justus Falckner, died 1723; Jehu Jones, died 1852; William Passavant, died 1894; pastors in North America

A native of Saxony, Falckner was the son of a Lutheran pastor and, seeing the stresses his father endured, did not plan on becoming a pastor himself, though he studied theology in Halle. Instead, he joined with his brother in the real estate business in Pennsylvania. Through this business he became acquainted with a Swedish pastor in America, and finally he decided to become ordained. He served congregations in New York and New Jersey. Not only was he the first Lutheran ordained in North America, but he published a catechism that was the first Lutheran book published on the continent.

Jones was a native of Charleston, South Carolina. Ordained by the New York Ministerium in 1832, he became the Lutheran church's first African American pastor. Upon returning to South Carolina he was arrested under a law prohibiting free blacks from reentering the state, so he was unable to join the group of Charlestonians he had been commissioned to accompany to Liberia. For nearly twenty years Jones carried out missionary work in Philadelphia in the face of many difficulties. There he led in the formation of the first African American Lutheran congregation, St. Paul's, and the construction of its church building.

William Passavant created and nurtured a new level of organized social ministry in western Pennsylvania. It was the seed of the system of social services that is now known as Lutheran Services in America. Passavant and his legacy sought to serve the poorest of the poor, providing shelter, medical, and living assistance.

Saturday, November 25
Isaac Watts, hymnwriter, died 1748

Isaac Watts was born in England to a family of nonconformists, people who thought the Church of England had not carried its reforms far enough. As a youth, Watts complained to his father about the quality of hymnody in the metrical psalter of his day. That was the start of his hymnwriting career. He wrote about six hundred hymns, many in a two-year period beginning when he was twenty years old. Some of Watts's hymns are based on psalms, a nonconformist tradition. When criticized for writing hymns not taken from scripture, he responded that if we can pray prayers that are not from scripture but written by us, then surely we can sing hymns that we have made up ourselves. Ten of Watts's hymn texts are in *Evangelical Lutheran Worship*, including "O God, Our Help in Ages Past" (ELW 632).

November 26, 2017
Christ the King
Last Sunday after Pentecost — Lectionary 34

On this final Sunday of the church year our gospel is Jesus' great story of judgment. In the end, the faithful are those who served Christ by ministering to those who are poor, hungry, naked, sick, or estranged. In the first reading God is the shepherd who seeks the lost, weak, and injured and feeds them with justice. We gather this day to celebrate the reign of Christ and his victory over death, yet awaiting the consummation of all things yet to come. Acknowledging Christ as our merciful ruler, we go forth that his reign may be known in our loving words and deeds.

Prayer of the Day

O God of power and might, your Son shows us the way of service, and in him we inherit the riches of your grace. Give us the wisdom to know what is right and the strength to serve the world you have made, through Jesus Christ, our Savior and Lord, who lives and reigns with you and the Holy Spirit, one God, now and forever.

Gospel Acclamation

Alleluia. Blessed is the one who comes in the name | of the Lord.* Blessed is the coming kingdom of our an- | cestor David. *Alleluia.* (Mark 11:9)

Readings and Psalm
Ezekiel 34:11-16, 20-24

Since Israel's kings proved to be bad shepherds, Ezekiel declares that the Lord will assume the role of shepherd in Israel. The Lord will also set over them a shepherd-messiah, "my servant David," who will feed and care for the people.

Psalm 95:1-7a

We are the people of God's pasture and the sheep of God's hand. (Ps. 95:7)

Ephesians 1:15-23

In this passage, God is praised for revealing ultimate divine power in raising Jesus from the dead. The resurrected, exalted Christ is Lord of both the church and the entire universe, now and in the age to come.

Matthew 25:31-46

Jesus compares himself to a king who moves among his subjects to see how he is treated: what is done for the least of those who belong to his family is truly done for him.

Semicontinuous reading and psalm
Ezekiel 34:11-16, 20-24

See above.

Psalm 100

We are God's people and the sheep of God's pasture. (Ps. 100:3)

Preface   Ascension *or* Sundays

Color   White *or* Green

Prayers of Intercession

The prayers are prepared locally for each occasion. The following examples may be adapted or used as appropriate.

Welcoming God's reign of righteousness and mercy, let us pray with people of every time and place.
A brief silence.
Almighty God, your merciful rule encompasses all the world. As we gather for worship in safety, we pray for places where the church is persecuted. Watch over your people as they witness to your good news. Lord, in your mercy,
hear our prayer.
Give bountiful pastures, safety, and health to herds, livestock, and all animals. May our care for all of your creation reflect your shepherding love for all that you have made. Lord, in your mercy,
hear our prayer.
We pray for international organizations that shine your light in places of strife (*especially*). Lead relief and aid workers, leaders and volunteers to seek the lost and provide safety. Lord, in your mercy,
hear our prayer.
Bind up the injured and strengthen the weak, abused, or ill (*especially*). Give wisdom to counselors, doctors, nurses, and all in professions that provide healing. Lord, in your mercy,
hear our prayer.
Shepherd your churches to welcome the stranger and immigrant in our midst. Call all your people to welcome, clothe, feed, and visit those in need just as you have provided for the lost and despairing throughout the ages. Lord, in your mercy,
hear our prayer.
Here other intercessions may be offered.

Give us the hope to which you call us, our glorious inheritance with all your saints. Enrich our lives with the faith and vision of those saints who have died (*especially*). Lord, in your mercy, **hear our prayer.**

Receive these prayers and the hopes and concerns of our hearts, O God, as we entrust into your loving care all for whom we pray, through Jesus Christ our Lord. **Amen.**

Images in the Readings

Calling this Sunday Christ the **King** may elevate that image above all others. Currently on the world scene some nations have rejected monarchies, some maintain figurehead monarchs, and some, while not using the term *king*, maintain heads of state with absolute, even ruthless, power over the people. The Bible promises that God's power and majesty differ radically from the reign of most human monarchs. Thus we need to use the image of king as correcting the image of king. Several hymns do a splendid job of playing the image against itself. As an example of how God's reign differs from that of human monarchs, the baptized saints receive riches and power from God. Some churches prefer the phrase "the reign of Christ" as stressing the activity rather than the status; unfortunately, English has the problem of the homonym *rain*.

In the Bible, written within a culture that treasured its pastoral past, **sheep and goats** are images of the life God gives to the people. Like sheep and goats, we are created by God to live together and offer ourselves for others. It is an urban prejudice to defame sheep as dirty and stupid.

Matthew's parable was depicted in sculptures over the main doorway and in wall paintings over the chancel of countless Christian churches, and one can imagine the fun that artists had in shaping the monsters on the left side of Christ the **judge**. As this imagery becomes less important for some Christians, it is important not to lose the biblical call that we saints are to live out the justice that God intends, serving each needy person who is Christ-for-us.

As the first-century decades progressed, *saints* became an increasingly common term for the baptized people of God. The usual English translation being "personally holy," the word *saint* is used differently by various Christian branches. In Ephesians everyone who is enlightened is called a "saint," the meaning most Protestants have retained.

Ideas for the Day

- Today's appointed prayer of the day was written especially for *Evangelical Lutheran Worship*. It names specific signs of the risen Christ (power, riches, wisdom, and strength) that we celebrate in the song "This is the feast of victory for our God." Today take notice of how our liturgies for Holy Communion point to the mysterious reign of Christ, the Lamb who was slain. Look for special opportunities within the liturgy to offer praise that is creative and innovative. Explore the diverse gifts of sacred arts that encourage our joy in the presence of Christ the king.

- How do faithful people behave in the presence of royalty? Three Old Testament stories demonstrate the complexities of this question. Joseph established a new identity by serving as an Egyptian governor. Esther also could not disclose her true identity, but when she became a queen, she risked everything to expose a wicked scheme to destroy the Jewish people. Daniel and his three friends were forced to change their names as they served in the royal court, but they always found a way to uphold their faith in the God of Israel. All of this comes to mind as Jesus tells the parable of a king who chooses the disguises of poverty, nakedness, and imprisonment to test the loyalty of those who have promised to serve him. How does Jesus reveal his presence in the ministries you support? What are the most intriguing surprises that have allowed you to recognize Christ among you in ways that you never expected?

- Mission strategists urge us to expect and prepare for seekers, people who want to connect with ministries that will help inform, nurture, and strengthen their faith. Ezekiel tells us today that God is a shepherd who seeks and searches for sheep that are lost, injured, or abandoned. Seeking is something that defines much of our activity as Christians. Our communities of faith are enriched as other seekers come and share our own hunger to better know and serve the Lord. What stories of seekers inspire and give shape to the ministries you know well?

Connections with the Liturgy

Annually on Good Friday, in the revised Solemn Reproaches, we conclude our litany of confession with a paragraph in which we repeat the words of today's Matthean parable: we gave Christ no food, no drink, we did not welcome him, we gave him no clothes. Remembering this parable, we beg for God's mercy, and we worship Christ who reigned from the cross.

Each Sunday that we sing the classic canticle of praise "Glory to God in the highest," we repeat Ephesians's language of the risen Christ "seated at the right hand" of power in the heavenly places.

Psalm 95, which in our lectionary marks the close of year A, was appointed by Benedict in the sixth century as the psalm with which all monks and nuns were to begin their praise each day. *Evangelical Lutheran Worship* continues this practice in Morning Prayer, in which Psalm 95 is the first option for the opening of our daily praise (p. 299).

Let the Children Come

Children know more about kings through movies and stories than through a lived reality. (Children probably know more about sheep that way too, for that matter.) The shocking aspect of Matthew's image of a king who has been hungry, thirsty, alone, naked, sick, and imprisoned doesn't have its full impact for children today. It may hit closer to home. Some children in your community may love, respect, and rely on people who are hungry, thirsty, alone, naked, sick, or imprisoned. Just as we are all saints and sinners, sheep and goats, the assembly is made up of folks giving and receiving help. How can our language help children live into the gospel's vision for the flock?

Assembly Song
Gathering

Crown him with many crowns ELW 855, LBW 170
Lord of glory, you have bought us ELW 707, LBW 424
Rejoice, for Christ is king! ELW 430, LBW 171

Psalmody and Acclamations

"Come, Let Us Sing to the Lord" (Venite) from ELW Morning Prayer, pp. 300–301.
D'Inverno, Ray. "Shout Joy to the Lord" from *Psalm Songs 2*. AFP 0800657713.
Houge, Ben. "Oh, Come, Let Us Sing." W&P 107.
ᴾ (GA) Haskel, Marilyn. "I Am Alpha and Omega." MSB2 S519.

Hymn of the Day

O Christ, what can it mean for us ELW 431 *ALL SAINTS NEW*
The head that once was crowned ELW 432, LBW 173
 ST. MAGNUS
Thine the amen ELW 826, WOV 801 *THINE*

Offering

The trumpets sound, the angels sing ELW 531, W&P 139
Soon and very soon ELW 439, WOV 744, TFF 38

Communion

O Savior, precious Savior ELW 820, LBW 514
O Christ the same ELW 760, WOV 778
As we gather at your table ELW 522

Sending

Lo! He comes with clouds descending ELW 435, LBW 27
Jesus shall reign ELW 434, LBW 530

Additional Assembly Songs

Come now, you blessed LS 141
Feed my lambs ASG 8
Ride on, King Jesus TFF 182
⊕ Bell, John, arr. "The Love of God Comes Close" from *Love and Anger: Songs of Lively Faith and Social Justice*. U. GIA G-4947.

⊕ South African traditional. "Amen. Alleluia!" from *Global Songs 2*. SATB. AFP 9780800656744.
☼ Cates, Jess/Mark Tedder/Anthony Skinner. "The King Is Coming" from CCLI.
☼ Egan, Jon/Jonathan Moos. "Jesus Reigns" from CCLI.
☼ Furtick, Steven/Chris Brown/Wade Joye/Mack Brock. "Only King Forever" from CCLI.
☼ Hughes, Tim/Martin Smith/Nick Herbert. "Hope and Glory" from CCLI.
☼ Liscum, David/Yochanan Marcellino. "He Will Reign" from CCLI.
☼ Stanfill, Kristian/Brett Younker/Ed Cash/Chris Tomlin. "Shout Hosanna" from CCLI.

Music for the Day
Choral

♫ Ferguson, John. "The Head That Once Was Crowned with Thorns." SATB, assembly, org, br qrt. GIA G-3750.
Jennings, Carolyn. "Climb to the Top of the Highest Mountain." SATB, opt children's choir, org. KJO 8118.
Mendelssohn, Felix. "The Lord Is a Mighty God (Psalm 95)." 2 pt mxd, kybd. KJO 0009.
ᴾ♫ Schalk, Carl. "Thine the Amen, Thine the Praise." SATB, org, opt assembly. AFP 9780800646127.

Children's Choir

Bryce, Ellen Woods. "Praise to the Lord, for the Lord Is Good." U, SAT(B), pno, opt tr, hb. CG CGA1044.
Leaf, Robert. "To the Glory of Our King." U, pno/org. CG CGA173.
Patterson, Mark. "Let All the World in Every Corner Sing" from *ChildrenSing: Seven Anthems for Elementary Age Singers*. AFP 9780800677695.

Keyboard / Instrumental

Buxtehude, Dietrich. "Nun lob', mein Seel', den Herren," BuxWV 214. Org. Various editions.
ᴾ Childs, Edwin T. "My Lord, What a Morning" (Burleigh) from *Spirituals for Organ: For Manuals Only*. Org. AFP 9781451401141.
Miller, Aaron David. "The Trumpets Sound, the Angels Sing" (The Feast Is Ready) from *Augsburg Organ Library: Autumn*. Org. AFP 9780800675790.
ᴾ♫ Rübsam, Wolfgang. "Thine the Amen" (Thine) from *Fourteen Chorale Preludes: A Guide to Liturgical Improvisation*. Org. AFP 9780806698038.

Handbell

ᴾ Hanson, Nicholas. "Triumphant Spirit." 2-3 oct, L3, CG CGB841. 3-6 oct, L3, CG CGB842.

⊕ = global song   ♫ = relates to hymn of the day
☼ = praise song   ᴾ = available in Prelude Music Planner
316

ᴾ Moklebust, Cathy. "Crown Him with Many Crowns." 2-3 oct hb,
opt B flat or C inst, L2, CG CGB771. 3-5 oct hb, opt B flat or
C inst, L2, CG CGB772.

ᴾ Raney, Joel/Arnold Sherman. "Crown Him with Many
Crowns." 3-6 oct hb, L4, HOP 2709. Opt full score (tpt),
HOP 2709T.

Thursday, November 30

Andrew, Apostle

Andrew was the first of the Twelve. He is known as a fisherman who left his net to follow Jesus. As a part of his calling, he
brought other people, including Simon Peter, to meet Jesus.
The Byzantine church honors Andrew as its patron and points
out that because he was the first of Jesus' followers, he was,
in the words of John Chrysostom, "the Peter before Peter."
Together with Philip, Andrew leads a number of Greeks to
speak with Jesus, and it is Andrew who shows Jesus a boy with
five barley loaves and two fish. Andrew is said to have died on a
cross saltire, an X-shaped cross.

Resources

Lectionaries

Lectionary for Worship Year A. Augsburg Fortress, 2008. The Revised Common Lectionary. Each reading is "sense-lined" for clearer proclamation of the scriptural texts. New Revised Standard Version. Available in study (includes reader helps) and ritual editions. Also available on sundaysandseasons.com.

§ *Revised Common Lectionary Daily Readings*. Consultation on Common Texts. Fortress Press, 2005.

Readings for the Assembly (A). Gordon Lathrop and Gail Ramshaw, eds. Augsburg Fortress, 1995. The Revised Common Lectionary. Emended NRSV with inclusive language. Available on sundaysandseasons.com

§ *The Revised Common Lectionary: Twentieth Anniversary Annotated Edition*. Consultation on Common Texts. Fortress Press, 2012. The most definitive source for the RCL and the most authoritative explanation of how it came to be developed. Includes marginal notes that identify sources and rationale for lectionary choices. With a foreword by Gordon Lathrop and a new historical introduction.

Worship Books

Evangelical Lutheran Worship. Augsburg Fortress, 2006. Available in pew, leaders ritual, leaders desk, gift, pocket, braille, and enlarged print editions.

Evangelical Lutheran Worship Accompaniment Edition: Liturgies. Augsburg Fortress, 2006. Complete keyboard accompaniments for all ten holy communion settings and additional music within liturgies. Simplified edition also available.

Evangelical Lutheran Worship Accompaniment Edition: Service Music and Hymns (2 vols; Compact Edition, 1 vol.). Augsburg Fortress, 2006. Full accompaniments to all hymns and songs in the pew edition, #151–893. Simplified Keyboard and Guitar editions for service music and hymns also available.

§ *Evangelical Lutheran Worship Occasional Services for the Assembly*. Augsburg Fortress, 2009. Rites and prayers for use on particular occasions in the worshiping assemblies of congregations and synods, such as ministry rites, dedications, and blessings.

§ *Evangelical Lutheran Worship Pastoral Care:* Occasional Services, Readings, and Prayers. Augsburg Fortress, 2008. An essential tool for caregivers conducting the church's ministry of care outside the worshiping assembly.

Evangelical Lutheran Worship Prayer Book for the Armed Services: For Chaplains and Other Military Personnel. Augsburg Fortress, 2013. Pocket-sized edition includes resources for individual daily devotion, prayers for various circumstances selected and composed especially for use by service members, several assembly service orders featuring ecumenical texts, and the texts of 26 psalms and 65 hymns and national songs. Intended for use by active and reserve service members and their families and friends, pastors and congregations who minister to them, chaplains, and veterans.

Libro de Liturgia y Cántico. Augsburg Fortress, 1998. A complete Spanish-language worship resource. Leader edition (2001) includes additional psalms and indexes.

New Hymns of Praise. Taosheng Publishing House, Hong Kong, 2011. Joint venture of the ELCA and the Evangelical Lutheran Church in Hong Kong. The majority of the 143 hymns and songs can be sung in either Mandarin or Cantonese and all include an English text. Keyboard accompaniments for all the hymns are also provided.

Ritos Ocasionales. Augsburg Fortress, 2000. Spanish language version of rites and prayers for various occasions and circumstances.

Santa Comunion / Holy Communion. Augsburg Fortress, 2014. Bilingual Spanish/English edition of Setting Seven from *Evangelical Lutheran Worship*, including texts and liturgical songs in both languages. Assembly and leaders editions.

This Far by Faith: An African American Resource for Worship. Augsburg Fortress, 1999. A supplement of worship orders, psalms, service music, and hymns representing African American traditions and developed by African American Lutherans.

Worship Planning Tools, Indexes, Calendars

∞ www.preludemusicplanner.com. A subscription-based online music planning tool. Create comprehensive plans. Browse, preview, and download music from multi-publisher library. Search music based on lectionary days, keywords, skill level and more. Store your usage history. Upload and organize your own library.

∞ www.sundaysandseasons.com. A subscription-based online worship planning tool. Browse, select, and download content for worship planning and worship folder preparation.

∞ Evangelical Lutheran Worship Liturgies CD-ROM. Augsburg Fortress, 2006. Liturgical material from pew edition in editable text files; assembly singing lines provided as graphics.

Indexes to Evangelical Lutheran Worship. Augsburg Fortress, 2007. Indexes the hymns and songs in Evangelical Lutheran Worship. Includes extensive lectionary, scripture, and topical indexes.

Choral Literature for Sundays and Seasons. Bradley Ellingboe, ed. Augsburg Fortress, 2004. A comprehensive listing of time-tested choral works, indexed to the readings for each Sunday and principal festival of the three-year lectionary. Includes information on voicing, instrumentation, composers, and publishers.

* *Calendar of Word and Season 2017: Liturgical Wall Calendar*. Augsburg Fortress, 2016. Features artwork by Rafael López. A reference tool for home, sacristy, office.

* denotes new or newer print resource
∞ denotes electronic or Web resource
318 § denotes print resource also available as an ebook

* *Church Year Calendar 2017.* Augsburg Fortress, 2016. A one-sheet calendar of lectionary citations and liturgical colors for each Sunday and festival of the liturgical year. Appropriate for bulk purchase and distribution. Also available in downloadable format.

*∞ *Words for Worship: 2017, Year A.* Augsburg Fortress, 2016. CD-ROM includes lectionary readings, worship texts, seasonal rites, and more for use in worship folders and other self-published materials.

* *Worship Planning Calendar 2017.* Augsburg Fortress, 2016. A two-page per week calendar helpful for worship planners, with space to record appointments and notes for each day. Specially designed to complement Sundays and Seasons. Features the CCT daily lectionary.

Westermeyer, Paul. *Hymnal Companion to Evangelical Lutheran Worship.* Augsburg Fortress, 2010. Background and insightful commentary on all 650 hymns, both text and music, together with biographical information on hymn writers and composers. Expanded indexes.

Worship Support

Boesenecker, Andrew, and James Graeser. *A Field Guide to Contemporary Worship: How to Begin and Lead Band-Based Worship.* Augsburg Fortress, 2011. A guide for anyone thinking about starting a contemporary worship service and an essential reference work for those wondering about the nuts and bolts of instrumentation, arranging, working with microphones and speakers, and much more.

§ Brugh, Lorraine, and Gordon Lathrop. *The Sunday Assembly.* Augsburg Fortress, 2008. A resource to guide leaders in their understanding and interpretation of the *Evangelical Lutheran Worship* resources. Focuses on holy communion.

§ Bushkofsky, Dennis, and Craig Satterlee. *The Christian Life: Baptism and Life Passages.* Augsburg Fortress, 2008. Contains detailed information on holy baptism and its related rites, as well as marriage, healing, and funeral.

∞ *Fed and Forgiven: Communion Preparation and Formation.* Augsburg Fortress, 2009. A comprehensive set of resources for leading children, youth, and adults into the sacrament of holy communion. Leader Guide with CD-ROM for all ages. Learner Resources for PreK-K, Grades 1-3, Grades 4-6, and adults. Supplementary DVD.

∞ *Go Make Disciples: An Invitation to Baptismal Living.* Augsburg Fortress, 2012. An ecumenical handbook offering a basic "how to" and a collection of updated resources for preparing adults for baptism or affirmation of baptism, and for Christian discipleship. Appropriate for a wide range of Protestant denominations, especially Lutheran, Episcopal, Anglican, United Methodist, Presbyterian, and Reformed. Supplementary CD-ROM available separately.

*§ Hoffman, Paul. *Welcoming to Worship: A Handbook for Ushers and Greeters.* Practical helps for ministers of hospitality and guidance for welcoming newcomers into the assembly. Augsburg Fortress, 2016.

§ Hoyer, Christopher G. *Getting the Word Out: A Handbook for Readers.* Practical helps and spiritual wisdom for those who serve as lectors in the assembly. Augsburg Fortress, 2013.

* *In These or Similar Words: Crafting Language for Worship.* Practical guidance for worship leaders and congregations wishing to craft new language for worship locally. Augsburg Fortress, 2015.

∞ *Leading Worship Matters: A Sourcebook for Preparing Worship Leaders* with accompanying DVD and CD-ROM. Augsburg Fortress, 2013. Practical, succinct, easy-to-use tools and resources to plan, execute, and evaluate worship leadership training. Covers assisting ministers, readers/lectors, altar guild/sacristans, intercessors, acolytes, ushers, greeters, communion ministers, and more.

Peace at the Last: Visiting the Dying (Augsburg Fortress, 2016). A beautifully illustrated liturgy that can be used by individuals or groups who visit those who are dying. Includes prayers, psalms, simple chants, and suggestions for ritual action, all accompanied by rich watercolor artwork.

*§ Ramshaw, Gail. *Praying for the Whole World: A Handbook for Intercessors.* Practical helps and guidance for those who prepare the prayers of intercession for the assembly's worship. Augsburg Fortress, 2016.

§ Ramshaw, Gail, and Mons Teig. *Keeping Time: The Church's Years.* Augsburg Fortress, 2009. Contains detailed information on Sundays, seasons, festivals, and commemorations, as well as daily prayer.

§ Scharen, Christian. *Serving the Assembly's Worship: A Handbook for Assisting Ministers.* Practical helps and spiritual wisdom for those who serve as assisting ministers in the assembly. Augsburg Fortress, 2013.

§ Stauffer, S. Anita. *Altar Guild and Sacristy Handbook.* Fourth revised edition. Augsburg Fortress, 2014. Revised and expanded edition of this classic on preparing the table and the worship environment.

∞ *Washed and Welcome: A Baptism Sourcebook.* Augsburg Fortress, 2010. Resources to support a congregation's total baptismal ministry and the participation of God's people in the lifelong gift of baptism. Includes CD-ROM.

Choral Collections

Assembly Required. Augsburg Fortress, 2010, 2014. Volume 1 includes four liturgical songs for choir and assembly. Volume 2 includes four songs for the Easter Vigil. Volume 3 includes liturgical music for holy communion.

Augsburg Choirbook, The. Augsburg Fortress, 1998. Kenneth Jennings, ed. Sixty-seven anthems primarily from twentieth-century North American composers.

Augsburg Choirbook for Advent, Christmas, and Epiphany. Augsburg Fortress, 2007. Thirty-three anthems, mostly easy-to-medium difficulty, for the Christmas cycle.

Augsburg Choirbook for Men. Augsburg Fortress, 2004. Fourteen anthems for two- to four-part male chorus.

Augsburg Choirbook for Women. Augsburg Fortress, 2006. Diverse selections for choirs of all ages and abilities from high school through adult.

Augsburg Easy Choirbook, vol. 1. Augsburg Fortress, 2003. Fourteen unison and two-part mixed anthems for the church year.

Augsburg Easy Choirbook, vol. 2. Augsburg Fortress, 2005. Sixteen anthems for the church year; accessible, quality music for the smaller, less-experienced choir.

Augsburg Easy Choirbook, vol. 3. Augsburg Fortress, 2016. Eleven unison and two-part anthems for the church year, most of them suitable for adult, youth, and children.

Augsburg Motet Book. Augsburg Fortress, 2013. Zebulon M. Highben, ed. Over thirty classic anthems and new motets, edited with optional accompaniments.

Bach for All Seasons. Augsburg Fortress, 1999. Richard Erickson and Mark Bighley, eds. Offers movements from cantatas and oratorios presented with carefully reconstructed keyboard parts and fresh English texts. Instrumental parts available.

Chantry Choirbook. Augsburg Fortress, 2000. Choral master works of European composers spanning five centuries, many with new English translations, and indexed for use in the liturgical assembly throughout the year.

Choral Stanzas for Hymns. 2 vols. Augsburg Fortress, 2010–2011. More than 150 reproducible arrangements of selected hymn stanzas for choirs to sing in alternation with assemblies.

GladSong Choirbook. Augsburg Fortress, 2005. Eleven titles for fall, Advent, and Christmas use, plus Reformation, Thanksgiving, All Saints, Christ the King, Epiphany, and communion.

Hear Our Prayer. Augsburg Fortress, 2007. A collection of sung prayer responses to be used between the petitions of the prayers of intercession or as a call or closing to prayer.

* *St. Olaf Choirbook for Men*. Augsburg Fortress, 2015. Christopher Aspaas, ed. Fourteen new and classic anthems scored for male voices.

The New Gloria Deo: Music for Small Choirs. Augsburg Fortress, 2010 (vol. 1), 2012 (vol. 2). Twelve anthems written with small ensembles in mind by Aaron David Miller and Thomas Keesecker.

Vocal Descants for the Church Year. Based on hymns in Evangelical Lutheran Worship. Augsburg Fortress, 2008. 250 descants, mostly reproducible, for adding color and brilliance to hymn singing.

Wade in the Water: Easy Choral Music for All Ages. Augsburg Fortress, 2007. A collection of two- and three-part choral music for the less-experienced singer.

Hymn and Song Collections

As Sunshine to a Garden: Hymns and Songs. Rusty Edwards. Augsburg Fortress, 1999. Forty-six collected hymns from the author of "We all are one in mission."

Come, Beloved of the Maker: Hymns of Susan Palo Cherwien. Augsburg Fortress, 2010. Thirty-four hymn texts by Cherwien, following up on her previous collection, *O Blessed Spring* (Augsburg Fortress, 1997). Each text is presented with a harmonized tune.

Earth and All Stars: Hymns and Songs for Young and Old. Herbert F. Brokering. Augsburg Fortress, 2003. A collection of hymn texts by the popular writer.

Justice like a Base of Stone. Bret Hesla. Augsburg Fortress, 2006. A collection of peace and justice songs in a variety of styles, easily taught to the congregation. Audio CD also available.

Pave the Way: Global Songs 3. Bread for the Journey. Augsburg Fortress, 2004. Eighteen songs from around the world, with performance notes. Also available: *Global Songs Local Voices* (1995) and *Global Songs 2* (1997).

∞ *Singing Our Prayer: A Companion to Holden Prayer Around the Cross. Shorter Songs for Contemplative Worship*. Augsburg Fortress, 2010. A collection of short, simple songs for worship. Available in full score and assembly editions, and audio CD.

Worship & Praise. Augsburg Fortress, 1999. A collection of songs in various contemporary and popular styles, with helps for using them in Lutheran worship.

Instrumental Collections

* *A New Liturgical Year*. Augsburg Fortress, 2015. John Ferguson, ed. Two volumes gather some of the best in 20th century organ settings of hymn and chorale tunes arranged in order of the liturgical year.

* *Augsburg Organ Library*. Augsburg Fortress, 2000–2016. A multi-volume collection of carefully selected organ music classics of the 20th and 21st centuries from a variety of publishers, organized according the seasons of the church year and primary liturgical contexts. Healing and Funeral (2013) is particularly useful for funerals, memorial services, services of healing, as well as Sundays when the lectionary explores themes of healing, death, and dying. Reformation (2016) offers settings of tunes primarily from Lutheran sources and is especially useful in this anniversary year.

* *Evangelical Lutheran Worship Festival and Ensemble Settings of Holy Communion*. Augsburg Fortress, 2008–2015. Additional instrumentation and choral elaboration for Evangelical Lutheran Worship Settings One, Two, Six, Seven, Eight, and Nine.

Hymns for Ensembles: Instrumental Accompaniments for Ecumenical Hymns. 2 vols. Augsburg Fortress, 2010–2011. More than 100 orchestrations of hymns old and new. Full score with keyboard part; parts for various instruments on CD-ROM, included.

In Heaven Above: Piano Music for Funerals and Memorials. Augsburg Fortress, 2011. More than fifty arrangements by various composers of favorite hymns of comfort, hope, and celebration of the saints.

Introductions and Alternate Accompaniments. Augsburg Fortress, 2007–2009. Two 10-volume series, one for organ and one for piano, covering every *Evangelical Lutheran Worship* hymn and song. Various composers.

Let It Rip! at the Piano (2 vols.) and *Pull Out the Stops* (2 vols.). Augsburg Fortress, 2000–2005. Collections for piano and organ respectively, each containing introductions and varied musical accompaniments by various composers for more than 100 widely used hymns and songs.

* *Organ Plus Anthology*, vol. 1, vol. 2. Augsburg Fortress, 2012, 2016. Hymn arrangements by various composers for organ and one or two instruments.

Piano Plus: Hymns for Piano and Treble Instrument, Advent/ Christmas. Augsburg Fortress, 2006. *Through the Year, 2009*. Arrangements by various composers that range in difficulty from simple cradle songs to jazz, and span numerous world cultures and several centuries.

* denotes new or newer print resource
∞ denotes electronic or Web resource
320 § denotes print resource also available as an ebook

Psalm Collections

See p. 326.

Preparing Music for Worship

∞ www.preludemusicplanner.com. A subscription-based online music planning tool. Create comprehensive plans. Browse, preview, and download music from multi-publisher library. Search music based on lectionary days, keywords, skill level and more. Store your usage history. Upload and organize your own library.

Boesenecker, Andrew, and James Graeser. *A Field Guide to Contemporary Worship: How to Begin and Lead Band-Based Worship.* Augsburg Fortress, 2011. A guide for anyone thinking about starting a contemporary worship service and an essential reference work for those wondering about the nuts and bolts of instrumentation, arranging, working with microphones and speakers, and much more.

Cherwien, David. *Let the People Sing! A Keyboardist's Creative and Practical Guide to Engaging God's People in Meaningful Song.* Concordia, 1997. Emphasis on the organ.

Bradley Ellingboe, ed. *Choral Literature for Sundays and Seasons.* Augsburg Fortress, 2004. A comprehensive listing of time-tested choral works, indexed to the readings for each Sunday and principal festival of the three-year lectionary. Includes information on voicing, instrumentation, composers, and publishers.

∞ *Evangelical Lutheran Worship* Liturgies Audio CD, vols. 1, 2, 3. Augsburg Fortress, 2006, 2010. Complete recordings of Holy Communion Settings One–Ten and Daily Prayer.

∞ *Evangelical Lutheran Worship Hymns* Audio CD, vols. 1 and 2. Augsburg Fortress, 2006, 2007. Recordings of four dozen hymns and songs from Evangelical Lutheran Worship, both new and familiar. Performed by choirs from St. Olaf and Lenoir Rhyne colleges.

Farlee, Robert Buckley, ed. *Leading the Church's Song.* Augsburg Fortress, 1998. Various contributors, with musical examples and audio CD, giving guidance on the interpretation and leadership of various genres of congregational song.

∞ *Favorite Hymns Accompanied.* John Ferguson, organist. Augsburg Fortress, 2005. A 2-CD set of 52 widely known hymns played without singing.

Highben, Zebulon M., and Kristina M. Langlois, eds. *With a Voice of Singing: Essays on Children, Choirs, and Music in the Church.* Minneapolis: Kirk House Publishers, 2007.

Musicians Guide to Evangelical Lutheran Worship. Augsburg Fortress, 2007. An introduction to the music, including specific suggestions for each liturgical music item, service music item, and hymn.

Soli Deo Gloria: Choir Devotions for Year A (Craig Mueller), *Year B* (Jennifer Baker-Trinity), and *Year C* (Wayne L. Wold). Augsburg Fortress, 2009–2011.

§ Westermeyer, Paul. *The Church Musician,* rev. ed. Augsburg Fortress, 1997. Foundational introduction to the role and task of the church musician as the leader of the people's song.

§ ———. *Te Deum: The Church and Music.* Fortress Press, 1998. A historical and theological introduction to the music of the church.

§ Wold, Wayne L. *Preaching to the Choir: The Care and Nurture of the Church Choir.* Augsburg Fortress, 2003. Practical helps for the choir director.

Preparing Environment and Art

Chinn, Nancy. *Spaces for Spirit: Adorning the Church.* Chicago: Liturgy Training Publications, 1998. Imaginative thinking about ways to treat visual elements in the worship space.

§ Christopherson, D. Foy. *A Place of Encounter: Renewing Worship Spaces.* Augsburg Fortress, 2004. An exploration of principles for planning and renewing worship spaces.

Crowley, Eileen D. *A Moving Word: Media Art in Worship.* Augsburg Fortress, 2006. An exploration of how visual elements in worship can enhance the assembly's understanding of the gospel.

∞ *Evangelical Lutheran Worship* Graphics CD-ROM. Augsburg Fortress, 2011. Contains more than 100 graphic images that appear in the *Evangelical Lutheran Worship* family of resources, including the pew edition, Pastoral Care, Occasional Services for the Assembly, and more. Color images are provided as both TIFF and JPG files; black-and-white versions of the images are provided as TIFF files.

Giles, Richard. *Re-Pitching the Tent: Reordering the Church Building for Worship and Mission.* Collegeville, MN: The Liturgical Press, 1999.

Mazar, Peter. *To Crown the Year: Decorating the Church through the Seasons.* Chicago: Liturgy Training Publications, 1995.

§ Stauffer, S. Anita. *Altar Guild and Sacristy Handbook.* Fourth revised edition. Augsburg Fortress, 2014. Revised and expanded edition of this classic on preparing the table and the worship environment.

Seasons and Liturgical Year

Of the Land and Seasons. Assembly and leader/accompaniment editions. Augsburg Fortress, 2013. A worship service connected to the change of the seasons in farming, orchards, or natural settings. Intended for quarterly use. This is a revised edition of the resource first published in 1990. The pattern and language have been reshaped to coordinate with the liturgies of Evangelical Lutheran Worship.

Worship Guidebook for Lent and the Three Days. Augsburg Fortress, 2009. A collection of insights, images, and practical tips to help deepen your congregation's worship life during the days from Ash Wednesday to Easter. A companion to *Music Sourcebook for Lent and the Three Days.*

Music Sourcebook for Lent and the Three Days. Augsburg Fortress, 2010. This collection includes 100 assembly songs, many of them reproducible, greatly expanding the repertoire for the assembly and its leaders during the days from Ash Wednesday to Easter.

Music Sourcebook for All Saints through Transfiguration. Augsburg Fortress, 2013. This collection offers a rich selection of assembly songs, mostly newly composed and many of them reproducible, for use during the days of November, Advent, Christmas, Epiphany, and the Time after Epiphany.

§ Ramshaw, Gail. *The Three-Day Feast: Maundy Thursday, Good Friday, Easter.* Augsburg Fortress, 2004. A little history and a lot of suggestions about how these services can enrich the assembly's worship life.

Children

* *ChildrenSing at Christmas.* Augsburg Fortress, 2015. Anne McNair and William McNair. Nine songs for young singers, useful independently or combined into a service of lessons and carols.

ChildrenSing Around the World. Augsburg Fortress, 2014. A collection of global songs that span the church year by various composers. Reproducible singer pages.

ChildrenSing in Worship. Augsburg Fortress, 2011–2013. Three volumes of anthems by various composers. Reproducible choral parts.

ChildrenSing Psalms. Marilyn Comer, ed. Augsburg Fortress, 2009. Collection of psalms for all seasons keyed to the lectionary.

Patterson, Mark. *ChildrenSing, ChildrenSing with Instruments,* and *Young ChildrenSing.* Augsburg Fortress, 2004–2006. Short anthems for young singers.

∞ *Fed and Forgiven: Communion Preparation and Formation.* (See Worship Support)

Kids Celebrate Worship Series. Augsburg Fortress, 2006–2007. A series of seasonal and topical 8-page booklets that introduce children and their families to worship and *Evangelical Lutheran Worship.* Pre-reader and young reader versions. Includes ideas and helps for parents, pastors, educators, and children's choir directors.

Our Worship Book (2006). A kid-friendly introduction to *Evangelical Lutheran Worship.*

Sunday Worship (2006). Focuses on the gathering, word, meal, sending pattern of Holy Communion.

Advent & Christmas (2006). Introduction to the Advent-Christmas season with activities.

Lent & Easter (2006). Introduction to the seasons of Lent and Easter with activities.

Three Amazing Days (2006). Introduction to Maundy Thursday, Good Friday, and the Easter Vigil.

Holy Communion (2007). Introduction to the sacrament of holy communion.

Baptism (2007). Introduction to the sacrament of holy baptism and baptismal living.

Our Prayers (2007). Focuses on how and when the assembly prays in worship, and prayer in the home.

The Bible (2007). Introduction to the ways in which scripture is used in worship.

LifeSongs (children's songbook, leader book, and audio CDs). Augsburg Fortress, 1999. A well-rounded selection of age-appropriate songs, hymns, and liturgical music that builds a foundation for a lifetime of singing the faith.

Living the Promises of Baptism: 101 Ideas for Parents. Augsburg Fortress, 2010. Concrete ideas for celebrating with children (infant to upper elementary) the gifts of baptism in daily living.

Ramshaw, Gail. *Every Day and Sunday, Too.* Augsburg Fortress, 1996. An illustrated book for parents and children. Daily life is related to the central actions of the liturgy.

———. *Sunday Morning.* Chicago: Liturgy Training Publications, 1993. A book for children and adults on the primary words of Sunday worship.

∞ *Washed and Welcome: A Baptism Sourcebook.* (See Worship Support)

Ylvisaker, Anne. Illustrated by Claudia McGehee. *Welcome, Child of God.* Augsburg Fortress, 2011. A board book about baptism for infants and toddlers.

Daily Prayer Resources

Briehl, Susan, and Tom Witt. *Holden Prayer Around the Cross: Handbook to the Liturgy.* Augsburg Fortress, 2009. Practical suggestions for planning and leading flexible orders for contemplative prayer. Includes fourteen liturgies in the Prayer Around the Cross format.

∞ *Singing Our Prayer: A Companion to Holden Prayer Around the Cross. Shorter Songs for Contemplative Worship.* (See Hymn and Song Collections)

*§ *Bread for the Day 2017: Daily Bible Readings and Prayers.* Augsburg Fortress, 2016. Daily scripture texts for individual or group prayer based on the daily lectionary in Evangelical Lutheran Worship.

Cherwien, David. *Stay with Us, Lord: Liturgies for Evening.* Augsburg Fortress, 2001. Settings for Evening Prayer and Holy Communion, full music and congregational editions.

Haugen, Marty. *Holden Evening Prayer.* Chicago: GIA, 1990. Revised edition including additional psalms and handbell parts, 2016.

Haugen, Marty, and Susan Briehl. *Unfailing Light.* Chicago: GIA, 2004.

Makeever, Ray. *Joyous Light Evening Prayer.* Augsburg Fortress, 2000.

Miller, Aaron David. *Behold Our Light: Music for Evening Worship.* Augsburg Fortress, 2013. Settings of the musical selections needed for evening prayer or an evening communion service, scored for cantor, assembly, piano, and optional C instrument. Includes a service of light, setting of Psalm 139, Magnificat, intercessory prayers, and blessing, as well as a gospel acclamation, Sanctus, and Nunc dimittis.

§ *Revised Common Lectionary Daily Readings.* Consultation on Common Texts. Fortress Press, 2005.

Worship Studies, series

Worship Matters Series. Augsburg Fortress, 2004–2011. The series explores a range of worship-related topics.

§ Christopherson, D. Foy. *A Place of Encounter: Renewing Worship Spaces* (2004).

Crowley, Eileen D. *A Moving Word: Media Art in Worship* (2006).

§ Dahill, Lisa. *Truly Present: Practicing Prayer in the Liturgy* (2005).

* denotes new or newer print resource
∞ denotes electronic or Web resource
322 § denotes print resource also available as an ebook

§ Lathrop, Gordon. *Central Things: Worship in Word and Sacrament* (2005).

§ Quivik, Melinda. *A Christian Funeral: Witness to the Resurrection* (2005).

§ Ramshaw, Gail. *A Three-Year Banquet: The Lectionary for the Assembly* (2004).

§ ———. *The Three-Day Feast: Maundy Thursday, Good Friday, Easter* (2004).

§ Rimbo, Robert A. *Why Worship Matters* (2004).

§ Stewart, Benjamin. *A Watered Garden: Christian Worship and Earth's Ecology* (2011).

§ Torvend, Samuel. *Daily Bread, Holy Meal: Opening the Gifts of Holy Communion* (2004).

§ ———. *Flowing Water, Uncommon Birth: Christian Baptism in a Post-Christian Culture* (2011).

§ Wengert, Timothy, ed. *Centripetal Worship: The Evangelical Heart of Lutheran Worship* (2007).

Ylvisaker, John. *What Song Shall We Sing?* (2005).

Worship Studies, individual titles

Worship Matters: An Introduction to Worship. Multiple authors. Augsburg Fortress, 2012. A 5-session adult course that illuminates the whys and hows of Christian worship so that worshipers might experience a deeper appreciation of their community's worship. Leader guide and participant book.

∞ *Go Make Disciples: An Invitation to Baptismal Living*. Multiple authors. Augsburg Fortress, 2012. An ecumenical handbook offering a basic "how to" and a collection of updated resources for preparing adults for baptism or affirmation of baptism, and for Christian discipleship. Appropriate for a wide range of Protestant denominations, especially Lutheran, Episcopal, Anglican, United Methodist, Presbyterian, and Reformed. Supplementary CD-ROM available separately.

§ *The Christian Life: Baptism and Life Passages*. Augsburg Fortress, 2008.

§ *Keeping Time: The Church's Years*. Augsburg Fortress, 2009.

* *More Days for Praise: Festivals and Commemorations in Evangelical Lutheran Worship*. Augsburg Fortress, 2016.

§ *The Sunday Assembly*. Augsburg Fortress, 2008.

§ *Inside Out: Worship in an Age of Mission*. Thomas Schattauer, gen. ed. Fortress Press, 1999. Lutheran seminary teachers address the mission of the church as it pertains to various aspects of worship.

§ Lathrop, Gordon. *The Four Gospels on Sunday: The New Testament and the Reform of Christian Worship*. Fortress Press, 2011. Lathrop demonstrates that the Gospels can remain a true catalyst for liturgical theology and liturgical renewal, as well as an inspiring link to the faith and convictions of the earliest followers of the Christian way.

§ ———. *Holy Ground: A Liturgical Cosmology*. Fortress Press, 2003.

§ ———. *Holy People: A Liturgical Ecclesiology*. Fortress Press, 1999.

§ ———. *Holy Things: A Liturgical Theology*. Fortress Press, 1998.

Principles for Worship. Renewing Worship, vol. 2. Augsburg Fortress, 2002. Principles for language, music, preaching, and worship space in relationship to the Christian assembly. Also available in Spanish.

Ramshaw, Gail. *Christian Worship*. Fortress Press, 2009. An engaging textbook on 100,000 Sundays of Christians at worship.

Senn, Frank. *Christian Liturgy: Catholic and Evangelical*. Fortress Press, 1997. A comprehensive historical introduction to the liturgy of the Western church with particular emphasis on Lutheran traditions.

§ ———. *Introduction to Christian Liturgy*. Fortress Press, 2012. This general introduction explores the meaning, history, and practice of worship in Eastern and Western, Catholic and Protestant traditions: the theology of worship, the historical development of the eucharist and the prayer offices, the lectionary and customs of the church year, other sacramental rites, and the use of music and the arts.

§ ———. *The People's Work: A Social History of the Liturgy*. Fortress Press, 2006. The first book to document the full history of ordinary Christians' liturgical expression.

Use of the Means of Grace: A Statement on the Practice of Word and Sacrament, The. Evangelical Lutheran Church in America, 1997. Also available in Spanish and Mandarin versions.

Web Sites

*∞ www.augsburgmusic.org. From adult choirs, large or small, to children's choirs beginning their musical journey; from organ and piano to keyboard with instruments; from solo vocal to liturgical music, Augsburg Music offers top-drawer, accessible music for every church.

*∞ www.evangelicallutheranworship.org. More than 150 resources for God's people, gathered in word and song around gifts of grace, sent with good news into the world.

∞ www.preludemusicplanner.com. A subscription-based online music planning tool. Create comprehensive plans. Browse, preview, and download music from multi-publisher library. Search music based on lectionary days, keywords, skill level and more. Store your usage history. Upload and organize your own library.

∞ www.sundaysandseasons.com. A subscription-based online worship planning tool. Browse, select, and download content for worship planning and worship folder preparation. Complements *Sundays and Seasons*. Add-on subscriptions to preaching and video content are also available.

∞ www.alcm.org. Association of Lutheran Church Musicians. Links to conferences and resources available through this pan-Lutheran musicians' organization. Also a bulletin board and placement service.

∞ www.elca.org/worship. Evangelical Lutheran Church in America. Monthly WorshipNews e-newsletter.

∞ www.theworkofthepeople.com. Visual media for worship based on the Revised Common Lectionary, including videos, loops, and stills.

∞ www.worship.ca. Lift Up Your Hearts: The worship and spirituality site of the Evangelical Lutheran Church in Canada. Contains a variety of resources and news about events related to Lutheran worship.

Preaching Resources

* Brown, Sally A. and Luke A. Powery. *Ways of the Word: Learning to Preach for Your Time and Place*. Fortress Press, 2016.

§ Brueggemann, Walter. *The Practice of Prophetic Imagination: Preaching an Emancipating Word*. Fortress Press, 2012.

Craddock, Fred, et al. *Preaching through the Christian Year*. Three volumes for Cycles A, B, C. Valley Forge, PA: Trinity Press International, 1992, 1993. Various authors comment on the Sunday readings, psalms, and various festival readings.

§ Elements of Preaching series. O. Wesley Allen, series editor. Fortress Press, 2008–. Guides to the art and craft of preaching. Authors include Ronald Allen, Teresa Fry Brown, Mary Foskett, Jennifer Lord, Marvin McMickle, James Nieman, Melinda Quivik.

*§ Fortress Biblical Preaching Commentaries series. Fortress Press, 2013–. With their focus on the biblical books themselves and working with the realities of the lectionary, these volumes are useful in tandem with more extensive commentaries as well as with seasonal lectionary materials.

§ Hedahl, Susan K. *Proclamation and Celebration: Preaching on Christmas, Easter, and Other Festivals*. Fortress Press, 2012.

§ Lose, David J. *Preaching at the Crossroads: How the World—and Our Preaching—Is Changing*. Fortress Press, 2013.

§ Ramshaw, Gail. *Treasures Old and New: Images in the Lectionary*. Fortress Press, 2002. A creative unfolding of forty images drawn from the lectionary readings.

§ Rhodes, David, H. Paul Santmire, and Norman C. Habel, eds. *The Season of Creation: A Preaching Commentary*. Fortress Press, 2011. Scholars who have pioneered the connections between biblical scholarship, ecological theology, liturgy, and homiletics provide here a comprehensive resource for preaching and leading worship in this new season.

∞ Sloyan, Gerard. *Preaching from the Lectionary: An Exegetical Commentary with CD-ROM*. Fortress Press, 2003. Exegetical analysis of each text from the RCL.

§ Stiller, Brian. *Preaching Parables to Postmoderns*. Fortress Press, 2005. An introduction to postmodern sensibilities and how it informs preaching the parables.

*∞ *Sundays and Seasons: Preaching*. Augsburg Fortress, 2014–. Multiple contributors. Encourages and provides helps for lectionary preaching, taking into account all the readings for the day, in addition to the rest of the worship service and the day itself in the church year. Features new commentary and ideas for proclamation, contributed by practicing preachers as well as scholars, together with succinct notes on each day and its readings. Also available as an add-on subscription to sundaysandseasons.com.

∞ www.homileticsonline.com. An online sermon preparation resource including illustrations and visuals.

∞ www.newproclamation.com. An online sermon preparation resource that combines in-depth exegesis with homiletic advice from practicing preachers.

∞ www.workingpreacher.org. A resource for preachers from the Center for Biblical Preaching at Luther Seminary.

Periodicals

Call to Worship: Liturgy, Music, Preaching, and the Arts. Offers insight and inspiration for pastors, church musicians, artists, and other worship leaders. Quarterly. Published by the Office of Theology and Worship of the Presbyterian Church (USA).

Catechumenate: A Journal of Christian Initiation. Chicago: Liturgy Training Publications. Published six times a year with articles on congregational preparation of older children and adults for the celebration of baptism and eucharist.

CrossAccent. Journal of the Association of Lutheran Church Musicians. Publication for church musicians and worship leaders in North America. www.alcm.org.

Faith & Form. Journal of the Interfaith Forum on Religion, Art and Architecture. www.faithandform.com.

Liturgy. Quarterly journal of The Liturgical Conference. Each issue explores a worship-related issue from an ecumenical perspective. customerservice@taylorandfrancis.com.

Worship. Collegeville, MN: The Order of St. Benedict, published through The Liturgical Press six times a year. One of the primary journals of liturgical renewal among the churches.

* denotes new or newer print resource
∞ denotes electronic or Web resource
324 § denotes print resource also available as an ebook

Key to Hymn and Song Collections

Augsburg Fortress publications

* Indicates resources whose hymns or psalm refrains are, at least in part, included in the online worship planning tool sundaysandseasons.com.

ASG*	As Sunshine to a Garden	LBW*	Lutheran Book of Worship	OBS*	O Blessed Spring: Hymns of Susan
BOL*	Bread of Life	LLC	Libro de Liturgia y Cántico		Palo Cherwien
CBM	Come, Beloved of the Maker	LS*	LifeSongs	SP*	Singing Our Prayer: A Companion to
DH*	Dancing at the Harvest	MSB1*	Music Sourcebook for Lent and the		Holden Prayer Around the Cross
ELW*	Evangelical Lutheran Worship		Three Days	TFF*	This Far by Faith
GS2*	Global Songs 2: Bread for the Journey	MSB2*	Music Sourcebook for All Saints	W&P*	Worship & Praise
GS3	Global Songs 3: Pave the Way		through Transfiguration	WOV*	With One Voice

Key to Music Publishers

ABI	Abingdon	ECS	E. C. Schirmer	LOR	Lorenz	RW	Ringing Word Publications
AFP	Augsburg Fortress		(MorningStar)	LP	The Liturgical Press	SEL	Selah
AG	Agape (Hope)	FB	Fred Bock Music	MAR	Maranatha	SF	SoundForthPublications
AGEHR	American Guild of English	FLG	Flagstaff Publications	MFS	Mark Foster (Shawnee)	SHW	Shawnee
	Handbell Ringers	FTT	From the Top Music	MMP	Masters Music Publication	SMP	Sacred Music Press
ALF	Alfred	GIA	GIA Publications	MSM	MorningStar Music		(Lorenz)
AUR	Aureole	HAL	Hal Leonard	NOV	Novello (Shawnee)	WAL	Walton
BAR	Bärenreiter	HIN	Hinshaw Music Co.	OCP	Oregon Catholic Press	WAR	Warner/Belwin
BP	Beckenhorst Press	HOP	Hope	OXF	Oxford University Press	WJK	Westminster/John Knox
CG	Choristers Guild	HWG	H.W. Gray (Warner)	PAR	Paraclete	WLP	World Library Publications
CPH	Concordia	INT	Integrity (Capitol CMG)	PET	C.F. Peters	WRD	Word Music
DUR	Durand (Presser)	JEF	Jeffers	PRE	Presser	WT	WorshipTogether.com
EAR	EarthSongs	KJO	Kjos	RR	Red River Music		

Key to Psalm Collections

The refrains included in the resources below may be reprinted with a OneLicense.net copyright license. Exceptions to this are *Psalms for All Seasons* and *Lift Up Your Hearts*, both of which contain psalm settings from a variety of publishers, some, but not all, of which are covered under the OneLicense.net license. In other cases (e.g., *Psalter for Worship* and *Psalm Settings for the Church Year*), permission to reproduce refrains is included with volume purchases. Psalm collections below that follow the Roman Lectionary are marked with [RL] at the end of the comments. Although the psalms appointed for the Roman Lectionary and the Revised Common Lectionary [RCL] are not identical, there is sufficient overlap to make these volumes very useful for those who follow the RCL.

ACYG   *Arise, Come to Your God: Forty-Seven Gelineau Settings of the Revised Grail Psalms*. GIA. This collection of psalm settings is an excerpted and edited volume of the Gelineau psalm settings included in the Psalter section of *Worship, Fourth Edition* (2011). Many of the original Gelineau collections are now out of print, so this new collection is a most welcome addition.

        ChildrenSing Psalms. Marilyn Comer, ed. Augsburg Fortress. This collection of 15 of the more well-known psalms is a must-have for anyone working with children's choirs. Reproducible singer pages and assembly refrains.

COJ:A   *Cry Out with Joy: Year A*. GIA. Verses are chanted rather than through-composed. Composers include David Haas, Kathleen Harmon, Stephen Pishner, Paul Tate, and Lori True. [RL]

COJ:S   *Cry Out with Joy: Christmas, Triduum, Solemnities & Other Celebrations*. GIA. [RL]

DH   Ray Makeever. *Dancing at the Harvest*. Augsburg Fortress. This collection of songs includes lyrical settings of selected psalms with refrains and through-composed verses.

LP:LG   *Lectionary Psalms: Lead Me, Guide Me*. GIA. Refrains and psalm verse accompaniments composed in gospel style. These settings work well with *Evangelical Lutheran Worship* Holy Communion Setting Six or another gospel setting of the liturgy. [RL]

LP:W4   *Lectionary Psalms: Joseph Gelineau, SJ and Michel Guimont* (as found in *Worship, Fourth Edition*). GIA. Psalms in this volume are presented with a single refrain that may be used with a Gelineau tone or a tone by Michel Guimont. [RL]

LUYH   *Lift Up Your Hearts: Psalms, Hymns, and Spiritual Songs*. Faith Alive Resources. Includes all 150 psalms in a variety of settings for assembly singing.

PAS   *Psalms for All Seasons: A Complete Psalter for Worship*. Calvin Institute of Christian Worship, Faith Alive Christian Resources, and Brazos Press. In addition to each of the 150 psalms and

several canticles presented in multiple sung settings, this volume contains extensive appendixes and indexes.

PCY   *Psalms for the Church Year*. Multi-volume. GIA. Each volume includes well-known psalm settings by various composers. This year, selections are recommended from volumes 1–4.

PRCL   Michel Guimont. *Psalms for the Revised Common Lectionary*. GIA. Responsorial psalms. May be accompanied by organ, piano, or guitar.

PS1   *Psalm Songs 1: Advent–Christmas–Epiphany*. Augsburg Fortress. This 3-volume set provides interesting settings of more common psalms. All settings include guitar chords and many have parts for other solo instruments.

PS2   *Psalm Songs 2: Lent–Holy Week–Easter*.

PS3   *Psalm Songs 3: Ordinary Time*.

Psallite *Psallite: Sacred Song for Liturgy and Life*. Liturgical Press. This set of resources includes an accompaniment edition for each lectionary year and one volume for cantor/choir. In addition to lectionary psalms, provides biblically based songs that can be used at other times in the liturgy. [RL]

PSCY   *Psalm Settings for the Church Year*. 2 vols. Mark Mummert, ed. Augsburg Fortress. A collection of psalm settings in a wide variety of styles and structures. Includes all psalms used in the RCL.

PWA   *Psalter for Worship: Year A*. Augsburg Fortress. The first of three volumes of psalm refrains by various composers with Evangelical Lutheran Worship psalm tones. Coordinates with Celebrate and Today's Readings inserts. Includes a CD-ROM with reproducible psalm texts, refrains, and tones.

SMP   Thomas Pavlechko, arr. *St. Martin's Psalter*. Augsburg Fortress. Refrains and psalm tones based on familiar hymns in Anglican chant style. Uses the *Evangelical Lutheran Worship* psalm version. Published on CD-ROM, it includes reproducible parts for choir.

TLP:A   Tony Alonzo/Marty Haugen. *The Lyric Psalter: Year A*. GIA. This set contains four editions, one for each of the three years of the lectionary and one for solemnities, feasts, and special occasions. Each has a companion volume of descants for C-instrument. Psalm verses are through-composed and can be sung by a cantor. [RL]

TLP:S   Tony Alonzo/Marty Haugen. *The Lyric Psalter: Solemnities, Feasts, and Other Occasions*. GIA. [RL]

TPP   *The People's Psalter*. MorningStar. Responsorial psalm settings that make use of folk tunes from around the world. Includes settings for every psalm in the three-year lectionary.

Key to Music for Worship

acc	accompaniment	fl	flute	oct	octave	tbn	trombone
bar	baritone	glock	glockenspiel	opt	optional	tpt	trumpet
bng	bongos	gtr	guitar	orch	orchestra	timp	timpani
br	brass	hb	handbells	org	organ	trbl	treble
bsn	bassoon	hc	handchimes	perc	percussion	tri	triangle
cant	cantor	hp	harp	picc	piccolo	U	unison
ch	chimes	hpd	harpsichord	pno	piano	UE	upper elementary
cl	clarinet	hrn	horn	pt	part	vc	violoncello
cont	continuo	inst	instrument	qnt	quintet	vcs	voices
cym	cymbal	kybd	keyboard	qrt	quartet	vla	viola
DB	double or string bass	LE	lower elementary	rec	recorder	vln	violin
dbl	double	M	medium	sax	saxophone	wch	windchimes
desc	descant	MH	medium high	sop	soprano	ww	woodwind
div	divisi	ML	medium low	str	strings	xyl	xylophone
drm	drum	mxd	mixed	synth	synthesizer		
eng hrn	English horn	narr	narrator	tamb	tambourine		
fc	finger cymbals	ob	oboe	tba	tuba		

A Note on Music Listings

Please note that some choral and instrumental music in the day listings may be out of print. We are unable to research whether musical pieces from other publishers are still available. Why do we still list music if it is out of print? Primarily because many music planners may have that piece in their files, and can consider it for use. If a planner wishes to use a piece that has gone out of print, that may still be possible. For Augsburg Fortress resources, call 800/421-0239 or e-mail copyright@augsburgfortress.org to inquire about onetime reprint rights or to see whether a piece may be available on preludemusicplanner.org, or by print on demand.